EX LIBRIS
DEPARTMENT OF MUNICIPAL AFFAIRS
ONTARIO
THIS BOOK MUST NOT BE REMOVED

THE ESTABLISHMENT

OF

Schools and Colleges
in Ontario, 1792-1910.

BY

J. GEORGE HODGINS, I.S.O., M.A., L.L.D., F.R.G.S.

OF OSGOODE HALL, BARRISTER-AT-LAW, EX-DEPUTY MINISTER OF EDUCATION,
HISTORIOGRAPHER TO THE EDUCATION DEPARTMENT OF ONTARIO.

VOLUME III.

PARTS XII. TO XV. INCLUSIVE.

PRINTED BY ORDER OF THE LEGISLATIVE ASSEMBLY OF ONTARIO.

TORONTO:
PRINTED AND PUBLISHED BY L. K. CAMERON,
Printer to the King's Most Excellent Majesty.
1910

Ministry of Education, Ontario
Information Centre, 13th Floor,
Mowat Block, Queen's Park,
Toronto, Ont.   M7A 1L2

Printed by
WILLIAM BRIGGS
29-37 Richmond Street West
Toronto.

PREFATORY NOTE.

I have devoted a good deal of space in this Volume to a general and historical account of the various Colleges and Universities in this Province, and have specified the date of their establishment.

To the University of King's College, the first among the most noted of these Institutions, I have given a good deal of attention, not only on account of its peculiar origin, but also of its Parliamentary record during successive years, which reach back to 1829.

So large a space in the public mind had the subject of King's College occupied in these early days that I have thought it well to prepare a somewhat extended sketch of that Institution, which I have named "The University of King's College and its Vicissitudes."

To the long and acrimonious agitation which took place on King's College questions is due the movement of the Methodist and Presbyterian Churches to found Colleges of their own, so that their youth would not have to depend for their higher education upon an Institution wholly managed by the Church of England. The Methodists therefore obtained a Royal Charter for an Academy at Cobourg, which shortly afterwards became a College and University. The Presbyterian Church of Scotland also obtained a Royal Charter to found Queen's College and University at Kingston.

For each of the other Universities established in more peaceable times, and for the various Theological Colleges, I have collected sufficient material to enable me to give a fairly full and interesting description of them.

From material which has been furnished me, I have inserted a very complete account of the means employed in the Normal and Model Schools to prepare the various grades of Teachers for their highly important work.

The subjects of Technical and Industrial Education, in their more elaborate and popular forms, have of late years received a great deal of practical attention. The testimony borne to their intrinsic value in a new country like Canada, by the various parties who were consulted on the subject by the Royal Commission, was both convincing and conclusive. Examples of the success of Industrial Education are given, and the Industrial Schools among the Indians are specially noted.

Details are also given of the various Professional Schools of Law, Music, Medicine and Art; and among the most useful and necessary institutions is the "School of Telegraphy and Railroading," the practical instruction given being of the highest value, especially the Branch dealing with "First Aid to the Injured," such knowledge being invaluable in case of the accidents which now and then occur on the Railroads.

I have been fortunate in securing a number of engravings to insert in this Volume in connection with the Papers and Persons to which they refer.

The record which this Volume presents of our Educational state and progress will no doubt be highly gratifying to all those who have taken an active part in promoting it, and to all who take an interest in our prosperity and success as an important part of the Empire.

J. GEORGE HODGINS,
TORONTO, 22nd November, 1910. *Historiographer.*

CONTENTS.

PART XII.

The Universities and Colleges of Ontario.

	PAGE
The University System of Ontario, by Doctor J. George Hodgins	1
University Representation in the Legislature, 1820	4
University of King's College and its Vicissitudes	5
The Charter of King's College as amended, 1837	16
Historical Address Relating to Toronto University	22
College and University Legislation, 1819-1884	24
Dates at which Colleges in Ontario were Established	28
The University of Toronto	28
The Toronto University Examinations—The University Fellowship, Medals and Scholarships	30
Details of Management of the University of Toronto	32
Ceremony of Placing the Coping Stone on the new University Buildings	33
Latin Inscription on the Interior Wall of Toronto University	36
Historical Facts Connected with the University of Toronto	46
The Library of Toronto University	49
The Museum of Toronto University	52
The Clinical Laboratory of the University of Toronto	53
Queen's Hall, the Women's Residence of University College	54
The School of Practical Science, Toronto	55
Denominational Colleges as Part of a System of Popular Education, by the Reverend Doctor Ryerson	57
Theological Education and Colleges in Ontario, by the Reverend Doctor A. H. Newman	58
Establishment of the Upper Canada Academy, afterwards Victoria College University	59
Characteristics of the System of Inspection to be Pursued in the Upper Canada Academy	62
Ceremony at Laying the Corner Stone of the Upper Canada Academy, 1832	63
Description of the Upper Canada Academy Building	65
The Charter of the Upper Canada Academy	66
The State and Financial Prospects of the Upper Canada Academy, 1835	67
The University of Victoria College	71
The Act to Incorporate Victoria College	71
The Granting of an Imperial Charter for the Upper Canada Academy, 1836	73
The Reverend Egerton Ryerson as President of Victoria University	74
Opening of the Upper Canada Academy as a Preparatory College, 1841	76
Upper Canada Academy and Victoria College—a Retrospect and Prospect, 1829-1892, by the Reverend A. L. Langford, M.A.	78
The Victoria College Faculty of Theology, by the Reverend J. G. McLaughlin, B.A., B.D.	81

CONTENTS.

	PAGE
The Reverend Doctor Nelles, President of Victoria University, Honoured by the Students	83
Annesley Hall, the Women's Residence of Victoria College University	85
The University of Queen's College, Kingston	88
Meeting held in Kingston to Promote the Establishment of Queen's College University	90
Sir John A. Macdonald's Recollection of the Queen's College Meeting of Fifty Years Before	91
Finances and Appliances of Queen's College University	92
The Constitution and Management of Queen's University	95
Queen's College School of Mining	97
The Establishment of Queen's College University	97
Golden Jubilee of Queen's College University	102
The Women's Residence of the Queen's University, by Alice A. Chown	105
Chancellor Fleming's Testimony to Queen's University	108
The Proposed Change in the Constitution of Queen's College University, 1905	110
The University of Trinity College, Toronto	113
Erection of Trinity College—Turning the First Sod, and Laying the Corner Stone, 1851	114
The Inauguration and Opening of Trinity College University	117
Bishop Strachan's Address—Continuance of the Home Life of Students in the Institution—Nature of the Discipline to be adopted at the College—Desirableness of this Necessary System of Salutary Vigilance and Control—What the Value is of a System of Education, Based upon Religion, Illustrated—The Bible as a Most Precious Guide to Spiritual Life—Appeal to Restore the Bible to its Rightful Place in Education—Address to the Newly Enrolled Students	117
Personal Address of Sir John B. Robinson to the Students of Trinity College University	123
Notice to Intending Students of Trinity College	127
The Church of England Theological Seminary Transferred from Cobourg to Trinity College	127
Transferance of the Church of England Theological Library from Toronto University to Trinity College	128
Installation of the Honourable John Hillyard Cameron as Chancellor of Trinity College	128
Historical Sketch of Trinity College University, by Reverend Provost Macklem	131
Address of Bishop Strachan on the Advantage of Trinity College to the Youth of the Country	134
St. Hilda's College, the Women's Residence of Trinity Univesity	136
McMaster University, Toronto	138
The Canadian Literary Institute, Woodstock	138
Woodstock College	141
Moulton Ladies' College, Toronto	141
McMaster Hall, or the Baptist Theological College, Toronto	142
Western University of London, Ontario	143
History of Huron College, London, Ontario	144
The Opening of Huron College, London, Ontario, 1864	145

CONTENTS.

vii

	PAGE
The University of Ottawa	148
New Science Hall of the University of Ottawa	150
The Physical Laboratory in the Science Hall, Ottawa University	152
The Lecture Hall, Chemical Laboratory and Mineralogical Laboratory, University of Ottawa	153
The Educational Facilities of Ottawa	153
Regiopolis College, Kingston	154
The Founding of Regiopolis College, Kingston	155
St. Michael's College, Toronto	155
Historical Sketch of Knox College, Toronto	157
Albert College, Belleville	162
Massey Hall and Residence, Albert College, Belleville	164
Courses of Study in Albert College, Belleville	166
The Protestant Episcopal Divinity School, Wycliffe College, Toronto, by the Honourable S. H. Blake, K.C.	172
The Evangelical Association of the Diocese of Toronto	175
The Church Association of the Diocese of Toronto	177
Incorporation of Wycliffe College	180
Position and Equipment of Wycliffe College	185
Connection of Wycliffe College with the University of Toronto	186
Regulations Relating to Courses of Study in Wycliffe College	186
Wycliffe College Bursaries	187
Granting Degrees in Divinity in Wycliffe College	187
Church Connection of Wycliffe College	188
Successful Work of Wycliffe College	188
Proposed Amalgamation of Trinity and Wycliffe Colleges, Toronto, 1910	189
Memorandum of the Honourable S. H. Blake, K.C., in regard to this Proposal of Trinity College	191
Adverse Decision of Wycliffe College to Amalgamate with Trinity College	195
Statement of the Reverend Provost Macklem in regard to the Proposed Union of Trinity and Wycliffe Colleges	198
Note on the State and Progress of Wycliffe College, addressed to its Graduates, by the President and Principal of the College	202
Inaugural Address of the Reverend Professor Thomas at Wycliffe College	203

PART XIII.

Facilities for Professional Education—Legal, Medical, Military, Etcetera.

	PAGE
Courses of Legal Study Prescribed by the Benchers of the Law Society, Toronto	204
Medical Education—General Regulations of the Medical Council	205
Medical Colleges and Schools in Ontario	206
The Toronto School of Medicine	207
Trinity Medical School, Toronto	207
Royal College of Physicians and Surgeons, Kingston	208
Ontario College of Pharmacy, Toronto	208
School of Dentistry of the Royal College of Dental Surgeons for Ontario	209
Women's Medical Colleges in Kingston and Toronto	209
The Royal Military College, Kingston	210

PART XIV.

The Education and Training of Public School Teachers and Directors of Kindergartens.

	PAGE
The Professional Training of Public School Teachers	212
The County Model Schools of Ontario	213
Syllabus of Courses of Study and Regulations	214
Duties of Prinicpals and Assistants	215
Duties of Teachers-in-Training	215
Subjects and Values of Examination	215
Teachers' Certificates	216
Programme of Studies	216
Observation and Practice of Teaching	217
Syllabus of Courses—Principles of Education and Methodology, School Organization and Management, Special Methodology, Language and Composition, Reading, Spelling, Literature, Grammar, History, Geography, Nature Study, Arithmetic, Writing, Art Work, Music, Physiology and Hygiene, Physical Training, School Law and Regulations	218
The Normal Schools of Ontario	228
Syllabus of Courses of Instruction and Regulations	228
Location and Purpose of the Normal Schools	228
Grades of Teachers-in-Training	229
Sessions and Vacations	229
Conditions of Admission	229
Duties of Principals and Assistants	230
Duties of Teachers-in-Training	230
Text Books, Library, Literary Society	231
Examinations—Groups I, II, III, IV	231
Certificates	232
Horticulture and Industrial Training at the Ontario Agricultural College, Guelph	233
Courses of Study at the Normal Schools	233
Order of the Courses	234
The Normal School and Affiliated Public Schools	235
Observation and Practice in Teaching	235
Details of Courses of Instruction—Science of Education, The Subject of Psychology, The Course in Child Study, General Methodology, History of Education, School Organization and Management, Special Methodolgy, Language and Composition, Reading, Spelling, Literature, Grammar, History, Geography, Nature Study and Agriculture, Elementary Science, Arithmetic, Algebra, Geometry, Writing, Art Work, Manual Training, Household Science, Music, Physiology and Hygiene, Physical Training, School Law and Regulations, Manners	237
Syllabus of Studies and Regulations for Kindergartens	256
The Kindergarten—Its Object and Purpose	256
Training Schools—their Sessions and Terms	256
Grades of Certificates	256
Conditions of Admission for Assistant Kindergartners	257
Conditions of Admission for Directors of Kindergartens	257
Certificates and Examinations of Assistants and Directors	257

CONTENTS.

	PAGE
Course for Assistants of Kindergartners	258
Kindergarten Gifts	258
Kindergarten Occupations	261
Songs and Games	264
Stories	264
Nature Study	264
Methods	265
Physical Training	265
Course for Directors of Kindergartens	265
Applied Psychology and the Philosophy of Froebel	265
Kindergarten Gifts	266
Kindergarten Occupations	267
Industrial Art	268
Mother Play	268
Teaching by means of Stories	268
History of Education	269
Nature Study	270
Child Study	270
Methods of Teaching	271
The Special Object of Music	272
Faculties of Education in the University of Toronto and in Queen's University, Kingston	272
General Information in regard to the Faculty of Education in the University of Toronto	272
Courses of Study for Provincial Certificates	273
Regulations of the Faculty of Education	275
Regulations of the Education Department	277
General and Advanced Courses—History of Education and Educational Systems, Principles of Education, Psychology and General Method, School Management and the School Law, Courses in Special Method, Part I., Part II.	279
Course for Public School Inspectors	282
Degrees in Pedagogy—General Information	283
The Summer Session of the University of Toronto	286
Courses Offered by the Faculty of Education	286
Information in regard to the Faculty of Education, University of Queen's College, Kingston	286
Courses of Study—General Course, Advanced Course, Special Course, and Courses for Degrees in Pedagogy	287
General Regulations of the Faculty of Education	289
Examination in the Faculty of Education	290
Details of Courses—History of Education and Educational Systems, Principles of Education, Psychology and General Method, School Management and School Law, Special Methods, Public School Courses for Specialists, Course for Public School Inspectors	291
Provincial Certificates	296
Degrees in Education—Bachelor of Pedagogy, Doctor of Pedagogy	297
Regulations of the Education Department for the Instruction of Teachers in Manual Training and Household Science	299
Course of Study in Manual Training	299
Course of Study in Household Science	300

CONTENTS.

	PAGE
Teachers' Training Courses in Elementary Agriculture and Horticulture and Industrial Arts	301
Course of Study in Agriculture and Horticulture	301
Course of Study in Farm Life and Allied Industries, Nature Study Literature, School Gardening, Botany, Horticulture, Field Husbandry, Soil Physics, Entomology, Soil Chemistry, Bacteriology	302
The Books in the Reference Library	304
Elementary Industrial Arts	305
Course of Study in Pedagogics, Drawing, Applied Art and Design, Wood Working, Constructive Work	306
Regulations of the Education Department for the Summer School for Teachers at the Agricultural College, Guelph	308
Terms and Courses, Fees, Supplies, etcetera	308
Syllabus of Study	308
Nature Study, Elementary Agriculture and Horticulture, Elementary Industrial Arts, Art and Constructive Work, Wood Working and Mechanical Drawing, Household Science	308
Regulations for Residence at Macdonald Hall	313
General Information	314
Agricultural Education in Ontario, a Paper by Doctor J. George Hodgins	314
Importance of Education to an Agricultural People, by the Reverend Doctor Ryerson	319
The Agricultural College and the Macdonald Institute and Hall, Guelph	327
The Departments and Equipments of the College	332
Advantages of an Agricultural Course of Instruction	337
The Various Courses of Instruction in the College	338
The Scholarships, Prizes and Medals	338
Short Courses in Practical Work	339
Terms and Examinations	339
Course of Instruction for an Associate Diploma	339
Special Students	340
Candidates for a B.S.A. Degree	340
Admission to Third Year Standing	340
Third Year (for the B.S.A. Degree) Course of Study	341
Outline of Work in Nature Study	341
Fourth Year (for the B.S.A. Degree) Various Options	341
The Macdonald Institute	347
Home Economics Department	347
Normal Course in Domestic Science	348
The Housekeeper's Course	349
The Home-Maker's Course	349
Short Course in Domestic Science	349
Regulations in Household Science	350
Macdonald Hall of the Ontario Agricultural College	350
Teachers' Training Courses	351
Manual Training Department	351
Department of Nature Study	351
Forestry, Farm Carpentry	352
Work in Summer Courses	352

	PAGE
Manual or Industrial Training in the Early Days of Upper Canada	353
Later Opinions of the Necessity for Manual Training in Our Schools	354
Departmental Regulations in regard to Manual Training	355
Manual Training, Household Science, and Special Technical Instruction	356

PART XV.

Miscellaneous Educational Institutions, comprising those of Agriculture, Art, Music, Telegraphy, Business and Technical Training, Etcetera.

	PAGE
Regulations and Courses of Study for the Agricultural Departments of the High School at Essex and the Collegiate Institutes at Galt, Collingwood, Lindsay, Perth, and Morrisburg	357
Eastern Dairy School, Kingston	360
Ontario Veterinary Association, Toronto	361
Business Colleges in Ontario	362
The British-American Business College	362
The Ontario Business College, Belleville	363
Technical Education and Industrial Schools	363
Technical Education in a Popular Form	364
Elementary Industrial Arts in Public and Separate Schools of Villages and Towns	366
Organization of Work	367
Accommodation and Equipment Provided	368
Details of the Courses	369
Supply of Teachers for Instruction in Elementary Industrial Arts	372
Industrial Schools in the Cities and Chief Towns of Ontario	372
Work Done by the Industrial School, Toronto	374
Industrial Schools Among the Indians	375
Mount Elgin Institution, Muncey Town	375
Shingwauk and Wawanosh Homes	377
Promotion of Industrial Education by the Universities	378
The Commission on Industrial Training and Technical Education, October, 1910	379
The Hamilton Scientific Association	381
The Hamilton Technical and Art School	383
The Queen's College School of Mining, Kingston	384
The Dominion School of Telegraphy and Railroading, Toronto	385
The Canadian Horological Institute, Toronto	386
Provision for the Promotion of Science, and a Provincial Observatory	387
The Magnetic and Meteorological Observatory, Toronto	389
The Duties of the Observatory Service	390
Instruments in the Toronto Observatory	391
The Practical Daily Work of the Toronto Magnetical Observatory	392
The Observing Stations	393
The Storm Signals	393
The Official Timekeeper	393

	PAGE
The Magnetic and Meteorological Observatory, Toronto—*Continued.*	
Practical Uses of the Reports	394
Some Weather Facts	394
Snowless Christmases	394
Curious Contrivances of Observers	394
Photographing an Earthquake	395
The Ottawa Observatory	395
Magnetic Observations	395
The Royal Astronomical Society of Canada, Toronto	396
Conservatories and Colleges of Music	397
The Toronto Conservatory of Music	397
The Toronto College of Music	398
The London Conservatory of Music and School of Elocution	402
Ontario Society of Artists	403
Art Schools	403
The Central School of Art and Design	403
Other Art Schools	403
Courses of Study for Commercial and Art Specialists	404
The Entomological Society of Ontario	404
Military Instruction of High School Cadet Corps	405

ILLUSTRATIONS.

		PAGE
1.	Lieutenant-Governor J. G. Simcoe	1
2.	Group of Universities and Colleges, Toronto	2
3.	King's College, Toronto	18
4.	The Reverend Doctor Egerton Ryerson	20
5.	The Honourable Francis Hincks	20
6.	The University of Toronto	29
7.	The Reverend Doctor Robert A. Falconer, President of the Toronto University	31
8.	The University of Toronto (Enlarged view)	34
9.	The Reverend Doctor John McCaul, First President of the University and College	40
10.	Sir Daniel Wilson, President of the University of Toronto	43
11.	The University of Toronto, Looking from the South East	47
12.	The Library of the University of Toronto	50
13.	The School of Practical Science, Toronto	56
14.	The Reverend Egerton Ryerson in 1836	61
15.	The Reverend Doctor Matthew Richey, First Principal of the Upper Canada Academy	64
16.	The Upper Canada Academy at Cobourg in 1842	65
17.	The Reverend Doctor James Richardson	66
18.	The Reverend Doctor Joseph Stinson	67
19.	The Reverend Doctor Ephraim Evans	67
20.	The Reverend William Lord	67
21.	The Reverend Doctor Anson Green	67
22.	The Reverend Egerton Ryerson, 1840	68
23.	The Reverend John Sunday (Indian)	70
24.	The Reverend Peter Jacobs (Indian)	70
25.	U.C. Academy, later Victoria College and Faraday Hall, Cobourg	72
26.	The Reverend Doctor Egerton Ryerson, Principal of Victoria College University, 1842	76
27.	Victoria College University	79
28.	The Reverend Doctor Nelles, President of Victoria University	81
29.	The Reverend Doctor Burwash, President and Chancellor of Victoria College University	83
30.	Annesley Hall, the Women's Residence of Victoria University	84
31.	Library of Victoria College University	86
32.	Victoria College University (Tail Piece)	87
33.	The Very Reverend Doctor Gordon, President of the Queen's University, Kingston	89
34.	Group of Past Presidents of Queen's University, Kingston	93
35.	Theological Building and Library of the Queen's University, Kingston	96
36.	Ontario Hall, Queen's University, Kingston	98
37.	Fleming Hall, Queen's University, Kingston	99
38.	Medical Laboratories, Queen's University, Kingston	100

xiii

ILLUSTRATIONS.

	PAGE
39. The Arts Department and Grant Hall, Queen's University, Kingston	103
40. Sir Sandford Fleming, Chancellor of Queen's University, Kingston	109
41. The University of Trinity College, Toronto	114
42. The Right Reverend Bishop Strachan, 1842	115
43. The Right Reverend Bishop Strachan, 1851	118
44. Sir John Beverley Robinson	123
45. The Reverend Doctor Whittaker, Provost of Trinity University	129
46. St. Hilda's College, the Women's Residence of Trinity University	137
47. McMaster University, Toronto	139
48. The Western University, London	143
49. Lieutenant-Governor Simcoe, 1791	146
50. The Ottawa University	149
51. Science Hall of the Ottawa University	151
52. Athletic Oval, Ottawa University	152
53. St. Michael's College, Toronto	156
54. Knox College, Toronto	158
55. Albert College, Belleville	163
56. Massey Hall and Residence of Albert College, Belleville	165
57. Wycliffe College, Toronto	172
58. The Reverend Doctor Sheraton, Principal of Wycliffe College, Toronto	174
59. Main Building of the Ontario Agricultural College, Guelph	328
60. The Consolidated School of the Ontario Agricultural College, Guelph	328
61. The Consolidated School and its Constituents, Ontario Agricultural College, Guelph	331
62. Part of the Experimental Grounds of the Ontario Agricultural College, Guelph	333
63. Example of Manual Training at the Ontario Agricultural College, Guelph	336

The Establishment of Schools and Colleges in Ontario.

PART XII.

THE UNIVERSITIES AND COLLEGES OF ONTARIO.

THE UNIVERSITY SYSTEM OF ONTARIO.

By J. George Hodgins, M.A., LL.D.

At present there are the following Universities in the Province, videlicet:

1. The University of Toronto, projected in 1798, opened as King's College University in June, 1843. Toronto University in 1850.
2. The University of Victoria College, Cobourg, founded as Upper Canada Academy in 1832, opened in October, 1841.
3. The University of Queen's College, Kingston, projected in 1839, opened in March, 1843.
4. The University of Trinity College, Toronto, founded in 1851, opened in January, 1852.
5. The (R. C.) University of Ottawa, founded in 1848, opened in 1866.
6. The Western University, London, founded in 1877, opened in 1878.
7. McMaster University, Toronto, founded in 1881, opened in 1881.

LIEUTENANT-GOVERNOR SIMCOE.

Before referring to these Universities in detail, I shall briefly glance at the early history of University Education in this Province.

Lieutenant-General J. Graves Simcoe, the first Governor of Upper Canada, arrived here in 1792. He was a man of comprehensive views and noble impulses

[1]

2 THE ESTABLISHMENT OF SCHOOLS AND COLLEGES IN ONTARIO.

in regard to University Education. He was educated at Eton College and partly at Merton College, Oxford, but entered the Army before taking his degree. He served with distinction under Wolfe at Quebec and during the American Revolutionary War.

GROUP OF TORONTO COLLEGES.

In April, 1795, Governor Simcoe addressed a Letter to the Protestant Episcopal Bishop of Quebec—then having jurisdiction in Upper Canada—urging him to seek to promote the establishment of a " Protestant Episcopal University " in

Upper Canada. The reasons which he gave for this appeal were characteristic of the English Churchman and of the times, and reveal somewhat of the social and religious state of the Colony. They showed, too, that he was a Statesman as well as a Churchman. He said:

The people of the Province enjoy the forms as well as the privileges of the British Constitution. They have the means of governing themselves; and, having nothing to ask, must ever remain a part of the British Empire, provided they shall become sufficiently capable and enlightened to understand their relative situation and to manage their own power to the public interest. Liberal education seems to me, therefore, to be indispensably necessary; and the completion of it by the establishment of a University in the Capital of the Country, . . . would be most useful to inculcate just principles, habits, and manners into the rising generation; to coalesce the different customs of the various descriptions of settlers . . . into one form. In short, from distinct parts and ancient prejudices to new-form, as it were, and establish one nation, and thereby strengthen the union with Great Britain and preserve a lasting obedience to His Majesty's authority.

I naturally should wish that the Clergy requisite for offices in the University, in the first instance, should be Englishmen, if possible. . . . I most earnestly hope that . . . by giving the means of proper education in this Province both in its rudiments and in its completion, and from ourselves we may raise up a loyal, and, in due progress, a learned Clergy, which will speedily tend to unite, not only the Puritans within the Province, but the Clergy of the Episcopal Church, however dispersed . . . and on all sides, to bring within the pale [of the Episcopal Church] in Upper Canada a very great body of sectaries, who, in my judgment, as it were, offer themselves to its protection and reunion.

These objects would be materially promoted by a University in Upper Canada, which might, in due progress, acquire such a character as to become the place of education to many persons beyond the extent of the King's dominions. . . . The Episcopal Clergy in Great Britain, from pious motives as well as policy, are materially interested that the Church should increase in this Province. I will venture to prophesy its preservation depends upon a University being erected therein. . . . I have not the smallest hesitation in saying that I believe if a Protestant Episcopal University should be proposed to be erected, (even in the United States), the British nation would liberally subscribe to the undertaking. . . . The Universities of England, I make no doubt, would contribute to the planting of a scion from their respectable stock in this distant Colony.*

---

*It is of interest to note that while the present generation owes so much to the foresight of the first Lieutenant-Governor of Upper Canada, General Simcoe, in anticipating the wants of elementary, higher, and university education in the Province of Upper Canada, which in 1791 was about being established by the Quebec Act, he sets forth in his letter to Sir Joseph Banks, Bart., President of the Royal Society, dated January the 8th, 1791, " his hope that he would be able to establish in the then virgin Province, among other means of civilization, a University"; and thus proceeds to speak of the locality which was to be the center of the new community : "For the purpose of commerce, union and power, I propose that the site of the Colony should be in that great peninsula between the lakes Huron, Erie, and Ontario, a spot destined by nature sooner or later to govern that interior world. I mean to establish a capital in the very heart of that country, upon the River La Tranche [Thames], which is navigable for batteaux 150 miles, and near to where the Grand River, which falls into Erie, and others that communicate with Huron and Ontario, almost interlock." Upon this spot the City of London, in which the Western University has just been established, stands, and while the site of Toronto was subsequently adopted as the capital, the views of Governor Simcoe in respect to the University remained the same, and have been literally fulfilled in the Provincial University at Toronto, and this one at London, according to his expectations as expressed in his Letter of the 16th of October, 1795, to Bishop Mountain : " My views in respect to a University are totally unchanged; they are on a solid basis, and may or may not be complied with, as my superiors shall think proper, but shall certainly appeal as my system to the judgment of posterity."—Appeal on behalf of the Western University.

There are two or three things worth noticing in this vigorous letter of the Governor:

(1) Among the objects sought to be attained by the establishment of a university were the conservation of "the privileges of the British Constitution"; (2) the fusing of the various nationalities represented in the colony; (3) the absorption of "Puritans" and "sectaries" into the Episcopal Church; (4) the growth and spread of loyalty to the King's authority.

Two things also are noticeable: First, the Governor did not ignore, or underestimate, the necessity of popular education, or "education in the rudiments"; second, he gives no hint of a desire to appropriate the public domain to the building up of an "Episcopal university." On the other hand, he assumes that, if done at all, it is to be aided by contributions from England. I call attention to these two points, from the fact that they were quite lost sight of by those who afterward took up the cause of university education in Upper Canada where he had left it.

University Representation in the Upper Canada Legislature, 1820.

With a view to emphasize the desire to have a University established in this Province the Legislature passed the following in 1820:

The fourth Section of the "Act to Provide for Increasing the Representation of the Commons of this Province in the House of Assembly," 7th March, 1820, 60th George III., Chapter 2, provides as follows:

IV. And be it further enacted by the authority aforesaid, that wherever an University shall be organized and in operation as a seminary in this Province, and in conformity to the rules and statutes of similar institutions in Great Britain, it shall and may be lawful for the Governor, Lieutenant-Governor, or person administering the Government of this Province, for the time being, to declare by proclamation the tract of land appendant to such University, and whereupon the same is situated, to be a Town or Township, by such name as to him may seem meet, and that such Town or Township so constituted shall be represented by one Member. Provided always, nevertheless, that no person shall be permitted to vote at any such election for a member to represent the said University in Parliament who, besides the qualifications now by law required, shall not also be entitled to vote in the Convocation of said University.

Governor Simcoe, having received a higher appointment in the colonial service, left soon after. The Bishop of Quebec, however, acted upon his suggestion and wrote to the Colonial Minister on the subject, in June, 1796. In November, 1797, the Legislature of Upper Canada addressed a Memorial to King George III., asking "that His Majesty would be graciously pleased to direct his Government in this Province to appropriate a certain portion of the waste Lands of the Crown as a fund for the establishment and support of a respectable Grammar School in each District thereof, and also of a College, or University, for the instruction of the youth in the different branches of liberal knowledge."

To this Memorial the King directed a gracious answer to be sent. The Duke of Portland, Colonial Minister, therefore instructed the acting Governor, President Russell, to give practical effect to the prayer of the Petitioners. In doing so he used the following language:

[His Majesty] being always ready . . . to assist and encourage the exertions of his Province in laying the foundation for promoting sound learning and a religious education, has condescended to express his [desire] to comply with the wishes of the Legislature . . . in such a manner as shall be judged to be most effectual—

First, by the establishment of free Grammar [classical] Schools in those Districts in which they are called for, and—

Secondly, in due process of time, by establishing other Seminaries of a larger and more comprehensive nature, for the promotion of religious and moral learning, and the study of the Arts and Sciences.

Such were the terms in which the King, through his Colonial Minister, intimated his desire that classical and University learning should be promoted in this Province. The very comprehensiveness and express terms of the Duke of Portland's Despatch on this subject gave rise to a protracted controversy in after years, especially as the controverted expressions were embodied in substance in the Royal Charter for a University obtained in 1828 by the Reverend Doctor Strachan (afterwards first Church of England Bishop of Toronto). Around the expressions —" religious education," " religious and moral learning," and " other Seminaries of a larger and more comprehensive nature," a fierce war was waged for many years, which, although virtually over now, has yet left traces behind of the bitter conflict.

The result of the instructions to President Russell was that 549,217 Acres of Crown Lands were set apart for the twofold purpose set forth in the Colonial Minister's Despatch. Of these Acres, 225,944 were, in 1827, devoted to the University that was virtually established, on paper, in that year, and by Royal Charter in 1828.

This Charter virtually placed the proposed University under the control of the Episcopal Church. When its terms were known in Upper Canada it was fiercely assailed. The Charter was subsequently modified, in deference to public opinion; but it was not until many years afterwards that the University was, by statute, declared to be free from denominational control. Out of the controversy which the Duke of Portland's Despatch and the Charter caused arose other Colleges and Universities, which will be referred to in detail hereafter.

THE UNIVERSITY OF KING'S COLLEGE AND ITS VICISSITUDES,
1827-1853.

SPECIAL NOTE.—Owing to the very decided objection to the denominational character of the Royal Charter of King's College University and the prolonged agitation and discussion on the subject from 1828 to 1853, during which time no less than eight special Bills were passed by the Legislature on the subject, I felt it to be desirable, under these circumstances, to give a Sketch, as briefly as I could, of these varied proceedings in regard to the King's College University before it assumed a settled form, under the title and designation of the Toronto University. The first three of these several University Bills were passed in the years 1832, 1835 and 1837.

Subsequently efforts were made to pass Bills to amend these Acts in 1843, 1845, 1849, 1850, 1851, (two separate Bills), and by final compromise, in 1853.

One of the many questions which engaged the attention of Lieutenant-Colonel Simcoe, the first Governor of Upper Canada, who arrived here in 1792, was the establishment of a College or University, which would, as he stated, " be most useful to inculcate just principles, habits and manners into the rising generation."

In a letter to Sir Joseph Banks, President of the Royal Society, in 1791, he stated that "if a College were established in Upper Canada it would be eminently useful, and would give a tone of principle and manners that would be of infinite support to the Government."

After the retirement of Governor Simcoe, the Legislature of Upper Canada presented an Address to the King in 1798, praying that a portion of the Crown Lands should be set apart for the maintenance of higher education, as proposed by Governor Simcoe. King George III., in the same year, gave a gracious answer to this Address, and instructed his Colonial Minister, the Duke of Portland, to issue directions to the Acting Governor, (President Russell), to have the Lands asked for set apart. This was done, and 549,217 Acres were devoted to the purposes set forth in the Address. The share which afterwards fell to the King's College University was 225,273 Acres.

The anxiety felt in these early days for the establishment of an Institution for giving higher education than that furnished by the District Grammar Schools manifested itself more than once in the House of Assembly, at first in 1797, then in 1816, and finally in 1825; when, as time progressed, so many young men were found turning their attention to the learned professions, the Reverend Doctor Strachan pointed out, in his Appeal for a University, that between forty and fifty young men were studying Law, while Medical Students had to go to the United States to study Medicine, that he, (the Reverend Doctor Strachan), was determined to make an effort to induce the Imperial Government to grant authority to establish a University in Upper Canada. He, therefore, went to England in 1826, and, after issuing a strong Appeal on the subject, succeeded in the object of his desire, and obtained a Charter for King's College to be established at York.

In response to his Appeal a Royal Charter was granted, dated the fifteenth of March, 1827, and the proposed College was endowed with a Grant of One thousand pounds sterling, (£1,000), a year, as the Colonial Minister, Earl Bathurst, informed Sir Peregrine Maitland, the Lieutenant-Governor, in a Despatch, dated the 31st of March, 1827. The Despatch stated that the King had graciously been pleased to grant this to the College, in addition to its share of the Imperial Grant of Lands made to the Province for educational purposes in 1797-8.

The Grant was payable to the College out of the yearly receipts of moneys, payable to the Province by the Canada Company for the Huron Tract, which was sold to that Company by the Government.

The Royal Charter authorized the establishment of an Institution at York to be designated the "University of King's College"; but owing to the opposition which the Charter received, on account of its exclusive Church of England character and other local causes, the College was not established until 1843, when the Corner Stone was laid with much ceremony in the Queen's Park.

On the terms of the Charter of King's College becoming known to the House of Assembly, the opposition which it received found expression in the formal Report of the House on the subject on the 20th March, 1828, which was afterwards embodied in the Address to King William IV., objecting to the exclusive character of the Charter.

In his evidence in regard to King's College before a Committee of the House of Commons in London, in June, 1828, the Reverend George Ryerson also stated that the opposition in Upper Canada to King's College was:

"On account of its being under the exclusive control of one denomination of Christians, and requiring Religious tests; and the large appropriation of Lands which is made for its support renders it unlikely that other Institutions will be founded,* (as provided for in the Imperial Grant of Land for Education in Upper Canada made in 1798.), open to other denominations of Christians."

The Address presented to the King by the House of Assembly in March, 1828, stated that:

"As the great body of your Majesty's Subjects in this Province are not Members of the Church of England, they have seen with grief that the Charter contains provisions which are calculated to render the Institution subservient to the particular interests of that Church, and to exclude from its Offices and Honours all who do not belong to it."

This Address to the King was, however, not sent to England by Lieutenant-Governor Sir Peregrine Maitland until the 22nd of May, 1828.

In reply to this Address, the Colonial Secretary in September, 1828, said:

"It would deservedly be a subject of regret to His Majesty's Government if the University recently established at York should prove to have been founded upon Principles which cannot be made to accord with the general feelings and opinions of those for whose advantage it was intended."

This reply was not communicated to the House of Assembly except in a semi-private manner to some Members, so that its terms were not publicly known.

As its purpose was not, therefore, known to the Public a Petition was presented to the House of Assembly on the subject, in January, 1830, which stated that:

"The appointment" (by the Local Government) of Trustees (of the District Grammar Schools) from one Communion alone has occasioned a jealousy in the minds of the people, and destroyed that confidence which should ever be placed in the Public Institutions of our Country."

In consequence also of this want of knowledge of the Colonial Secretary's reply to the Address of the House of Assembly to the King, the opposition to the King's College Charter of 1827 finally culminated in December, 1830, in the holding of a Public Meeting of the "friends of Religious Liberty in the Town of York and its vicinity to consider the propriety of petitioning the Imperial Government respecting General Education, and the enjoyment (in it) of equal Religious privileges by all classes of His Majesty's Subjects."

This meeting, after an animated discussion on the subject, agreed to Address a petition to the Imperial Parliament on the subject, the concluding portion of which was as follows:

"May it, therefore, please Your Honourable House to take the subject of promoting Religion and Education in Upper Canada into your serious consideration and to modify the Charter of King's College established at York in Upper Canada, so as to exclude all Sectarian tests and preferences, and to appropriate the proceeds of the Sale of Lands, heretofore set apart for the support of a Protestant Clergy, to the purposes of General Education, etcetera."

(Signed by upwards of ten thousand inhabitants of the Province.)

A copy of this Petition was entrusted to Mr. (afterwards the Reverend) George Ryerson for presentation to the House of Commons. He also personally presented a copy of it to the Colonial Secretary, with such remarks on the subject

*The University of Victoria College was founded in 1841, and that of Queen's University in 1843.

of King's College Charter as he thought desirable. He afterwards wrote the following Letter to the Secretary of State on the subject:

Your Lordship intimated to me that the difficulties in Upper Canada respecting General Education might be compromised by leaving King's College for the Members of the Episcopal Church, and endowing another College, (on a more extensive scale), for the country generally. . . . You expressed a wish that an unworthy jealousy would not make us, the Petitioners, object to the existence of King's College, that is, as an Episcopal College, provided liberal provisions were made for others, etc. . . . But I assure your Lordship that many of the most powerful opposers of the Institution, in its present character, and of the system of an ecclesiastical establishment, with which it is identified, are Churchmen. . . . I then repeat it, that, constituted as the population of Upper Canada is, every independent man feels and acknowledges that it would be impolitic and unjust to confer upon any religious class such emoluments, power and literary or other advantages as would virtually constitute that denomination the established religion. . .

We therefore oppose King's College, and every approximation towards an exclusive religious or ecclesiastical establishment, not only from feelings of patriotism, but from principles of loyalty. . . . I unite with my countrymen in resisting every encroachment upon our equal rights and liberties, and the attempts of those who wish to . . . mingle with the fountains of knowledge the bitter waters of sectarian strife and jealousy. . . .

I am well assured that the only certain security and permanent protection for British power in North America will be to give those Colonies a Liberal Government, free and popular institutions, and full power to regulate and manage all their internal concerns, civil, literary and ecclesiastical, themselves.

In September, 1831, the Methodist Conference, in an Address to Sir John Colborne, the Lieutenant-Governor, requested him to transmit to the King a Memorial and accompanying documents of a like character, on the subject of the King's College Charter, such as the Petition adopted at the Public Meeting held in Toronto in December, 1830, and also the proceedings of the House of Assembly in regard to King's College of 1831. The Lieutenant-Governor having complied with the request of the Conference, he received from the Colonial Secretary the following reply:

1. Among the subjects which your Correspondence, public and private, with this Office, has brought under my notice, there is none more important than that of Public Education, and particularly that part of it which relates to the existing constitution of King's College, at York.

2. There can be no doubt that the Institution was established with a view of giving to the Province of Upper Canada the benefit of complete instruction in all the higher branches of knowledge, and of connecting in the minds of the youth of the Province those associations which belong to the seat of early Education with their future progress in life; and it is greatly to be regretted that anything in the Constitution of the (College) establishment should have tended to counteract, if not to defeat, this laudable design, and practically to deprive the Province of the advantage which was anticipated from its adoption. It cannot, however, be denied that the exclusive and restrictive character given to King's College has had this effect, and a plan which was intended to bring together and to harmonize in the pursuit of the common object of useful knowledge all classes of His Majesty's subjects has had the opposite effect of causing uneasiness, complaint and dissension. It is obvious, in this state of things, too notorious to require detailed proof, that it is the duty of His Majesty's Government to consider what course of policy is most likely to remedy the evil, and to insure to the Province a real enjoyment of the advantages intended to be conferred on it. Had the recommendations of the Canada Committee of the House of Commons upon the subject been successfully

followed up at the time they were submitted by you to the Provincial Legislature, under the instructions given to you by my predecessor, and had the restrictive clauses of the Charter been then removed, there is every reason to presume that such a course would, at once, have proved satisfactory and effective. Even now, that measure appears to afford the most easy and simple means of meeting the difficulty of the case; and, without entering into a discussion of the probable causes of the delay in carrying the recommendations of the Committee into effect, some additional facility for now adopting them may be found in the circumstance that, whilst no positive steps have been taken for giving to King's College any practical existence, the new College which you have established has been forwarded with considerable activity, and is now open for the instruction of youth. It may, therefore, be assumed that experience has demonstrated that, under the peculiar circumstances of Upper Canada, a College with restrictive tests is altogether inoperative for any useful purposes; and that all that is wanted is such a system of regulations to be established by a law of the Province for the management of the Institution of Upper Canada College as may give to it the requisite extension and development without subjecting it to any qualifications calculated to render it unpopular in the eyes of those various classes of the community for whose benefit, as well as for that of the Church of England, it is established.

3. I am confirmed in this latter observation by referring to a Resolution of the House of Assembly of 2nd March, 1829, in which the following opinion is pronounced upon the advantage likely to result from the establishment of the Upper Canada College:

Resolved, that this House trusts that no hope for modifications of the present Charter will suspend the exertions of His Excellency to put into operation "Colborne College," and by the observance of those liberal principles which His Excellency has already been pleased to patronize, and recommend to open, with as little delay as possible, opportunities of Education no way inferior to those contemplated by the proposed University.

4. Under these circumstances, I am to convey through you to the Members of the Corporation of King's College, at the earnest recommendation and advice of His Majesty's Government, that they do forthwith surrender to His Majesty the Charter of King's College of Upper Canada, with any lands that may have been granted them. I persuade myself that the counsels which are thus given to that body, in the spirit of the most perfect respect for all the individuals of whom it is composed, will not be disregarded; and it is on this assumption that I proceed to notice the ulterior measures which, upon such a surrender, it will be convenient to adopt. It can scarcely be necessary to say that no part of the Endowment of King's College would ever be diverted from the great object of the Education of youth. It must be regarded as a fund sacredly and permanently appropriated to that object. I presume that the general concurrence of all classes of society may be anticipated in favour of a new College upon a more enlarged basis.

5. As it is the intention of His Majesty to manifest his desire that the internal concerns of the Province should, as far as possible, be regulated by its own Legislature, I abstain from instructing you, with any particularity, on the subject of the general regulations which it may be expedient to apply to the Government of the new College. They will, doubtless, be well considered by the Legislature, and adopted in a spirit of justice, mutual harmony and good will. But there is one object to which I must direct you attention, and which you will not fail specially to recommend to the consideration of the Legislature, I mean the permanent establishment in the College, upon a secure footing, of a Divinity Professor of the Church of England. This is a matter of great importance to those of His Majesty's subjects in Upper Canada who belong to the Church of England; and His Majesty, as Head of that Church, can not be insensible to the duty which belongs to him of protecting it in all parts of his Dominions.

6. It is not from any desire to give an undue preponderance to the Colonial Members of that Church, either as regards the College in particular or the concerns of the Province generally, that His Majesty has this object at heart; but, when His Majesty

cheerfully recommends the surrender of a Charter, which the Crown was lawfully and constitutionally entitled to grant, on account of the dissatisfaction which its exclusive character has created, he feels an entire confidence that his faithful subjects, the Members of the two Houses of the Legislature of Upper Canada, will see nothing in his anxiety for the specific object to which I refer, but a proof that, whilst he is most desirous of remedying all real grievances, and removing all just grounds of discontent, he is not forgetful of those interests to which he is peculiarly bound to attend, and which His Majesty is sure can be attended to in this instance without prejudice of any kind to any other of his subjects.

7. I shall await, with much solicitude, your report of the result of the communication which I have now made to you. I am well aware of the jealousies, not to say animosities, which have been engendered in the Province by the agitation of this question; and it is scarcely to be expected that those feelings can, all at once, subside with the cause which gave them birth, nor can I conceal from myself that there may be prejudices and habits of thinking which may not be easily reconciled to the adoption of the new system, but it cannot be to the interest of any class of Christians to be an object of jealousy, perhaps of dislike, to those who, differing upon certain points of doctrine and discipline, find themselves debarred, by the effect of that difference, from an equal share in advantages universally desired, because universally beneficial.

8. It will be your special duty to use every exertion to impress upon all classes the incalculable importance of looking at all questions of this description with moderation and forbearance. The members of the Church of England should remember the peculiar situation in which they stand, in the midst of a population of whom so large a proportion differs from them in religious opinions; how much that situation exposes them to the chance of painful collision with large masses of their fellow Subjects; and how much the extension of their own Church depends upon the absence of all grounds for such collision.

9. Those who, on the other hand, differ from them, ought not to forget the causes which drew to the Church of England the marked countenance of the British Parliament, when, on the first establishment of a Legislative Assembly in Canada, many ancient and laudable associations of feeling and long attachment to the Established Church, whose rights and privileges centuries of legal and constitutional possession had consolidated, created a natural predilection in the English Parliament for the National Church, even in the more remote Possessions of the Crown; and, if difference of circumstances in Upper Canada has prevented such sentiments from taking extensive root there, every religious man,—be his mode of faith and his views of Church discipline what they may,—must feel that the interests of Religion, and its concomitant morals, cannot prosper among heart burnings and jealousies. If, therefore, it be fitting to call upon the Church to forego the exclusive advantages which the present Charter confers upon it, it is no less incumbent upon all other classes of Christians to receive the boon now tendered them in that conciliatory spirit by which alone His Majesty's Subjects can be united, by those common ties of mutual attachment which constitute the strength and mature the prosperity of a nation.

DOWNING STREET, 2nd November, 1831.   GODERICH.

This Despatch having been laid before the King's College Council, that Council, in an elaborate and comprehensive reply, stated, that, while modification in the Charter might be considered reasonable, it was not prepared to surrender so valuable a trust as the Charter graciously granted to them years ago by His Majesty the King.

In 1832, the question of the modification of the Charter was brought up in the Legislature, and a "Revised Charter Bill" was submitted to the House of Assembly by a Select Committee of that Body. It provided that the Lieutenant-Governor should not be the Chancellor of King's College, but that the Chancellor should be elected by Convocation; that the Judges of the Superior Courts should be Visitors of the College, instead of the Lieutenant-Governor, and that the President of the University should not be an Ecclesiastic, and that Upper Canada College should be an appendage of the University.

In 1832 the payment of the Imperial Grant of £1,000 Sterling per annum to the University of King's College was suspended by order of the Colonial Secretary until the Canadian Legislature should pass an Act amending the Charter of the University.

In January, 1833, the House of Assembly again resumed consideration of the "King's College Revision Bill," but the "Committee of the Whole House" to which it was referred adjourned for want of a quorum. The House did not meet again during the session, so that the Bill failed to be again considered or to pass.

In March, 1835, the question of the amendment of King's College Charter again occupied the attention of the Legislature, and it was passed by the House of Assembly on the 2nd of April of that year, but was rejected by Legislative Council.

The reasons given by the Legislative Council for dropping, and thus practically rejecting, the Bill modifying the Charter of King's College, passed by the House of Assembly on the 2nd of April, 1835, and sent up to the Council on the same day, are contained in the Report of a Select Committee of the Council, dated the 18th of April, 1835, and are as follows:

A careful examination of the Bill will show how far its provisions are " in conformity with His Majesty's gracious instructions," as the Address (of the House of Assembly to the King) asserts, and how far also they are consistent with the opinions formerly expressed by the House of Assembly.

If there is, in any Country, a University resting upon principles similar to those which this Bill would establish, it is not known to this Committee; and everyone can decide for himself the speculative question how far it would tend to promote the interests of Science, to advance Religion, Morality and Social Order, and to maintain Discipline within the University, and how far it would be likely to add to the harmony and good understanding between the Government and the Legislature, to have a University of which the Principal Officers should be appointed and removed by votes of Legislative Assemblies, and of which the interests and affairs must, in consequence, become mixed up with party politics and dissensions:—a University, of which the Directors are to choose not only the President, but the Visitor, that is the Superior, by whom they are to be themselves controlled, and in which, above all, as it is expressly declared: "Religion shall not be taught according to the Creed, or Faith, of any Christian Church."

The Lieutenant-Governor having, on the 6th of May, 1835, sent to the Colonial Secretary a copy of this King's College Charter Amendment Bill, as passed by the House of Assembly, the Secretary replied, under date of the 17th of June, 1835, in the following Despatch:

I have received your Despatch, dated the 6th May last, enclosing the copy of a Bill for amending the Charter of King's College, Upper Canada, which was passed by the House of Assembly and rejected by the Legislative Council in their last Session. You express your persuasion that no law for the amendment of the College Charter will be enacted by the Provincial Legislature; but state that you "entertain no doubt that the existing Charter may be so modified by the interposition of His Majesty's Government, as to leave, in essential points, no just grounds for dissatisfaction on the part of either House." You state that you have informed the Legislative Council and House of Assembly that you would strongly recommend to His Majesty's Government to sanction the opening of King's College, and express the hope that the course which you have suggested may be adopted.

As I find it impossible to act upon the recommendation which you have thus tendered to His Majesty's Ministers, I think I shall best discharge my duty by announcing to you that decision, without delay or hesitation.

I am not aware what may be the grounds on which you anticipate the acquiescence of the House of Assembly in such an amended Charter as you have proposed; on the other hand, the reasons for apprehending their strenuous resistance are obvious, and to me, at least, appear conclusive.

First: Your plan departs in every one essential particular from that which the House of Assembly, in their last Session, sanctioned by their votes. It is not likely they would be satisfied to have their judgment overruled by the direct interposition of the Royal authority.

Secondly: The Earl of Ripon, (lately Lord Goderich), referred the matter to the discretion of the Provincial Legislature. They would scarcely otherwise than be displeased with the retraction of His Lordship's order.

Thirdly: The decision of such a question by His Majesty's advisers in this Kingdom would be condemned with plausibility, and not indeed without justice, as a needless interference in the internal affairs of the Province.

Finally: The supposed amendments, even if they had not been preceded by any controversy, or debate, on the subject, could hardly fail to give umbrage to the House of Assembly. Without, of course, claiming a very intimate acquaintance with the state of public opinion in Upper Canada, but chiefly adverting to the accounts which have reached me through the public journals, of the proceedings of the Assembly in their last Session, (and, except from those journals, I am without the means of forming such a judgment), I should think it impossible that the scheme which you have proposed could ever be carried into execution. It is contrary to the whole tenor of the recent Resolutions of the Representatives of the people (of Upper Canada) to suppose that they would acquiesce in giving to the Church of England, permanently, so many as five members in the governing body of the College, of which, according to your plan, the entire number would only be seven; especially when the Lieutenant-Governor of the Province is to occupy one of the two remaining seats, and Archdeacon Strachan is, for the present at least, to fill the seventh. The magnitude of this trust is enhanced by the consideration that it is proposed to place under the control of the Council the management of all the revenue and expenditure of the College, and the establishment of all rules for granting Degrees of Divinity, while to His Majesty is confided the making of all such rules as are to regulate the education of the pupils. I cannot hesitate to express my opinion that this plan claims for the Established Church of England privileges which those who best understand and most deeply prize her real interests would not think it prudent to assert for her in any British Province on the North American Continent.

It is with the most lively regret that I have heard of the dissensions on this subject, between the Legislative Council and the House of Assembly. I would respectfully and earnestly impress upon the Members of both those Bodies the expediency of endeavouring, by mutual concessions, to meet on some common ground. Especially would I beg the Legislative Councils to remember that, if there be any one subject on which, more than others, it is vain and dangerous to oppose the deliberate wishes of the great mass of the people, the system of national instruction to be pursued in the moral and religious education of youth is emphatically that subject. It remains for me only to acquaint you that His Majesty refers back again to the House of Assembly and Legislative Council the consideration of the subject of amending the Charter of King's College. If there should prevail between those Bodies an irreconcilable difference of opinion, and, if they should concur in addressing His Majesty to assume the decision of the controversy, His Majesty will be most happy to interpose as a mediator for the adjustment of the question, upon such principles as appear to him best adapted for promoting the general interests of all classes of his subjects in the Province, and in a manner the most consonant with the general views and feelings of the inhabitants at large. Except in compliance with such a joint application His Majesty will not think it expedient to resume the decision of a question which, by His Majesty's commands, Lord Ripon referred to the judgment of the Provincial Legislature.

DOWNING STREET, 17th June, 1835. GLENELG.

In reviewing the proceedings of the House of Assembly and of the Imperial Government in regard to King's College from 1829 to 1832, the Reverend Doctor Strachan, in an address on the subject, states that:

No further proceedings appear to have been had regarding King's College University until the Sessions of 1831 and 1832, when another Address to the King was adopted bearing date the 28th of December, 1831; praying that the Charter of King's College might be cancelled on account of its exclusiveness, and another granted, more open in its provisions. On the 4th of January, 1832, his Excellency replied:

That he has reason to believe that, either the exclusive privileges considered exceptionable in the Charter of King's College have been cancelled, or that such arrangements have been decided upon by His Majesty's Government as will render further application to this subject unnecessary; but that a Charter solemnly given cannot be revoked, or its surrender obtained, without much delay.

This language evidently alluded to a Despatch from Lord Goderich, (now Lord Ripon), of the 2nd November, 1831, (page 8), which was soon laid before the College Council, proposing to the Members of the Corporation to surrender the Charter granted by the Imperial Government, together with the endowment, on the assurance from the Secretary of State for the Colonies that no part of the endowment should ever be diverted from the education of youth.

In an able Report, the College Council stated their reasons for refusing compliance with this request, and that they did not think it right to concur in surrendering the Charter of King's College or its endowment. The College Council further observed, that they did not feel, or profess to feel, a sufficient assurance that, after they had consented to destroy a College founded by their Sovereign, under as unrestricted and open a Charter as ever had passed the Great Seal of England, for a similar purpose, the different branches of the Legislature would be able to concur in establishing another that would equally secure to the inhabitants of the Colony, through successive generations, the possession of a seat of learning, in which sound Religious instruction should be dispensed, and at which care should be taken to guard against those occasions of instability, dissension and confusion, the foresight of which had led, in our present state, to the making of uniformity of Religion in each University throughout the Empire an indispensable feature of its constitution. The Report proceeded to say:

If the objections entertained by the College Council against the surrender of the Charter were not insurmountable, no stronger inducement could be offered than the request which his Lordship's Despatch conveys; for the Council cannot fail to be sensible that such a request can have been dictated only by a supposed necessity for departing from established principles, in order to promote the peace and contentment of the Colony.

With the opinions, however, which the Council entertain, and with the opportunity of forming those opinions which their residence in the Colony affords them, they could never stand excused to themselves, or to others, if they should surrender the Charter, supposing it to be within their power, so long as there is an utter uncertainty as to the measures that would follow.

The moral and Religious state of more than three hundred thousand, (300,000), British subjects is at present involved in the proper disposal of these questions; and, before many years will have elapsed, more than a million, (1,000,000), will be affected by them. The Council, therefore, whatever results may be obtained by other means, could not justify to themselves the assuming of the responsibility of endangering the very existence of the Institution. They feel bound to look beyond the movements and discussions of the passing moment, and could not, even if they concurred in the views of the present expediency, consent to pull down the only foundation which at present exists in Upper Canada for the advancement of Religion and learning upon a system which has not yet been repudiated by the Government in any part of Her Majesty's dominions.

The College Council then proceeded to state that, "for the sake of peace, they were disposed to concur in some such modifications as have been since forced on the Institution by the Legislature [in 1837]; not that they considered them improvements, but because the Government seemed to give them countenance; it being their conviction that a College for the education of youth in the principles of the Christian Religion, as well as in Literature and the Sciences, is less likely to be useful, and to acquire a lasting and deserved popularity, if its Religious character is left to the discretion of individuals, and to the chance of events, and suffered to remain the subject of un-Christian intrigues and dissensions, than if it is laid broadly and firmly on its foundation by an authority that cannot, with any reason, be questioned. . . .

ADVERSE COMMENT ON THIS PROCEEDING AND REFUSAL OF THE COLLEGE COUNCIL.

In a Pamphlet published in 1844* by Mr. John Macara, on the "Origin, History and Management of the University of King's College, Toronto," he thus refers historically to the proceedings of the Lieutenant-Governor in the matter, and to the refusal of the Council of King's College to surrender the King's College Charter of 1827:

Before the opening of the next Session, Sir John Colborne applied himself with energy, in obedience to the instructions which he had received from His Majesty's Ministers, to effect a modification of the Charter. Anxious still that this should be done with the friendly co-operation of the College Council, and, aware that, without that co-operation, any attempt to liberalize the Institution would be defeated in the Legislative Council, he renewed his urgent entreaties to have the Charter surrendered. His efforts, however, having proved unavailing, he was at length compelled to suspend the operations of the Charter,† and to direct his energies to such ameliorations in the defective system of Education, which then prevailed in the Province, as would best remedy the evils which, in his opinion, the obstinate conduct of the College Council might inflict upon the Country, etcetera.

Mr. Macara then proceeds to comment on the further proceedings of the College Council in regard to King's College, and of the Reverend Doctor Strachan in particular. In the light of to-day, and of the explanations which were given, in regard to these proceedings, such comments were scarcely just, and the narrative of these proceedings themselves, as detailed by Mr. Macara, was too highly coloured by him.

In transmitting a copy of this refusal of the Council of King's College to surrender the Charter of the University, Sir John Colborne wrote a Despatch to Lord Goderich, the Colonial Secretary, dated the 2nd of April, 1832. In it he suggested the expediency of the issue of a new Charter by the Imperial Government,

---

* In the First Volume of the Documentary History, page 254, I have already quoted from this Pamphlet— the date of which is incorrectly printed there as 1854, instead of 1844. It is of too partisan a character to be entirely trustworthy; but its historical facts are of course correct.

† In reference to this suspension of the Charter of King's College, Sir George Murray, in 1831, then Colonial Secretary, said: "While I was in office, I suspended the operations of the Charter, having it in contemplation to abolish entirely the distinction [in the Charter on the score of Religion]; and, had I remained in office, I should certainly have done so." (Macara's Pamphlet on the Origin, etcetera, of King's College, etcetera, page 41.)

and the subsequent cancellation of the former Charter of 1827 by the Provincial Legislature, or its formal surrender by the College Council, as then no longer operative.

It is evident from the Despatch of Lord Goderich to Sir John Colborne, dated the 8th of November, 1832, (page 112 of the Second Volume of the Documentary History), that the Colonial Secretary declined to act upon this suggestion of Sir John Colborne; for, in the Despatch of the date mentioned, (8th November, 1832), he said: " Every possible measure has been taken to refer to their [the Canadian people's] Representatives the decision of the question, in what form, and upon what principles the College should be founded."

In 1835, upon the failure of the Legislative Council to concur in the Charter of King's College, as amended by the House of Assembly, Sir John Colborne practically made the same suggestion to the successor of Lord Goderich in the Colonial Office, (Lord Glenelg), and said:

I am persuaded that no law for the amendment of the College Charter will be enacted by the Provincial Legislature . . . and I entertain no doubt that the existing Charter may be so modified by the interposition of His Majesty's Government as to leave in essential points no just grounds for dissatisfaction on the part of either House.

The reply of Lord Glenelg on these points was equally conclusive with that of Lord Goderich, his predecessor, for, in his Despatch of the 17th of June, 1835, he said:

As I find it impossible to act upon the recommendation which you have thus tendered to His Majesty's Minister, I think I shall best discharge my duty by announcing to you that decision without delay or hesitation.

I am not aware what may be the grounds on which you anticipate the acquiescence of the House of Assembly in such an amended Charter as you have proposed; on the other hand, the reasons for apprehending their strenuous resistance are obvious, and to me, at least, appear conclusive.

First: Your plan departs in every one essential particular from that which the House of Assembly, in their last session, sanctioned by their votes. It is not likely they would be satisfied to have their judgment overruled by the direct interposition of the Royal authority.

Secondly: The Earl of Ripon, (lately Lord Goderich,) referred the matter to the discretion of the Provincial Legislature. They would scarcely otherwise than be displeased with the retraction of His Lordship's Order.

Thirdly: The decision of such a question by His Majesty's advisers in this Kingdom would be condemned with plausibility, and not indeed without justice, as a needless interference in the internal affairs of the Province.

From this time, until 1837, the practically adverse decision of the Imperial Government to deal with the King's College Charter in any way led to a good deal of local dissension on the subject, and finally to a movement in the House of Assembly to modify the terms of the Charter, provided it could be shown that a Colonial Legislature was competent to alter the terms of an Imperial Charter. This having been declared by a number of legal gentlemen, who were consulted, to be quite within the province of a Colonial House of Assembly, a Bill was introduced into that House in 1837 to so modify the Charter, as practically suggested by the Colonial Minister, so as to make it acceptable to the people of Upper Canada.

Prompted by their sagacious Leader, and the Chief Officer of the College Council—the Reverend Doctor Strachan—the Council wisely, yet unwillingly, suggested such modifications in the Charter as would take away its alleged objectionable character of denominational exclusiveness, and thus it passed both Houses and became the law of the land in 1837.

"THE CHARTER OF THE UNIVERSITY OF KING'S COLLEGE, UPPER CANADA; AS AMENDED."

Such is the title of an old printed Pamphlet, which I have in my possession. It is without date, but, from internal evidence of its style, it must have been prepared about the year 1835. It was printed in Toronto, "by R. Stanton, Printer to the King's Most Excellent Majesty." It suggests the incorporation of Upper Canada College with the University, as an appendage to it. This was suggested in a Report of the House of Assembly in 1832. It declares that the Judges of the Court of King's Bench shall be Visitors; Sir John Colborne, Chancellor; the Reverend Doctor Strachan, first President; the Principal of Upper Canada College, and the Speaker of the House of Assembly, to be Members of the College Council, and the Reverend Doctor Joseph Harris, to be the first Principal of Upper Canada College. It bears internal evidence of being the modified Charter, proposed to the Colonial Secretary by Sir John Colborne, in his Despatch of the 6th of May, 1835.

Owing to many causes, and chiefly want of sufficient funds with which to erect the proposed building for King's College, nothing was done in that direction until 1842, when the Reverend Doctor Strachan addressed a Letter to Sir Charles Bagot, the Governor-General, on the subject. In reply he was requested to submit to the King's College Council the necessary Statutes providing for the expenditure of a sum not exceeding Twenty Thousand Pounds, (£20,000), of the Funds of the College in the erection of a suitable Building for it and that, while this was being done, the temporary occupation of the Parliament Building be respectfully solicited from His Excellency the Governor-General.

Although the Royal Charter was amended by the Canadian Legislature in 1837, the Imperial grant of £1,000 sterling per annum, which was made to the College in 1827 and suspended in 1832, until the Charter was amended, was not renewed as expected. The Bursar of King's College was directed to address a Letter to the Governor-General, Lord Sydenham, on the subject, which he did in 1840. No action having been taken in response to this Letter, another was addressed by the Council to the Provincial Secretary in 1842, urging the restoration of the grant, as the reasons for its suspension no longer existed; but even then the grant was not restored. Years afterwards some arrangement was made in regard to it.

The 23rd of April, 1842, was indeed a memorable day in the history of King's College University. Elaborate preparations were made by the Council of that College to make St. George's Day, 1842, a red letter day, and one long to be remembered in the annals of King's College. It certainly was a gala day in Toronto. The procession, which formed in the grounds of Upper Canada College, embraced a full representation of all the National and other Societies, Public Bodies, and Public Functionaries, as well as the Educational Institutions of the city.

At one o'clock His Excellency, Sir Charles Bagot, M.A., of Oxford University, the Chancellor, arrived at the gate of the College Avenue in an open carriage and four, escorted by a party of the First Incorporated Dragoons. Here he was received by the Right Reverend Doctor Strachan, President of the University, the Principal and Masters of Upper Canada College, and the Esquire Bedel, William Cayley, M.A., of Christ Church, Oxford, and conducted to a Chair of State at the front door of the College, which was placed on a slightly raised platform, over which was suspended a canopy decorated with evergreen boughs.

The following Address was then read by the Reverend Principal McCaul, of Upper Canada College, His Excellency standing, and attended by his Chief and Private Secretaries—Thomas W. C. Murdoch, Esq., and Captain Henry Bagot, R.N.:

Rejoicing in the honour which Your Excellency has conferred upon this City, we feel deeply grateful that you have condescended to visit this Institution.

We commend this College to your favour, not doubting that you will gladly undertake the office of Patron, and that looking benignantly upon these youthful votaries of religion and learning, you will foster their abilities and encourage their studies. We would indulge the hope that he,—by whose prompt and energetic action the Province of Canada, earnestly desiring so great a boon, has been blessed with the princely gift of King's College,—will also deign to be our Macænas.

We congratulate the Province, we congratulate yourself, O most Excellent Chancellor, upon this day, the birthday of the University, a day which the present age will treasure up in grateful and retentive memory and which will also be remembered by—

"Our children's sons, and each successive race."

May Your Excellency, through the favour of Almighty God, long continue to afford to this Province the enjoyments of the arts, as well as the blessings of peace, and as on this day so may it ever be Your Excellency's characteristic, "to wear as the chaplet on your brow the classic ivy twined round the olive, happy emblem of peace."

His Excellency's reply was as follows:

It is with no ordinary feelings of pleasure that I receive your cordial congratulations. Be assured that your College shall receive my countenance and support, and that I will gladly extend protection and fostering care to the pupils of the institution. I can indeed undertake no duty more excellent or more congenial to my feelings than to cherish those studies to which you so zealously devote yourselves, for they inculcate the rendering of allegiance to the Queen, attachment to the Father-land, and profound reverence to God. This day will forever be imprinted on my memory; and I hope that it will ever be regarded by the inhabitants of Canada, whilst enjoying the blessings of the University of Toronto as a most auspicious and memorable anniversary.

It is my earnest prayer to Almighty God that this Province, which at once strengthens and adorns the British Empire, may long be blessed with Peace, that it may flourish alike in wealth, learning and religion.

Immediately on the termination of these proceedings the procession moved on to the Site of the proposed University in the Queen's Park, where the Corner Stone of the King's College was duly laid by Sir Charles Bagot, the Governor-General. Before doing so, the Right Reverend Doctor Strachan, President of the College, presented him with an Address, in which he stated that:

The University of King's College is designed to be strictly Collegiate, both in discipline and character, as the circumstances of this new country will admit: and, for this purpose, it will keep in view in its progress the glorious models, furnished by the Parent State, to which Science, justly so-called, and Christian truth are so much indebted; and it will raise, on a like basis, such a superstructure as shall fully meet the wants and circumstances of this great Colony, as well as the particular destination of each of the numerous students by whom it will be attended.

At the formal opening of the College on the 8th of June, 1843, inaugural addresses were delivered by the Right Reverend Doctor Strachan, the President, the Reverend John McCaul, Vice-President, and the Honourable Chief Justice J. B. Robinson, and Mr. Justice C. A. Hagerman, Visitors.

In October, 1843, the Honourable Robert Baldwin, seconded by the Honourable Francis Hincks, introduced into the House of Assembly a Bill " to amend

KING'S COLLEGE, QUEEN'S PARK, TORONTO.

the Acts relating to King's College, and to provide for the incorporation with it of Victoria, Queen's and Regiopolis Colleges with it." To this Bill, Doctor Strachan took exception and presented a Petition against it in November of that year, which he stated was: " Subversive of the sacred rights of conscience . . . and altogether repugnant to the British Constitution and to Civil and Religious liberty."

The introduction of the Baldwin University Bill marked a new era in educational affairs in Upper Canada. The Bill did not pass, but it embodied the principle that provincially endowed Institutions must be free from Denominational control.

In February, 1845, the Honourable W. H. Draper introduced a Bill into the House of Assembly " for erecting a University by the name and style of the University of Upper Canada." He also introduced another Bill which was intended to enlarge and popularize King's College, and a third Bill to vest the Imperial Grant of Land of 1797 in the proposed University of Upper Canada.

These Bills were opposed by Bishop Strachan, and he presented a Petition against them to the House of Assembly as contemplating "the transfer to a new University of the privileges granted to this (King's) College by the Royal Charter of 1827."

The Draper University Bills having failed to receive the concurrence of the Legislature, the Honourable Attorney-General Draper in 1849 introduced an elaborate Bill into the House of Assembly to repeal all former University Acts, and to constitute the University of Toronto. This Bill was strongly opposed by the Honourable Attorney-General Baldwin, who, in 1849, introduced an elaborate Bill into the House of Assembly, designed to repeal all former University Acts, and to constitute in their place the University of Toronto. This Bill was favourably received by the Council of King's College, and it became the law of the land on the first of January, 1850.

This Toronto University Act of the Honourable Robert Baldwin of 1849-'50, not having subsequently proved satisfactory to a number of members of the Legislature, the Honourable Henry Sherwood introduced into the House of Assembly a Bill in 1851 to amend that Act. His reasons for doing so he declared to be his objection that, by the proposed affiliation of existing Universities in different parts of the Province with that of Toronto, the Act limits the University area, and confines to one place the University privileges now possessed in common by each of these Institutions. Besides, by the very act of affiliation, each University is required to surrender some of the most valuable of its chartered rights, and the young men now being educated in these outlying Colleges are required, on graduation, to proceed to Toronto to take their earned Degree. Notwithstanding these popular objections being strongly urged in the House of Assembly, the Bill failed to pass, and was withdrawn.

On the withdrawal of Mr. Sherwood's Bill, Mr. William H. Boulton introduced a Bill on the same subject—his object, as he stated, having been to popularize the University and model it on that of the University of London, so as to make it "acceptable to all classes of Her Majesty's subjects." This Bill, however, never came to a second reading and was withdrawn.

After the change made in the management of the Institution effected by the Baldwin Act of 1849-'50, and its separation into University College and the University of Toronto, the Reverend John McCaul, LL.D., was appointed President of University College. He had taken high rank in classics in the University of Dublin and had been Professor of Classics in King's College. He gave to University College a prestige in that department of learning which it has maintained ever since.

Nothing further was done on the University question for a year. In July, 1852, therefore, the Reverend Doctor Ryerson, after consultation with the Honourable Francis Hincks, drafted a third Bill on the subject "for the Establishment of an University, and the promotion of a System of Liberal and General Education in Upper Canada." It, too, was based upon the London University Charter. From various causes the Bill was not acceptable to many Members of the House of Assembly. Finally, however, a compromise measure was agreed to by the Legislature, and it became the law of the land in April, 1853.

In regard to this Act, the Reverend Doctor William Leitch, President of Queen's University, in a statement on University Affairs, drawn up at the request of the Board of Trustees of that University, in which, while expressing approval of the Spirit and purpose of its practical provisions with a view to extend and popularize University education, yet, (as he particularly pointed out), it unjustly narrowed the application of the generous financial provisions of the Imperial Grant of 1797-'98, to one University, or College, only, and not, as the Grant specified, to the other [Colleges, or] Seminaries, of a larger and more "comprehensive nature [than Grammar Schools] for the promotion of Religious and Moral Learning and the Study of the Arts and Sciences" which might be "established in due process of time."

In justice, however, to the framers of the University Act of 1853, the Reverend Doctor Leitch points out that in this University Bill of 1853 fixed sums were allotted to the various Colleges affiliated to the Toronto University, but that, in its passage through the Legislature, objectors to the making of these Grants to the outlying Colleges had this just and equitable provision struck out and the obnoxious clause was substituted, which "completely destroyed the national character of the Measure."

REVEREND DOCTOR RYERSON.   HONOURABLE FRANCIS HINCKS.

Doctor Leitch's remarks, in regard to this University Act of 1853, were as follows:

The Act of 1853, under which the University of Toronto now exists, gives evidence of enlightened and generous purpose. It was evidently the original aim of the Bill to found a great National Institution embracing the various Collegiate Institutions of the Country. It provides for Colleges throughout various parts of the Country, but they were all to be united under one University or Superintending and Examining Board. By the Act, Victoria College, Queen's College, Trinity College, and Regiopolis College, were, as well as University College, to be affiliated to the University of Toronto, and were as much to form part of the University of Toronto as University College, with the exception of sharing the Endowment. This fact has been very much overlooked in the controversy, and it has been assumed that University College is the only College of the University of Toronto, but the others by the Act equally form part of the Institution. These Colleges have Representatives in the Senate, and, if they choose, they can take advantage of the privileges of affiliation. Academically, they form an integral part of the University: it is only financially that they are excluded. But how should such an anomaly exist, that all the various Colleges should be put on the same level in relation to the University, and that one College, videlicet, University College, should alone monopolize all the funds? There is perfect consistency in the whole of the Act except on this one point. It exhibits all the elements of a great national scheme of higher education without reference to religious differences. The Act does not, academically, draw any invidious and sectarian distinction between the various Colleges. It does not recognize the superior rights of a non-religious College over a religious one. A College whose corporation holds a negative creed in Religion is not acknowledged as having any claim superior to that of a College whose Corporation holds a positive Religious creed. Creeds are entirely ignored, and regard is had only to the work done; and the University is appointed to test that work, from whatever quarter it may come. The Act assumes that if there is a danger in beliefs, the belief in no Religious doctrine may be quite as dangerous as a belief in some Religious doctrine, that a godless College may be as much fraught with evil as a godly one. Hence, as far as the Colleges are related to the University, there is no sectarian partial dealing. But it is far otherwise with the provision in the Act for the support of the several Colleges affiliated to the University. The preamble fully and explicitly acknowledges the importance of having Colleges in various parts of Canada for the accommodation of the people who could not, and would not, send their sons to one College at Toronto; and in the body of the Act the various chartered Colleges are made part and parcel of the University of Toronto, quite as much as University College itself. Strange that, while all this is conceded, the financial provisions should be such as entirely to negative this grand, magnanimous, and national scheme for the University Education of the Country. How should the financial element clash so entirely with the academic as totally to neutralize the good in the latter? Why rear a magnificent fabric, and at the same time place a mine under it to destroy it as soon as it is erected? The clause which has thus acted ruinously upon the whole academic structure is to the effect that one of the affiliated Colleges, videlicet, University College, should have, in the first place, all its wants supplied, and that, if there should be a surplus, it was to be applied to aid the cause of higher education in other Institutions. It is easy to conceive how such a clause as this should operate. It developed enormously, not the teaching, but the spending power of the Institution. The grand problem was, with a mere handful of Students, to spend the enormous revenue without leaving a Surplus. To accomplish this it was necessary to resort to acts of extravagant and wasteful expenditure which have no parallel in older and richer Countries.

In his criticism of the same Act of 1853, the Reverend Doctor Ryerson stated:

The Legislature in passing the Provincial University Act of 1853 clearly proposed and avowed a threefold object. First, the creation of a University for examining candidates and conferring degrees in the Faculties of Arts, Law, and Medicine. Secondly, the establishment of an elevated Curriculum of University Education, conformable to that of the London University in England. Thirdly, the association with the Provincial University of the several Colleges already established, and which might be established, in Upper Canada, the same as various Colleges of different denominations in Great Britain and Ireland are affiliated to the London University—placed as they are upon any equal footing in regard to any aid from the State, and on equal footing in regard to the composition of the Senate, and the Appointment of Examiners.

Doctor Ryerson proceeds:

The result of this wide legislation was a great disappointment to the friends of University Education.

The curriculum of the University studies, instead of being elevated and conformed to that of the London University, has been revised and changed three times since 1853, and reduced by options and otherwise below what it was formerly, and below what it is in the British Universities, and below what it is in the best Colleges in the United States. The effect of this narrow and anti-liberal course is, to build up one College at the expense of all others, and to reduce the standard of a University Degree in both Arts and Medicine below what it was before the passing of the University Act in 1853.

In the draft copy of the University Bill of 1853, as I have shown, the objectors to Parliamentary grants to the outlying Colleges set aside and entirely ignored the comprehensive terms of the Royal Grant of 1797-'98, to promote, (as it was bound to do, on accepting the grant), the establishment of other Seminaries, (in addition to its single College, or University), "of an equally large and comprehensive nature," by making Grants out of the original Fund to Colleges in various parts of the Province. This it did in the shape of Parliamentary Grants to Colleges for many years.*

The Act of 1853, while it prohibited the making of these Grants in the future, provided that any Surplus remaining over, after paying the expenses of the University and University College, should, by the Legislature, be devoted to the promotion of Collegiate Education in Upper Canada.

Soon after this Act was passed, it became apparent to the friends of the outlying Colleges that the Senate of the University had so largely increased the expenditure that apparently no Surplus would be available for distribution by the Legislature. The consequence was that the Authorities of both Victoria and Queen's Colleges made such strong representations to the Legislature on the subject that the House of Assembly, in 1860, appointed a Select Committee to inquire into the matter. This Committee having heard a large amount of evidence on the subject was nevertheless unable to come to any conclusion, and failed, therefore, to make any report to the House on the subject. The result of this failure to settle the University Question was that, in 1861, the Government appointed a Visitorial Commission of three Members to take evidence on the subject and endeavour to settle it,—one from the University of Toronto, and one from each of the Universities of Victoria and Queen's College. That Commission, having made an exhaustive inquiry into the various details of the University Question, submitted to the Government an elaborate Report, in which they made a number of practical suggestions.

This Report was strongly opposed by a number of the graduates of the Toronto University, who held a public meeting in Toronto to give expression to their dissent to the financial recommendations of the Commissioners, and maintained that the whole of the University endowment should be preserved intact and applied solely to the maintenance of the University of Toronto and its adjunct, University College.

The Report also led to a good deal of discussion in the Public Press and in the annual meetings of the various Church Synods, Conferences and other gatherings, chiefly in favour of the recommendations in the Report. In addition an elaborate Report on the subject was drawn up, as the result of a meeting held by Representatives of these Churches. The Reverend Doctor Leitch also drew up in 1863 an extended Report on the "Plan of University Reform," which had been adopted by the Senate of the University of Toronto.

Historical Address, Relating to the University of Toronto, by the Reverend Doctor McCaul.

The distribution of Prizes at the Convocation held on the 8th of June, 1860, having been completed, Doctor McCaul said:

In order to remove a misapprehension which seems to prevail very generally I wish to explain the distinction between the two Institutions, whose home is within these walls,—the University of Toronto, and University College, Toronto.

It was in the year 1827, that His Majesty George IV. chartered the Institution called "King's College," at Toronto, then called York. For ten years no step was taken

---

* In 1860 the Reverend Doctor Ryerson prepared the draft of a tentative University Bill for the consideration of the colleges concerned, but he did not propose it for adoption by the Government at the time.

to carry the Royal Patent into effect. In the year 1837 an Act of our Legislature was passed amending the Royal Charter, and it is probable that the Institution would have been brought into operation, had it not been for the troubles caused by the Rebellion in the Winter of that year, which entirely prevented anything of that sort being done. It was not until the year 1843,—sixteen years after the Charter had been granted,—that the Institution, then called King's College, was brought into operation; and June the 8th is the honoured anniversary of the opening of that Institution. Six years afterwards,—in 1849,—an Act of the Legislature was passed abolishing the name of King's College, and also abolishing the Faculty of Divinity; and the Institution then received the designation of the University of Toronto. Under that Statute the Institution was conducted for four years. In the year 1853 another Statute of the Provincial Parliament was passed; and the Institution originally called King's College (but then called the University of Toronto) was separated into two Establishments,—one the University of Toronto, and the other called University College, Toronto, whose anniversary we are now engaged in celebrating. The Statute of 1853 also provided for the abolition of the Faculties of Law and Medicine,—the Faculty of Divinity having been abolished in 1849. In this Institution then,—University College,—there is but the one Faculty, of Arts, with the Departments of Civil Engineering and Agriculture. There are no Students in Law and none in Medicine, recognized as such; although Gentlemen pursuing these Studies attend such Classes as may suit their purposes. By all of these Statutes making these changes, the Endowments, which had been graciously given us from the Grant by George IV. of 1797, remained untouched, and, up to the present day, remain untouched; but it is no longer under control of any of the academic Bodies, but of a Bursar, appointed under the Great Seal of the Province, by the Governor of the Province, the property being vested in the Crown as Trustee.

The office of the University of Toronto, as constituted by the University Act of 1853, is simply to prescribe subjects for Degrees, to appoint Examiners, to conduct Examinations, and to confer Degrees, Scholarships, and Certificates of Honour on those entitled to them. But there is no instruction or teaching of any kind given in the University of Toronto. All such instruction or teaching is given in University College.

Having made these preliminary remarks, I would turn to the Statistics, which will give the best idea of the condition of University College. As I have said, the Institution, in its present form, was established in 1853. I cannot give the Statistics of 1853, because that was a year of transition, and nothing could be inferred from them. In 1854 we had but twenty-eight matriculated Students in attendance. I omit reference to occasional Students,—I mean those who have attended particular classes without going through the whole Course as Matriculated Students,—because it may be justly said that their numbers would furnish no test of the position of such an Establishment as this. It is exceedingly desirable that they should attend. We rejoice to see them attend in the number they do; but I omit them on this occasion so that I may put the Statistics in the simplest and fairest form. The numbers of the Matriculated Students, then, have been:

In 1854............ 28   In 1856............ 37   In 1858............ 63
In 1855............ 35   In 1857............ 56   In 1859............ 80

And at the commencement of the present academic year, 1860, the Students who have matriculated reach the number of 110. In 1854, counting all Students, occasional as well as matriculated, the number was 110. In the present year we have precisely the same number of Matriculated Students as we had then, counting all who came to the Classes, whether matriculated or not. I think this justifies me in saying that the course of this Institution has been prosperous, and we have gained in the confidence of the public.

This was at once a Provincial and a Non-denominational Institution, as had been intended by the Legislature. No fewer than fifteen Religious Denominations were represented among the present 110 Matriculated Students. Of the fifteen, eight had but one Representative each. Of the other seven, the following were the numbers:

Presbyterians—
Free Church	25
United Presbyterians	16
Church of Scotland	11
	52
Church of England	30
Methodists (of all kinds)	15
Baptists (of all kinds)	3
Congregationalists	2
Eight other Denominations, 1 each	8
Total	110

As regards the prospects of the Institution, if they looked at its present condition as a guarantee of what it might yet attain to, he thought they would be justified in saying that the prospects of the Institution were very good.

In regard to the charges made against the administration of the University of Toronto before the Legislative Committee at Quebec, he would say that he had only now to deal with charges against the Institution of which he was the head. The College Council, neither collectively nor individually, were responsible for the charges brought against the University. They were not responsible, for example, for the standard which had been selected by the University, nor for the too liberal use of Options, nor for some of the Members of the Council being placed on the Senate of the University. There could not be a doubt that it was the intention of the Legislature by passing the Act of 1853, that the University should be Non-denominational and form, as it were, the highest of the series of Educational Institutions of the Country; and in this connection he must say, whatever difference might now exist between them, that the thanks of every lover of education were due to the Chief Superintendent of Education, Reverend Doctor Ryerson, to whose valuable aid and constant care we are indebted for a System of Education, —the establishment of which did honour to the Country. He (Doctor McCaul) would ask the warmest advocate of a change in the University to test the allegations that have been made, and if there were evils he believed they would be remedied. He would never shrink from what was called innovation, provided it accomplished good.

College and University Legislation in Ontario, 1819-1909.

Before giving a detailed account of the Provincial University, and the other Universities and Colleges of the Province, a brief summary of the different Legislative enactments made from time to time may be interesting:—

1819.—It has been already noted that the project for a College, which had engaged much attention, was abandoned at the close of last century. But in 1819 the Executive Council again took the matter into consideration, and recommended that 500,000 Acres of land be disposed of for the purpose of establishing a University. The estimate of the Council comprised £10,000 for buildings and appliances, with £4,000 per annum for salaries, scholarships and contingencies.

1820.—In 1820 it was enacted that on the establishment of a Provincial University it might be duly represented in Parliament. In March, 1827, the charter of King's College was obtained and Lord Bathurst's Despatch promised a Grant of £1,000 per annum for the College Buildings. The Governor was directed to endow King's College from the Crown Reserves.

1828-9.—In 1828-9 the Wesleyan Methodists began to move for the establishment of their Upper Canada Academy in Cobourg, which, in the year 1841, became the University of Victoria College, under the presidency of the Reverend Doctor Ryerson, and received an annual grant of £500 from the Legislature. The College opened with the Faculty of Arts; Medicine was added in 1854, Law in 1862, and Theology in 1872.

1835.—In 1835, by the will of the Right Reverend Bishop Macdonell, of Kingston, four Acres of land were devised for a proposed Roman Catholic College, which was afterwards incorporated as Regiopolis College, and was opened at Kingston in 1846.

1837.—In 1837 the Provincial Legislature, having been authorized by the Imperial Government to deal with the Charter of King's College, passed an Act amending the same and connecting Upper Canada College with the University.

1840-1.—In 1840 an Act incorporating a Presbyterian College at Kingston was passed and reserved for the Queen's pleasure, but in 1841 Her Majesty granted a Royal Charter to the Institution, as "Queen's College at Kingston." The Faculties of Theology and Arts were thereupon established; Medicine was added in 1854, and Law in 1861.

1842.—In 1842 the Foundation Stone of King's College was laid by Sir Charles Bagot, Governor, and in June, 1843, the University was formally opened under the Presidency of the Right Reverend Bishop Strachan.

1843.—In 1843 an effort was made to affiliate King's College and Queen's College, but it failed, and an agitation began under which King's College Charter was again amended by the Act of 1849, and the Toronto Institution was denuded of its Theological Faculty.

1848.—In 1848 St. Joseph's College was established at Bytown (Ottawa). It is now known as the University of Ottawa.

1849.—The University of King's College was, by the Baldwin Act, changed into the University of Toronto with University College as its adjunct. A change was made in the Senate, the Faculty of Divinity was abolished and a Caput consisting of the President, the Deans of the three Faculties and a fifth member appointed by Convocation was formed.

1851-2.—The authorities of the Church of England in this Province, having determined upon the establishment of another University on the abolition of the Faculty of Theology in King's College, obtained an Act of Incorporation in 1851 for a new College, and in 1852 a Royal Charter issued to the University of Trinity College, Toronto, and the Diocesan School of Theology, at Cobourg, which had been in existence for several years under the Venerable Archdeacon Bethune, who subsequently became the second Bishop of Toronto, was thereupon merged in it.

1853.—In 1853 the Legislature again amended the Charter of the University of Toronto (the new name of King's College), and separated the University from the College, depriving it at the same time of the Professors of Law and Medicine. By this Act the University became the examining body, also conferring degrees in Arts, Law and Medicine, and the College was constituted a teaching institution for the faculty of Arts. Convocation was abolished, and the government was vested in a Senate appointed by the Crown.

1857.—In 1857 the Methodist Episcopal Church established a Seminary at Belleville for the education of students of both sexes, which in 1866 and 1871 was incorporated as the University of Albert College (afterwards affiliated as Albert College with Victoria University).

1868.—In 1868 the annual Legislative Grants, which had been long enjoyed, were withdrawn from the following Institutions: Victoria College, $5,000, and $750 for the Medical Faculty; Queen's College, $5,000; Regiopolis, $3,000; St. Michael's College, $2,000; Trinity College, $4,000; Ottawa College, $1,400; L'Assumption College, $1,000; and $750 each for the Medical Faculties of Kingston and Toronto.

1873.—In 1873 another Act modifying the Constitution of the University of Toronto was passed.

1874.—In 1874 the Charter and Acts relating to Victoria College were repealed, and a new Act passed for the appointment of the College Board by the General Conference of the Methodist Church of Canada. By this same Act the Senate was composed of the President and the Professors of the different Faculties, with power to confer degrees in Arts, Science, Law, Divinity and Medicine. The Board of Trustees of Queen's College was made a self-perpetuating body, and the University became the University of the Presbyterian Church in Canada. Convocation was composed of Trustees, Lecturers, Tutors, Fellows, Graduates and Alumni, or Students, being Undergraduates; a Council was organized; provision made for the registration of Graduates, or Alumni, as might desire to vote for elective Members of the Council and for the Chancellor; the Principal was declared to be Vice-Chancellor, and the Board of Trustees were empowered to elect a Vice-Principal.

1878.—In 1878 the Western University of London, Ontario, was incorporated, and power given to Huron College to affiliate with it.

1879.—In 1879 provision was made by Act of Parliament that the Dean of the Faculty of Theology should be nominated by the "Board of Victoria College" and appointed by General Conference. In the election of representatives of the Alumni to the Senate all graduates of three years, and registered, were entitled to vote and declared eligible for election.

1880.—McMaster Hall was established. McMaster Hall was erected into McMaster University.

1881.—Power was given to Knox College to confer Degrees in Divinity.

1883.—In 1883 certain changes were made in the "Board of Victoria College" by the addition of six representatives of the Graduates and of the President. The Senate was also increased by the addition of the Principal and Professors from the Wesleyan Theological College, Montreal.

1884.—In 1884 Victoria University was formed by the amalgamation of Victoria College and Albert College. All powers and functions were vested in the General Conference of the Methodist Church. The title of the Board was changed to "The Board of Regents of Victoria University." The President was constituted Chancellor, and a Vice-Chancellor was to be elected by the graduates every two years. The number of representatives of the graduates was increased to eight and affiliated Institutions were allowed representatives. By an Act passed this year High School Masters were allowed two representatives on the Senate of the University of Toronto, and that University was empowered to grant the Degree of LL.D. *honoris causa*.

1887.—Provision was made for the Government of Upper Canada College.

1887.—Federation of the University of Toronto and University College with other Universities and Colleges.

1887.—The Toronto Baptist College and Woodstock College united under the name of McMaster University.

1887.—The Toronto University Property vested in the Crown. A Site provided for Upper Canada College and a Permanent Fund provided for it as an Endowment.

1888.—The foregoing Act amended in several of its Sections.

1889.—An Agreement between the University of Toronto and the City Corporation validated.

1889.—The University Federation Act of 1887 further amended in several Sections.

1890.—Cities of 100,000 inhabitants can make grants to the University of Toronto.

1890.—Aid was provided by the Legislature to erect New University Buildings after the Fire of 1889.

1890.—Institutions of Learning, not supported in whole, or in part, by a Legislative Grant, are liable to Taxation.

1891.—The University Federation Act of 1887 amended in several of its sections.

1892.—The University Federation Act of 1887 amended in several of its sections.

1892.—The Act of 1887 in regard to the University of Toronto Property amended in several of its sections.

1892.—The University of Toronto authorized to deal with certain Upper Canada College Lands.

1892.—The Western University Incorporation Act of 1878 amended.

1894.—Part of the Property of the University of Toronto in the Queen's Park granted for a Site of Legislative and Department Buildings.

1894.—The Property and Effects of Upper Canada College vested in the Crown, and the College placed under the management of Trustees.

1895.—University of Toronto to deal with certain Upper Canada College claims.

1897.—Senate of the Toronto University to appoint members of the Educational Council of the Education Department.

1901.—Government and Management of the University of Toronto.

1901.—Sale of the Upper Canada College Block on King Street with the consent of the University of Toronto.

1902.—The University of Toronto Act of 1901 amended in several of its sections.

1903.—Wild Lands set apart for the use of the University of Toronto.

1904.—The Act of the University of Toronto of 1901 amended by several additions.

1904.—Public Educational Institutions exempt from Taxation.

1905.—Students' University Residence exempt from Taxation.

1905.—University Wild Land's Grant Act amended.

1905.—Toronto University authorized to assist in reorganizing the Toronto General Hospital.

1906.—An Act relating to the University of Toronto and University College.

1907.—An Act to amend the University of Toronto Act and University College.

1909.—An Act to amend the University Act of 1906.

Very few changes occurred after this date.

As to the growth and extension of University Education, Mr. James H. Coyne, M.A., of St. Thomas, writes as follows:

The century is remarkable for the growth of Universities. Even when Queen Victoria ascended the Throne there was not a University in all British North America in actual operation except McGill in Montreal. The commencement of the University of Toronto, under its former name of King's College, when its first students were enrolled, took place on the 8th day of June, 1843, six years after the Queen's accession. Victoria College obtained authority to confer Degrees in 1841. In the same year Queen's obtained its Charter from the Imperial Government. The other Universities are of later date: Trinity, Western, McMaster, Regiopolis and Ottawa, in Ontario (see further on). The universal instinct for consolidation and expansion has affected our great educational Institutions. The University of Toronto has gathered about it a number of affiliated Colleges, and federated with Victoria University and Trinity. The provincial educational system of Ontario includes practically in one organism Kindergartens and Public Schools, Collegiate Institutes, Classical Preparatory Colleges and Schools and the Universities.

The bequests in our Province of Messieurs William Gooderham and Hart A. Massey to Victoria; the gifts to the University of Toronto by Messieurs E. Blake and W. Mulock, J. Macdonald and others, and the endowments of Trinity, Queen's and McMaster Universities, and Knox, Wycliffe, and various Ladies Colleges, make a good beginning of similar generous support of Educational Institutions in our Dominion.

Dates of the Establishment of Colleges of Various Kinds in Ontario.

(Note.—The dates of the establishment of the Universities of Ontario will be found on page 1).

Provincial	Upper Canada College	1828
Presbyterian	Knox College	1845
Roman Catholic	St. Michael's College	1852
Roman Catholic	Assumption College	1856
Methodist	Albert College	1857
Baptist	Woodstock College	1857
Incorporated	Veterinary College	1862
Church of England	Huron College	1863
Incorporated	Royal College of Physicians and Surgeons	1866
Incorporated	College of Pharmacy	1868
Incorporated	Royal College of Dentistry	1868
Provincial	Agricultural College	1874
Incorporated	College of Physicians and Surgeons for Ontario	1874
Church of England	Wycliffe College	1877
Baptist	McMaster Hall, afterwards McMaster University	1880

Ladies Colleges in Ontario.

Methodist	Alexandra College, Belleville	1857
Methodist	Wesleyan Ladies College, Hamilton	1860
Church of England	Bishop Strachan School, Toronto	1867
Church of England	Helmuth Ladies College, London	1869
Presbyterian	Ottawa Ladies College	1872
Methodist	Ontario Ladies College, Whitby	1874
Presbyterian	Brantford Ladies College	1874
Non-denominational	Demill Ladies College, St. Catharines	1876
Methodist	Alma Ladies College, St. Thomas	1877

THE UNIVERSITY OF TORONTO.

This University was originally established under the Royal Charter obtained by the Reverend Doctor Strachan as King's College in 1827. The proceeds of the Endowment were for many years so small that the University existed only on paper until 1842-43.

In April, 1842, the Corner Stone of the new Institution was laid by Governor-General Sir Charles Bagot, M.A., (of Christ's Church, Oxford). In June, 1843, it was opened under the style and title of the "University of King's College," Toronto. In October of that year, an effort was made by the Honourable Attorney-General Baldwin to introduce a comprehensive scheme of University reform, but it was defeated in the Legislature. In 1845 and 1847, other abortive attempts were made to "reform" the University; but, in 1849, a comprehensive measure was introduced into the Legislature by the Honourable Attorney-General R. Baldwin, and passed into a law, by which it was re-incorporated under the name of "The University of Toronto," and made a purely national Institution, by placing it and its adjunct University College under the sole control of the Legislature, and of a Senate and Officers appointed by the Government.

Part XII.   THE UNIVERSITY OF TORONTO.   29

Under this Act the University of Toronto and University College are now constituted. The University prescribes the requirements for Degrees, Scholarships, and Prizes; appoints Examiners; and confers Degrees in the Faculties of Law, Medicine, and Arts. University College gives instruction in the Departments of Arts and Science prescribed by the University for the Degrees of B.A., M.A. and LL.D.

THE UNIVERSITY OF TORONTO.

The governing body of the University is the Senate, composed of:

1. *Ex-officio* members.
2. Members appointed by the Government.
3. Members elected by Convocation.
4. Representatives of Affiliated Institutions.
5. Representatives of High School Masters.

Under the control of the Senate are:

1. University College.
2. School of Practical Science.
3. Upper Canada College.
4. The University Library.
5. The University Museum.

Functions of the University of Toronto.

The Functions of the University comprise the Examinations of Candidates for standing, Scholarships and Degrees in the several Faculties. It prescribes the Curriculum of Study, and appoints the Examiners and conducts the respective Examinations; it also maintains a Library and Museum.

Co-Education.—The Legislature of the Province, in 1884, passed the following Resolution on this subject, videlicet:

That inasmuch as the Senate of the Provincial University, having for several years admitted women to the University Examinations and Class Lists, and inasmuch as a considerable number of women have availed themselves of the privilege, but labour under the disadvantage of not having access to any Institution which affords tuition necessary in the higher years in the Course; in the opinion of this House provision should be made for that purpose as early as practicable in connection with University College. (This was done.)

Instruction.—The work of instruction is performed by University College through its Professors and Lecturers. This College and the University are maintained out of the common Endowment of the Provincial University, which is administered by the Bursar's Department, under the control of the Lieutenant-Governor-in-Council. University College is governed by a Council composed of the President and Professors. The following Chairs have been established in the College, namely: Classical Literature, Logic and Rhetoric, Mathematics and Natural Philosophy, Chemistry and Experimental Philosophy, History and English Literature, Mineralogy and Geology, Metaphysics and Ethics, Meteorology and Natural History, and lectureships on Oriental Literature, in German and French.

The Course of Instruction follows that prescribed by the Curriculum of the University of Toronto, and involves four academic years, each consisting of two terms each.

The students are required to pass a Matriculation Examination before being recognized as regular students of the University, or entitled to its Degrees. They are required to pass annual Examinations in the University, so as to gain standing year by year, as well as for the particular Degrees. Students who are not matriculated may attend Lectures in the different departments. The Junior Matriculation Examination is prescribed by the University Statutes.

The University Examinations.

1. All Matriculated Students are required to attend the College Examinations in every department, or branch, prescribed by the University of Toronto as necessary for their respective standings.

2. Prizes and Honours in the College are awarded in each department on the result of the Examinations at Easter, with additional Examinations at Christmas, at the discretion of each Professor, or Lecturer.

3. Candidates for Prizes and Honours are arranged, according to their Proficiency, in two classes, and those who are not Candidates for Prizes and Honours, or who fail to obtain Honours, are similarly arranged in the Third Class; but no name of a Candidate for Honours shall be entered on the Class Lists until he has passed in all the prescribed subjects.

4. Certificates of Honour in each department are awarded to those Students who have been placed in the First Class at the Examinations.

5. The Examinations for both Pass and Honours in the University for all Students of the Second and Third Year attending Lectures in University College will be conducted by the Professors, Tutors, and Lecturers of the College, and conjointly with Associate Examiners appointed by the Senate, at the same time as the University Examinations for the First and Fourth Years.

THE REVEREND ROBERT ALEXANDER FALCONER, Litt.D., LL.D.. D.D.,
President of the University of Toronto.

6. Non-matriculated Students are not required to attend the Examinations, unless they are Candidates for Prizes, or Honours, or desire to obtain Certificates of attendance.

Matriculation Examinations for the Provincial and other Universities and Colleges may be held, under the direction of the Education Department, at the same places as the Examinations for Certificates to First and Second-class Teachers.

The University Fellowships.

Seven Fellowships, of the value of $500 each, are open for appointment each year, on the recommendation of the College Council. The selection will be made immediately after the publication of the result of the University Examinations in May, from among the Graduates of the University of Toronto.

The Statute requires that each Fellow shall be appointed annually; but he may be reappointed for a period not exceeding in all three years.

Each Fellow is required to assist in the teaching and practical work of the Department; to pursue some special line of study therein; and to devote his entire time during the College Terms to the work of the Department, under the direction of the Professor or Lecturer.

The Statute provides that "The Fellows shall be appointed from among the Graduates of the University of Toronto, on the recommendation of the College Council, and shall be selected with a special view to their aptitude for teaching, along with their acquirements in the work of the Department to which each Fellowship is attached." And also that "Every Fellow on accepting his appointment shall come under an obligation to fulfil the duties of his Fellowship during the College Terms of the Academic Year in which he is appointed, unless specially exempted by resolution of the College Council."

The University Medals and Scholarships.

The Governor-General (Lord Lansdowne) presented a Silver Medal for annual competition in University College, which is open to the competition of Honour students of the third year. Mr. John Macdonald donated an annual Scholarship of $50 for general proficiency to second year students. Prizes in Books are also awarded. The Prince of Wales' annual Scholarship of $50 is open to competition to junior matriculants of the University. The Mary Mulock Scholarship is awarded for proficiency in classics. In addition to these special Scholarships, there are also a number of other University Scholarships and Prizes open to competition.

By the will of the late Mr. Richard Noble Starr, a valuable Farm in the Township of Caradoc, in the London District, was bequeathed to the University of Toronto, the annual income derived from which is expended in providing three silver, or gold, Medals, as the Senate sees fit, to be competed for by the Graduates of the University. The special subjects named in Mr. Starr's will are Anatomy, Physiology, and Pathology. And should the income derived from the property exceed, as it is likely to do, the cost of the Medals, the surplus will be devoted to provide Scholarships in the Faculty of Medicine.

Details of Management of the University.

The most striking feature of the organization consists undoubtedly in the division of the whole academic work of the institution, introduced in principle by the Act of 1853, between the Senate, the Councils of the University and of University College, and the federated institutions. Each of these bodies is entirely independent of the control of the others.

1. *The Crown*—The supreme authority in all matters is vested in the Crown, represented by the Government of the Province. The property is vested in the Crown in trust, and is managed by the Bursar, a Crown officer. Annual appropriations are authorized by the Crown, as also expenditure of endowment, subject in the latter case to the Legislature. The Crown exercises veto power as to statutes of Senate and Councils, and makes all appointments in the University and University College.

2. *The Board of Trustees*—Consists of Chancellor, Vice-Chancellor, and President, five members appointed by Senate, and two by University College. It advises the Crown through the Bursar as to conservation, increase, and expenditure of endowment and income, and management of property in general.

3. *The Senate*—This body makes curricula, examines, grants degrees, and standing, but does not teach. It has sixty members—nine ex-officio, namely, the Minister of Education, the President of University College, the President of each federated institution, the Chancellor, and Vice-Chancellor, and all past Chancellors and Vice-Chancellors; twenty-six appointed members from various educational bodies, and nine members appointed by the Crown; twenty-three members elected by graduates, and two elected by the High School Teachers.

4. *Convocation*—Consists of the whole body of graduates, and elects representatives to Senate in Arts, Medicine, and Law.

5. *The University Council*—Consists of the President and Professors of the University in Arts, Medicine, and Law. It is entrusted with teaching and discipline of students.

6. *The University College Council*—Consists of the President and Professors of University College. Duties and powers parallel to those of Number 5.

7. *Federated Universities and Colleges*—These assist in teaching the arts curriculum, and exercise discipline over their own students.

W. H. FRASER.

The total income of the University is $80,000; endowment, about $1,000,000; amount invested in buildings, $500,000. Scholarships have been founded by a number of persons, videlicet, by the Trustees and by the Council, the Honourable Edward Blake, Sir William Mulock, Mr. John Macdonald and others. There is also the Honourable George Brown Memorial Statue Fund, and the Lansdowne Silver Medal.

CEREMONY OF PLACING THE COPING STONE ON THE NEW BUILDINGS OF THE UNIVERSITY OF TORONTO AND UNIVERSITY COLLEGE.

On the Fourth day of October, 1858, the highly interesting Ceremony of placing the Coping Stone on the Turret of the Toronto University Buildings took place. The Ceremony was performed by His Excellency Sir Edmund Head, Governor-General, who was *ex-officio* Visitor of the University.

It was on the Turret, which rises from the north-east corner of the massive Norman Tower in the centre of the southern Front, that the Ceremony took place of laying on it the Coping Stone, as shown in illustration on next page. The Ceremony is described as follows:—

Early in the afternoon, a procession, consisting of the Boys of Upper Canada College, with their Masters, the Graduates and Undergraduates, and the Officers of

34 THE ESTABLISHMENT OF SCHOOLS AND COLLEGES IN ONTARIO.

THE UNIVERSITY OF TORONTO.

the University of Toronto and University College, proceeded to the New Buildings. The Heads of the University and College took their place on a Platform, at the entrance of the Tower, so as to receive His Excellency, the Graduates, Undergraduates, etcetera, being ranged on either side, while the Upper Canada College Boys were drawn up in an enclosure. Lady Head, Miss Head, and other Ladies, were received by the Vice-Chancellor and the President of the University College. The Governor-General having taken his place on the platform, Mr. John Langton, M.A., the Vice-Chancellor, read to him the following address:—

May it Please Your Excellency:—

On this auspicious occasion, when we are assembled for the purpose of placing the Top-most Stone on the Building dedicated to the uses of the University and College, of which Your Excellency is the Visitor, we, the Members of the Senate of the University of Toronto, and of the Council of University College, with the Graduates and Students, beg leave to express to Your Excellency, with the utmost respect, the high gratification with which we recognize in our Visitor, not only the Representative of our Gracious Sovereign, but one who alike in the most ancient University of the Empire has achieved distinguished honours, and in the wider arena of Literature, has maintained the well earned distinctions won in Academic Halls.

We now unite in praying Your Excellency to lay for us the Crowning Stone of this Edifice, which, while we hope it may prove the happy emblem of many future triumphs to be achieved within the walls, will, we also trust, ever be associated with one whose generous sympathy in the progress of our University and College has so materially contributed to the prosperity they now enjoy.

The Governor-General replied as follows:—

Doctor McCaul, Mr. Vice-Chancellor, and Gentlemen of the University of Toronto, and University College, I thank you very sincerely for the flattering terms you have made use of in your Address to me, and I shall have great pleasure in complying with your request, but, before proceeding to this work, let us join in supplicating the Divine Blessing.

The Reverend Doctor McCaul then offered up the following prayer:—

O most gracious Lord God, we humbly offer unto Thee our unfeigned praises for all the mercies which Thou hast vouchsafed to us; especially do we desire to thank Thy Holy Name for permitting us to carry on successfully the great work in which we have been engaged, and enabling us on this occasion to celebrate the approaching completion of the Structure intended for the use of our University and College. It is of Thy favour, most Merciful Father, that the work of our hands has so far prospered; it is on Thee alone that we depend for the future success of our Institutions. Pour down, we beseech Thee, an abundant measure of Thy Grace on those who are to impart, and to those who are to receive, instruction within these walls, and grant that successive generations may here acquire such information and form such habits as may enable them to discharge the duties of the stations to which it may please Thee to call them, to Thy Honour and Glory, with credit to themselves, and with benefit to their fellow creatures. And now, O Lord, we pray Thee to bless Our Sovereign, Her Majesty's Representative, and all that are set in authority under him, and to grant that each of us, in our several stations and employments, may live in the fear of God, in dutiful allegiance to the Queen, and in brotherly love and Christian charity, each towards the other; and this we humbly beg in the Name and for the sake of Jesus Christ, Our Lord. Amen.

The Reverend Doctor McCaul then repeated the Lord's Prayer, and pronounced the Apostolic Benediction, after which His Excellency proceeded to the top of the Tower. Thence His Excellency, accompanied by several Officials, the Architects, and Contractors, ascended a temporary stairway to the top of the Turret, erected on the North East corner of the Tower. A Bottle containing the College Calendar and other Documents, connected with the History of the Institution, having been duly deposited in it, a plate, bearing the following Latin inscription, by the Reverend Doctor McCaul, was inserted on a stone slab in the wall:

HOC· LAPIDE·
OMNIUM INAEDIBUS· ACADEMICIS·
SUMMO·
TURRI· IMPOSITO·
OPUS· ABHINC· BIENNIUM· SE· AUSPICE· INCHOATUM·
CORONAVIT·
EDMUNDUS· WALKER· HEAD· BARONETTUS·
A·M· OXON·
E· SECRET· REGIN· CONSIL·
VICE· REGIA· RERUM· SUMMAM·
PER· PROVINC· BRITANN· IN· AMERICA· SEPTENTR·
ADMINISTRANS·
IDEMQUE· UNIV· ET· UNIV· COLL· APUD· TORONTONENSES·
VISITATOR·
IV· NON OCTOBR·
A·D· MDCCCLVIII·
ET·
VICT· REG· XXII·

HON· ROBERTO· E· BURNS·   REV· JOHANNE· M'CAUL· LL·D·
    UNIV· CANC·   UNIV· COLL· PRAES·
JOHANNE· LANGTON· A·M·
   UNIV· V· CANC·

F· GUL· CUMBERLAND· ET· GUL· G· STORM·
ARCHITECTIS·
JOHANNE· ET· JACOBO· WORTHINGTON·
REDEMPTORIBUS·

A very handsome silver Trowel, with a similar Latin inscription, was handed to His Excellency. The Cope Stone was then lowered to its place, and His Excellency, having applied the Square and Plummet and struck the Stone with the Mallet, formally declared:—"The Cope Stone is now laid,"—and, on a signal being given, a salvo of artillery was then fired by the Field Battery under the command of Lieutenant Colonel Denison in the Park, to announce the completion of the Ceremony. His Excellency and the rest of the company then descended to the Museum, where the dejeuner took place.

The Governor-General took the Chair, in his capacity as Visitor to the University.

After the Reverend Doctor McCaul had said the Latin Grace, Mr. J. Langton, M.A., Vice-Chancellor, rose and said the toast he had to propose needed no preface, —"The Queen." The Band played "God Save the Queen."

The Reverend Doctor McCaul then said that he had to propose the Toast which usually stood next in order. It was a toast to the "Prince Consort and the rest of the Royal Family."

If Prince Albert had no other claim than the relation which he bears to the Queen, it alone would be sufficient to secure for him the respect and regard of all loyal subjects, but he does not require to shine by reflected light, for he had strong personal claims. Without reference to his attainments and accomplishments, which rather grace private life than the exalted station which he occupies, I would specially call attention to that remarkable judgment, that discretion, that tact with which he has so conducted himself, since he came to England, that in a Country characteristically jealous of foreign influence near the Throne he has won the esteem of all parties, and is regarded with the same affection as if he had been British by birth. With him also originated the great English Exhibition of 1851. Another claim upon them was that he was the Chancellor of the ancient University of Cambridge. Of the other Members of the Royal Family I would say no more than that our warmest good wishes attend the Princess Royal, the Fair Rose of England, transplanted, we trust, to bloom in the genial soil of Prussia, and that our earnest prayers are that they all may follow the footsteps of their illustrious Parents, for by so doing their course will be alike honourable to themselves and beneficial to the Community.

Mr. John Langton, the Vice-Chancellor, then said:

I have now the honour to propose "The health of His Excellency the Governor-General"; not alone, however, as the Representative of our Sovereign, but also as the joint Visitor of the University of Toronto and the University College. I do not propose it as merely an official toast, but one which was intended as an acknowledgment of the interest taken by His Excellency and the peculiar attention which he had shown to the University, and his special care with regard to it. Sir Peregrine Maitland and Lord Elgin had done much to encourage the erection of the Building, but there had been no one had shown more special care concerning it than His Excellency Sir Edmund Head. At the very critical period, when the University was left without a Head, His Excellency had afforded them his valuable assistance and advice. It must be to His Excellency a matter of satisfaction that he could see the University in its present stage of completion, and it is gratifying to myself to present the Trowel, with which His Excellency has laid the Topmost Stone, as a memorial of the celebration of that event.

His Excellency the Governor-General said:

I have much pleasure in accepting the Trowel, with which I have laid the Top-most Stone of the Building. I shall, as long as I live, preserve this Memorial of the day on which the last stone of your University has been laid, and I shall long remember the kind manner in which the Vice-Chancellor has been pleased to speak of my services in connection with the University. The good sense of the people of this Country acknowledged the necessity for such a University, and the advantages of the education to be afforded by it, and I have only acted in the discharge of my duty in doing what I have been enabled to accomplish in promoting the progress and, I hope, in consolidating the foundation of this great Institution.

I have a thorough conviction that Academical Institutions, such as are calculated to afford the means of acquiring a superior education, are of the highest value, especially in new Countries. They are of value in all Countries. But in new Countries, which are beset with peculiar difficulties, their results are of great importance to the whole Community. Such Institutions are doubly important, where the rougher elements of society are called upon, at an early age, to go into the wilderness, there to earn their daily substance,—they are doubly important in every case where it is necessary that the young men of the Country should go forth with those resources which may enable them to pass their leisure free from vice and in a manner befitting a Christian and a Gentleman. You have to contend with circumstances which make it doubly difficult to apply a remedy for the softening down of that surface which is necessarily more, or less, refined by contact with the world, because in new Countries, such as this, men are called into active life at an earlier period of life than in old Countries, and they have not, therefore, the means of receiving the full benefit of a University education. It is also clear that however sound may be the basis of Classical learning,—that however much you may wish to refine those with whom your lot is cast,—you must rear an enduring superstructure, or the mass of the Community will not be able to receive at your hands the instruction which you desire to put before them. I consider that the instruction inculcated in a University ought to extend a practical influence over a man's life, to enable him to go forth a better citizen, and more able to earn his own bread in whatever walk of life he may be placed. In order to discharge these important duties successfully all kinds of appliances are necessary.

The University of Toronto had, no doubt, in the times referred to by the Vice-Chancellor, to struggle with many difficulties; but I have felt a deep conviction that, amongst the means most essential to its future welfare was that of a Building alike worthy of the City in which the University is situated and of the University itself. Such a Building was greatly needed, and I did not hesitate, as the Visitor of the University, to sanction the outlay of the money necessary for the erection of the present Structure. In so doing, I felt convinced that the result would fully justify the step then taken. Such a Building is important in many respects. There is a general disposition to depreciate that of which there is no outward visible sign. The existence of a Building like this, of an important character, commensurate with the growth of the University itself, tends to remove such an impression. In the next place, the appliances connected with the Building are of first-rate importance, not only to the Students of the University, but also to the Community amongst whom the University is situated.

A few months, or at least a year, or two, may pass, and the Room, in which we are now assembled, will be filled with Volumes of Books; and in this Room the Citizens of Toronto, whether they are, or are not, Members of the University, may, if they choose, seek recreation and information. The influence of such a Library as this is a most important matter. It is not only so with regard to what the young men take away, but it is so in its general humanizing spirit—in the feeling of respect for Literature which grows by the possession of such an Institution as this.

With regard, also, to another Room, which we have just left,—the Museum,—I shall hope to see collected in this Museum such Remains as may, from time to time, be found, (and which would otherwise be scattered about and lost), of the Aboriginal Inhabitants of the Country,—Remains which my friend Professor Wilson is as well able to conserve and explain as any man I know. Again, in Natural History, a Museum of that sort, constantly open for the reception of Specimens, affords the certain prospect of the accumulation of that which is of the utmost importance in the History of Science. You have amongst you men, (such as Professors Hincks and Chapman), who are in every way qualified to occupy a high position in this branch of science.

Another feature, in connection with this Building, which I look upon as of great importance, is that of providing accommodations within the walls of the College for some portion of the Students. This is undoubtedly one of the most powerful means of forming the character and maintaining, through the influence of the College discipline, that decorum and that sense of propriety with which you would wish to see the Students leave the walls of the Institution. I do not know that the time would allow me to go more into detail on the points connected with the Building, as bearing upon the success of the University itself. I cannot, however, sit down without adding a few words in reference to the object of the Building.

I congratulate the Architect upon having dealt with the structure in the successful manner he has done. So far as my knowledge extends, I am not aware of any other instance of the Norman, or Romanesque, style of Architecture on this Continent. There may be such instances; but I know of none. I believe that style is capable of the most useful results. To my own mind, it suggests a variety of analogies, some of them bearing particularly on the nature of the duties of the Members of the University here assembled.

In the first place, I never see a Building in this style of architecture—whether it be ecclesiastical or civil—but I regard it as a type of modern civilization. It is the adaptation to modern purposes of forms which originated long ago,—it is the adaptation of Roman architecture to modern civilization. Where did you get these forms? Where did you get these ceremonies, under which Municipalities were formed,—those Municipalities, which, under different names, are creeping through the Continent of America carrying the principles of local self-government with them? They are from Rome, from whence comes this kind of Romanesque Architecture,—they are the adaptation of Forms derived from Rome to the wants of modern society. Many things in modern Europe are precisely analogous to the style of the Building in which we are assembled. I say, moreover, that the style of the Architecture of this Building suggests some reflections upon the duties of the University itself, for it is the business of the University to give a sound Classical education to the youth of our Country. and to impart to them that instruction and information which are essential to the discharge of their duties as Citizens, both in Public and private life, according to the wants and usages of modern society. I say, Sir, that we may take the Building in which we are assembled as the type of the duties standing before the University to discharge. I repeat my thanks for the handsome manner in which you have acknowledged the little I have done in connection with this University. I would express my best wishes for its future success. Whereever I may be, I shall ever look with interest on the success of the University of Toronto. I have now to propose "Success to the University and to the University College in connection with it."

Mr. John Langton, the Vice-Chancellor, in responding on behalf of the University, alluded to the intimate connection existing between the two Institutions, which were together in the same Building and supported by the same Endowment:

The prosperity of the one was ever connected with the prosperity of the other. It is gratifying to me, on the present occasion, to announce that the University had hitherto gone on so steadily progressing, that very little doubt could be entertained as to its future prosperity. The year before last the number of Students increased at the rate of twenty per cent., and the last year showed a further increase of seventeen per cent. Such an increase made them look forward to the possibility of their being hardly established in the present building before they would have to make additional preparation to provide further accommodation in that portion set apart for the residence of the Students. I am glad that His Excellency did propose the two Institutions in connection with each other, because he felt that they were necessarily dependent the one upon the other. As their Arms were inscribed upon the Windows side by side—as Doctor McCaul and myself, representing these two Institutions, sat on the present occasion on the right hand and on the left of His Excellency, as their common Visitor—so I hope the Institutions will continue to go on hand in hand until they fulfil those high designs which I believe they are destined to realize.

The Reverend Doctor McCaul responded on behalf of University College:

It will readily be believed that it was with no ordinary feeling I have taken part in the proceedings of the day, intended as they are to celebrate the completion, for such I might call it, of the great work which I have for so long and so anxiously striven,— a day in which I have seen the realization of hopes, often disappointed, but never abandoned—of intentions, often frustrated, but never given up. In truth, my feelings are such as those of the mariner, when he passes from the surging billows of a storm swept sea to some calm, unruffled haven of rest, and the festivities of the occasion seem to be as the rejoicings of "the gladsome sailors as they place the garlands on the poops." During the past year it had been blest with great success, and the entries at the Matriculation Examination, which had just terminated, indicated a continuance of this prosperity for the present year. Last year the number of Students in attendance had almost

THE REVEREND JOHN McCAUL, LL.D.,
First President of the University of Toronto

reached two hundred, being considerably more than had ever attended either University, or College, and I feel persuaded that, when they are in the new Buildings, with the additional accommodation which it affords, that number will be considerably increased. If I were asked, what were the causes of this success, I would trace it, under God, to the facts, that I have associated with me, as Colleagues, men able and willing to discharge their duty, and that I have under my charge Students, at once apt to learn, and prompt to obey, talented, diligent, and tractable. But five years have passed since this vigorous stripling commenced its legal existence, and yet it has already attained a magnitude and achieved a reputation, such as usually attend only on mature age. And to what cause should this be traced? To the additional fact, that the College has with it the warmest sympathies and the cordial co-operation of the Graduates, of those who have been connected with the establishment from its infancy from the memorable 8th June, 1843, when the doors of King's College were first opened for the admission of Students up to the present time, in which we are engaged in rejoicings, that herald the approaching occupation of our permanent Buildings; in a celebration, the harbinger of those ceremonies, wherewith we shall shortly inaugurate, in our Hall of Convocation, the home which we have achieved for our University and College. It but remains for me now to express the hope that the College may still continue to prosper,—*Esto perpetua!*—that it may still continue faithfully to discharge the important duties committed to it,—that it may long send forth loyal subjects, good citizens and useful Members of society,—men that are qualified to serve their Country in whatever position she may require their services, whether professional or otherwise, as Magistrates, as Legislators, as Statesmen, as Judges. And I trust that long after the wild grass waves over the grave that wraps my bones, and those bones are mingled with their kindred dust, successive generations may hand down, for the benefit of posterity, an Institution which freely offers the advantages of an education of the highest order to all who are qualified to avail themselves of its benefits, and enables the Son of the poorest and humblest man in the land to compete on equal terms with the Children of the most affluent and the most influential.

In the next toast which I have to propose, I ask you to do honour to our Soldiers and Sailors, to those gallant Heroes who have held up the Red Cross Flag in triumph in many a hard-fought contest. I ask you to do honour to those whose types are Nelson and Wellington,—honoured names, that shine out on this bright roll of British glory. I ask you to do honour to the Heroes, who have proved in the late terrible mutiny in India that the sons of our Island Homes possess both those qualities so proudly claimed as characteristic of the ancient warriors,—"*Et facere et pati fortia Romanorum est,*"— for their bravery and their endurance have been equally heroic. I give you, Gentlemen, "The Army and Navy."

The toast was received with unbounded enthusiasm, during which the band played "The British Grenadiers" and "Rule Britannia."

Colonel Irvine, though he did not belong to the regular Army, begged to return thanks on their behalf, and he knew they would be always ready to do their duty when required.

Professor Croft proposed the next toast, "Prosperity to Upper Canada College":

Independently of the interest which every Canadian must feel in the Educational Establishments of the Province, the University of Toronto was particularly interested in Upper Canada College, inasmuch as a very large proportion of its Students were derived, or had been derived, from Upper Canada College; and at present, as regarded the Members sent to the University, Upper Canada College disputed the prize with the Grammar Schools—and within the last few months no fewer than four of the Masters of Upper Canada College were Graduates of this University. Of all the Students who had entered University College since its commencement, sixteen years ago, none had been more successful in winning its honours than Stennett, Wedd, Brown, Evans, and Moss.

The Reverend Walter Stennett, Principal of Upper Canada College, responded:

The boys from the Institution over which I preside have taken the first places of honour in the University—and I consider every fresh acquisition of University distinction by a Boy of Upper Canada College is a new cord to bind together the higher Educational Institutions of the Country. It is to the awards of the University that we look for a recognition of the soundness of our Educational System, while at the same time we have the higher and better aim of sending forth to the world youths in whom we have endeavoured to infuse principles which should make them honest men and useful Members of society. On behalf of my Colleagues and the Boys, I heartily tender thanks for the compliment which has been paid them.

Professor Cherriman said:

The toast which has been entrusted to me is, "The Schools of Upper Canada"—one which seems peculiarly fitting on an occasion like the present, for when we have assembled to lay the Cope-stone of our chief National Educational Institution, we should, at the same time, gratefully commemorate those Institutions which lie at the base of the whole system. The more widely and solidly that foundation was laid, the higher would the superstructure rise, and with it our welfare as a people. It is our boast that in Canada we possess a School System, whose machinery and organization are unsurpassed, if not unequalled, in any other Country, and that its practical working should be as yet below its theoretical perfection may well be excused. Rome was not built in a day, neither could the education of a whole people be achieved in one generation. I would connect with the Toast the justly venerated name of the Reverend Doctor Ryerson, the Founder of our System of Public Schools.

The Reverend Doctor Ryerson, Chief Superintendent of Education for Upper Canada, responded:

The manner in which the Toast had been received was one of those encouraging indications of the intellectual advancement of this Country, that must warm and cheer the heart of those who were most intimately connected with its educational Institutions. Years ago, when making my Official Visits to the various Counties, the greatest obstacle which I had to encounter was the disposition of the people to undervalue their own Institutions and advantages; but, as soon as they began to respect themselves, their Institutions began to flourish. The People of Upper Canada, more than those of any other Country, had now learned to cherish their Institutions, and more particularly to entertain feelings of the deepest interest for their Common Schools. During the past years, not a single year had elapsed without an advance of at least Twenty per cent. in the amount of taxes imposed by the people on themselves for educational purposes, and of nearly Twenty per cent. in the number of Pupils, and I think I can say, without the slightest exaggeration, that there has been a corresponding improvement in the character and quality of the education given in the Schools. During the past year, a year of unusual depression, the increase of Pupils in the Schools had been about 20,000, and the increase in the amount of money raised for the salaries of Teachers and other appliances connected with the work, was upwards of £23,000. For the support of Grammar Schools, the amount raised by the Municipalities during the past year exceeded by £4,000, the amount raised in any previous year. Looking at these facts, nothing could be more encouraging than the proof they afforded of the intellectual progress of the Country. With regard to the Common Schools, though no perfection was assumed for the system, yet it was a noteworthy fact, that, throughout the length and breadth of the land not a single complaint had been preferred against the System by any Municipality in the Province, and only two Municipalities in all Upper Canada had desired a different adjustment from that which now prevailed with regard to the power of the Trustees. The only theory I have ever heard propounded for the improvement of our School System in Upper Canada, was to introduce the Irish National System—a System in which "Mixed Schools" were the exception and Separate Schools were the general rule. I think the subversion of our System for the introduction of a system of that kind would scarcely be an improvement. Of these Irish National Schools 1,600 were Mixed, 3,000 Separate Roman Catholic Schools, 800 Presbyterian, 80 Church of England, and 100 of other Persuasions. And I would ask, would the introduction of that system into Canada be an improvement? The Common School System of this Country was the property of the Municipalities, and was closely and indissolubly connected with the rights, privileges and duties of those Municipalities, and was inseparably interwoven with those principles which are destined to be the life-spring of future generations. I hope the Common School System of this Country will be conserved inviolate;—but, whatever might be the future fate of the System of Public Instruction in this Country, I shall have the satisfaction at least of feeling that, up to the present time, it had advanced without the slightest abatement. I thank the assembly with all my heart for the manner in which the Toast has been received.

Professor Wilson proposed the next toast, "The Architect":

This day we accomplish one important stage in the history of this magnificent Building,—destined, we trust, through long centuries to be the nursery of the young intellect of this Province,—and it would ill become us, on such an occasion, to be forgetful of those Architects whose intellect has been especially occupied in rearing so noble an Edifice,

SIR DANIEL WILSON, LL.D., F.R.S.C.,
President of University College.

worthy of so noble an employment. It is, therefore, with peculiar pleasure that I beg you to join with me in toasting the Architects of this Building. Your Excellency has already anticipated what I might have desired to say in reference to this Toast, in the commendations you passed on this intellectual work of one of the Architects of the Province. Nor is it an unimportant thing that an Institution, where intellect is to be cultivated, the aesthetic faculty of the young minds of Canada should be specially nurtured by gazing, through every stage of such development, on works of gorgeous sculpture and beautiful architecture, showing the adaptation of intellect wrought in stone, for such purposes as this Building is to be devoted to. All great Nations in past times have sought to establish memorials of their intellectual power in the architectural structures that they have handed down to other generations. These will survive to us in the grand old monolithic memorials of the early Britons,—the evidence of that struggle with rude power which showed itself in later times in the fierce conflict with aggressive Rome. There still are reared for us, in the old Nile Valley, the time-baffling monuments of Egypt, which perpetuate the results attained in that cradle of the World's civilization. And still more the chaste purity and intellectual power of the marbles of Greece commemorate to us, in another form, that truth which has fed the mind of the world in all later centuries. Nor is there wanting in the sensuous magnificence of the gorgeous palaces of old Rome something of the intellectual power of that nation, which wrought with its plough-share to prepare the soil of Europe and the world for the introduction of Christianity.

We look forward to a glorious future for this Institution, a noble destiny for this Building, upon which Your Excellency has laid that Crowning Stone, the evidence of the glory which, we trust, awaits us. I refer with sincere pleasure to the refined taste, the intellectual power, the true genius which our Architect has manifested in the erection of this magnificent Structure. Your Excellency has referred to its admirable adaptedness to the purposes for which it is intended. More than this, it is peculiarly emblematic of this Province and the adaptations of our Institutions to it. It belongs to an old period, coeval with the laying of the foundations of British freedom, and it is exhibited here with a wise adaptation to modern uses. The Architect has achieved the highest triumph an Architect can accomplish,—he has finished a beautiful Structure, consistent in all respects with the style he has adopted, but in no one point sacrificed its wise and fitting adaptation to the modern purposes to which it is to be devoted.

Mr. Cumberland, the Architect, acknowledged the compliment in a brief but graceful speech, in the course of which he gave credit to His Excellency for having suggested the particular architectural style of the Building.

The Reverend Doctor McCaul next proposed "The Contractors":

For evidence of the success which had attended their operations, it was only necessary to look around. I might apply to them the old quotation—" *Si monumentum quoeris, circumspice,*"—which however conformable to the ancient custom of the living erecting their own Monuments, there was this happy propriety, according to existing usage, that whereas it was originally applied to commemorate the excellence of a dead Architect, I apply it to mark the worth of living Contractors.

Mr. Worthington, on behalf of the Contractors, briefly and suitably responded.

The Honourable James Patton said he had been requested to propose the next toast, "The late Professors in the Faculties of Law and Medicine":

When we next meet, on an occasion like this, I hope we shall be in a position to toast the Faculties of Law and Medicine as actually in existence, and the Professors of those Faculties in their proper places.

Doctor Skeffington Connor responded:

I thought that, as it was a toast to the "memory of the departed," it would be drunk in solemn silence, and that all that would be required of me in responding would be to stand up, remain silent for whatever time might be thought proper, and then resume my seat. And I was rather strengthened in that conviction, than otherwise, when I heard the President of University College, in proposing a Toast to the Contractors, pronounce upon them the epitaph of a departed Architect. I thought my learned friend was then preparing the mind of the assemblage for the solemn scene next to be enacted. I must say, however, that I have been most agreeably disappointed, when I listened to the sentiments expressed by the honourable Gentleman who proposed the toast, and the connection in which he uttered them, I am well satisfied, will give them in the eyes of the country at large a far greater value than in other circumstances might have been attached to them. But I had come here rather to listen than to speak. And as I have been listening, I have heard one sentiment, which I was extremely proud and happy to hear, and which I fully endorse. It was a sentiment expressed by the Reverend Doctor Ryerson, when speaking of the educational establishments of this Country. That Gentleman clearly traced their progress and their present highly commanding and respectable position in this Country, and in the eyes of the people of the whole continent of America, and of England, too, to this fact, that, as the people advanced in self-respect, in other words, in respect for their Institutions, their Institutions then began to flourish. That was a noble doctrine, and one which I fully endorse. . . . I am proud and happy to see that from one end of the Country to the other, that feeling is growing strong in the breast of every Canadian,—that it is on his own self-respect, the respect he paid to himself and his Institutions, that his rights and liberties could alone be firmly based. The expression of such a sentiment was well worthy of the great occasion for which they were now assembled, that of aiding to open one of the most important Institutions in Canada. I fully agree in the views expressed by my Honourable friend, Mr. Patton, and most sincerely and cordially hope to see the Faculties of Law and Medicine soon restored.

Reverend Doctor McCaul then proposed the health of the Nobleman who was the head of a branch of the noble house of Waldegrave, and a distinguished honourman of the University of Oxford. He begged to give "Lord Radstock and the British Universities."

In responding, Lord Radstock said:

I regret my inability to do justice to the subject. It was a great subject, for it not only treated of the connection between this University and the Universities of Oxford, but I hope also the connection between this young Colony and the Mother Country. There was a strong link of interest and of sympathy which bound the two closely together, and there was a unity of principle and of action which would ever keep the two firmly united. In coming across the water—in leaving one's native land— one naturally looked for British Institutions, and I was glad to see them when I came to Canada. But it was not until I came into this Room and heard the band play " The Roast Beef of Old England," and saw the good cheer around me, that I realized how essentially I was among Englishmen. I felt it was not the climate which made the nation, nor the territory, but the People,—" *Coelum non animum mutant, qui trans mare currunt.*" I was going to say that I found here a " chip of the old Block." But that was altogether a wrong expression, because it conveyed the idea of separation. I prefer to regard it as a branch of the same tree, spreading its branches far and wide, and bearing an abundance of fruit. I would ask to be permitted to constitute myself the Delegate, not only of the English Universities, but of English public feeling, which I can assure them is strongly affectioned towards them.

In conclusion he wished prosperity to the Colony and to its Universities.

Mr. Langton, the Vice-Chancellor, proposed the health of Sir Allan MacNab:

The honourable career of Sir Allan MacNab afforded an example to the young men of the present day of what energy, unassisted by any foreign aid, might do. He had excelled in the Military profession, in the practice of the Law, and, as a Legislator, he had risen from the post of a junior writing Clerk in the House of Assembly to the high and honourable office of Speaker and left it as Prime Minister. His genial temperament made him friends everywhere, and I doubt if there is a man in Canada who does not honour him in his dignified retirement, or who grudges him the distinctions he has so honourably achieved.

Sir Allan MacNab, in reply, said:

I feel proud at being an invited Guest on this occasion, and am doubly grateful for the hearty and generous manner in which you have been pleased to respond to the Toast. I must disclaim a great deal of the credit which the kind will of the Vice-Chancellor had been pleased to ascribe to me. I had the advantage of being a Canadian. My Father was one of those who came to this Country in order to avail themselves of the bounty which the King was pleased to offer to them in the shape of Lands; and when I was called upon by the inhabitants of the Town in which I had the happiness to reside to represent them in Parliament, all I could say was that I did so to the best of my ability; I could say no more. There were those in the Room who could recollect the time when the City of Toronto did not contain two hundred people, and when, I believe I might say, there were not half a dozen Public Schools in the Province; and I would say to the young gentlemen who had the good fortune to be able to attend and receive the advantages which this Institution would confer upon them, that they who were born at an earlier period of the Country's history had never ceased to regret that such advantages were beyond their reach. It was, however, a matter of great consolation to me, at this period of my life, to find that, in the discharge of the duties I have been called upon to fulfil, I have received the commendation of such an assembly as surrounded this festive board.

Sir Allan MacNab then proposed "The Graduates and Students of the University," and said that he had no doubt that, if they availed themselves of the advantages afforded by this University, they would hereafter take the positions in public life which many of those present had left, and be able to fill them with still greater advantage to the Country.

Mr. McMichael replied for the Graduates, and Mr. Bernard for the Undergraduates.

The last toast, by the Vice-Chancellor, "Lady Head and the Other Ladies," was then cordially received.

His Excellency responded:

Having had to return thanks once already for the manner in which you have drunk my health, I have now, on behalf of Lady Head, and the Ladies with whom you have coupled her name, only to express my thanks for the honour you have done her. I feel extremely glad that she has been able to witness this interesting Ceremony, and I acknowledge sincerely the kind manner in which you have drunk her health.

HISTORICAL AND OTHER FACTS CONNECTED WITH THE UNIVERSITY OF TORONTO, AND ITS NEW HOME.

The original Site of the University consisted of various Lots in the Township of York, and comprised portions of the property of Mr. D'Arcy Boulton, the Honourable John Elmsley, Chief Justice Powell, and Sir J. B. Robinson,—in all one hundred and sixty-eight Acres. The first portion of the Site was deeded to the University in December, 1828, and the remainder in May, 1829. The Avenue leading from Queen Street comprises about Ten Acres, and is nearly three quarters of a mile in length. The Yonge Street Avenue is a quarter of a mile long, and contains about Two Acres. Both Avenues are well laid out, and planted with Trees on each side, which afford to the Citizens an agreeable drive, or promenade. The Grounds connected with the University extend to the northern boundary of the City.

PART XII. THE UNIVERSITY OF TORONTO. 47

About two-thirds of the whole Property, now called "The Queen's Park," has been taken possession of by the Government, under authority of a Provincial Statute, with the view of erecting thereon hereafter suitable Parliament Buildings and a Government House. The rest of the Park was set apart for "the use and purposes of the University," in February, 1856. It comprises the portion west of Queen Street Avenue, about one hundred and four Acres. His Excellency the Governor General in Council, by on Order-in-Council, bearing date the 22nd of February, 1856, authorized the Senate of the University of Toronto to erect suitable Buildings, and to expend on such Buildings, out of the University Funds, a sum not to exceed seventy-five thousand pounds (£75,000). In addition to this, the sum of twenty thousand

THE UNIVERSITY OF TORONTO.
(Looking from the south-east.)

pounds (£20,000) was also granted for the erection and establishment of a Library and Museum. With the view of carrying out these objects, the Senate engaged Mr. F. W. Cumberland, an Architect, to prepare Plans, and as soon as they were approved, contracts were entered into for the erection of the Building, the Foundation Stone of which was laid on the 4th of October, 1856.

The chief Facades of the University Building are those of the South and East, the former has a massive elevation for distant effect from the Lake and City, the latter of more broken and picturesque outline for combination with the Ravine lying between it and the main Park Avenue, from which it will be chiefly viewed. The general outline of the Buildings approaches the form of a square, having an internal Quadrangle of about Two hundred feet square, the north side of which is left open to the Park. One great peculiarity in the appearance of the Building is the constant break and change, which is everywhere apparent. View it from what side you will, the Roofs, Mouldings, and other Enrichments are in pleasing variety. The Architecture of the Building is Norman Gothic, the Carvings and Mouldings being in the character of that period. The principal Entrance is under the massive Tower at the south side. The main Porchway, with its Mouldings and Carvings, is quite elaborate. This Porchway leads to the Vestibule, which is the ground floor of the main Tower,—having the President's Ante-room and Porter's Waiting-room on the right and left. Having passed through a second Archway, in a decorated screen, the main Hall is gained. This Hall is forty-three feet long, twenty-five feet wide, and thirty feet high. It is lighted by five windows, with richly carved frames, and a Gallery, which runs along the south end. The Hall is paved with encaustic Tiles, and from it the Main Corridor and principal Stone Stairs open right and left. On the ground floor, opening from the Corridor, are eleven Lecture Rooms and the President and Professor's private Rooms.

The Museum is situated on the first principal Floor in the west end of the Building. It is Seventy-five feet long by Thirty-six feet wide, and Thirty-six feet high, and has a pannelled Ceiling and highly decorated Corbels. Adjoining it is the Natural History Department and the Professors' Rooms.

The Library is on the east side of the Central Hall, and is of the same dimensions as the Museum. In decoration it is, however, different. It has enriched timber Ceilings, with appropriate Corbels. Connected with the Museum and Library are Galleries, at the end nearest the Central Hall. Over the Central Hall, and in connection with the Galleries and these Rooms, is the Geological Museum. The upper portion of the main Tower contains the Mineralogical Collections. From the main Tower, on a clear day, the Shore on the opposite side of the Lake can be distinctly seen.

At the extreme west of the Building is the Chemical School and Laboratory,— with a Bell Turret attached.

The total length of the main Front of the new Building is 384 feet and the average height about Fifty-three feet.

The East Wing of the Building is about 260 feet long, and has two Towers (capped with Spires), the one octagonal and the other square. On the Ground Floor are Lecture Rooms, Professors' and Registrar's Rooms, and the Convocation Hall. This Hall is eighty-five feet in length by thirty-eight in breadth, with an average height up to the leading-beams of forty-five feet. At its northern end is the Dais, for the Members of the Senate and other Official Personages on State Occasions. On the upper Floor of this Wing are the Reading Rooms for the public and for the Students, Senate Chamber and Chancellor's Apartments—the approach to which will be by a large and elaborately worked oak Staircase. The stone carvings of the Senate Hall are of the most elaborate description. Above these are Rooms for the accommodation of the Beadle and Sub-Librarian.

The West Wing, 336 feet long, contains Lodging Rooms for Students, together with the College Society Room and residence for the Officer in charge of the Students. Here will be, also, the Dining-Hall, having an open timber Ceiling, and a Gallery at each end. Stretching away from this Hall are the Domestic Offices, Steward's Room, etcetera. Attached to the south-east corner of the Dining Hall is a Porch leading to the Cloister, which runs along the whole of this Wing. This

Porch is surmounted by a Clock Tower, where a handsome Clock with Chimes will be conspicuous.

The main Porches, Entrance Halls, Corridors, Convocation Hall, Museum, and Library have tasteful enrichments and carvings.

The Quadrangle has a raised Terrace,—having flights of steps to the central area. This area is laid out in Grass plots, with Shrubs.

The whole of the Grounds around the new Buildings and the Observatory are laid out with Walks and planted. About forty, or fifty, Acres are devoted to a public Park for the use of the Citizens, and provision has been made for a Botanical Garden, in addition to the Experimental Farm already at the North of the Park.

The Library of the Toronto University.

After the disastrous fire of February 14th, 1890, in which the entire Library of the University was destroyed, a new policy was adopted. The Library, instead of being housed in the main University Building, was to be provided with a special Building, of fire-proof construction and of the most approved modern pattern, with Reading-rooms, Offices, and special Study-rooms attached. The mode of administration was also modified. The charge of the Library, no longer a supplementary office to one of the Lectureships, was filled by the appointment of a Librarian who was to devote his whole time to the duties of the position, and the clerical assistance required was no longer to be rendered by Undergraduates for a small emolument, but by regular salaried clerks.

The separate Library Building was soon commenced, and was occupied in the autumn of 1892. It consisted of a fire-proof stack-room, calculated to contain upwards of 100,000 Volumes, a Reading-room capable of seating from 150 to 175 readers, seven special Study-rooms, to be used after the manner of the Seminars in German Universities, both as Reading-rooms and as Class-rooms for the Honour Classes in certain departments, and offices.

The acquisition of a new collection of Books had proceeded rapidly. Through the generosity of Governments, Universities, Scientific Institutions and individuals, particularly in England, but also in most of the other European Countries and in the United States, about 20,000 Volumes had been received as gifts. A fund, subscribed by graduates and friends, and added to from the insurance money on the old collection destroyed by fire, was expended by degrees under the supervision of the Library Committee, and in a few years the Books in the New Library amounted to over 60,000 Volumes, nearly double the number of the former collection at the time of its destruction. The principle adopted in making purchases was to lay a solid foundation of the most necessary Books of Reference in each subject taught in the University. Thus, in the departments of pure Science the first purchases were of complete sets of the principal periodicals and publications of learned societies. In the literary departments, the complete works of authors of first and second rank were provided, together with selected works of less important writers. A similar idea was carried out in the historical subjects. By this means, the additions made in subsequent years were chiefly to fill in the gaps inevitably left at the outset, and to keep abreast of the more important of the recent publications in each subject.

As the University grew in the number of Students in attendance and also in the new Faculties and departments embraced in its Courses of Study, the demands upon the Library became increasingly urgent. The Teachers and Students of each

THE LIBRARY OF THE UNIVERSITY OF TORONTO.

new subject contained in the Curriculum had to be furnished with the Books they needed, and in most cases a considerable outlay had to be made on the fundamental literature of each subject to place it on an equality as far as possible with the subjects that were provided for in the original expenditure after the fire. The number of Students using the Reading-room greatly increased. The work of administration became more onerous and complicated. Finally, in about fifteen years from the first use of the Library Buildings, it became obvious to the Authorities that the Building in all its purposes had been completely outgrown. Complaints were made of the inadequacy of the Reading-room for the number of Students who wished to use it. The Stack-room was choked with the accumulation of Books, and large drafts to departmental libraries established in other buildings gave only a temporary alleviation. The members of the Faculties had no room in which they could sit, even to look through the periodicals in their respective departments. The Library Staff was working under the greatest disadvantages, three and four being accommodated in a room originally designed for one or two.

In 1907 the first instructions were given to prepare plans for a comprehensive enlargement of the Library Building, and the additional wings are expected to be completed by the end of 1910. The new construction involved a considerable rearrangement of the Rooms in the original Building. To describe the new accommodation briefly it will be advisable to give an outline of the divisions of the entire Building, including what is old as well as what is new. The new Stack-room is calculated to hold 250,000 Volumes. Above it, in order to be included in the fire-proof portion of the Building, is a large well-lighted Room where folio volumes on Art and Archaeology will be kept in suitable cases, and likewise the collection of Maps and Charts. On the same floor with this Art-folio Room there are ten private Study-rooms for the use of research Students in the historical and literary subjects or in scientific subjects where laboratory research is not necessary. There are two Reading-rooms, one for men (the old Reading-room), the other for women, the two together being capable of seating 360 Readers. Besides these two Reading-rooms, the entire Basement storey under the men's Reading-room will be converted into a single Room to be used as a supplementary Reading-room as occasion requires. A new Reading-room for the Members of the Faculties is provided, which will contain the current numbers of the periodicals; it will have a seating capacity of about seventy-five persons at Reading-tables. The same Room, having a special entrance from outside and capable of being shut off from the rest of the Building, may be used at night without necessitating the opening of any other part of the Library. The special Studies (formerly seven) are now eight in number. The Basement of the Building provides, besides the supplementary Reading-room already described, accommodation for the Students' Book Department, a kind of university Book-shop conducted under the supervision of the University for enabling Students to obtain their Text-books on the most reasonable terms, and space for the University Press and Bindery. The Rooms occupied by this latter institution are fire-proof and entirely cut off from the rest of the Building. Office Rooms have also been provided on a scale commensurate with the increased Staff now required, and, in the same wing, a suite of Rooms is fitted up for a Caretaker.

The Staff of the Library now includes a Librarian, the Librarian's Secretary and Typewriter, a Chief Clerk in charge of ordering and accession work with two Assistants, a chief Cataloguer with two Assistants, two Clerks in charge of periodicals and binding, and three Clerks in charge of the circulation and Reading-room.

TORONTO, 15TH JULY, 1910.   H. H. LANGTON, *Librarian.*

THE UNIVERSITY MUSEUM, TORONTO.

PRELIMINARY NOTE.—Up to the time of the Fire, which took place at the University of Toronto in 1890, the University Museum contained a very interesting collection, chiefly of Minerals,—especially the Ferrier Cabinet, the Mounted Corals, Cases of Insects and Birds, and a few Animals, including the " Canada Beaver," presented by Mr. B. E. Walker. This collection had been made under the direction of Professor W. Hincks, a naturalist; Nicholson, Ramsay Wright, and their Assistants.

The Biological specimens and the various models in the Museum are also of interest and value, not only to the University Student, as affording him an opportunity for practical Study, but they also illustrate the great value of Museums in an educational point of view, and as an educational factor in systems of University training.

THE NEW MUSEUM OF THE UNIVERSITY OF TORONTO.

By PROFESSOR MONTGCMERY, Ph.D., Curator of the Museum.

For many years past there has been felt a great need for suitable Buildings in which the Scientific Collections of the Provincial University could be properly preserved and studied, and also other and larger collections brought together, classified for practical use, and exhibited to the general public. Accordingly, this subject has received much consideration by the Authorities, the latest and best information has been obtained regarding the important University and Public Museums in America and Europe, and plans for a Building have been submitted and approved. These latter have been prepared with a view to alterations and enlargement in the future. The Site chosen is the southwest corner of Bloor Street and Queen's Park, a location both beautiful and convenient of access. The rear, or western, portion of the Museum Building was begun last Autumn, and is now in course of erection. This is three hundred and twelve feet long, that is, from north to south, and sixty feet in width. There will be two and one-half storeys above the Basement. The Building is expected to be ready for occupation before the end of the year. The entire Museum is to be fireproof, and great attention is being given to the lighting of the Rooms for exhibition as well as to the construction of the Cases. The ordinary teaching collections are to remain in the Geological and Biological Buildings. But large collections of Minerals, Fossils, and Rocks and also extensive Archæological and Ethnological Collections will be placed in the new Museum Building now being constructed. Eventually the Museum will contain large and interesting Collections, representing all the various departments of Science, and these will be labelled and will be exhibited to the public without charge. For want of room there are now about fifty thousand Geological and Mineralogical Specimens stored, or inadequately exhibited in the University Buildings. There are also large Ethnological and Archæological Collections in storage; thus more than one-half of the entire Collections of the University are at the present time without proper Museum accommodation for either exhibition or study. Therefore, the progress being made in the erection of the new building is hailed with delight and satisfaction by those conversant with the work and needs of the departments of Science and the great and far-reaching benefits derived from a Public Museum.

THE CHEMICAL LABORATORY OF THE UNIVERSITY OF TORONTO.

The new Chemical Laboratory of the University of Toronto is a commodious Building of red pressed brick and Credit Valley stone, situated on the southwest corner of the University Grounds, just west of McCaul Street, and a little north of College Avenue. It consists of a ground floor, upper storey, and basement, and is constructed in the form of a hollow square, with central Courtyard for light and ventilation, the west side being occupied by the large lecture-room, and the east by the Students' Laboratories, while the north is devoted to the entrance, staircase, and approaches, and the south to the Storerooms, Caretaker's Residence, private Laboratories, Library, and Professors' Rooms. Electricity is the lighting agent throughout, and the heating is effected by means of coils of steam pipe, over and amongst which the cold air must pass before entering the Rooms, while three large fans, driven by electric motors, insure thorough ventilation. All wires and pipes for the conveyance of electricity, gas, water, etcetera, are fully exposed on the walls and ceilings, thus facilitating repairs to the plumbing, while fire—that other ever-present danger in all large buildings—is guarded against by four separate hydrants.

From each side of the main entrance short flights of steps diverge, leading, on the right hand, to the large Lecture-room, and on the left to the Rooms devoted to practical instruction.

The Lecture Theatre is large, occupying two storeys of the Building; is fitted with Chairs for an audience of three hundred and eighteen, and is lighted altogether from the top, either by the skylight (which may be closed by curtains from above), or by means of groups of electric incandescent lamps suspended from the ceiling, thus avoiding all confusing reflections in the glass part of the Lecture Apparatus.

The Lecture Table has been the subject of careful thought. It is forty feet long by three wide, and is divided in the middle into two independent parts, each on its own foundation of three brick piers to protect it from vibrations proceeding from the Auditorium. This Lecture Theatre is the largest in the University, and the care spent in its design, and the careful work in its execution, have resulted in a great advance in the art of making things comfortable for both Lecturer and Hearers. Behind the Amphitheatre, on the south side of the Building, is the Preparation room, where Apparatus and material are got ready for the Lectures, and on either side of this are conveniently-arranged Store-rooms for the specimens, Chemicals, Glassware, Instruments, and all the thousand and one things which go to make up the equipment of a large Chemical Institute.

The east wing of the Building (at the left of the main entrance) is devoted to the Working-places of the Students, the "Laboratories" in the narrower sense of the term.

On the ground floor of this wing is a suite of three large Rooms, fitted with work places for in all 100 men. Each Student has for his own use about five feet of Table, two gas Taps, a Water Tap, a Sink, and a set of Reagent Bottles (there are nearly 5,000 of these in the Laboratory), connected with the ventilation system in front, the Student is provided with his own particular fume closet, whose work in the Laboratory is a necessary supplement to that of the Lecture-room if the student is to obtain any real familiarity with the facts of the science.

The first of the three rooms, counting from the main entrance, is set apart for the beginners,—the test-tubers of the lower years,—the second for those more advanced—doing quantitative work—and the third for practical work in Organic Chemistry. Conveniently accessible from the Quantitative Laboratory is the Balance-room, with twelve delicate Instruments, on independent brick piers. The upper storey of the south wing is occupied by the small Lecture-room, and by a large Laboratory, capable of accommodating ninety-six men at one time.

It is here that the large class of the medical faculty receive their practical instruction.

The remainder of the upper storey contains the Caretaker's Rooms, with private staircase leading to the Street, the Library, etcetera. In the basement (floored with asphalt) are placed the Lavatories, the various Meters, the Furnace for heating the Building, with its Coal-bin and Ash-pit, the Electric fans of the ventilating system, the Air-compressing machine and the sixty cells of the storage battery.

On the west and south, where the basement floor is but little, if any, under the earth level, there have been constructed fire-proof unpacking and Store-rooms, an "equal temperature" Room, a Gas analysis Room, with Pier, Furnace Rooms, for assaying and mineralogical work and for organic combustion analysis, also a small fire-proof Room, with all the usual appliances of a Laboratory, where experiments may be left going over night. And lastly, on the west side, underneath the large Lecture-room, is a commodious Chamber for use in making Physico-chemical measurements, with piers and stone Tables for Galvanometers and other delicate Instruments. The impression gained by a visit to this building is that of a structure eminently suited to the work for which it is designed, and the precautions taken against fire all show careful thought on the part of those responsible for the plans.

Economy has been practised in grouping the working rooms, so as to necessitate the least possible number of Instructors, the general effect of the plain brick and wood finish, with the interlacing pipes and wires, is far from unpleasant.

The mere existence of gas pipes and electric mains recalls the immense advance of knowledge within the last few years, the methodical arrangement and careful design of the Building itself, and all that pertains to it, is singularly appropriate in the home of that Science which, more than any other, is noted for its systematic and methodical compilation and arrangement of its material.

If the University main Building, of which College and City are alike proud, can educate the finer feelings of the Student by its mere presence in the grounds, surely the influence of the new Chemical Laboratory on those who work in it cannot fail to be equally important in making them more purposeful, more earnest, and more systematic.

Queen's Hall—The Women's Residence of University College.

For many years University College lacked a Women's Residence; our *Alma Mater* sheltered only the Alumnus and could not foster the Alumna. The need was keenly felt by many Women Students, but it was not until the spring of 1893 that a number of Ladies, feeling the same necessity, and recognizing the value of such an Institution as a humanizing force in a University, formed an organization called the "University Women's Residence Association," with the object of arousing interest in the question, and collecting, if possible, the necessary funds for its erection. Subscriptions were solicited, and an attempt was made to spread the knowledge of the effort by forming auxiliary Committees in various places in Ontario. The Fund thus started was augmented by the proceeds of Lectures given under the auspices of the Association from time to time, and a dramatic presentation of scenes from Homer, in the original Greek. As the money obtained in these ways was by no means sufficient for the object, the matter was brought before the Government, with the result that four Townships in Northern Ontario were set apart for the purpose. These had not yet been sold; but, in the meantime, the University fitted up the former Howland Residence in Queen's Park, and opened it as the "Queen's Hall" in January, 1905—the funds of the Association contributing to its support. In consequence of the untiring efforts of devoted Graduates, and the Wives of the Members of the Faculty, who have ever been its tutelary Goddesses, the Women Students now enjoy comforts which are at once artistic and gratifying. On the actual establishment of the Residence, great interest was shown by gifts of Books, Pictures and other furnishings that contribute much to the home-like atmosphere that prevails. Success followed so immediately that in the following Summer a large wing was built, which stands in a commanding position, and serves daily as a reminder that, in the future, a new body will be added to this unattached Member, and then, it is hoped, there will be a Building quite adequate for all the Women Students of University College. At present nearly fifty Students are accommodated, and, under the able direction of Mrs. Campbell, are happy to find that now, at last, *Alma Mater* truly deserves her ancient cognomen "gracious."

The Townships set apart for the Women's Residence are the following: Currie, Egan, McCann and Warden; together with such portions of Walker and Milligan as may be necessary to replace the lands in the other four Townships which have been taken up under the Veterans' Allotments Act.

To Miss L. Hamilton the establishment of the Women's Residence Association was due; and to her untiring energy and devotion the present condition of Queen's Hall may be justly, in a large measure, ascribed. The Hall was so named in honour of Her Gracious Majesty, Queen Alexandra; who was pleased to signify to the College Council her willingness that her interest in this, as well as in all other Institutions for the benefit of Women, should be so recorded.

Dean.—Mrs. Campbell, (widow of the late Reverend John Campbell, Professor in the Presbyterian College, Montreal).

Board of Control.—John Hoskin, LL.D., K.C., President Loudon, Mr. C. S. Gzowski, the Principal of University College, Professor Van Der Smissen, Professor Squair and Professor Fletcher.

Advisory Committee of Ladies.—Miss L. Hamilton, Mrs. R. Ramsay Wright, Mrs. J. F. McCurdy.

THE SCHOOL OF PRACTICAL SCIENCE, TORONTO.

Prior to the year 1871 there was no institution in the Province for practical instruction in the industrial sciences. In 1870 the Government of the Province issued a Commission to Doctor Hodgins, Deputy Superintendent of Education, and to Doctor Machatti of London, directing them to proceed to the United States for the purpose of inspecting and reporting upon any Technical, or Science Schools, or Colleges, there established, as to their Buildings, Departments of

Study and general appliances. On their return a Report was submitted to the Government, with full details as to the cost of the proposed Institution. The Government acted upon the information contained in their Report, and with a grant of $50,000 established a "College of Technology" in Toronto. In 1877 the name was changed to the School of Practical Science, and the Honourable Adam Crooks, Q.C., Minister of Education, had a suitable Building for it erected close to the Provincial University. Four of the University Professors were engaged in Departments of the School. The new Building was opened for students in September, 1878.

SCHOOL OF PRACTICAL SCIENCE, TORONTO.

Course of Study.—The Course embraces three departments: 1. Engineering —Civil and Mining. 2. Assaying and Mining Geology. 3. Analytical and Applied Chemistry.

Special Course.—A Course in Biology, for the benefit mainly of Medical Students, is conducted partly by Lectures in University College, and partly by Practice in the School. The subjects of the former: Elementary Botany; Cryptogamic Botany; Zoology; Comparative Anatomy of Vertebrata. Of the latter: Elementary Practical Biology; Advanced Course; Specialized Course for Study of Vertebrate Anatomy; Histology.

Diplomas and Certificates.—Diplomas are issued in each of the three Departments on a student's completing a regular Course of three years. Certificates of attendance and standing are, on certain conditions, issued for any separate Course or group of Courses. In the Department of Engineering, the University of Toronto confers the Degree of Civil Engineering on holders of the School's Diploma who have practised their Profession for three years after receiving such Diploma.

Prizes.—Books to the value of $45 are awarded as Prizes in each year of the Course.

Laboratory.—The Physical Laboratory is furnished with a large collection of Apparatus for Lecture experiments in the Departments of Mechanics, Sound, Light and Heat. It is also well supplied with instruments for individual work in the same Departments. In addition, there are special Laboratories which offer unusual facilities for conducting experiments in Sound and Heat. There is also a special Optical room.

DENOMINATIONAL COLLEGES AS PART OF A SYSTEM OF POPULAR EDUCATION.

By the Reverend Doctor Ryerson.

The Denominational Collegiate System which I advocate is in harmony with the fundamental principles of our Common School System. . . . The fundamental principle of that School System is two-fold. First, the right of the Parent and Pastor to provide Religious instruction for their children; and to have facilities for that purpose. While the law protects each pupil from compulsory attendance at any Religious reading, or exercise, against the wish of his Parent; it also provides that within that limitation "pupils shall be allowed to receive such Religious Instruction as their Parents and Guardians shall desire, according to the general Regulations which shall be provided according to law." The general Regulations provide that the Parent may make discretionary arrangements with the Teacher on the subject; and that the Clergyman of any Church shall have the right to any School House being within his charge for one hour in the week, between four and five, for the Religious Instruction of the pupils of his own Church. Be it observed, then, the supreme right of the Parent and the corresponding right of the Pastor in regard to the Religious instruction of youth, even in connection with day Schools, where children are with their parents more than half of each week day, and the whole of each Sunday, is a fundamental principle of the Common School System. The less, or greater, extent to which the right may be exercised in various places does not affect the principles or right itself, which is fundamental in the System. The second fundamental principle in the School System is the co-operation and aid of the State with each locality, or section, of the community as a condition of and in proportion to local effort. This is a vital principle of the School System, and pervades it throughout, and is a chief element of its success. No public aid is given until a School House is provided, and a legally qualified Teacher is employed, when public aid is given in proportion to the work done in the School; that is, in proportion to the number of children taught and the length of time the School is kept open; and public aid is given for the purpose of School Maps and Apparatus, the Prize Books and Libraries, in proportion to the amount provided from local sources. To the application of that principle between the State and the inhabitants of localities there is no exception whatever, except in the single case of distributing a sum not exceeding £500 per annum in aid of Poor School Sections in new Townships, and then their local effort must precede the application for a special grant.

Such are the two fundamental principles of the School System, on which I have more than once dwelt at large in official reports.—*Story of My Life.*

THEOLOGICAL EDUCATION AND COLLEGES IN ONTARIO.

BY THE REVEREND PROFESSOR ALBERT H. NEWMAN, LL.D., OF THE TORONTO BAPTIST COLLEGE.

In no department of education has progress been so marked within the last twenty years, in Ontario, as in the Theological. Most of the progress really falls within the last six years. Of the six leading Protestant Theological Institutions, two of the most flourishing have been founded within the latter period, one having been fully equipped and virtually endowed, and the other already taking rank alongside of the older institutions. Of the four older Institutions, all have added largely to their resources, and we may suppose that their efficiency has correspondingly increased. There is every reason to expect that the next twenty years will be a period of even greater progress than the last. A generous rivalry prevails among the Denominations in this, as in other departments of Christian work, and each can rejoice in the prosperity of the Theological Institutions of the rest, if for no higher reason, because of the stimulus which is imparted thereby to its own Institutions.

1. *Conservative Character of Theological Education in Ontario.*—So far as I am aware, no new system of Theology or Ecclesiology has been developed on Canadian soil. Whatever of unorthodox teaching and practice has appeared has come from without, and the spirit of conservatism has been so dominant from the first that little encouragement has been given to innovators. Naturally, the Theological Colleges reflect this spirit of conservatism, and are themselves bulwarks of orthodoxy, each according to the standard of the Denomination it represents.

2. *Faculties.*—The Theological Faculties of Ontario are none of them large as compared with those of some of the wealthier Institutions of the United States, or in proportion to the actual need. The various Theological Faculties have each from three to five Members, and in some of the Institutions even these are able to devote only a portion of their time to Theological teaching. Only one Institution has a faculty of five, all of whom give their entire time to the work. In this particular there is abundant opportunity for progress, and there are indications that some of the faculties will soon be reinforced by the establishment of new Chairs. The fact is becoming more and more widely recognized that two or three men, however able, cannot satisfactorily master or teach the whole circle of the Theological Sciences, and that the necessity of distributing one's energies among several departments and of devoting an excessive number of hours to Class-room work forbids the highest attainment in any department. . . .

3. *Endowments.*—Hitherto all of the Theological Institutions have been supported almost entirely by annual contributions of the Churches and of generous individuals. Of our six Institutions, one is supposed to be, virtually, well endowed, another has an endowment of about $150,000, and the rest have each less than $75,000. . . .

4. *Libraries.*—In scarcely any other particular are the Theological Institutions of Ontario more deficient than in Libraries. These range from 3,000 volumes or less to 10,000 volumes. No one of them is endowed to any considerable extent, and the growth of most of them has been slow and precarious. . . .

5. *Students.*—The number of Students in these six Institutions ranges from 15 to 50, the latter being probably the largest number of strictly Theological Students ever present at the same time in any of these institutions. The degree of preparation required varies, one Institution insisting upon the completion of a University

Course, one upon University matriculation, and others, while urging upon all the importance of completing a University Course if practicable, receive Students for special Courses of Study who have only ordinary school education. The tendency throughout seems to be toward gradually raising the standard of admission.

6. *Courses of Study.*—The three years' curriculum prevails in most of the colleges with special advanced Courses of reading for the Degree of B. D. The Degree of D. D. is likewise conferred on examination by several of the Colleges, and some of them have the power of conferring the honourary degree of D.D. Little has been attempted as yet in the way of resident Graduate Courses of Study.

7. *Affiliations of the Theological Colleges.*—The Theological Colleges of Ontario may be divided into two classes, as regards their connection with Literary Institutions: *First,* those that are affiliated more or less closely with the Provincial University, or with the College maintained by the University (University College, Toronto); and, second, those that form departments of denominational Universities. To the former class belong Knox College (Presbyterian), the Protestant Episcopal Divinity School (Wycliffe College), and Toronto Baptist College (McMaster Hall), all of Toronto. To the latter class belong the Theological department of the University of Trinity College, Toronto (Anglican), Queen's College University, Kingston (Presbyterian), and Victoria University, now Toronto (Methodist). The institutions thus connected with the Provincial University, besides making use of the Arts course for fitting their Students for Theology, avail themselves of the lectureship in Oriental Languages maintained by the University, and are thus able to dispense, either wholly or in part, with instruction in Hebrew and Aramaic as languages. Moreover, theological students who have not enjoyed the advantages of University training have the privilege of attending any of the Courses of Lectures provided by the University, while pursuing their Theological Studies. The large University Library is also accessible to the Students of the affiliated Theological Colleges. The theological departments of the Denominational Universities are, of course, much more intimately related to the Arts department, the same Professors lecturing in Theology and in Arts.

ESTABLISHMENT OF THE UPPER CANADA ACADEMY, AFTERWARDS VICTORIA COLLEGE, COBOURG.

At a meeting of the Methodist Conference in 1829 the subject of an Educational Seminary was taken into consideration, and a Committee was appointed on the subject. At the Conference of 1830 another Committee was appointed to consider the matter, as the Committee of 1829 had failed to report. It brought in a Report on which a series of Resolutions was based, as follows:

Resolved, 1. That it is expedient to establish a Seminary of Learning, to be under the direction of the Conference of the Methodist Episcopal Church in Canada.

Resolved, 2. That the plan and Constitution of said Seminary be published; and that each Preacher belonging to the Conference be furnished with a copy of the same, and a form of subscription also; and that he be requested to use his best endeavours to obtain funds for the Institution.

Resolved, 3. That a Committee of nine persons be appointed by the Conference—three from each Presiding Elder's District—to fix upon the location of said Seminary; to meet at Hallowell, on the 27th of January, 1831, at 9 o'clock, a.m.

Resolved, 4. That the above Committee have authority to determine the place at which to locate said Seminary; and if, in the judgment of the Committee, the amount secured by subscriptions, or otherwise, be sufficient to justify the undertaking, they shall have power and authority to purchase, or otherwise obtain, a suitable situation for a site; to choose Trustees for the time being; to appoint a Building Committee, and to transact all other business necessary to forward the building, as far as practicable, before the session of the next Conference.

Resolved, 5. This Academy shall be purely a Literary Institution. No system of Divinity shall be taught therein; but all students shall be free to embrace and pursue any Religious creed, and attend any place of Religious Worship which their Parents, or Guardians, may direct.

The Conference, after full consideration, finally adopted the following as the Constitution of the Academy:

1. *Resolved*, That nine Trustees be appointed by the Conference, three of whom, the first on the list, shall go out of office annually, who shall hold and manage, in trust, all the property belonging to the Institution

2. *Resolved*, That a Board of Visitors, consisting of five persons, be chosen annually by the Conference, who shall be associated with the Trustees in appointing the Principal and Teachers of the Academy; in fixing their salaries and in framing the regulations and by-laws; in fixing the course of study, and in all other matters which relate to the proper regulation, government, discipline, and instruction of the students.

3. *Resolved*, That to this joint Board of Visitors and Trustees, the Principal and Teachers of the Academy shall be amenable.

4. *Resolved*, That the above Board of Trustees and Visitors shall examine annually both the financial and literary state of this Institution, and furnish a full and detailed account of the same to the Conference.

The Reverend Doctor Ryerson, who was at this time Editor of the *Christian Guardian,* called the attention of the Public to this effort on the part of the Methodist Church to provide the young people of all Denominations with a means of intellectual improvement under careful and anti-sectarian oversight and supervision:

To assist many Parents and Guardians of children in the several parts of the Province to give their children an education, and to assist the youth and children to acquire that education, is the object contemplated by the Conference in attempting to erect and establish a Seminary of Learning.

The object of this proposed Seminary is not to compete with any College [University] which may be established in this Province; but rather to be tributary to it, when one shall be established for the general benefit of the Province under the several branches of the Provincial Legislature, by imparting to youth and children the elements of a classical education, and by preparing them to enter the halls of a College, or University. The promoters of this measure, however, principally intend the contemplated Seminary to be a place of learning, where the stream of educational instruction shall not be mingled with the polluted waters of corrupt example; where the public shall be guarded against the infection of immoral principles and practices; where a good English and classical education may, with all possible facility, be acquired; where the rudiments of the several Sciences will be taught; where habits of industry will be encouraged; where scholars of every Religious creed will meet with equal attention and encouragement; and where the terms will be made as moderate and easy as the circumstances of the Province will admit. The urgent necessity of such an Institution must be apparent from the fact that there is not one embracing all these important objects in the whole Province, in which there are, probably, from twenty to thirty thousand youths and children who might, and ought to, possess an education that would entitle them to transact any kind of business, and be qualified for public stations in society.

The great advantage resulting from the establishment and successful operation of such an Institution, under the management of faithful and able Masters, may very easily be inferred from the salutary influence of similar Institutions in the United States. The acquirement of a good education is thus brought within the reach of hundreds of promising youths, to whom it would be otherwise inaccessible. The probable cost of the Site and Buildings will be from £4,000 to £6,000; and may not an appeal be confidently made to the Canadian public on behalf of this object? Who will refuse a donation according to his means when respectfully called upon? We humbly hope no one.

THE REVEREND EGERTON RYERSON, D.D.

From a painting in England by Gush in 1835.

Cobourg having been selected as the Site of the proposed Seminary, the Methodist Conference appointed a Building Committee and passed the following Resolutions for its guidance:

1. That the Building Committee proceed to provide materials for building, as soon as Two thousand pounds (£2,000) are subscribed, and one-fourth of it collected.

2. That the Presiding Elders of Districts be authorized to employ Agents in their respective Districts, to aid in procuring Subscriptions; and that the said Agents be instructed to provide in the subscription papers for the first payment to be made on, or before, the first of May next.

3. That the Presiding Elders of Districts obtain information respecting the proper persons to be employed as Teachers in the Academy.

4. That the Building be erected of Stone for the ground storey, and Brick for the remainder; and that the Building Committee provide materials for a House, one hundred feet long, by thirty-six feet wide, three storeys high; the two lower floors to be of white oak, or ash, if it can be conveniently obtained.

5. That the said Seminary be designated the UPPER CANADA COLLEGE.

In order to promote the success of the canvas for Subscriptions for the proposed Academy, the Reverend Doctor Ryerson issued the following appeal on the subject:

I. The Site is central, and one of the most healthful and delightful in the Province.

II. It is located in a district of moral and intelligent people, who highly prize the advantages of education, and manifest, without distinction of party, a praiseworthy zeal and liberality towards the erection of the necessary Buildings, and the speedy and successful operation of the Institution.

III. Its being established under the special and active patronage of a numerous Religious Body will be likely to combine a more general interest for its support and a much larger attendance of pupils, and, consequently, render it more extensively useful to the rising generation in Upper Canada, than any similar Institution established by a few private individuals. And, in proportion to the probable public usefulness of the Institution should be the liberality of the friends of education towards its establishment.

IV. It is the first literary Institution which has been commenced by any body of Ministers in accordance with the frequently expressed wishes of the people of Upper Canada. The Methodist Conference have not sought endowments of Public Lands for the establishment of an Institution contrary to the voice of the people as expressed by their Representatives; much less have they sought to acquire such endowments to erect "essentially a Missionary College" as others have done for the purpose of carrying on an extensive proselyting warfare upon the territories of their Religious neighbours. But the Methodist Conference in the manner in which they have commenced and are proceeding in the establishment of this Institution say, in effect, to the people of Upper Canada: "We have not laboured among you for the promotion of selfish and party purposes, but for the diffusion of pure and undefiled religion; nor have we sought, or received, any other subsistence than the voluntary offerings of your liberality. Desirous of promoting more extensively the interests of the rising generation and of the country generally, we have resolved upon the establishment of a Seminary of Learning—we have done so upon liberal principles—we have not reserved any peculiar privileges to ourselves for the education of our own children; we have published the Constitution for your examination; and now we appeal to your liberality for assistance—we feel confident you will not withhold it—we believe your good wishes are with us in this undertaking, and we submit to your decision for the success or failure of it."

CHARACTERISTICS OF THE SYSTEM OF INSTRUCTION TO BE PURSUED.

1. On the characteristics of the system of education which it is contemplated to pursue in the proposed Seminary, we may observe that it will be such as to produce habits of intellectual labour and activity; a diligent and profitable improvement of time; bodily health and vigour; a fitness and relish for Agricultural and Mechanical as well as for other pursuits; virtuous principles and Christian morals. On the importance of education generally, we may remark, it is as necessary as the light—it should be as common as water, and as free as air. A young man commencing life without education is like a mariner going to sea without any knowledge of navigation. There is a possibility of his getting into some desired port, but it is only a possibility. Education to

the mind is like hands to the body—they are essential to most of the pursuits of ordinary life, though they may be sometimes abused to the worst of purposes. Education among the people is the best security of a good government and constitutional liberty; it yields a steady unbending support to the former, and effectually protects the latter. An educated people are always a loyal people to a good government; and the first object of a wise government should be the education of the people. An ignorant population are equally fit for and are liable to be the slaves of despots, and the dupes of demagogues; sometimes, like the unsettled ocean, they can be thrown into uncontrollable agitation by every wind that blows; at other times, like the uncomplaining ass, they tamely submit to the most unreasonable burdens.

2. Education, like seeing, is one of the most fruitful sources of public, social and individual happiness. We may see many things that are hurtful and painful, yet the pleasures of observation are inexhaustible; so it is with the pleasures of knowledge. Education is the handmaid of religion. "It is the will of God (says Doctor Adam Clarke) that Christians should be well instructed; that they should become wise and intelligent; and have their understanding well cultivated and improved. Sound learning is of great worth even in religion; the wisest and best instructed Christians are the most steady and may be the most useful. If a man be a child in knowledge, he is likely to be tossed to and fro and carried about with every wind of doctrine; and often lies at the mercy of interested designing men; the more knowledge he has, the more safe is his state. If our circumstances be such that we have few means of improvement, we should turn them to the best account. Partial knowledge is better than total ignorance; he who can not get all he may wish, must take heed to acquire all that he can. If total ignorance be a bad and dangerous thing, every degree of knowledge lessens both the *evil* and the danger."

Laying the Corner Stone of Upper Canada Academy, Cobourg, 1832.

Notwithstanding the many discouragements experienced by the promoters of the Upper Canada Academy at Cobourg, yet the Corner Stone of that Institution was successfully laid on the 7th of June, 1832.

The following is the detailed account of the ceremony, copied by the Editor of the *Christian Guardian,* then the Reverend James (afterwards Bishop) Richardson, from *The Reformer,* a local paper, then published at Cobourg:

The Foundation Stone of the Upper Canada Academy was laid on Thursday last by Doctor John Gilchrist, accompanied by the Building Committee of which he is Chairman. We witnessed the ceremony with unmingled delight, regarding it as the commencement of an undertaking which promises incalculable advantages to the rising generation and reflects the highest honour on the Province, the District of Northumberland and the Methodist Episcopal Church generally. A leaden box was imbedded in the under part of the Stone, in which were deposited several Coins of the Realm, the first number of *The Reformer:* a Number of the *Christian Guardian*, Number 6 of *The Watchman* (Kingston), a number of *The Star,* Cobourg; a Report of the York Bible Society, a Report of the Missionary Society of the Methodist Episcopal Church, and lastly the following Memorial:

The Upper Canada Academy.

By the favour of
Almighty God,
On the 7th day of June, A.D. 1832, and in the Second
Year of the Reign of
Our Most Gracious Majesty,
King William the Fourth,

THE CORNER STONE.

Of this Edifice, erected by the Conference of the
Methodist Episcopal Church in Canada,
Was laid by the
Committee and Builder.
Major-General Sir John Colborne, K.C.B,.
Lieutenant-Governor of Upper Canada.

BUILDING COMMITTEE:

Messieurs Ebenezer Perry,
John McCarty,
John Gilchrist, M.D.,

Messieurs L. S. Church,
J. W. Cleghorn,
Wilson S. Conger.

Edward Crane, Architect and Builder.

On the 18th of June, 1836, the formal opening of the Upper Canada Academy took place. A preliminary service was held in the Church in town by the Reverend Joseph Stinson. After which a procession was formed and it proceeded to the Academy.

THE REVEREND MATTHEW RICHEY, D.D.,*
Principal of the Upper Canada Academy.

On arriving at the Academy, the Keys were given up by the Architect to the Reverend Anson Green, Chairman of the District, and the procession entered the Institution, and proceeded to the Chapel set apart for Divine Worship. After prayer being offered by the Reverend Ephraim Evans, the Keys of the Institution were presented to the Principal by the Reverend Anson Green, accompanied by a short Address, containing a condensed relation of the commencement and progress of the Building—the difficulties which had been encountered in bringing it to its present state of preparation for the reception of pupils, and concluding by formally investing the Reverend Matthew Richey with the charge of the Academy, and introducing him to the audience as its Principal. The ceremony was followed by an able address from Doctor Richey, the Principal.

---

*The Reverend Matthew Richey was a native of the North of Ireland, where he was classically educated After emigrating, he found a situation in an Academy in Saint John, New Brunswick . . . He had power and pleasantness of voice, ease and gracefulness of elocution, ready command of . . . language . . together with a rich variety of theological lore. . . He was tall and slender, but straigh and graceful as were all his movements. He received the honorary degrees of M.A. and D.D. *(Carroll's Case and his Contemporaries, pages 108 and 109.)*

THE UPPER CANADA ACADEMY.

The following were the Officers of the Academy: The Reverend Matthew Richey, Principal; Mr. H. Baldwin, Classical Master; Mr. Henry Evans, English Teacher; Mr. James O'Loane, Mathematical Master; Mrs. Smith, Preceptress; the Reverend C. R. Allison, Steward; the Reverend John Beatty, Agent.

DESCRIPTION OF THE UPPER CANADA ACADEMY BUILDING.

The ground floor of the Upper Canada Academy Building, which had been approved by the Committee in charge, embraced an area of 11,700 feet, of which

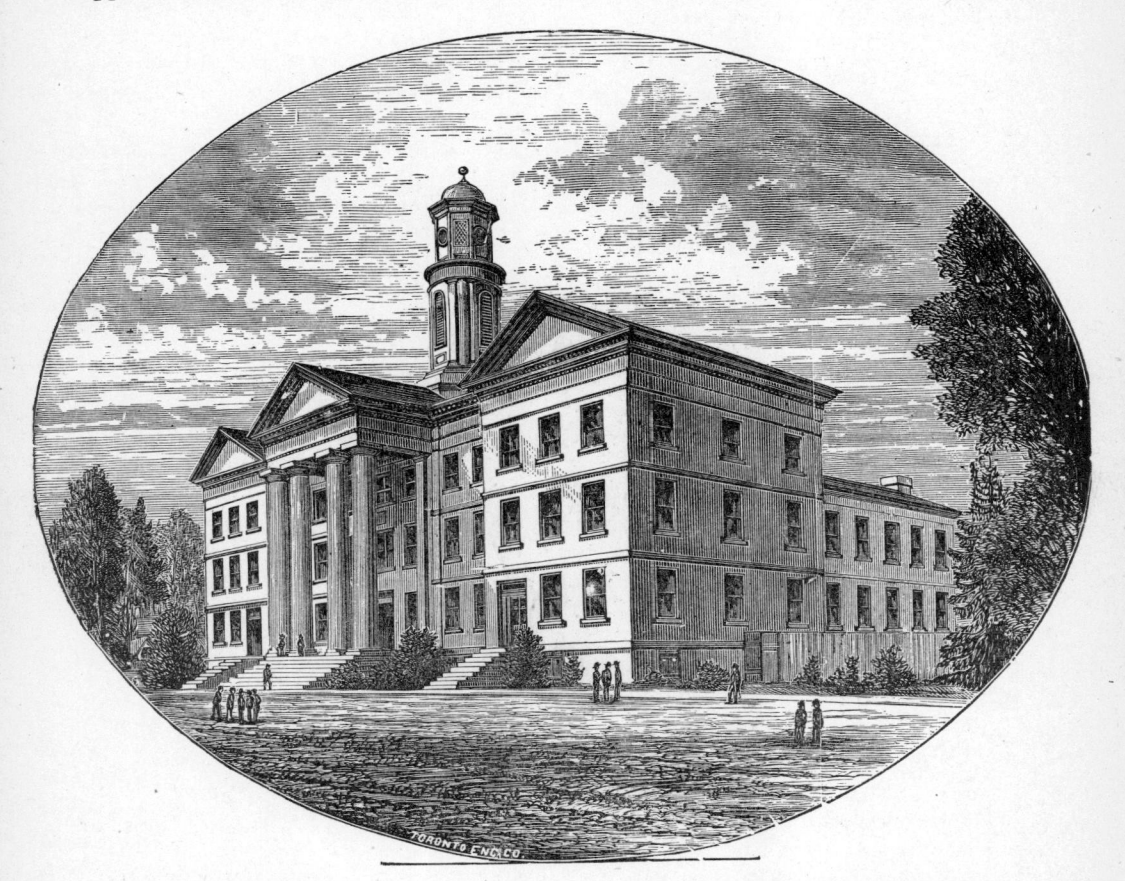

THE UPPER CANADA ACADEMY, AFTERWARDS VICTORIA COLLEGE, COBOURG, 1832-1842.

the following was the contemplated arrangement, videlicet: The main Building in front 130 feet long and 40 feet deep, with two Wings, extending from either extremity to the rear, each 50 feet by 24, leaving a Court Yard of 82 feet by 50. The front Building was intended to be three storeys high, and the Wings two storeys. Particularly pleasing was the attention paid to the convenience and comfort of the students as shown in the interior arrangements, which appropriated for their use a variety of small studys, so constructed as to place them under the immediate inspection of the different Professors. The right, or west,

Wing, constituted the female department. The left, or east, Wing, (in which was an extensive Dining-hall), that of the Males. There was a Chapel, Professors' Room, etcetera, in the centre.

The Charter of the Upper Canada Academy, Cobourg, 1835-36.

Owing to the stringency of the times, pecuniary embarrassment very soon overtook the newly erected Upper Canada Academy, at Cobourg. It was, therefore, necessary that an effective Agent should be despatched to England to

THE REVEREND JAMES RICHARDSON, D.D.*

obtain the necessary funds there, either by a direct appeal for subscriptions, or by way of loan.

The Reverend William Lord, President of the Academy Board of Trustees, having reported to the Board the embarrassed state of the Academy funds, a meeting was called to consider ways and means, so to extricate the Trustees from their difficulties. The Reverend Anson Green in his *Life and Times,* (1877), thus refers to this financial crisis in the affairs of the Academy. He says:

July 19th, 1835.—I was summoned to Toronto by the President for the purpose of attending . . . the Board Meeting of Upper Canada Academy; to prepare for the

---

* The Reverend James (afterward Bishop) Richardson, D.D., was for many years a prominent public man and a Minister. In 1833 and 1834 he was elected Editor of the *Christian Guardian.* In the War of 1812 he lost an arm in a Naval encounter at Oswego. After the War he received a pension of $500 a year. For many years he was Agent of the Upper Canada Bible Society, and subsequently he became Bishop of the Methodist Episcopal Church in Canada.

opening of that Institution, and to provide funds to pay off the debt incurred by its erection. We resolved to send the Reverend Egerton Ryerson to England to procure assistance, while at the same time we were to petition the Upper Canada Parliament to make us a grant of Four thousand one hundred pounds (£4,100), this being the amount of our indebtedness. . . . 740,275 Acres of Land were set apart (in 1791) for higher Education (in Upper Canada); . . . 225,944 Acres of these Lands have been given to King's College, and 66,000 to Upper Canada College; and why should not Upper Canada Academy have some assistance from the same quarter? . . .

The main object of the meeting of Trustees was, however, to select an efficient Agent to collect the necessary funds in England, and also to obtain a Royal Charter for the Academy in England.

The choice of this Agent naturally fell upon the Reverend Egerton Ryerson, who, two years previously, had successfully negotiated the union between the English and Canadian Methodist Conferences. He was, therefore, well known to the leaders of the English Conference, who could, and did, give him effective aid in his mission.

THE REVEREND JOSEPH STINSON, D.D.   THE REVEREND EPHRAIM EVANS, D.D.   THE REVEREND WILLIAM LORD.   THE REVEREND ANSON GREEN, D.D.

MINISTERS WHO TOOK PART IN THE OPENING OF THE UPPER CANADA ACADEMY, COBOURG, 1832.

Another important object of this mission was to obtain from the King through his Ministers a Royal Charter for the Academy, which had just been established at Cobourg. This was the more necessary from the fact that it was not found possible to obtain from the Upper Canada Legislature either pecuniary assistance, or an Act of Incorporation for the Academy such as its promoters could accept.

THE STATE AND FINANCIAL PROSPECTS OF UPPER CANADA ACADEMY, 1835.

The Reverend Egerton Ryerson finally retired from the Editorship of the *Christian Guardian* on the 17th of June, 1835. On that day his final valedictory appeared in the *Guardian,* and, in it, he thus referred to the financial state and prospects of the Upper Canada Academy:

An encouraging circumstance, which will be hailed with gratitude and delight by every friend of Christian Education, is the prospective completion and operation of the

Upper Canada Academy. The establishment of a Seminary of learning has been long meditated by the Conference with anxious solicitude, and great and generous exertions have been made the last four years to accomplish this object. Subscriptions to the amount of Seven, or Eight, thousand pounds (£7,000 or £8,000) have been obtained, and about Three thousand pounds (£3,000) collected. This is the most noble and patriotic effort yet made by any Religious denomination in this Province for the advancement of Education. The pressure upon the currency of the Country, to a very considerable extent, for the last two years, together with other circumstances of opposition and difficulty, has greatly retarded the completion of the Academy Buildings, until with an accumulated debt of between Two and Three thousand pounds (£2,000 and £3,000), an exhausted treasury, and without available sources to meet pressing demands, there appeared grounds to apprehend the failure of the philanthropic enterprise, and the loss of all the labour and expense and anxiety bestowed upon it. In this extremity, the President of the Conference, now feeling perfectly assured of the stability of the Union of the Methodist Churches, and witnessing the sacrifices and exertions made by the

THE REVEREND EGERTON RYERSON.

Preachers and a great portion of the Members of the Church, and after having become jointly responsible for a large sum of money, in behalf of the Institution, during the past year, generously came forward and offered to draw upon friends in England to the amount of Ten thousand dollars to complete the Buildings and bring the Institution into operation as soon as possible, relying upon the establishment itself and the subscriptions due, together with the exertions of the friends of Religion and Education, for the repayment of the money thus advanced. We confidently look to the operations of this Institution as the source of invaluable Literary and Religious advantages to Upper Canada, if not to the Canadas. May it go on and prosper; and may the friends of Education and Religion rally around it with more efficient support than ever, and with a patronage commensurate to its claims upon their confidence.

On leaving for England to collect funds on behalf of the Upper Canada Academy, Doctor Ryerson was furnished with a strong appeal to the British public for aid for the Academy, in which it was stated that:

For want of such an Institution upwards of sixty of the youth of Canada are now attending Seminaries of Teaching, under a similar management, in the United States, where nearly two hundred Canadian youth have been taught the elementary branches of a professional education during the last eight years. There is good reason to believe that nearly, if not quite, all the Canadian youth now being taught in the United States Seminaries of Learning will return to Canada as soon as this institution shall have been brought into operation. . . .

In behalf, therefore, of this Institution—most important to the best interests of a healthy, fertile, and rapidly improving British Colonial possession, the inhabitants of which have in this, as in other instances, shown the strongest desire to help themselves to the utmost of their very limited means—a respectful and earnest appeal is made to Britsh liberality, an appeal which it is devoutly hoped will be responded to in a manner that will contribute to draw still closer the bonds by which the loyal Province of Upper and the British population of Lower Canada are united to the Mother Country.

This appeal was indorsed by the Governor of the Province, Sir John Colborne (afterwards Lord Seaton), in the following terms:

The Reverend Egerton Ryerson proceeds to England . . . to solicit subscriptions . . . to enable [the conference here] to bring into operation a Seminary established at Cobourg, in Upper Canada. . . . As I am persuaded this Colony will derive the greatest advantage from the Institution and from the exertions of the Conference to diffuse Religious Instruction, I cannot but strongly recommend that it may receive encouragement and support from all persons interested in the welfare of Upper Canada.

The "appeal" was also heartily indorsed by the Honourable Peter McGill, founder of McGill College University, Montreal, and by other distinguished gentlemen and merchants in Montreal. In his letter Mr. McGill referred to Doctor Ryerson as "a Gentleman who has distinguished himself in Upper Canada by his writings in defense of religion, order, and good government."

On his arrival in England, Doctor Ryerson, (in 1835), stated the "specific objects of the Institution" to be as follows:

1. To educate, upon terms equally moderate with similar Institutions in the neighbouring Republic of the United States, and with strict attention to their morals, the youth of Canada generally.

2. To educate for Common School Masters, free of charge, poor young men of Christian principles and character, and of promising talent, who have an ardent thirst for knowledge.

3. To educate the most promising youth of the recently converted Indian Tribes of Canada as Teachers to their aboriginal countrymen.

In behalf, therefore, of this Institution—most important to the best interests of a healthy, fertile and rapidly improving British Colonial possession, the inhabitants of which have in this, as in other instances, shown the strongest desire to help themselves to the utmost of their very limited means—a respectful and earnest appeal is made to British liberality, an appeal which it is devoutly hoped will be responded to in a manner that will contribute to draw still closer the bonds by which the loyal Province of Upper and the British population of Lower Canada are united to the Mother Country.

Several of these Indian youths were educated at the Academy, among whom were John Sunday and Peter Jacobs, who became afterwards Teachers and Missionaries among the Tribes.

After much delay and great discouragements Doctor Ryerson succeeded in his Mission, but any financial aid from the Canadian Revenues of the Imperial

Government was at first absolutely refused; but a recommendation was sent to the Colonial Legislature asking them to make a grant. The Charter was held in suspense, and would have failed to pass the Great Seal had not Doctor Ryerson been skilful enough to deal with perplexing questions in regard to it as they arose, and had he not been able to prove to the satisfaction of the distinguished Law Officers of the Crown in England that the principles which the Charter embodied were quite in harmony with those that prevailed in Canada and were acknowledged by all parties in England. He was further able to show that the status which the Charter accorded to the Methodist Church in this Country had previously been granted to it, and was so recognized by the Statute law of Upper Canada. It is of interest to know that a most important step, as Doctor Ryerson at one time stated to the present Writer, in this victory for equal rights was the securing of this Charter, which was, we believe, the first Charter ever granted to a Dissenting body by the Imperial Government of England for such a purpose.

JOHN SUNDAY.
(Shahwundais.)

PETER JACOBS.
(Pahtehsega.)

The old parchment is treasured in the vaults at Victoria College as a magna charta of religious equality.

The Charter passed the Great Seal on October the 12th, 1836, and Doctor Ryerson continued his labours in collecting funds until May, 1837, realizing, over and above the entire expenses of his mission, about £1,000 for the funds of the Academy. Meantime, in June, 1836, the Academy had been opened for pupils, under the Reverend Matthew Richey, M.A., as Principal. In June, 1837, Doctor Ryerson returned to his Country, bringing with him an Order from Lord Glenelg for a grant of £4,100 to the funds of the new Institution.

Thus, after much delay and great discouragement, Dr. Ryerson succeeded in the objects of his mission—Money and a Royal Charter. At the close of his mission he writes to the Academy Committee as follows:

Thus terminated this protracted [business], . . . although I had to encounter successive, discouraging and almost insurmountable difficulties [in obtaining the charter]. Not having been able to effect any loan . . on account of the agitated state of the Canadas, and being in suspense as to the result of my application to the Government, I was several months pressed down with anxiety and fear by this suspense and by reason of the failure of my efforts to obtain relief.

I have given these particulars somewhat in detail, as they afford a striking narrative illustration of the almost insurmountable difficulties which the early pioneers of education in this Province encountered in endeavoring to found these valuable Institutions which have been so useful to this Country, and which have shed such lustre upon their founders' names. It is also due to Victoria University and (as I shall show) to Queen's University also to state these particulars, from the fact that the first practical, yet entirely abortive, attempt to make King's College a Provincial University was made in 1843, two years after the Methodists and Presbyterians had been compelled to found Universities of their own. This they did at a great sacrifice.

By the time that the liberation of King's College took place, in 1849-'53, the really Provincial Universities at Cobourg and Kingston had become recognized as most important factors in our Educational System; and from them alone, up to that time, could students of all denominations obtain a University Education.

In connection with the Victoria University, Faraday Hall, or School of Practical Science, was erected in 1877. It was a handsome and spacious building, and was admirably fitted up for the purpose of Science teaching.

THE UNIVERSITY OF VICTORIA COLLEGE.

Proposed Charter to "Upper Canada Academy" as "Victoria College."

The continued success of the "Upper Canada Academy" induced its promoters to seek for it a higher position and status in the Country. They, therefore, applied to the Legislature in 1841 to grant them an Act of incorporation for the Academy, under the name and style of "Victoria College."

The request was complied with, and the following Act of Incorporation of the College was passed in the Session of the Legislature of 1841:

An Act to Incorporate Victoria College, Cobourg.

I. Whereas, by the Petition of the Board of the Upper Canada Academy, it appears that the said Academy has been in continuous operation during the last five years, and that its success and usefulness would be greatly increased if it were incorporated with the style and privileges of a College; and whereas the said Board have prayed for the incorporation of the said Academy under the name and style of "Victoria College" at Cobourg, with such privileges as were intended to be conferred upon a College about to be established at Kingston, in connection with the Church of Scotland, by an Act of the Legislature of the late Province of Upper Canada, intituled: "An Act to establish a College by the name and style of the University at Kingston"; Be it therefore enacted by the Queen's Most Excellent Majesty, by and with the advice and consent of the Legislative Council, and by the Legislative Assembly of the Province of Canada constituted and assembled by virtue of and under the authority of an Act passed in the Parliament of the United Kingdom of Great Britain and Ireland, intituled: "An Act to Re-unite the Provinces of Upper and Lower Canada, and for the Government of Canada"; and it is hereby enacted by the authority of the same, that, for and notwithstanding anything in the said Charter contained, the said Academy shall hereafter be called and known as "Victoria College" at Cobourg: and that all the provisions of the said Charter, hereinbefore recited, shall be in full force and apply to everything which appertains to the Constitution, Government, Management, Proceedings and Interest of the said College, as they have heretobefore applied to the said Academy.

II. And be it enacted, that the Annual Meeting, or Conference, of the Ministers of the Wesleyan Methodist Church, mentioned and provided for in the hereinbefore recited Charter, for the filling up of vacancies in the Board of Trustees and Visitors, and for other purposes, shall be held each year at any time and place the said Meeting, or Conference, may from time to time appoint.

III. And be it enacted, that the Principal and Professors of the said College, together

UPPER CANADA ACADEMY (LATER VICTORIA COLLEGE) AND FARADAY HALL, COBOURG.

with the Members of the Board (a majority of whom shall form a quorum), shall constitute "the College Senate," which may be assembled as occasion may require by the Principal, by giving one month's notice in the Official Gazette of this Province; and which, whenever there shall be a Principal and four Professors employed in said College, shall have power and authority to confer the degrees of Bachelor, Master and Doctor in the several Arts and Faculties.

IV. And be it enacted, that the President of the Executive Council, the Speakers of the Legislative Council and Legislative Assembly, and the Attorney and Solicitor-General for Canada West, shall be *ex-officio* Visitors of the College, and, as such, Members of the Senate and Board.

V. And be it enacted, that the words "Canada West" in this Act shall be understood to mean all that part of the Province which formerly constituted the Province of Upper Canada.

THE GRANTING OF AN IMPERIAL CHARTER FOR THE UPPER CANADA ACADEMY IN 1836.

The *Christian Guardian,* in giving an account of the Establishment of the Upper Canada Academy at Cobourg, thus makes reference to an article written by the Editor of this Volume for the Second Volume of the Documentary History of Education in Upper Canada:

This Second Volume of Doctor Hodgins' able and most important work . . . commits to the immortal custody of the Press documents of rare . . . interest to Canadian Methodism as containing: 1st, the inception of Upper Canada Academy in 1830-31; 2nd, the laying of the corner-stone of the building in 1832; 3rd, the completion and opening of the institution, and the obtaining of a Royal Charter and financial aid in 1836. The story of the faith, labour, self-sacrifice, energy and almost suffering implied in these doings of sixty years ago, which laid the foundation of Methodist education in Canada, is of course not written here; but here are the original documents from which one may easily gather a vivid conception of the whole scene, as step by step it became history. We can give but an epitome of the facts which are contained in nearly sixty closely printed pages of Doctor Hodgins' work:

1. The first definite steps were taken by Resolutions passed at the Kingston Conference in 1830. The Constitution of the Academy in five articles was adopted, and a Committee of nine persons appointed to decide upon the location, name, etcetera, of the Institution.

2. On the 27th of January, 1831, this Committee selected Cobourg as the location, appointed Trustees and a Building Committee, who were authorized to proceed as soon as £2,000 were subscribed, and one-fourth of the amount paid, made arrangements for Agents, for the approximate form of Building, and gave the Institution the name of Upper Canada Academy. On the 10th of May, 1831, Tenders were called for by Mr. Conger, Secretary of the Building Committee. In September of that year the subscriptions amounted to £3,954, the Reverend John Beatty was appointed General Agent for the collection of subscriptions, and the Committee were finally instructed by Conference to proceed with the Building, the Plans of which had been adopted. At this same conference an address was adopted to Sir John Colborne, the Lieutenant-Governor of Upper Canada, the reply to which is a curiosity in our day. It speaks of the Methodist Ministers who had undertaken this work as "leaders of societies who, perhaps, have neither experience nor judgment to appreciate the advantages of a liberal education." The reply of Mr. Egerton Ryerson, Editor of the *Christian Guardian*, was characteristic and to the point. On the 7th of June, 1832, the Corner-stone of the new Building was laid with appropriate ceremonies.

In the Autumn of 1835 the Building, after the most strenuous labours of Agents, Trustees, Committee and Conference, was approaching completion. In the month of June of that year, £7,000 or £8,000 had been subscribed and less than £3,000 collected, and the Trustees were already nearly £3,000 in debt. Mr. Ryerson was sent to England with a Petition to the Imperial Government for pecuniary aid and a Royal Charter. When he prepared his appeal for the Government and people of England, the home contributions had reached £4,000 and the debt stood at £2,000. Mr. Ryerson was furnished with Letters of introduction and commendation from Sir John Colborne and from that patron of learning, the Honourable Peter McGill, the founder of McGill University in Montreal, and others. Mr. Ryerson reached England in December, 1835, and then commenced a long "weary and disheartening effort" to accomplish the task assigned. Any financial aid from the Canadian revenues of the Imperial Government was at first absolutely refused; but a recommendation was sent to the Colonial Legislature asking them to make a grant. The Charter was held in suspense, "and would have failed to pass the Great Seal had not its promoter been skilful enough to deal with perplexing questions in regard to it as they arose, and had he not been able to prove to the satisfaction of the distinguished Law Officers of the Crown in England that the principles which the Charter embodied were quite in harmony with those that prevailed in Canada and were acknowledged by all parties in England. He was further able to show that the status which the Charter accorded to the Methodist Body in this Country had previously been granted to it, and was so recognized by the Statute law of Upper Canada." The arguments by which all this was accomplished are now for the first time printed at length in Doctor Hodgins' work, and furnish a valuable chapter not only in our educational history but also in that weary conflict by which perfect religious equality before the law was secured for our Country. It is of interest to know that a most important step, as Doctor Ryerson at one time stated to the present Writer, in this victory for equal rights, was the securing of the Charter of Victoria University, which is, we believe, the first Charter ever granted to a Dissenting Body by the Imperial Government of England for such a purpose. The old parchment, which is treasured in our vaults at Victoria, thus stands as Britain's Magna Charta of religious equality.

The Charter passed the Great Seal October 12th, 1836, and Mr. Ryerson continued his labours in collecting funds until May, 1837, realizing, over and above the entire expenses of his mission, about £1,000 for the funds of the academey. Meantime, in June of that year, the Academy was opened for pupils, under Reverend Matthew Richey, M.A., as Principal. In June, 1837, Mr. Ryerson returned to this country, now in need of his services in another way, bringing with him an order from Lord Glenelg for a grant of £4,100 to the funds of the new Institution, thus completing at every point the full success of his mission.

The Reverend Egerton Ryerson as President of Victoria College.

On the establishment of the Upper Canada Academy in 1832-36, the Reverend Matthew Richey, an eloquent and noted Wesleyan Methodist Minister, was appointed as its first Principal, (page 64). He continued as such until about 1840, when the Reverend Jesse Hurlburt, the Senior Master, was appointed temporarily as Acting Principal, in the hope that, as soon as circumstances would permit, the Reverend Egerton Ryerson would accept the office. A strong effort was made, in March, 1841, to induce him to do so, by the Reverend Daniel C. Van Norman, and Mr. William Kingston, Masters in the Upper Canada Academy, and prospective Professors in Victoria College. In a joint Letter written to him by these Gentlemen, on the 31st of March, 1841, they say:

We, as a Body, could scarcely be placed in more favourable circumstances to benefit the Country than those at present occupied by our Church. In comparison with other Christian Denominations, God has placed us on vantage ground, inasmuch as we occupy at present the field of Education almost without a rival.

Now, Reverend Sir, to you and to you alone, do we look, under these peculiar circumstances. It remains for you to decide whether the Academy shall rank amongst the first Literary Institutions of the Country, and become an important agent in forming its future character and controlling its destiny, or have a mere nominal existence.

With one, to whom Canada is already so greatly indebted, and who has for years been made the "Servant of the Public," duty alone (or where can I be most useful?), will turn the scale in matters of this nature. The present generation will soon have passed away; and, whether you can ever so effectively and extensively promote the interests of the rising and future generations in any other field of labour as at the head of such an Institution as this, appears, at least to us, not at all problematical.

Notwithstanding that we used our influence to have another placed at its head, *pro tempore*, still we supposed that upon you, as soon as the circumstances of the Church and of the Country should become favourable, would devolve the superintendence of the Upper Canada Academy.

We speak the honest conviction of our minds, when we say, that from our acquaintance with Literary Institutions, and the qualification necessary for those who have their direction, we believe no person can be found in whom so many of these qualifications are combined as in yourself. Those peculiar intellectual endowments, and other various qualities,—which have already gained for you an amount of influence and popularity, possessed by no other man in Canada,—are admirably suited to the situation of President of a Literary Institution, and would go far towards establishing the character of our Academy for permanent prosperity—investing it with attractions possessed by no other School in the Country. . . .

You have at heart the welfare of our Church; and, in what relation can you so fully subserve her interests as by occupying a situation in which you would have the direction of the education of those whom God may call to minister in her Sanctuaries? All circumstances being considered then, does not Providence seem clearly to point out this place as the principal scene of your future labours?

D. C. VAN NORMAN.
W. KINGSTON.[*]

COBOURG, 21st of March, 1841.

At a meeting of the Board of Trustees of the newly constituted College, held in the early part of October, 1841, it very cordially approved of the recommendation of the Committee, and the Reverend Egerton Ryerson was unanimously appointed by it to be Principal of Victoria College. He did not agree to accept the appointment, except with a view to the provisional opening by him of the Institution as a College in October, as he did not desire to give up the pastoral charge of the Adelaide Street Church—to which he had been appointed at the Conference of 1840—until the Spring of 1842, but as he said:

At the end of two years labours in the Station of Adelaide Street Church, I was again wrested from my loved work (as a Pastor) by an official pressure brought to bear upon me to accept the Presidency of Victoria College, which was raised from being Upper Canada Academy to be a College, opened and incorporated, in 1842, as a University College.

The Letter of Mr. Wilson S. Conger, M.P.P., and a Member of the Board of Victoria College, announcing this appointment, was written to Doctor Ryerson on the 3rd of September, 1841, as follows:

I have the satisfaction to inform you that at our Committee Meeting held on Wednesday last (all the Members being present), you were, by their unanimous voice, recommended to the "Board" to fill the Principal Chair in "Victoria College," and I must beg of you not to throw any obstacle in the way of your appointment to that important trust.

---

[*] Mr. William Kingston eventually retired from Victoria College and became one of the Officers of the Civil Service at Ottawa. A few years ago, two or three of his old pupils waited on him, to tender their heartfelt thanks for his efforts to make mathematics an agreeable study to them in the old days at Victoria College. The ex-students were Senator Brouse, J. L. Biggar, M.P., and the Writer. He was deeply touched by this personal tribute from his old pupils.

I need not say to you that our hope of success depends entirely upon raising the character of the College above that of the Upper Canada Academy. To do this, we must place at its head a person holding a commanding influence over that portion of society from whom we expect to receive support; and, allow me to say that the Committee believe they are only doing you justice, when they say that they know of no person so likely to accomplish that end, or to satisfy public expectations, as yourself.

I have written to several members of the Board, informing them of what we have done, and requesting them to attend a Board Meeting to be held here at the close of the Session. At this Meeting, the Committee will lay before the Board a statement of their affairs, and arrangements will, of course, be made for the ensuing year.

COBOURG, 3rd of September, 1841.   W. S. CONGER.

THE REVEREND EGERTON RYERSON, D.D.,
First Principal of Victoria College.

OPENING OF THE UPPER CANADA ACADEMY AS A PREPARATORY COLLEGE, ON THE 21ST OF OCTOBER, 1841.*

On the 21st of October, 1841, the formal opening of the Upper Canada Academy, as a "Preparatory College," prior "to its commencement as Victoria College" took place. At the time appointed, the Professors, Officers and Students being present, the Reverend Egerton Ryerson, the Principal elect, delivered an Address on "The Kind of Education which Canadian Youths require; and Hints to them for its Attainment." Only portions of this Address which refer to this preliminary opening of the College—to the history and circumstances of the Institution, and to the recent Legislative proceedings on its behalf—are given below:

In opening this Institution, (the Principal said), as a preparatory College, with a view to its commencement as a College proper, at the beginning of the next Academic

---

* It was my good fortune to be present on this occasion, having been a student of Upper Canada Academy.—J.G.H.

year, I deem it advisable to make a few observations on the leading features of that kind of education which it is intended to impart at the Victoria College, and to offer you a few principal suggestions for your present assistance and encouragement, as Students, in your ordinary and preparatory studies.

Gentlemen and Young Friends,—I cannot conclude these remarks without adverting to the new and elevated character with which this Institution has been invested by the Parliament of Upper Canada.

His late Most Gracious Majesty William IV., of precious memory, first invested this Institution, in 1836, with a corporate Charter as the Upper Canada Academy—the first Institution of the kind established by Royal Charter unconnected with the Church of England, throughout the British Colonies. It is a cause of renewed satisfaction and congratulation that, after five years operation as an Academy, it has been incorporated as a University and financially assisted by the unanimous vote of both branches of the Provincial Legislature—sanctioned by more than an official cordiality, in Her Majesty's name, by the late lamented Lord Sydenham, Governor-General, one of whose last Messages to the Legislative Assembly was a recommendation to grant £500 as an aid to the Victoria College. . . . We have buoyant hopes for our Country when our Rulers and Legislators direct their earliest and most liberal attention to its Literary Institutions and educational interests. A foundation for a Common School System in this Province has been laid by the Legislature, which I believe will, at no distant day, exceed in efficiency any yet established on the American Continent;* and I have reason to believe that the attention of the Government is earnestly directed to make permanent provision for the support of Colleges also, that they may be rendered efficient in their operation and accessible to as large a number of the enterprising youth of our Country as possible. . . .

It will be my province and aim to occupy the moral and more practical departments, by connecting the acquisition of knowledge with the duties and interests of private life so that you may go forth from this Institution not merely sound scholars but qualified and disposed to discharge your duties as Christians and citizens in all the relations to which the guidance of Providence, the authorities of your Country, and the voice of your fellow-subjects may call you.

Two of the best and most laborious years of my life have been employed in promoting the establishment of this Institution; and if my humble labours will in any way contribute to its successful operations and usefulness, they shall be freely and unreservedly bestowed—deeply convinced as I am of its infinite importance to the educational, moral and general interests of a large portion of my fellow-subjects, if not of the Province at large.

The present session, commencing with the attendance of a larger number of Students than have attended at the commencement of any previous Session, augurs well for the future. Had we even commenced upon a scale more limited, and with an attendance less numerous, there would still have been ground for encouragement and hope. The University of Glasgow began in 1450, with one Professor in Theology and three in Philosophy. Mareschal College, Aberdeen, began with a Principal and two Professors. At the first foundation of the University of Edinburgh, only one Professor was appointed, and he the Minister of the city. And the celebrated University of Cambridge itself commenced in the twelfth century under the auspices of an Abbott and two Monks, who hired and delivered public lectures in a barn! Encouraged by such examples, and animated by our present prospects, we confidently anticipate extensive success and usefulness in the future operations of this Institution. For your success and happiness, my Young Friends, I feel the deepest solicitude; with the parents of several of you I have been a school-fellow in my boyhood; and it is my earnest wish and prayer, and will, I am sure, be the united endeavour of your Instructors, that your attendance here may be eminently useful to you all, and be followed by lives of virtue, honour and usefulness.

---

* This memorable prophecy, made by Doctor Ryerson in 1841, was abundantly verified in after years, chiefly as the result of his own labors in maturing the School System, of which he was the Founder.

The "Provisional" Officers of Victoria College, as appointed by the Board of Trustees at the time, were as follows:

The Reverend Egerton Ryerson, Principal, with the Department of Moral Philosophy and Rhetoric.

The Reverend Jesse Hurlburt, A.M., Professor of Hebrew, and the Natural Sciences.

The Reverend Daniel C. Van Norman, A.M., Professor of the Greek and Latin Languages.

Mr. William Kingston, Professor of Mathematics, with the charge of the English Department.

Mr. Crowley, Assistant in the English Department.

The Reverend John Beatty, General Agent and Treasurer.

Mr. Robert Webster, Steward of the College.

The Curriculum of the College proper, (omitting the English Department), was as follows:

Freshman Class.—Algebra completed; Geometry; Geometrical Drawing; History of England; French; Virgil, Livy, Latin Exercises; Roman Antiquities; Græca Majora, Xenophon's Memorabilia, Cyropœdia, Anabasis, Herodotus, Thucydides; Physiology.

Sophomore Class.—Geometry completed; Logarithms, Plane Trigonometry, Mensuration of Superficies and Solids; Isoperemetry, Mensuration of Heights and Distances; Navigation, Surveying, Levelling; French; Cicero de Amicitia et de Senectute; Horace: Lysias, Isocrates, Demosthenes, Plato; Latin and Greek Exercises; Rhetoric; Evidences of Christianity.

Junior Class.—Spherical Trigonometry, Conic Sections; Natural Philosophy; Chemistry; Cicero de Oratore, Tacitus; Homer's Iliad and Odyssey, Greek Tragedies; Latin and Greek Exercises; Hebrew; Intellectual Philosophy.

Senior Class.—Differential and Integral Calculus, Astronomy, Latin and Greek; Chemistry reviewed; Logic, Moral and Political Philosophy, British Constitution; Natural Theology, Hebrew; Natural History; and the Philosophy of the Bible.

The Reverend Doctor Nelles, President of Victoria University, states that only two special donations have been made to this University, videlicet:

1st. A gift of $635, made in the year 1856, by J. George Hodgins, LL.B., for establishing two annual prizes in English Composition, and one in Scripture History. By investment this amount was increased in value.

2nd. A donation of $800, in the year 1860, by his Royal Highness the Prince of Wales, the interest of which is annually appropriated to the Prince of Wales gold and silver Medals.

Victoria College—A Retrospect and Prospect—1829-1892.[*]

By A. L. Langford, M.A.

A student of the educational events which occurred in the early days of this Province might very fairly wonder why it seemed necessary to the men of that time to found three Universities—Toronto, Queen's and Victoria. The duties of the early settlers were necessarily far removed from higher education, and only a small proportion of their sons could be spared for an advanced scholastic course.

---

[*] Owing to the fact that this interesting sketch of Victoria University contained a good deal of information already given in these previous pages, relating to Victoria University, I was necessarily obliged to omit the parts of this paper which stated the same facts and related to the same incidents in the history of the University.

It would hence seem to us to have been the part of wisdom in those days to concentrate work and economize resources. What were the circumstances, therefore, that can be cited in justification of this seemingly needless extravagance?

The answer to this question will take us at once into the midst of contestants who, though their weapons were always keen, yet wielded them generally with

VICTORIA COLLEGE, TORONTO.

courtesy. To understand aright the questions in the debates of 1820 and the immediately succeeding score of years, one must state briefly what had preceded this time of conflict. Governor Simcoe, the first Governor of the Province, arrived in this country with at least two definite ideas in his mind for the betterment of its citizens: Religion and Education. By education he had in view not only the rudimentary schools, but also an endowed " University, which would be most useful to inculcate just principles, habits and manners into the rising generation." He further stated as his forecast for the proposed University in Upper Canada, that it might " prevent the youth of the Province going to the United States, and thus pervert their British principles." . . .

The first mention of a Methodist College was at a Conference held in Ancaster in 1829. . . . Next year at Kingston, at a similar gathering, a " committee of seven devised and reported a plan for establishing Upper Canada Academy." Their report was adopted by Conference. . . . " The object," as stated by Doctor Ryerson, " of this proposed Seminary is not to compete with any College which may be established in this Province, but rather to be tributary to it." . . . At the following Conference, September, 1831, owing to the success attending the effort to obtain subscriptions, it was recommended " that the Building Committee at Cobourg proceed with the building." . . . The utmost efforts of all concerned up to 1836 could raise only £4,000, leaving £2,000 for which the trustees had to become personally responsible to the bank in order to complete the payments on the building. At this crisis the Legislature, in 1837, came to their aid and granted as a loan £4,150. . . . That the leaders in the Legislature were adherents of the Anglican, Presbyterian and Roman Catholic Churches made this generous aid all the more gratifying. This relieved the promoters of the College from all immediate anxiety, but meantime " the formal opening of Upper Canada Academy " had taken place on the 18th of June, 1836, under the Reverend Matthew Richey as Principal, with one hundred and twenty Students.

From 1836 to 1841 Upper Canada Academy played an important part in supplying a rudimentary education to the young men and women of the Province, and in some parts of it one can still find old pupils of Upper Canada Academy. . . .

Between 1836 and 1841 the Academy had the usual experiences incident to such institutions, growing attendance, and in consequence deficits and shrinking funds. Still, owing to the efforts of the laymen and ministers, often at a very great personal sacrifice, the Academy was kept in operation and grew till 1841. Then, owing to King's College maintaining its sectarian attitude, an Act was passed by both branches of the Provincial Legislature, enlarging the powers of the Academy to those of a University, with the name of Victoria College. At the same time a grant of £500 was made. . . .

On October the 21st, 1841, the formal opening of Victoria College took place, with Doctor Ryerson as Principal and Professor of Moral Philosophy and Rhetoric. . . . The first Graduates of Victoria University in course were: Oliver Springer, '46; William Ormiston, '48; Wesley P. Wright, '48; Charles Cameron, '49; and James Campbell, '49.*

In 1850 the Reverend S. S. Nelles, M.A., was appointed Principal, and he at once set to work to increase the number of the Faculties connected with the University. The Faculty of Medicine, in Toronto, was added in 1855, the Faculty of Law in 1860, and later the Faculty of Theology.

The next long step in advance made by Victoria was in 1871, two years after the Legislative grant was cut off. The Faculty of Theology was established largely by the generous help of the late Mr. and Mrs. Edward Jackson, of Hamilton. . . .

---

* It is a gratifying fact that Victoria College was the first University in Upper Canada whose doors were open to receive students. The first Session commenced in October, 1841 ; that of Queen's College University in March, 1842, and King's College University in June, 1843. The first Graduate in arts who received a diploma in Upper Canada was sent out from Victoria College in 1845-46.—J.G.H.

The last matter to be dealt with in this statement of the crises in Victoria's history is the cutting off of the Legislative grant of $5,000 in 1869. . . . It should be borne in mind that Victoria at least, in accepting this money, had at the same time put herself under governmental inspection. Doctor Ryerson said in 1842: "The Charter of Victoria College provides that the Speakers of the two Houses of the Legislature and the Law Officers of the Crown for Canada West shall be members of the Victoria College Board and of its Senate, and as such they have the right to visit and examine into the affairs of the College at any time. We have not asked aid from the Government without giving it ample supervision, and, if it chose, a paramount influence in the operations of the College." . . . Notwithstanding this protection to the public interests, the Legislature voted to cut off these

THE REVEREND S. S. NELLES, D.D., LL.D.,
President of Victoria University.

grants. . . . Victoria, since getting rid of governmental aid and depending wholly on her natural friends and supporters, has made steady progress in equipment, staff, endowment and buildings.

With now more than seventy years of honourable service behind her, and with prospects that seem to promise a much wider field of service in the future, why should not Victoria students and graduates feel proud and confident? *Conscientia facti satis est.*

THE VICTORIA COLLEGE FACULTY OF THEOLOGY.

BY THE REVEREND J. F. McLAUGHLIN, B.A., B.D.

Previous to 1871 Victoria University had no Faculty of Theology, but many students in preparation for the ministry had received instruction in the Arts course, taking their Theological studies elsewhere. Biblical History, Biblical Greek and Hebrew, Ethics, and Christian Evidences, formed a part of the Victoria College Arts curriculum. . . .

In 1871 the Faculty of Theology was established largely as the result of the generous gifts made for that purpose by Mr. and Mrs. Edward Jackson, whose memory is gratefully cherished in our Halls. The Reverend N. Burwash, B.D., our present Chancellor, was made Dean and Professor of Biblical Literature and Theology. Associated with him were Reverend Chancellor Nelles; John Wilson, M.A., and Reverend A. H. Reynar, M.A. Doctor Burwash was formerly Professor of Chemistry and Natural History in the Faculty of Arts, and he continued for some years to occupy the dual position, giving instruction in Hebrew and Aramaic, Old and New Testament Exegesis, and Systematic Theology, in addition to his lectures in Natural Science. The other Professors also held positions in the Faculty of Arts, yet they cheerfully undertook the additional labour now imposed upon them.

From the beginning a broad Curriculum was framed, in which Biblical studies had a central and important place, and a high standard of excellence was sought. A course of four years was offered in Arts and Theology, leading to the degree of Bachelor of Divinity. This, however, was replaced in 1874 by a course similar to that now provided, requiring three years study in Theology, at least two years of which must be taken after graduation in Arts. Instruction was also given in the subjects of the ordinary course prescribed for probationers. Then, as now, the close association of students in Arts and Theology, due to the intimate relationship of the two Faculties, was regarded as of the highest value in promoting a broad and truly Christian culture.

In the first year twenty-five students were enrolled in Theology. In 1874 the first class graduated, and the degree of B.D. was bestowed upon three candidates— Hugh Johnston, M.A.; J. R. Ross, M.A., and A. L. Russell, M.A.

In 1883 Rev. G. C. Workman, M.A., became Adjunct Professor in Theology, and in 1885 he was made Professor of Old Testament Exegesis and Literature, which position he held until his resignation in 1892. In 1884, upon the union of Albert College with Victoria, the Reverend Doctor Badgley, formerly Professor in Albert College, became Professor of Mental and Moral Philosophy, and Adjunct Professor in Theology. He continued a highly esteemed member of the Faculty of Theology until his death, in 1905.

In 1887 the Reverend Doctor Burwash became Chancellor of the University. In the same year the Reverend F. H. Wallace, M.A., was made Professor of New Testament Exegesis and Literature, and subsequently Secretary of the Faculty. Upon the removal of the University to Toronto the Faculty was enlarged. The Reverend John Burwash, M.A., D.Sc., became Professor of Homiletics and English Bible, and Professor Wallace was made Dean. Doctor Wallace, who is a Graduate of the University of Toronto, brought to his new position not only a fine reputation for exact scholarship, which he has amply sustained, but also a practical knowledge of the work of the ministry drawn from his previous experience as pastor of several of the most important churches in Ontario Methodism. The number of students enrolled this year in Theology, and under his care, is upwards of one hundred and fifty.

In 1906 the Reverend Doctor Blewett was appointed Professor of Ethics and Apologetics, in succession to the late Reverend Doctor Badgley, and the Reverend

R. P. Bowles, M.A., Professor of Homiletics and Pastoral Theology. The present Staff consists, therefore, of seven professors.

I cannot conclude this brief sketch without paying a warm tribute of respect and admiration to the four men to whose faith and courage the establishment of this Faculty was due. Two of those men are still with us, occupying honoured places in the College and in the Church—the Chancellor and the Dean of the Faculty of Arts.

THE PRESIDENT OF VICTORIA COLLEGE HONORED.

At the close of one of the Sessions of Victoria University in 1860, the Students, in order to testify the warm regard for their Principal and Chancellor, presented

THE REVEREND NATHANAEL BURWASH, S.T.D., LL.D., F.R.S.C.,
President and Chancellor of Victoria University.

the Reverend Doctor Nelles with a Silver Service, and a highly complimentary address, to which the Reverend President and Chancellor of the College replied as follows:

1. I accept with great pleasure this flattering expression of your regard. For the last ten years my thoughts and labours have been devoted, amid many discouragements, to the preservation and improvement of our College, and it cannot but be gratifying to me to receive from the students of the present year so kind and valuable a proof that my labours are not wholly unappreciated. In the character of our Alumni, in the number, gifts, and diligence of our Under-graduates, and especially in the liberal and Christian principles upon which our University has been conducted, we have a strong security for its future. So long as Christianity continues to flourish in our Land, so long Victoria College and similar Seminaries will also flourish, and they, who, amid opposition and obloquy, now toil to establish such Institutions, will hereafter reap an abundant reward.

2. In closing the exercises of the present Academic Year, I am affected to think that I have of late been so much separated from you, and that now, from many of you, I am

ANNESLEY HALL, THE WOMAN'S RESIDENCE OF VICTORIA COLLEGE, TORONTO.

to be separated most widely and permanently: I can only say that my good wishes and prayers will follow each of you through life. It saddens me to remember how little of the future career of any one of you can be foreseen. The uncertainty of your several destinies, after leaving these Halls, is perhaps less than that which attended your entrance. Your characters have become somewhat matured and settled, and you have been brought, I trust, under the guidance and principles which will lead you on to usefulness and honour, yet nothing can save you from the severe and perilous conflict of life. Much of joy and sunshine may await you, but also disappointment and sorrow. These are wisely intermingled in the system of Divine discipline under which we live. Ardently as I could desire for you a joyous future, I do not pray that you should be wholly free from "the days of darkness." I pray rather that each of you may become wise, and strong, and sure, and that you may cultivate, in sunshine and in shade, that essential principle of all strength and excellence,—a true faith in God.

What is called a prosperous life is commonly the most beset with dangers. With a proper interpretation I may commend to you the paradoxical lines of Lover:—

> O watch you well by daylight.
> By daylight you may fear.
> But keep no watch in darkness,
> The Angels then are near.
> O watch you well in pleasure,
> For pleasure oft betrays,
> But keep no watch in sorrow,
> When joy withdraws its rays.

Remember that the goal of life is spiritual perfection, and those who have most fully attained to this great object have come round by the rough and thorny road of sorrow.

> Then in life's goblet freely press,
> The leaves that give it bitterness,
> Nor prize the coloured waters less,
> For in thy darkness and distress,
> New light and strength they give.

I thank you, my young friends, for your costly and beautiful gift, with your affectionate Address. They will ever remain as precious Memontoes in my Family. They will remind me that Victoria College has many devoted Sons scattered through the Land. They will ofttimes serve to cheer me and my dear Companion amidst future toils and trials, and will inspire me with new ardour for the advancement of our beloved University.

Annesley Hall—The Woman's Residence of Victoria College.

The movement to erect a Women's Residence in connection with Victoria University received its first important impetus in the year 1896, when the will of the late Mr. Hart A. Massey bequeathed the sum of $50,000 for the purpose. The money for the purchase of the Land Site was afterwards raised by an Association of Ladies interested in the University, of which Mrs. George A. Cox was Treasurer. The original gift of Mr. Massey was also supplemented, while several others contributed largely to the Furnishings. The Hall was opened to the Students in October, 1903. It has proved to be a most popular Institution, and has more than fulfilled the objects which its Founders had in view.

In May, 1902, the Corner Stone was laid, on behalf of Mrs. Eliza Phelps Massey, by Mr. Chester D. Massey, and the Building was completed and occupied in the Autumn of 1903.

The cost of the Building and furnishing was approximately Ninety Thousand Dollars, ($90,000). It is not surpassed by any such Residences in the extent of its accommodation and the completeness of its appointments. It provides for the resi-

LIBRARY OF VICTORIA UNIVERSITY, TORONTO.

dence of fifty-six Students, besides Officers and Servants. Another step in the same direction is the proposal of Mrs. Massey-Treble to erect and equip a University Laboratory for Household Science.—*Communicated.*

New Library for Victoria College.

The friends of Victoria College throughout our Province will rejoice that the College has recently been made the beneficiary of munificent gifts for the building and equipment of a Students' Residence and for the building and endowment of a College Library.

It was found, however, that Mr. Andrew Carnegie's generous appropriation of $50,000 for the Library Building was not sufficient to enable the Committee to erect a Library that would harmonize with the group of stone Buildings which eventually will adorn our College grounds. The endowment of $50,000, provided chiefly through the beneficence of Mr. Cyrus A. Birge, could not be used for building purposes.

After competitive plans from three architects had been submitted, very favourable tenders were obtained for the Building, from which it was ascertained we would need $86,000 to complete the building and equip it with modern fireproof Book-stacks. Toward this amount generous friends of the College have added $25,000 to Mr. Carnegie's gift.

For the balance required the Professors of the College and others have become personally responsible rather than delay a work so greatly needed.

The Building is now nearing completion, as will be seen from accompanying illustration. The style is perpendicular Gothic. It will be an attraction to the College, an ornament to the Queen's Park, and a credit to Canadian architects and workmen. The Oxford type and flavour have been creditably reproduced.

The Library will give a permanent home to our priceless possessions of Documents and Books, and place them beyond ordinary risk of destruction, by fire or otherwise.

In the new building it is intended to provide not only for accommodation of Students, but also to have facilities provided and a special Room set apart for Members of the ministry, not only in Toronto, but throughout the Province, and for the Alumni of the College. It is proposed to make the Library a useful centre for reference and research work on a scale more nearly adequate than has been possible heretofore.

VICTORIA COLLEGE, TORONTO.

THE UNIVERSITY OF QUEEN'S COLLEGE, KINGSTON, 1829-1910.

As early as 1829 it was felt among the Members of the United Presbytery of Upper Canada that a Seminary, or College, for the training of their Ministers was highly desirable. As the management of King's College at Toronto was in the hands of the adherents of the Church of England, it was felt that such an Institution could not be made available for Presbyterian Theological Instruction. A Committee of the British House of Commons, to which had been referred petitions from Canada in 1828 and 1830 against the exclusive character of the Charter of King's College, Toronto, were disposed to solve the difficulty by suggesting that two Theological Chairs be established in King's College, (and did so recommend)—one each for Students of the Churches of England and Scotland, respectively. Nothing, however, of the kind was done; nor was there any Arts College then open on equal terms to all the youth of the Country. The Presbyterians, like the Methodists, had, therefore, to found an Institution of their own for this purpose.

On the 11th of January, 1830, a meeting of the Presbytery was held at Brockville, at which the Committee on a Literary and Theological Institution, in reporting the result of their enquiries, stated that they were happy in informing the Presbytery that the erection of a Literary Institution, embracing a Course of appropriate Studies for such as are assigned for the Christian Ministry, meets with the most decided and individual approbation of the friends of Christ, and of the public generally.

In June, 1831, the United Presbytery of Upper Canada issued an appeal for aid to establish a Literary and Theological Seminary, and deputed Mr. Eliakim Cory of Prince Edward County to collect subscriptions in the United States and Canada. The *New York Evangelist* of the 13th of August, 1831, issued the following notice on the subject, which was copied into the *Christian Guardian* of September the 3rd, 1831:

We would invite the attention of our readers to the appeal of the United Presbytery of Upper Canada which we publish below. We cannot but think that the interests of sound doctrine and of vital religion in Canada are very intimately connected with the establishment of the proposed institution. We hope that the Christian public will contribute liberally for an object of so high importance. Mr. Cory appears before the public with well attested credentials, as the agent of the Presbytery to collect donations. We commend Mr. Cory and the object of his mission to the generous and sympathizing consideration of our Christian friends, and trust that the appeal now made to them will not be in vain. The Presbytery feels deeply convinced that such an Institution as is now contemplated is of vital importance, not only to the prosperity of Religion in that part of the Country, but to the Province at large, especially as there is no public Seminary in the Province where young men, as Presbyterians, can be trained for the work of the Gospel Ministry. In the intended Institution provision will be made for such pious and devoted young men as may give themselves to the work of the Lord in the public ministry of His Word in Canada.

An Institution such as is contemplated by the friends of the Redeemer, at Pleasant Bay, is essentially necessary for the spread of the Gospel in Upper Canada—yet, however desirable and important such an Institution is believed to be, it cannot be carried into effect without the kind aid and co-operation of the friends of science and religion in the Province and the United States. Mr. Cory, therefore, and the object of his mission are commended to the care and blessing of the Great Head of the Church, and to the kind offices, attention and liberality of all good men.

WILLIAM SMART, Clerk of the Presbytery.   ANDREW BELL, Moderator.
Dated at Brockville, Upper Canada, this 16th of June, 1831.

Part XII. Queen's College University, Kingston. 89

A session of the Synod, in connection with the Church of Scotland, was held in Kingston the 18th of August, 1832. . . . A reference from the Presbytery of York respecting King's College and an Overture from the Reverend William Rintoul on the training of young men for the Ministry were laid before the Synod. The substance of the Overture was that the Synod recognize the great importance of a Seminary for educating and training young men for the ministry within the bounds of the Synod; that the Synod should

VERY REVEREND D. M. GORDON, D.D., LL.D.,
Principal of Queen's University, Kingston.

make an immediate and urgent application to the Government to found an Institution, or to endow Professorships in connection with the Synod; and that, in the event of the Government not founding or indefinitely delaying to found an Institution, or Professorships, the Synod should take into serious consideration the importance of adopting a permanent measure for the education and training of ministers. The Synod resolved to adopt the first two articles of the Overture, and appointed a Committee to prepare a Memorial on the subject to the King. (Page 466 of the Reverend Doctor Gregg's History.)

The Presbyterian Church continued to discuss the question of establishing a College from 1831 onward. The idea kept growing, but the undertaking seemed too great. A few students for the Ministry were in Hamilton, receiving instruction in literary subjects from Doctor Rae, Grammar School Master, under the direction of the Presbytery of Hamilton.

In a note from the Reverend George Bell, Registrar of Queen's College, dated the 23rd of November, 1893, he says:

If King's College had been opened on equal terms to the public previous to 1838, Queen's College would not have been founded at all,—the prevalent idea being from 1831 to 1838 to found only a Theological College for Students for the ministry. But the uncertainty about the opening of King's College and the pressing necessity for having something done led to a determination . . . to found some kind of an Institution . . . for the training of Ministers for the Presbyterian Church.

This feeling led to the idea of establishing such a training school at Pleasant Bay in Prince Edward District, should funds warrant it.

Sandford Fleming, Esquire, C.E., C.M.G., afterwards Chancellor of Queen's University, in his Address on the same occasion said:

The Church of Scotland in Canada . . . took every means to promote the establishment of a College which would be generally accessible to all classes of the people, and which would command the confidence and support of all Denominations of Christians.

At a meeting held in Hamilton, in November, 1839, the Commission which had been appointed for that purpose prepared the draft of a Charter for the proposed College. Kingston was selected by the Synod as the Site for the new Institution.

Meeting Held in Kingston to Promote the Establishment of Queen's College.

A Public Meeting was held in Kingston on the 18th of December, 1839. Its object was to promote the establishment of Queen's College in that City. The Reverend John Machar acted as Chairman, and Mr. Roderick M. Rose as Secretary. The following Resolutions were adopted at the Meeting:

Moved by Major Logie, seconded by John A. Macdonald, Esquire, and

Resolved, 1: That this Meeting deeply regret the limited means afforded the youth of this Country of acquiring a liberal education, founded on Religious principles, and more especially the total want of an Institution for educating and preparing young men for the Ministry in connection with the Church of Scotland.

Moved by Thomas Greer, Esquire, and seconded by Reverend Henry Gordon, and

Resolved, 2: That this Meeting learns with great satisfaction the proposal by the Commission of Synod to erect a College in Kingston for the instruction of young men, with a view to the Holy Ministry in connection with the Church of Scotland, and the education of youth generally in the various branches of Literature and Science, upon sound Religious principles.

Moved by the Reverend James Williamson, seconded by Mr. Francis A. Harper, and

Resolved, 3: That this Meeting pledge themselves by every means and exertions in their power, to forward the views and intentions of Synod.

Moved by Mr. William Ferguson, seconded by Mr. Joseph Bruce, and

Resolved, 4: That a Committee of six be appointed, with power to add to their number, to collect subscriptions from Members of the Congregation of St. Andrew's Church, Kingston, and from others friendly to the proposed Institution, and to exert themselves in such a way as may best promote its successful completion.

Moved by Mr. John A. Macdonald, seconded by the Reverend William Reid, and *Resolved*, 5: That the Committee consist of Messieurs Francis A. Harper, A. Pringle, John Roy, Robert Matthews, Thomas Greer, and Roderick M. Rose.

SIR JOHN A. MACDONALD'S RECOLLECTION OF THE QUEEN'S COLLEGE MEETING OF FIFTY YEARS BEFORE.

One of those who took part in the Meeting in St. Andrew's Church in December, 1839, was Sir John A. Macdonald, who thus referred to it, in a pleasant speech, which he made at the Jubilee Meeting of Queen's University held in December, 1889:

This morning, after my arrival from Ottawa, I was informed that I was expected to make some allusion to the events of fifty years ago. Since that memorable occasion, when a small party, small, as compared with recent gatherings, assembled in St. Andrew's Church, many events of importance have occurred to me, which might naturally be expected to impair somewhat my recollection of what occurred in that Church, on the 18th of December, 1839. But, I am happy to say, that my recollection of that Meeting is perfect.

I was a young man, just commencing my practice, and, being a Kingstonian, and a Presbyterian, I was exceedingly anxious that my native City, practically, should have the honour of being a University City,—a Seat of Learning. I was one of those who assembled in St. Andrew's Church, now gone, like most of those who, that day, gathered within its walls.

His Excellency, the Governor-General, Lord Stanley, was kind enough to say that he had no doubt that those who were present on that occasion could give a more historically correct statement of the events of that time, than, in his position, he could do. But, he ventured to state, that I, among the rest, with the youthful energy of the time, spoke eloquently. Now, I must confess that His Excellency did me more than justice . . . and, when I arose to move the Resolution that was placed in my hands,—and although I had prepared myself for the effort,—I was in such a mortal fright that I did not say a single word of what I had intended to say—*Obstupui steteruntque comœ faucibus hæsit* —I just placed the Resolution in the Chairman's hands, and sat down. My silence was golden; and I was cheered more than if I had made a speech, or had courage enough to deliver it.

It was, however, an occasion of great pride to me to see the successful laying of the foundation of this University. It was still more gratifying to me to see its almost immediate success. The Presbyterians of Upper Canada, and the Protestant portions of Lower Canada, came forward at once, and, with great liberality and generosity, contributed to the success of this Institution. It was also a great pleasure to me subsequently to invite to my Drawing Room the Medical men of the City, with old Doctor Sampson at their head, and settle the basis of the School of Medicine, affiliated with the University. . . .

It is very gratifying to me to meet, in my old days, at this very remarkable gathering, my old friends, a pleasure not unmixed with melancholy recollections of those who are gone. I am delighted to meet my old friend, Mr. Roderick M. Rose, who was the Secretary of that Meeting of fifty years ago, and who, I may tell you, was my first client. He is here this evening, still vigorous. We are here in our health and strength, and on this occasion I am glad also to refer to the Reverend Doctor Reid, who took part in that Meeting, and seconded a Resolution of mine.

I look forward with great hope to the future of the University. I stood at its cradle, and am proud to see it such a healthy child. I may say to it: You are yet young, but you are healthy, strong and active, and can look forward with hope to the years of strong, vigorous manhood before you in the future. Allow me to say again, that I am pleased to think that whatever I have done has been so kindly remembered by those who, in their good-will, value it so much.

An Act embodying the charter was passed by the Provincial Legislature in February, 1840, incorporating the "University of Kingston." The Act was, however, disallowed by the Imperial authorities, on the ground that it conflicted with the royal prerogative of granting charters. A Royal Charter was, however, issued in 1841, incorporating the Institution under the name of Queen's College, with "the style and privileges of a University."

The opening of the Queen's University took place on the 7th of March, 1842. The Reverend Thomas Liddell, D.D., of Edinburgh, was appointed the Principal and Professor of Divinity, and the Reverend P. C. Campbell, of Brockville, Professor of Classics. The Reverend James Williamson, D.D., LL.D., in 1842, became Professor of Mathematics and Natural Philosophy.

After the opening of King's College, Toronto, in 1843, an agitation commenced with the view to unite the three Universities then in operation, (Toronto, Victoria and Queen's), into a single provincial Institution. Many plans were proposed, and several measures tending to that end were introduced into Parliament and fully discussed. In 1843 the Honourable Robert Baldwin introduced a University Bill, which, although it presented many popular features, was strongly objected to by the Churches named and others also, chiefly because it did not provide for Religious Instruction.

A Bill was introduced by Honourable W. H. Draper, in 1845, to amend Mr. Baldwin's Act, so as to make it more generally acceptable to the Religious bodies of the Country; and, in 1847, the late Honourable John Hillyard Cameron introduced a Measure in which it was proposed to devote a large part of the Endowment to increased support of High Schools and also to largely subsidize the Denominational Colleges. The measure failed to be carried in Parliament, however, and this practically ended the agitation for the union of Colleges for many years.

In 1846 the Reverend Doctor Liddell resigned his position as Principal and returned to Scotland. The Reverend J. Machar, D.D., was next appointed Principal, and under his administration there was slow but real improvement.

The Reverend Doctor Cook, of Quebec, occupied the position of Principal for a time, but he refused to accept the position permanently. The Reverend Doctor Leitch was next appointed, but his early death deprived the Institution of his services. He was followed by the Reverend Doctor Snodgrass, and on his retirement the Reverend George Monro Grant, D.D., of Halifax, was appointed. Doctor Grant entered on his arduous duties with his accustomed energy, and occupied that position with great acceptance. He is an able speaker and a wise administrator. Queen's College has now Faculties of Arts, Theology, and Law, and there are affiliated with it the Royal College of Physicians and Surgeons, also in a prosperous condition, and the Kingston Women's Medical College.

FINANCES AND APPLIANCES OF THE UNIVERSITY OF QUEEN'S COLLEGE, KINGSTON.

The Reverend Doctor Snodgrass, President of the University, in his reply to a letter from the Editor, writes as follows:

Original Foundation.—Donations to the University began to be received in December, 1839, and ultimately amounted to $34,955, in money. After the incorporation of the Board of Trustees, in 1841, there were conveyed, by different owners, 2,264 acres of Land, in various parts of Upper Canada, and several Lots in the City of Toronto. These Lands

REVEREND GEORGE MONRO GRANT, D.D., LL.D., C.M.G.
Principal of Queen's College, Kingston.

were valued at $6,982; but sales have shown the estimate to be considerably in excess of their real value.

Building Fund.—In October, 1854, a Building Fund was formed, and, between that date and April, 1858, donations were received which amounted to $12,622. With this sum, and funds belonging to the original foundation, the Site and Buildings now occupied, formerly known as the "Summerhill Property," were purchased at a cost of $35,993.

General Fund.—(1856) Mrs. T. Wilson, Montreal, donation, $40; (1864), Mr. John Watkins, Kingston, donation, $100; (1886), Executors of the late Mr. George Michie, Toronto, intimated a legacy of $2,000.

Bursary and Scholarship Fund.—(1849 and 1854) the Reverend John Machar, D.D., two donations, $280; (1854) Honourable Oliver Mowat, Toronto, $50; Students of St. Andrew's University, $48, continued annually; (1854) Ladies of St. Andrew's Church, Toronto, $60, continued annually until 1858, when they gave an endowment of $800; (1856) Students of Aberdeen University, $34, continued annually; (1857) the Reverend David Watson, Thorah, donation, $40; Mr. Hugh Allan, Montreal, $50, continued annually; (1858-9) Mr. John Paton, Kingston, donation, $116; (1860) Mr. J. Mowat, Kingston, legacy, for an endowment, $800; Principal Cook, donation, $50; (1861)) Ladies of Kingston, endowment, $1,113; (1862) the Honourable Alexander Campbell, Kingston, $80, continued annually; Mr. John Watkins, Kingston, $80, continued annually, with another donation of $60, for that year; (1863) Anonymous, $40; (1864) Donald Ross, Montreal, Fellowship, $200; (1865) Mr. E. H. Hardy, Kingston, $50, and (1866) by the same Gentleman, $50, both grants to be continued annually; Sabbath Schools, Missionary Associations, Congregations, and Presbyteries contribute annually about $600. To the present time, donations, amounting to $1,684, have been received for the endowment of Scholarships in memory of the late Reverend Principal Leitch.

In 1869 it was resolved to make an appeal to the Country for aid. The people of Kingston raised about $25,000, and the result of the whole effort was that about $103,000 was raised for the equipment of the College.

In 1878, Principal Grant made the proposition to raise $150,000, in order to provide new Buildings, additional Professors, and Apparatus. The appeal was successful; additional ground of about twenty acres was purchased— a Site of rare beauty and convenience—and the present fine Building was erected.

Special Prizes.—(1860), Endowment by Prince of Wales, $800; (1861), A Gentleman in Toronto, $20; Mr. James Douglas, Quebec, $40; (1865) Parties in Ottawa, $40; Mr. J. Smith, Montreal, $40; (1866) Offered by Mr.. J. Carruthers, Kingston, $50; Mr. R. Cassels, Toronto, $40; Mr. J. Smith, Montreal, $40; Mr. J. Croil, Morrisburg, $25.

The Library.—Donors have been very numerous. It is estimated that the Volumes presented at various times amount to 3,500, the probable value being $3,000. The following are some of the largest and most valuable contributions: the late Reverend Principal Leitch, 570 volumes; the late Mrs. McGill, Montreal, 310; Mr. J. Smith, Montreal, 490; Mr. W. Dow, Montreal, 145; Mr. J. Fotheringham, Montreal, 176; Mr. Charles Low, Montreal, 123; Mr. Donald Ross, Montreal, "Liberatti Impronte."

The Museum consists almost entirely of Donations. The following are among the most extensive and valuable: Canadian minerals and fossils, 3,040 specimens, bequeathed by the late Reverend Andrew Bell, of L'Orignal; from Sir William Logan, 209 minerals and Rock specimens, 467 Fossils, characteristic of the Canadian rocks, also a collection of the Invertebrate Animals of the Gulf of St. Lawrence; Mr. A. T. Drummond, European and American Coins, 300, Canadian Minerals, Shells, Fossils, Insects, Fishes, and Reptiles, 182 Specimens; Doctor Thibodo, Walla-Walla, valuable collection of Minerals, Silver, Mercury, Gold, Copper, etcetera, from California, Oregon, British Columbia, etcetera, also a collection of Dried Plants; Professor Williamson, an extensive series of Fossils and Minerals, mostly Canadian.

Observatory.—Reflecting Telescope, by the late Reverend Principal Leitch; Achromatic Telescope, by the late Mr. A. J. Macdonell.

The Constitution and Management of Queen's University.

The new College building is of stone, and was erected mainly through the energy of the Principal, the Very Reverend G. M. Grant, D.D. It is fully equipped with Laboratories, Museums, and a well-stocked Library. (See illustrations on page 96.) In addition to these, the Kingston Astronomical Observatory, which had been built in 1855 by private subscription, aided by the City Corporation, was in 1861 conveyed by Deed to the College, on condition that the College give every year a Course of not fewer than six Popular Lectures on Astronomy, open to the public. This Observatory is one of those which are connected with the Magnetical Service of the Dominion—the headquarters of which are at Toronto. The other is at Montreal.

The Council.—This Body consists of the Chancellor, the Trustees, twelve Ministers of the Presbyterian Church in Canada, and fifteen Laymen in full communion; the Senate, *i.e.,* the Principal and all the Professors, and thirty-three Members elected by the registered Graduates.

Trustees.—At the time of the union between the different Presbyterian Churches of Canada, and of the formation of the " Presbyterian Church in Canada," Queen's University became, in 1874, by Act of Parliament, the College of that Church; the Board of Trustees was made self-perpetuating, instead of being appointed as heretofore by the Synod, and they were empowered to appoint a Vice-Principal to take the place and discharge the duties of the Principal in his absence.

Convocation and Council.—By this same Act, Convocation was organized and a Council established, having power to pass By-laws for the registration of graduates, for the appointment of Officers, and for the election of a Chancellor by the Council, if there is but one candidate; otherwise he is elected by the registered Graduates and Alumni.

Senatus.—The Members of the Faculties of Theology and Arts form one Board, with the title " Senatus." This Board awards the Scholarships and apportions the Bursary Fund.

Faculty Boards.—The Professors of each Faculty meet as a Board and administer the affairs of the Faculty.

Affiliated Institutions.—The Royal College of Physicians and Surgeons and the Women's Medical College, both situated in Kingston, are affiliated with this University.

Faculties.—When the College opened in 1842 there were but two Faculties—Arts and Theology—to which the teaching work was confined. In the year 1854 the Faculty of Medicine was added, which afterwards (1866) became a separate Corporation under the name of the " Royal College of Physicians and Surgeons." The Faculty of Law was added in the year 1860.

Course of Study.—*Arts*—Classics, Mathematics, Mental and Moral Philosophy, Political Economy, Chemistry, Natural Science, History, Rhetoric, English Literature and Modern Languages. *Medicine and Law*—The usual Courses as generally prescribed. *Theology*—The Inspiration and Authority of the Scriptures, Systematic Theology, the Pastoral Office, Homiletics, Hebrew and Chaldee, Apologetics, Biblical Criticism, Church History.

Degrees.—A complete Curriculum of Study in these four Faculties, covering a period of four years, leads to the usual degrees—in Arts, B.A. and M.A.; in Law, of LL.B.; in Medicine, of M.D.; and in Theology, of B.D. The Degree of D.Sc. is conferred on Masters of two years' standing who shall have taken first-

THEOLOGICAL BUILDING AND LIBRARY, QUEEN'S UNIVERSITY, KINGSTON.

class Honours in any two departments of the Honour Course—Literature, Philosophy, Mathematics and Science. The Honourary Degree of D.D. and LL.D. are given for literary, scientific, or professional, distinction.

Scholarships.—Of these there are two classes—in Arts and in Theology. In each class there are two kinds—Matriculation and Sessional Examination Scholarships; the former tenable during the first Session, the latter during the following Session.

Bursaries.—Besides the Scholarships—a few of which are close, *i.e.,* tenable only by students having in view the Ministry of the Presbyterian Church—there are Bursaries, which are awarded to Divinity students who have not obtained Scholarships.

Prizes.—The University Prizes are money Prizes for literary articles, Essays, etcetera.

Medals.—Gold and Silver Medals are also awarded to successful Candidates after examination in various subjects—Classics, Physics, Mathematics, etcetera.

The Queen's College School of Mining.

Up to 1893 very little had been done for mining education in Canada. While several Canadian Universities had mining Courses in their Calendars, it cannot be fairly stated that there was anywhere in the Dominion any equipment for that department of engineering education. The School of Mining was founded in that year with a separate Charter and a Board of Governors of its own. The funds at first available were (1) a subscription list of about $35,000, and (2) an annual grant of $5,000 from the Ontario Government. For several Sessions all the departments were housed in Carruthers Hall, but in 1894 there was built the Mining Laboratory, with funds provided by the Government of Ontario. In 1900 the School of Mining had grown to such an extent that, an appeal being made to the Ontario Government, the Legislature voted $112,500 to erect two large buildings (Ontario Hall and Fleming Hall) for the departments of Mineralogy, Geology and Physics, and for Civil, Mechanical and Electrical Engineering.

In 1895, the University constituted its Faculty of Practical Science and built a Mechanical Laboratory which was available for the Students of Mining as well as for those of other branches of Engineering. The two Institutions co-operated informally until the year 1900, when they were amalgamated as the School of Mining, which then became a College of Applied Science affiliated to the University. The teaching Staff has grown until it now numbers ten Professors, three Associate or Assistant Professors, four Lecturers, and nine Demonstrators, twenty-six in all. Last Session, (1905-6), there were 192 Engineering Students enrolled.

One feature of work of the Mining School is Summer work in Mining Camps, (with a view to stimulate the study of elementary Mineralogy and Geology), also to take part in railway surveys, electrical works, and in machine shops, and thus spend at least part of the Summer holidays. Students have found it to be very useful and interesting, if not stimulating.

The Establishment of Queen's University.

From the Queen's Quarterly.

Like the Colleges of Yale, Harvard, and Princeton, Queen's was a true product of the social, political and religious conditions from which it arose. The founders of these Institutions were University men, who had brought with them

ONTARIO HALL (GEOLOGY, MINERALOGY AND PHYSICS), QUEEN'S UNIVERSITY, KINGSTON.

to America ideals, traditions, and associations, which made a University to them one of the necessaries of life. The obligation upon them was irresistible to provide for the generations to come the wherewithal by which they also might become men. " Following the Universities of our native land as a model we shall take up the pupil at the farthest point to which the District Grammar School has conducted him and introduce him to those higher studies that may qualify him for public and professional avocations." These were the words in which the Reverend Doctor McGill, the Moderator of the Church of Scotland's Synod, outlined the scheme of the Queen's University in a pastoral Address to his people in 1835. From that time the movement went earnestly forward. Steps were taken to raise an endowment. About £20,000 were raised in various places for the purpose. In 1841 the Royal Charter was obtained incorporating the College " for the educating of youth in the principles of the Christian religion and for their instruction in

FLEMING HALL (ENGINEERING), QUEEN'S UNIVERSITY, KINGSTON.

the various branches of science and literature " and providing further " that no Religious test or qualification shall be required of or appointed for any persons admitted or matriculated as scholars within our said College." The Charter provided a governing Board of twenty-seven trustees, and under this constitution work was begun and continued until 1874. Principal Liddell, a man of eminent ability and great force of character, had been sent from Scotland, specially designated to take charge of the infant Institution, and Professor A. C. Campbell, afterwards the able Principal of Aberdeen University, taught classics. The next Session came the Reverend Doctor James Williamson, and began his fifty years of devoted service. The struggle for existence was strenuous from the first—no buildings, no adequate endowment, nothing but a small band of Teachers and scholars made the College of those days. In 1853 the Buildings and Grounds were acquired which are now Professors' residences. The Reverend Doctor Liddell had resigned the Principalship in 1846. For the next eleven years the difficulties were great. The Reverend Doctor Machar, the much-beloved minister of St. Andrew's Church, held the post until 1852, then the Reverend Doctor George, the able Professor of Mental and Moral Philosophy, took hold until 1857. The Reverend Doctor Cook, of Quebec, followed him till 1860, when the Reverend Doctor Leitch came from Scotland to accept the position and devote his life to its duties. He entered upon the office with great enthusiasm and much promise of success, but his health gave way under the stress of things and he died, greatly lamented, in 1864.

The Medical Faculty was instituted in 1854 and from the first its success was assured by the quality of the Professors and the large number of students they attracted. They were Doctors Sampson, Stuart, Dickson and Yates. They set up a standard which the men of to-day still find perhaps their best inspiration. Queen's led the way in co-education as in other things. As early as 1870 special

MEDICAL LABORATORIES, QUEEN'S UNIVERSITY, KINGSTON.

Classes in English and other subjects were arranged for women, but the academic career leading to a Degree was not definitely provided until 1878. In 1880 co-education was extended to the medical course and continued until 1894, when Toronto established a Women's Medical College, which rendered it unnecessary to continue a separate Medical School here.

The Reverend Doctor Snodgrass succeeded the Reverend Doctor Leitch as Principal in 1864, and if the Trustees had had a pre-vision of the dark days which were coming to the University they could not have made a better choice of a pilot to weather the storms. In 1868 the failure of the Commercial Bank and the withdrawal of the Government Grant left the College without visible means of support. Even so heroic a soul as the Reverend Doctor Mackerras despaired. He wrote to a friend that "it seemed as if the only thing remaining to do for Alma Mater was to bury her decently," but it was the Reverend Doctor Mackerras himself who turned the tide by his inspiring words. Some of us still remember his impassioned speech at the meeting of Corporators held in 1869 to determine whether Queen's should live or die. The Endowment movement of 1869 was the outcome of that speech. Principal Snodgrass and Professor Mackerras successfully appealed to men of all creeds and opinions; and $100,000 were raised. From that time the future of Queen's was assured. In 1874 the union of the Presbyterian Churches of Canada called for a change in the constitution, which was amended, and the Trustees provided for by it have since then been elected by the Board itself. At the same time the first expansion of the constitution took place in the establishment of a Representative University Council, devised by the wisdom and sagacity of Snodgrass and Mackerras, thus giving Graduates a voice in the College Councils. No important step for the past thirty years has been taken without the advice, approval and support of the University Council.

In 1877 the Reverend Doctor Snodgrass retired from the principalship. A new endowment was required, and a new man must undertake it, and as Doctor Snodgrass felt himself unequal to the strain of another Financial Campaign, and as the growing interests of the College required a younger and more vigorous hand at the helm, he had taken the measure of the Reverend Doctor G. M. Grant, and saw how ideal a man he was for the place, and so he named him as his successor, and Doctor Grant was chosen Principal in 1877. What he did for Queen's would fill one or more books. Such energy and ability, sagacity and tact, kindly sympathy and strong force united in one man made a unique personality which is rarely found. The progress in his time may be thus noted: In 1880 the now old Arts Building; in 1891 Carruthers Hall; in 1900 Kingston Hall, the gift of Kingston City; in 1902 Fleming Hall and Ontario Hall, the gifts of the Ontario Government to the School of Mines, in recognition of the great work of Queen's notable Principal. Crowning all is Grant Hall, the gift of his Students and Graduates and friends. These buildings are the visible witnesses that testify to the work he did, but they are only an external index of it. In 1889 he broadened the Constitution by empowering the University Council to elect five trustees, and the Church Synod has authorized the election of five additional Trustees to represent the graduates. These ten men are chosen irrespective of their church affiliations.

Before Doctor Grant came to the University as Principal it had barely held its own. From the time that he took charge it rapidly advanced. In 1878 the total number of students was 170. When he died there were 805, and now there are over 1,000. There were crises of which little was known to the public. Take, for example, the federation movement of 1884. Only the strongest man could have resisted the pressure brought to induce Queen's to enter into confederation. His characteristic answer was that " Queen's roots were in the ground, not in the air, and that to move her would be to sever her from traditions, associations and affections, the very source of her growth and life." His last efforts for Queen's were to still further nationalize her. He brought the matter before the General Assembly at Halifax in 1900 and the Assembly approved of " any well considered change in the constitution of the University which would still further increase its public usefulness by making a body of Trustees more completely representative of the undenominational character of the work it is doing." With that deliverance Doctor Grant proceeded to frame a measure to nationalize the University, and he was still working at it when death stayed his hand. At Vancouver, the Church changed its mind and resolved to retain Queen's, whilst at the same time broadening its constitution by granting further representation to its graduates in its government and providing for an endowment to be raised of $500,000.—From the *Queen's Quarterly*.

Golden Jubilee of Queen's College University.

On the occasion of celebrating the Golden Jubilee of Queen's College, on the 18th of December, 1889, quite a number of addresses were given. From that of the Chancellor, Sir Sandford Fleming, I select the following:

In 1831 the Presbyterian Synod of Upper Canada experienced great difficulty in obtaining a sufficient number of Ministers from the Mother Country, and it became impressed with the necessity of educating young men in the Colony. It was accordingly proposed that a College should be established in Canada, and Kingston, being the most central and generally the most eligible point for such an Institution, was selected by the Synod as the Site where it should be placed.

The Church of Scotland in Canada felt the importance of a thoroughly educated Ministry. They knew that Literature, Science, Philosophy and all that constitutes the Arts Course of a University are the legitimate handmaidens of Divine Truth, and they desired the highest standard in every branch of learning. They, therefore, took every means to promote the establishment of a College which would be generally accessible to all classes of the people, and which would command the confidence and support of all Denominations of Christians. The Government was memorialized and the most strenuous efforts were made for years to achieve this great and nationally important work. . . . The Synod, feeling that higher education in Upper Canada should no longer be neglected, determined to appeal directly to the Presbyterians of the Province, numbering then about a hundred thousand, and it entreated the friends of the cause to assist by contributions as bountiful as their circumstances would permit. The appeal which was made explained very clearly that, although the primary object of the Synod was to obtain a high standard of education for their own Ministers, it was also the desire and purpose to provide for a complete course of literary and scientific training, open to all; from $120,000 to $160,000 was asked for, to make a commencement.

Following this Appeal the first meeting to raise funds was held in St. Andrew's Church, in the City of Kingston, on December 18th, 1839. The meeting was marked by enthusiasm and success, a large sum was subscribed, and thus the endowment of the College was practically commenced.

Contributions came in also from many quarters in all sections of the Country, notwithstanding that the large majority of the population were yet clearing the forest and struggling to gain the means of living. It is the more astonishing, therefore, that the response to the general Appeal made was so generous. In a few months Legislative authority was sought and a Bill was assented to entitled " An Act to establish a college by the name and style of the University at Kingston." The year following, Her Majesty was graciously pleased to grant a Royal Charter conferring on the Institution the rank and title of Queen's College and University.

To Sir John A. Macdonald the Chancellor extended a hearty welcome, and was requested to address the meeting. The veteran chieftain, who was cheered again and again, in his remarks said:

Your Excellency, Mr. Chancellor and Gentlemen,—This morning, after my arrival here from Ottawa, I was informed that I was expected to make some allusion to the events of fifty years ago, at the meeting which was called in Kingston for the establishment of the then projected University of Queen's College. I was a young man then, just commencing my practice, and being a Kingstonian and a Presbyterian I was exceedingly anxious that my native city should have the honour of being a University city—a seat of learning. As has been explained, I was one of those of her citizens who assembled in St. Andrew's Church, now gone, like most of those who that day assembled within its walls.

His Excellency was kind enough to say that he had no doubt that those who were present on that occasion could give more historically correct statements of the events

THE ARTS DEPARTMENT AND GRANT HALL, QUEEN'S UNIVERSITY, KINGSTON.

than in his position he could do, but he ventured to state that I, among the rest, with the youthful energy of the time, spoke eloquently. Now I must confess that his Excellency did me more than justice, for when I arose to move the Resolution that was placed in my hands, and although I had prepared an eloquent oration, I was in such a mortal fright that I did not say a single word. "*Obstupui, steteruntque comæ, vox faucibus, hæsit.*" I just placed the Resolution in the Chairman's hands and sat down, as I could not say a single word! . . .

The Reverend W. T. Herridge, in uncovering the Brass Memorials in the College to the Donors of Funds and Benefactors of the University, said:

In the early days of the College its foundation may well have seemed a hazardous experiment, for the Country was young and its resources limited.

The growth of Queen's has more than kept pace with the growth of the country. She has been true to her good name, loyal in her love of letters and loyal in her devotion to the British crown, and believing that this Dominion has before it a glorious future she has always been marked by a contagious patriotism, and stands to-day by no means the least important factor in developing a national sentiment, and filling us with a just pride that we are Canadians.

The tablet which we have placed here in memory of these early benefactors is but a feeble acknowledgment of the gratitude of succeeding generations. We unveil it more for our sake than for theirs, for the fathers of this University do not need any formal memorial. They have raised a monument more lasting than brass, and while the love of learning remains among us their noble deeds can never pass into oblivion. They will live in these college halls; they will live in the annals of Canada; they will live in the unfeigned homage of thankful hearts.

The Tablet, which is of beautiful workmanship, bears the following inscription:

Royal Arms.	In Memoriam of the Benefactors who Laid the Foundation of Queen's University.	Queen's Arms.

The Reverend Doctor Williamson rose to unveil the second brass, and in so doing said:

You have just heard of the circumstances in which the founders of Queen's College took the first practical step for its establishment in 1839, and of its being thereafter opened in March, 1842, with two Professors and eleven students, in a small frame House still standing on Colborne Street.

It was then like a pioneer settler in the Canadian forest, in his small and scantily furnished Log House, with little help for preparing the ground, sowing the seed, and reaping the fruits of the harvest, and no facilities by road, or rail, for marketing the produce. It was yet but a little and tender Plant, keenly sensitive to every chilling wind that blew. How different the scene is now, when we behold the same Plant grown through the Winters and Summers, the Clouds and Sunshine, of fifty years, to its present fair proportions! How would it have gladdened the hearts of those, its beneficent first founders, on whose wisdom time has thus set its seal, but who have long since passed away, if it had been given to them, as it is to us, to see its wonderful and healthful growth and its stately form to-day! The University is now housed in this beautiful and commodious abode, and instead of two we have now sixteen Professors to carry on, with the many-sided and able Principal, the work of the University.

As the annual subscriptions to revenue, which had been given by friends years ago, were about to terminate, it was unanimously resolved to appeal to the Country for an addition to the Endowment Fund of $250,000, to be known as the Jubilee Endowment Fund, so as to enable the Trustees to provide for additions to the Teaching Staff, and to equip and erect a new Science Hall.

The scheme thus inaugurated by the Principal and carried into effect mainly by his own appeals and indefatigable exertions in visiting the different parts of the country in its behalf, met with a most hearty and gratifying response, Kingston nobly answering to the call and leading the van. He had thus the satisfaction in March, 1888, of reporting to the Trustees its complete accomplishment. Since then four new Professors, of superior qualifications and tried ability, have been appointed to important Chairs, and the Carruthers Science Hall will be opened in the beginning of next College Session.

It is, then, most fitting that we should do all honour to those generous donors who, most of them not rich in means, gave out of the riches of their hearts to a Fund so needful, and which has already so largely contributed to extend the intellectual domain occupied by the University. This Memorial Tablet, which I now unveil, is a token of our grateful remembrance.

This was the design of the second memorial:

Royal Arms.	In Honor of 500 Benefactors who in 1887-88, Contributed $250,000 to the Endowment Fund of Queen's University.	Queen's Arms.

Other addresses on this interesting occasion were delivered by the Reverend Provost Body of Trinity University, the Reverend Doctor Wardrope of Guelph, the Reverend Doctor Milligan of Toronto, the Reverend John Burton and Mr. R. V. Rogers of Kingston.

In the evening Addresses were delivered by Lord Stanley, Governor-General; Sir Alexander Campbell, Lieutenant-Governor; Sir James Grant, Major General Cameron, the Reverend J. A. Macdonald, President MacVicar, the Honourable W. McDougall, Major Derbeshire, Warden Tilson, Warden Rankin, Mr. R. W. Shannon, Mr. Cuthbertson, and others.

THE WOMEN'S RESIDENCE OF THE QUEEN'S UNIVERSITY.

(NOTE.—This sketch of the Women's Residence of the Queen's University is taken from the *Queen's Quarterly* for July, 1910. The Editor of this volume has slightly altered it in some instances and made a few additions, as the result of his experience.)

The ideal of to-day is the commonplace of to-morrow—we attain the heights to which we aspire, only to perceive higher peaks beyond. For centuries a narrow idea of Woman's sphere had been accepted, she was regarded as the Home-maker, but her function was largely industrial, which demanded neither intelligent comprehension of her work, nor of life. As social changes relieved her of some of the routine management of the House, she sought opportunity to study, and her first contention was for equality of opportunity with Man. To gain this equality she had to prove that she could pursue the same Studies as effectively, and do the same work as he did. Having proved her point and gained access to all the intellectual privileges open to Men she is commencing to see that she needed, not a different sphere, but an enlarged conception of her sphere. She is not so ready, as a rule, as others are, to assert to-day her demand for equality with Man, as to plan that the enlarged opportunities of the Classroom shall not rob her of her womanly prerogatives. Her entrance to College Halls has enlarged the general and former conception of College life.

Twenty years ago, when the first Woman Students gained admission to Queen's University, the educational ideal was intellectual training, and culture for culture's sake. The first College Women were eager for learning, but their ideal of education included little beyond the mere acquisition of knowledge. Twenty years, however, have largely widened the nature and purpose of a College training. To-day, the ideal College Course aims to fit the individual for better personal success in life, and for better service for Society. If the College is to fulfil this enlarged ideal, the training of the Classroom must be supplemented by elevating æsthetical, physical and social influences. General Courses in Art and Music, in Household Science and Manual training, as well as Literature, with pictures and illustrations by scholarly performers in these things, must be provided, not as the regular subjects on the Curriculum, but as part of the cultural and homelike atmosphere of the College. The Levana, the Women's Undergraduate Society of Queen's College, took a step in this direction two years ago, when it then arranged the Course of Lectures on Music. This was followed by a more extensive Course of Lectures on Music and Art last Session, and larger plans have been made for the coming year, which we hope will embrace the practical subjects to which we have referred, and thus widen the sphere for women in the University. The Play given each Year by the Modern Language Society and the Shakespearean Recitals of the Dramatic Club have done much to awaken an interest in the æsthetical side of College life. The effort to create a cultured Home for the Woman Students was the next evidence that a more comprehensive educational ideal was gaining ground at Queen's, as has been herewith referred to and suggested.

In July, 1901, Principal Grant sanctioned an experiment which a few Women who were interested in the Residence question desired to make. A furnished House was rented for the seven Months of the College Session, a Lady was secured to take the management, and ten Girls spent last Winter there. The receipts from the Students paid all the expenses except the rent of the Furniture, and, true to traditions of Queen's, the House was self-governing. This experiment having proved a success, plans are now being made to furnish a House capable of accommodating twenty Students. The Residence will aim to provide the best conditions for maintaining the physical life of the Students. The House that has been leased stands in spacious Grounds, so the sun will have access to every Room, the sanitary conditions are receiving due consideration, the plumbing is effective and the plans for heating and ventilation complete. Much care will be given to the proper selection and dainty serving of the Food. The external advantages of the Residence are so obvious that many People think that the features which are simply incidental are the main object, but Domestic, or Household, Science, and other subjects will not, we trust, be overlooked.

Too many Students leave College with their theories of music, science and art in one corner of their Brain, and in another corner their theories of life, or rather for the practice of it they have far too often no intelligent theory. Truthfulness, simplicity, harmony, subordination, or ornament to purpose and adaptability are among the cardinal principles of all art. The Student, for instance, in her Art Course is learning how these principles found expression in various phases of life and how success, or failure, followed as they were obeyed, or ignored. She ought to find the effort to incorporate them and other important practical principles of action in her daily life more easy in a community where all were and are at least conscious of their effort to do so, than in a Community where some of the Members had not grasped their significance. These principles may be taken as a criterion by which to measure the culture to which a Household, or an Individual, has attained. The Classroom has taught the worthlessness of merely external forms of morality, and has also taught that all moral and Religious observance should spring from the Spiritual Life rather than from authority. The aspiration of the Residence would naturally be to inculcate that in conduct, as in Religion, the highest incentives are from within, and from the heart to provide an environment where there will be an intellectual appreciation of beauty and a spirit that seeks its expression in the practical details of daily life, rather than the observance of social forms, and to unite the Women who feel the need of working out a higher Home Life than is possible in the average Boarding House. The idea of the value of such an environment as has been provided for Queen's is not a new one; the old Greek Educator never conceived of intellectual training separated from a harmonious environment for the Student-beauty of thought found expression in the æsthetic relations of every-day Life.

According to the statistics of the American Alumnæ, fifty per cent. of College Women marry and their life work becomes the creation of their helpful, healthy environment. Although the first difficulty which confronts the Home Maker of to-day is the industrial one, which needs knowledge as well as experience to solve, more and more the problem of Homemaking will become the problem of creating conditions physical, mental and moral that will develop the best Citizens. The necessity for the application of intelligence to all the details of daily living will, here in the Residence, or Home, be recognized. The first steps towards an ideal seemed at first so far from the goal sought that one hesitated to point it out. Not only in providing helpful surroundings for the Student, but in emphasizing the importance of the Home and the wide sphere a Woman in developing it has, will have an important bearing on her education; and the Residence, however imperfectly it may fulfil its object, nevertheless it illustrates the increasing importance that educated Women are placing on such a Home. The whole trend of College life is almost inevitably towards criticism, rather than action. This habit of criticising rather than endeavouring to act is bad in every way, for so soon as one commences to act one discovers the difficulties in the way of any successful achievement. It is in the effort to overcome difficulties that principles are strengthened. Art is the fruit of the union between struggle and knowledge, and in some way the College must endeavour to inculcate the necessity for the effort as well as the knowledge, in order that the Student may leave College with more faith in the lessons taught there and determination to persevere in the attempt to carry them into practice. At present the majority of Graduates give over the struggle too quickly when they do not succeed in attaining the ends they seek. The Residence will be one attempt to emphasize the necessity for persistent, intelligent effort by Women to work out the highest ideal in their future life work.

> "Who seeks for Heaven, alone to save his Soul,
> May keep the Path, but still not reach the Goal."

The struggle after a higher life must be shared to yield its highest rewards. The ideal which unites a household in an effort to put theories into practice has a higher value and a success beyond the attempt of the individual to attain this end alone, for the culture is not only "a passion for perfection but a passion for making it prevail." To unite the Students in a corporate home life which one and all are interested in maintaining at a high point of efficiency is one of the fundamental aims of the Residence. Last year, it had to prove that it could be self-governing and self-supporting, which it did. After furnishing the Home the Committee will be free to direct its attention to the cultural side of the Residence. We do not anticipate much difficulty in doing so, as the goal kept in view is the creation of a cultured Home, which shall be helpful to the expression of the theories of the Class-room in every-day life.

KINGSTON, July, 1910.   ALICE A. CHOWN.

CHANCELLOR SANDFORD FLEMING IN REGARD TO THE CHANGE OF THE CONSTITUTION OF QUEEN'S UNIVERSITY.

To the Friends of Queen's University:—

As Chancellor of Queen's University, I have felt it incumbent on me to place before the entire constituency of Queen's the following brief explanation. The unexpected action of the General Assembly at Vancouver in 1903 and at St. John in 1904 affords proof of the re-awakening of an intense interest and feeling in favour of the aims which inspired the founders of Queen's.

The Presbyterians of Canada, following the tradition of their fathers, have always sought to foster liberal education. Nearly three-quarters of a century ago the Scotch settlers began a movement which eventually led to the establishment by Royal Charter at Kingston of a seat of learning, where education, while not divorced from Christian influence, would be open to every Canadian of whatever race or creed.

In more recent years the progress of the University, owing to the foresight of its founders and the wise guidance of far-seeing men, has been distinctly gratifying. Evidence of its rapid development may be found in the steady increase of students and the yearly necessity of enlarging the staff of Professors. There are at the present time, (1905), nine buildings, which form an imposing group within a spacious College park of twenty acres. A special interest is attached to the last building, completed only a few weeks ago. It stands on the western side of the quadrangle, and its lofty campanile adorns the whole group. On 7th November, 1904, the Students, numbering with their friends more than two thousand, assembled within its walls to present it formally as a free gift to the University, and to ask that it be dedicated as a Memorial Convocation Hall in honour of Principal Grant. The erection of this magnificent Hall resulted from a spontaneous movement of the students, who earnestly desired to express in this form their regard and affection for their late beloved Master. The Building was formally received from the Students, was solemnly dedicated, and will be known as Grant Hall. It is a fitting monument to the memory of a man who, imbued with the spirit of the founders, laboured to carry out their patriotic aims. It is a tribute of affection for one who was an inspiration to the Graduates, and has left behind him an influence for good which will long endure.

SIR SANDFORD FLEMING, C.E., K.C.M.G., LL.D.,
Chancellor of Queen's University, Kingston.

I may be allowed to allude to one other building which has come into use within the last two years. Its origin is unique, being the gift of the City of Kingston as a municipality. Other buildings within the College park owe their existence to private beneficence, but the funds in this instance were granted by public vote of the whole people of Kingston. The vote was given with substantial unanimity, a majority coming from every ward in the city. What higher testimony could be proffered to Queen's? What better evidence that her teaching has always been carried on without a tinge of sectarianism? This building must itself be regarded as convincing testimony to the broad catholicity of Queen's. Equally it bears testimony to the intelligence and character of the citizens among whom so many students find homes. No other city in Canada has such a record. Kingston is probably the first municipality within the Empire to erect a University building.

I have touched on two instances only of the virility and powerful influence of Queen's, but they indicate among other things the esteem in which she is held by those who know her best, and should go a long way to satisfy the people of Canada at a distance as to the character and value of the work done and the position held by Queen's in the life of this young nation.

OTTAWA, January, 1905.   SANDFORD FLEMING.

PROPOSED CHANGE IN THE CONSTITUTION OF QUEEN'S COLLEGE UNIVERSITY.

The following is the Report of the Joint Meeting of the Committees of the Commission of the General Assembly of the Church and of the Board of Trustees of Queen's University to further consider the proposed changes in the Constitution of the University, and the future maintenance of the Faculties of Arts and Theology therein.

The Commission of the General Assembly, after conference with the Board of Trustees in October, 1909, resolved as follows:—

"That the Assembly's Commission sympathizes with the Board of Trustees of Queen's University in the difficulties that confront them in providing for the expansion of the University, and feel that this expansion calls for some reconstruction of the Constitution and Governing Body of the University, and the Commission would welcome from the Trustees a more detailed outline of their proposals for the future character, management and maintenance of the University, especially with regard to the Faculties of Arts and Theology, and feel constrained to defer a final decision until such outline can be considered at an adjourned meeting of the Commission to be held at a convenient time, and to that end are willing to appoint a Committee to co-operate with a similar Committee of the Trustees in framing such a plan."

In compliance with the request of this Resolution, the Committee of the Board of Trustees submitted to the Committee of the Assembly's Commission a Statement regarding,—

I. Proposed changes in the Constitution and Management of the Faculties of Arts and Theology.

II. The future maintenance of those Faculties.

The proposed changes affect only the departments of Arts and Theology. These originally constituted "Queen's College." The School of Mining, which is affiliated to the University, is practically a Faculty of Applied Science, but is under a separate Board of Governors. Certain Professors' Chairs (Physics, Geology, Mineralogy, Chemistry and part of Mathematics) were transferred to it, and have been maintained in connection with it. Arts Students attend those Classes, and Science Students attend some Arts Classes. The Medical Faculty (originally the Royal College of Physicians and Surgeons) is to a large extent under the management of the Members of the Medical Staff. The appointments to the Faculty of Education are under the joint control of the Board of Trustees and the Provincial Department of Education. If the proposed constitutional changes are carried into effect, it would be possible to have these various Faculties of Science, Medicine and Education brought into much closer relation to the Faculty of Arts than at present.

I. In regard to changes in the Constitution and Management of the Faculties of Arts and Theology:—

In the Memorandum submitted by the Board of Trustees to the Commission of Assembly on 5th October, 1909, it is stated " That in the opinion of the Trustees there are certain Denominational restrictions which tend to impede the development of the University, videlicet, (1) that all Members of the Presbyterian Church in Canada constitute the Corporation of the University; (2) that of the thirty-seven Members at present constituting the Board of Trustees, twenty-seven must be Members of the Presbyterian Church; (3) that the Principal must be a Minister of the Presbyterian Church."

Members of the Committee of the General Assembly's Commission.—The Reverend Doctor Lyle, Moderator of General Assembly; The Reverend Doctor Ramsay, Knox Church, Ottawa; The Reverend D. W. Best, Beaverton, Ont.; Mr. Hamilton Cassels, K.C., Toronto; Mr. Edward Brown, Winnipeg.

Members of Committee of Board of Trustees.—Sir Sanford Fleming, K.C.M.G., Ottawa; The Reverend Principal Gordon, Kingston; The Reverend Doctor Herridge, St. Andrew's Church, Ottawa; Mr. Adam Shortt, Ottawa; the Chairman, the Honourable Mr. Justice McLennan, was prevented by illness from being present.

After full consideration of the foregoing statement and of all the matters involved, the unanimous recommendations of the Joint Committee are as follows:—

Attention is first directed to the fact that, by Royal Charter Queen's College was founded, " for the education of youth in the principles of the Christian Religion and for their instruction in the various branches of Science and Literature." It is agreed that shall continue to be the character of the University.

The following changes in the Constitution are proposed:—

1. It is proposed that the Corporation shall consist of the Members of the Board of Trustees, the Professors, the Graduates, and the Benefactors.

2. It is proposed that the Board of Trustees shall be constituted as follows:—
   (*a*) The Chancellor to be elected as at present by the University Council.
   (*b*) The Rector, who shall be elected by the Students every three years.
   (*c*) The Principal.
   (*d*) The Minister of Education for the Province of Ontario.
   (*e*) An Assessor, appointed by the Minister of Education.
   (*f*) Two Members, to be appointed by the Corporation of the City of Kingston.
   (*g*) One Member from each affiliated College.
   (*h*) Six Members to be elected by the University Council.
   (NOTE.—The Council consists of the Trustees, the Senate and an elected number of Graduates equal to the combined number of the Trustees and Senate.)
   (*i*) Six Members, to be elected by the Graduates, according to By-laws that have been or that may be made for this purpose by the University Council. (There are over three thousand Graduates.)
   (*j*) Four Members, to be elected by those Benefactors who have contributed one hundred dollars or upwards to the Endowment of the University. (There are over six hundred such Benefactors.)
   (*k*) Twelve Members, to be elected by the present Board of Trustees. These twelve Members, or any of them, may be chosen from amongst the present Members.

After the first election of these twelve Members the Board of Trustees shall fill vacancies in this number by co-optation.

(*l*) Of the Members elected by the University Council, two shall retire annually; similarly with those elected by the Graduates. Of those elected by the Benefactors, one shall retire annually, and of those elected by the Members of the Board, three shall retire annually. Retiring Trustees shall be eligible for re-election.

3. The Senate shall continue as at present constituted, subject to the following provision, videlicet: the Board of Trustees, acting in consultation with the Senate, shall have power to enact any Statute that they may, from time to time, think proper, to add to the Senate Professors of any School, or College, that may be connected with the University, or to change the present Constitution of the Senate.

At present the Senate consists of all the Professors and Assistant professors in Arts and Theology, the Dean of the Faculty of Medicine, and those Professors of the School of Mining whose Chairs were connected with the Arts Faculty prior to the existence of the School, and the Professors of the Faculty of Education. These shall continue to be Members as at present. It may, however, be necessary, on account of the increase of the Staff, to make the Senate consist of Representatives of each Faculty; and it is proposed that authority to do this be vested in the Board of Trustees.

4. The Theological Faculty of the University shall be known as "Queen's College," and shall be governed by a Board of Management consisting of twenty-five Members appointed by the General Assembly of the Presbyterian Church in Canada; five to retire annually and to be eligible for re-appointment. Until the appointment of the Board of Management by the General Assembly, the Faculty of Theology shall be governed by the Board of Trustees of the University.

5. The position of Principal should be separated from that of Primarius Professor of Divinity, and Laymen, as well as Ministers, should be eligible for it.

II. In regard to the future maintenance of the Faculties of Arts and Theology:—

If the proposed changes were carried into effect, some of the subscribers to the present Endowment Fund might desire to change the destination of their contributions. Accordingly, the Trustees, on the 6th of October last, resolved "that, in the event of the proposed Constitutional changes in Queen's University being carried into effect, the whole facts of the case be set before the subscribers to the last Endowment Fund, enquiring what change, if any, they desire to have made in the disposal of their contributions."

The maintenance of the Faculty of Theology would be dependent on revenue from Endowment and on annual congregational contributions.

When it was proposed eight years ago to change the relations of the University to the Church, it was agreed by the University to set apart for the maintenance of the Theological College, $150,000, with proper accommodation, Light, Heat and Attendance. This amount was regarded as fairly representing the proportion contributed for Theological Education of the successive Endowment Funds that had been raised in aid of Queen's College, and this appropriation was concurred in by the joint Committee representing the Church and the University.

Although the present Endowment Fund was specially intended for the Arts Department, yet some subscribers did not exclusively restrict their contributions to the maintenance of Arts. It might, therefore, be suitable that the sum of Fifty thousand dollars be allowed for the Theological Department from the amount received in the present endowment campaign, and that the total amount of $200,000 be set apart by the University for the maintenance of the Theological College with Accommodation, Light, Heat and Attendance satisfactory to the Board of Management of Queen's College.

The contributions received from the Church for the Theological Faculty have been about $3,500 annually. They should amount to $6,000. And if the maintenance of the Theological College were the only purpose for which we appeal to the Church, this latter sum would be a very moderate annual contribution. It is necessary that the Staff of the Theological Department should be increased at an early date, and that existing salaries should be increased, but the revenue from the proposed Endowment, along with the contributions of congregations, should meet the requirements of the Theological College, even with such an increase of the Staff.

Note.—At the Meeting of the General Assemby in 1910 this matter of the change in the Constitution of Queen's College University was deferred for a year, in the hope that, in the meantime, a harmonious conclusion might be arrived at regarding the best course to be pursued for the settlement of this question.

THE UNIVERSITY OF TRINITY COLLEGE, TORONTO.

Erection of Trinity College—"Turning the First Sod," and "Laying the Chief Corner Stone," 1851.

The Founding of Trinity College in 1851 was an event of great interest and importance, as it added one more to the three Universities then in successful operation in Upper Canada, one of them—Toronto University—as King's College, was also founded by Doctor Strachan nearly ten years before the period at which he, in the case of Trinity College, assisted at the laying of the Corner Stone. The following is an account of the Ceremony of turning the first sod for the foundation of Trinity College:

On the Twenty-third of January, 1851, the Provisional Council of the proposed "Church University" passed a Resolution to the effect that Mr. Kivas Tully and Messieurs Cumberland and Ridout should be applied to for designs for the intended Building, the estimated cost to not exceed Eight Thousand pounds, (£8,000 = $32,000). Mr. Tully's design was adopted by the Council, and Tenders were advertised for. On the Thirteenth of March, the Tender of Messieurs Metcalf, Wilson and Forbes was accepted for the sum of Seven Thousand eight hundred and forty-five pounds, (£7,845 = $31,380), and orders were given to commence the work forthwith. On Monday, the Seventeenth of March, 1851, the first Sod was turned; at noon Doctor Strachan, the Bishop, accompanied by the Council of the College, the Architect, and the Contractors, with others, proceeded to the Site of the College, when the Bishop thus addressed them:—

We are met, according to appointment, to commence this important undertaking. It is our intention to confine ourselves strictly to breaking the Ground, as we shall soon, if it please God, find a more fitting occasion, when we come to lay the Foundation-stone, for some of those forms and ceremonies which ancient usage has prescribed and hallowed for such occasions. It is, nevertheless, becoming that we should mark the beginning in such a manner as to convince our friends that we are in earnest in the matter. . . .

We may seem, to those who look only to earthly and outward appearance, as a feeble band; and, because we have a little or no Endowment, to be in danger of passing away like the Summer cloud; but it is a work which has for its object the Glory of God, and the extension of His Kingdom; and, therefore, if we prosecute it in the right spirit, it will obtain the Divine Blessing, and be sure to prosper.

We have indeed much already for which to be thankful; the contributions of the Members of the Church, both here and at home in England, have enabled us to contract for a noble Edifice, which will, it is hoped, not only adorn, but become the channel of many blessings to this City and Diocese. . . .

UNIVERSITY OF TRINITY COLLEGE, TORONTO.
(Looking from the south-west.)

And why should we not look for like results? Why should we despond in this, which may be termed our "day of small things"? The offerings already received, when our plan was deemed by the cold and thoughtless as merely imaginary, will, we trust, be increased ten-fold, now that there can be no longer any doubt of our going forward; and not only this, but our own Alumni will soon arise with their gifts and offerings. They will gather round the sacred Structure, in which they have acquired the most precious treasures of knowledge, sacred and profane; feeling the blessedness of those holy principles by which their lives are directed, and their felicity here and hereafter secured, they will provoke one another to heap benefits upon their Alma Mater, and thus will her power of doing good be increased, and her blessed influence be extended through the whole Diocese.

After some further remarks the Bishop took the Spade from the Architect, and, having filled it with the soil, said,—"We begin this work in the name of The Father, and of The Son, and of The Holy Ghost." He then threw it into the Barrow, which was soon heaped over by the Council, each throwing into it one or more spadefulls; the High Sheriff, F. W. Jarvis, wheeled it to the place of deposit, amid much cheering.

Thus ended this simple, but yet very interesting, preliminary step towards the erection of Trinity College.

On Wednesday, April 30th, 1851, the Corner-stone of the Building was laid with all the solemn observances usual on such occasions.

At one o'clock, the procession, marshalled by Major George T. Denison, proceeded to St. George's Church. When the Service was ended, the Bishop, the Clergy and the Congregation formed in procession and proceeded to the Site of the College. On entering the Grounds, the procession, headed by the Bishop, proceeded to the appointed Site, where a large platform had been erected, and which was crowded with Ladies anxious to witness the interesting Ceremony from the commanding position which it gave them.

THE RIGHT REVEREND BISHOP STRACHAN, D.D., LL.D.

ADDRESS OF DOCTOR STRACHAN, ON LAYING THE FOUNDATION STONE OF TRINITY COLLEGE, 1851.

It would not be very easy for me to address you on this occasion without briefly adverting to the fact, that, on the Twenty-third of April, 1842, little more than nine years ago, some of us assisted at the laying of the Foundation Stone, by Sir Charles Bagot, the Chancellor, of the University of King's College, with promising hopes and sincere prayers. The day was exceedingly fine and the Ceremony was conducted with solemnity and dignity. It was, perhaps, the most imposing and interesting spectacle that had ever been seen in Upper Canada, and was hailed as the harbinger of many benefits to the Colony. . . . To found a common Seat of Learning is a proud object of ambition; but to establish a College devoted to the cause of God and the diffusion of Science, sound Learning, and the true Religion through so vast a region as Upper Canada is one of those precious distinctions which are seldom attained; and associated in our imaginations, as it must be, with so many gifts and blessings to young and old, it cannot fail to become a source of delightful reflection through life to all of us who now enjoy the privilege of being present on this happy occasion.

This projected Institution is peculiarly the child of the Church; from her it springs, and under her wing it desires to nestle; it will breathe as she breathes, and acquire life and energy from the spiritual nourishment which she is ordained to dispense.

So soon as the Buildings are completed, Trinity College will become, in all her proceedings, as strictly collegiate in discipline and character as the circumstances of this new Country will permit; and its Authorities will ever keep in view the glorious models of the Parent State, to which pure Science and the Christian Faith are so much indebted. From them she will borrow a spark of that living flame by which they have been animated for so many centuries, in order that she may, with God's Blessing, kindle similar inspiration in the Colony. And I trust that many around me will be permitted to see Trinity College taking an honoured place among the more celebrated Schools of Learning, and doing for Canada what Oxford and Cambridge have done for England.

Allow me, in conclusion, to congratulate you,—the City of Toronto, and the whole Province,—that God has put into the hearts of Churchmen, both here and in the Mother Country, to establish this College " on the foundation of the Apostles and Prophets, Jesus Christ Himelf being the Chief Corner Stone."

It will constitute a great Christian Household, the domestic home of all who resort to it for instruction, framing them in the Christian graces, and in all sound learning, and sanctifying their knowledge, abilities and attainments to the service of God and the welfare of their fellow-men. . . .

A Bottle containing the Coins and Documents intended to be placed under the Foundation Stone was then handed to the then Bishop by Doctor Burnside.

The Honourable Chief Justice Robinson read the inscription engraved in Latin on the brass plate, which was then cemented into its place.

Professor Doctor Edward Hodder read a translation of the inscription, as follows:—

In the name of the Father, and of the Son, and of the Holy Ghost. Amen.

On the Thirtieth of April, 1851, in the Fourteenth Year of the Reign of Victoria, by the Grace of God, Queen, Defender of the Faith, and while the Right Honourable the Earl of Elgin and Kincardine was Governor-General of British North America, this Foundation Stone of Trinity College, Toronto, an Institution established for the furtherance of the Christian Religion, and all the Liberal Sciences, was laid by the Honourable and Right Reverend John Strachan, D.D., LL.D., Bishop of Toronto.

The College, now commenced, is built through the munificence of those who, at his earnest instigation, both in Britain and in this Diocese, gave with willing minds, as to the Lord, gifts of money and lands, for the accomplishment of this object.

To this devoted and persevering Prelate, who, throughout an extended life, labours that the youth of Canada may, at all times, be trained in Christian principles, let posterity render grateful thanks.

With the Bishop, who is deservedly the first President of the College, have been associated the Council of the College.

God grant a prosperous issue to the begun labour! May He, who is at once the Founder and Foundation-stone of His Church, be ever present with those who shall, within these walls, devote themselves to Christian Learning and the Liberal Sciences.

The Bishop having offered up a fervent and appropriate Prayer, the Architect handed him the Trowel, and the Stone having been adjusted the Bishop said:

Our help is in the name of the Lord. "Answer. Who hath made Heaven and Earth." Except the Lord build the house, they labour in vain that build it.

Upon which, the Bishop, having struck the Stone three times with the Mallet, said:

In the name of the Father and of the Son, and of the Holy Ghost. Amen. I lay this Corner Stone of an Edifice to be here erected by the name of Trinity College, to be a place of sound learning and religious Education, in accordance with the principles and usages of the United Church of England and Ireland. Other foundation can no man lay than that which is laid, even Jesus Christ, who is God over all, blessed for evermore; and in whom we have redemption through His blood, even the forgiveness of sins. Amen.

After laying the Corner Stone, Sir Allan Napier McNab addressed the Bishop as follows:

It affords me great satisfaction to congratulate you, and, through you, all the Churchmen of your extensive Diocese, upon the auspicious commencement of a work, the completion of which is ardently prayed for by all who desire the dissemination of sound Religious and Secular Education; combined, as on the very highest considerations they ought to be, in order that all things may work together for the glory of God, and the advancement of Christ's Kingdom on Earth.

The realization of these hopes must prove likewise the accomplishment of what a long, active, and useful life among us abundantly shows us as the great object you have for many long years devoutly and zealously laboured to effect. I trust that the Blessing of God will attend the exertions of yourself and supporters to the end, and that we have here laid the foundation of an Institution that shall extend its blessed influence to the latest posterity. . . .

We contemplate the happy issue of the present work, not only in its construction, but still more in its efficient operation, as of vital importance to the prosperity and well being of the Members of our Church in particular, and also of all classes of society in general; inasmuch as whatever contributes to the one necessarily proves beneficial to the other.

(*Note.* Other addresses in Latin followed, and the Ceremony was concluded by a Prayer by the Reverend H. J. (afterwards Dean) Grasett and the "Bidding Prayer" by Doctor Bethune, (afterwards the second Bishop of Toronto), and the Benediction by Bishop Strachan of Toronto.)

The Inauguration and the Opening of Trinity College, 1852.

On Thursday, the 15th day of January, 1852, the Ceremony of opening the First Session of Trinity College took place, under the Presidency of Doctor Strachan, the Founder of the College. In opening the proceedings he delivered the following address. After referring to the many varied aspects of the question of the founding of the College, Doctor Strachan deals with the more serious and interesting subjects of the good influences of College life on Students, and on what constitutes an enduring foundation for the life and future career of a Christian Gentleman. His references to the Bible and its blessed truths, as forming the true basis of all elementary and Collegiate education, are quite in harmony with the opinion on this subject of enlightened Christian Statesmen. The Bishop said:

I feel it impossible to address so respectable an audience on this occasion, auspicious as it is, without experiencing a strange mixture of painful, as well as pleasing, emotions, or, as the ancient Poet has expressed it, "The joy of grief."

On laying the Foundation Stone of King's College about ten years ago, I declared, as I then truly felt, that it was the happiest moment of my life, and that I had been anxiously looking and working for it during more than forty years, as a consummation of the greatest importance, and which, under Divine Providence, was eminently calculated to advance the glory of God and the best interests of man.

Again in June, 1843, I was called upon to take a prominent part in the proceedings at the opening of the same Institution for the business of Instruction and in my Address I remarked that we were assembled to celebrate an event to which many had been looking forward for nearly half a century,—that it was a work of infinite value to the well-being of Canada,—and that the proceedings, with which it was attended, would hence-

THE RIGHT REVEREND BISHOP STRACHAN,
Founder of Trinity College University.

forth become a matter of history, while the College itself would shed the most precious blessings on the whole Country. . . .

On the Seventh of February, 1850, or about five weeks after King's College had ceased to exist, I sent a Pastoral Letter to the Clergy and Laity of the Diocese, informing them that we had been deprived of King's College, the gift of our Sovereign, and that a University had been substituted in its stead. . . . . It became a matter of necessity, as well as duty, to establish a University from our private resources, in close connection with the Church to which we had the happiness to belong. To this appeal my people nobly responded, and subscribed in money, lands, and stock in Building Societies, about twenty-five thousand pounds currency (£25,000 = $100,000). . . .

Encouraged by what was actually done within the Diocese, and fully persuaded that much more would be done when the College was seen in successful operation, I prepared to visit England, being convinced that the cause I had to advocate could not fail to command the sympathy of all who belonged to our Communion, and awaken their best affections in its favour.

On the Thirtieth of April I reached London, and lost no time in addressing Letters to the Archbishops, Bishops, Clergy and Laity Members of the Church, telling them, that, under the pressure of what I felt to be a great necessity, I had ceased, for a short time, my pastoral labours in the Diocese of Toronto, to appeal, I hoped not in vain, to their sympathy in behalf of their brethren in Upper Canada. The full explanation of the causes of my visit, my objects and wants, was most favourably received, and munificent donations granted. . . .

On my return to the Diocese, on the second of November, 1850, I called as many of our subscribers together as possible, and communicated to them a full account of my journey and the gratifying results, which proved, as might have been anticipated, highly satisfactory to all our friends and benefactors. . . .

The next step was to choose an eligible Site, and after a little search we had the good fortune to secure one of twenty acres, fronting on Queen's Street, Toronto, and commanding a view of Lake Ontario. It is considered, by every person capable of forming a correct judgment, to be the most beautiful and convenient for the purpose that could have been selected in all the neighbourhood.

Having purchased the Site, another question arose, as to building; but, as our College was to be one of residence, there was no alternative, for we could not even commence until we had suitable accommodation for the Students.

Plans were accordingly advertised for, and contracts entered into for erecting such a portion of the College as our funds would enable us to meet, postponing the remainder until our increased numbers and resources made it convenient to complete the whole.

And now that we are assembled in a large and finished portion of this fine structure, which is allowed by all to be an ornament to the Capital and creditable to the Diocese, we may honestly congratulate ourselves and one another on the great and rapid progress which we have made in our undertaking,—and lift up our hearts in thankfulness and prayer to Almighty God that as He has so far blessed our endeavours, He will continue to bless them to the end. . . .

While we were actively employed in preparing for the opening of Trinity College and the commencement of instruction, a Committee of four of the most eminent Clergymen in London were prevailed upon, at the Bishop's request, to undertake the selection of the Gentlemen who were more especially to preside over and conduct the Institution. This Committee have discharged their onerous, but most important, duty in a manner highly creditable to themselves, and, it is believed, to the great benefit of the Institution. The Provost, who is a Professor of Divinity and Head of the College, the Professors of Classical Literature and of Mathematics, are now present and prepared to begin the discharge of their respective duties. They bring with them the highest testimonials, and reputations of which we may be proud, and which cannot fail of calling our infant Institution into speedy notice; but I dare not, in their presence, proceed any farther on this part of my subject.

Suffice it to say, that we shall commence the business of instruction in greater efficiency than has yet been attempted in any of the British-American Colonies, under five departments—Theology, Classical Literature, the Mathematical Sciences, the Faculty of Law, and the Faculty of Medicine, including Chemistry. All our arrangements are of the most liberal and satisfactory kind. The care bestowed in making our various appointments, whilst proving our great anxiety for the success of the College, offers a sure pledge of future watchfulness over its interests. Cherishing the hope of conferring a lasting benefit upon the Church and the Country, we shall proceed with double confidence in every department; for, though we make Religion the basis of all our teaching, there will be no neglect of any of those secular branches of knowledge which are embraced in the most extensive and approved Systems of Academical Education.

Having thus brought the history of Trinity College down to the present hour, I will now proceed to make a few general remarks on the beneficial results which we anticipate from the discipline, training and instruction which are to be employed in the College.

This is, perhaps, the more necessary, because the larger portion of our young men will come to us from a distance, and it will gladden the hearts of their parents to know that, though not immediately under their eye, everything will be done to supply the place of paternal counsel and maternal tenderness. As there is no system of education to be compared with that which is carried on at the domestic fireside, so that which, in advanced years, comes nearest to it, is unquestionably the next best.

Continuance of the Home Life of Students in this Institution.

Now, one of our principal objects in this Institution will be to bring back to the hearts and affections of our youth the fresh and innocent impressions of early infancy. With what deep emotions do we find the best and greatest of men recalling, in after life, the blessed influences which they imbibed under the parental roof, the holy truths communicated and the first faint accents of prayer, which a pious and tender mother whispered in their ears, invoking the protection of their God and Saviour before she kissed them and consigned them to their night's repose. On such sweet and pure recollections they delight to dwell, for at home all our best and holiest charities and affections begin, and from this centre they extend through an ever widening circle. Our desire then is to build up this holy foundation, to form ourselves, as far as possible, into a larger Household, and to keep as near as may be practicable to the order and economy of a well regulated family. There will be daily and hourly intercourse between the youths and their Instructors—reverence for superior age and attainments, and a prompt obedience to all their reasonable commands.

There will also be among the young men themselves an affectionate brotherhood, confidential and salutary companionship, noble resolutions, aspiring hopes, useful conversation and a friendly intimacy, on terms and with an intensity which nothing but a College life will admit. But, were they scattered about and living here and there in lodgings, these advantages, great and precious as they are, would be altogether lost.

Nature of the Discipline to be Adopted in the College.*

In regard to discipline, we can not surely be required, in 1852, to show that it is unnecessary,—on the contrary, the experience of all ages and countries points out the advantage of subjecting the passionate and enthusiastic period of youth to salutary control, as well as the great difficulty of rendering it effectual. This difficulty it will be our endeavour to surmount,—not that we entirely hope to reduce to order those who are determined to be vicious, for, to a certain degree, all plans of restraint, however judiciously carried out, will be found deficient,—yet a steady and just system of control, firmly but affectionately exercised, will do much. Even residence alone will be found highly conducive to the encouragement and preservation of correct moral conduct.

It removes many from temptation who are weak, or timid, to resist,—It keeps others from vicious practices who were at first open to no higher motives;—and, even where offences may have been committed, it prevents the habits of vice by the watchful supervision employed,—the certainty that those who persist in evil courses will at length be discovered, condemned, disgraced and expelled. Moreover, it sets up and establishes, if not always the highest, yet a respectable standard of morals and behaviour, which will become purer and more elevated as they advance in life.

Desirableness of this Necessary System of Salutary Vigilance and Control.

Let it be added, that the young men who come here, and who may, in future years, become leading men in society, as Clergymen, Lawyers, Physicians, Statesmen, Merchants,

---

* With remarkable clearness and precision Doctor Strachan laid down the rules of the disciplinary measures which were to be adopted in the "Household" of Trinity College, which commend themselves as most desirable and judicious in all seats of learning.

and Landed Proprietors, etcetera, are to be subjected to this salutary vigilance and control, not in boyhood, but from sixteen to twenty-two, or during the whole of their residence in College. To be thus under a well regulated restraint for several years, during the most critical period of their lives, is an advantage of great value, and gives the surest guarantee which is possible to obtain that they will leave the Institution with characters and attainments honourable to themselves and full of promise to their Country.

On the other hand, we may rest assured that even to young men naturally well disposed the effect will not only be calamitous, but, in many instances, blast their prospects in life, if they be cast loose, as it were, in a large City like this, without a friend, or counsellor, whom they revere, without any moral discipline, left to choose their abode, and their hours and companions as they please,—to attend, or not to attend, the Worship of God, and fall a prey to every corruption. Doubtless in some cases under all these disadvantages early impressions of Religion, through God's grace, may preserve them from evil, and bring them out of the fiery trial, corrected, strengthened and improved. But is this the natural result that we are entitled to expect from the total absence of vigilant supervision, discipline and control?

It would, therefore, seem that nothing is more likely to benefit Students than to afford them an opportunity of living together in society—of which the regular attendance upon religious ordinances, the observance of correct and gentlemanly habits, and obedience to a wholesome restraint, would form prominent features. Thence we infer that, without residence within the College, the full benefit of collegiate life and education cannot be obtained.

The facts of attending Daily Service in the Chapel, morning and evening,—listening to the religious Lectures,—dining together in the Hall,—conversations on their progress in their studies,—cheerfully conforming to the rules of order and regularity prescribed, will seldom fail to produce good habits; and, as we are the children of habit, we may, by God's help, gain those that are good more easily than the wicked learn such as are evil.

WHAT THE VALUE IS OF A SYSTEM OF EDUCATION BASED UPON RELIGION ILLUSTRATED.

When we speak of education based on Religon we mean, by Religion, the Gospel of the Lord Jesus Christ, and that instruction in this, the most important of all knowledge, shall not be confined to Public Worship, but shall enter largely into the daily studies and training of every department of the College. Thus the Students in the Arts and Sciences, as well as in Theology, are required to attend Lectures on the Holy Scriptures, and the doctrines and duties of Christianity, in conformity with the teaching of the Church of England, several times a week, and be, from time to time, examined on what they have heard and learned.

And it will be well for Students who are attached to the Law and Medical departments, though not required to reside within the walls of the College, to attend the Religious Instruction thus afforded them as often as possible—for such instruction is necessary to all men, to sanctify their thoughts and actions, and qualify them for a higher state of existence.

For the embodiment of the doctrines of Holy Scripture, as they have been universally received in all ages by the Catholic Church, and their adaptation to Public Worship and teaching, we point to the Book of Common Prayer as our guide,—that is the whole Prayer Book,—the Creeds—the Catechism,—Articles, etcetera,—but in doing this the Church of England neither supersedes the supreme authority of the Holy Scriptures nor adds to them, for they contain "all things necessary to salvation"; she merely seeks, in the most approved and certain manner, to lead us to the right understanding of the Christian Faith. Hence we find the doctrines taught by the Bible expressed in nearly the same words in the Prayer Book, and feel assured that we are in possession of the truth. In no branch of the Catholic Church are the Scriptures so extensively used in the Public Services as ours. We hold the Book of Revelation in special reverence; and no person

THE BIBLE AS THE MOST PRECIOUS GUIDE TO SPIRITUAL LIFE.

can attend on the ministration of our Church, for any length of time, without becoming intimately acquainted with its contents.

Associated with the Book of Common Prayer, the Bible, as has been beautifully said, fits every fold of the human heart, and is felt to be God's Book. It is also felt to be man's Book, because it satisfies all our thoughts and feelings, and leads us willingly to receive it as divinely authorized, and the scheme of human and divine things which it presents as essentially true.

How comes it then, that this, the most precious of all Books,—the Rule of Faith,—the Light that guides to Eternal Life, and which, until lately, was revered by all professing Christians, is now excluded from our Schools and Plans of Education, or only doled out "in shreds and patches," and even these deprived of all vitality by the divorce of the doctrines,—the sum and substance of Revelation. We answer that it is a fearful sign of the times, and of the prevalence of infidelity. It is true that some few of what are called the good and wise of this world are not unfavourable to this proceeding, because they are labouring under a delusion, and they perceive not the hidden purpose of the Man of Sin to deprave the heart,—corrupt the moral taste,—and keep Religion and the Holy Scriptures constantly out of view. And yet, no man can open the Bible, with a sincere desire to find it true, without being convinced that it is a revelation from God. Does he look for a ground of veneration,—he finds it in an antiquity unrivalled. Does he search for evidences of its truth,—he meets them in the testimony of miracles and prophecy,—in the ministry of men and angels,—yea, even in "God manifest in the Flesh, blessed for ever more." Does he ask for its authority?—it speaks from heaven in vision, in prophecy, directed by the Creator of all things, and "the giver of every good and perfect gift." In regard to its truths, we find them lovely, sublime and holy,—as God is holy. Are we anxious to know what benefits it offers?—all who read it will reply with one voice, that humility, resignation, purity, order and peace, faith, hope, charity, are its blessings upon earth.*

APPEAL TO RESTORE THE BIBLE TO ITS RIGHTFUL PLACE IN EDUCATION.

Now, if we are really sincere in our Christian profession, we ought to exert ourselves to the utmost of our power,—nay, at the hazard of our lives,—to remove this profanation and restore the Bible to its true position in education from the first School to the highest Seat of Learning. But, if we stand aloof and surrender our children to a system of instruction which not only excludes the Book of Life, but places it under a ban, and permit them to be fed with the husks, instead of the bread of Heaven, we are guilty of a serious offence before God and expose ourselves to His just displeasure.

In Trinity College I trust that the Bible will ever occupy its true place, as containing the whole revelation of God, the source of all our hopes, and the safe foundation of all our teaching.

ADDRESS TO THE NEWLY ENROLLED STUDENTS OF TRINITY COLLEGE.

In turning to you, my young friends, who are now about to commence your studies in this College—and in it, I trust, I shall have many opportunities of conferring with you on your duties, hopes and prospects,—suffer me to remind you that in this College you will enjoy every facility and incentive to active exertion which you can desire,—and do not forget that the spirit of the times in which you live has pronounced knowledge, power,—and ignorance, degradation. Nor can the youngest among you fail to perceive that he who wastes in idleness the opportunity of early life will lose caste in after years, and fall back from the honourable companionship of his former associates and

---

* The Bishop is here very strong in the utterance of his views on the great value of Bible truths being made the basis of all schemes of Education. His tribute to the "Great Book of Life," is very beautiful indeed.

from the station in society which he might have claimed. Above all, whether you pursue your studies with the view of advancing in the several Professions to which you are destined or merely for the cultivation of your minds, never omit to improve the means of regulating your moral conduct and forming your hearts in truth and righteousness. Hold fast the conviction that you are following the allotted path of duty, under the guidance and protection of One with whom is the result of your labours, and under a deep responsibility to One, " with whom is no variableness neither shadow of turning."

To you whose destination is the sacred Ministry, I would say: To what nobler aim can you dedicate your faculties and acquirements than to vindicate the great principles of your common faith, and defend them from the assaults of infidelity. Be not content with mediocrity;—aspire to that eminence which has been attained by the great preachers of other ages, the honoured champions of the Protestant Faith.

SIR JOHN BEVERLEY ROBINSON,
Chief Justice of Upper Canada.

Sir John Beverley Robinson, the Chief Justice, spoke as follows:*

You have, my Lord, from the fulness of your heart, addressed this Assembly on an occasion in which you may be supposed to feel a stronger personal interest than in any other public event of your life.

From Doctor Bethune, the Venerable Archdeacon of York, and from the Reverend George Whittaker the Provost, we shall hear with pleasure the observations suggested to them by a day so full of encouraging hopes for the Church of England [in Upper Canada], and for this Country; and I trust I shall not be thought to be assuming a part in this gratifying Ceremony which does not properly belong to me, if I venture, on behalf of a large body of my fellow-Churchmen in Upper Canada, to say some few things which I believe they would desire to have said, in connection with the scene before us.

And first: I am persuaded that I speak what is uppermost in the minds of all who are around me, when I assure your Lordship of our cordial sympathy with those feelings which must possess your mind when you look upon the Building in which we are assembled, and consider the occasion which has called us together within its walls. . . .

---

* In addition to a reference to the circumstances which led to the establishment of Trinity College, the Chief Justice also addressed salutary counsels to the matriculated students. He was afterward the first Chancellor of Trinity College University.

It has been long ago said, in a noble spirit of philanthropy, that it ought to be the aim of every man, while passing through life, to leave behind him some enduring proof that he has not lived in vain; some useful monument of his labours, by which his name may be favourably known in future generations. We thankfully acknowledge that your Lordship, standing under the roof of Trinity College, and in the presence of its duly appointed Professors, has fully acquitted yourself of this debt to posterity, while it is, at the same time, our peculiar advantage to know that as failures have not deterred, so success will not slacken, your services in this good cause. There is no one, we are convinced, who can be so influential as yourself in whatever remains to be done for placing this Institution on a secure and adequate foundation; nor is there one, of whom all of the friends of the Church can say, with so much reason, that they are sure his utmost exertions will, to his latest moment, be devoted to its service.

Our prayer is, that it may be permitted to your Lordship to witness, for many years to come, the growing usefulness of this Seat of Learning; and to assist with your countenance and advice those who have been selected to lay the foundation of its systems of instruction. To these gentlemen we can readily believe that this day has been one of anxious interest; for they cannot but feel that our chief dependence is on them for the success of what has been undertaken in so hopeful a spirit; while on that success must again, in a great measure, depend the satisfaction and comfort which are to attend them through the remainder of their lives.

We may be assured that those friends of your Lordship, who kindly undertook, in England, the very delicate and difficult task of selecting our first Professors, proceeded under deep and anxious sense of the responsibility which attended it; and that they were most solicitous to acquit themselves faithfully of the trust. As one of the College Council, appointed under the Statute, I may be permitted to say that we acknowledge ourselves as under a great obligation to them for the successful manner in which they appear to have fulfilled it.

Of the higher qualities necessary for the discharge of such duties as are to be performed here, I do not take upon myself to judge, but there are others of which I can form an opinion, and which are so far essential that there could be no hope of success without them. Speaking in reference to these, which will be understood to include disposition, judgment, and discretion, I have sincere pleasure in stating my conviction that the learned Professors, whose duties in the Institution are to begin this day, will be found possessed of excellent qualifications for the charge they have undertaken.

They are, I believe, as fully satisfied as we can be, that in those who are relied upon for preparing the minds and dispositions of youth for the business and duties of life, moderate exertion would be no more suited to this time and Country than moderate attainments; and, on the other hand, it will be satisfactory to them to feel assured, as they doubtless may, that they can in no other way so strongly recommend themselves to the friendship and confidence of the Members of the Church of England in Upper Canada, as by bringing up the youth committed to their charge, to be zealous, faithful, and undoubting Members of their Church, and firm and consistent supporters of her rights,—loyal subjects of their Queen, lovers of order, cheerfully, and from principle, obeying the constituted authorities, and the laws; and just and kind in all their intercourse with their fellow subjects, of whatever class,—religious or political.

And it cannot but be most satisfactory to these Reverend Professors to reflect that, not distracted, or checked, by considerations of political expediency, they will be under no obligation to withhold from God any portion of what they believe to be His true and reasonable service, from deference to the dissensions, jealousies, or prejudices, of men, but can teach sincerely, and without reserve, as they know they will be expected to do, " all things which our Church instructs " us a Christian ought to know and believe to his soul's health.

Personal Counsels to the Matriculated Students of Trinity College.

I do not for a moment imagine it to be any part of my province to offer counsel to our young friends who have just matriculated in Trinity College. They will have better and abler instructors. But, as it does sometimes happen that advice is more kindly received when it does not come attended with authority, I will venture, in a few words, to express an earnest hope that the young gentlemen who will be sent here to receive the inestimable advantages of a sound Religious Education, may, at all times, so conduct themselves as to prove to their Instructors that, in regard to their disposition, deportment, and moral conduct, the youth of Upper Canada stand in no disadvantageous contrast with the youth of other Countries, as, it is admitted, they do not in point of natural endowments.

And, in particular, I trust that they will bear constantly in mind of what consequence it is that they should be careful no less for the sake of the College than for their own sakes, to repress all disposition to insubordination, to vicious indulgences or degrading habits, convinced, as they must be, that while these cannot fail to bring discredit on themselves, and the most bitter disappointment to their parents and friends, they must also prove injurious to the reputation of this College, and in a great measure frustrate the benevolent intentions of its Founders.

It may be admitted to be true that in the course of the liberal studies to which they will be invited within these walls they will find some instances, (though they may be few in proportion), of men in whom the light of genius will shine so brightly as to be seen, though with greatly diminished lustre through the unlovely mists which their vices and follies throw around them; but they will also find that those who, by common consent, are spoken of as "lights of the world," and have been remembered from age to age as the benefactors of mankind, were men to whom the restraints of early discipline were never irksome,—who had no youthful excesses to repent of, or youthful extravagances to deplore, but who left the seats of learning as they had left the parental roof, with minds uncontaminated and characters unspotted. How enviable the lives of such men, who, haunted by no reproaches for time wasted, or energies abused, or faculties perverted, can look back with grateful and affectionate remembrance on the years spent in their College as the period when the foundation was laid of an honourable career in life, and of those Christian dispositions and principles which can best afford to them a happy immortality, and best prepared them for its enjoyment.

The Conditions and Prospects of this, the Church University of Upper Canada.

I have yet something to add, with your Lordship's permission, upon the condition and prospects of this Institution, not however descending to details, for which this would not be a fitting occasion. It must have been evident to all who have duly reflected upon it, that the most formidable difficulty attending its establishment is the difficulty of proceeding gradually in such a design, on account of the necessity that exists for making the system of instruction sufficiently comprehensive from the first. Whatever preference parents might feel for the sound principles on which it is founded, it could not be expected that, in order to sustain it, they would consent to place their sons under present disadvantages, which could never afterwards be repaired. An imperfect system of education would scarcely be accepted at first, and would not be tolerated long. When we look around us, we see that, in all that regards Public Instruction, the progress is rapidly onward.

Late Legislative Efforts to Improve Our Common and Grammar Schools.

The great effort which our Legislature has of late years made to improve and extend the System of Common School education, is a highly honourable distinction of the present time. The revenue raised expressly for that object—Ten thousand pounds per Annum for both Provinces—is large in proportion to the population of the Provinces; and the System of Instruction which it supports is conducted with acknowledged ability and zeal. The many Grammar Schools, besides, which are being established throughout this portion of Canada cannot but greatly assist in raising the standard of intellectual attainments throughout all classes of the community. It must follow, as a consequence, that those who are to fill the learned Professions, or who are likely, from their position, or property, to aspire to a lead in public life, will require superior qualifications. If they are to be eminent, it must be above those who will stand upon a higher level than the great bulk of the people could before attain to.

THE PRESENT AGE DEMANDS A HIGH STANDARD OF ATTAINMENT IN KNOWLEDGE.

There seems to be then a strong necessity for commencing at and upon such a scale as shall be reasonably suited to the requirements of an age remarkable for its rapid advancement and wonderful discoveries in the Science and Arts, and for the practical adaptation of those discoveries to the useful purposes of life. And besides, the pursuits of Commerce have become of such increased importance, its interests so varied, its arrangements so multiplied and complicated, and the competition they give rise to so keen and so incessant, that not a quicker application of the faculties, but a much wider range of knowledge, has become indispensable for those who are engaged in the active business of life.

The Professions demand higher qualifications. Wholly new departments of Science and Art have been created; old errors have been exploded, new processes and combinations adopted; what a few years ago were subjects of speculation and cautious experiment have become established facts, and engage attention and claim observance in the current transactions of the day.

MEMBERS OF THE CHURCH OF ENGLAND IN THIS PROVINCE CANNOT BE SILENT SPECTATORS OF CURRENT MOVEMENTS IN IT.

The Members of the Church of England, cannot, if they would, withdraw, for the sake of Religious harmony and peace, into a sequestered haven, and let the great current of human affairs flow by them; they must, like others, adventure upon the waters, prepared to bear their parts, with the best equipments they can provide,—studious above all things "not to make shipwreck of their faith," and, therefore, careful to take with them the chart which is to direct their course.

Relying upon the blessing of Providence in so good a cause, the Council of the College has concurred with the Bishop in going to the limit of their means in appointing the scale on which the College is to commence its operations; and they feel it to be their peculiar good fortune that the Faculties of Medicine and Law, for which they would otherwise have been at present unable to provide, will at once be placed on a highly efficient footing by the zealous services of Gentlemen whose experience and talents are most favourably known. To sustain the College in this state, and gradually to increase its efficiency, will require a hearty and very general co-operation from the Members of the Church. And why should not this be looked for?

We ought, perhaps to congratulate ourselves that the course of events, inauspicious as it has seemed to be to the United Church of England and Ireland in this Province, has at least this effect, that it has led to the establishment of this College, for the education of her sons in perfect and unreserved communion with her faith,—standing, in that respect, on a footing more entirely satisfactory than King's College did, even under its original Charter of 1827. That this principle of avowed and unreserved connection is that on which such institutions can be conducted with the best prospect of harmony and efficiency, seems to be a truth as clearly acknowledged and acted upon by the other large Religious Communities into which the population of this Province is divided as by us; and surely it would ill become the Church of England in Upper Canada to be less earnest in preserving the integrity of her doctrine, and the purity of her worship.

Ours is no new faith. It is not from the Reformation that the Church of England dates her existence. We are not separated from other Christian Communities in consequence of any recent adoption on our part of a doubtful interpretation of some text of Scripture, or any modern scruple in regard to forms. Nothing else that we most fondly venerate,—not the glorious flag of England, nor the great Charter of our liberties in the olden time,—has, from its antiquity, so strong a claim to our devotion as our Church. It is the Church which, from age to age, the Sovereign has sworn to support; centuries have passed since holy martyrs have perished at the stake, rather than deny her doctrines; and the soil of England is hallowed by the dust of countless worthies who have sunk to their rest professing her creed, and invoking blessings on her labours, after lives illustrated by piety and learning, and devoted in the purest spirit to the welfare of mankind.

May the honour be conceded to Trinity College, in the progress of time, of having produced men who, by their learning and virtues, may establish as strong a claim to the grateful admiration of posterity.

Notice to Intending Students of Trinity College, 1851.

Previous to the opening of Trinity College the following notice to Grammar Schools and to intending Students was issued:

Arrangements having now been made to open "Trinity College—Church University"—for the business of instruction, on the first of October next, information is hereby given to all whom it may concern that Grammar Schools in any part of Upper Canada will be received into union with the College, upon application to the Council.

1. Testimonials will be required to afford evidence that provision is made in the Regulations of such Schools for the systematic instruction of the Scholars in the doctrines and duties of Christianity, as taught by the United Church of England and Ireland, and also the Head Master and regular Assistants are Members of that Church.

2. Pupils educated in the Grammar Schools "in union" with Trinity College will become entitled to certain privileges, not conferred upon those from other Schools, such as becoming Associates of the College in shorter time, etcetera.

3. An Annual Prize will also be given by the Council of Trinity College to the best Pupil from each Grammar, or other, School.

Toronto, 26th February, 1851.   Thomas Champion, Secretary.

The Church of England Theological Seminary at Cobourg Transferred to Trinity College.

In his Address, in April, 1851, to the Clergy and Laity of the Diocese of Toronto by the Bishop he thus referred to the Establishment in 1842 of the Church of England Theological Seminary at Cobourg and its transferrence to Trinity College, Toronto, in 1851. He said:

You are aware that our Theological Seminary at Cobourg, (which has been conducted with so much ability and has been of so great benefit to the Church by the great number of zealous and active Clergymen which it has furnished), was intended from the first to be only temporary.

But so long as King's College existed and enjoyed a Religious Character, and had not only a Professor of Divinity to prepare our youth, inclined to the Church, for Holy Orders, but also to conduct regular service evening and morning and on Sundays and Holidays,—there was no urgent necessity for making any alterations in its constitution, or efficiency.

But when the Legislature of this Colony passed an Act in 1849, suppressing King's College, and excluding from the new University which it established all Religious Instruction, according to any form of doctrine; prohibiting any form of Prayer and every act of Public Worship;* . . . the Members of the Church of England thus deprived of a University, with which they could co-operate, determined to use their utmost efforts to establish a University in direct connection with the Church of England in Upper Canada, from their private means, and which should recognize the principles of Christianity as the basis of education.

An appeal was first made to the clerical and lay members of the Church of the Diocese, which was nobly answered by contributions in land and money amounting to the value of something more than Twenty-five Thousand pounds, (£25,000 = $100,000).

Encouraged by this generous liberality, which proved that the Church of England in this Diocese was wholly with me, I proceeded to England and renewed my appeal to our brethren, the Members of the Mother Church there; and they, applauding the object and confiding in the faith and sincerity of our supporters here, gave largely of their bounty, the two great Church Societies and the University of Oxford taking the lead in this work of Christian love.

Since my return to the Diocese, a temporary College Council has been organized, a Site has been purchased for the proposed College, which is to be called "Trinity College," and contracts entered into for the erection of the Buildings. The Institution is intended for the whole Diocese; and, in case of division, it is proposed to give the new Bishop, or Bishops, the same authority and interest in its proceedings as the Bishop of Toronto.

The position chosen as a Site is most beautiful; and the College, when completed, will present a striking object and a great ornament to the rising City.

TRANSFERENCE OF THE CHURCH OF ENGLAND THEOLOGICAL LIBRARY FROM THE UNIVERSITY OF TORONTO TO TRINITY COLLEGE.

The Society for Promoting Christian Knowledge in London decided to transfer to Trinity College the Library of Theological and other Books which it had previously granted to King's College.

INSTALLATION OF THE CHANCELLOR OF TRINITY UNIVERSITY, 1864.

The Annual Meeting of the Convocation of the University of Trinity College was held in the College Hall on the 17th of January, 1864. After morning Prayers in the Chapel the newly-appointed Chancellor, the Honourable John Hillyard Cameron, proceeded to the Convocation Hall, attended by the Vice-Chancellor, the Reverend Provost Whittaker, and other Members of the Convocation, where he was received by the Right Reverend Doctor Strachan, Bishop of Toronto, and where the Graduates, Undergraduates, and a large number of the friends of the College were assembled.

The Vice-Chancellor addressed the Chancellor, as follows:

Mr. Chancellor: In rising to address you on this occasion, one thought is especially present to my mind, and I am satisfied that the place of our assemblage and the purpose for which we are assembled have suggested that thought to the minds of all present. I am persuaded, Sir, I shall be best consulting your own feelings, by giving expression to that thought, before the utterance of a single word of congratulation, to yourself, or to our University, on your acceptance of the Chief Office in our Body. We cannot but recall, with grateful and affectionate regret, the remembrance of the Honourable Sir John Beverley Robinson, the former occupant of your Chair, whose name was associated with

---

* After the passage of this Supplementary University Act of 1850, Doctor Strachan favourably modified this expression of his opinion in regard to the Christian Character of the University of Toronto.

Trinity College from its foundation,—who may, indeed, be regarded, in connection with the venerable Prelate on your right hand, as one to whom it mainly owes its existence. On every occasion of the annual assembling of our Body, except the last, when illness had incapacitated him for discharging the duties of his office, we have enjoyed his dignified and kindly presence, and old and young must have alike recognized the tone which was imparted to our proceedings by the moral worth and refinement of character of which he was so signal an example. The congratulatory Address presented to him on the occasion of his installation, in June, 1853, closed with the following words:—"*Longe autem id tempus distet, quum mutua hæc amoris societas casu ullo aut necessitate dissolvatur.*" The "*suprema necessitas*" has dissolved our union far earlier than we, who

THE REVEREND GEORGE WHITTAKER, D.D.
Provost of Trinity College, Toronto.

cannot read the Book of God's Providence, could have desired; and it now remains that we should both cherish the remembrance of the departed, and strive to imitate his virtues. Our College and University has lost in him one of its wisest counsellors,—one of its steadiest friends; a man who never swerved for a moment from the course which he felt to be right, because that course might seem to involve unpopularity or a sacrifice of material interests; who had embraced exalted principles of action, and firmly adhered to those principles. We have lost one who gave most patient attention to any subject on which his counsel was sought, bestowing on it indeed what others might esteem, in regard either of its absolute, or relative, importance, undue thought and labour. We have lost one whose equable temper, whose cheerful urbanity, made it, at all times, a pleasure to hold communication with him. I must be permitted to add that I believe that any person coming from the Old Country must have been struck by the faithfulness with which he presented amongst us the type of an English Gentleman, not only in respect of the more important points of moral principle and feeling, but also in respect of the minor graces of demeanor—those small details of conduct, which scarcely admit of being particularized, but which collectively impart an inexpressible beauty to the life, and do assuredly indicate that a man has learned, by a delicate spiritual perception, to recognize what is due, before God, both to his neighbour and to himself. . . . During the twelve years for which the College has now been in operation it cannot be said wholly to have failed in accomplishing the intentions of its Founders. The number of Students matriculated up to the present time, inclusive of those who will be admitted to-day, is 195, besides a large number of Occasional Students, who attend the Medical Classes. Of Students in Arts, or Divinity, 83 have proceeded regularly to the Degree of Bachelor of Arts, exclusively of sixteen, who, without attendance on Lectures, have been admitted to that Degree after due examination. Of the 83, 37 have received Holy Orders; the remainder, with only one, or two, exceptions, are engaged in the study, or practice, of the Law, or Medicine, or are in charge of Schools. The total number of Students of the College who have been admitted to Holy Orders is 48; some Students, especially during the first few years, having been unable to accomplish the double object of passing through the Divinity Course and graduating in Arts. Many satisfactory proofs of the interest taken in the College have been afforded since its opening, by the establishment of Scholarships, or by other donations. The last instance of an endowment of this kind is the foundation of the Hamilton Memorial Prize, to be awarded according to the result of an annual examination in Scripture History.

The Chancellor, in reply to this Address, said:

Mr. Vice Chancellor: I feel deeply the congratulatory remarks you have addressed to me, as I felt deeply the confidence reposed in me by the Corporation of Trinity when they conferred upon me the honour of Chancellorship. You have well described the character of the late Chancellor. In every relation in life he stood pre-eminent, and to those who, like myself, for upwards of twenty years enjoyed the privilege of close communion with him, as their Chief, there is no power in language to pourtray their high estimate of his ability. His sweetness of temper, his gentleness of manner, his courtesy, were proverbial, and in the long roll on which this University shall write the names of her future Chancellors no name will ever be found of brighter lustre than the first. It is now upwards of twenty years since the venerable Prelate at my side, on the opening of King's College, congratulated himself that he had lived to see the work of forty years accomplished. But clouds were already rising in the distance to obscure the glorious prospect, and a storm soon burst upon him, which swept that inheritance of the Church away for ever. Did your noble Bishop despond, when he saw his cherished hopes in the dust? Did he give up his efforts to establish a Church University, because that Endowment was taken away? No, with the energy and determination which have ever marked his character through his long life, he resolved at three score years and ten to buckle on his armour again, and, in conjunction with our late Chancellor, those two great men, reflecting back light and lustre each upon the other, Churchmen in Canada and in the Mother Country contributed of their means, a Royal Charter was obtained, and the University of Trinity College arose from the ashes of the former King's College. You have told me, Sir, how much success has attended this Institution; that in twelve years we had nearly three hundred Students, and half that number of Graduates; that thirty-seven men have taken Holy Orders directly from this College, while eleven more, I believe, who have been at the College, have entered the Ministry, making forty-eight in all. Our Matriculants for the last three years have averaged twelve, which is not much inferior to the number in the separate Colleges in Cambridge, with the exception of St. John, Trinity, and another. We are about to appeal to the Churchmen in England to sustain our efforts, and we have very reason to hope that our appeal will be successful. As Chancellor of this University, I shall endeavour faithfully to fulfil my duty to it by doing all in my power to uphold the views which I have expressed, and I shall ever expect that each and all of those who hold office in it, or claim, or hope to claim, it as their Alma Mater, shall bear their part, both at home and abroad, within the walls of the College, without in the world, to establish Toronto as

Pulcherrima, honestissima, optima.

HISTORICAL SKETCH OF THE UNIVERSITY OF TRINITY COLLEGE.

BY THE REV. T. C. STREET MACKLEM, PROVOST.

"The best security of a just Government must consist in the morality of the people, and such morality has no true basis but Religion."

This wise utterance, which General Simcoe, first Governor of Upper Canada, made in November, 1792, indicated the basis upon which King's College was established at York, (now Toronto), as a Royal foundation in 1827, under a Charter granted by King George IV. Under the terms of this Charter, Religious learning and secular instruction went hand in hand in the University of King's College. But unhappily for the peace of that institution, the terms of the Charter provided also for its close connection with the Church of England and Ireland, which was then practically the Established Church in Upper Canada, as it was in reality in the Home Land. The conditions in the New World, however, were altogether different from those obtaining in the Old World, and the close union between King's College and the Church of England in Upper Canada caused much dissatisfaction amongst that part of the population which belonged to other communions. One result was that religious dissensions broke out in connection with the early history of the young University, and combined with other difficulties to hinder its development. But this is not the place to enter into a detailed account of the fortunes of King's College. Suffice it to say very briefly that its Charter was modified in 1837 with a view to placating the opposing interests, but without avail, and after a troubled period of several more years King's College ceased to exist, and the University of Toronto took its place. This momentous change led up directly to the establishment of Trinity College. For when the change came, it was not only the Church of England which was ejected from the counsels and teaching of the re-organized University; it was practically religion itself. The original King's College, with its sound union of religious and secular education, ceased to exist, and the University of Toronto, which took its place, was established as a purely secular institution, in which no Minister of religion of any denomination was allowed to hold office, as such, and the worship of God, according to the forms of any Religious body whatsoever, was forbidden. The Faculty of Divinity, which in King's College had been exclusively connected with the Church of England, was abolished. These changes were effected in 1849, and in the following year the University of Toronto entered upon its career as a secular institution.

The Church of England in Upper Canada, being thus deprived of the rights and privileges which it had enjoyed under the modified form of the original Charter of King's College, was obliged to make separate provision for the training of Candidates for the Ministry of the Church of England; while, in respect of the higher education of its youth generally, in order to fit them for various walks in life, the members of the Church of England were obliged either to be content with such a secular institution or to establish another University in which secular education would again be combined with Religious teaching and influences. Without hesitation they chose the latter alternative, and Bishop Strachan, although now past seventy years of age, addressed himself with characteristic energy and vigour to the founding of another University. In a Pastoral Letter which the Bishop issued to the Members of his Church in the Diocese he called on them for loyal support in this new endeavour, and shortly afterwards proceeded to England to plead his cause before Her Majesty's Government. How strongly the good Bishop felt about the act which had brought about the present situation, may be gathered from one paragraph of his Pastoral Letter.

This measure is so wicked and inconsistent, that, sooner or later, a serious reaction will take place. Its three leading features—contempt for the people, enmity to Religion, and disloyalty to their Sovereign—are each of them offensive to large and influential parties. The sentiments of the people are set at nought, to gratify the few, who neither value nor regard schools of learning. Religion is suppressed, and ecclesiastics proscribed, to please the enemies of property and order. And the very name "King's College" is abolished, for fear that some attachment to the Sovereign might, in the generous minds of youth, be associated with a Royal foundation.

While men to-day may not be prepared to echo all that the Bishop said, we can readily understand the strength of his feelings. He had expended the best energies of his life in the cause of education in Upper Canada and in aiding in the establishment of a University in which secular education should be built up upon the foundation of religious faith, and it was hard to face the destruction of the best fruits of his labour at a time of life when a man may reasonably hope for some repose and the enjoyment of the fruit of earlier years of toil. Yet he was nothing daunted by the prospect. With the least possible delay he founded Trinity College, obtaining from the Provincial Legislature an Act of Incorporation. He then proceeded to England, where he obtained generous support for the College from Churchmen there, to supplement the noble efforts made by Members of the Church of England in Upper Canada. He also procured from Her Majesty's Government a Royal Charter, conferring upon Trinity College the rights and privileges of a University. The Provincial Act of Incorporation was obtained in 1850, the Royal Charter in 1852, and in the same year the College was opened as a University.

Associated with the good Bishop in his arduous task were men whose names stand high on Canada's Honour Roll. The Honourable Sir John Beverley Robinson, Chief Justice of Upper Canada, was his staunch supporter throughout, becoming first Chancellor of the University of Trinity College, and other names prominent in the movement were those of the Venerable Doctor Okill Stuart, Archdeacon of Kingston; the Venerable Doctor A. N. Bethune, Archdeacon of York, and afterwards Bishop of Toronto; the Reverend H. J. Grasett, Rector of St. James' Cathedral and Dean of the Diocese; Doctor Alexander Burnside, the Honourable J. B. Macaulay, the Honourable J. G. Spragge, the Honourable Philip VanKoughnet, the Honourable George Crookshank, the Honourable William Allan, and Sir Allan MacNab.

While the Bishop was in England, seeking to obtain the Royal Charter, steps were taken on this side of the Atlantic for the establishment of a School of Medicine. Doctors Hodder and Bovell were the chief organizers of the School, and associated with them were Doctors Badgely, Hallowell, Bethune, and Melville. When the Bishop returned from England these gentlemen offered themselves and their School to become the Medical Faculty of the new Church University. Their offer was gratefully accepted, and the teaching of Medicine continued from that time on to be a strong department of Trinity's work. Later on, Trinity Medical College was established under a separate Act of Incorporation, but in close connection with the University of Trinity College, and it gained for itself an enviable reputation throughout the American continent. Eventually, as late as 1904, this Medical College was merged into the Faculty of Medicine of the University of Trinity College, and almost immediately afterwards was amalgamated with the Faculty of Medicine in the University of Toronto in connection with the Federation of these two Universities.

But to return to the earlier days and the establishment of the Arts College of Trinity University. The site selected was a large tract of land on Queen Street West, which in that day commanded an uninterrupted view of the Lake and Harbour; and when the College Buildings were erected they presented a striking picture to anyone approaching the City by water.

Bishop Strachan returned from England on the 4th of November, 1850, and on the 7th day of the same month the Medical Faculty of Trinity College was formally inaugurated. Then the Bishop turned his attention to the erection of the Arts College. With as little delay as possible, plans were called for, and those submitted by Mr. Kivas Tully were accepted. On the 13th of March, 1851, Contracts were signed for the erection of the Building by Messieurs Metcalfe, Wilson and Forbes. On the 17th of March the first Sod was turned by the Bishop, who, as he began the work, said, "We begin this work in the name of the Father, and of the Son, and of the Holy Ghost." The Corner-stone was thus laid on the 30th of April with solemn and imposing ceremony. The Bishop then delivered an address from which the following extracts are taken:

It would not be very easy for me to address you on this occasion, without briefly adverting to the fact that, on the 23rd of April, 1842, little more than nine years ago, some of us assisted at the laying of the foundation stone of the University of King's College, with promising hopes and sincere prayers.

But vain and fleeting are the works and hopes of men unless the Divine blessing rest upon them. The noble Seminary . . . from which so great results were expected, found itself immediately assailed. . . . And after maintaining a feeble and troubled existence for little more than six years, it was swept away. . . .

But forgetting those things that are behind, and reaching forth to those things that are before, let us not be dismayed, but seek with increasing faith the Divine aid in this our second . . . undertaking to raise a Christian Seminary where God's Holy name may ever be blessed and praised. . . .

Trinity College is a burst of Christian benevolence, to remedy an intolerable act of injustice. . . . It is peculiarly the child of the Church. I trust that many around me will be permitted to see Trinity College take an honourable place among the more celebrated Schools of Learning, and doing for Canada what Oxford and Cambridge have done for England. . . .

It will constitute a great Christian household, the domestic home of all who resort to it for instruction, framing them in the Christian graces, and in all sound learning, and sanctifying their knowledge, abilities and attainments to the service of God and the welfare of their fellow-men.

Other ceremonies being concluded and prayer having been offered, the Bishop receiving the trowel from the Architect said:

"Our help is in the name of the Lord,"

and the large assembled gathering responded,

"Who hath made heaven and earth."

Then, the stone being adjusted, the Bishop continued:

"Except the Lord build the house, their labour is but lost that build it."

Then, striking the stone three times with the mallet, he said:

"In the name of the Father, and of the Son, and of the Holy Ghost. Amen. I lay this corner stone of an edifice to be here erected by the name of Trinity College, to be a place of sound learning and religious education in accordance with the principles and usages of the United Church of England and Ireland. Other foundation can no man lay than that which is laid, even Jesus Christ, who is God over all, blessed for evermore; and in Whom we have redemption through His blood, even the forgiveness of sins. Amen."

The next important gathering was held on the 15th of January, 1852, when the Ceremony of Inauguration took place. On this occasion the Bishop reviewed the history of the establishment of Trinity College, in an admirable and most valuable Address which has been reproduced on pages 117 to 123 of this volume. Passing on to speak of the actual work of instruction, the Bishop said:

We shall commence the business of instruction in greater efficiency than has yet been attempted in any of the British American Colonies, under five departments—Theology, Classical Literature, the Mathematical Sciences, the Faculty of Law, and the Faculty of Medicine, including Chemistry. All our arrangements are of the most liberal and satisfactory kind. The care bestowed in making our various appointments, whilst proving our great anxiety for the success of the College, offers a sure pledge of future watchfulness over its interests. Cherishing the hope of conferring a lasting benefit upon the Church and the country, we shall proceed with double confidence in every department; for though we make religion the basis of all our teaching, there will be no neglect of any of those secular branches of knowledge which are embraced in the most extensive and approved systems of Academical education.

The Bishop then proceeded to speak of the advantages which Trinity College would offer to the youth of the country.

When we speak of education based on Religion, me mean, by Religion, the Gospel of the Lord Jesus Christ, and that instruction in this, the most important of all knowledge, shall not be confined to public worship, but shall enter largely into the Studies and training of every department of the College. Thus the Students in the Arts and Sciences, as well as in Theology, must attend Lectures on the Holy Scriptures, and the doctrines and duties of Christianity, in conformity with the teaching of the Church of England.

Let it be added, that the young men who come here, and who may, in future years, become leading men in society, as Clergymen, Lawyers, Physicians, Statesmen, Merchants, and Landed Proprietors, etcetera, are to be subjected to this salutary vigilance and control during the whole of their residence in College. To be thus under a well regulated restraint for several years, during the most critical period of their lives, is an advantage of great value, and gives the surest guarantee which it is possible to obtain that they will leave the Institution with characters and attainments honourable to themselves and full of promise to their country. . . .

It would therefore seem that nothing is more likely to benefit Students than to afford them an opportunity of living together in society—of which the regular attendance upon Religious ordinances, the observance of correct and gentlemanly habits, and obedience to a wholesome restraint, would form prominent features. Thence we infer that without residence within the College the full benefit of collegiate life and education cannot be obtained. . . .

In Trinity College I trust that the Bible will ever occupy its true place as containing the whole revelation of God, the source of all our hopes, and the safe foundation of all our teaching.

In turning to you, my young friends, who are now about to commence your studies in this College, . . . suffer me to remind you that in this College you will enjoy every facility and incentive to active exertion which you can desire—and do not forget that the spirit of the times in which we live has pronounced knowledge, power—and ignorance, degradation. Nor can the youngest among you fail to perceive that he who wastes in idleness the opportunities of early life will lose caste in after years, and fall back from the honourable companionship of his former associates and from the station in society which he might have claimed.

Above all, whether you pursue your Studies with the view of advancing in the several professions to which you are destined, or merely for the cultivation of your minds, never omit to improve the means of regulating your moral conduct and forming your hearts. Hold fast the conviction that you are following the allotted path of duty, under the guidance and protection of One with whom is the result of all your labours, and under a deep responsibility to One with whom is no variableness, neither shadow of turning.

Other notable Addresses were given, but I close with a brief extract from that delivered by the Honourable Sir John Beverley Robinson, Chief Justice of Upper Canada and first Chancellor of Trinity College:

The Members of the Church of England cannot, if they would, withdraw for the sake of Religious harmony and peace into a sequestered haven, and let the great current of human affairs flow by them; they must, like others, adventure upon the waters, prepared to bear their parts, with the best equipments they can provide—studious above all things "not to make shipwreck of their faith," and, therefore, careful to take with them the chart which is to direct their course.

Relying upon the blessing of Providence in so good a cause, the Council have concurred with the Bishop in going to the limit of their means in appointing the scale on which the College is to commence its operations; and they feel it to be their peculiar good fortune that the Faculties of Medicine and Law, for which they would otherwise have been at present unable to provide, will at once be placed on a highly efficient footing by the zealous services of gentlemen whose experience and talents are most favourably known.

To sustain the College in this state, and gradually to increase its efficiency, will require a hearty and very general co-operation from the Members of the Church of England. And why should not this be looked for?

Ours is no new faith. It is not from the Reformation that the Church of England dates her existence. We are not separated from other Christian communities in consequence of any recent adoption on our part of a doubtful interpretation of some text of

Scripture, or any modern scruple in regard to forms. Nothing else that we most fondly venerate,—not the glorious Flag of England, nor the great Charter of our liberties,—has, from its antiquity, a stronger claim to our devotion than our Church. It is the Church which, from age to age, the Sovereign has sworn to support; centuries have passed since holy Martyrs have perished at the stake, rather than deny her doctrines; and the soil of England is hallowed by the dust of countless worthies who have sunk to their rest professing her creed, and invoking blessings on her labours, after lives illustrated by piety and learning, and devoted in the purest spirit to the welfare of mankind.

May the honour be conceded to Trinity College, in the progress of time, of having produced men who by their learning and virtues may establish as strong a claim to the grateful admiration of posterity.

Thus was Trinity College launched upon her fateful and successful history, which, although it has numbered to itself more than half a century of years, stands only at the threshold still of that to which its friends of to-day, like its founders of half a century ago, look forward with confidence and faith.

The original subscription list of Trinity College contains a host of names familiar in the early days of Upper Canada—Burnside, Mercer, Strachan, Robinson, Draper, Esten, Macaulay, Gordon, Allan, Crookshank, Denison, Ridout, Dixon, Hagarty, Baldwin, Moffat, VanKoughnet, Brock, Paterson, Grasett, Melville, Henderson, Bovell, McKenzie, Turner, Gooderham, Rolph, Beard, Cameron, Lett, Lefroy, Cayley, Spragge, Boulton, Bevan, Harman, Sherwood, Rowsell, Jarvis, Champion, O'Brien, Brent, Magrath, Sanson, Nanton, VanNostrand, Boyd, Darling, Patton, Ardagh, MacNab, O'Reilly, Geddes, Mackelcan, Street, Gates, Clemow, Crickmore, Kerby, McMurray, Nelles, Parsons, Macklem, Cumming, Leeming, Ingles, Taylor, Fuller, Hamilton, Farmer, Fauquier, Millman, Bethune. Ruttan, Boyer, Daintry, Beck, Jones, Kirkpatrick, and many others.

The later history of Trinity College, and how a union was at length brought about with the University of Toronto, on terms which are honourable to all, and do no violence to the principles for which the Church University was founded—all this is too well known, and too recent, to need any record in the present volume.

TORONTO, 1910.   T. C. STREET MACKLEM, *Provost*.

ST. HILDA'S COLLEGE—THE WOMEN'S RESIDENCE OF TRINITY UNIVERSITY.

St. Hilda's College, the Women's Residence of Trinity University, was founded in 1888 by the then Provost, the Reverend C. W. E. Body, D.C.L. At that time there was no Residence for Women connected with any University, or College, in Ontario, but when the first Woman Student had been enrolled at Trinity, Doctor Body, with that practical wisdom characteristic of his operations, decided that the time had come for a Women's Hall of Residence to be opened in connection with Trinity University. A House was, therefore, taken, where intending Female Students could be received, and could obtain the advantages of that collegiate life and discipline which it has always been the aim of Trinity College to afford. Here the Women Students were taught for the most part—separate Lectures being given by the Professors and Lecturers of Trinity College, except in Honours, when both classes of Students worked together.

In 1899, largely through the influence of the Reverend Doctor William Jones, Professor, and afterwards Bursar, of Trinity College, a Building was erected in the grounds of Trinity, Her Excellency Lady Minto laying the Foundation Stone in April, 1899. About the same time, the plan of separate Lectures at Hilda College was abandoned; Students of that College now receive all instruction at Trinity College University, and, since Federation with the Toronto University, they attend also certain Lectures furnished by that University.

The Building of St. Hilda's College, with its Common, Drawing and Dining Rooms, Chapel, Library and excellent Students' Rooms, is, in every way, admirably adapted to its purpose. The Founders felt that, in order to obtain the full benefit of life in residence, a small society was best, and the present Building, which accommodates about twenty-five Students, is one where the life of the Home need not be lost in that of the Institution.

ST. HILDA'S COLLEGE, TORONTO

Besides the round of study, the Students observe many activities—intellectual, athletic and social. They take part in the debates and games of the Inter-College League of Women Students. They take an active part in the work of Evangelia House, where a St. Hilda's Chapter has been formed; they manage and edit a College paper.

One Graduate of Trinity College is a permanent Member of the Staff of Evangelia House; one is a Missionary of the Women's Auxiliary, at Nagano, Japan; many are engaged in teaching and other professions; and, through them, as we hope, St. Hilda's College is exercising a real influence for good in the outside world and upon the rising generation. Miss Cartwright is the Principal of St. Hilda's College.—*Communicated.*

TORONTO, 1907.

McMASTER UNIVERSITY, TORONTO, INCLUDING WOODSTOCK AND MOULTON COLLEGE.

McMaster University is the product of a long struggle on the part of the Ontario and Quebec Baptists to give effect to their conviction as to the importance of the Higher Education. That conviction busied itself first with making provision for an educated Ministry, and looked only to the establishment of a Theological School. Such was the Montreal College, which did useful work from 1836 to 1849, under the successive Principalships of the Reverend Doctor Benjamin Davies and the Reverend Doctor J. M. Cramp. Its failure was due to its distance from the centre of its constituency, divided counsels, and the general financial depression of 1848-1850. The following year the Baptist Union of Canada West considered a plan for a Theological School in Toronto, but nothing came of it. In 1852, the Maclay College scheme for a like purpose was floated, and pledges for $25,000 were secured; but difficulties arose, delays ensued, pledges lapsed, and, in 1856, that enterprise was abandoned.

THE CANADIAN LITERARY INSTITUTE, WOODSTOCK.—Soon afterwards the Reverend R. A. Fyfe, D.D.,—a notable figure in Canadian Baptist history,—suggested a new plan which should combine Literary and Theological Departments, and offer to young men and women the opportunity of obtaining a general education under Christian influences in a Residential School. The plan was received with favour. In 1857, an organization was effected, and, by an Act of the Canadian Parliament, (20th Victoria, Chapter 217), incorporated under the name of the **Canadian Literary Institute, Woodstock.*** Slight amendments were made in 1864, (27th and 28th Victoria, Chapter 143) and 1877 (Ontario Legislature, 40th Victoria, Chapter 63). Fourteen Trustees were named in the Act, and provision made for the election of Successors by the subscribers to the College funds. Control was thus vested, not in the Churches, or Convention, but in the Subscribers. By their voluntary gifts it was supported and, although offers of Municipal aid were made, they were always courteously, but promptly, declined, even in times of great financial embarrassment. The Institute was opened in 1860, and was immediately successful in attracting Students. The Literary course covered the work of the Public and High Schools, and was later extended to cover half the course of the University of Toronto, with which for some years it was affiliated.

After the Reverend Doctor Fyfe's death in 1878, Professor J. E. Wells, M.A., became Principal of the Literary Department, and the Reverend John Torrance, M.A., of the Theological, and suggestions for the removal of the latter Department to Toronto became more frequent. Through the munificence of Senator William McMaster this was effected; and, in 1881, the Toronto Baptist College was comfortably housed in McMaster Hall, Queen's Park, and was opened with twenty Students and a staff of three Professors, under the Presidency of Reverend John H. Castle, D.D.

The Act of Incorporation, (44th Victoria, Chapter 87), named twenty Trustees and gave them "full power and authority, (a), to appoint, dismiss, or remove Trustees and to appoint new Trustees from time to time," and, (b) "as to the appointment and dismissal of all Professors, Tutors and Teachers, and all Officers

---

* For a description of this Institute, as Woodstock College, see a page further on.

of the said College, and for and in respect of every matter and thing connected with the control, maintenance and regulation thereof." The Faculty, with the concurrence of the Trustees, were empowered to confer Degrees in Divinity. Thus the

McMASTER UNIVERSITY.

Toronto Baptist College was a close corporation, conducting the work of Ministerial Education for the Regular Baptists of Ontario and Quebec, and, later, for all Canada; for, in 1883, the Theological Department of Acadia University was closed, and, in 1885, Prairie College, Manitoba, completed its brief career.

In 1885, the Institution was affiliated with the University of Toronto and in the same Year by an Act of the Legislature (48th Victoria, Chapter 96), a Senate was created, composed of Representatives of (1), the Board of Trustees, (2), the Faculty, (3), the Faculty of Acadia College, (4), the Faculty of Woodstock College, (5), the Alumni and (6), each of the four Baptist Conventions of Canada. The Senate was given "concurrent power in the appointment and dismissal of Teachers" and "the control and management of the system and course of education." Meantime the Institute at Woodstock had changed its name to Woodstock College; an endowment of $40,000 had been raised for it, and much prosperity was enjoyed under the principalship of the Reverend N. Wolverton, B.A.

McMASTER UNIVERSITY.—The general policy of the Toronto Baptist College was to urge intending Students to take their literary preparatory Course in Woodstock College and the University of Toronto. Notwithstanding their efforts, however, a considerable number of men of defective education attended the College, and literary work was added, and the College Staff increased to meet their needs. For this work recognition was sought in the University of Toronto, and at the same time similar recognition was being sought by other Theological Schools in the City. In the course of the discussion of these adjustments the matter of University Federation was broached in 1884. The Reverend Doctors Castle and MacVicar and Principal Wolverton represented the Baptist Colleges in the negotiations that followed. At the Baptist Union in Brantford, in 1885, Senator McMaster offered $180,000 for such a Federated Arts College, provided the Denomination should increase the endowment of Woodstock College; but, in 1886, the Federation Scheme was abandoned. Mr. McMaster agreed to transfer this money to Woodstock, and Professor Theodore H. Rand, D.C.L., accepted the Principalship of that institution, on the express understanding that it should be free to develop to the full status of an independent University. In 1887, a Charter was obtained from the Ontario Legislature (50 Victoria, Chapter 45), abolishing the separate Corporations, uniting the two Colleges under the corporate name of McMaster University, and empowering it to grant degrees not only in Theology, but in the various Arts, Sciences and Faculties. During the struggle for the Charter, Mr. McMaster greatly increased his gifts, and, after his death, in the Autumn of that year it was found that he had left about $900,000 for the endowment of the University. An important feature of the Charter is that control of the University was entrusted unreservedly to the Baptist Convention of Ontario and Quebec. The Convention appoints the Board of Governors of sixteen Members who are given by the Statute "full power and authority to fix the number, residence, duties, salary, provision, and enrolment of the Chancellor, Principal, Professors, Tutors, Masters, Officers, Agents, and Servants of the said University, including any preparatory, or academical, Departments" and to appoint, or remove, any such Officials,—appointments, however, being made only on the recommendation of the Senate. The Senate, since the amendment of 1893, (56 Victoria, Chapter 114), consists of, (1), the Members of the Board of Governors, (2), six Representatives of the University Faculty, (3), five Representatives elected by the Graduates in Theology, (4) five Representatives elected by the Graduates in Arts, (5), two Representatives elected by the Teachers of Woodstock College, (6), two Representatives elected by the Teachers of Moulton College, and, for Theological purposes, only, (7), eight Representatives are elected by the Baptist Convention of the Maritime Provinces, (8), the President and two Professors of Acadia University, and, (9), two Representatives elected by the Baptist Convention of Manitoba and the North-West. The Senate was given "control of the system and Course of Education pursued in the University, and of all matters pertaining to the management and discipline thereof, and of the examination of all departments thereof, also the right to confer Degrees and to determine the Courses of Study and qualifications for Degrees, subject to the proviso that the standard for the Matriculation and subsequent Examinations should be as thorough and comprehensive as that maintained in the University of Toronto." The Senate is also authorized to nominate to the Board of Governors all Members of the Teaching Staff, and to prescribe the terms on which other teaching Institutions may affiliate with the University.

In October, 1887, the Toronto Convention unanimously voted to " accept the trust on the basis of the Will and Charter," and elected the first Board of Governors. The Guelph Convention of March, 1888, resolved, (1), that the University " should be organized and developed as a permanently independent Christian School of Learning, with the lordship of Christ as the controlling principle," and, (2), to locate the Arts Department in Toronto.

A month later Professor M. MacVicar, Ph.D., LL.D., was appointed Chancellor and the work of organization was begun forthwith.

Woodstock and Moulton Colleges.

Co-education was discontinued at the Woodstock College, and it was re-organized, so as to "provide for Males a thorough and practical general education." Through the generosity of Mrs. Susan Moulton McMaster, the Senator's widow, (who presented the McMaster Residence on Bloor Street East, Toronto, for the purpose), it was made possible to open Moulton College for Girls in September of the same year. Both Colleges are under the direction of the Senate and Board, and have preparatory, Matriculation, and other Literary and Scientific Courses of equal strength. A Manual Training department, the first in Canada, was opened in Woodstock in 1889; and since then a Domestic Science Department has been established in Moulton College. In the latter thorough Musical and Art Courses are also provided. Considerably over $100,000 has been expended in new Buildings, re-fitting, Scientific Apparatus and general equipment; the Collegiate Departments are in the hands of the University Graduates and the result is that these Schools stand unexcelled in Canada for equipment and efficiency.

The Arts Department began work in McMaster Hall in October, 1890, its Classes being open to women as well as men. Chancellor MacVicar resigned in the previous spring, and for the next two years Professor Theodore H. Rand, M.A., D.C.L., was Chairman of the Arts, and the Rev. Professor Calvin Goodspeed, D.D., LL.D., was chairman of the Theological Faculty. In 1892, the Faculties were united and Doctor Rand became Chancellor, and Principal, *ex-officio,* of the United Faculty. He was succeeded in 1895 by the Reverend O. C. S. Wallace, M.A., D.D., LL.D., and he, in turn, in 1905, by Professor A. C. McKay, B.A., LL.D., who has been identified with the University from the beginning. In 1903, Deans in Arts and Theology were appointed.

The University has been successful beyond the most sanguine expectations of its promoters. The Arts attendance has grown to 145; the Graduates in course already number 287; 36 have received the Degree of M.A. and 10 that of B.D. on examination; 29 have taken post-graduate work abroad; and 10 have already arisen to the position of Professors in Universities. The total numbers of Students in all the Departments is about 500.—There are nineteen Professors and Lecturers on the University Staff, five of whom belong to the Theological Department; in Woodstock College seven, and in Moulton College eight, Teachers give their time wholly to Literary work. The University Buildings, Grounds and equipment are valued at $250,000, the endowment at $900,000. Castle Memorial Hall was opened in 1901; and a new Science Hall is to be added this year.

It should be added that in keeping with the character of McMaster University, as a Christian Institution, the English Bible is, by Charter, a required subject in every Course in each Department, and all Teachers must be Members in good standing of some Evangelical Church. At the same time the University is non-sectarian and no religious tests are demanded of any students except in the Theological Department.—*Communicated.*

January, 1906.

McMaster Hall, or the Baptist Theological College, Toronto.

This College was founded in order to increase the number and efficiency of the Baptist Ministry in the Dominion of Canada. In 1883 it became the Theological Seminary of the whole Dominion of Canada, the Theological departments of the Woodstock College, Prairie College, Manitoba, and of Acadia College, Nova Scotia, having, by vote of Conventions, been transferred to Toronto.

This College is one of the few Theological Institutions that have entered upon their career somewhat fully equipped. It was founded in 1881 by the Honourable William McMaster, who erected the commodious Building known as McMaster Hall, at an expense of $100,000, and who has contributed largely towards the expense of the College. During 1883, the Faculty of the College was increased from three to five. These Professors devote themselves entirely to Theological teaching. The College also avails itself partially of the lectureship in Oriental Languages provided by the McMaster University. The Library of the College has been most carefully selected, and consists of nearly 7,250 volumes. It embraces the entire set of Migne's Greek and Latin Patrology, the works of the German, Swiss, English, Scotch, and Polish reformers, etcetera. It is well supplied also with the most important works in all departments of Theological Science. The equipment of the Colleges embraces a well-furnished Gymnasium. Candidates for the degree of B.D. must be Graduates in arts, and pass examinations on a prescribed course of reading at least one year after the completion of the College Course. Those who have secured the degree of B.D. may, after an interval of five years, proceed to the degree of D.D. on examination. Students support themselves by missionary work performed under the direction of the Faculty during Vacation and in Term time, the compensation received on their fields of labour being supplemented to a certain minimum amount. Those who do the full amount of mission work prescribed receive at present $200 per annum, clear of traveling expenses and board, while on the mission fields.

The number of students pursuing Theological Studies varies each session. Besides these, a considerable number of students for the Ministry who are pursuing University studies are enrolled among the students of the College and are under the care of the Faculty.

THE WESTERN UNIVERSITY OF LONDON, ONTARIO.

The Western University of London, Ontario, was established in 1878 by an Act of the Legislature, 41st Victoria, Chapter 70, and empowered to confer Degrees in Arts, Divinity, Laws, Medicine and Science—subject to the provisions of Section 10 of said Act. Like all Canadian Universities down to a very recent date, it owed its foundation to the needs of a Church, and was primarily intended to supply educational advantages to the Students of Huron Theological College. No Denominational test, however, was required of Students, and, almost from the first, the other Religious Churches were more largely represented than the Church of England which established the College. Through the energy and liberality of the late Bishop Hellmuth, the first Chancellor, a considerable sum of money was raised for endowment, partly in England, partly in Canada and the United States.

WESTERN UNIVERSITY, LONDON.

The work of instruction in the Arts Department began in 1881, with Huron College in affiliation as the Divinity School. The Medical Faculty began its operations in October, 1882, and has been in successful operation ever since. In 1887 a Law Faculty was established, with the late Judge William Elliot as Dean, and an able staff of professors. Owing to an unfortunate investment in Real Estate, it was found necessary to suspend work in the Arts Department in the year 1885. Ten years later, in 1895, this Department was re-opened, Principal Watkins of Huron College being made Provost. The Chancellor was then the Reverend Doctor Peach, of England, and the Vice-Chancellor, Sir William R. Meredith. Since that date, there has been, on the whole, a steady growth in the number of Students, although for some years the Institution had to depend upon private subscriptions for its maintenance. The Reverend Provost Watkins, having resigned in 1901, was succeeded by N. C. James, Ph.D., the present President of the newly organized University. In 1906 the government of the University was remodelled. Up to that time, Members of the Senate had to be Members of the Church of England. By the new Act this restriction was removed; but, owing to the relatively large representation of Huron College and the Diocese of Huron, the great majority of Members still belonged to that Church.

Finally, by the Act of the Ontario Legislature passed in 1908, the University became entirely undenominational and its government was reorganized. There are two governing bodies—a Board of Governors and a Senate. The Municipal Council of the City of London appoints four Members of the Board of Governors, the Lieutenant-Governor-in-Council appoints four, and these eight elect four others. The Senate consists of the Professors in the Arts' Faculty; two Members appointed by each of the other Faculties, or affiliated Colleges; two by the City Council; one by each of the School Boards of the City; one by the Graduates of each Faculty, or Affiliated College; one may be appointed by each County Council, or City Council, in the following Counties: Videlicet, Brant, Bruce, Elgin, Essex, Grey, Huron, Kent, Lambton, Middlesex, Norfolk, Oxford, Perth, and Waterloo. At the present time, January, 1910, nine of these Counties and five of the Cities have elected Senators. The Chancellor of the University is Mr. R. M. Meredith.

HISTORY OF HURON COLLEGE, LONDON.

Huron College was founded as a Divinity School in 1863 by the Right Reverend B. Cronyn, D.D., first Bishop of Huron. It was primarily intended to furnish a supply of men for the ministry of the Church of England in his own Diocese, but it has never been a merely Diocesan College. His efforts were ably seconded by the Venerable Archdeacon Hellmuth, who became the first Principal of the College, and who secured a gift of Five thousand pounds (£5,000) from the Reverend Doctor Peache of England, towards the endowment of the Divinity Chair. A most suitable property was secured in the North End of the City of London, and the first Buildings of the College consisted of the old Ridout House, with a slight addition to provide accommodation for Students, in addition to the Residence for the Principal, and a Chapel, which was used as a place of Worship for the Congregation then forming in the north end of the City.

The Addresses given on the occasion of the opening of this Chapel show that it was already in the minds of the Founders of the Institution to develop, not merely a Theological College, but an Institution of higher learning. Some slight provision was already made at that time for a Professorship of Mathematics, and it was with the intention of developing these plans that the Charter of the Western University was secured. The failure then to establish that Institution on a sufficiently solid foundation, coupled with the resignation of Bishop Hellmuth as Principal, prevented the development of Huron College, and it was continued for many years for the purpose of providing a Theological College for such Students as it could simply prepare for the Ministry without having the usual University training in addition.

The revival of the Charter of the Western University in 1895 gave a new stimulus to Huron College as the Theological School, but its own resources were somewhat handicapped by the effort to aid the University. In 1908, both Institutions were put on a broader basis. The government of Huron College was changed so as to give the Synod of Huron the direct control over its affairs, and, about the same time, the Western University was made absolutely undenominational and placed on an entirely separate financial basis. It is now proposed to mark the Jubilee of Huron College by a large increase to its endowment, and possibly also to its Buildings.

The Opening of Huron College, London, 1864.

The Huron College was formally opened for the reception of Students on the second of January, 1864. It was intended for the education of Young Men for the Ministry of the Church of England in the Anglican Diocese of Huron.

The Reverend Doctor Isaac Hellmuth, Archdeacon of Huron, was commissioned by the Bishop of Huron (Doctor Cronyn), in 1863, to proceed to England, to collect funds for the erection of the College. He was successful in his mission, and obtained Twenty-three thousand dollars ($23,000) as the result. The Reverend Doctor Hellmuth having been appointed Principal, he again visited England, and obtained a grant of Twenty thousand dollars ($20,000) from the Reverend Alfred Peache there, for the endowment of the Divinity Chair of the College. In his Address at the opening of the College, the Bishop of Huron said:—

On my consecration to the Episcopal Office I found a great demand for Clergymen in the Diocese of Huron. Out of 138 Townships not more than 30 were supplied with the administration of the Church of England, and there was no adequate supply of Candidates for the sacred office. I was, therefore, under the necessity of applying to friends in England and Ireland, and by their means a few young men were induced to come to this Country. Still the wants of the Diocese were but partially supplied, and at the present time over fifty Townships are not yet supplied with the ministrations of the Church of England.

I have received several proofs of the deep interest which is felt in our College by friends in this country both near and at a distance. A Gentleman in Kingston some time ago transmitted to me $400, and a Colonel C. S. Gzowski, who was for many years a resident amongst us, has evinced the interest he still takes in our welfare by contributing £120 per annum for five years towards the endowment of the University equivalents of Classical and Mathematical Chairs. A Gentleman connected with the College has liberally contributed $320 per annum toward the same object. And I received within the last week a Letter from which I extract the following passages:—

"I am requested by a 'Friend of the Gospel' to forward to you the enclosed order upon the Bank of Upper Canada for $4,000, as a donation to your Theological College, for the training of young men for the Ministry, who may go forth and preach Christ and him crucified. That the blessing of God may attend the Institution, and that the Lord may graciously spare you to see some fruits of your labours is our earnest prayer."

I will conclude my Address with the recital of a pleasing incident which occurred when the Reverend Doctor Hellmuth was soliciting aid for Huron College, in England. He called upon two Ladies residing near Bath; they are the daughters of the late General Simcoe, who was the first Governor of Upper Canada. These Ladies have ever taken a lively interest in Canada, and they have evinced their earnest desire to promote the progress of Huron College, by contributing to its funds, and by presenting to it the picture of their Father, to be placed in the College; that picture is now before you. Governor Simcoe explored this Country before roads were formed, or Townships surveyed. He encamped on the forks of the Thames, and it was he who fixed upon the Site of this City, and called it "London," and, in his Journal, which is in the possession of his Daughter, and which Doctor Hellmuth has seen, it is recorded that he and his Staff at one of their encampments, it may be on the site of our City, knelt and prayed that God's light and truth might penetrate these regions, and that His blessing might rest upon the Country. On that occasion Governor Simcoe was attended by the late General Evans, as one of his

Staff, and it was by advice which he kindly gave me before I left Ireland to come to Canada that my course was directed to the London District as being in his opinion and in that of Governor Simcoe, the part of Canada best adapted for settlers from England and Ireland. By this chain of coincidences, then, my presence here to-day is thus linked with the visit of Governor Simcoe to the Site of the City of London.

The Right Reverend Doctor McIlvaine, Bishop of Ohio, said:—

He was happy to be present on the occasion of such an interesting ceremony as the inauguration of the Huron College, coming, as he did, from across the lines, and pleased

GOVERNOR SIMCOE.

(From "Lieutenant-Governors of Upper Canada," by D. B. Read, Q.C.)

he was to congratulate the Bishop of the Diocese and the Venerable Archdeacon of Huron, for the active part they had taken in bringing the Huron College to such a satisfactory position. To the Bishop of Huron was due the origination of this noble design, and to Archbishop Hellmuth was due much for commending the cause which he had so nobly pleaded for in England. He had had the pleasure of being present in England at the time the Archdeacon was collecting funds for the Huron College, and he could say with all confidence that much self-sacrifice, energy, and attention was given to the noble work which he had to accomplish. He was glad to learn that the teaching of this Institution was to be purely evangelical. He liked the term evangelical, although many Ministers of the Gospel did not like it.

The Bishop's Address was received with the greatest attention and respect, and was warmly applauded.

It is of interest to notice that while the present generation owes so much to the foresight of the first Lieutenant-Governor of Upper Canada, General Simcoe, in anticipating the wants of Elementary, higher and University Education in the Province of Upper Canada, which in 1791 was about being established by the Quebec Act, he sets forth in his Letter to Sir Joseph Banks, Bart., President of the Royal Society, dated January the 8th, 1791 "his hope that he would be able to establish in the then virgin Province, among other means of civilization, a university"; and thus proceeds to speak of the locality which was to be the centre of the new community:—

For the purpose of commerce, union and power, I propose that the Site of the Colony should be in that great peninsula between the Lakes Huron, Erie and Ontario, a spot destined by nature, sooner or later, to govern that interior. I mean to establish a capital in the very heart of that country, upon the River La Tranche [Thames], which is navigable for batteaux 150 miles, and near to where the Grand River, which falls into Erie, and others that communicate with Huron and Ontario, almost interlock.

Upon this spot the City of London, in which the Western University has just been established, stands, and while the Site of Toronto was subsequently adopted as the Capital, the views of Governor Simcoe in respect to the University remained the same, and have been literally fulfilled in the Provincial University at Toronto, and this one at London, according to his expectations as expressed in his Letter of the 16th October, 1795, to Bishop Mountain:

My views in respect to a University are totally unchanged; they are on a solid basis, and may or may not be complied with, as my superiors shall think proper, but shall certainly appear as my system to the judgment of posterity. (Appeal on behalf of the Western University.)

The Honourable M. H. Foley said that having been honoured with the, to him, pleasing duty of introducing and carrying of the Act of Incorporation through Parliament, he could speak with a personal knowledge of the actions of Archdeacon Hellmuth, and to them in conjunction with that of the Bishop were the Churchmen of the Diocese indebted for the unanimous passage of the Bill in the very shape required. About thirty years ago there were within its limits, comprising an area of some 13,000 square miles, scarcely a dozen Ministers of the Church of England; now they number between seventy and eighty. Then the number of Houses of Worship were yet more limited—now nearly all the Towns and Villages have their numerous Temples erected to the living God. Then the Log School Houses, few and far between, were the only places where even the rudiments of an ordinary education could be obtained,—now the Country is covered with suitable and commodious Buildings, in which not only a fair, but in many cases a superior education might be had. Mr. Foley then moved the following Resolution:

That this Assembly desires to record its devout thankfulness to the Great Head of the Church, for the success which he has vouchsafed to the efforts made to establish Huron College.

The Reverend S. B. Ardagh, of Barrie, seconded the Resolution in a speech, congratulating the Chairman on the Institution of a College which would enunciate the true principles of the Church of England in this Country. He had come several hundred miles to identify himself with it. He felt confident, if the simple preaching of the Cross were made the basis of their faith, that the English Church would rank first in purity among the Churches in the world.

Further addresses were made by the Reverend Doctor Boomer of Galt, the Reverend Doctor O'Meara of Port Hope and the Reverend Doctor Hellmuth.

THE UNIVERSITY OF OTTAWA.

The University of Ottawa, originated by Bishop Guigues, is conducted by the Oblat Fathers of Mary Immaculate, began with the infancy, and has developed with the growth of the City of Ottawa.

Incorporated in 1849, under the title of the "College of Bytown," this Institution received, in 1861, the title of "College of Ottawa," and, in 1866, was granted the power of conferring University Degrees. All the Degrees conferred are officially recognized in the Dominion and in all other British possessions.

By a Brief, dated February the 5th, 1889, the Sovereign Pontiff, Leo XIII., raised the University of Ottawa to the rank of a Roman Catholic University, with all the privileges conferred on such an Institution.

The Degrees of B.A. and B.L., which the University confers in virtue of its University Charter, besides being honourable testimonials of high and varied attainments, entitle those who study Law to exemption from preliminary examinations and to a reduction of two years from the ordinary course of five years. These Degrees also exempt those who study Medicine from preliminary examinations.

A Certificate that the holder thereof has passed the examination held at the end of the first year in Arts, entitles such holder to registration as a Medical Student, within the meaning of the Ontario Medical Act.

A Certificate that the holder thereof has passed an examination on the subjects required for entrance to the Ontario College of Pharmacy, entitles such holder to registration as a Student in Pharmacy.

The observance of Discipline and good order being indispensable to insure the success of Students in their Studies, the observance of the Rules of the University is enforced. Moral influence is resorted to, especially as an incentive to the performance of the duties prescribed.

Reports are sent by the Prefect of Studies to Parents, showing the conduct, application and standing of their sons, and giving information about matters of special interest.

Parents are earnestly requested to impress upon their sons the importance of practising economy while at the University.

Students are strictly forbidden to lend, borrow or exchange personal effects of any kind.

The Government Museum, the Dominion Observatory, and the Parliament Library at Ottawa furnish the Professors and Students of the College with the means of elucidating questions in Literature, Science, and Art. Moreover, the Students enjoy the advantage of occasional attendance at the Debates of the Dominion Parliament, and thus become familiar with those political contests in which they may afterwards be called to take part.

PART XII. THE UNIVERSITY OF OTTAWA. 149

THE OTTAWA UNIVERSITY.

Besides these, and other educational advantages, spacious Grounds for Athletic Sports, well-ventilated recreation Halls, and an Infirmary with Doctors in daily attendance, recommend this Institution to parents who consult both the intellectual and physical advancement of their sons.

The New Science Hall of the University of Ottawa.

One bright morning in the early fall of 1856 a few dozen lads gathered for the first formalities of an academic year's work in the new stone Building which to most of them, as to most of the people of Bytown, seemed a stately College home. The new Building was not indeed palatial, but compared with the humble quarters provided for the Faculty and Students in the College of Bytown since its inception, eight years before, the five storeyed structure, 84 by 40 feet, on Wilbrod Street, looked quite imposing.

When Bytown became Ottawa, the College of Bytown became the University of Ottawa; the new Capital grew, and its leading educational institution more than kept pace with it. The Stone Building was erected thirty years previously, and had, by 1885, been enlarged to more than seven times its original size, and in that year the Theological Students, who could no longer find room in that main edifice, moved into a new Building on the banks of the Rideau River, truly splendid in dimensions, style and surroundings. Before ten years more had rolled by, another colony, this time collegiate students attending the Apostolic School of the Oblat Fathers, went to occupy the fine modern annex on Theodore Street, opposite to the College Block.

These extensions and annexes, however, failed to permanently supply ample room for all departments of the University. Great inconvenience has been occasioned, of late years, by the insufficiency of space allotted to the Laboratories and Museum, and by the fact that this space was very much needed for Class Rooms. There was but one remedy for the inconvenience, and the application of the remedy brought into existence the new Science Hall.

Every old Student will remember the two small Log Houses that stood on the north side of Wilbrod Street facing the Statue of Doctor Tarbaret. They had some interest in serving to recall a style of habitation that belongs to bygone days, but standing in the midst of a modern residential quarter, and just in front of a remarkably fine Building, they seemed, to say the least, not in harmony with their surroundings. A little over two years ago they became the property of the College Corporation, and their demolition speedily followed. The lot on which they stood is occupied to-day by the latest University Building, a solid stone structure, 98 by 85 feet high.

Its lofty storeys, and many windows, high and wide, at once impress upon the visitor the fact that the Science Hall comes up to the modern Educationist's standard of a plentiful supply of natural light and pure air. Pleasing architectural effect has been equally well compassed. The monotonous, massive appearance that is often a feature of structures of this kind, is obviated, and grace of outline attained by an ornamental Tower with Turrets, as well as by other attractive features.

The Museum, with the Offices and Workrooms connected with it, occupies the entire second floor. The main room, 80 by 65 feet, and 20 feet high, is finished and furnished in an elaborate and tasteful style that makes it peerless among Canadian Museums.

SCIENCE HALL, OTTAWA UNIVERSITY.

The Physical Laboratory.

The Physical Laboratory is a room 60 by 40 feet. Communicating with it are a Workroom, also a dark Room and a Room for specialty work. In the location

ATHLETIC OVAL, OTTAWA UNIVERSITY.

and general arrangement of all these Rooms, the special purpose which each is to serve has been kept closely in view, and the plans of the principal Laboratories in **the country** made a subject of careful study. Gas, water at high and low pressures, and the electric current, alternating or direct, as desired, are available. The experienced eye will certainly see in the general features of the Department of Physics possibilities for thorough demonstration and exhaustive research.

THE LECTURE HALL.

This capacious Room for public, or semi-public, scientific Lectures and Demonstrations supplies a want long felt by students and lovers of Science in Ottawa. The new Science Lecture Hall will enable the University Scientific Society and other Scientific Clubs, using it, to offer to Lecturer and audience unusual advantages.

THE CHEMICAL LABORATORY.

Easy of access from this Room are a Private Laboratory, a Lecture Room and a Storeroom for chemicals and other materials. In the new home of the Chemical Department the student is provided with facilities for doing his experimental work in a thorough manner and under most favourable conditions. In location and finish the Rooms leave nothing to desire; they are heated and lighted perfectly, and the system of ventilation effectively prevents the accumulation of foul odours and noxious gases.

THE MINERALOGICAL LABORATORY.

In this Room fifty Students may find working space, and each has before him Apparatus, Water, Gas, Reagents and all else necessary for Blowpipe analysis. Every Student also has Shelves and a Locker for the storage of articles used by him. Desk wall Cases, conveniently placed, contain samples of a great variety of Minerals. These are distributed amongst Students for experimental work. The study of the Mineral Products of the Dominion is facilitated by the large collection of Canadian Minerals in the Museum.

THE EDUCATIONAL FACILITIES OF OTTAWA.

The University is only one of the City's many educational advantages—it is well equipped in Elementary and Classical Residential Schools for the education of the rising generation. Ottawa University, one of the leading Roman Catholic Colleges in the Dominion, has power to confer Degrees in Theology, Philosophy, Law, Medicine, Arts, Music, Science, and Civil Engineering, and its Graduates in these several departments rank high in the professional world. There are also a Normal School and Model Schools under the control and supervision of the Provincial Government, from which a large class of highly trained Teachers is turned out annually. Public School education is amply provided for from the Kindergarten through all intermediate grades to the High School, or Collegiate Institute, from which latter pupils matriculate to the Universities, the Military College, and other Institutions. There are at the present time fifty-two Public and Separate Schools in which about 13,000 pupils are instructed by 300 Teachers.

There are branches of the Grey Nuns, (the Convent of the Sacred Heart), and Congregation de Notre Dame; the Ottawa Ladies' College; the Carleton School for Girls; Ashbury College for Boys; the Conservatory of Music and several Business colleges. (See also page 48 of Volume I.)

REGIOPOLIS COLLEGE, KINGSTON.

In 1825, the Right Reverend Bishop Macdonell* established a Seminary at St. Raphael. In 1835, he and others petitioned for an Act of Incorporation for a Seminary, or College, at Kingston, and, in 1837, it was incorporated, and had a piece of land set apart for it as a new College. In that year Bishop Macdonell, Vicar-General Angus Macdonell and Doctor Thomas Rolph of Ancaster went to England for the purpose of collecting money for the new Seminary at Kingston. After a time this Seminary was established there as Regiopolis College.

In 1835, the Honourable and Right Reverend Bishop Macdonell gave . . . four acres of land to a projected Roman Catholic College . . . a College established (in 1830) in the County of Glengarry. The Site (of St. Raphael's) of the College was afterwards removed to Kingston, as Regiopolis College.

Regiopolis College . . . was opened in 1846, by the Very Reverend Angus Macdonell, Vicar-General, who was its President (1863). The general course in the College embraces Classics, Mathematics, Philosophy and Theology.†

Bishop Macdonell endowed it with a grant of nearly four acres within the limits of the City of Kingston, and afterwards by a legacy of real and personal estate. In 1837, it was incorporated, under the title of *The College of Regiopolis*, (7th William IV, chapter 56); and, in 1845, the Trustees under the Will were authorized by the Act, (8th Victoria, chapter 79), to convey the legacy of the Bishop to the College Corporation, and the latter was authorized to hold real property to the value of Three thousand pounds, (£3,000), currency per annum. The Officers were: The Reverend Angus Macdonell, Vicar-General, President; the Reverend J. B. O'Brien, B.A.; H. Burns, Isaac McCarthy and Michael Stafford, Professors.‡

Doctor D. A. O'Sullivan, D.C., LL.D., in his Essays on the Roman Catholic Church in Canada, says:

Doctor (Thomas) Rolph . . . states that Bishop Macdonell has long since desired to erect a College for the Education of Youths for the Priesthood, in a beautiful and commanding piece of ground . . . overlooking the Town and suburbs of Kingston. . . .

Dr. O'Sullivan says further:

A gift of One thousand pounds sterling, (£1,000), by Cardinal Weld, for the purpose of building a College at Guelph, is mentioned in early days; and the same writer, (Doctor Rolph), says that there was, in Prescott, a very elegant Stone Building erected by the (Roman) Catholics, denominated "Grenville College," over which the Reverend J. W. Campion presided. (Pages 132, 133.)

---

*In his Essays on the (Roman Catholic) Church in Canada, Doctor D. A. O'Sullivan thus refers to the first Bishop of Regiopolis (Kingston): "Bishop Macdonell did missionary work in Canada for thirty-six years, and died in 1840. He is a martial figure in the history of the Church in this Country, and had many difficulties to encounter. He had been Chaplain in Ireland during the trouble of '98; . . . . he was missionary in Canada during the War of 1821, and Bishop of Kingston during the Rebellion of 1837. . . . . He was named a Legislative Councillor in 1834, shortly after the creation of his See, and was in receipt of a considerable pension for his loyal services from the (British) Government of the day. In speaking to the late Bishop Strachan, many years ago, about his early School life at Cornwall, he incidentally mentioned to me that he and his countryman, Bishop Macdonell, were very friendly with each other, and that the Bishop used to stop with him on returning to Glengarry from the mission journeys.

†The Educational Directory and Calendar for 1857-8, edited by Thomas Hodgins, B.A., Univ. Coll., Toronto, page 89.

‡This gentleman was afterward well known as the excellent Priest at Lindsay, to whom I was authorized to speak in regard to his acceptance of the post of Principal of the Normal School at Ottawa, when it was established.

The Foundation of Regiopolis College, Kingston.

In March, 1862, the Reverend John O'Brien, Director of Regiopolis College, sent to the Editor of this Volume the following account of the establishment of that Institution:

Regiopolis College was founded in the year 1846 by the Very Reverend Angus MacDonell, Vicar General, its present Superior. It is now a very flourishing institution. Already many have gone forth from it who are distinguished in the professions of Law and Medicine, and within its walls were educated a large portion of the Roman Catholic Clergy of this Diocese, who are noted for their piety and learning, and whose Missionary labours have been crowned with signal success. This Institution advancing gradually in its career of usefulness from its first foundation, received an additional impulse on the arrival of Bishop Huron in Kingston. Having been engaged all his life in the cause of Education in the most flourishing Institutions of Lower Canada, he was intimately acquainted with the proper manner of conducting a college, and resolved on his first advent to Kingston to employ the experience he had gained in making Regiopolis rank among the first Colleges of the country. In this he has fully succeeded; for the College has now a staff of able Professors, and already counts within its walls a hundred Students from different parts of Canada and the United States. The Studies embrace a complete Classical and Mercantile course, together with Mathematics, Philosophy and Theology. The College is situated in one of the most beautiful sites of the city, and is remarkable for the health of the Students. Although it is a Roman Catholic College, yet students of other Denominations are admitted, and there are at present several Protestant Boarders in it.

SAINT MICHAEL'S COLLEGE, TORONTO.

This College was established in 1852, by the Basilian Fathers from Annonay, France, at the request and under the patronage of the Most Reverend Doctor Charbonnel, Roman Catholic Bishop of Toronto. It was incorporated in 1855. In 1861 the College was affiliated with the University of Toronto, on a basis similar to that of the affiliation of the Roman Catholic Colleges of England and Ireland with the University of London. The students are considered as matriculated upon passing the University Examination. At the end of the first and the third year, Certificates from the College are accepted in lieu of the University Examinations. At the end of the second and the fourth year, the Examinations are passed before the University Examiners. Throughout the Course, all the Lectures in Mental and Moral Science, Civil Polity and History are given at St. Michael's College.

The Directors of Saint Michael's College are men devoted by Profession to the training of youth; they certainly exert themselves to the extent of their ability, and the means at their disposal, to improve the Institution of which they have charge, and in this they have been highly successful.

In his note, enclosing the following Sketch, the Reverend J. M. Soulerin stated, that the:

College received its first Students in a small House on Queen Street—near Church Street. It was soon afterward transferred to a portion of St. Michael's Palace. The number of Students increasing rapidly, the project of a larger Building, to be erected on Clover Hill, was formed in 1854.

This Institution was established in 1852, by some Clergymen of the Order of Saint Basil, which has for its immediate object the training and instruction of youth. It was incorporated in 1854 by an Act of our Provincial Parliament. A success, as decided as unexpected, considering the brief period of their career, has crowned the endeavours of these Gentlemen, in the cause of imparting a sound and substantial education. Already no less than Four hundred Students have received, if not the whole, at least the greater part, of their education in this Establishment; some of these embraced the ecclesiastical state, and propose to devote their lives to administering to the spiritual wants of their fellow men; others are to be found discharging the arduous duties of the liberal professions, whilst many are engaged in a mercantile career.

This Institution possesses all the advantages that could be desired with respect to both its situation and its course of study. 1st. With regard to its situation, it has a fine, healthy and picturesque location, being on a slight eminence 125 feet above Lake

ST. MICHAEL'S COLLEGE, TORONTO.

Ontario, and surrounded by a beautiful grove which affords the students a pleasing and refreshing retreat during the heat of Summer. 2nd. As respects the Course of Study pursued in this Establishment: It is such as to meet the exigencies of all classes, consisting of two distinct branches, videlicet, the one Commercial, and the other Classical. The first is for such pupils as require only sufficient education to carry them through the ordinary pursuits of life. . . . The second is adapted to those who wish to follow a learned profession. . . . Students can also receive lessons in German, Drawing and Music, if their Parents or Guardians desire it. Religious training, the basis, or foundation, of all Education, receives that particular attention which its importance demands. The Professors, being a Teaching Fraternity, have been trained in the school of experience, and, consequently, are fully capable of imparting a good sound education. Every means is taken to insure the health of the pupils; the different apartments are spacious and airy; the splendid ball alleys and a gymnasium are placed at their disposal during the hours of recreation, that there they may relieve their minds from the monotony of study and develop their physical strength.—J. M. S.

The General Course of Studies in Saint Michael's College is as follows:

Classical Course.—Besides certain English branches, this Course embraces the Greek and Latin Languages, Belles-Lettres, History, Mathematics and Natural Sciences; German optional. This course extends over five years.

Higher Course.—A further Course, covering two years, embraces Mental and Moral Philosophy, Natural Theology, Natural Philosophy and Inorganic Chemistry. Special Lectures are delivered on Mental and Moral Science and History, as prescribed by the University of Toronto.

Theological Course.—In addition to these Courses of Study, there is a Theological Course, in which Candidates for the Ministry are in part prepared for their work, the Course being completed at the "Seminary" in Montreal, Province of Quebec.

Societies.—Besides two Religious Societies, or Sodalities, there is a Literary Association—"The St. Michael's Society" and "The St. Charles Literary Society."

HISTORICAL SKETCH OF KNOX COLLEGE, TORONTO.

In 1844, arrangements were made for the training of young men for the Ministry in connection with the (Free) Presbyterian Church of Canada; and, in 1855, the Reverend Henry Esson, Minister of the St. Gabriel Street Church, Montreal, was appointed Professor. He was aided by several Ministers from Scotland; and, in 1846, the Institution was put on a more permanent basis, and was designated "Knox College." The Reverend Doctor Robert Burns, the first Pastor of Knox Church in the City of Toronto, acted as Professor of Theology for a time; but, in 1847, the Reverend Michael Willis, D.D., of the Free Church of Scotland, in Glasgow, was appointed Professor of Theology—the duties of which Chair he continued to discharge until 1870, when he resigned. The Reverend Alexander Gale, M.A., the Reverend William Rintoul, and the Reverend G. P. Young were connected with Knox College for a longer, or shorter, time.

Its charter of incorporation, under the Seal of the Province, is only dated in 1858. It was then the only Theological School of the Presbyterian Church of Canada, as it now is of the "Canadian Presbyterian Church." Its professorial Staff consists of three—one of these being Principal, as well as Professor of Divinity. To the other two Professors are assigned the departments of Church History, with the evidences of Christianity; and Exegetical Theology, and with the oversight of the Philosophical Studies of the Students.

The latter part of the arrangement was only provided for, in what was intended as a purely Theological College, to meet the case of a large class of Students, when the arrangements of the University College were not found to be so adapted to its needs as was desirable.

For a like reason Classes in the Department of the Languages and Mathematics were also, for a time, taught in Knox College. But the desire of the Founders of the Institution being, as far as possible, to affiliate their College with the public Universities, they did not contemplate—nor does the Canadian Presbyterian Synod contemplate—a permanent provision, at the expense of one Church, of the means of preparatory education already provided for at the expense of the country in common.

The governing bodies of the College are, for the purpose of internal discipline and daily government, the Senate, the Professors, with a few Assessors, appointed by the Synod; and a larger body called the College Board, which is for the conduct of its secular and general affairs. Both report to the Synod of the Church, to which ultimately belongs the choice of the Teachers, the arrangement of the Curriculum and the care of its whole interests.

The present Curriculum extends to six years, the latest three of these being given to Theological Studies proper. Students are permitted to join at any stage of the Course, on producing satisfactory proofs of attendance elsewhere, and of proficiency. The admission to the College is through the Presbyteries, with whom lies the right of examination in order to enter.

KNOX COLLEGE, TORONTO.

The number of Students attending the College, including the preparatory Students, or prospective Students of Divinity, has kept pace with the growth of the Church. The number was very much increased after the union of the several Presbyterian Churches.

From the account of the Jubilee of Knox College in 1894, I have selected the following historical data:

Knox College at first, like some other Institutions, such as the Log School, began in a somewhat humble style, having been conducted in a Room in the House occupied by the Reverend Henry Esson, on James Street. In 1846 it was transferred to Front Street, where a house, now included in the Queen's Hotel, was rented, and here it remained till 1854. Having to leave these quarters, the College authorities had some difficulty in securing a suitable location, but attention having been directed by a gentleman, still living, who has always been a good friend of the College, Mr. A. M. Smith, to Elmsley

Villa, then in the market, negotiations were begun, which issued in the purchase of the Building which had been previously occupied by Lord Elgin, the Governor-General. The cost of Elmsley Villa was about $28,000. Assistance was given by the Free Church of Scotland, and by the Presbyterian Church in Ireland, but the greater part was contributed by friends in Canada. For twenty years Knox College had its home in Elmsley Villa, and I have no doubt some who were then youthful Students, now in maturer years, may remember not a few happy gatherings, and some innocent interludes amidst graver studies, in the old and somewhat homely Building. *Forsan et haec olim meminisse juvabit.* But, by-and-bye, we began to search for some building of a more Academic style, and after looking out for a Site farther west, our attention was directed to the circle in Spadina Avenue, which was secured at the price of $10,000. The Foundation Stone was laid on the 3rd of April, 1874, and the College was opened here in October, 1875. Liberal subscriptions were made for the erection of the Buildings. Several years were spent in canvassing the congregations, which was largely done by the Professors, and still longer time in collecting the amounts subscribed, thus adding largely to the interest and expenses. There is still a debt for which a mortgage was given for $26,500. The hope is entertained that a Jubilee offering will be raised in token of gratitude for all the goodness which the Great Head of the Church has manifested to the College, and for the very large number of labourers which the College has supplied for the work of the Ministry in our own Province and in the regions beyond.

An Act of Incorporation was obtained for the College in 1858, and in 1881 an Act was passed amending the Act of Incorporation, and giving power to the Senate to confer Degrees in Divinity. The College has been for some years affiliated with the University of Toronto, and is now a Member of the University Confederation.

Support of the College.—The support of the College came at first from congregational contributions, aided for some years by a grant of £300 from the Free Church of Scotland, but this was given up by the Church here in 1854. The annual expenditure at first was about $2,500, and in 1861 it was about $4,750. An Endowment Fund was commenced, but amounted to very little until 1875, when from the estate of the late Mr. William Hall, of Peterboro, there was received the amount of $40,000; from the late Mr. James MacLaren $50,000 for the endowment of the Chair of Systematic Theology; subsequently there was received from the estate of the late Mr. Bowman upwards of $20,000; and from the estate of the late Mrs. Nicholls of Peterboro, $20,000. A number of smaller sums were devised by individuals, and a general canvass of congregations for the Endowment Fund was begun and well responded to. It took a considerable time to complete the canvass and collection of funds, but the amount available for the support of the College, after deducting expenses and an amount of arrears which had accumulated on the Ordinary Fund, is fully $20,000. In consequence of the general fall of interest from seven and seven-and-a-half per cent. to five and five-and-a-half per cent. the amount from the Endowment has considerably decreased. This makes it all the more necessary to raise, if possible, the amount aimed at for removing the mortgage on the Building. In connection with both the Building Fund and the Endowment Fund, the services of the Reverend W. Burns were most valuable.

Scholarships.—From time to time generous Members of the Church have contributed amounts for the help and the encouragement of young men studying for the Ministry. The Senate is enabled to give at present, as annual Scholarships, the following:—For students of the first year in Theology, seven Scholarships of the aggregate value of $300; for Students in the second year, seven Scholarships, $365; for Students of the third year, six Scholarships, $340. Besides these there are the Bayne Scholarship, for proficiency in Hebrew, $50; Prince of Wales Prize, $60, tenable for two years; Smith Scholarship, $50; Brydon Prize, $30; two prizes given by Mr. W. M. Clark, (Lange's Commentary), one in Old Testament Hebrew and one in New Testament Greek; also three Scholarships by the late Mr. James Henderson, Hamilton, being the interest of three sums, $800, $600 and $600, respectively, to be at the disposal of the Senate in aid of deserving Students, apart from competition. Five Scholarships are offered for Students, Candidates for the Ministry, who are taking a University Course.

Library.—There was little at first in the shape of a Library in Knox College. The Reverend Mr. Esson kindly gave the use of his splendid Library for the Students who at first attended, and Ministers and other friends assisted in the same way. The Reverend Doctor Burns, who from the very first took a lively and practical interest in everything connected with the College, collected in Scotland from various friends a valuable Library of from two to three thousand volumes. From time to time additions were made to the Library, in some instances by purchase, but more largely by donations. Efforts were made from time to time by Students and by Ministers to collect money for the enlargement and improvement of the Library, but little comparatively was effected in this direction until the death of the late Mr. James MacLaren, already mentioned as a liberal benefactor, when the sum of $20,000 was bequeathed by him for the purchase of Books for the Library. This amount has been invested, the interest to be used from year to year in the purchase of Books. The amount available will be about $1,100 a year, an amount which although not very large will prove a very great benefit, and will in time put the College in possession of a valuable Library.

The Library possesses the following valuable volumes: (1) The Paris Polyglot in ten volumes, the gift of the late Reverend Alexander Black, D.D., of the New College, Edinburgh, per Reverend Doctor Burns. (2) Codex Sinaiticus (fac simile) 4 volumes, presented by Mr. W. M. Clark, M.A., Q.C. (3) Codex Alexandrinus (Auto type copy), 3 volumes. (4) Aristotles Constitution of Athens, (Auto type copy of MS.). 5 Poems of Herodus (Auto type copy), from Papyri in British Museum. These three also by Mr. Clark, besides other valuable works.

Museum.—From an early period of the history of the College, there has been a nucleus of a Museum, but circumstances prevented much being done towards its improvement. Recently, through the energy of some of the Graduates and Alumni, there has been stirred up a greatly increased interest in the Museum. A very large collection of interesting objects from Formosa has been presented to the Museum by the Reverend Doctor G. L. MacKay, the present Moderator; a moderate grant was made by the College Board for its improvement, and the hope is entertained that the Museum will become, before long, worthy of the College. . . .

On looking back on the past fifty years of the existence of the Knox College, since it was established in 1846, we have abundant cause for gratitude to the Great Head of the Church for the very large degree of favour bestowed on our Seminary. For the sound, able and evangelical men whom He has qualified and sent as teachers for our candidates for the Ministry, for the large number of Students who have passed through our Hall, for the self-denial, fidelity and zeal which they have manifested in their work, and for the measure of liberality which our people have shown, we are truly grateful. We thank God for what He has done for us. May His blessing, notwithstanding our unworthiness and our unfaithfulness, be still continued, and may those who may see the completion of another period of fifty years have still more abundant reason to bless and praise our faithful and covenant keeping God. Grateful for the past and hopeful for the future, we would say:—

"The Lord of us hath mindful been
And He will bless us still."

The Reverend Doctor Grant, President of Queen's College University, in representing the Sister Colleges at its Jubilee, said:

I have been asked to speak on the relation of sister Theological Colleges to each other, a subject to which the Jubilee Committee attaches great importance, if we are to judge from the number of addresses bearing upon it in one way or another which are to be given to-night. These relations, he said, it seemed to him must be largely determined by the origin of the Institutions and the nature of their work, and on such occasions as that which they were celebrating it was more fitting to reflect upon and to gather instruction, inspiration, warning and hope from the past. Just as a free state was infinitely more complex than a despotism and could, therefore, preserve its stability only by having its Institutions deeply rooted in antiquity, so was it with a Free Church. It must not abandon any real treasure of the past. They must drink from the same fountains which inspired their fathers, while keeping their eyes open to the necessities of a new age and a new land. The learned Principal then proceeded to give a brief review of the origin of the various Colleges, pointing out the distinctive features of each and also their close relations to each other. The daughters of one mother must love, trust, frankly recognize and heartily co-operate with each other. This applied not only to sister institutions in the same Church but to all Colleges. All rejoiced in a common parentage. All, too, were engaged in the same work. All Colleges now professed to study the Bible carefully, lovingly and scientifically, and the Churches, therefore, must accept conclusions arrived at in accordance with canons of universal validity, or perish morally in the presence of the scientifically educated world. In the settlement of the question at issue regarding the nature and extent of the human elements in the Bible, votes of general assemblies, or of Conferences, or of Bishops, or the Encyclicals or Decrees of Popes, avail nothing. These only darken counsel and confuse the souls of tender and timid people.

All the Colleges have a common origin and common work to do. They stand on common ground, and are bound together by spiritual sympathy. There is therefore mutual recognition and the conviction that they are embraced in a world-wide union. So shall it be in due time with the Churches also.

Further historical references to Knox College:

During the twelve years which have elapsed since the Jubilee of Knox College was celebrated, the work has gone on steadily; and the number of Students, while varying from year to lear, has, on the whole, been gradually increasing. Many and important changes have taken place in the staff of Teachers. The Workers have changed, but the work has gone on.

Professor R. Y. Thomson, M.A., B.D., closed a short but brilliant career in 1894. His early death was felt to be a great loss to the Institution, to which he had devoted his high gifts.

Reverend Professor W. Gregg, D.D., retired in 1895 from the Chair of Apologetics and Church History, which he had filled for so many years with marked ability and success.

In 1896, the Reverend G. L. Robinson, M.A., Ph.D., of Boston, Massachusetts, was inducted into the Chair of Old Testament Literature and Exegesis, in which he rendered excellent service for two years, when he accepted a similar position in Chicago. On the same day as Doctor Robinson was inducted into Knox College, the Reverend James Ballantyne, B.A., of Ottawa, was installed as Professor of Church History and Apologetics. At a later date, the subjects taught by him were changed to Church History and Government. And in this congenial work he continues still to do excellent service.

In 1898, the Reverend John E. McFadyen, M.A., B.A. (Oxon.), was appointed to the vacant Chair of Old Testament Literature and Exegesis, which he still fills with marked ability.

In 1901, the Reverend Halliday Douglas, M.A., of Cambridge, was appointed to the Chair of Apologetics and Homiletics, and, for one Session, he filled the Office with the highest promise of success. But, the following Summer, when on a visit to his native land, he died suddenly in Edinburgh, and a career of great promise closed.

In 1903, the Reverend J. D. Robertson, M.A., D.Sc., was appointed to the Chair left vacant by the death of Professor Halliday Douglas, and, in October of that year, entered on his work, which he still continues to discharge with growing success.

The lamented death of the Reverend Principal Caven, which took place on the first of December, 1904, left a great blank in Knox College. He had been forty years connected with the Institution, as Lecturer, Professor and Principal. No man could have left a deeper impress on his Students.

The Reverend Doctor MacLaren, who for thirty-one years had been Professor of Systematic Theology, was chosen by the Senate to discharge the duties of the Principalship *pro tempore*, and the General Assembly in the following June appointed him Principal, relieving him, at the same time, of the heavier portion of his Class work. The same Assembly appointed the Reverend T. B. Kilpatrick, D.D., of Manitoba College, to the Chair of Systematic Theology, and Reverend H. A. A. Kennedy, M.A., D.Sc., of Callendar, Scotland, to the Chair of New Testament Literature and Exegesis. These Gentlemen entered upon their duties last October, and have gained for themselves a good report.

During the sixty-two years that have elapsed since Knox College was founded, it has encountered many difficulties, but it has overcome them, and has continued to do an important work for the Presbyterian Church. It has prepared and sent out eight hundred and twelve Graduates to enter on the Christian Ministry, a larger number than probably has been trained by any other Theological School in Canada. And its friends still regard its outlook for the future as hopeful and promising.—*Communicated.*

TORONTO, 1907.

ALBERT COLLEGE, BELLEVILLE.

This Institution, founded in 1854, was the result of the active zeal and wise policy of the Methodism of that early day, and grew out of the conviction that Schools for the Christian education of the youth of the Church should be maintained and encouraged by the Church. The position of the College is exceedingly favourable. The City of Belleville is one of the most noted and enterprising Cities between Toronto and Montreal. It has a population of about 10,000, and is situated on the historic Bay of Quinte, on the direct line of the Grand Trunk Railway, and is the southern terminus of the Midland Division of that Railway. Its advantages as a location for a seat of learning had long been noticed before steps were taken for forming one in its vicinity. When the prosperity of Canada began to make the multiplication of facilities for higher education a necessity, the General Conference of the Methodist Episcopal Church, in 1854, adopted a scheme—initiated in the Bay of Quinte Conference in the preceding year—for the erection and maintenance of an Educational Institution in Belleville, " designed to teach a system of Classical, Scientific and Commercial instruction, free from sectarian tenets and Religious tests, while its moral government is based on Religious principles, as revealed in the Holy Scriptures."

Having been chartered by Parliament in 1857 as the " Belleville Seminary," it was opened in July of the same year, and entered upon its work under very favourable circumstances, with a superior staff of Instructors and a large number of students. In the year 1866, by Act of Parliament, the name was changed to " Albert College," and a Senate was created with ample powers. By the terms of the Union of the Methodist Churches of Canada, Albert College was retained in Belleville and adopted by the General Conference of the United Church as a Church College. The Charter was afterwards amended, and the College was affiliated to the Victoria University, Cobourg. As now constituted it has an ample teaching Staff for imparting instruction to Young Men and Women in the advanced branches of a liberal education—and its Senate has full power to examine and

PART XII. ALBERT COLLEGE, BELLEVILLE. 163

grant Prizes, Scholarships, Medals, Honour Certificates and Diplomas in Domestic Science, in Music, Fine Arts, Commercial Science and Collegiate Courses, etcetera.

ALBERT COLLEGE, BELLEVILLE.

Albert College is, by Act of Parliament, in affiliation with Victoria University and with Toronto University, and is especially fitted to prepare Students for both Junior and Senior Matriculation in the different Arts and Faculties of these Universities.

Large and ever-increasing numbers enter Victoria University from the Halls of Albert every year.

Ample opportunity is afforded to those preparing for the examinations of the Board of Provincial Surveyors, the College of Physicians and Surgeons of Ontario, the Ontario College of Pharmacy, the Law Society of Ontario, and the Literary and Scientific portions of the various Theological Examinations, of which advantages many have availed themselves with marked success.

Albert College possesses excellent advantages for the preparation of Candidates for Teachers' Certificates. Large Classes are annually prepared for these examinations, and with gratifying results. The College has Chemical and Physical Laboratories, also a splendid Museum. The Departmental Examinations are held every year in the College Building.

Students are admitted into Albert College without examination.

Special attention is given to the preparation of Candidates for Examination in the Preliminary Course for the Ministry of the Methodist Church. Classes are formed in all of the subjects required, and the Certificates of Albert College are accepted in the subjects of the Conference Preliminary Course by the several Annual Conferences. The College also affords the very best instruction in Elocution, including Bible and Hymn reading, and singing.—*Communicated.*

BELLEVILLE, 1910.

MASSEY HALL AND RESIDENCE, ALBERT COLLEGE, BELLEVILLE.

Massey Hall.—This Building was commenced in June of 1895, and was opened in January of 1896. It is erected on the west side of the Residence, and the two are connected by means of a covered passage-way thirty-four feet long. To the rear of the passage in the Basement is placed a row of Bedrooms and Bathroom, which are intended for the use of the Employees of the College. The extreme length of the new Building proper is 94 feet, and the extreme width through hall 75 feet. Through the centre of the Building in Basement and ground floors runs a spacious Hall, which gives free access to the various parts of the structure. There is an easy flight of stairs to each end of the Hall, which not only affords more direct and easier communication to the different portions of the Building, but is also a decided advantage in case of fire, giving an additional means of exit. In the Basement, which is high, airy and well lighted, besides the Bedrooms before mentioned, are a large Sitting-room, Store-room, Natural History Class-room, Museum and Lavatory. On the ground floor are an Office, four large Class-rooms, a Cloakroom, and a spacious Vestibule. All these Rooms have high ceilings, and are thoroughly well lighted and ventilated.

On the next floor is the Chapel and two large Class-rooms, which can be opened into the Chapel by means of folding doors. Assembly Chairs are used for seating, and will accommodate over 500 persons. The Chapel has large Gothic windows, and is in every way adapted for the purpose for which it was erected.

The front elevation of the Building presents an imposing appearance, with its Tower and Turrets, and spacious entrance to the Vestibule.

The interior wood finish is in ash, in Queen Anne style, with moulded architraves and handsome dadoes. The hardware is of bronze, and is rich in appearance and substantial. Leaded cathedral glass is used in all the windows of the first and second floors. The Class-rooms are seated with automatic single Desks, or

Assembly Chairs, and are in every way up-to-date. A large Regulator has been placed in the main Hall, to which electric Bells are attached, and which regulate the change of Classes.

MASSEY HALL AND RESIDENCE, ALBERT COLLEGE, BELLEVILLE.

The Residence.—The Building is large, substantial and convenient, of brick and cut stone, with a total length of 230 feet, including wings. It was erected originally for College purposes, and is situated in a quiet and healthy part of the

City. During the Summer of 1888 it underwent a thorough system of repair, a fifth storey with new Roof was added, a new steam heating Apparatus was placed throughout the whole Building, and the older portions were thoroughly renovated. It has been still further improved during the recent enlargement of the College Buildings, and is now devoted entirely to Residence. Throughout the Building, Lavatories, with steel-clad Baths and Closets of the newest and most approved designs, have been placed, and the work done in the best style of the plumber's art. The drainage and sanitary conditions are the very best. The Building also contains a handsome and well furnished Reception Room, Library and Reading Room. The large Room, 50 x 52, which was formerly used as the Chapel, has been fitted up with Banking Offices, Merchants' Emporium, etcetera, and is now used as the Commercial Hall.

Courses of Study in Albert College.

I. *Collegiate Course.*—Embodying Elective Undergraduate Studies.

II. *Junior or Senior Matriculation.*—In Arts, Civil Engineering and Royal Military College, Law, Medicine and Theology.

III. *Teachers' Courses.*—To prepare for Teachers' Examinations.

IV. *Preliminary Course of Studies.*—As prescribed by the General Conference of the Methodist Church.

V. *Business College Courses,*—Comprising Theoretical and Practical Bookkeeping, Practical English, Shorthand, Typewriting, Telegraphy, Civil Service and Chartered Accountants.

VI. *Musical Courses in Musical Academy.*—Comprising Full Conservatory Courses in Piano, Pipe Organ, Vocal, Violin, Harmony and Theory of Music.

VII. *Course in Fine Arts.*—Embracing Painting, Drawing, etcetera.

VIII. *Course in Elocution.*

IX. *Course in Physical Culture.*

X. *Courses in Domestic Science and Art.*

XI. *Alexandra Ladies' College Courses.*—Leading to Degrees of M.L.A. and M.M.L.

The Collegiate Course.—The Literary Department of the College is conducted in exactly the same way as in the High Schools and Collegiate Institutes of Ontario, and embraces: Form IV. (Fourth Book) of the Public School Course of Study and Forms I., II., III. and IV. of the High School Course. Classes are thus provided to prepare Students for entrance into the High School, and covering all the work for Junior and Senior Matriculation, and also for Junior Leaving and Senior Leaving Teachers' Certificates. No examination is required to enter the College. Beginning Classes are organized in the Public School Arithmetic and English Grammar, and special attention is given to backward Students.

Semi-terminal examinations are held throughout the College year in all forms of work, and are compulsory upon all Students in attendance.

Annual examinations are held during the closing days of the College in Forms I., II., III., to test the ability of Students to enter upon advanced forms of study, and the names of those successful in passing these examinations appear upon the Programme of the annual College Convocation. A Certificate of having passed in the College Examination in the subjects prescribed for Junior Matriculation into the University is accepted by the Conference of the Methodist Church as equivalent to the Conference Preliminary Examination prescribed for Candidates. Persons desiring a clear Certificate for registration to the College of Physicians and Surgeons in Ontario, ecetera, are required to write on the regular Departmental Examinations held each year in the College Buildings under a presiding Examiner appointed by the Education Department. The examination in Form IV. (Senior Matriculation, Pass and Honour) is conducted by the Senate of Toronto University, and is held in the College Buildings, commencing on the second Tuesday in June, and successful Candidates secure both the Diploma of graduation of the College and first year standing upon the Arts Course at the University.

In June, 1894, the first class of six Candidates wrote at this Examination, and all were successful, two of whom made first-class Honours. In 1895 eleven Candidates wrote, ten of whom were successful, and two secured Honours. Classes varying in number from six to thirteen have written each year since that time, with most gratifying success. This excellent record is due to the fact of a longer College year, and the close contact of Teacher and Student in Class-room grind. These years have fully proven the ability of the College to prepare Students in both Pass and Honour work of the first year in the Arts Course of the University.

Valuable Matriculation Scholarships have been won by Albert College Students.

Teachers' Courses.—The College each year prepares Candidates for the different grades of Teachers' Certificates. In 1894, six out of eight Candidates were successful. In 1895, the College prepared three Candidates for the Senior Leaving Examination, two of whom took Science and the Moderns as optional subjects, and all three were successful; and of the Candidates for Primary and Junior Leaving Certificates, 50 per cent. were successful. In 1896, two out of three Candidates for Senior Leaving were successful, and over 80 per cent. of the Junior Leaving and Primary Candidates were successful. In 1897, of eight Candidates for Senior Leaving were successful, and of eight Candidates for Junior Leaving, all were successful. Since that time large Classes have written annually with gratifying success. This high percentage of successful Candidates at once stamps the College work as thorough and efficient. Every department is in charge of an Honour Specialist of experience and teaching ability.

The College has separate and specially fitted Class Rooms for Biology, Chemistry and Physics, so that Students have splendid facilities for practical work. Regular semi-terminal Examinations are held, which are made severe and thorough, and every care and attention is given to the Candidates to insure their success. Students will write in July on both Junior and Senior Leaving work. The Examination is held each year in the College Building.

Conference Preliminary Course.—The General Conference of 1894 made the College requirements for Conference Preliminary as follows: (*a*) Candidates for the Ministry shall be required to present a Certificate, or other evidence, of matriculation (with the Greek option) in a Canadian, or British, University; or (*b*), an equivalent Certificate from one of our Colleges.

The Collegiate Course of Albert College provides an exact equivalent for matriculation, and offers just such advantages as young men in preparation for the Ministry require. This Examination is held in June, and all Candidates are recommended to take the regular Examination coming at that time, as a full College year is necessary to do the work justice.

Special Lecture Courses.—Missionary Course and Bible Study, etcetera: Regular Classes are organized under the direction of the Principal, supplemented by special Lectures for the systematic study of the English Bible and Missionary Literature, and known as the (*a*), *Missionary Course.* While specially designed for the benefit of Students in preparation for the Ministry, these Classes and Lectures are open to all Students without additional fee.

Business College Courses.—Since 1877 a Commercial Department has been conducted in connection with Albert College, and with good success. The College is prepared to give a practical business training, combined with a thorough English Course, unexcelled by any Business College in Ontario, and at moderate rates. One of the paramount reasons why young men and women should take their Commercial Course in Albert College is because they are allowed to take any subjects they wish that are embraced in the Albert College Commercial Course of Study. It is confidently believed that no other Canadian College possesses more complete facilities for promoting the success of its Students.

Musical Courses.—Full Conservatory Courses are provided in the following: Pianoforte, Pipe Organ, Voice Culture, Violin, Harmony and Theory Music. This department has been in affiliation with the Toronto Conservatory of Music for the past six years, and over 300 Certificates and Diplomas have been secured in that time, and several Students have graduated with first Honours at the Conservatory. Students are also prepared for the Toronto University local Examination in Music. This department is growing in strength every year, and was never as prosperous as at present. It is now thoroughly equipped as a "College of Music," with Professors and Assistants, providing teaching for every grade of student, from the Preparatory to the "Bach. Mus." Degree. The Director of the Department is a Graduate of the Royal Conservatory of Music, Leipsic, Germany, and was for sixteen years a Teacher in the Toronto Conservatory of Music. He has adopted the Syllabus of the Conservatory in all the work of the Department, and gives special attention to the preparation of students for Conservatory and University Examinations in Music. The Department has been further strengthened by the addition of a Baritone Soloist, who has full charge of Voice Culture and of the Choral Classes. The aim of this Department is to give an artistic, correct and graceful performance, combined with feeling and expression, and also to impart a thorough theoretical and practical musical education to those who wish to fit themselves as Teachers, or who desire to thoroughly understand the great Masters of analysis and practice. A splendid new Pipe Organ of superior tone, with water motor attachment, was placed in the College Building in 1901.

The Pianos in use in the College are furnished and kept in order by Messieurs A. and S. Nordheimer, of Toronto, and are not surpassed by those in any College in Ontario.

The Students in this department are expected to furnish music for the various College Societies which meet weekly throughout the year, and all in turn appear on the Programme.

An important advantage that a College Course affords to pupils in music is an opportunity for ensemble playing, *i.e.,* playing together in Duets, Trios, Quartettes, etcetera, by which exactness and uniformity in time and methods are acquired. Full Musical Recitals are given by the Graduating Class during the closing exercises of each year, in which every Member of the Class must take part.

Fine Arts.—During the Summer of 1901 a new and most attractive Art Room was fitted up in "Massey Hall," and thoroughly equipped with Statues, Busts, etcetera. It will be used as an Art Gallery to contain specimens of the work in Oils,

Water Colors, etcetera, of Graduates of the department, and also as an Art Studio. The Course of Study in this department is that prescribed by the "Ontario School of Art," which conducts the Examination under the general supervision of the Honourable Minister of Education of Ontario. As Albert College is in affiliation with the "Ontario School of Arts," all Certificates, Prizes, Honours and Awards offered to the Students of the School are open for competition to Students of Albert College. The work of the Students is sent each year to the Department of Education for examination, and successful Students receive their Diplomas or Certificates from the Education Department. Albert College has taken place in the very front rank, both for the number of Diplomas, or Certificates, and Medals secured, and from the high character of the work done. The Albert College Exhibit, placed side by side with the Exhibits from other Ladies' Colleges and Art Schools, has always been one of the most attractive, and has received unstinted praise. The work of the Students of Albert College was among that chosen by the Department of Education to be sent to the World's Fair at Chicago, and with other similar Schools secured Medals and Diplomas. Instruction is provided in every subject of Fine Art:—Drawing, Painting in Oils, Water Colours, China Painting, enlargement of Photographs, Pastels, etcetera.

Elocution and Physical Culture.—The Courses of Study in Elocution and Oratory include the following:—Voice Culture; the Principles and Philosophy of Expression; Public Reading and Speaking; Sight Reading; Extempore Speaking; Description Analysis, Interpretation of the best Authors, and Gesture. Special attention is paid to Breathing, Voice Placing, Distancing (that is, how to be heard with the least effort), Articulation and Enunciation.

This department has won for itself even more than Provincial Reputation, from the fact that its Students have won prize after prize in Elocution at the different Universities in competition with Students from all parts of the Dominion. It is the aim of this department to afford such thorough instruction in Elocution that its Students may be able to analyze any form of literature, and to apply artistically to each style of composition an appropriate form of delivery; in a word, to make natural, elegant and forcible Readers for the Home circle, the Drawing Room, the Pulpit and the Public Platform. Special attention is given to Candidates for the Ministry in Bible and Hymn Reading, as well as Elocution and Oratory.

The course in Physical Culture (Swedish and Delsarte) includes exercises both for strength and grace. As through the outer (the body) we get the expression of the inner (the psychic), so the outer must be brought into subjection before the inner can express itself. A well balanced body is a necessity to a well balanced mind and soul. "A sound mind in a sound body" is a good adage.

Diplomas are awarded upon completion of course, in both Elocution and Physical Culture.

Domestic Science and Art.—Domestic Science is a combination of Manual Training and Applied Science, as will be seen from the following Course of Study given to the pupil in a simplified form. The subjects embodied in the Domestic Science Course are as follows: Bacteriology, Hygiene, Household Economy, Dietetics, Food Economics, Cookery, Marketing, Home Nursing and Emergencies, and Laundry Work.

The Course in Domestic Art gives the Student a knowledge of Hand and Machine Sewing, and includes talks on materials used, choice in purchasing, etcetera. A systematic series of Models is made, covering the ground of plain needle-work, followed by Machine Sewing and the draughting, fitting and making of Undergarments.

These Courses of Instruction are carefully graded to give a thorough knowledge of the subjects and to teach the pupils the value of economy, accuracy and order. The aim is to make better and more useful women, and not only to increase their love for work, but to give it a dignity of its own, and thus to counteract all false ideas of labour.

Three specially equipped Rooms have been prepared for this department: Demonstration, Working and Dining Rooms. The Working Room is provided with individual Tables, Electric Stoves, Chart, Cabinet of analyzed Foods, etcetera.

Beside the different courses in Cooking and Sewing, special attention is paid to artistic serving, etcetera.

At regular periods throughout the year the Students give Luncheons and Full Course Dinners, using the regulation Menu and Place Card. Regular Lectures are also given to the Young Women Students on Table Etiquette and general deportment.

Two Diploma Courses are provided in Domestic Science: (I.) The Normal Course; (II.) The Housekeeper's Course.

I. The Normal Course covers a period of two years, and upon completion of this Course the Education Department of Ontario awards the Student a full Teacher's Certificate in Domestic Science, entitling the Student to teach Domestic Science in any Public, Separate, or High School in Ontario. The Government Regulations provide that such Teacher must also hold Matriculation standing, and, in case of a Normal Graduate, only one year is required instead of two. The outline of the Course at Albert College embraces:—Cooking, Sewing, Sanitation, Household Economics, Emergencies and Home nursing, Physiology, Bacteriology, Biology, Chemistry, Methods, Demonstration of Work, Practice Teaching, English Literature, History of Education, Sewing.

II. The Housekeepers' Course covers a period of one year, and consists entirely of practical work. The outline embraces:—Cooking, Sewing, Chemistry of Foods, Household Economics, Physiology.

Alexandra Ladies' College Course.—All the departments of Albert College are open to young women as well as to young men. Upon completion of the regular Collegiate Course young women receive the Diploma of M.L.A., which gives them full first year standing at the University, so that it is of Provincial, as well as Collegiate, value.

Library.—The College Library owes its maintenance and increase to the exertions of friends of the College. During the year 1871 a number of gentlemen formed themselves into a society for the purpose of increasing the number of the volumes by making and soliciting contributions. This society obtained some important and valuable donations, in both scientific and general reading.

The Library contains much matter useful to the student, and its utility renders its enlargement a matter of personal interest to all in any way connected with the College. Any person desirous of donating Books, Periodicals, etcetera, will kindly send the same to Miss Ella Gardiner, B.A., Librarian.

Museum.—The Museum has been gradually increasing in importance for the last ten years, and now, in the elegant new Rooms, which have been specially fitted for this purpose, is a matter of large interest. The Botanic Department comprises over two thousand specimens of North American species, contributed by Professor Macoun. The Mineralogical Department has been augmented by contributions from the Theological Survey and by purchase from Mr. Legatt, of Montreal, and now contains 10,000 specimens of economic and other minerals, also 200 specimens of French rocks, obtained by Mr. Legatt from the French Government. The Geological Department has been enlarged by the purchase of a cabinet of Geological Casts of the most noted Fossils of the European and American Museums.

To these may be added the Canadian Archaeological contributions by the late Reverend Thomas Webster, D.D., and others, besides many articles of interest and instruction to Students.

It is the intention to make a collection which shall embrace, as far as possible, all the products of the Country, and it is, therefore, greatly desired that any having specimens will contribute them to the Museum, and thus help to increase its value and interest.

The Gymnasium.—This Building was completed in January of 1896. It is 60 x 32 feet, two storeys high, with Gallery, and is composed of Brick and Trenton Limestone. The Basement is fitted up as an Armoury, and also contains Shower Baths, Lavatory, with Water Closets and every modern convenience. The main floor is used as the Gymnasium proper, and has a Gallery running the entire length of the Building. It has a 20-foot ceiling, and is thoroughly fitted with all the latest Apparatus, including Basket Ball, Parallel Bars, vaulting Horse, travelling Rings, flying Rings, horizontal Bar, Ladders, Chest weights, etcetera—in fact, everything to be found in the largest and best Gymnasiums. The young women, as well as the young men, have the use of the Gymnasium at regular and assigned hours, and under a competent Instructor.

Reading Rooms.—Reading Rooms, well supplied with Newspapers and Magazines, are provided in both the residences of the young men and young women, under the management of a Committee of the College Council and the Philomathian and Polymnian Societies. They are free to the use of all Students, subject to such Regulations as may be made by the Committee.

Exercise.—The well-equipped Gymnasium, which is used by both sexes on different days, under competent Instructors, gives opportunity for Physical Culture. Attention is given to out-door exercise on the College Campus—Football, Lawn Tennis, Skating Rink, etc., are provided in season. In the month of May the young men hold an annual Field Day, which is always of great interest. A five-acre field for athletic purposes has recently been purchased.

College Societies.—The following societies annually, or semi-annually, elect officers and contribute greatly to the life and progress of the College: Alumni and Alumnae, Philomathian and Polymnian Literary Societies, Y.M.C.A. and Y.W.C.A., Missionary Society and Mission Band, and the Athletic Societies. No secret society is allowed to meet in the College.—(Extracts from the College Calendar.)

THE PROTESTANT EPISCOPAL DIVINITY SCHOOL, WYCLIFFE COLLEGE, TORONTO.

By the Honourable S. H. Blake, K.C.

The name of this Institution was carefully chosen by its Founders to express the causes which brought it into existence, the principles on which it was based, and the work which it was intended to carry on.

The Founders were men who believed with Archbishop Whately that " It makes all the difference in the world where we put truth—in the first place, or in

WYCLIFFE COLLEGE, TORONTO.
(Looking from the west.)

the second place." They resolved that it should be put in the first place—and there it has, as understood by them, remained. They determined that it was their duty to do their part to preserve it in the Protestant Church of England, and from this determination they have never wavered. The intention was to form a College, the teaching of which should be in harmony with the principles laid down by the Reformers, holding, as they did most strongly, the Protestant Evangelical view of the Church of England.

These men publicly declared the great first Century fundamental truths of the Christian Religion, and, in their teaching, brought the Church of the twentieth, into harmony with the teaching of the first, Century.

The Church of England is thus linked together by these great truths and is truly Apostolic and Catholic.

They loved the Protestantism of the Church of England, the great truths that are the basis of the religious and civil liberty, which are to-day the glory of Great Britain.

It is necessary to glance at the great questions which had arisen on the subject of University Education, and which had from the early part of the last century divided Christians in Canada into two hostile camps. The King's College Charter of 1827, at length issued, in which provision was made for the teaching of Anglican Theology only. This was eminently unsatisfactory to the other Churches, and efforts were made by Presbyterians to obtain peace and harmony in the Province by obtaining a Professorship in Divinity, in King's College, or by a grant of funds for the establishment of a Theological Seminary of their own.

By the Baldwin University Bill of 1843, and the Draper University Bills of Upper Canada of 1845, provision was made for the establishment of Denominational Theological Colleges, to be founded and supported by private beneficence, in connection with the University. By the Baldwin Act of 1849, which changed King's College into the University of Toronto, the Faculty of Divinity was abolished.

By the University Bill of 1853, provision was made for the affiliation of Denominational Colleges.

From among the vast mass of material produced on the one side and the other during the prolonged period of heated controversy connected with University matters it is instructive to peruse the clear solution presented over sixty years ago, and which our University is now working out, by the Reverend P. C. Campbell, D.C.L., who afterwards became the Principal of the University of Aberdeen. He there enunciates what ought to be the "leading principle." "That while Theology shall form no part of education in the University as such, Colleges, principally Theological and Denominational, shall be placed beside the University and incorporated with it, and in which students of each Denomination while receiving in common the general literary and scientific instruction provided by public endowment, shall reside, enjoying simultaneously with the benefits of the University the advantage of religious superintendence, and in which after their preliminary studies in the public classes and obtaining the degree of B.A.,—those who are intended for the clerical profession in each Denomination, shall proceed under Professors in the foundation of the various Colleges, with their strictly Theological Studies."

The above views were shared by a large body of Churchmen, who were much opposed to the efforts of Bishop Strachan in his unceasing attempts to found another University in the Province. In this, however, he succeeded, and on the 15th January, 1852, Trinity College was formally opened, not merely as a Theological College, but with full University powers, having the Reverend Doctor Whittaker as its first Provost, and the Reverend Professors Irvine and Parry as Members of its Teaching Staff.

Two paragraphs of contemporaneous literature will give some idea of the tone then assumed by the Founders and supporters of Trinity College in their continuous remarks on Toronto University:

We object further to a system which would recognize the lawfulness of Religious division, and strike at the foundation of the unity of the Church, in countenancing an assemblage of sects and parties, with an equality of claim and pretension, around, what we are constrained to term, a gorgeous temple of infidelity.

As it was impossible for us, great as the sacrifice might be, to hold connection with an Institution essentially anti-Christian, though originally bearing the honoured name of its loyal founder, George the IV., and established expressly for Religious purposes, it became a matter of necessity, as well as duty, to establish a University from our private resources, in close connection with the Church to which we had the happiness to belong.

To the dissatisfaction which arose from the founding of another University was shortly added the very powerful reason, of the clearly marked divergence of

THE REVEREND DOCTOR SHERATON,
Principal of Wycliffe College.

opinion on Theological questions caused by the introduction by Trinity University of what was then called "the teaching of the Tractarian Movement." It was shown that a sum of $65,860 was given to Trinity for endowment out of the Commutation Fund, which had been realized from public lands set apart expressly by the Imperial Acts of 1774 and 1791: "For the encouragement of the Protestant Religion and for the maintenance and support of a Protestant Clergy within the Province."

Fault was found with "The Society for the Propagation of the Gospel" for applying $5,000 of its funds contributed by Churchmen generally to the support of this Institution. A portion of the donations of money and lands furnished for the building and support of the College was supplied by members of the Evangelical Party. For these reasons it was said that the peculiar views there propounded should not be found in Trinity College.

A heated controversy continued from the period of the first attack of the Evangelical Party upon Trinity College. In 1857, the attempts made to alter the teaching of Trinity having failed, the authorities in the Diocese of Huron determined to found an Independent College based upon the principles for which they were contending. From 1860 to 1863 the centre of this attack was the "Provost's Catechism," the teachings of which were alleged to be erroneous according to the Evangelicals' standpoint, and were upheld by those who supported Trinity.

In the Synod of the year 1861, Bishop Strachan entered into an elaborate justification of Trinity College from recent attacks. The lines between the two parties in the Church were drawn with greater distinctness and precision. In 1863 Huron College was opened under the Presidency of the Reverend Doctor Hellmuth, then Archdeacon of Huron. The feeling of distrust because of the belief that some of the Clergy in the Diocese of Toronto were not true to the principles of the Reformed Church and that they were spreading Ritualistic doctrines, increased from year to year, and its effect was so marked that in the address of the Bishop to the Synod in 1869 he thus refers to the subject:

I advert with sorrow and mortification to the fact that the liberality of contributions to our missionary objects has been in some quarters seriously damped by the suspicions and distrust awakened as to the management of our Church enterprises.

The explanations given and the position taken were, however, entirely unsatisfactory to those who were dissatisfied with the teaching of Trinity College and with the non-Anglican features which were rapidly being introduced to its teaching and services.

No changes having been made in these respects, the "Evangelical Association of the United Church of England and Ireland in the Diocese" was formed. Dean Grasett was appointed President; Archdeacon Fuller, Canon Givens, Doctor Daniel Wilson and Mr. B. H. Dixon were appointed Vice-Presidents; Reverend Canon E. Baldwin and Mr. F. W. Kingston, Secretaries; and Mr. H. Mortimer, Treasurer.

On the 16th of March, 1868, its first appeal was made to the Lay Members of the Church in the Diocese of Toronto. The object of the Association was stated to be "to maintain the principles of the Reformation." It issued an elaborate address calling attention to the non-recognition in all Church matters of those "who count the name of Protestant a distinguished honour, and regard the Reformation as the richest blessing ever vouchsafed to our Church."

The election of Delegates to the Provincial Synod, as well as membership in the Executive Committee, was given exclusively to the High Church, or Trinity College, Party. The teaching, which began secretly, but afterwards was openly carried on, culminated in 1871 in the announcement that the "Manual of the Confraternity of the Blessed Sacrament" was in use in the city, and that a Branch of that fraternity existed presided over by a licensed Clergyman of the Diocese. The Honourable W. B. Robinson handed this book to Mr. Clarke Gamble, K.C., who took counsel with Chief Justice Draper, Professor Daniel Wilson, and Colonel C. S. Gzowski.

An address was presented to the late Bishop Bethune upon the subject, meetings were held, investigations were made, and the dissatisfaction which ensued on ascertaining the Ritualistic teaching which was being introduced into several Parishes of the Diocese, and by four of her Ministers, caused the determination that active measures should be taken to protect the Church from these Ritualistic invasions.

In 1872, in the first charge of the Reverend Doctor Hellmuth, then Bishop of Huron, he strongly condemned Hymns Ancient and Modern, and stated of them: That "If all the hymns were unsound they would at once be detected, and very few would have been deceived. It was, therefore, a skillful masterpiece of the Ritualists to administer the poison in small doses, not to be perceived immediately, but to effect, nevertheless, their purpose, of undermining the spiritual constitution of our Reformed Church."

He warned the Church of the growing evils of the trend toward Ritualism. which he termed the "Catholic Revival." A fierce controversy, especially between Doctor Hellmuth and Doctor Whittaker, as Provost of Trinity College, in which, however, many others took part, had been going on, in which the views of Trinity on the one side and the Evangelical Party on the other had been fully presented and a large measure of education as to the teaching of their respective parties and its effects had been given to the members of the Church in the Diocese of Toronto and throughout the Dominion generally. A large measure of interest was taken in these discussions. As a result, in 1873, "The Church Association of the Diocese of Toronto," was brought into existence, with the following objects in view, as then expressed in its constitution:

1. To maintain the principles and doctrines of our Church as established at the Reformation, and to preserve the simplicity of her Protestant worship and the purity of her scriptural teaching as derived from the Holy Scriptures, and set forth in the Liturgy and Articles of the Book of Common Prayer.

2. To oppose the dissemination of doctrines contrary to those authoritative standards of our Church; and to resist all unauthorized changes or innovations in her services as prescribed in the Prayer Book; and all novelties in vestments, decorations or practices, whether revived from pre-Reformation times, borrowed from the Church of Rome, or introduced as rites and ceremonies hitherto unknown amongst us as a Church.

3. To cultivate an earnest spirit of brotherly union in accordance with the Apostolic precept; "that there be no divisions among you: but that ye be perfectly joined together in the same mind and in the same judgment," and so to foster hearty co-operation in all efforts for the spread of the Gospel, the extension of the Church, the enkindling of a devoted missionary spirit among its members, and the maintenance of the doctrines for which so many noble martyrs of our Church, Bishops, Clergy and Laymen, witnessed a good confession in the dungeon and at the stake.

4. To diffuse information on all subjects specially affecting the welfare of the Church, and to aim at uniting all her members in a hearty and uncompromising maintenance of our most holy faith: alike against tractarianism, ritualism, rationalism, or whatever other movements threaten to undo the great work of that Reformation to which we owe alike our English Bible, our English Prayer Book and that liberty of conscience which is our prized inheritance.

5. To extend co-operation throughout the Diocese, by forming branches of this the Evangelical, or Church Association; by public meetings and by the agency of the Press; so that the members of our Church may be confirmed in the great principles which were reasserted in her Articles at the Reformation; and "looking unto Jesus, the author and finisher of our faith," all may be encouraged and strengthened to "hold fast the profession of our faith without wavering."

The following were the first Officers of the Church Association:

President—The Honourable Chief Justice W. H. Draper, C.B.

Vice-Presidents—The Very Reverend H. J. Grasett, B.D., Dean of Toronto; the Honourable Vice-Chancellor Blake; Professor Daniel Wilson, LL.D.

The Executive Committee—The Reverends F. A. O'Meara, Port Hope; A. Sanson, A. Stewart, the Honourable James Patton, Colonel C. S. Gzowski, Lieutenant G. H. Grierson, and Messieurs. A. H. Campbell, C. J. Blomfield, Peterborough; J. George Hodgins, Kivas Tully, Toronto; William Magrath, Credit; William Powis, Hamilton; B. H. Dixon, Toronto, Honorary Secretary and Treasurer.

In the same year a number of Clerical and Lay gentlemen formed themselves into a society called the "Church Union," of which the Bishop (Bethune) was the President, and Archdeacon Fuller and the Honourable George W. Allan, the Vice-Presidents. It carried on its work for two or three years.

The appeal of the Church Association of 1874 contained the following statements:

Many members of the Church of England have felt compelled, much against their inclination, to withhold their contributions from the funds of the Church. They feel that it is impossible for them to assist in maintaining a Students' Fund for the support of young men who are carefully trained to look with aversion on our Church as a Church of the Reformation, and to abhor the name Protestant; or to build up a Mission Fund for the support of men who become worthy disciples of such teaching, and propagators of these and more extreme views.

These reasons combined to make many lukewarm and to deter others from having anything to do with the temporal affairs of the Church.

In answer to a very general demand for some objects connected with the Church in which her members might heartily co-operate, the Church Association has resolved to undertake a training establishment for young men of sound evangelical views, where they will be prepared with the utmost care for the Ministry of our Church. The Association has likewise undertaken the formation of a Mission Fund to aid in parts of the Diocese where such assistance is needed, in the support of faithful men not ashamed to preach the Gospel of Christ and to make known His finished work.

The Bishop strongly disapproved of this action of "The Church Association." He brought the matter before the Synod. He issued two pastorals on the subject— one in 1873 and another in 1874. He held a Visitation of the Clergy in December, 1874, which resulted in the impeachment of the Clerical members of the Executive Committee of the Church Association, who were by direction of the Bishop "presented" and were tried for "depraving the government and discipline of the Church" by a commission consisting of the Reverends Canon Read, and Rural Deans Allen and Brent. The Reverend Doctor Fuller and Clarke Gamble declined to act.

The names of those against whom these proceedings were taken are: The Very Reverend Dean Grasett, the Reverend Rural Dean Stewart, the Reverend Rural Dean Givens, the Reverend Rural Dean Cooper, the Reverend Canon Edmund Baldwin, the Reverend Doctor F. A. O'Meara, the Reverend S. J. Boddy, the Reverend Alexander Sanson, the Reverend W. F. Checkley, the Reverend H. H. Waters, the Reverend G. H. Moxon.

During the trial the charges were narrowed down to that of "establishing a separate Mission Fund tending to cripple the resources of the Synod Mission Fund." The judgment was that:

The Commissioners cannot find that any Canon, or other law, of the Church in this Diocese has been violated. They do not recommend the institution of further proceedings.

During the pendency of this matter an address was presented to those who were the subjects of the presentment by over 2,000 Laymen, who thus expressed their views on the subject:

We, the undersigned Members of the Church of England in the Diocese of Toronto, beg to express to you our deep regret at the unprecedented course taken in the recent attack made upon you by the Ritualistic party in this Diocese.

We beg to express our warm sympathy with you, and our great thankfulness that you have stood forward as champions of our Church at a period when she so much needs her sons to battle for her.

We beg to assure you of the strong feeling of indignation with which we have heard of the inquisitorial proceedings taken against you; we believe you have the approval of the great body in the Laity in the part you have taken in the struggle to support the principles of the Reformation and the Protestant character of our Church.

Our earnest prayer is that with the blessing of God the present crisis may be so overruled as the more firmly to build up in our Church the principles of the Reformation.

Dated this 2nd of January, 1875.

Among some of the well-known names appended to this document are found:

Chief Justice Draper.
B. Homer Dixon.
J. G. Worts, Sr.
The Honourable Adam Crooks, K.C.
Mayor Medcalf.
The Honourable S. H. Blake, K.C.
Henry Pellatt.
Sir C. S. Gzowski.
Arthur B. Lee.
Ogle R. Gowan.
William Magrath.
J. Maughan, Jr.
George J. Boyd.
J. Herbert Mason.
F. A. Ball.
David Lewis.
Colonel George H. Grierson.
Kivas Tully.
Samuel B. Smith.
Ernestus Crombie.

Sir Daniel Wilson.
The Honourable James Patton.
Walter S. Lee.
Sir Thomas Galt.
James Bennett.
D'Arcy Boulton.
Judge Gwynne.
Doctor J. G. Hodgins.
Samuel Platt.
R. N. Gooch.
H. F. Godson.
Vice-Chancellor Strong.
R. L. Denison.
Stephen Heward.
Thomas Hodgins, K.C.
George M. Evans.
Philip and James Brown.
Frederick Wright.
C. S. Ross.
John Boyd.
Stephen Radcliff.

A. Shaw.
Colonel George T. Denison.
William Gooderham, Sr.
The Honourable Edward Blake, K.C.
Sheriff Jarvis.
Colonel Durie.
Colonel Robert M. Denison.
A. Thornton Todd.
Clarke Gamble, K.C.
A. H. Campbell.
D. Delamere.
J. K. Kerr, K.C.
W. R. Mulock, K.C.
W. T. Boyd.
J. F. Lash.
John J. Vickers.
John Gillespie.
W. F. McMaster.
James Graham.
Thomas H. Lee.

As no laymen were permitted to be present at the Visitation held by the Bishop, the Lay members presented a communication to the Bishop, which is found in the *Globe* and *Mail* of the 8th of January, 1875, from which it is necessary to take a few sentences in order to understand the grievances, supposed or real, from which the Laymen of that day considered that they were suffering. They said:

(a) "In referring to Trinity College, we deal with it solely as a Theological College for training Candidates for Holy Orders, and as such we cannot help but pronounce it unworthy of its pretensions."

(b) The doctrine of Apostolic Succession as taught leads "to no other result than that of begetting a narrow-minded exclusiveness and stimulating a sacerdotal spirit among our Clergy, the revival of which has largely contributed to the evils which we deplore."

(c) Looking at the longer course and the Staff of Professors and Tutors in Knox College for training Ministers for the Presbyterian Church, and comparing it with one Theological Professor in Trinity, "it is manifest that wholly apart from objection to his doctrinal teachings the actual instruction furnished to the Ministers of our Church must be miserably small as compared with that given by the Staff of Knox College."

(d) The charges of "erroneous teaching preferred against Trinity College are not now made for the first time." The late Venerated Bishop Hellmuth of Huron pressed them in a way that carried conviction to thousands; and failing to meet with any satisfaction, he established a Theological Institution in his own Diocese, the head of which is a life member of the Church Association. But the tree is known by its fruit; and we shall best test the question in brief form by referring to a work not unknown to your Lordship. "The Christian Manual," published in 1872, is set forth as, with your Lordship's permission and approval, dedicated to you by one of your Clergy, a graduate of Trinity College, who now as one of the Masters in the Port Hope Church School uses it there as the Manual for Religious Instruction.

In this manual we read of the Holy Eucharist: "do" strictly means "make," videlicet, "this offering"; in other words "offer this." The Lord's Body is there, independent of the faith, or conduct, of the receiver. The reader is warned against "the most erroneous view of the Holy Sacrament," wherein no body and blood of Christ was held to be really present in any strict sense; or, to express it in a grosser form, the body and blood of Christ were really absent.

"During the prayer of consecration it is that particularly the Eucharistic sacrifice is being made."

In this book there is found the very same unscriptural Ritualistic teaching which is more openly promulgated in "The Path of Holiness," the Manual of the Confraternity of the Blessed Sacrament, and the like pernicious works.

This we believe to be the teaching of Trinity College, as it is the teaching of Port Hope Church School, and we do not "insinuate," but say plainly and expressly, that any College where such Theology is taught "is an unsafe Institution for the religious training of young men, and specially of aspirants for the Ministry."

In 1866 the Provost sought election for the position of Coadjutor Bishop of the Diocese of Toronto, notwithstanding the strong feeling that then existed on the part of the Laity against him.

It was out of this state of matters that the Protestant Episcopal Divinity School came into existence in October, 1877. It began its work of instruction of students in a small and humble way in the School House of St. James' Cathedral. Its name was liked by its supporters and they have ever insisted on the two words, "Protestant" and "Episcopal," with the full meaning that is attached to them. The principles of the Divinity School, as presented to its supporters, and as then adopted, have never been varied. Shortly put they are as follows:

1. The Bible, the Sole Rule of Faith; in opposition to the error that would make the Bible and tradition the joint rule of faith *

2. Justification by Faith in Christ alone; in opposition to the Sacramentarian system.

3. The Sole and Exclusive Priesthood of Jesus Christ; in opposition to the sacerdotal assumption which would convert Christ's Ministers into an order of sacrificing and meditating Priests (heireis).

4. The Real presence of Christ by Faith in the hearts of worthy recipients of the Holy Communion; in opposition to the figment of His presence corporally, or spiritually, on the Communion Table, under the form of bread and wine, after the consecration of the elements.

5. The Church of Christ is the "Holy Catholic Church."—(Creed.) "The Holy Church Universal."—(Prayer for Church Militant and Litany.) "The mystical body of Christ, which is the blessed company of all faithful people."—Communion Service.

6. "The visible Church (visibilis Ecclesia) of Christ is a congregation of faithful men, in which the pure Word of God is preached, and the sacraments be duly administered according to Christ's ordinance, in all those things that of necessity are requisite to the same."—Article XIX.

7. An Historical Episcopate, traceable to apostolic direction, as conducive to the well being but not necessary to the being of the Church; in opposition to the dogma of a tactual succession, "a fiction," asserts Dean Alford, "of which I find in the New Testament no trace."

In 1879, the Institution was incorporated and now bears the name of "The Protestant Episcopal Divinity School—Wycliffe College." From its inception it adopted the principle suggested in the formation of Toronto University and took advantage of the opportunity given for obtaining there the secular education of its Students.

Those interested in the history of the Church of England in Canada are under great obligations to the late Archbishop Sweatman of Toronto for his Historic Charge of 1879. This deals with those aspects of the state of the Church of England in Canada, and its members for the last sixty years, reference to which gives, with conciseness and accuracy, its true position, and explains the reason of the action taken by the Evangelical Party in founding Wycliffe College. In this Charge he says:

It is fruitless for us to deny, brethren, it would be unworthy for us to apologize, that there are parties in the Church. I trust we have learned enough wisdom from the past, frankly to accept the position. I am not advocating compromise, which is a weak and futile expedient for evading difficulties, but tolerance.

There can be no question in the mind of anyone acquainted with the religious aspect of the Country, that the heart of the great bulk of our laity is staunchly, jealously, Protestant. I thank God for it. And in the endeavour to fulfil the difficult task that lies before me, my first and most earnest efforts will be directed to supply the Missions of the Diocese with Clergymen of sound Protestant views.

There are those who have grown to be ashamed of the honest name of Protestant, and think it necessary to speak quite apologetically of the Reformation. But, I would ask, what existence have we as a Church duly constituted, with a polity of its own, with

---

* In his address at the opening of Trinity College University, the Reverend Doctor Strachan, in referring to the "rightful place of the Bible in Education," said: "Associated with the Book of Common Prayer, the Bible, as has been beautifully said, fits every fold of the human heart, and is felt to be God's Book. It is also felt to be Man's Book, because it satisfies all our thoughts and feelings, and leads us willingly to receive it as divinely authorized, and the scheme of human and divine things which it presents as essentially true." It is the most precious guide to spiritual life.

prescribed liturgy and authorized standards, except through the Reformation? It is true that we trace back the independent autonomy of our branch of the Church Catholic far beyond that struggle which was as the throes of a secondbirth ; beyond its subjection to the Papal Primacy; beyond the accession to it of the Saxon converts of Augustine, and its consequent first connection with the See of Rome, back through the persecutions and depressions of the British Christians, who also had their Bishops and their Liturgy, to the very Apostolic age.

We cannot deny, if we would, that what we are as a Church to-day, was the work of the Protestant Reformers. To these noble, holy and learned men—even if they were erring, who shed their blood to purchase with it for us the priceless heritage of a pure faith, enshrined in a form of worship that is sublime in its dignity, venerable for its antiquity, and glorious with the beauty of holiness—we owe a debt which we cannot over-estimate, a debt which it were the climax of base ingratitude for us to repay, as some who call themselves Anglican Churchmen have done, by casting approbrium upon their blessed memory.

The heritage they have bequeathed to us is indeed a rich one—a faithful version of the Holy Scripture in our own tongue, that the unlearned may have free access to the Word of Life, "the Book of Common Prayer and Administration of the Sacraments and other rights and ceremonies of the Church"—the Thirty-Nine Articles of Religion, forming a complete summary of the Reformed Faith on the Cardinal Doctrines of Christianity, and specially on those points which were matters of controversy with the Church of Rome.

In avowing myself a Prayer Book Churchman, I vindicate my title to be held a Protestant Churchman; for the Prayer Book is, as I regard it, the very bulwark of Protestant principles.

I am one of those who are satisfied with what the Reformers have done, regretting nothing which they have abolished; and not wishing to see anything abolished which they have thought worthy to be retained.

Why should any clergyman wish to make his Church such that a common man placed suddenly within it would not be able to say whether he was in a Church of England or a Church of Rome place of worship?

This Charge which the Archbishop called his "Declaration of Faith," went into the details of Sacerdotalism and Ritualism practised in the Church in Canada, to which it is not necessary now to refer further. What has been given has been only presented as showing the antagonistic views which then, as now, were held in the Church of England in Canada, and which are found in innumerable pamphlets and letters which issued from the press during the twenty-five preceding years. It also shows how largely the Diocesan was prepared to rely on a College, existing for the express purpose of furnishing men of the type needed to answer the urgent demands of congregations.

These extracts, short although they be, give in essence the position and teaching of the Evangelical members of the Church foremost in founding Wycliffe, and which embrace such well-known names as Dean Grasett, Dean (afterwards Archbishop) Bond, Dean (afterwards Bishop) Baldwin, Sir Daniel Wilson, Chief Justice Draper, Mr. A. H. Campbell, Sir Casimir Gzowski, the Honourable Edward Blake, K.C., and the Honourable James Patton, K.C.

At the time of the election of Bishop Sweatman it was agreed that "The Church Association" should cease to exist, and that "Wycliffe College" should continue its work. In pursuance of this arrangement on the 11th of June, 1879, the closing meeting of the Association was held. On the 13th day of June the second annual meeting of the Protestant Episcopal Divinity School took place, when His Lordship the Bishop was present, and then among other words of kindly approval said:

The great complaint throughout this Diocese was the lack of money, but another and even greater want was the want of men, of good and suitable men, who had the love of the Saviour in their hearts, and the love of those for whom the Saviour died. He hoped the School would send forth well-trained and educated men to engage in the work of the Church. Other Denominations—all praise and honour to them for it—were sending out such men, and the Church of England in these days could not afford to be behind. He was pleased to learn that great care was being exercised in the education of the young men in this Divinity School. He trusted that through the means of this School much good would be done for the Church, not only in this Diocese, but throughout the Country. The report which had been made by the Principal was most satisfactory, and he sincerely looked forward to the time when he would be able to ordain and send out to the Missions of the Diocese men from this Institution thoroughly well fitted both in head and heart. He wished the School every success and would give it all the fostering care he could, so long as the circumstances of the Diocese required that it should be conducted as a separate Institution.

On the resignation of the Reverend Doctor Whittaker as Provost of Trinity College, it was felt that an opportunity had at length arrived for remodelling the College and for the formation of a strong Divinity School to provide for the training of Theological Students in accordance with the principles of the Reformation as embodied in the Articles of our Church.

In order to do its part in the accomplishment of this purpose, on the 7th of February, 1880, the Board of Management of Wycliffe passed the following resolutions and sent them to Trinity College:

Resolved, That in the opinion of the Members of the Board of Management of the Protestant Episcopal Divinity School, an opening is now afforded for compliance with the expressed wish of the Lord Bishop of Toronto, that an effort should be made for the union of the School with Trinity;

Resolved, That the terms of union which commend themselves to the judgment of the Members of the Board are as follows:

(1) That the office of Provost should be filled by someone who shall be pronounced by the Bishop to be entirely acceptable to him, and to be by him approved as fitted to meet the special exigencies of the Church at this time.

(2) That an additional Theological Chair should be at once established in the College, to which Chair the Reverend Doctor Sheraton, the present Principal of the School, should be appointed.

(3) That within a reasonable time one or more additional Chairs in the department of Theology should be established in the College.

(4) That the members of the Church holding Evangelical views shall receive a fair representation in the Council of the College.

(5) That the School should be merged in the College.

Resolved, That although in the opinion of the members of the Board they might fairly ask that the salary of the new Professor should be paid out of the resources of Trinity College, which have been contributed by the Church at large, yet they will take the responsibility (in case the proposed union is accomplished) of agreeing that the Evangelical members of the Church shall themselves provide that salary, without trenching on the resources of Trinity College.

Resolved, That a copy of the foregoing resolutions be transmitted by the Secretary to the proper officer of Trinity College, with the request that they be laid before the Council of that Corporation, and that any communication it may be pleased to direct in reference to them be transmitted to the Secretary.

TORONTO, February 7th, 1880.   S. H. BLAKE, *Chairman*.

With these resolutions in the hands of the Bursar of Trinity, that College proceeded to the choice of a Provost and elected the Reverend Doctor Lobley to that office, although it was stated by one of the Members of the Board of that Council that such " appointment would be received with disfavor by those whom it was desirable to conciliate, if not regarded by them as a challenge direct."

The views of the Evangelical Party were well-known, having been expressed when the name of Doctor Lobley was proposed as a candidate at the recent election for Bishop of the Diocese. Thereupon, and on the 6th of March, the following resolution was passed by the Board of the Protestant Episcopal Divinity School and sent to Trinity College:

Resolved, That having regard to the course pursued by Trinity College since the proposal made by this Board for union with that College, the Secretary do immediately write to the Bursar of Trinity College, informing him that it is unnecessary for him to submit the proposals to the Board for the consideration of the Council of Trinity College.

And thus ended the effort for the founding of a first-class Theological College out of the materials then at hand.

From that time onward Wycliffe College has continued its work, until to-day it is honoured in having His Grace the Archbishop of Rupert's Land, the Primate of all Canada, His Lordship, the Bishop of Toronto, and ten Bishops of other Dioceses of Canada its Visitors.

Its history has been markedly one of progress. It was most fortunate in having for its first Principal the Reverend Doctor Sheraton, who remained in this office until his much lamented death.

The latest addition to the Staff, composed of seven Professors and two Tutors, is the Reverend Doctor Griffith-Thomas, late Principal of Wycliffe College, Oxford, England. Wycliffe is to be congratulated, and the Church in Canada generally, on the advent to our land of this scholar of deservedly world-wide reputation.

It was at first thought that twenty-five Students would be the largest number that it would be necessary to provide for; and in 1882 a Building was erected on College Street, within the Toronto University grounds, to supply the accommodation for carrying on the work. Soon, however, the contemplated number was exceeded, and in 1885 the Building was enlarged to accommodate over fifty. In 1890, when further additions were needed for seventy Students, an opportunity was found for moving from the College Street location to one on Hoskin Avenue, where the Buildings of the College at present stand. This was completed in the Autumn of 1891 and the work of the College was transferred to it, with an attendance of seventy Students. From time to time, the number increasing, it became necessary to enlarge. In 1902 extensive additions were made; but, the increase in pupils continuing, it became necessary again to build, and a new wing, Dining Hall and Faculty Room were opened by His Grace the Archbishop of Toronto on the 21st of February, 1908. During the last year the number of Students in attendance was one hundred and ten.

Since the commencement of its work, the College has sent one hundred and ninety-six men to the work of the Ministry in Canada and foreign parts.

In 1885 Wycliffe College was affiliated to the University of Toronto. In 1889, by Act of the Legislature, it was federated and made a constituent part of the great Provincial University.

The benefits derived from this intimate relationship are great. Wycliffe College thereby obtains the incalculable benefit of a life spent in immediate association with a very large body of Students.

The whole resources of this University, with its splendid Biological and Scientific Apparatus, its Library, its Gymnasium and Athletic Grounds, its band of more than one hundred Professors, Lecturers and Assistants, are open to its Students.

Wycliffe College enjoys the unique advantage of being the only Theological College connected with the University of Toronto, which possesses its residential and teaching equipment within the University grounds—thus enjoying the advantage of an intimate relationship with the daily life and teaching of the University. With the ample resources of the University placed at its disposal through its federation, all the resources and funds of Wycliffe College can be devoted to Theological training.

Wycliffe College forms an integral part of the Educational System of the Church of England in Canada. By Resolution of the Provincial Synod of 1899 it became, with those at other centres of educational and Church life in Canada, one of the recognized Theological Colleges of the Church. Its Graduates are received by all Bishops of Canada (of whom twelve are its Visitors), as Candidates for Holy Orders. The Course of Study throughout the period of training is so arranged as to lead up to the examinations for the degrees of B.D. and D.D., set by the Board of Examination of the Provincial Synod, upon which body Wycliffe College has its representative and which are open to its Graduates.

In addition to the many Associations of Toronto University open to this College, it has its own " Alumni Association," " Wycliffe Prayer Circle," " Students' Mission Society," " Young Men's Christian Association," " Brotherhood of St. Andrew," " Literary and Theological Society," and " Athletic Association."

Its Building, Library, etcetera, are valued at $193,000, and are now free of debt. Its Endowment Fund amounts to over $150,000. Its annual Expenditure now reaches the sum of $40,000.

An effort is now being made to increase largely the Endowment Fund. The most generous offer of a sum of $200,000, to be increased to $250,000 if necessary, recently made by a Layman of the Church, to procure a union between the two Theological Colleges of Toronto, was, of course, a very great temptation to Wycliffe, thus easily to place itself in funds. It wanted the money, and disliked much to display even apparent discourtesy to one ready to make so handsome a donation— but the College felt that it could not honourably be partaker of a gift, accepted on terms against which its Founders had most carefully provided—that it deserved deep reprobation if, while it professed to teach righteousness, it practised unrighteousness; that it would be disastrous to the Church to imperil the Protestant teaching, which the Laity loved, and for want of it drive them out of the Church of England to other Churches; that there was no offer to change in any respect the teaching of Trinity; that this teaching for nigh sixty years, and its results, constituted an object-lesson to which only unwise people could close their eyes; that every reason assigned for the founding of Wycliffe is now present for its retention, and that at no period was it more necessary that the Church of England should be a faithful witness against Ritualism and the Anglican form of it than the present. The inducement offered, therefore, failed to lead Wycliffe to abandon its position, and it still remains true to its original foundation.

The College has the satisfaction of meditating upon the fact that, at large cost to itself, it has pondered over the weighty words of Archbishop Whately and has determined that, at all times, Truth is to be placed in and retain the first place.

TORONTO, August 3rd, 1910.

The writer of the above sketch is largely indebted for his facts to Doctor J. George Hodgins' "History of the Diocese of Toronto," and to the many contemporary documents which he kindly placed at his disposal.

POSITION AND EQUIPMENT OF WYCLIFFE COLLEGE.

Wycliffe College is conveniently situated in a beautiful open space on Hoskin Avenue, Toronto, and just on the border of Queen's Park, being north-west of the Provincial Parliament Buildings, and forming the north-east end of the crescent of University structures which surround the main building of the University of Toronto. It is built of Stone and pressed Brick, in collegiate style. The whole Building is heated with Steam and lighted with Electricity throughout. It has every modern convenience for the comfort of the Students and is at present in the most thorough state of repair and efficiency.

The College Building contains: Residential accommodation in separate Rooms for seventy-three Students. Separate residences for the Principal, and one Member of the Teaching Staff. Chapel, Faculty Room and Office. Convocation Hall capable of seating 700. Lecture and Assembly Halls. Dining Hall. Missionary Museum and Reading Room. A commodious Library, situated beneath the Convocation Hall, and well equipped for the convenience of the Students. Housekeeper's Apartments.

The leading features of other than Theological work in Wycliffe College consist of:

(a) *The University Library* of 100,000 Volumes and accommodation for upwards of 400 Readers, with a periodical room, seven departmental Libraries.

(b) *The Biological and Medical Buildings,* which contain the Biological Museum and Lecture Rooms where Students of Wycliffe take work in Biology.

(c) *The University Y.M.C.A.,* organized in 1873, and incorporated in 1892. The objects of the Association are: (1) The promotion of Christian fellowship amongst the men, and (2) The carrying on of aggressive spiritual work among all the Students of the different Colleges. The Canadian Colleges' Mission in connection with the Y.M.C.A. seeks to interest the Students of the Universities in foreign mission work.

(d) *Gymnastic and Athletic Grounds.*—The Gymnasium contains a Running Track, Shower Baths and Swimming Baths. A competent Instructor is in constant attendance.

Connection of Wycliffe College with the Toronto University.

From its relationship with the University of Toronto, Wycliffe College derives great advantages.

1. *The Official Status.*—In 1889, Wycliffe College was, by Act of the Legislature, federated, and made a constituent part of the University of Toronto.

2. *University Course in Arts.*—The teaching of the entire Curriculum in Arts, including the general Course, and the thirteen Honour Courses in Classics, Philosophy, Modern Languages, Semitic Languages, etcetera, is provided by the University and is open to every Student of Wycliffe College.

Regulations Relating to Courses of Study.

The Courses leading to the Diploma of the College are four:—

A. *The Seven-Year Graduate Course:*

(*a*) The full four years' Course in Arts at the University of Toronto or other recognized university.

(*b*) A three years' Course in Theology at Wycliffe College.

B. *The Six-Year Graduate Course:*

(*a*) The full four years' Course in Arts in the University of Toronto; followed by

(*b*) A two years' Course in Theology in Wycliffe.

Note.—Candidates pursuing this Course are required to take, if possible, one subject in Theology, or one of the permitted Theological Options, in each year of the Arts Undergraduate course.

C. *The Five-Year Combined Course:*

(*a*) The full four years' General Course in Arts in the University of Toronto (with the permitted Theological options); and concurrently with it:

(*b*) The Theological Course in Wycliffe College as prescribed in the appended prescription of Courses.

Note.—Students cannot enter the Five-Year Course without the permission of the Committee on Students, and the Committee reserve the right to direct a student at any time to transfer to the Six-Year Graduate Course.

D. *The Four-Year Non-Matriculant Course:*

(*a*) Selected portions of the four years' Course in Arts in the University of Toronto.

(*b*) Special work in Latin and Greek at Wycliffe College.

(*c*) The full Regular Course in Theology in Wycliffe College.

Note.—Certain subjects in the Curriculum of Wycliffe College are constituted options, and are thus made a portion of the ordinary Course required for the B.A. Degree. A necessarily high uniform standard of teaching is thus maintained throughout the departments of the College.

Wycliffe College Bursaries.

The following Bursaries of $120 each per annum have been established by friends of Wycliffe College:—

The Mortimer Bursary.—Given by the late Mr. Herbert Mortimer, Toronto.

The Ridout Brothers Bursary.—Given by the late Mr. J. D. Ridout, Toronto, his Widow and Sons, (Messieurs. Percival F. Ridout and Walter L. Ridout).

The London, England, Bursary.—Given by friends in England, through the Honourable S. H. Blake, K.C.

The Worthington Bursary.—Given by the widow of the late Mr. John Worthington, Toronto.

The Bishop Cronyn Bursary.

The Catharine Hume Blake Bursary.—Given by the Honourable Edward Blake, K.C., M.P.

The Robert Baldwin Memorial Missionary Bursary.—Given by the family of the late Mr. Robert Baldwin, Toronto, for the assistance of a Student in training for foreign Missionary work. The Bursary is only presented on the recommendation of the Board of the Canadian Church Missionary Society.

The Gurd Bursary.—Given by the late Mr. R. S. Gurd, Sarnia.

In Memoriam Bursary "R.E.A.P."—"*Have Faith in God.*"—Given by the late Mrs. Robert Phelps, Leamington, England.

The Phelps Memorial Bursaries.—Given by the late Mrs. Robert Phelps.

The James F. Robertson Bursary.—Given by Mr. James F. Robertson, St. John, New Brunswick.

The Wm. Grey Bursary.—Given by the late Mr. Wm. Grey, Woodstock, Ontario.

The Jones Memorial Bursary.—Endowed by Mr. R. A. A. Jones, Guildford, England, in memory of the Honourable Robert and Caroline Jones.

The Stapleton Caldecott Memorial Bursary.—Established by Mrs. Caldecott, of Toronto, in memory of her husband, for many years the esteemed Treasurer of the College.

Besides the above, there are available four Bursaries of the same amount through the kindness of a warm friend of Evangelical and Protestant truth, Tunbridge Wells, England.

In addition to these Bursaries, all of which are endowed, the Colonial and Continental Church Society, of London, England, have agreed to contribute £30 sterling per annum for the assistance of a Student in training for Missionary work in North-west Canada.

Granting Degrees in Divinity.

The Course of Study in the College is so arranged as to lead up to the Examinations for the Degrees of B.D. and D.D., as set by the Board of Examiners appointed by the Provincial Synod. The Board, so appointed, for the years 1907-1910 is as follows:—

The Archbishop of Ottawa, Chairman; the Reverend Professor Vroom, representing King's College, Windsor, Nova Scotia; the Reverend Professor Allnott, representing Bishop College, Lennoxville, Quebec; the Reverend F. H. Cosgrove, B.A., B.D., representing Trinity College, Toronto, Ontario; Reverend Principal Waller, M.A., representing Huron College, London, Ontario; Reverend Professor Abbott-Smith, M.A., D.D., representing the Diocesan College, Montreal, Quebec; Venerable Archdeacon Cody, M.A., D.D., D.C.S., representing Wycliffe College, Toronto, Ontario. The Reverend Professor Abbott-Smith, Diocesan College, Montreal, Secretary.

Church Connection of Wycliffe College.

Wycliffe College forms an integral part of the educational system of the Church of England in Canada. By Resolution of the Provincial Synod in the year 1889 it was given its place as one of the recognized Theological Colleges of that Church, on an equal basis with those at other centres of Educational and Church life in Canada. Its graduates are received by all the Bishops as Candidates for Holy Orders. The Course of Study throughout the period of training is so arranged as to lead up to the Fxaminations for the degrees of B.D. and D.D., set by the Board of Examiners of the Provincial Synod, upon which body Wycliffe College appoints its Representative from year to year.

Candidates have the option of taking the examinations at any of the Universities or Theological Colleges connected with the Church in the Ecclesiastical Province. The examinations will be held simultaneously at these various centres, or at other centres which may be appointed by the Board, and will be conducted oy written papers only, commencing on the third Tuesday in May.

Candidates who have passed this examination shall be entitled to receive from the Board of Examiners a Certificate. Such Certificate shall authorize the holder after ordination to wear the prescribed hood, on payment of the fee of $10.

Successful Work of Wycliffe College.

From the Annual Report of the Reverend Doctor O'Meara for 1910 it appears that the year's work has been very successful. He states that there was an enrollment of Students for the year of 110—of which three were extra-mural Students, studying and doing Missionary Work in the Northwest.

Requests had come from the various Bishops for thirty-six men, but they had been able to send out only twelve to them.

At the Convocation President Falconer of Toronto University complimented the College on its remarkable growth and prosperity, and stated that he was glad, as a Canadian, that there was such an institution to turn out strong men, the kind of men that Canada needed.

The Reverend Canon Plumptre, in delivering the message to the Graduates, urged them always to follow the truth, to love Jesus Christ, and rewards to labour would come in abundance.

The Reverend W. H. Vance referred to the strong foothold which the doctrines of universal brotherhood and of the missionary spirit had gained, and he also spoke of the importance of the laity as a factor in the active work of the Church of England in Canada.

PROPOSED AMALGAMATION OF TRINITY AND WYCLIFFE COLLEGES, TORONTO.

An Anglican Clergyman asks *The Globe*, in view of the approaching Meeting of the Synod of Toronto, to give prominence to the following statement of the present position of the movement for the union of Trinity and Wycliffe Colleges:—

1. For twenty-five years or more it has been a constant reproach to the Church of England in the Dominion of Canada, and more especially in the Diocese of Toronto, that there should be in existence, side by side, two Divinity Schools operating for the same purpose, videlicet: Training men for Holy Orders.

2. The fact of such a condition being undesirable has been constantly in the minds of the Church's well-wishers, and has been brought acutely to the fore by the splendid work of unification which is being done by the Laymen's Missionary Movement.

3. So greatly has been the necessity of unification felt by many in the Church, that the question has been broached over and over again—Why should these two Colleges exist as they do at present?

4. One Churchman has made the offer that if the Colleges above mentioned will unite in one he will give toward the maintenance of the work of the new institution a quarter of a million of dollars.

5. No Theological platform is laid down by this generous son of the Church, because he states that his one idea is that of unification, and that it is surely possible when the Laity show such tangible proof of their longings that the Clergy who represent the doctrinal side of the Church will be able to get together and meet upon a common platform which will be acceptable to all.

6. The statement has been made by the Head of one of the Institutions that there do not now exist any differences between the two Institutions of such essential character as would preclude such *rapprochement*, but that a cordial meeting and endeavour to understand each other's point of view on the part of the supporters of these Institutions would result in the consummation so earnestly desired.

7. One College at the present time has one hundred and ten students, the other College has twenty-five students, all preparing for the work of the Ministry.

8. One condition of the gift being made is that one Building and one Staff of Professors should do the work which is now being done by the double equipment. So far only Committees of the two Institutions have gotten together to discuss the possibilities, and the discussion has been, at least on the one hand, most vague and general, with the result that to those who long for the ideal, only discouragement is felt.

9. Is it not time that a matter of such vital importance to the Church at large should be taken out of the hands of the few and submitted to the great body of the Clergy and the Laity throughout Canada.

10. If this were done surely the conscience of the Anglican Church in this Dominion would be so unanimous in perceiving the power and blessing which would accrue from such a union that the sentiment evoked would force the hands of the few who are allowing what they feel, or claim, to be non-essentials to stand in the way of this magnificent result.

TORONTO, June, 1910.

Communicated.

The Toronto *Globe* commented on the foregoing Letter as follows:—

Announcement is made by a Correspondent in *The Globe* to-day that a Member of the Anglican Church in Canada offers $250,000 for the purposes of Theological education and ministerial training in Toronto on condition that Wycliffe College and the Theological Faculty of Trinity College be united in one Divinity School. That announcement will provoke interest far beyond the Corporations of the two Colleges concerned, and beyond the confines of the Church with which those Colleges are identified. All who are interested in the promotion of Church union among the Denominations and who deplore the facts of overlapping and duplication and consequent competition throughout the country must be interested in a proposal to unite two Institutions belonging to one Church whose separate existence in the same city cannot be defended unless the causes for their continued disunion are stronger and more immovable than the causes which keep the Denominations apart. Unionists among the Anglicans must do what was done by Presbyterians in 1875 and by Methodists in 1884. Unite the fountain springs of the Church's leadership and the streams of the Church's membership will not be charged with division, distrust, and strife.

But there is a larger question. Those who have at heart the best interests of the Church in Canada and of the higher Theological learning see in Toronto under present conditions an opportunity almost unmatched elsewhere either in America, or in Britain. It is possible to establish and develop here a centre of Theological Education and of broad and efficient ministerial training such as is not to be found on either side of the Atlantic. The conditions here are more favourable. The University of Toronto is not only larger in numbers than any of the Universities in Britain, but its constitution and attitude are more favourable to the Theological Colleges than is ordinarily found in other great University centres. The co-operation of the Colleges has been not only a strength to the Provincial University, but on more than one critical occasion was its salvation. For years past the international reputation for scholarship and power won by men in the various Theological Professoriates has added to the prestige of the University. The policy of the Colleges in securing Professors of the very highest type has given the study of Theology an academic standing in Toronto which no University man can afford to disregard. No department in the Provincial University is more strongly manned than is Theology in the Denominational Colleges.

Even better results might be achieved were Church union to secure the amalgamation of Knox College with the Theological Faculty of Victoria College, and were there a union of the two Divinity Faculties of the Anglican Church. These are questions of far more than Denominational interest. Those who have to do with their settlement should not be unmindful of the wider issue.—*Toronto Globe of the 10th of June, 1910.*

The Toronto *Mail and Empire,* in referring to the proposed union of Trinity and Wycliffe Colleges, states that:

The negotiations looking towards the amalgamation of Trinity and Wycliffe Colleges have fallen through, and in a Letter written by Mr. N. W. Hoyles, K.C., and the Reverend T. R. O'Meara, President and Principal respectively of Wycliffe College, the reasons for the collapse of the negotiations are given. The Letter reviews the plan which was discussed as a good one on which to base the amalgamation of the two Institutions, and concludes by stating that there would have to be a compromise if the union were decided upon, which could not be agreed to by Wycliffe, and it would be unfair to alienate or divert funds contributed towards the maintenance of Wycliffe. . . .

During the early part of 1910 a movement was made on the part of the Council of Trinity College to effect a union of Wycliffe with Trinity College University. With that view the Provost of Trinity College opened a correspondence with the Honourable S. H. Blake, one of the Treasurers of Wycliffe College. The result of this movement led to the publication of certain explanatory statements and papers on the subject, which are herewith appended in the consecutive order in which they were issued. They include a Memorandum by the Honourable S.

H. Blake, co-Treasurer of Wycliffe College, of the 18th of April, 1910; a Circular from the Council of Wycliffe College to the Graduates of that College of the 20th of July, 1910; and a statement of the Provost of Trinity College of the 29th of July, 1910.

Memorandum of the Honourable S. H. Blake in Reference to the Proposal of Trinity College for a Merger or Union of Wycliffe College with it.

To the mind of the Writer it is impossible to exaggerate the necessity of distinct Evangelical teaching to the welfare, if not the very existence, of the Church of England in Canada.

The majority of our Laymen desire such teaching, and the effort to replace it with Sacerdotalism and Ritualism and a non-Anglican form of service is generally disliked and resented.

It is essential to the life of the Church of England in Canada to continue and strengthen any provision whereby the Anglican, rather than the Anglo-Roman, system of worship should be preserved, and an earnest missionary spirit cultivated in every member of our communion.

It is because of the effort which is now being diligently made to introduce into Canada such Societies as "The English Church Union," "The Confraternity of the Blessed Sacrament," "The Kilburn Sisterhood," otherwise called "The Sisters of St. John the Divine," with their Convents, Sisterhoods, and all the surroundings of the Church of Rome, and such of her doctrines as Transubstantiation, with the various phases of the Real Presence in the elements, Altar worship, the Confessional, and the long list of false teaching that follows in their train, that our Church, most unfortunately, is throughout our Dominion generally decreasing in numbers and consequently losing her power.

It cannot, therefore, be a matter of surprise to the members of this Committee to be told that I view with the utmost alarm any suggestion that has for its object the interference with the instruction which is being given in those clearly defined principles of Evangelical truth, based on the Bible, which are found in our Book of Common Prayer and the Thirty-nine Articles. These I conceive to be necessary, not only to the well-being, but to the very existence of the true Church. While prepared to make large sacrifices in the cause of union in non-essentials, I am not prepared to sacrifice one iota in favour of a uniformity obtained by the abandonment of some matter essential to our Evangelical Church of England, or by the introduction of error that mars the simplicity of her service.

Therefore, in any union, or merger of Wycliffe with Trinity, I consider it to be absolutely necessary, in the true interests of our Church, that the doctrines and teachings which represent these views should be preserved and safeguarded. We, as a Committee, are wanting in our duty to the Church, which in this matter we are representing, and which should be of far higher moment than the mere existence or non-existence of a Theological College, if we fail in devising the proper means for preserving and propagating these foundation principles of our Church.

Now, both Trinity and Wycliffe, as Theological Colleges of the Church of England, claim that their principles are those of the Book of Common Prayer and the Thirty-nine Articles. But with these two Colleges, as with others erected on the same foundation, the structures built differ most materially and in most vital points. Some lean strongly towards Rome, with her ornate, spectacular architecture, and with a strong mediæval bias, embracing altars, confessionals, and an elaborate paraphernalia suitable to such erections; while others lean from Rome and prefer the Reformed style and build accordingly.

Now, knowing all this, especially developed since the year 1850, let us face the question honestly and seek to ascertain what is, as before God, in the true interest of our Church, and conscientiously refuse to close our eyes to the vital differences that exist to-day in this very City of Toronto, and thence throughout our Dominion. Then let us seek to ascertain their causes, and thereafter proceed to find out whether, or not, we can agree so entirely to remove these causes that complete harmony may be established. Then shall our Church not only cease to retrograde, but begin an onward movement as a leader among Churches.

The class of matters to which I refer, as interfering sadly with the progress of our Church, without giving an exhaustive list, may be placed under the following enumeration of innovations:

1. The Bible not treated as the Word of God, our sole Guide, but to be modified by tradition, the voice of the Church, etcetera.
2. Societies such as the C. B. S., the E. C. U., the Kilburn Sisterhood, not only permitted but patronized in our midst.
3. The Altar permitted to replace the Table of the Lord.
4. The Eastward position, and back of the Minister to the Congregation while consecrating the elements, thereby concealing the acts of the consecrating Minister.
5. Eucharistic vestments.
6. Wafer bread.
7. The Reserved Sacrament and its adoration.
8. The Real Presence in the elements taught by word, or act.
9. Symbolical lights.
10. Morning fasting Communion.
11. The anathematizing Evening Communion.
12. The Confessional, penance, Priestly absolution.
13. Vespers of the departed and prayers for the dead.
14. The use of incense.
15. The blessings of the holy oil and extreme unction.
16. The invocation of saints, or angels.
17. The stations of the Cross in the Church.
18. The mixed chalice at the time of celebration.
19. The placing of the "Body of Christ in the hand."
20. The ablutions.
21. The consumption by the Minister alone of what remains of the consecrated Bread and Wine.
22. The change of stoles at the sacrament of baptism.
23. The procession and blessings of palms.
24. Bowings, genuflections, crossings, and adorations of the Table and the elements on it.
25. Convents and Sisterhoods, with all their surroundings.
26. All attempts to introduce non-Anglican ceremonies from the Church of Rome under the plea of bringing back Catholic worship.

I do not mean to say, as I have above stated, that the list given is exhaustive. I have only referred to those matters in respect of which complaints have been made to me within the last year, by those who have felt so aggrieved at their introduction into the services of the Church, that with some it is a cause for leaving the Church of England, and with others a matter of grave consideration as to whether they can honestly remain in her, or what the action taken by them should be.

When I refer to the above grounds of complaint, so largely disturbing our Church at present, it must be borne in mind that it will not satisfy those to whom I am referring that these matters be treated in a Laodicean fashion. They are vital matters, as to which the answer will not be accepted, " Let those that like them have them, and those that dislike them reject them." They must be considered as proper subjects for distinct teaching, and the distinct teaching as to them must be that they are non-Anglican, alien to our Reformed Church of England, do not represent the Evangelical teaching for which our Church has stood for over 300 years, and are the outward visible signs of the Anglo-Roman movement, which has determined to unite the Church of England with the Church of Rome, and to assimilate the doctrines and standards of our Reformed Church with those of the Church from which we have separated.

Our Church has now a College in which for over thirty years this distinct teaching has been given with a large measure of acceptance. It is affiliated with Toronto University, and has the great academic and financial strength that flow from this union. The Laymen of our Church approve of this College and of this union, and express their liking and sympathy, not only in words, but by the support which they generously and freely give. So heartily have they from time to time up to the present appreciated the arrangement and its result that almost the whole endowment of Wycliffe has been given on the disinct understanding that it shall continue; and, if it is varied, or ceases, that the moneys conditionally given shall revert to the donors.

It is said that it will be in the interest of our Church to enter into a merger, or union, with Trinity, and that to accomplish this all necessary sacrifices by Wycliffe should be made.

But is it in the interest of our Church to ask the Council of Wycliffe now to make such a change, that the present system, tested, tried, and found eminently successful, shall be brought to a termination? And would the Trustees be justified in answering such request by abandoning this sacred trust, and enter into other undefined and untried alliances, which might result in seriously interfering with the present crying need of our Church—a supply of Clergymen for all parts of the Dominion?

In looking at this matter simply from the standpoint of the best interests of our Church, the following considerations strike me as most important:

As Wycliffe stands at present she has:

(*a*) Buildings admirably situated and fitted to carry on her work.

(*b*) An endowment, in these Buildings and in money, which amounts to nearly $300,000. This will be lost to the Church if the proposed merger be carried out, as it will revert to the Donors.

(*c*) An arrangement whereby through the Toronto University education in all subjects but Theology is given to the Students.

(*d*) This enables the College to devote all its time, money, and energy to instruction in Theological and kindred subjects.

(*e*) A staff of Professors who command the love and respect of her Students, and the confidence of her supporters.

(*f*) An income reaching almost $40,000 a year—sufficient to answer her present requirements—and a body of subscribers prepared to help in extensions as the need for them may from time to time arise.

(*g*) A Board of Trustees in absolute harmony with her principles and teaching, and ready, with God's blessing, to continue to carry on Wycliffe so as to make her, from year to year, an increased help to our Church.

Now, so far as the vague presentation of the arrangement proposed enables one to form a conclusion, it would appear to place the Church in this position:

(*a*) Wycliffe to cease to exist as a College.

(*b*) Complete large expensive buildings to be erected in the neighbourhood of Queen's Park, to replace those at present on Queen Street, which will cease to be used for College purposes.

(*c*) The Students at present at Wycliffe to be withdrawn from Toronto University and to receive their education at Trinity.

(*d*) To effect this a complete Teaching Staff to be introduced into Trinity to give the instruction at present found in Toronto University.

But in considering these matters of vital moment the following questions naturally arise:—

1. If the Wycliffe Students part from Toronto University, what guarantee is given that the education which Trinity promises will equal that given by the former University and shall continue to be given free of charge?

2. Will there be provision in the new Buildings for Wycliffe Students, and will these Buildings replace the present Wycliffe College Buildings, and where will they be situated?

3. **Will** Trinity College undertake to finance annually the present $40,000, all of which must be made up, as the endowments will be lost? What **guarantee will** be given for the fulfilment of this undertaking?

4. What guarantee is proposed that the teaching of the Church as above defined, and as at present given to Wycliffe Students, will be continued; and, if not continued, what is to be the result? This is to me a very vital **consideration, as** the eliminating of such teaching would be a fatal blow to our Church.

To me it is immaterial whether the proposed Theological College be called Trinity, St. Paul's, St. Latimer, or Wycliffe. I will agree to any of them. This is a non-essential. The teaching is essential, and must be safeguarded.

I still trust that you may, in the interest of our Church, end the question you raise, and that you will see your way to have but one Theological Institution, and to permit Wycliffe to be the educating College for all Divinity Students who will come to her from this Diocese or elsewhere. A reasonable addition on the vacant ground to the east of Wycliffe would give the needed accommodation, and enable this proposal to be carried out at a very small cost, giving all Divinity Students the great benefits now found at Wycliffe.

If there be not essential differences to interfere with union, then permit Wycliffe to continue the work on the above defined lines in the present location, so well situated, and with the free use to all of the great advantages given freely next door, by the Toronto University. Let us thus work together and save to the Church the very great cost of additional buildings, Professorial staff, and the display of a want of harmony in our work.

If there be differences which prevent a union, let us honestly admit it and live apart.

" Can two walk together except they be agreed? "

I recognize the courtesy which caused the offer to be made to me of the position of Chancellor of the proposed Institution. I feel, however, it would be my duty to decline it, as my acceptance thereof must necessarily be most distasteful to many Trinity College Graduates and supporters, whom I would not like to place in so false a position.

S. H. BLAKE.

TORONTO. 18th April, 1910.

ADVERSE DECISION OF WYCLIFFE COLLEGE TO AMALGAMATE WITH TRINITY COLLEGE.

The question of the amalgamation of Trinity and Wycliffe Colleges, having been referred to a representative Committee of Wycliffe College, it decided adversely to the proposal, and the following Circular, containing that decision, was addressed by the Committee to the Graduates of Wycliffe College, and also to its other Friends and Supporters:—

You have all doubtless noticed in the daily Papers Letters and Reports of interviews upon the subject of a suggested union between Trinity University and Wycliffe College. You have a right to expect a full statement in regard to what has taken place, and without going too much into details, the following we trust will supply you with the information desired.

It is true that there have been conferences between certain Members of Trinity University and certain Members of the Council of Wycliffe College. This was the result of an offer made, as you have seen, by a man of wealth to give $250,000 to promote a union of the two Colleges. In consequence of this a Letter was addressed by the Provost of Trinity College to the Honourable S. H. Blake, suggesting a consideration of terms of union; after some little correspondence between them it was suggested by the Provost that in addition to Mr. Blake the following members of Wycliffe College Council should be asked to take part in a conference—The Co-Treasurer, Archdeacon Cody, the President and the Principal of the College. After anxious consideration it was thought by those named by the Provost to be wise to take part in the suggested conference, and not to refuse to listen to any proposition that might be made on behalf of Trinity College. These gentlemen did not profess to represent Wycliffe officially. They were suggested by the Provost himself as persons whom it was desirable to have present at the Conference, and their action could not in any way bind, or compromise,

Wycliffe College, inasmuch as they were not there in any official or representative capacity.

The plan of union proposed was shortly this—

(1) Wycliffe and the Theological Faculty of Trinity University were to be merged into a new Theological College.

(2) Wycliffe Students were to take their Arts Course in Trinity University, instead of, as at present, in University College, Toronto. New Buildings for the occupation of Trinity were to be erected in Queen's Park.

(3) The proposed new Theological Faculty was to be governed by a Body, or Council, in which, as originally suggested, Trinity was to have 43 out of 55 Members.

(4) For the present the teaching staff of each College, with any exceptions which might be made in particular instances, was to be retained in the proposed new College.

(5) All questions of discipline, teaching and government were to be under the control of the Governing Body above referred to.

(6) In favour of the proposition it was urged that there would be great gain to our Church if the different schools of thought would agree to unite in one large Divinity College; that there would be a considerable financial saving if this were done; and that a more harmonious spirit would pervade the whole Church if, instead of two rival Colleges, one strong Institution were formed for the Theological training of all students.

Several conferences were held. The positions taken by those invited to be present on behalf of Wycliffe were briefly as follows:—

(a) What guarantee is there that the students of Wycliffe College shall receive the distinctive Protestant and Evangelical teaching that is called for by the statement of "Distinctive Principles," to be found in the College Calendar of 1883, which formed the basis of the College.

(b) What guarantee is there that they shall not receive the sacramental and sacerdotal teaching which has usually been associated with the traditions and teaching of Trinity?

(c) What guarantee is there that the teaching in regard to the Word of God shall be in accordance with the views insisted on by the Evangelical party of the Church of England?

(d) The teaching in regard to vital matters to be given in a College where it is sought to fuse together mechanically views so far apart as those of the High Church and Evangelical parties undoubtedly are, would either be absolutely colourless, or would be tinged in one way or the other. Neither result would be satisfactory to earnest and intelligent members of these two Schools of Thought.

(e) Students graduated from a Theological College where the teaching must necessarily be so indefinite as would be the result of the union proposed could hardly be real leaders of thought in the Parishes to which they might be called.

(f) Moreover, those who have come to Wycliffe College as Students had their own strong convictions and sympathies in favour of Protestant and Evangelical views, and would probably refuse to attend a College where such views were not definitely held and taught.

It was further pointed out that by the terms of the Trust Deed, under which large sums of money have been contributed by friends and supporters of Wycliffe College, three conditions have been laid down—

(a) The College must be carried on wholly independent of and unconnected with any other place or Theological Institution.

(*b*) It must be conducted on the distinctive principles laid down in the College Calendar for 1883.

(*c*) No change can be made in the principles of instruction, or in the doctrinal standards of teaching hereinbefore referred to.

A breach of these conditions, or any change in the distinctive teaching, or any union with other Theological Colleges, would create a forfeiture of the bequests and donations in favour of the Donors, or their representatives, and would involve the loss of the whole endowment of the College.

To endeavor to evade the terms of the Trust would be an immoral and dishonest act and a grievous wrong to the Donors of the moneys. These were men of deep and intelligent convictions who would never have given a cent to Wycliffe had there been any danger that these funds should be diverted from the purposes for which they were given, and the Council of Wycliffe College would be untrue to its duty if it were to be in any way a party to alienating, or diverting, funds given under such circumstances.

It was further stated that since Wycliffe College had been established and had been recognized as having a legitimate status and function in our Church, there had been increasing harmony between the different Schools of Thought in the Diocese of Toronto and throughout the Dominion, and a corresponding development and advance had been manifested by the Church in its various departments.

It was pointed out, in answer to the statement made on behalf of Trinity that there was no difference between the two Colleges at the present time, certainly nothing that should keep them apart, that it was unfortunate that this view had not been taken by the supporters of Trinity at the time of the recent Episcopal Election. On that occasion nearly all the clergy of the Diocese were marshalled as a compact body in opposition to the election of one who was in the estimation of the whole Canadian public brilliantly fitted for the position, simply because he was a Wycliffe Graduate and Wycliffe Professor.

No result has come from the Conferences in question, nor indeed can there come one which would gain the consent of Wycliffe to a merger such as was proposed. The members of the Council of Wycliffe College attending the Conference were, and are, deeply convinced of the absolute importance for the sake of our Church in this Dominion of maintaining Wycliffe College free and untrammeled as it stands at present.

They believe that the vital differences between Trinity and Wycliffe, which were the cause of bringing the College into existence thirty years ago, are just as real to-day as then. It is idle to say that there is no distinction between the different parties or Schools of Thought in our Church. In the language of the late lamented Archbishop Sweatman:—

"It is fruitless for us to deny, brethren, it would be unworthy for us to apologize, that there are parties in the Church. I trust we have learned enough wisdom from the past frankly to accept the position; and that each party is willing honourably to concede to the other the right to exist and to claim a just recognition—so long, of course, as its doctrines and usages are within the legitimate limits of a fair and honest interpretation of the formularies acknowledged by both."

The late Archbishop also said:—

"I hold most strongly the Protestant Evangelical views of our Reformed Church as opposed to the Sacerdotal and Sacramentarian views which are characteristic of Ritualism."

Firmly agreeing with these views of the late Archbishop, believing that the maintenance of Wycliffe College is as essential to the *bene esse* of our Church as it was when it was first founded, and believing that the proposed change, instead of promoting true union and harmony, would accentuate our differences and perpetuate our unhappy divisions, those who took part in the Conference on behalf of Wycliffe can never consent to any compromise, and will never agree to any union which will weaken or diminish the clear unshaken position of Wycliffe as holding and teaching the "Protestant Evangelical views of our Reformed Church." . . .

We believe that not only must this distinctive teaching continue to be the message of Wycliffe College, but that the time has come when the Clergy and Laity, who value the Reformed Faith and Worship of our Church, must be prepared to speak out clearly and decidedly in opposition to the very dangerous and wide-spread Sacerdotalism now being openly taught in so many of our Parishes.

The prospects before the College were never more encouraging; we call upon its Graduates to remain unflinchingly true to those Protestant and Evangelical principles which the College was founded to teach, and which its Founders believed, and its friends and supporters at the present day are convinced, are the true principles of our Reformed Church of England.

In closing may we urge upon each and every Graduate to continue instant in prayer for the great cause which centres at Wycliffe College. Those of us who bear the more direct responsibility for administration and teaching depend, as the work grows ever increasingly, upon the earnest co-operation in prayer on the part of all who feel the importance of our great and holy undertaking.

May we take this opportunity of thanking most heartily those who have so generously contributed the necessary means for carrying forward this branch of the work of Christ. Nothing, we believe, will bring greater blessing and more lasting results in our Church and land than the thorough training of godly young men in the great truths of the Word of God and of our Reformed Church of England.

TORONTO, July 20th, 1910.

N. W. HOYLES, *President.*
T. R. O'MEARA, *Principal.*

THE PROPOSED UNION OF TRINITY COLLEGE AND WYCLIFFE COLLEGE—A STATEMENT

BY THE REVEREND PROVOST MACKLEM.

At this juncture it is permissible, and it is deemed advisable, for Trinity College to issue a Statement, for the information of its Graduates and of Church people generally, of the facts relating to a recent effort made by its Friends and Authorities to bring about a union with Wycliffe College. This Statement, which is based upon Memoranda and Correspondence now on fyle with the Minutes of the Corporation of Trinity College, is a succinct recital of events in the order of their occurrence.

In December, 1909, a prominent Churchman of this Province, upon being approached on behalf of the Endowment campaign of Trinity College now in progress, made the spontaneous and munificent offer of $200,000, or more if necessary, for the Theological work of the two Colleges, Trinity and Wycliffe, provided their union could be effected. This generous offer, untrammelled by any restriction or condition other than that of union, was made in the first instance to the Reverend Doctor Llwyd, Vice-Provost of Trinity College, who communicated it to the Provost. At the same time the Donor entered into correspondence on the subject with the Honourable S. H. Blake, as a representative of Wycliffe College; and subsequently the Provost was asked to submit a scheme of union as a basis for discussion.

At the January meeting of the Corporation of Trinity College, the Provost asked for an expression of opinion as to union with Wycliffe College, but in deference to the Donor's wish he made no mention of the proposed benefaction. The Corporation expressed itself enthusiastically and unanimously in favor of closer relations with Wycliffe College, and appointed a Committee to co-operate with the Provost in ascertaining what practical steps might be taken in this direction. The Committee consisted of the Archbishop of Ottawa, the Bishop of Toronto, the Vice-Provost, Doctor J. A. Worrell, K.C., Mr. E. B. Osler, M.P., Mr. W. R. Brock, and Mr. N. F. Davidson, K.C.

After consultation with Members of the Committee, the Provost submitted a plan for union embracing the following features:—

1. Wycliffe College and the Theological Department of Trinity College to be amalgamated so as to form a new Theological College, for which the name St. Paul's College was tentatively proposed.

2. The Staff of the new College to be composed of the Staffs of the two Colleges at the time of union, unless in respect of any of them for whom other arrangements might be mutually agreed upon.

3. Trinity (Arts) College and St. Paul's (Theological) College to work together harmoniously as integral parts of the University of Trinity College (in federation with the University of Toronto), so as to provide by their united work for the complete education of their Students in both Arts and Theology.

4. Trinity College to provide suitable Buildings and equipment, in close proximity to the University of Toronto, for the Theological Students during their Arts Course, and Wycliffe College to provide similarly for them during their Theological Course.

5. The new Theological College to be governed during the period of transition and fusion by a Provisional Council consisting of all the Bishops of the Province of Ontario, the Chancellor and Vice-Chancellor of the University of Trinity College, the Principal of the new College, and forty-six other members, of whom one-half were to be nominated by the Council of Wycliffe College and one-half by the Corporation of Trinity College.

After the period of transition, the Provisional Council to be replaced by a regular Council constituted as follows:—

(a) The Bishops of all the Dioceses in the Province of Ontario.

(b) The Chancellor and Vice-Chancellor of the University of Trinity College and the Principal of St. Paul's College.

(c) Two Clerical and two Lay members representing each Diocese and elected by the Synod of the Diocese every third year, to hold office till the next such election.

(d) Two Laymen nominated by each of the Bishops, and not necessarily members of any Synod nor resident in the Diocese of the Bishop so nominating; the Members thus nominated to hold office for three years.

(e) Ten Members, Lay or Clerical, to be elected by the Council.

The foregoing proposal was criticized by a mutual friend on the ground that the name of Wycliffe College should be retained, and this point was immediately conceded. It was criticized also by the Honourable S. H. Blake on several grounds, and especially in respect of the composition of the regular Council. According to Mr. Blake's contention, all the Bishops of the Province, six in number, and the two Laymen appointed by each of them, making twelve more, with at least one-half (namely twelve) of the Members elected by the Synods, and the ten Members named by the Council itself, togeher with the Chancellor and Vice-Chancellor of Trinity College and the Principal of the new Theological College, would be favorable to Trinity College; and, he contended, the administration of a Council so composed would have the effect of blotting out Wycliffe College and the teaching for which it stands. Mr. Blake further drew attention to the Trust Deed of Wycliffe College, which sets forth that the moneys given under the Trust revert to the Donors, in case Wycliffe College should "cease to be carried on as a place for Theological instruction wholly independent of and unconnected with any other place for Theological instruction."

The Trinity College Committee was unable to see why Mr. Blake should suppose that Bishops of the Province and their nominees on the Council, with all those elected by the Council itself, and at least one-half of the members elected by the Synods, would be opposed to the teachings and principles of Wycliffe College. Nevertheless, the Committee was anxious to allay all fears (even groundless ones) and to establish the fullest mutual confidence. Accordingly, the Provost wrote again to Mr. Blake to express an earnest desire for a College so governed that the Evangelical principles of Wycliffe College would be properly protected, and for a Council so constituted as to safeguard all the interests concerned. This letter, dated 22nd February, 1910, reads in part as follows:—

I have carefully considered your Letter of the 14th instant, and, as I understand the matter, there are two main objections in your mind to the proposal made in my Letter of the 7th instant, namely, (1), that "it blots out Wycliffe College," and (2) that the Trust Deed of Wycliffe College stands as a serious difficulty in the way of a merger of any kind.

As to the former, (Number 1), I would say that I have no desire at all to blot out Wycliffe College. On the contrary, I regard its continuance (under whatever name) as being essential to a real and permanent consolidation of the interests we are discussing, and I shall be glad to assent to any fair and reasonable proposition for safeguarding the interests of both Colleges in the proposed merger.

If you desire the retention of the name Wycliffe College, I have no objection to offer on the point.

As to the Council, I feel sure it could be so constituted as to give fair and proper representation and safeguards to all the interests concerned.

. . . What is aimed at is the elimination of all old controversies and differences, and the establishment of a state of things in which all shall work together in the fullest harmony and with perfect mutual confidence. For the present, then, let it suffice to say that I am prepared to consider favourably any reasonable proposition for a Council so composed as to command the confidence and support of all parties.

As to the other objection, (Number 2), The Trust Deed certainly constitutes a formidable difficulty, but if both Colleges really desire to come together—and I can answer for Trinity College in this regard—surely the contributors of Wycliffe College could agree to waive the conditions under which their gifts were originally made, since there has risen an incentive so great as the concentration of the forces of our Church in support of one strong Institution for the education of our youth and the training of men for the Ministry. If, after this, any legal difficulty still remains, surely this might be met by suitable legislation, on application of the parties concerned.

May I, therefore, beg of you very earnestly, in the interests of our Church, that you will give this whole matter your careful consideration and support, and that you will allow me hereby to vary the proposal made in my former Letter by the contents of this Letter. I do so in the honest desire and earnest hope of meeting every reasonable objection on your part, or on the part of Wycliffe College, feeling well assured that both you and Wycliffe College will respond in a generous spirit and with an equal readiness to meet the views and difficulties of Trinity College. Thus taking counsel all together, in a spirit of mutual regard and conciliation, there may be devised some suitable plan whereby the educational interests of the Church of England in Ontario will be consolidated and existing differences done away.

Mr. Blake in his reply to this Letter, having expressed a desire to consult other representatives of Wycliffe College, the time seemed opportune for the Provost to suggest a conference between the representatives of the two Colleges, for a friendly discussion of the whole question. The representatives subsequently named for the conference were (*a*) for Trinity College, Mr. E. B. Osler, Doctor J. A. Worrell, Mr. N. F. Davidson, the Provost, and the Vice-Provost; and (*b*) for Wycliffe College, the Honourable S. H. Blake and Mr. F. C. Jarvis, Co-Treasurers; Doctor N. W. Hoyles, President of the Council; the Reverend Canon O'Meara, Principal of the College; and the Venerable Archdeacon Cody.

The conference met first on Saturday, 19th March, 1910, in Mr. Blake's office, when Trinity College submitted a brief memorandum embracing the following statement:

Trinity College has asked for this conference because,

(*a*) We are convinced that the proposed union would be highly beneficial to the Church in the Dominion and to the Colleges themselves.

(*b*) Such a union is heartily desired by Trinity College and would be welcomed by practically all of its supporters.

(*c*) The difficulties, legal and other, standing in the way of a union, great although they admittedly are, can surely be overcome if there be on both sides a strong desire for union.

At this, and subsequent meetings, the representatives of Wycliffe College took the position that a union of the Colleges was in their opinion not desirable, and would probably prove the reverse of beneficial. Naturally, therefore, they had no suggestion to make looking immediately towards union, the questions they offered for discussion being chiefly matters of doctrine and ritual. These were partly certain Evangelical doctrines, which they supported as being essential to the continuance of "Wycliffe teaching," and which are practically common to both Colleges, being fundamentals of Anglican Christianity; and partly certain other doctrines and practices from which they dissented, and which for the most part have never had any relation to Trinity College, or its practices and teachings. The discussion of such questions—although of undoubted importance and, in the right time and place, necessary—seemed to the Representatives of Trinity College to be out of place and practically futile so long as the Wycliffe Representatives adhered to their opinion that union was in no case desirable. Under these circumstances progress seemed impossible, and the Provost had no alternative but to notify the Donor that the negotiations had failed to give any promise of effecting the union, which was the condition of his proposed gift.

In conclusion it may not be out of place to remind the Graduates and Friends of Trinity College that although federated with the University of Toronto in so far as its Arts teaching is concerned, that College remains still the Church College for the Province of Ontario—the College of the whole Church, not merely of any part, or section, thereof, and guaranteed as such not only by its foundation, but also by its government. It is still charged, as at its foundation, with the teaching of the principles and practices of the Christian Religion as laid down in the Bible and in the authorized formularies of the Church of England, without reference to, or distinction between, any of the historic Schools of Thought existing in the Anglican Communion. It has never been better equipped than it is at the present time to carry out the aims of its Founder, and to obey the call of the Church, whose University it is. Whether in union with Wycliffe, or alone, the University of Trinity College is bound to maintain the whole teaching of the Church of England including the wealth of Evangelical truth and learning. Its government is under the control of the Bishops and authorized Representatives of the various Dioceses of the Church, as the surest guarantee of loyalty to the essentials of faith and order on the one hand, and of breadth and comprehension on the other. Its doors are always open to Churchmen of every School of Thought, and among the Graduates trained within its walls Evangelical Churchmen are largely represented. It desires, not the emphasis of "party," but the unification of the Church; it entertains no feelings of enmity; it remains ready to welcome overtures from Wycliffe College, at any time, looking towards closer relations or towards organic union.

Signed on behalf of the Corporation,

T. C. S. MACKLEM,
Provost and Vice-Chancellor.

TRINITY COLLEGE, TORONTO,
29th July, 1910.

NOTE ON THE STATE AND PROGRESS OF WYCLIFFE COLLEGE ADDRESSED TO THE GRADUATES OF THE COLLEGE.

BY THE PRESIDENT AND PRINCIPAL OF THE COLLEGE.

As a result of not having any Church paper of a distinctively Evangelical character, or other regular means of communication, we feel that often those who represent Wycliffe College in the Parishes and Missions of our own and other lands are not kept as fully informed regarding the progress of the work as would be possible under other circumstances. At the close of the Academic year we feel that there are matters of vital interest connected with our beloved College concerning which we would like to write to you, as we know that you will be interested in hearing something from us of the work which has been done.

The year which has just closed has been one of the most successful and promising which the College has ever enjoyed. We have had the maximum number of students in attendance, 111 having been registered in preparation for the Christian Ministry during the year, and the spirit of our College life has been most encouraging and full of promise for the future. Our Students are now scattered literally

Part XII. Note on the State and Progress of Wycliffe College.

from one extreme of our great Dominion to the other, a larger number of them than ever before being engaged in the active missionary work of the Church. Twelve men, having satisfied the requirements of the course, were granted the diploma at our Commencement Exercises a few weeks ago. This number, however, entirely failed to supply the urgent demands of the Bishops, and three times as many could have been located in important Parishes and Missions had they been forthcoming. You will be glad, we feel sure, to know that the promise of students for the opening of next term is most encouraging.

The item of outstanding importance in the year has been the appointment of the Reverend Doctor Griffith Thomas, Principal of Wycliffe Hall, Oxford, to serve upon our staff. For many months past we have been on the outlook for just such a worker. We had but little hope, however, that it would be possible for us to obtain the services of so able a man. His visit to Canada in the interests of the Bible League last March proved to be our great opportunity. Shortly after his return to England a formal invitation was sent to him by the Council, and we are glad and thankful to inform you that he accepted without hesitation, feeling that the call was indeed from God. The possibility of obtaining the services of such a man as the Reverend Doctor Griffith Thomas arose from the wonderful response made to the Special Appeal of the Council for increased revenue last Winter—one gentleman alone guaranteed $3,000.00 per annum—many others promised handsome annual contributions to the College. Doctor Thomas will, we trust, enter upon his new duties at the opening of the Term. He will relieve Mr. Cotton of the subject of Old Testament, allowing the latter to devote much more time and strength to Apologetics and Hebrew. It is also hoped that Mr. Cotton will be able to assist the Principal to a larger extent than in the past in the College administration. Doctor Thomas will also take charge of the department of Ecclesiology, leaving Canon Hague the subject of Liturgics. Two subjects—" Outlines of Christian Doctrine " and the " English Bible "—up to the present taught by the Principal, will also be in the charge of Doctor Thomas.

In his inaugural Address, Reverend Doctor G. Thomas, the new Professor of Theology at Wycliffe College, stated that before the Bible was reduced to writing the Church had the spoken Word of the Apostles. The Word created the Church, not the Church the Word. The Word of God in the Bible was supreme over Church tradition or Church custom. It was the final testing ground for all doctrine, and in that he held that it was of supreme authority.

PART XIII.

FACILITIES FOR PROFESSIONAL EDUCATION—LEGAL, MEDICAL, MILITARY, ETCETERA.

LEGAL EDUCATION: COURSES OF LEGAL STUDY PRESCRIBED BY THE BENCHERS OF THE LAW SOCIETY.*

1. That after Hilary Term, 1877, Candidates for admission as Students-at-Law, (except Graduates of Universities), be required to pass a satisfactory examination in the following subjects:

Classics.—Xenophon, Anabasis, Book I.; Homer, Iliad, Book I.; Cicero, for the Manilian Law: Ovid, Fasti, Book I., Verses 1-300; Virgil, Æneid, Book II., Verses 1-317; Translation from English into Latin; Paper on Latin Grammar.

Mathematics.—Arithmetic; Algebra, to the end of Quadratic Equations; Euclid, Books I., II., III.

English.—A paper on English Grammar; Composition; an examination upon "The Lady of the Lake," with special reference to Cantos v. and vi.

History and Geography.—English History from Queen Anne to George III., inclusive. Roman History, from the commencement of the second Punic war to the death of Augustus; Greek History, from the Persian to the Peloponnesian wars, both inclusive; Ancient Geography—Greece, Italy, and Asia Minor; Modern Geography; North America and Europe.

French.—A paper on Grammar. Translation of simple sentences into French prose. Corneille, Horace, Acts I. and II.

German.—A paper on Grammar. Musaeus; Stumme Liebe. Schiller, Lied Von der Glocke.

2. That after Hilary Term, 1877, Candidates for admission as Articled Clerks, (except Graduates of Universities and Students-at-Law), be required to pass a satisfactory examination in the following subjects—

Ovid, Fasti, Book I., vv. 1-300,—or
Virgil, Æneid, Book II., vv. 1-317.
Arithmetic.
Euclid, Books I., II., and III.
English Grammar and Composition.
English History—Queen Anne to George III.
Modern Geography—North America and Europe.
Elements of Book-keeping.

---

* The Law Society of Osgoode Hall was established in 1797 by Act of the Parliament of Upper Canada. In 1881 the Society formed a Law School with a Staff of Lecturers for the admission of Students-at-Law as Barristers and Attorneys.

3. That a Student of any University in this Province who shall present a Certificate of having passed, within four years of his application, an examination in the subjects above prescribed, shall be entitled to admission as a Student-at-Law, or Articled Clerk, (as the case may be), upon giving the prescribed notice and paying the prescribed Fee.

4. That all Examinations of Students-at-Law and Articled Clerks be conducted before the Committee on Legal Education, or before a Special Committee appointed by Convocation.

THOMAS HODGINS, *Chairman.*

Adopted by the Benchers in Convocation, August 29th, 1876.

OSGOODE HALL, Trinity Term, 1876.   J. HILLYARD CAMERON, *Treasurer.*

MEDICAL EDUCATION—GENERAL REGULATIONS BY THE MEDICAL COUNCIL.

In 1866, an Act was passed by the Legislature of Canada, reorganizing the Medical Council of Upper Canada, under the new title of "The General Council of Medical Education and Registration in Upper Canada." It was composed of Representatives from "the University of Toronto, the University of Queen's College, or Body, in Upper Canada, by law authorized, or hereafter to be authorized to grant Medical, or Surgical, Degrees, or Certificates of Qualification to practise Medicine, Surgery, or Midwifery, or either," and of twelve persons to be elected from among the registered Medical Practitioners of Upper Canada. It was empowered to establish a uniform standard of Matriculation for the admission of Students to all the Medical Schools, and to make By-laws and Regulations for determining the admission and enrolling of Students in them. It shall also have power to determine, from time to time, a Curriculum of Students to be pursued by the Students. The Regulations up to that time for obtaining a Medical Education were as follows:

1. That 21 years be the earliest age at which any professional License, or Degree, shall be obtained.

2. That four years' Study be required after Examination in General Education, except as hereinafter provided.

3. That the Professional Examination be divided at least into two distinct parts; that the first be undergone after two years' study, and the final Examination after four years' study.

4. That the Professional Examination be conducted partly in writing and partly *viva voce*; and that such parts as admit of it be made as practical and demonstrative as possible.

5. That the second Examination be conducted partly in writing and partly *viva voce*, and practically so far as may be convenient and attainable.

6. That professional examinations by the various professional and licensing bodies be given due notice of to the Registrar, so that one, or more, Members of the Medical Council may be present.

7. That Returns from the various Medical Schools and Licensing Bodies be made annually, on the first of May, to the General Medical Council, stating the number of Candidates who have passed their first as well as their second Examinations respectively; the number of those who may be entitled to Registration who shall not have attended Lectures, for at least three Sessions of six months each, in a University, College, or School of Medicine, approved of.

9. Candidates for final Examination shall furnish Testimonials of attendance in the following branches of a Medical Education, namely: Anatomy, Chemistry, Theory and Practice of Medicine, Principles and Practice of Surgery, Midwifery and Diseases of Women and Children, Materia Medica and Pharmacy, Institutes of Medicine, General and Practical Anatomy, of which two Courses will be required of six months each; Chemical Surgery, Medical Jurisprudence, Botany, Practical Chemistry, of which one Course of three months will be required.

10. Candidates must also give proof by ticket, of having attended at least twelve months' practice of a General Hospital, or that of some other Hospital approved of, and certified to.

11. Moreover, no one shall be permitted to attend any other Lectures, during their first year, than those in the following primary branches, videlicet: Final and Practical Anatomy, Chemistry, Materia Medica and Physiology; nor will the Certificates of any Teachers who lecture on more than one branch of Medical Science be recognized; and more than one Lecture each day shall not be delivered by the same person, on these primary branches. The Professor of Surgery may lecture on Clinical Surgery; the Professor of Medicine, and the Professor of Materia Medica may lecture on Botany and Medical Jurisprudence.

12. Each Candidate to be required to produce a Certificate of having compounded Medicines for two periods of six months each, or one period of twelve months, in the

MEDICAL COLLEGES AND SCHOOLS IN ONTARIO.

1. COLLEGE OF PHYSICIANS AND SURGEONS OF ONTARIO, TORONTO.

The Medical Profession in Ontario was first incorporated by an Act of Parliament in the year 1866, and the name given to it in its corporate capacity was The College of Physicians and Surgeons in Ontario. As every legally qualified Medical Practitioner in the Province is a member of this College, it is not, as its name might indicate, an Institution for the teaching of Medicine.

The Council.—The business of this Corporate Body is managed by a Council composed of (1) a Representative from each of the Universities in the Province,

(2) Twelve Territorial Representatives who are elected by the Registered Practitioners of Medicine residing within the territorial division, and (3) Five Representatives from the Homœopathic Practitioners. The Council regulates all matters connected with Medical Education; determines the Curriculum of Studies to be pursued by Students; appoints a Board of Examiners. Candidates passing a satisfactory examination before the Board are enrolled as Members of the College —the prerequisite for being legally qualified to practice their profession in Ontario. In the case of Practitioners duly qualified in other Countries, the Council fix the terms on which they may be admitted and become legally qualified Practitioners. In all cases, however, they must undergo the examination.

2. Toronto School of Medicine.

This Medical School, recognized by the several Colleges of Physicians and Surgeons in Great Britain, was established as the Rolph School in 1843, and incorporated by Act of Parliament in 1851. It is in affiliation with the University of Toronto and Victoria University. The Staff of Lecturers is composed of seventeen Physicians. The School is in close proximity to the General Hospital. The Students have also access to the various public charities of the City.

Course of Study.—As fixed by the College of Physicians and Surgeons of Ontario, the Course of Study extends over four Winter Sessions of six months each.

Summer Session.—A Summer Session is held in the General Hospital. The teaching is entirely practical and demonstrative, and is intended to supplement the Winter Session.

3. Trinity Medical School, Toronto.

This School was originated in 1850 by Doctors Hodder, Bovell, Badgley and Bethune, and then became a Faculty of the University of Trinity College. In 1855-6 it ceased to be a Faculty of the University. In 1871, it was reorganized under a Faculty differently constituted, but with many of the original Professors. In the year 1877 the School, instead of being one of the Faculties of the University of Trinity College, became an affiliated Body.

Course of Study.—The Curriculum embraces all the subjects required by the College of Physicians and Surgeons of Ontario; and besides these, Lectures on Medical Psychology, Biology, Zoology, etcetera, are provided for those Students who desire to graduate at the University of Toronto, or wherever else these courses are demanded.

Affiliation, Etcetera.—This School is in affiliation with the Universities of Trinity College, Toronto, and Manitoba, and is recognized by the Royal College of Surgeons, England; the Royal College of Physicians of London; the Royal College of Physicians and Surgeons, Edinburgh; the Faculty of Physicians and Surgeons of Glasgow; the King's and Queen's College of Physicians of Ireland, and by the conjoint Examining Boards in London and Edinburgh.

Summer Session.—A Summer Session of eight weeks, consisting of Didactic and Clinical Instruction, Lectures, and Demonstrations, is given at the Toronto General Hospital by the Professors of this School, conjointly with the Professors of the Toronto School of Medicine.

4. Royal College of Physicians and Surgeons, Kingston.

This Medical College was incorporated in 1854, and, possessing independent powers and privileges, is entitled to confer upon its own students and others the Diplomas of "Licentiate" and "Fellow." In consequence of its affiliation with Queen's University, its Students obtain the Degree of "Doctor of Medicine and Master of Surgery," by passing the requisite examination.

Foreign Recognition.—Certificates of attendance at this College are recognized by the Royal College of Surgeons, London and Edinburgh.

Curriculum.—The Course of Study embraces all the subjects required by the Royal College of Physicians and Surgeons of Ontario, and may be pursued either at the College, or partly there and partly at some other recognized Medical School, provided that at least one full Session has been spent at the College. Full courses in the subjects of instruction for at least three (3) Sessions must be attended before a Student can present himself as a Candidate for either the Diploma of the College or the Degree of the University. In either case the Candidate must have completed a period of four (4) years' study, and have passed the Matriculation Examination of Queen's University, or its equivalent.

5. Ontario College of Pharmacy, Toronto.

The Ontario College of Pharmacy is established in Toronto, having been incorporated by Act of Parliament in 1871. It is designed for the education of those who desire to carry on the business of Chemist, or Druggist.

The Council.—The College is under the control of the Pharmaceutical Council. It has authority to grant Certificates of competency, and the Holders of these Certificates must be registered. The qualification for such Certificates is that the Candidate shall furnish to the Council satisfactory evidence of having served an apprenticeship, under a written contract, for not less than three years, to a regularly qualified Pharmaceutical Chemist. He must also satisfy the Council that he has passed an examination entitling him to admission to a High School, Collegiate Institute, or to a fourth class of a Public School.

Course of Study.—The Course of Instruction pursued in the College includes all the subjects prescribed by the Council for Certificates, and embraces Chemistry, Elementary and Pharmaceutical; Pharmacy; Materia Medica; Botany; Practical Dispensing; Reading and Translating Prescriptions.

6. School of Dentistry of the Royal College of Dental Surgeons for Ontario.

The Royal College of Dental Surgeons, incorporated in 1868, was empowered to establish a School of Dentistry in the City of Toronto.

Requirements.—The Authorities of this School require, as a preliminary, that the Candidate shall have passed the High School, or an equivalent examination. He must also enter into indentures with a Licentiate for two years and a half, during which time he must attend two full courses, of four months each, in the School of Dentistry.

Examinations.—At the end of the first Course of Lectures he must pass an examination in Operative Dentistry; Mechanical Dentistry; Anatomy; Surgery; Physiology; Chemistry and Materia Medica. An Infirmary furnishes subjects for practical work. This Examination constitutes the Primary. The Final Examination, leading to the Diploma of Licentiate of Dental Surgery (L.D.S.), embraces the same subjects treated more minutely. A further Diploma of Master of Dental Surgery (M.D.S.) is conferred, after thorough examination in the same subjects, but of a more advanced character, and the writing of a Thesis on some prescribed subject, on Licentiates of not less than five years' standing.

7. Women's Medical Colleges, Kingston and Toronto.

Although Colleges for the instruction and graduation of women in Medicine have long been in operation in Great Britain and the United States, the first step in that direction was not made in this Province until the year 1880, when the principle of Medical co-education was attempted at the Royal College of Physicians and Surgeons, Kingston. As this did not prove satisfactory, a School for Medical Education of Women only was established in 1883. The City Council of Kingston placed at the disposal of the School apartments in the City Buildings, and by means of generous donations the School was placed upon a permanent basis. A similar School was established in Toronto the same year, and it is the aim of each to give all the Students a thorough grounding in the scientific and practical rudiments of Medicine.

The Course of Lectures in each College is equivalent in all respects to the ordinary Winter Course delivered in other Medical Colleges and Schools. The requisites for graduation differ in no sense from what is required from the male students. Several have already graduated from the Kingston College; two of whom have gone as missionaries to India; the others have built up good practices, and one of them is a Professor in her Alma Mater. The College in Toronto has not been established long enough to send out any graduates.

Statistics of the Medical Schools, Etcetera, in Ontario.

Name.	Date of Incorporation.	Subjects of Study.	Length of Course.	Number of Staff.	Institutions with which affiliated.
Toronto School of Medicine, Toronto.	1843	Those prescribed by the College of Physicians and Surgeons, Ontario.	4 Years.	17	1. University of Toronto. 2. Victoria University.
Trinity Medical School, Toronto	1850	Do do	Do	14	1. University of Trinity College. 2. University of Toronto. 3. University of Manitoba
Royal College of Physicians and Surgeons, Kingston.	1854	Do do	Do	10	Queen's University.
Medical Department of Western University, London.	1882	Do do	Do	15	1. Western University. 2. University of Toronto.
Women's Medical College, Kingston.	1883	Do do	Do	11	Queen's University.
Women's Medical College, Toronto	1883	Do do	Do	13	University of Trinity College.
School of Dentistry, Royal College of Dental Surgeons, Toronto.	1875	Anatomy, Physiology, Dental Pathology and Histology, Clinical and Operative Dentistry.	2 Sessions of 4 months each.	4	
College of Pharmacy, Toronto..	1871	Chemistry, Pharmacy, Materia Medica, Botany, Prescriptions and Practical Dispensing.	2 Courses of 3 months each.	3	
Ontario Veterinary College, Toronto.	1863	Anatomy, Physiology, Pathology, Chemistry and Materia Medica.	....	7	

THE ROYAL MILITARY COLLEGE, KINGSTON.

(*Under the Direction of the Dominion Government.*)

The primary object of the establishment of this College, which was opened on June 1st, 1876, was to secure such a complete Military and Scientific education to young men belonging to the country as would qualify them to fill all the higher positions in the Canadian Military Service. At the same time, owing to the breadth and general scope of the Curriculum of Study, the Graduates are fitted equally for any civil business, or profession, public or private.

There are few national institutions of more value and interest to the country than this Royal Military College. It is a Government Institution, designed primarily for the purpose of giving the highest technical instructions in all branches of Military Science to Cadets and Officers of the Canadian Militia. In fact, it is intended to take the place in Canada of the English Woolwich and Sandhurst and the American West Point.

The Commandant and Military Instructors are all Officers on the active list, and, in addition, there is a complete staff of Professors for the civil subjects which form a large proportion of the College Course. Medical attendance is also provided.

Whilst the College is organized on a strictly Military basis, the Cadets receive, in addition to their Military Studies, a thoroughly practical, scientific and sound training in all subjects that are essential to a superior and general modern education.

The Course in Mathematics is very complete, and a thorough grounding is given in the subjects of Civil Engineering, Civil and Hydrographic Surveying, Physics, Chemistry, French and English.

The strict discipline maintained at the College is one of the most valuable features of the system.

In addition, the constant practice of Gymnastics, Drills and outdoor exercises of all kinds, ensures good health and fine physical condition.

Seven commissions in His Majesty's regular Army are annually awarded as prizes to the Cadets.

Three Commissions in the Permanent Force are given annually, should vacancies exist, to the Graduating Class, videlicet: Every year one in the Infantry; and each alternate year:

One in the Engineers and one in the Horse Artillery.

One in the Cavalry, or Mounted Rifles, and one in the Garrison Artillery.

Further, every three years a Commission in the Ordnance Corps is given to the graduating Class.

Three Second Class Clerkships, or appointments with equivalent pay, are offered annually to the graduating Class, such appointments to be in the following Departments, videlicet: Public Works, Railways and Canals, Inland Revenue, Agriculture and Interior.

The length of the Course is three years, in three terms of nine and a half months' residence each.

The total cost of the three years' Course, including Board, Uniforms, instructional material, and all extras, is from $750 to $800,

The annual competitive examination for admission to the College takes place at the Headquarters of the several Military Districts in which Candidates reside, in May of each year.

NOTE.—An historical sketch of the establishment of the Military College at Kingston is given on pages 62-65 of the First Volume of "The Establishment of Schools and Colleges in Ontario."

PART XIV.

THE EDUCATION AND TRAINING OF PUBLIC SCHOOL TEACHERS AND DIRECTORS OF KINDERGARTENS.

PREFATORY AND EXPLANATORY NOTE.—In providing that part of this Volume relating to the Training of Teachers of the Public Schools, and the Directors of Kindergartens, I have included in it as large a portion of the programme of Study and the official Applications of the Education Department on the subject as would give a clear and connected view of the comprehensive scheme adopted by the Department for the official training and preparation of Teachers and Directors for their important work. I have done so for two reasons. First, that I might thus be able to present a complete and connected view of the whole subject of the Training of Teachers, and, Secondly, that I might be able to furnish the prospective and more youthful Teachers with a valuable *Vade Mecum* to assist the former in coming to a decision as to whether they would adopt Teaching as a Profession, and to aid and stimulate the latter, by the valuable suggestions, examples and illustrations contained in these papers, to renewed efforts—make his, or her services a success in the profession as complete as possible.

It can be well understood that the Education Department, in presenting so comprehensive a scheme, could not avoid a good deal of explanatory detail. I have, however, wherever practicable, condensed these details as much as possible, while not lessening the value of the suggestions, or information, contained in them.

THE PROFESSIONAL TRAINING OF SCHOOL TEACHERS.

The following is a brief description of the means under the control of the Education Department of Ontario for preparing young men and women in the Province for the teaching profession. They are:

(1) The Provincial Model Schools, at Cornwall, Durham, Kingston, Orillia, Renfrew, and North Bay.

(2) The Normal Schools at Hamilton, London, North Bay, Ottawa, Peterborough, Stratford, and Toronto.

(3) The Faculties of Education of the Universities of Toronto and Queen's.

The necessity for providing properly trained Teachers for the Public Schools of the Province was recognized by the establishment of the Toronto Normal School, in 1847, where Students received Academic and Professional Education for First, Second and Third Class Teachers. Other Institutions of the kind were needed, and the Ottawa Normal School was accordingly opened in 1875. In 1908, additional Normal Schools were established at Hamilton, Peterborough and Stratford, and, in 1909, at North Bay.

The Professional Education of Teachers is now given at the Normal Schools for those only who hold a Second Class Certificate. There are Provincial Normal Model Schools at Toronto and Ottawa, where the Normal School Students get practice in Teaching. There are no Provincial Model Schools at any of the other Normal Schools, but the Public Schools are used for the purpose as a substitute.

County Model Schools were established in 1877 for training Teachers for the Elementary Schools. They were discontinued in 1907, except those that were retained for special purposes

In 1908, Model Schools for the Professional Education of Teachers were established by the Department of Education at eight different centres, and in 1909 at six and in 1910 at six.

The rapid growth of the High Schools and Collegiate Institutes made an increasing demand for properly trained Teachers. This was met to some extent by the establishment of Training Institutes at four of the leading Collegiate Institutes, such as Guelph, Hamilton, Kingston and Strathroy in 1886 and Owen Sound in 1888. Graduates from these and other Schools who had the necessary scholarship were given a course of training in Methods of Teaching for four months of the year, after which Certificates were awarded, as the result of a written and practical examination.

It was soon felt that Student-Teachers needed a course of training in the Science of Education and Psychology before the best advantages could be secured from observation and practice in teaching.

The establishment of the School of Pedagogy in Toronto, in 1890, was the outcome. The removal to Hamilton in 1897 of that Institution as a Normal College secured the advantages of both features of a High School Teachers' professional training. In the Normal College, therefore, the benefits of Training Institutes and the School of Pedagogy were combined. The facilities were ample for enabling candidates to obtain not only a theoretical but a practical knowledge of all that pertains to High and Public School work.

The Course of Instruction and Training in the Normal College comprehended, (1) Educational Psychology; the History and Criticisms of Educational Systems; the Science and Art of Education. (2) School Organization and Management; Lectures on Kindergarten principles and practice; Lecture, with practical illustrations, on the best methods of teaching the subjects in the several departments of Mathematics; English, Classics, Science and Modern Languages; Observation and Practice in the Collegiate Institute, and affiliated Schools; Criticisms and suggestions upon the practice lessons of the Teachers in training. (3) Instruction in Reading and Elocution; Temperance and Hygiene; Writing and Drawing; Drill, Gymnastics and Calisthenics.

In May, 1907, the Normal College was discontinued and the Course of Instruction and Training was then given at the University of Toronto, and Queen's University, Kingston, under the name of the Faculty of Education. The first Session commenced at the Universities in October, 1907.

THE COUNTY MODEL SCHOOLS.

The establishment of County Model Schools dates back to the year 1843. The first Schools Act for Upper Canada, passed in that year, declares:

That it shall and may be lawful for the Court of Wardens of any County in Upper Canada . . . to raise and levy by County rate a sum not exceeding £200, ($800), and to appropriate and expend the same for the maintenance of one or more " County

Model Schools," within such County, and to constitute, by By-law, or By-laws, to that effect, any Township, Town, or City, School, or Schools within the County, to be for any term not less than one year, such County Model School, or Schools, etcetera.

The 66th Section of the same Act declares:

That in every such Township, Town, or City Model School, gratuitous instruction shall be given to Teachers of Common Schools.

The Schools Act of 1846 also provided for the establishment of District Model Schools, in which "instruction shall be afforded to all Teachers of Common Schools within the District." They were thus Normal Schools in miniature, for the persons under instruction were already Teachers.

In 1850, when the whole machinery of the School System was revised and reorganized, the Act provided for the establishment and maintenance of Township Model Schools in place of County ones.

SYLLABUS OF COURSES AND REGULATIONS FOR THE COUNTY MODEL SCHOOLS OF ONTARIO.

(1) The Model Schools are situated at Cornwall, Durham, Kingston, Orillia, and Renfrew. Provision is also made at the North Bay Normal School for Model School Work.

(2) The purpose of the Model Schools is to prepare Teachers of the Third Class, in the Theory and the Art of organizing, governing, and instructing the Pupils of the Public and the Separate Schools; and to improve the general culture of such Teachers and, in particular, their academic preparation for teaching the subjects prescribed in the Programme of Studies.

(3) The attached Urban Public and Separate Schools, and the attached Rural Schools, are used, as required, to afford the Teachers-in-training adequate means of observing well-conducted Schools, and of securing practice in Teaching, Discipline, and Management. Application for admission shall be made to the Deputy Minister not later than August 15th, on a form to be supplied by him.

(4) (1) The Applicant shall forward with his application to the Deputy Minister, the following Certificates:—

(*a*) A Certificate from competent authority that he will be at least eighteen years of age before December 31st.

(*b*) A Certificate from a Clergyman, or other competent authority, that he is of good moral character.

(*c*) A Certificate from a Physician that he is physically able for the work of a Teacher, and, especially, that he is free from serious pulmonary affection and from seriously defective eyesight or hearing.

(2) The applicant shall also submit one of the following:—

(*a*) A Certificate of having passed the District Certificate Examination of 1904, or any subsequent year.

(*b*) A Certificate of having passed the Examination for Entrance into the Model School.

(*c*) A Certificate of having passed the July Examination for Entrance into the Normal Schools, or Faculties of Education, or of having obtained 50 per cent. of the aggregate marks in either of these Examinations, with 34 per cent.

in each Paper; provided that in all such cases the Candidate satisfies the Principal of the Model School that he is competent in the subjects of the Model School Entrance Examination, which are not required at the said July Examinations. For either of the above Examinations 40 per cent. of the aggregate and 25 per cent. in each Paper to be accepted.

Duties of Principals and Assistants.

(1) Subject to the Regulations and to the approval of the Minister of Education, the Principal of each Model School shall prescribe the duties of his Staff and shall be responsible for the efficiency of the Model School.

(2) The Members of each Staff shall be subject to the authority of the Principal.

Duties of Teachers-in-Training.

(1) Teachers-in-training shall board and lodge at such Houses only as are approved of by the Principal.

(2) They shall attend regularly and punctually, and shall submit to such discipline and directions as the Principal may prescribe.

(3) Teachers-in-training who, in the opinion of the Staff, are unduly defective in scholarship, or whose conduct, or progress, is unsatisfactory, may be dismissed by the Principal at any time during the Session from further attendance at the Model School.

(4) All Applicants are strongly advised to review carefully before entering, the work of the Lower School and of the High Schools.

7.—(1) The Text-books for the academic work shall be those prescribed in such subjects for the High Schools.

(2) The Text-books for the professional work shall be those prescribed for the Public Schools.

8.—A Literary Society for general culture and for professional advancement shall be established in each Model School, and shall be fostered.

Subjects and Values of Examination.

9.—(1) (a) The final standing of the Teacher-in-training shall be determined on the combined results of his sessional records (including Class Tests and Observation and Practice-teaching) and the prescribed final Examination.

(b) The final Examination Papers shall be uniform for all the Model Schools, and shall be based upon the Courses as laid down in this Syllabus.

(2) (a) The Examinations in Groups II. and III. shall include a thorough test of the academic qualifications of the Teacher-in-training.

(b) At the Examination in Groups I. and II. there shall be one paper on each of the following subjects, and the maximum marks for each subject of the examination shall be as follows: the marks for the Sessional Records in each subject being 20 per cent. of the maximum.

Group I.—Professional.—Principles of Education, School Organization and Management, each 100.

Group II.—Academic and Professional.—Arithmetic, Literature, Grammar, History, Composition, Geography, and Nature Study, each 100.

Group III.—(3) The marks counted in estimating the final standing of the Teacher-in-training in the following subjects shall be those awarded him during the Session, more especially towards the close thereof, for the oral, written, and practical tests in matter and, where applicable, in method, the maximum for each subject being as follows:—

Academic and Professional.—Art, Music, Reading, Spelling, Writing, Physical Training, and Physiology and Hygiene, each 100; School Law and Regulations, 50.

Group IV.—(4) The marks counted in estimating the final standing of the Teacher-in-training in Observation and Practice-teaching shall be those awarded him in these subjects during the Session, and more especially towards the close thereof, after an introductory Course of Lessons in each. The maximum marks for Practice-teaching shall be 1,000, and those for Observation lessons 200.

Certificates.

10.—(1) A Teacher-in-training who at the final Examination obtains 40 per cent. of the marks in each subject and 60 per cent. of the aggregate of the marks for each of Groups I., II., III., IV. may on the recommendation of the Staff be awarded a Limited Third Class Certificate valid for five years.

(2) A Teacher-in-training who fails at the final Examination in either or both of Groups I. and II., but who passes in Groups III. and IV., may, on the recommendation of the Staff and Board of Examiners, obtain a Limited Third Class Certificate, without attending a second Session, by passing at a subsequent Examination in the Group, or Groups, in which he has failed. All other Candidates who fail shall attend a second Session.

(3) Candidates who are exempt from attendance at a Model School and who are actually engaged in teaching shall be exempt from an Examination in Group IV., provided they submit to the Minister a Certificate from their last Inspector that they have taught successfully for at least six months. The pass standard shall be 40 per cent. of the marks for each subject and 60 per cent. of the aggregate of marks for each of Groups I., II., and III.

Programme of Studies.

11.—(1) The Courses of Study for Teachers-in-training shall consist of the following:—

(*a*) A review, as far as time will permit, of the Public School Course and of the academic subjects, from the standpoint of Pedagogy and the requirements of the Public and Separate Schools, including special instruction in Reading, Writing, Art, Physical Training, Physiology and Hygiene, Music, School Law and Regulations.

(*b*) The Principles of Education and General Methodology, Special Methodology, and School Organization and Management.

(*c*) Supervised Observation in the Public Schools.

(*d*) Supervised Practice Teaching in the Public Schools.

12.—(1) In order that the Teacher-in-Training may begin early the Observation work and the Practice-teaching, the following introductory Courses shall be taken up in the following order:

(*a*) The prime essentials of the Course in the Principles of Education and General Methodology.

(*b*) A Course of Observation in the different forms of the Public Schools.

As soon as the Course begins, one Lesson a day shall be given in the Course in (*a*) and in (*b*), the total number in each being from ten to fifteen.

(2) To prevent the dissipation of energy which would result from the concurrent study of a large number of subjects diverse in contents, the system of intensive study should be followed so far as circumstances will permit. In the order of the Courses and the grouping of the subjects, due regard should be had to the character of each subject and its natural relations, and to the logical development of the Courses and their relative functional value in the Pedagogy of the Public School Programme. When a subject has been finished, it should from time to time be reviewed with a further extension of the most important parts, having due regard to its character and importance.

(*a*) On the professional side, after the completion of the Introductory Course [12 (1) (*a*)] the Course in the Principles of Education should be taken up three times a week until finished. The Course in School Organization and Management should be taken up from the first three times a week until finished.

(*b*) The minimum number of periods for each of the professional and academic subjects should be as nearly as practicable as follows:

The Principles of Education, including the Introductory Course, 35; School Organization and Management, 30; School Law and Regulations, 5; Arithmetic, 20; Grammar, 15; Literature, 15; History, 10; Geography, 15; Language and Composition, 20; Spelling, 8; Reading, 20; Nature Study, 15; Physiology and Hygiene, 8; Art, 15; Music, 10; Physical Training, 8; Writing, 15.

Observation and Practice Teaching.

13.—(1) The Introductory Courses provided for in Regulation 12 (1) (*b*) shall be followed by systematic Observation and Practice-teaching, the minimum number of Observation lessons being 30 and of Practice-teaching lessons 20; but these numbers shall be increased to meet the necessities of individual Teachers-in-training.

(2) (*a*) The Teachers-in-training shall be divided into suitable groups, and the work of Observation and Practice-teaching shall be taken up systematically per time-table arranged from time to time.

(*b*) At least that group to which the Teacher-in-Training belongs shall be present at the discussions on his Observation and Practice-teaching Lessons.

(3) The Observation and Practice-teaching Lessons for each Teacher-in-training shall, as far as practicable, be arranged so as to cover the work of the Public Schools in all subjects and in all grades.

(4) (*a*) Teachers-in-training shall be notified by the Principal of the subject and the scope of the Observation Lesson, and shall prepare the Lesson beforehand.

(*b*) After observing the Lesson, they shall submit a report upon it to the Teacher concerned.

(5) (*a*) Teachers-in-training shall be notified of the subject and the scope of the Practice-teaching Lesson, by the Teacher of the Public School, after consultation with the Principal.

(*b*) Teachers-in-training shall prepare a plan of each Practice-teaching Lesson for submission to the Teacher concerned.

(6) Model Lessons for Observation by the Students shall be taught by the Teachers of the School in accordance with the regular Programme of the Model School.

(*a*) The necessary applications of the Principles of Education and of Special Methodology shall be made systematically by the Model School Principal in connection with the Model and the Observation Lessons and the Practice-teaching; so that the Course may be taken up in terms of the child's mind and growth.

(*b*) Concerted work on the part of the Teachers in the Model School shall be secured by frequent conferences, especially before the work concerned begins.

Syllabus of Courses.

Educational Principles and General Methodology.

14.—The object of this Course is to provide Teachers with such a working conception of the nature of Education and of Methodology as will improve natural tact and skill by determining procedure and forming ideals.

(1) **Aim of Education**: Examination of some of the current definitions of Education; relation of aim to procedure in Education.

(2) **Function of the School**: The relation of the School to other social institutions—the Home, the Church, the State, the vocation.

(3) **Subject Matter of Instruction**: Purpose and value of subjects of study.

(4) **Methods of Instruction**: Purpose of methods of instruction; necessity of basing methods of instruction on the knowledge of the laws of mental development.

(5) **Instincts and Interests**: The place of natural tendencies in the development of mental life; a study of some of the more significant of the child's instincts and interests; methods of eliminating, strengthening or modifying instincts, or interests.

(6) **Habit and Association**: Nature of habit; relation of habit to instinct; condition of the formation of habits; the laws of habit applied to school studies, especially to those involving the acquisition of skill, such as Writing, Reading, **Manual Training**, Art, etcetera; the place of habit in character formation; nature of association; conditions of association; relation of association to habit; how to form permanent associations.

(7) **Apperception**: Nature of apperception; necessity for making subjects taught meaningful; the process of interpreting the new in terms of the old applied to School Studies; significance of the maxim, " Proceed from the known to the related unknown."

(8) **Attention**: Nature of attention as a process; conditions of attention; relation of attention to habit and association; interest in its relation to attention; voluntary and non-voluntary attention distinguished; attention in young children

and in adults compared; methods of securing and retaining attention; obstacles to attention.

(9) **Retention:** Conditions of retention; the relation of retention and apperception; the factors in efficient recall; functions of the drill lesson and of the review lesson; methods of conducting drill and review.

(10) **Individual and General Notions:** How they are distinguished from each other; how individual notions should be approached and presented; how to proceed from individual to general notions; the value of types in the development of general notions; how general notions should be applied.

(11) **Laws underlying the Process of Teaching:** The relation of analysis to synthesis, of induction to deduction.

(12) **Impression and Expression:** Their interdependence; importance of this **interdependence as the basis for the constructive side of School work; its bearing upon the development of character.

(13) **The Plan of the Recitation:** Adjustment to the needs of the capacities of the pupils; relation of previous work; examination of the "five formal steps" of the Herbartians.

(14) **Teaching Devices:** Use of questioning in the development of the individual and general notions; right and wrong methods of questioning; examination of the so-called Socratic method; answers; qualities of a good answer; treatment of faulty answers; mistakes in dealing with answers; illustrations; their office and value.

Books of Reference.—McMurry—Method of the Recitation.   Gordy—Psychology.   Tilley—Methods of Teaching.

School Organization and Management.

15.—The object of the Course is to give the Teacher, in the light of the **principles of education, a knowledge of the technique of School Management and Organization, which shall enable him to secure the smooth and efficient working of his School.** The Course includes the following topics:

(1) **The Teacher:** Natural qualifications of a good Teacher; importance of **scholarship, of training, of experience, of professional studies, of wide culture, of Teachers' Associations, etcetera; the Teacher's relations with the Principal, the Inspector, Trustees and Parents; civic and social duties; personal power and influence in the School, in the community;** daily preparation for teaching; correcting written exercises; care of health.

(2) **Classification:** The meaning and the problems of School organization; promotions, when and how ma**de;** in graded Schools the division of subjects and pupils among the several Teachers.

(3) **The Daily Programme:** Its purpose and value; principles involved in the construction of a Time-table; Seat work; individual Blackboard work; the ques**tion of** fatigue; typical Time-tables for graded and for ungraded Schools; School records.

(4) **Written Examinations:** Good effects; bad effects; School results that **cannot be tested by examinations;** how to set Examination Papers; reading and valuing the answers; Examinations as related to promotions.

(5) School-room Routine: Chief varieties of mechanizing routine, their advantages and disadvantages; appointment of Monitors.

(6) Desirable School Habits: Punctuality; neatness in person and in work; accuracy; quietness; industry; obedience; the relation of the preceding to moral training.

(7) School Incentives: Kinds and office; effects on character, on School work, on health.

(8) Order and Discipline: What is meant by good order; the chief elements of governing power; faults and how to avoid them; co-operation of School and Home; punishment; ends and necessity; right conditions; characteristics of judicious punishment; injudicious punishment; the discipline of consequences.

(9) Physical Education: Relations of physical and intellectual development; importance of change of work; value of plays and games; organized, or unorganized, play; dangers of fatigue; the Teacher on the playground; physical exercise within the School.

(10) The Kindergarten: Its essential principles; relation to the School System as a whole.

Special Methodology.

16.—The object of the Course is to prepare the Teachers-in-training for intelligently observing and teaching in all grades of the attached Public Schools, by enabling them to apply the principles of education and, in particular, to adapt to the work in each subject the principles of General Method. The work in the special method of each subject is introduced by a few lessons of a general character, embracing the application of the principles of General Methodology to the teaching of the subject. These introductory Lessons are followed by a series of a more detailed character, dealing with:

(1) The selection and the organization of material for the Public School Forms, taken in order, from the standpoint of presentation to the pupil.

(2) The discussion of special methods of instruction concurrent with the academic review of the subject matter.

The Courses shall be taken up in terms of the Public School Programme of Studies, the provisions of which shall be constantly kept in mind.

General Books of Reference.—Chubb—Teaching of English. Hodge—Nature Study and Life. Dearness—How to Teach Nature Study. Silcox and Stevenson—Nature Study. Geikie—Teaching of Geography. Annandale—The Concise Imperial Dictionary.

Language and Composition.

17.—The special object of the Course in Language and Composition is to prepare the Teacher to train his Pupils to speak and to write good English as a fixed, unconscious habit. The Course includes the following topics:

The importance of language training; the place of a knowledge of the mother tongue in education; the value of clearness, force and grace of expression.

Oral and Written Composition: Their relation; how habits of speaking and writing correctly are formed; the effect of the Teacher's example upon the pupil's language; importance of Libraries for supplementary reading; influences opposed to good usage; incidental work in language training; expression as a stage in the development of every Lesson; necessity for special exercises in oral and written Composition.

Methods in Oral and Written Composition: Methods of encouraging pupil's free natural expression and of extending his vocabulary through oral exercises; principles governing criticism of oral work; the dangers connected therewith and the means of avoiding them; value of formal linguistic exercises; the relation of a knowledge of grammatical rules to the development of correct forms in speech; method of correcting common errors; relative value of pupil's own language and of special exercises in false syntax as material for criticism; the principles to be kept in view in conducting exercises in written composition; supervision and aid during writing; value of topical outlines; the place of Home-work in written Compositions; methods of correcting Compositions; value of re-writing.

Mechanics of Written Composition: Sentence and paragraph structure; paragraph Compositions; the use of capitals, punctuation marks, quotation marks, abbreviations, etcetera.

Materials for Written and Oral Composition: Principles governing choice of topics; gathering, selecting and arranging material; class answers as material for oral composition; importance of framing questions that will require answers of considerable length; the reproduction of fairy and folk stories, Fables, Poems, Biographies; relative value of reading and telling Stories; transition from reproduction to originality; descriptions of personal experiences, real and imaginary; pictures suggestive of stories, School games, autobiographies of familiar things; developing themes from minor incidents, themes connected with School studies, general themes; Letter Writing, with special attention to form and style; invitations and replies thereto; bills, receipts, promissory notes, etcetera.

Reading.

18.—The special object of the Course in Reading is to prepare the Teacher to train his pupils to get the writer's thought and feelings (*intelligent reading*) and to communicate them to the listener so that he may appreciate them (*intelligible reading*). The Course includes the following topics:—

The Scope of Reading: Its correlation with other subjects; importance of training in reading and the principles of vocal expression to pupil's ordinary speech and general culture; the limitations of the pupil's ability to interpret words; his previous preparation.

Forms of Reading: The function and value of silent reading, sight reading, dramatic reading, elocution, declamation.

Methods in Reading: Examination of the various methods of teaching beginners to read; advantages and disadvantages of each; devices for securing rapid word recognition and for fixing attention on the thought as well as upon the word forms in the earlier stages; means of securing natural expressive reading; the place and limitations of imitative reading; common faults on the part of both pupil and Teacher and how to correct them; criticism by Teacher and by pupils. Change in purpose and methods of reading as determined by the development of the pupil's experience and powers; the necessity for giving attention to expression in all stages; the objects of advanced reading; methods of developing in pupils the habit of reading for thought and pleasure; reading as a means of creating and fostering a taste for good literature.

Spelling.

19.—The special object of the course in Spelling is to prepare the Teacher to secure accuracy in the mechanism of written word-expression. The Course includes the following topics:

Scope of Spelling: Its correlation with other subjects; causes of the difficulties experienced by pupils in learning to spell; causes of incorrect spelling.

Methods in Spelling: Necessity for teaching, not merely testing, spelling; examination of the various methods of teaching spelling; the adaptation of each to the nature of the words and to the individual mental characteristics of pupils; phonic exercises and word-building in relation to spelling; syllabication; the place of transcription and dictation; methods of checking and correcting errors; value of re-writing; prevention *versus* correction; the character of drill and review exercises in spelling; methods of varying the spelling recitation; value of rules in spelling.

Materials for Spelling: Principles of selection of material for spelling; grouping of words for the purpose of spelling; incidental spelling; uses of the Dictionary and of the Spelling-book.

Literature.

20.—The special object of the Course in Literature is to prepare the Teacher to create in his pupils a taste for good literaeure, while broadening their knowledge, moulding their characters, and aiding them to appreciate the beauty and the power of artistic expression of thought and feeling. The Course includes the following topics:—

Selection of subject-matter for Literature Lessons: Qualities of literature that appeal to children of different ages; basis of selection of material for different grades; lists of suitable fairy tales, fables, nature stories, etcetera, adapted to children of lower grades, and of general works for pupils in the higher forms; complete wholes *versus* extracts.

Methods in teaching Literature: Methods of dealing with primary Literature; comparison of values of reading and telling; the application of the general principles of method to the teaching of Literature; method in supplementary reading contrasted with that in exact study; the importance and method of memorizing selections; the value of oral reading in the interpretation and appreciation of Literature; the importance of the Teacher's own ability to read well.

Lesson Procedure: Preparation of the pupils; necessity for preparing a suitable mood for the Lesson; how far the Author's biography has a place here; preliminary reading of the selection; the main thought of the Lesson grasped in a more or less indefinite way through a reading of it; the analysis of a selection into its wider thought-elements and the analysis of these again into their elements; the place of explanation of words and phrases; the use of the Dictionary; the relation of the subordinate thoughts to the unity of the whole; the main thought of the selection as made definite by the analysis; the oral reading of the selection by pupils after study; the value of oral and written reproduction; suitable seat work.

Examinations in Literature: Difficulties of examining in Literature; specimen Examination Questions.

Teacher's preparation: Special importance of Teacher's own qualifications; sessional private Reading-courses for Teachers-in-training; suggestions for their future reading.

School Library: Principles to be kept in view in selecting works for the School Library; methods of making use of School Library; means of securing the co-operation of the Home in the pupil's reading.

Grammar.

21.—The special object of the Course in Grammar is to prepare the Teacher to secure precision of expression on the part of his Pupils, to train them in habits of logical analysis, and to give them a basis for self-criticism in language by developing the principles of language structure. The Course includes the following topics:—

Meaning of Grammar; the relation of Grammar to Speech; correlation with other subjects; reasons for and against retaining it in elementary Schools; reasons for deferring the formal study till Form IV.

The sentence as the starting point; basal value of function; order and method of teaching the parts of speech; principles of classification as applied to Grammar; inflection, use and value of our remaining inflections; rules of syntax, their value; use of grammatical terminology; definitions, their value; how to be obtained, how to be applied; analysis and parsing, aim and value of each; value of diagrams; oral and written exercises; treament of false syntax.

History.

22.—The special object of the Course in History is to prepare the Teacher to train pupils to adapt human experiences to present situations. In the elementary stages the chief objects are to arouse an interest in historical studies, to enable the pupils to appreciate the logical sequence of events, and to give them a knowledge of their civil rights and duties; also to stimulate a love of Country. The Course includes the following topics:—

The scope of History: The correlation of history with other subjects, especially Geography; the special value of Canadian and of British history; the proper perspective in the development of the subjects; parts enlarged in the academic review; what makes an event important.

Methods: The Recitation, its form and purposes; the place of oral teaching and of Blackboard work by Teacher, and of written exercises at Seat and at Blackboard by pupils; methods in oral and in written work; the use of Pictures, Maps, etcetera; of Readers and of the Text-book; relation of method to the personality of the Teacher and his knowledge of the subject; special importance of preparation of Lesson by Teacher owing to mass of detail; errors to be avoided.

The selection and arrangement of material suitable for different grades; the place and purpose of each of the following:—

History of the Aborigines, Pioneers, local History.

Biography: The natural attractiveness of Biography; the relation of biography to history; the effects of a study of biography on the development of character; selection of suitable biographies for pupils of different grades, as the lives of Explorers, Navigators, and Soldiers for primary grades; of Statesmen, Poets, Scientists, etcetera, as representing more complex conditions, for pupils of higher grades.

Civics: Ends to be kept in view in teaching Civics; consideration of work to be undertaken in Civics; study of Civic Institutions as appearing in their lowest forms among primitive peoples; the beginnings of governments, of Courts, of School Systems, of Factories, of means of Transportation, etcetera, study of present forms of Civic Institutions.

Epochs: Their relation to biography; systematic chronological study of history; its value and its dangers; the casual sequence of events.

Supplementary material: The use of Mythology, Ballads, Orations, Epics, Legends, tales of Chivalry, narrative Poems, and historical Novels; character of history Readers and of supplementary works for the different grades. Significance and value of the National Flag.

Geography.

23.—The special object of the Course in Geography is to prepare the Teacher to extend the pupils' knowledge of the earth and its relation to life thereon, and to assist them in interpreting and utilizing their physical environment in accordance with their needs. The Course includes the following topics:—

The scope of Geography: Its relation to other subjects, especially to Nature Study, History, and Elementary Science.

The review of the Course should lay special emphasis on the study of the Earth's Surface and the changes wrought thereon by the various agencies; rock formation and Soils; distribution of Mineral products; Plant and Animal Life; the Earth's relation to other Heavenly Bodies; Weather and Climate; Man's relation to the rest of the world; Commercial and Political Geography.

Methods: Consideration of the order of development of the subject in rural and urban Schools; the use of Maps, Globes, Pictures, Blackboard Drawings, Natural Objects, specimens of Products, Stereoscopic views; Modelling, Map Drawing, Scales and Projections; Weather observations and records, simple experiments in explanation of Natural Phenomena (See course in Experimental Science); Excursions in connection with the observations in local Geography; the use of Reference Library, Books of Travel, Geography Readers, etcetera; common mistakes in teaching Geography and means of avoiding them; special importance of preparation of Lesson by Teacher owing to mass of details.

Nature Study.

24.—The special object of the Course in Nature Study is to broaden and deepen the Teacher's sympathies and interests, and, through him, those of his pupils, by training them to observe and interpret the common Phenomena of the World about him. The Course includes the following topics:—

The character and scope of Nature Study: Its relation to formal Science; its correlation with other subjects.

Material for Nature Study: Conditions determining the choice of material for Nature Study Lessons for pupils of different grades, and for varying conditions in rural and urban Schools; uses and limitations of Books, Pictures, Models, Collections, etcetera; supplementary materials, such as Stories, Literature, etcetera.

Methods in Nature Study: Nature Study as a method; special characteristics of a typical Nature Study Lesson; directions for conducting School Excursions. The study of special topics dealing with materials of Nature Study and illustrating methods of presentation in all grades of Public Schools, the topics to be typical and to be selected from various grades and departments of the Public School Course of Study.

NOTE.—Teachers-in-training should make frequent local excursions for the purpose of studying materials in their natural environment and relations. They should make collections of different kinds for their own use as well as to enable them to direct as Teachers the practical side of Nature Study. The nature of the collections will be regulated by the kind of School in which the Student will likely teach; rural Teachers should make collections of Weeds, Weed Seeds, economic plants, diseased plants, injurious and beneficial insects, etcetera; urban Teachers, of Factory Products, Garden flowers, etcetera.

Arithmetic.

25.—The special object of the Course in Arithmetic is to improve the Teacher's knowledge of the subject that he may use it effectively as a means of logical training, and more particularly that he may be prepared to give his pupils such instruction in the various arithmetical processes, as will enable them to make with accuracy, rapidity, and facility the calculations and computations which their future life may render necessary. The Course includes the following topics:—

The scope of Arithmetic; its relation to the other subjects of the Curriculum; importance of its practical aspects as related to the lives of the pupils; danger of over-estimating its value as training in logic; the various steps involved in the development of the number idea; the unit, its nature and use; the necessity for standard units; number, a ratio.

Methods in Arithmetic: Analysis and Synthesis, Induction and Deduction, compared, illustrated, and applied; graphic methods; use of concrete material in making clear new processes and in verifying and interpreting operations performed; the use of Text-books and of prescribed Apparatus; the importance of training in, and devices to secure, neatness, accuracy and speed in computation; the importance, place, and treatment of Oral Arithmetic; the value of Problems; the essentials of proper solutions; solutions by full analysis, and by performing operations only; "unitary" method and method of direct measurement; grading of Problems; interest in Problems for which the pupils themselves furnish the material; Blackboard work; Drill and examination work in Arithmetic.

A thorough treatment of the various arithmetical operations and their applications with special stress upon the requirements of Teachers engaged in Public School work. They should include the following:—

Counting; measuring with standard units; numbers 1 to 10, from 10 to 20 etcetera; number Pictures; Notation and Numeration; Addition-tables, exercises, devices; subtraction by decomposition, by equal additions, and by complementary additions; multiplication, relation to other operations, tables, exercises, factors; division, short and long, factoring, cancellation, division by factors; measures and multiples.

Fractions: How and when to be introduced, different interpretations, notations, rules for operations deduced and applied; decimal fractions, correspondence of methods of numeration, notation, and operations with those of integers, recurring decimals.

Applied Arithmetic: Percentage, Trade Discount, Commission, Insurance, Taxes, Interest, Discount, Stocks, Exchange; Tables of Weights and Measures; the Metric System; Mensuration, including the Areas of Rectangles, Triangles, Parallelograms, and Circles, and the volume of Rectangular Solids, Cylinders, and Prisms; Square root.

Writing.

26.—The object of the Course in Writing is to train the Teacher to write rapidly and legibly, and to make him familiar with the best means of securing the most satisfactory results in the teaching of the subject. This Course includes the following topics:—

The purpose of writing; its correlation with other subjects.

Penholding; position at the Desk; position of the Paper; the proper formation of the small and the Capital Letters and the figures; various movement exercises; practice on Paper and on the Blackboard.

Use of Headlines and Copybooks; use of Blank paper; its ruling; value of transcription, dictation and composition in writing; use of the Blackboard to teach the correct form of each Letter singly and in combination; how general and individual faults are corrected; the formation of a characteristic hand; how to deal with pupils having some physical disability.

NOTE.—After the Teacher-in-training has mastered in Class the proper formation of the letters, etcetera, and the movement exercises, the Master should require him to hand in from time to time exercises for criticism until his handwriting is satisfactory.

Art Work.

27.—The special object of the Course in Art is to give the Teacher such a knowledge of the subject, such a training of his æsthetic nature, and such facility in the use of Art as a means of expression, as will enable him to develop like tastes and powers in his pupils. The Course includes the following topics:—

The scope of Art: Art as a mode of expression and a means of æsthetic culture; its correlation with other subjects in the School Course.

Freehand Drawing: How to use the various mediums: pencil, charcoal, crayon, ink with pen or brush; the drawing of common flat objects, such as leaves, grasses, brooms, shovels, saws, hammers, in an appropriate medium; the drawing of common spherical, cylindrical and rectangular solids, illustrating the principles of reehand perspective; the grouping of objects; simple landscapes from nature and imagination; illustration of games, occupations, nursery rhymes and stories, pose drawing; drawing from casts.

Blackboard Drawing: The use of white, black and coloured crayons on the Blackboard and on large pieces of paper; rapid illustrative sketches to aid in the teaching of all subjects; Blackboard drawing specially important to the Teacher as a means of expression; the representation in colour, neutral values, and sepia, of leaves, grasses, flowers, fruits, trees, insects, pet animals, birds, and common objects; the grouping of objects; simple landscapes from nature and imagination; elementary composition of pictures.

Books of Reference—Prang's Text Books of Art Education; 7 books, $2.40. Prang's Drawing Course.

Music.

28.—The special object of the Course in Music is to train the Teacher in the use of Music as a means of self-expression and of æsthetic culture. The Course includes the following topics:—

Tunes: Practice in singing from the staff and tonic-solfa modulators; intervals of moderate difficulty, contained in the major diatonic scales; modulation from any given key to its relative minor, and its dominant and subdominant.

Time: Practice in singing rhythmical studies in simple or compound duple, triple, or quadruple time; the pulse as the unit of measurement in time, with its divisions into halves, quarters, or thirds in varied combination.

Voice Culture: Practice in correct tone production; vowel formation; enunciation of consonants; breath control; correct intonation; and the equalization of the various registers of the voice.

Songs: The study of Songs suited to the requirements of pupils in all grades of Public and Separate Schools, with special attention to development of power in musical expression.

Notation: Elements of notation, both tonic-solfa and staff; the formation of the major and minor diatonic scales; elements of modulation and transposition.

Methods: Concurrently with the foregoing Course, a practical knowledge of recognized systems of teaching the tonic-solfa and staff notations.

NOTE.—Teachers-in-training who, from any cause, consider themselves incapable of learning to Sing should present their cases to the Teacher of Music at the beginning of the Term. If, on examination, it should be found necessary, special instruction will be provided, adapted to their needs; and their efforts to overcome any natural disability which may be found to exist will be taken into account at the oral examination at the close of the Term. The written examinations, however, are compulsory for all students, and, if the Teacher-in-training is unable to sing, his Certificate will state so.

Physiology and Hygiene.

29.—The object of the Course in Hygiene is to train the Teacher in the knowledge requisite for the maintenance of the health of both himself and his pupils, and to qualify him for supervising the sanitary conditions of the School and its surroundings. The Course includes the following topics:—

Contagious and Infectious Diseases: How to detect existence of common infectious and contagious diseases; modes of preventing spread of these diseases; sanitary legislation; duties of the Teacher.

Personal Hygiene: Care of teeth, skin, eyes and ears; relation of exercise to health; effects of alcohol and tobacco.

Accidents and Emergencies: First aid in such cases as fainting, suffocation, drowning, hemorrhage, fractures and dislocations, venomous stings, poisoning, frost-bites, sunstroke and heat-stroke; burns; bandaging.

Physical Training.

30.—The special object of the Course in Physical Culture is to enable the Teacher to make proper provision for the physical training of his pupils.

Series of graded exercises to be used as recreation in Class-room in intervals between Classes.

Recreative gymnastics, or Gymnastic games: indoor and outdoor games.

School Law and Regulations.

31.—The Ontario School Law and Regulations so far as they deal with the duties and obligations of teachers and pupils.

THE NORMAL SCHOOLS OF ONTARIO.

Date of Establishment.—The establishment of a Normal School for the Training of Teachers as a part of a Provincial System of Education engaged attention in Upper Canada (now Ontario) in 1836. Nothing definite, however, was done until the year 1846, when, in compliance with the recommendation of the Reverend Doctor Ryerson, Chief Superintendent of Education, in his Report, the Legislature appropriated funds for furnishing suitable Buildings, and an annual grant for the support of a Normal School at Toronto, under the management of a Board of Education and the Chief Superintendent. As the seat of Government was at this time in Montreal, the Government House at Toronto became the Normal School, and, at the disposal of the educational authorities, was opened on November 1st, 1847. The removal of the seat of Government to Toronto, in 1849, necessitated the adoption of measures for the immediate erection of the necessary permanent Buildings. The requisite money having been voted by the Legislature, the corner-stone was laid July 2, 1851, by His Excellency the Earl of Elgin and Kincardine, Governor-General; and, in the month of November in the following year, the Normal and Model Schools were opened in the Buildings which were erected on St. James Square, but Offices for the Education Department were also provided in the new Building. In the year 1858 the Normal School was transferred to the present building, and its former apartments were applied to the purposes of an Educational Museum and a projected School of Art and Design, which is now the Ontario School of Art.

Syllabus of Courses of Instruction and Regulations.

(1) The Terms of the Normal Model Schools shall correspond with those of the Public Schools in Cities. The Regulations of the Department of Education with regard to Pupils and Teachers in Public Schools shall apply to the Teaching Staff and to Pupils of the Model Schools.

(2) The Head Master of each Normal Model School and the Director of the Provincial Kindergarten shall act under the direction of the Principal of the Normal School to which their respective departments are attached, and shall be responsible to him for the order, discipline, and progress of the Pupils, and also for the accuracy and usefulness of the Lessons conducted by the Teachers-in-training.

Location and Purpose of the Normal Schools.

1.—(1) The Normal Schools are situated at Hamilton, London, North Bay, Peterborough, Ottawa, Stratford, and Toronto.

(2) The purpose of these Normal Schools is to prepare Teachers of the Second Class in the theory and the art of organizing, governing, and instructing the pupils of the Public and the Separate Schools; and to improve the general culture of such Teachers and, in particular, their academic preparation for teaching the subjects prescribed in the Programme of Studies.

Note.—In addition to the work prescribed for the other Normal Schools, the School at North Bay prepares Teachers-in-training for Third Class Certificates. For this School and its special conditions a separate announcement is made, which may be obtained on application to the Deputy Minister.

(3) The Normal Model Schools, the Model School, attached Public Schools, and the attached Rural Schools, are used, as required, to afford the Teachers-in-training adequate means of observing well-conducted Schools, and of securing practice in Teaching, Discipline, and Management.

GRADES OF TEACHERS-IN-TRAINING.

2.—There shall be two grades of Teachers-in-training.

GRADE A.—Those who hold professional Third Class Certificates with at least Junior Teachers' academic standing and who have taught successfully a Public, or a Separate, School for one year, or for six months, under the supervision of the Inspector of a City where there has been a Model School.

GRADE B.—All others who hold Junior, or Senior, Teachers' academic Certificates, or have passed the full Examination for Entrance to the Faculties of Education, or to the Normal Schools.

SESSIONS AND VACATIONS.

3.—(1) The Sessions of the Normal School will begin and end as follows:

(a) For all applicants who are required to pass the September examinations in the prescribed Lower School subjects it will begin on September the 20th at 9 a.m.

(b) For applicants with the prescribed Certificates from Approved Schools and for Applicants belonging to Grade A., it will begin on Monday, September the 26th, at 9 a.m.

(c) For Teachers-in-training belonging to Grade A., who may qualify at Easter for Second Class Certificates, it will end at a date to be fixed hereafter.

(d) For all other Teachers-in-training it will end on June the 16th.

(2) There shall be two Vacations as follows:

(a) At Christmas, beginning on December 17th, and ending on January 2nd.

(b) At Easter, beginning on the Thursday before Good Friday and ending on the Monday following Easter Monday.

CONDITIONS OF ADMISSION.

4.—(1) Application for admission shall be made to the Deputy Minister not later than September 6th, on a form to be supplied by him.

(2) Candidates who have appealed against the result of the July examination should apply for admission as above. If their appeals are successful they will be admitted on the same terms as other Applicants.

NOTE.—To those who have complied with the prescribed conditions, a card of admission will be sent. Without this card no one will be admitted.

5.—(1) The Applicant shall forward with his application to the Deputy Minister, on official forms supplied by him, the following Certificates:

(a) A Certificate from competent authority that he was at least eighteen years of age before October 1st.

(b) A Certificate from a Clergyman or other competent authority that he is of good moral character.

(c) A Certificate from a Physician that he is physically able for the work of a Teacher, and, especially, that he is free from serious pulmonary affection and from **seriously** defective eyesight, or hearing.

(2) The Applicant shall also submit one of the following:

(a) A professional Certificate, an academic Certificate, and a Certificate of successful experience from an Inspector, entitling the Applicant to become a member of Grade A.

(b) A full Junior, or Senior, Teachers' Academic Certificate.

(c) A Certificate of having passed the July Academic Examination for Entrance into a Faculty of Education.

(d) A Certificate of having passed the July Academic Examination for Entrance into the Normal Schools, having endorsed thereon the prescribed Certificate from the Principal of an Approved School that the Applicant has completed satisfactorily the Lower School subjects of the High School Course prescribed for entrance into the Normal Schools.

(3) Other applicants than those holding the qualifications prescribed in (2) above, shall present, beside the Certificates required in (1), (a) (b) (c) above, a Certificate of having passed the July Academic Examination, and shall pass in addition at the Normal School an Examination in the prescribed subjects of the High School Lower School in accordance with the Time-table, the pass standard being 40 per cent. of the marks for each subject and 60 per cent. of the aggregate.

Duties of Principals and Assistants.

6.—(1) Subject to the Regulations and to the approval of the Minister of Education, the Principal of each Normal School shall prescribe the duties of his Staff and shall be responsible for the efficiency of the Normal and the Model School.

(2) The other Members of each Staff shall be subject to the authority of the Principal.

(3) Subject to the direction of the Minister, each Normal School Master, in company with the Public School Inspector, shall visit each year Rural Schools in the district in which the Normal School is situated. He shall submit a report of his observations for the consideration of the whole Staff of the Normal School.

(4) Each Principal shall submit to the Minister of Education, not later than December 31st of each year, a report in detail upon the character of the preparation of the Teachers-in-training in attendance who have been admitted on Certificate from the Principal of each Approved School.

(5) Subject to the direction of the Minister, each Member of the Normal School Staff shall take part in the work of the Teachers' Institutes at such dates as the Minister may arrange.

Duties of Teachers-in-Training.

7.—(1) Teachers-in-training shall board and lodge at such houses only as are approved of by the Principal.

(2) They shall attend regularly and punctually, and shall submit to such discipline and directions as the Principal may prescribe.

(3) Teachers-in-training who, in the opinion of the Staff, are unduly defective in scholarship, or whose conduct, or progress, is unsatisfactory, may be dismissed by the Principal at any time during the Session from further attendance at the Normal School.

(4) All Applicants are strongly advised to review carefully, before entering, the work of the Lower School of the High Schools.

TEXT-BOOKS.

8.—(1) The Text-books for the academic work shall be those prescribed in such subjects for the High School.

(2) The Text-books for the professional work shall be the Text-books prescribed for the Public Schools.

LIBRARY.

9.—Under the direction of the different Hembers of the Staff, the Library shall be constantly used for consultation by the Teachers-in-training. To this end it contains a supply of Books of general literature, and a sufficient number of copies of each of the most important professional Books of Reference.

LITERARY SOCIETY.

10.—A Literary Society for general culture and for professional advancement shall be established in each Normal School, and shall be fostered by the Staff as an important part of the Course of Study. It should begin immediately after the work of organization has been completed, and should meet once each week until the special preparation for the final examination begins. The Programmes should include essays, debates, recitations, and the reproduction of suitable scenes from standard plays. Suitable Lecture Courses also will be arranged for under the direction of the Minister of Education.

EXAMINATIONS.

11.—(1) (*a*) The final standing of the Teacher-in-training shall be determined on the combined results of his sessional records and his prescribed examinations.

(*b*) In addition to oral and written class tests in each subject, and the Observation and Practice-teaching records, there shall be a written examination in the subjects of Groups I. and II., below, immediately before the Christmas Vacation.

(*c*) There shall be two Final written examinations in Groups I., II., and III., one at Easter for the Teachers-in-training belonging to Grade A., and one at the close of the Session in June for the Teachers-in-training belonging to Grade B., and for those of Grade A who fail to qualify at Easter or who postpone their examination.

(*d*) Each of the Easter and June examinations shall be based on the work preceding it. The final Examination Papers in Groups I. and II. shall be uniform for all the Normal Schools, and shall be based upon the Courses as laid down in this Syllabus.

(e) The Examinations in Groups II. and III. shall be based on the Courses as laid down in this Syllabus, and shall include a thorough test of the academic qualifications of the Teacher-in-training for teaching all grades of Public School work.

(2) At each Examination in Groups I. and II. there shall be one Paper on each of the following subjects, and the maximum marks for each subject shall be 100; the marks for the Christmas Examination and the Sessional Records in each subject being 40 per cent. of the maximum.

Group I.

Professional: Science of Education, History of Education, School Organization and Management.

Group II.

Academic and Professional: Arithmetic, Algebra and Geometry, Literature, Grammar, History, Composition, Geography, Elementary Science, and Nature Study and Agriculture.

Group III.

(3) The marks counted in estimating the final standing of the Teacher-in-training in the following subjects shall be those awarded him during the Session, more especially toward the close thereof, for the oral, written, and practical tests in matter and, where applicable, in method, the maximum for each subject being 100 each, except for Manners, for which the maximum shall be 50 (25 for the Paper, and 25 on the report of the Staff as to the general deportment of the Teacher-in-training).

Academic and Professional: Art, Music, Reading, Spelling, Manual Training, Household Science, Physical Training, Writing and Book-keeping, Hygiene, and Manners.

Group IV.

(4) The marks counted in estimating the final standing of the Teacher-in-training in Observation and Practice-teaching shall be those awarded him in these subjects during the Session and more especially toward the close thereof, after an introductory Course of Lessons in each. The maximum marks for Practice-teaching shall be 1,200, and those for Observation Lessons 200.

CERTIFICATES.

12.—(1) A Teacher-in-training belonging to Grade A, who at the Easter or the June final Examinations obtains 40 per cent. of the marks in each subject and 60 per cent. of the aggregate of the marks for each of Groups I., II., III., and IV., may on the recommendation of the Staff be awarded a permanent Second Class Certificate, provided he is then twenty-one years of age, or an Interim Certificate valid until he reaches that age, when a permanent Certificate may be issued on application.

(2) A Teacher-in-training belonging to Grade B, who at the June final examination obtains 40 per cent. of the marks in each subject and 60 per cent. of the aggregate of the marks for each of Groups I., II., III., and IV., may on the recommendation of the Staff be awarded an Interim Second Class Certificate,

which will be made permanent at the end of two years' successful experience duly certified on an official form by the Inspector concerned, provided the Teacher is then twenty-one years of age. An Interim Second Class Certificate which expires before the Teacher is twenty-one years of age, or before the holder has taught two years thereon, may be renewed until that date, on the recommendation of the Inspector concerned.

(3) (a) A Teacher-in-training who at the June final examinations fails to obtain a Second Class Certificate but who makes at least 60 per cent. in Group IV., and 35 per cent. of the marks in each subject and 55 per cent. of the aggregate of the marks in each of Groups I., II., and III., may on the recommendation of the Staff be awarded a Third Class Certificate valid for two years.

(b) Such Teacher-in-training who at the following Easter or June examination passes at one examination in the Group or Groups in which he failed may be awarded an Interim Second Class Certificate on the conditions prescribed in (2) immediately preceding.

(4) All other Teachers-in-training shall be required to attend a second Session.

(5) Candidates who have not attended a Normal School, who are exempt from such attendance, and who are actually engaged in teaching, may take Groups I., II., and III., at the same examination, or at different examinations, and shall be exempt from an examination in Group IV., provided they submit to the Minister a Certificate from their last Inspector that they have taught successfully. The pass standard shall be 40 per cent. of the marks for each subject and 60 per cent. of the aggregate of marks for each of Groups I., II., and III.

Horticulture and Industrial Training at the Ontario Agricultural College, Guelph.

13.—(1) Beginning in April, at a date to be settled, a Course of about ten weeks will be provided at the Ontario Agricultural College, Guelph, in Elementary Agriculture and Horticulture and in Elementary Industrial Training, with concurrent discussion of methods, supplementary to the Courses in these subjects in the Normal Schools, for Teachers-in-training who pass the April Examination for Second Class Certificates. The object of the Course is to provide duly qualified Teachers for the Public and Separate Schools in (a) Elementary Agriculture and Horticulture, and (b) Elementary Industrial Training.

(2) The above Courses at the Agricultural College are optional, and Teachers-in-training may take either, but not both.

Courses of Study at the Normal Schools.

14.—(1) The Courses at the Normal Schools shall consist of the following:

(a) A review of the Public School Course and of the academic subjects prescribed for admission into the Normal Schools, especially those of the Lower School, from the standpoint of Pedagogy and the requirements of the Public and Separate Schools, with such an extension of said subjects for the purpose of culture as time will permit; also special instruction in Reading, Writing, Art, Physical Training, Physiology and Hygiene, Music, Household Science, Manual Training, Manners, School Law and Regulations.

(b) The Science of Education, including Applied Psychology and Ethics, Child Study, and General Methodology; the History of Education; Special Methodology; and School Organization and Management.

(c) Supervised Observation in the Model Schools, also in the affiliated Rural Schools of the adjoining County, or Counties.

(d) Supervised Practice-teaching in the Model Schools.

(2) For Teachers-in-training of both Grades, A and B, the main details of the Courses shall be the same.

Teachers-in-training belonging to Grade A will be assumed to have made themselves familiar with Bett's "The Mind and its Education," and McMurry's "The Method of the Recitation," before entering the Normal School.

Order of the Courses.

15.—(1) In order that the Teacher-in-training may begin early the Observation work and the Practice-teaching, the following introductory Courses shall be taken up in the following order, having due regard to the requirements of Grades A and B respectively:

(a) The introduction to the Science of Education, and those parts of the Applied Psychology, and Child Study which bear most directly upon General Methodology, the prime essentials of which shall be discussed in this connection. To this Course shall be added a discussion of the functional value of each of the Normal School Courses.

(b) A Course of Observation in the different forms of the Model Schools.

(2) To prevent the dissipation of energy which would result from the concurrent study of a large number of subjects diverse in content, the system of intensive study should be followed so far as the special qualifications of the members of the Staff will permit. In the order of the Courses and the grouping of the subjects due regard should be had to the character of each subject and its natural relations, and to the logical development of the Courses and their relative functional value in the Pedagogy of the Public School Programme.

(a) On the professional side, after the completion of the Introductory Course [15 (1)], the Course in the Science of Education should be taken up three times a week until finished. The Course in School Organization and Management should be taken up from the first three times a week until finished. The History of Education should not be taken up until after Christmas.

(b) The total number of periods for each of the professional subjects should be as nearly as practicable as follows:

The Science of Education, including the Introductory Course, 70; School Organization and Management, 65; the History of Education, 32; Manners, 5.

(c) The number of Lessons per week for each of the professional and academic subjects shall be, as nearly as practicable, as follows: Mathematics, 3; English (Grammar, Literature, History, Language and Composition, Spelling, and Reading), 7; Science (Physics, Chemistry, Biology, Geography, and Physiology and Hygiene), 5; Art, 2; Music, 2; Manual Training, 1½; Physical Training, 1; Writing and Book-keeping, 1; Domestic Science, 1½; Literary Society, 1; Observation and Practice-teaching (minimum), 4; Religious Instruction, 1.

(3) The foregoing principles of selection and order should also be observed in the Special Methodology and the academic treatment of the other subjects of the Course:

(*a*) In the Mathematical group, Arithmetic should be taken up before Algebra and Geometry, being taken three times a week for about the first six months. It should then be continued with one lesson a week to the end of the session, the other two periods being given to Algebra and Geometry.

(*b*) The subjects of the groups, Geography and History; Language, Grammar, and Composition; and Phonics, Voice Culture and Reading should respectively be related in organization as are the subjects of the Mathematical group; Geography, Language and Grammar, and Phonics and Voice Culture preceding in their respective groups.

(*c*) In the Science group, the Biological side should be given special attention during the Autumn and the Spring, and the Science subjects should be taken up first from the Nature Study point of view. On account of their relations to parts of the courses in Art, Domestic Science, and School Management, suitable introductory Courses bearing directly on these subjects should be provided in Chemistry and Physics. So, too, on account of its basal relations to Psychology, Physical Training, Music, and School Management, the course in Physiology should be taken up at the beginning and completed as soon as practicable.

(*d*) The Courses in Music, Art, Writing, Physical Training, Literature, Manual Training, and Domestic Science should continue throughout the Session.

(*e*) Short courses should be provided at the beginning of the Session in Spelling and Manners; and, toward the close, in School Law and Regulations.

The Normal Model Schools and Affiliated Public Schools.

These are adjuncts to the Normal Schools and are used as Practice Schools for the Teachers-in-training. The course of study is in harmony with that of the Public Schools. After the Students in the Normal Schools have observed the Methods employed in the Model Schools, and have, in the presence of the Masters, managed classes formed amongst themselves, they are detailed to perform similar work in the Model Schools under the immediate direction and criticism of the regular Teachers. From the Reports emanating from the Head Teachers of these Schools, and from those of their Assistants in the Normal Schools, the Principals of the Normal Schools frame their report as to the Candidates' qualifications to receive permanent Certificates.

Observation and Practice Teaching.

16.—(1) The Introductory Courses provided for in Regulation 15 shall be followed by systematic Observation and Practice-teaching, the minimum number of Observation Lessons being 40 and of Practice-teaching Lessons 25 for Grade B, and 20 for Grade A, Teachers-in-training, but these numbers shall be increased to meet the necessities of individual Teachers-in-training.

(2) (*a*) The Teachers-in-training shall be divided into suitable groups, and the work of Observation and Practice-teaching shall be taken up systematically per time-table arranged from time to time.

(*b*) At least that group to which the Teacher-in-training belongs shall be present at the discussions on his Observation and Practice-teaching lessons.

(3) (*a*) The Observation and Practice-teaching lessons for each Teacher-in-training shall, as far as practicable, be arranged so as to cover the work of the Public Schools in all subjects and in all grades.

(*b*) The Observation and Practice-teaching lessons provided for in the logical development of the Normal School course shall be supplemented by other lessons in such forms of the Model School as may be available.

(*c*) Continuous Practice-teaching for several periods toward the end of the course shall be required, the teacher-in-training being wholly responsible for the discipline of the class.

(*d*) Teachers-in-training shall be available as substitutes in the Public or Separate Schools of the locality (urban or rural) in which the Normal School is situated, subject to arrangement with the Principal of the Normal School.

(4) (*a*) Teachers-in-training shall be notified by the Principal of the subject and the scope of the Observation lesson, and shall prepare the lesson beforehand.

(*b*) After observing the Lesson, they shall submit a report upon it to the Model School teacher concerned.

(5) (*a*) Teachers-in-training shall be notified of the subject and the scope of the Practice-teaching lesson, by the Model School teacher, after consultation with the Normal School Master concerned.

(*b*) Teachers-in-training shall prepare a plan of each Practice-teaching lesson for submission to the Model School teacher concerned.

(6) (*a*) Model lessons shall be taught by the teachers of the Model School in accordance with the regular programme of the Model School.

(*b*) The Normal School Masters in charge of the academic work in a subject shall develop its details in their teaching order, and after each suitable step shall also themselves teach model lessons in special Public School classes in the Normal School and in the Model School itself. At these lessons, the Model School teacher in charge of the subject shall be present.

(7) (*a*) The necessary applications of the Science of Education and of Special Methodology shall be made systematically by both the Normal School Masters and the Model School teachers in connection with the Model and the Observation lessons and the Practice-teaching; so that the course may be taken up in terms of the child's mind and growth. From time to time the Master in charge of the Science of Education should formally illustrate by actual teaching the principles he has discussed in class.

(*b*) As far as practicable, it shall be the duty of the members of both the Normal School and the Model School staffs, in accordance with the Time-table, to be present at the Observation lessons and Practice-teaching of the Teacher-in-training, and to make jointly the criticism and the valuation of his work.

(8) Concerted work on the part of the Normal and the Model School shall be secured by frequent conferences of the Staffs of both Schools, especially at the beginning of the session.

Details of Courses of Instruction.

Science of Education.

17.—The object of the Course in the Science of Education is to provide the Teacher with a working conception of the nature of education which will be useful to him in forming ideals and determining procedure, to give him a rational basis for intelligently evaluating and selecting subject matter and methods of instruction, and to improve natural fact and skill through the acquisition of experience, with the least expenditure of time and energy. The Course, which shall be as practical as possible, includes Applied Psychology, Child Study, and General Methodology.

18.—The Aim of Education: Provisional statement of the aim of education to be used as a working definition.

Function of the School: Function of the School in directing the development of the child's experiences during the plastic period; relation of the School to other social institutions—the Home, the Church, the State, the Vocation.

Subjects of Study: School Studies as typical forms of experience that the race has found valuable in meeting its needs; basis for determining the functional value of a subject in a Course of Study.

Methods of Instruction: The purpose of method; necessity for basing methods of instruction on a knowledge of the characteristics and the conditions of mental life; the problem of method a psychological problem. A preliminary outline of the general principles of method.

Books of Reference.—McMurry—The Method of the Recitation—75 cts. Bagley—The Educative Process.

The Subject of Psychology.

19.—Problems and Methods of Applied Psychology: The subject-matter of psychology; the essential characteristics of mental life; contrast between mental and physical phenomena; "stream of consciousness" and its "contents"; knowing, feeling, and willing; their interdependence.

Methods of studying the facts of mental life; the meaning of introspection; the limitations of introspective methods; methods of observing and interpreting the expressive signs of mental life; the attitude of the Teacher as an observer; the place of experimental methods.

Nervous System and Mental States: Body and Mind, general nature of their connection; illustrations to show that mental life is dependent on physical conditions; outline study of the structure and functions of the nervous system in so far as it is related to mental processes; relation of mental growth to the development of the nervous system; conditions of sensory and motor development; development of the nerve centres through natural growth and through use; effects of disuse on nerve cells; connection between sensory and motor action; development of nerve connections; the "reflex arc"; automatic and reflex acts; the process of the growth of motor control; importance of a knowledge of the growth of the nervous system to the Teacher.

Instincts: The place of natural tendencies in the development of mental life; the nature of instincts; outline study of some of the more important human instincts; transitory character of many instincts; necessity for utilizing instinctive tendencies at the time of their appearance; the adaptation of the subject-matter of instruction to the stage of natural development of the child; the dangers of introducing subjects too soon or too late; useful and injurious instincts; methods of strengthening and modifying instincts through use, and of weakening or eliminating them through disuse, substitution or repression; transformation of instincts into habits.

Habit: Nature of habit; physical basis of habit; the functions and limitations of habit: the dangers of mental "fossilization"; the relation of habit formation to School Studies, especially those involving the acquisition of skill, such as Writing, Reading, Manual training, Art, etcetera; Pedagogical rules for the formation of new habits, or the breaking up of old ones.

Interests: The nature of interests; interests as tendencies to thought and action.

Interest as a means in education; tendencies as the starting points in acquisition of desirable and suppression of undesirable tendencies; instinctive interests; a classification of the more common instinctive interests; the relation of acquired to instinctive interests; the reciprocal character of knowledge and interest; growth of purposes and plans from natural instincts.

Interest as a means in education; tendencies as the starting points in acquisition of knowledge or the formation of habits of action; practical teaching rules for applying the principle of interest in gaining knowledge; the relation of interest to effort; distinction between the interesting and the easy, and between the interesting and pleasureable.

Capacities and Activities: Examination of some of the more fundamental capacities.

Sensitivity: The relation of sense impressions to the growth of knowledge. Retentiveness: The importance of retention in the growth of experience; conditions of retention. Relating Activity: First steps in thinking; dissociation, discrimination and association as activities. Expression: Process of giving significance to motor movements; relation of impression to expression.

The development of capacities through experience; the place of formal discipline as an end in education.

Apperception: Mental states, or acts, as dependent on original tendencies and previous experience; the development of mental life as conditioned on the interaction of the "old" and the "new"; learning as the development of experience into experience; necessity for making experiences meaningful; the process of interpreting the new in terms of the old; the necessity for studying the child's tendencies and capacities in selecting and presenting the subject matter of instruction; significance of the pedagogical maxim, "Proceed from the known to the related unknown."

Attention: The nature of attention; the selective character of attention; meaning of concentration of attention, dispersed attention and inattention; conditions of non-voluntary, or spontaneous, attention; the relation of habit to attention; methods and devices for securing spontaneous attention; the conditions of voluntary attention; growth of purpose and plans; the importance of an aim on the part of the learner; the development of aims and ideals as an end in education; methods of securing voluntary attention; the application of the law of derived interest to school studies; the relation of voluntary to non-voluntary attention; gaining and holding attention; physical conditions favourable and unfavourable to attention.

Sensation and Perception: Sensation as a mental process; the physical conditions of sensation; classification of sensations; sensation qualities; the nature of perception; the presented and reproduced factors in perception; the functions of sensation and perception as forming the basis for thought; the development of perception; the growth of percepts in richness and definiteness through the detection of new features connected with old things; the meaning of observation; the relation of observation to alertness and keenness of sense activity and to knowledge, interests and purposes; methods of cultivating habit and observation.

Imagination: Relation of imagery to sensory experiences; the function of imagery in interpreting the present by the past and in forming aims, purposes, and plans; power of imagery as varying in different people; types of imagery; the reconstruction of images; reproductive and productive imagination; their relation to each other; simultaneous association of images, as in perception; successive association of images in the train of thought; laws of association; physical basis of association; training the imagination as involving the storing of the mind with a rich stock of usable images and giving facility and dexterity in grouping images into new wholes for the sake of a definite purpose; school studies and activities as a means of training the imagination; study of children for the purpose of determining the "mind stuff" in which they think.

Memory: The characteristic features of Memory; the relation of memory to reproductive imagination; retention, recall and recognition as factors in memory; characteristics of a good memory: recency, vividness, frequency and association as factors in efficient recall; training of memory; cultivation of memory as improvement in methods of recording facts; methods of securing vividness of original impression; relation of attention to retention; rules or proper use of repetition; methods of securing association and organization; cramming and its effects.

Thinking: The importance of consciousness of meaning in the development of mental life; meaning dependent on relations; thinking as the process of grasping relations; thinking of the child and the adult compared; analysis of conceptional thinking; nature and growth of a concept; the place of the image in conception; the relation of conception to language; judgment as a phase of thinking; sound judgment as an end in education; reasoning as purposive thinking; deductive reasoning; inductive reasoning; the interrelation of induction and deduction; principles involved in training in thinking; school studies as a means of training in thinking.

Feeling and Emotion: Various uses of the term feeling; feeling as the tone of a conscious state; qualities of feeling; relation of feeling to cognition and to motor reaction; nature of emotion; relation of emotion to instinct and to feeling; conditions upon which the appearance of emotion depends; functions of feeling and emotion, their influences on attention, judgment and effort; outline study of some of the more significant emotions; directions along which emotional development should take place; place of habit in emotional development, the growth of moods, sentiments, temperaments, and dispositions; significance of school studies and activities in the growth of feeling and emotion.

Will: Involuntary and voluntary action compared; a voluntary act as the attentive selection of one way of action as against another; the place of deliberation, effort and choice in a voluntary act; factors in a well-balanced will; study of volitional types which vary from the normal, such as the impulsive type and the obstructed will; relation of involuntary action to voluntary in the training of the will; methods of developing normal will through the activities of the School and the Home; methods of dealing with abnormal types of will; education in its relation to conduct; elements involved in moral training; the function of the School in moral training; effects of methods of instruction on morals; moral effects of School Studies; value of specific moral instruction; character development as the full aim of education; factors in character development; the function of the School in character development.

Books of Reference.—Betts—The Mind and its Education. Angell—Psychology. Halleck—Education of the Central Nervous System. James—Talks to Teachers.

The Course in Child Study.

20.—The object of the Course in Child Study is to enable the Teacher-in-training to adapt intelligently his methods in each subject to the child's mind at the different stages of its growth. The Course includes the following topics:—

The scope of Child Study; methods of investigation; importance to the Teacher of the study of the child mind. Physical growth and development during infancy, childhood, and adolescence. Mental development during the same periods. Mental types and variations from normal mental conditions. Differences in individual children. The study of children along the lines suggested in the course in Applied Psychology.

Book of Reference.—Kirkpatrick—Fundamentals of Child Study.

General Methodology.

21.—The object of the Course in its final stage is to gather up the main facts and principles bearing most directly on methods of instruction which have been developed in connection with the various topics in Applied Psychology and Child Study; and, by dwelling on connections and relations, to organize the whole into a comprehensive and logical system of General Methodology and so to form a basis for the Special Methodology. The Course includes the following topics:—

The Problem of General Method: The relation of general method to special methods and teaching devices; the relation of method to subject matter.

Planning for the Lesson: Principles to be observed in dividing the subject matter into topics or units of instruction; the adjustment of the Lesson to the tendencies, needs and capacities of the pupils; the relation of the Lesson to previous work and to the stage of development of the pupils; necessity for the Teacher to study the Class as well as the subject matter of the Lesson.

Means of Presentation of the Lesson: Lecture, Text-book, and question-and-answer methods of presentation; advantages and limitations of each; graphic representation as a means of presentation; diagrams, etcetera; nature and functions of objective teaching; limitations of objective teaching; principles governing successful use of Objects, Pictures, Models, Maps, etcetera.

The Aim of the Lesson: Aim of the Lesson from the Teacher's standpoint; aim of the Lesson from the pupil's standpoint; tendencies as the starting point in the growth of knowledge, or the acquisition of skill; relation of the child's interest to native instincts and capacities and to the development of aims and purposes;

the relation of interest to self-activity; the use of interest in the School-room; the normal attitude of the learner as an attitude of inquiry; the necessity for connecting the Lesson with some pre-existing need of the child or of making it fit into some of his purposes or plans; the place of the statement of the aim of the Lesson; the nature and purpose of the preview.

Preparation of the Class for the Lesson: Necessity for revival and reconstruction of the old experiences of the pupil in giving meaning to the new Lesson; the aim of the Lesson as a purpose in the recall of old experiences; means of recalling and utilizing old experiences in the presentation of the new Lesson; "preparation" as a formal step in method.

Development of the Lesson: The effect of the preview, the statement of the aim and the preliminary stage of preparation to fix in the mind of the learner a vague mental whole within which mental movement in the Lesson takes place; the purpose of the development of the lesson to give definiteness to this whole; the development as a process of analysis, focussing attention on particular phases within the whole, and of synthesis, instituting relations among these particulars; typical illustrations from varied subjects to show the meaning and the universality of application of this principle; the interdependence of analysis and synthesis; learning as an analytic synthetic process; the place of comparison and contrast in the development of the Lesson.

The analytic phase in learning; the principle of selection of relevant analysis; the place of sense-perception, telling and inference in the development of individual notions; meaning of "analytic methods" of teaching.

The synthetic phase in learning; the adaptation and use of selected material; the development and application of universal notions; meaning of "synthetic methods" of teaching; inductive and deductive methods of teaching; "presentation," "comparison," "abstraction," "generalization," and "application," as formal steps in instruction.

Expression as a Stage in Method: Necessity for expression as a stage in rational method; interdependence of impression and expression; the importance of this interdependence as the basis for the constructive side of School work.

Typical Lesson Forms: The Study Lesson; the recitation Lesson; the development Lesson; the drill Lesson; the review Lesson; the construction of Lesson plans.

Teaching Devices: Use of questioning in the development of the Lesson; right and wrong methods of questioning; examination of the so-called Socratic method; answers; qualities of a good answer; treatment of faulty answers; mistakes in dealing with answers; illustrations, their office and value; uses of the Blackboard.

Books of Reference.—McMurry—The Method of the Recitation. Bagley—The Educative Process. Thorndike—Principles of Teaching.

History of Education.

22.—The object of the Course in the History of Education is to widen the professional outlook and rationalize School practice through the discussion of the development and of the merits and the defects of educational theories. It presupposes an historical background and discusses movements rather than individuals.

The Course includes the following topics, and deals only with the most important points:—

Education Prior to the Fifteenth Century: A very brief survey of significant movements, with reference to the following topics: Education among primitive peoples; education in Sparta and Athens, the idea of a liberal education; education in Rome, the idea of practical education; education and monasticism, education and chivalry, the early Universities.

The Renaissance: The relation of the Renaissance to modern civilization; its origin and educational significance; Erasmus, Vittorino da Feltre, and Sturm; influence of Renaissance upon subject matter, methods and purposes of Schools; humanistic conception of education: humanism and realism.

Reformation and Counter Reformation: The Reformation and the Renaissance; Luther and Elementary Education in Germany; Schools of the Jesuits and other Religious Orders.

Realism in Education: Verbal realism as represented by Rabelais and Milton; social realism as represented by Montaigne; sense realism as represented by Bacon, Mulcaster and Comenius.

Education according to Nature: Development of the new conception of education; Locke and Rousseau.

Modern Educational Theories and Movements: Pestalozzi and the Elementary School; Herbert and Methodology; Froebel and the Kindergarten; Spencer and scientific tendencies in Education; education as social adjustment; Public Education in Great Britain: the development of Public Education in Ontario.

Books of Reference.—Monroe—A Brief Course in the History of Education. Quick—Educational Reformers. Kemp—History of Education.

School Organization and Management.

23.—School Organization and Management: The object of the Course is to give the Teacher, in the light of the Science of Education, a knowledge of the technique of School Management and Organization which will enable him to secure the smooth and efficient working of his School. The Course includes the following topics:

School Management: Its scope and its return to the Science of Education.

The Teacher: Natural qualifications of a good Teacher; importance of scholarship, of training, of experience, of professional studies, of wide culture, of broad sympathies, of sense of responsibility, and of earnestness of purpose; the Teacher's relations to the Principal, Inspector, Trustees, Parents; his civic and social duties; his personal power and influence in the School and in the community; his daily preparation for teaching; the care of his health.

Classification: Principles governing the classification of Pupils in the School; the advantages and disadvantages of graded and ungraded Schools; number and size of Classes in urban and rural Schools; common defects in Class instruction; effects of over-teaching; advantages of Class instruction; defects of a rigid Class instruction; the value of the individual system; examination of various methods of promotion; the division of subjects and Pupils among the several Teachers in Graded Schools.

Daily Programme: Its purpose and value; principles involved in the construction of a Time-table; Seat work; individual Blackboard work; question of fatigue;

typical Time-tables for Graded and for Ungraded Schools; registration and School Records.

School-room Routine: Chief varieties of mechanizing routine; their advantages and disadvantages; the appointment and duties of Monitors; Fire drill.

Desirable School Habits: Methods of securing desirable School habits such as punctuality, neatness in person and in work, accuracy, quietness, industry, obedience, etcetera.

Order and Discipline: Characteristics of good order; the relation of authority to Discipline; the chief elements of governing power; Rules, their value and enforcement; common faults and how to avoid them; discussion of methods of dealing with typical offences; the relation of incentives and penalties to order and Discipline; co-operation of School and Home in matters of Discipline.

School Incentives and Penalties: Classification of incentives; the effects of each on School work and on health and character; the values of punishment; characteristics of judicious and injudicious punishment; the discipline of consequences.

Physical Education: Relation of physical to intellectual development; importance of change of work; value of play and games; organized and unorganized play.

The School Building and Premises, and School Hygiene: The Grounds; Situation, aspect, area, Drainage, ornamentation, protection, Water-supply, its sources, impurities, modes of purification.

The Outbuildings: Location, structure, and supervision.

The School House: School Architecture, size, shape, and suitability of Rooms, Hall, etcetera; importance of proper lighting; how to secure proper lighting, position of Pupils with reference to windows; heating, warming by stoves, by hot air, by hot water, by steam, the advantages and disadvantages of each method, the jacketed Stove; the Thermometer, the Hygrometer; Fire-escapes and like appliances; Ventilation; necessity for good Ventilation; signs of vitiated Air, moistening of Air, quantity of fresh Air needed, different methods of Ventilation; furniture and equipment; Desks and Seats; necessity of adjusting the height to the pupil; Blackboards, their size, situation, and kinds; Cloak rooms and clothing; Maps, Globes, Library, and other necessary apparatus and equipment; Pictures and decoration of Walls.

School Law and Regulations: The Ontario School Law and Regulations in so far as they deal with the duties and obligations of Teachers and Pupils.

Books of Reference.—Bagley—Class Management. White—School Management. Landon—Principles and Practice of Teaching and School Management.

Special Methodology.

24.—The object of the Course is to prepare the Teachers-in-training for intelligently observing and teaching in all grades of the Model Schools, by enabling them to apply the principles of education and, in particular, to adapt to the work in each subject the principles of General Method. The work in the special method of each subject is introduced by a few lessons of a general character, embracing the application of the principles of General Methodology to the teaching of the subject. These introductory Lessons are followed by a series of a more detailed character, dealing with:

(1) The selection and the organization of material for the Public School Forms, taken in order, from the standpoint of presentation to the pupil.

(2) The discussion of special methods of instruction, concurrent with the academic review of the subject matter.

The courses shall be taken up in terms of the Public School Programme of Studies, the provisions of which shall be constantly kept in mind.

General Books of Reference.—Carpenter, Baker and Scott—Teaching of English. Chubb—Teaching of English. MacClintock—Literature in the Elementary School. Arlo Bates—Talks on the Writing of English. Arlo Bates—Talks on the Teaching of Literature. Hodge—Nature Study and Life. Dearness—How to Teach Nature Study. Silcox and Stevenson—Nature Study. Scott—Nature Study and the Child. Coulter—Practical Nature Study. Geikie—Teaching of Geography. Arnold Foster—This World of Ours. Morang & Co.—The Study of Geography. Smith—Teaching of Elementary Mathematics. Young—The Teaching of Mathematics. Annandale—The Concise Imperial Dictionary.

I. *Language and Composition.*

25.—The special object of the Course in Language and Composition is to prepare the Teacher to train his Pupils to speak and to write good English as a fixed, unconscious habit. The Course includes the following topics:

The importance of language training; the place of a knowledge of the mother-tongue in education; the value of clearness, force and grace of expression.

Oral and Written Composition: Their relation; how habits of speaking and writing good English are formed; the effect of the Teacher's example upon the Pupil's language; value of reading and of memorizing good Literature; importance of Libraries for supplementary reading; incidental work in language training; expression as a stage in the development of every Lesson; necessity for special exercises in oral and written Composition.

Methods in Oral and Written Composition: Methods of encouraging Pupil's free natural expression and of extending his vocabulary through oral exercises; principles governing criticism of oral work; the dangers connected therewith and the means of avoiding them; value of formal linguistic exercises; method of correcting common errors, relative value of pupil's own language and of special exercises in false syntax as material for criticism; the principles to be kept in view in conducting exercises in written Composition; supervision and aid during writing; value of topical outlines; the place of Home work in written Compositions; method of correcting Compositions; value of re-writing.

Mechanics and Written Composition: Sentence and paragraph structure; paragraph Compositions; the use of capitals, punctuation marks, quotation marks, abbreviations, etcetera.

Materials for Written and Oral Composition: Principles governing choice of topics; gathering, selecting and arranging material; class answers as material for oral Composition; importance of framing questions that will require answers of considerable length; the reproduction of Fairy and Folk Stories, Fables, Poems, Biographies; relative value of reading and telling Stories; transition from reproduction to originality; descriptions of personal experiences, real and imaginary, and of places, operations and processes of personal interest; striking incidents in the history of the families of the pupils; Pictures suggestive of Stories, School Games, autobiographies of familiar things; developing Themes from minor incidents, themes connected with School studies, general Themes; Letter writing, with special attention to form and style; invitations and replies thereto.

II. *Reading.*

26.—The special object of the Course in Reading is to prepare the Teacher to train his pupils to get the Writer's thought and feelings (*intelligent reading*) and to communicate them to the listener so that he may appreciate them (*intelligible reading*). The Course includes the following topics:

The Scope of Reading: Its correlation with other subjects; importance of training in reading and the principles of vocal expression to pupil's ordinary speech and general culture.

The Processes Involved in Reading: The relation of ideas to symbols; the associations of visual, auditory, and motor images in reading; conditions of the formation of accurate visual and auditory impressions; constant necessity for connecting the printed symbol directly with the idea.

Forms of Reading: The function and value of Silent Reading; Sight Reading, Dramatic Reading, Elocution, Declamation.

Methods in Reading: Examination of the various methods of teaching beginners to read; advantages and disadvantages of each; devices for securing rapid word-recognition and for fixing attention on the thought and feeling as well as upon the word forms in the earlier stages; means of securing natural expressive reading; the place and limitations of imitative reading; common faults on the part of both Pupil and Teacher and how to correct them; criticism by Teacher and by Pupils. Change in purpose and methods of reading as determined by the development of the Pupil's experience and powers; the necessity for giving attention to expression in all stages; expression to be based on impression; the objects of advanced Reading; methods of developing in pupils the habit of Reading for thought and pleasure; Reading as a means of creating and fostering a taste for good Literature.

Mechanics of Vocal Expression: The necessity for attention to the principles of vocal expression; time, inflection, pitch, force, quality, pause, phrasing, emphasis, stress; and to exercises for rendering the organs of speech subservient to the will—vocalization, articulation, breathing, development of chest and lungs, vocal training for pure tone; the connection between the reading lesson and the singing lesson.

III. *Spelling.*

27.—The special object of the course in Spelling is to prepare the Teacher to secure accuracy in the mechanism of written word-expression. The Course includes the following topics:—

Scope of Spelling: Its correlation with other subjects; nature and origin of peculiarities of English Orthography; causes of the difficulties experienced by pupils in learning to spell; causes of incorrect spelling.

Methods of Spelling: Necessity for teaching, not merely testing spelling; examination of the various methods of teaching spelling; the adaptation of each to the nature of the words and to the individual mental characteristics of pupils; phonic exercises and word-building in relation to spelling; syllabication; the place of transcription and dictation; methods of checking and correcting errors; value of re-writing; prevention *versus* correction; the character of drill and review exercises in spelling; methods of varying the spelling recitation; value of rules in spelling.

Materials for Spelling: Principles of selection of material for spelling; grouping of words for the purpose of spelling; incidental spelling; uses of the dictionary and of the spelling book.

IV. *Literature.*

28.—The special object of the Course in Literature is to prepare the Teacher to create in his pupils a taste for good literature, while broadening their knowledge, moulding their characters, and aiding them to appreciate the beauty and the power of artistic expression of thought and feeling. The Course includes the following topics:—

The nature and elements of Literature.

Selection of Subject Matter for Literature Lessons: Qualities of Literature that appeal to children of different ages; basis of selection of material for different grades; lists of suitable Fairy Tales, Fables, Nature Stories, etcetera, adapted to children of lower grades and of general works for Pupils in the highest forms; complete wholes *versus* extracts; the correlation of Literature with Nature Study, Geography, History, etcetera.

Methods in Teaching Literature: Methods of dealing with primary Literature; comparison of values of reading and telling; method in supplementary reading contrasted with that in exact study; the extensive and intensive study of Literature; the importance and method of memorizing selections; the value of oral reading in the interpretation and appreciation of Literature; the importance of the Teacher's own ability to read well; the futility of attempts to develop formally the critical sense.

Lesson Procedure: Preparation of the pupils; necessity for preparing a suitable mood for the Lesson; how far the Author's biography and the experience of the Pupils have a place here; preliminary reading of the selection; the main thought of the Lesson grasped and the main feeling of the Lesson impressed in a more, or less, indefinite way through a reading of it; the analysis of a selection into its wider thought elements and feeling elements, and the analysis of these again into their elements; the place of explanation of words and phrases; the use of the Dictionary; the relation of the subordinate thoughts and feelings to the unity of the whole, the main thought and feeling of the selection as made definite by the analysis; the oral reading of the selection by pupils after study; the value of oral and written reproduction; suitable seat work.

Examinations in Literature: Difficulties of examining in Literature; specimen examination questions.

Teacher's Preparation: Special importance of Teacher's own qualifications, a Class Course in Literature, in part based on the poetic selections in the Readers; the literary study of portions of the Bible prescribed by the Department of Education; sessional private Reading Courses for Teachers-in-training; suggestions for their future reading.

School Library: Principles to be kept in view in selecting works for the School Library; methods of making use of School Library; means of securing the co-operation of the home in the pupil's reading.

NOTE.—Teachers-in-training having conscientious objections to the literary study of the Bible shall be excused therefrom by the Principal. Religious instruction by local clergymen of the different Denominations is provided in each Normal School.

V. *Grammar*.

29.—The special object of the Course in Grammar is to prepare the Teacher to train his Pupils in habits of logical analysis, and to give them a basis for self-criticism in language by developing the principles of language structure. The Course includes the following topics:—

Meaning of English Grammar; the relation of Grammar to speech; correlation with other subjects; reasons for and against retaining it in elementary Schools; reasons for deferring the formal study till Form IV.; introductory work of Forms II. and III.

The sentence as the starting point; basal value of function; order and method of teaching the parts of speech; principles of classification as applied to Grammar; inflection, use and value of our remaining inflections; rules of syntax, their value; use of grammatical terminology; definitions, their value, how to be obtained, how to be applied; analysis and parsing, aim and value of each; value of Diagrams; oral and written exercises; treatment of false syntax; elementary etymology, the derivation and composition of words.

VI. *History*.

30.—The special object of the Course in History is to prepare the Teacher to train Pupils to adapt human experiences to present situations. In the elementary stages the chief objects are to arouse an interest in historical studies, to enable the Pupils to appreciate the logical sequence of events, and to give them a knowledge of their civil rights and duties; also to stimulate a Love of Country. The Course includes the following topics:—

The Scope of History: The correlation of History with other subjects, especially Geography; the special value of Canadian and British History; the proper perspective in the development of the subject; arts enlarged in the academic review; what makes an event important.

Methods: The recitation, its form and purposes, the place of oral teaching and of Blackboard work by Teacher, and of written exercises at the Seat and at Blackboard by Pupils; methods in oral and in written work; the use of Pictures, Maps, etcetera, of Readers, of Source Books, of the Text-book, and of current Journals and Periodicals.

Stages in the Course: Special necessity for the adaptation of the teaching of history to the Pupil's growing knowledge and logical capacity. The Picture and Story stage, a methodically arranged series of picturesque Biographies graphically narrated; no Text-book. The information stage; an introduction to History proper, methodically presented; external and picturesque side made prominent, with emphasis on biographical and social aspects; introduction of History Readers and Biographies in the Library. The reflective stage; the study of casual relations and of the origin, development, and inner life of our Institutions.

The selection and arrangement of material suitable for different grades; the place and purpose of each of the following:—

History of Aborigines, Current History, Pioneers, Local History.

Characteristics of Peoples, as those of the United States, Japan, China, Germany, France, Italy, Quebec.

Biography: The natural attractiveness of Biography; the relation of Biography to History; the effects of a study of Biography on the development of character; selection of suitable Biographies for Pupils of different grades, as the lives Explorers, Navigators, and Soldiers for primary grades; of Statesmen, Poets, Scientists, etcetera, as representing more complex conditions, for Pupils of higher grades.

Civics: Ends to be kept in view in teaching Civics; consideration of work to be undertaken in Civics; study of Civic Institutions as appearing in their lowest forms among primitive peoples; the beginnings of Governments, of Courts, of School Systems, of Factories, of Routes and means of Transportation, etcetera, study of present forms of Civic Institutions.

Epochs: Their relation to Biography; systematic Chronological study of History; its value and its dangers; the casual sequence of events.

Supplementary Material: The use of Mythology, Ballads, Orations, Epics, Legends, Tales of Chivalry, Narrative Poems, and Historical Novels; character of History Readers and of supplementary works for the different grades. Significance and value of the National Flag.

VII. *Geography.*

31.—The special object of the Course in Geography is to prepare the Teacher to extend the pupils' knowledge of the earth and its relation to life thereon, and to assist them in interpreting and utilizing their physical environment in accordance with their needs. The Course includes the following topics:—

The scope of Geography; its relation to other subjects, especially to Nature Study, History, and elementary Science.

The review of the Course should lay special emphasis on the study of the Earth's Surface and the changes wrought thereon by the various agencies; Rock formation and disintegration; origin, formation and composition of Soils; distribution of Mineral deposits, not overlooking local deposits of building material, as Marl, Limestone, Brick, Clay, and Sand, and also of Plant and animal Life; the relation of the Earth to other Heavenly Bodies; Weather and Climate; Man's relation to the rest of the world; interdependence of Nations; Commercial and Political Geography.

Methods: Consideration of the order of development of the subject in rural and urban Schools; the use of Maps, Globes, Pictures, Blackboard Drawings, Natural Objects, specimens of Products, Lantern Slides and Stereoscopic Views; Modelling, Map Drawing, Scales and Projections; Weather Observations and records, simple experiments in explanation of Natural Phenomena (see course in Elementary Science); Excursions in connection with the observations in Local Geography; inter-school correspondence; the use of Reference Library, Books of Travel, Geography Readers, Newspapers and Periodicals, etcetera, common mistakes in teaching Geography and means of avoiding them.

VIII. *Nature Study and Agriculture.*

32.—The Special object of the Course in Nature Study is to broaden and deepen the Teacher's sympathies and interests, and, through him, those of his pupils, by training him to observe and interpret the common Phenomena of the world about him. The Course includes the following topics:—

The character and scope of Nature Study; its relation to formal Science; its correlation with other subjects.

Materials for Nature Study: Conditions determining the choice of material for Nature Study Lessons for pupils of different grades, and for varying conditions in rural and urban Schools; uses and limitations of Books, Pictures, Models, Collections, etcetera, supplementary materials such as Stories, Literature, etcetera.

Methods in Nature Study: Nature Study as a method; special characteristics of a typical Nature Study Lesson; uses and limitations of records of observations; directions for conducting School Excursions. The study of special topics dealing with materials of Nature Study and illustrating methods of presentation in all grades of Public Schools, the topics to be typical and to be selected from various grades and departments of the Public School Course of Study; the relation of feeling to knowledge in Nature Study work.

School Gardens: The purpose of School Gardens; School Gardens as a phase of Nature Study work; their relation to Agriculture and Horticulture; the discussion of the purpose and possibility of the study of Agriculture and Horticulture in urban and rural Schools; care of School Gardens.

Practice in planning and plotting a Garden; planning School Grounds for Tree planting in accordance with the principles of Landscape Gardening; preparation and planting of experimental Plots in the School Grounds to illustrate the benefits of Rotation, Fertilizing, Spraying, Mulching, etcetera.

NOTE.—Teachers-in-training should make frequent excursions for the purpose of studying materials in their natural environment and relations. They should make collections of different kinds for their own use as well as to enable them to direct as Teachers the practical side of Nature Study. The nature of the collections will be regulated by the kind of School in which the Student will likely teach; rural Teachers should make collections of Weeds, Weed Seeds, Economic Plants, Diseased Plants, injurious and beneficial Insects, etcetera; urban Teachers, of Factory Products, Garden Flowers, etcetera. Besides acquiring experience in planning and planting Gardens, Teachers-in-training should visit Schools where successful Garden work is being done.

IX. *Elementary Science.*

33.—The special object of the Course in Elementary Science is to give the Teacher a better appreciation of its general principles, a more accurate knowledge of its facts, and greater familiarity with Apparatus; so that he may be able to teach natural and experimental Science systematically. The Course includes the following:—

The scope of the Experimental and Natural Sciences; their correlation with other School Studies.

A comprehensive and practical review of the Course in Elementary Science prescribed for the Lower School of High Schools, the emphasis in Experimental Science being placed on those facts and principles of Chemistry, Mechanics, Heat, Sound, Light, and Electricity which are essential to the understanding of common Natural Phenomena.

The construction of simple Apparatus. (See Manual Training Course.)

The Microscope: Its construction and use; selection and preparation of material for Microscopic work, having direct reference to Bacteriology,—a brief Course.

Methods of Teaching: The meaning and value of observation and experimentation; inductive and deductive methods of investigation; the place of Class Room discussion; demonstration by the Teacher and Laboratory work by the Pupil; the use of Note-books and Text-books.

NOTE 1.—The work in Elementary Science should be carried on through Class-room discussions and Laboratory work, with emphasis on the latter. Teachers-in-training should become familiar with methods of experimentation and should attain skill in Instrument manipulation. They should also be required to keep neat and accurate records of observation and experimental work.

NOTE 2.—In both the nature study and the elementary science course the subject matter of biology should receive more attention than that of physics and chemistry, which are subjects of the July Entrance Examination. The course in nature study is of more importance than that in experimental science.

X. *Arithmetic*.

34.—The special object of the Course in Arithmetic is to improve the Teacher's knowledge of the subject that he may use it effectively as a means of logical training, and more particularly that he may be prepared to give his Pupils such instruction in the various arithmetical processes as will enable them to make with accuracy, rapidity, and facility the calculations and computations which their future life may render necessary. The Course includes the following topics:—

The scope of Arithmetic; its relation to the other subjects of the Curriculum; importance of its practical aspects as related to the lives of the Pupils; danger of over-estimating its value as training in logic.

The origin of Number as the result of the necessity for the valuation or limitation of quantity by Measurement; the various steps involved in the development of the Number idea; the Unit, its nature and use; the necessity for standard Units; Number, a ratio.

Methods in Arithmetic: Analysis and synthesis, induction and deduction,—compared, illustrated and applied; graphic methods; use of concrete material in making clear new processes and in verifying and interpreting operations performed; the use of Text-books and of prescribed Apparatus; the importance of training in, and devices to secure, neatness, accuracy, and speed in computation; the importance, place and treatment of Oral Arithmetic; the value of Problems; the essentials of proper Solutions; Solutions by full analysis, and by performing operations only; "Unitary" method and method of direct measurement; grading of Problems; interest in problems for which the pupils themselves furnish the material; Blackboard work; drill and examination work in Arithmetic.

A thorough treatment of the various Arithmetical operations and their applications with special stress upon the requirements of Teachers engaged in public School work. This should include the following:—

Counting, measuring with standard units; numbers from 1 to 10, from 10 to 20, etcetera; number Pictures, Notation and Numeration; Addition Tables, Exercises, Devices; Subtraction—by decomposition, by Equal Additions, and by Complementary Additions; Multiplication—relation to other operations, Tables, Exercises, Factors, Division—Short and Long, Factoring, Cancellation, Division by Factors; Measures and Multiples.

Fractions: How and when to be introduced, different interpretations, Notations, rules for operations deduced and applied; Decimal Fractions, correspondence of methods of Numeration, Notation, and operations with those of Integers, recurring Decimals.

Applied Arithmetic: Percentage, Trade Discount, Commission, Insurance, Taxes, Interest, Discount, Stocks, Exchange; Tables of Weights and Measures; the Metric System; Mensuration, including the areas of Rectangles, Triangles, Parallelograms, and Circles, and the volume of Rectangular Solids, Cylinders and Prisms; Square Root.

XI. *Algebra.*

35.—The special object of the Course in Algebra is to familiarize the Teacher with its fundamental conceptions and to prepare him to present the various processes of the subject in the most effective way. Having regard to the fact that Algebra is Arithmetic generalized, its special object is the same as that of Arithmetic. The course includes the following topics:—

The scope of Algebra when the subject should be introduced.

Relation of Algebra to Arithmetic; a comparison of the nature and application of its symbols and operations with those of Arithmetic; the Equation as a means of connecting the subject with Arithmetic and of introducing its symbols; the origin and explanations of Algebraical Symbols; the relation of Algebra to Geometry.

The use of Induction, Deduction, and Mathematical Induction in Algebra.

Methods of Teaching Algebraic Notation, Addition, Subtraction, Multiplication, Division, Formulæ, Factoring, Measures, Multiples, Fractions; Testing Algebraic operations by "Checking."

The Equation: Its nature; identities; the solution of Equations of one and of two unknowns, and of easy Quadratics; the Mathematical Axioms employed in these solutions; the interpretation of results; the Equation applied to the solution of problems; comparison, where possible, of Algebraic with Arithmetical Solutions.

XII. *Geometry.*

36.—The special object of the Course in Geometry is to prepare the Teacher to train his Pupils to attain skill in the use of instruments, in accurate measurements, and in drawing; and, through these, in inductive and deductive reasoning. The course includes the following topics:

The scope of Geometry; when it should be begun; methods of treatment—inductive and deductive; the relation of Inductive Geometry to Deductive Geometry; the Inductive Course for beginners.

Method of introducing the Definitions.

The use of simple instruments, Compass, Protractor, Divider and Set Square, in the measurement of lines and angles; the construction of lines and angles of given magnitude; the construction of Geometrical Figures.

The inductive method of proving some of the leading propositions of Euclid, through the accurate construction of figures; the deductive application of principles reached through Induction.

Throughout the Course, accuracy in construction shall be insisted upon as co-ordinate with exactness of thought.

XIII. *Writing.*

37.—The object of the Course in Writing is to train the Teacher to write rapidly and legibly, and to make him familiar with the best means of securing the most satisfactory results in the teaching of the subject. The Course includes the following topics:

The purpose of writing; its correlation with other subjects.

A brief outline of the different methods of teaching the subject.

Penholding; position at the Desk; position of the Paper; the proper formation of the small and the Capital Letters and the figures; various movement exercises; practice on Paper and on the Blackboard.

Use of Headlines and Copy-books; use of Blank Paper; its ruling; value of transcription, dictation, and Composition in Writing; how general and individual faults are corrected; the formation of a characteristic hand; how to deal with pupils having some physical disability. Business Forms, including Bills, Receipts, Promissory Notes, Cheques, Drafts.

A brief review of the Lower School Course in Book-keeping, also affording practice in writing.

NOTE.—After the Teacher-in-training has mastered in class the proper formation of the letters, etcetera, and the movement exercises, the master should require him to hand in from time to time exercises for criticism until his handwriting is satisfactory.

XIV. *Art Work.*

38.—The special object of the Course in Art is to give the Teacher such a knowledge of the subject, such a training of his æsthetic nature, and such facility in the use of Art as a means of expression as will enable him to develop like tastes and powers in his Pupils. The Course includes the following topics:

The scope of Art: Art as a mode of expression and a means of æsthetic culture; its correlation with other subjects in the School Course.

Freehand Drawing: How to use the various mediums—pencil, charcoal, crayons, ink with pen or brush; the drawing of common Flat Objects such as leaves, grasses, brooms, shovels, saws, hammers, in an appropriate medium; the drawing of common spherical, cylindrical, and rectangular Solids, illustrating the principles of freehand Perspective; the grouping of Objects; simple Landscapes from nature and imagination; illustration of games, occupations, nursery rhymes and stories; pose drawing.

Blackboard Drawing: The use of white, black, and coloured Crayons on the Blackboard and on large pieces of Paper; rapid illustrative sketches to aid in the teaching of all subjects; Blackboard drawing specially important to the Teacher as a means of expression.

Water Colours: Theory of Colour; the Solar Spectrum; the six standard colours, red, orange, yellow, green, blue, and violet; the intermediate hues, red-orange, yellow-orange, yellow-green, blue-green, blue-violet and red-violet; the tints and shades of each colour in graduated scales; the pigmentary theory; primary, secondary, and tertiary colours; complementary colours; colour harmony, dominant, analogous, and complementary; the neutral value scale; the making and applying of graduated and uniform washes; the representation in colour, neutral values, and sepia, of Leaves, Grasses, Flowers, Fruits, Trees, Insects, pet Animals, Birds, and common Objects; the grouping of Objects; simple Landscapes from nature and imagination; elementary composition of Pictures.

Decorative Design: The principles that determine the rhythm, balance, and harmony of tones, measures, and shapes; borders, surface designs, designing of Christmas Cards, Programmes, Book Covers; Lettering; designs to be done in neutral value first and then carried out in colour.

How to study a Picture; the critical study of a few masterpieces of painting.

Books of Reference.—Prang's Text Books of Art Education; 7 books, $2.40. Prang's Art Education for High Schools. Prang's Drawing Course. Atkinson, Mentzner and Grover—Applied Arts Drawing Books. D. C. Heath & Co.—The Parallel Course Drawing Books. H. W. Poor—How to Draw. Practical Drawing—Arts and Crafts Course, 8 parts.

XV. *Manual Training.*

39.—The special value of the Course in Manual Training is to train the Teacher to appreciate the educational value of various forms of constructive work, and to select and use in the most effective ways constructive exercises in the varying conditions of urban and rural Schools. The Course includes the following topics:

The scope of Manual Training; its correlation with other subjects in the Curriculum; the selection of exercises based on the requirements of the School and the Home; outlines of courses in the different forms of hand work. The practical Course includes the following, with concurrent Methodology:

Handwork for Primary Grades: Typical forms of constructive work adapted to the capacities of children in the lower grades, including Weaving, elementary paper and cardboard work in Modelling.

Drawing: A short Course in Mechanical Drawing with and without instruments; Plans and Blue Prints.

Advanced Cardboard work; Book-binding, simple repair of Books; trimming and mounting of Pictures.

Modelling: Materials used for Modelling and how these are kept; Modelling natural forms; Plotting, Modelling as a means of teaching Geographical concepts; supplementing observation of the topography of School neighbourhood; supplementing Word Pictures in Readers, etcetera; Models used in conjunction with Drawing, etcetera; in teaching principles of Design.

Woodwork: Tools and how to keep them in good working order; designing; a short Course in Bench work; uses of Woods and their suitability to such uses.

The construction of simple forms of School Apparatus in Wood, Metal, Glass, and their combinations.

Co-operative exercises in the above forms of work.

XVI. *Household Science.*

40.—The special object of the Course in Household Science is to enable the Teacher to relate the work of the School to the activities of the Home. It is a form of Manual Training, and possesses the same educational value. The Course includes the following topics, with concurrent Methodology:

The Home: Purpose; use, furnishing, and care of each Room; methods of Cleaning.

Foods: Elements of Food required by the body; digestibility of these; analysis of Common Foods—milk, eggs, meat, fruit, vegetables, cereals; effect of Heat on these as to food value, digestibility, and flavour.

Cookery: Principles of combustion; care of Stoves; Fuels; economy in the use of Fuel; principles and practice of each method of cooking—Boiling, Simmering, Steaming, Steeping, Toasting, Broiling, Frying, Baking, etcetera; food combinations; flour mixtures, lightening agents used in these; Table service.

Bacteriology: Occurrence and nature of Bacteria; Sanitation based on this knowledge; preservation of Foods.

Needle Work: A study of each stitch on different textures and fabrics; application of these in making simple articles as Bags, Aprons, Handkerchiefs, Needlecases, Towels, etcetera; Mending, Darning, Patching, using different textures and fabrics; Button-hole making, sewing on Buttons, Hooks and Eyes; colour combinations; making Dolls' Clothes.

XVII. *Music.*

41.—The special object of the Course in Music is to train the Teacher in the use of Music as a means of self-expression and of æsthetic culture. The Course includes the following topics:—

Tune: Practice in Singing from the staff and tonic-solfa modulators; intervals of moderate difficulty, contained in the major Diatonic Scales; modulation from any given key to its relative minor, and its dominant and subdominant.

Time: Practice in singing rhythmical studies in simple or compound duple, triple or quadruple times; the pulse as the unit of measurement in time, with its divisions into halves, quarters, or thirds, in varied combination.

Ear Training: Development of the power to recognize by ear, and to transcribe the tonal and rhythmic elements of short musical phrases, when sung, or played.

Voice Culture: Practice in correct tone production; vowel formation; enunciation of consonants; breath control; correct intonation and the equalization of the various registers of the voice.

Songs: The study of Songs suited to the requirements of Pupils in all grades of Public and Separate Schools, with special attention to development of power in musical expression; the study of Part Songs of recognized merit, arranged for adult voices.

Notation: Elements of Notation, both tonic-solfa and staff; the formation of the major and minor Diatonic Scales; elements of modulation and transposition.

Vocal Physiology: Comparison of abdominal, intercostal, and clavicular breathing; the Larynx; action of the Vocal Chords in the production of the various vocal registers; influence of the mouth and nasal cavities on vocal resonance and vowel quality.

Methods: Concurrently with the foregoing Course, a practical knowledge of recognized systems of teaching the Tonic-solfa and Staff Notations shall be acquired; also of the relative importance of the Staff and Tonic-solfa systems and the grading of musical studies.

NOTE.—Teachers-in-training who, from any cause, consider themselves incapable of learning to Sing should present their cases to the Teacher of Music at the beginning of the Term. If, on examination, it should be found necessary, special instruction will be provided, adapted to their needs; and their efforts to overcome any natural disability which may be found to exist will be taken into account at the oral examination at the close of the Term. The written examinations, however, are compulsory for all Students.

XVIII. *Physiology and Hygiene.*

42.—The object of the Course in Physiology and Hygiene is to train the **Teacher in the knowledge requisite** for the maintenance of the health of both himself and his Pupils, and to qualify him for supervising the sanitary conditions of the School and its surroundings. The Course includes the following topics:—

School Hygiene: School sanitation.

Contagious and Infectious Diseases: Common facts of Bacteriology, how to detect existence of common infectious and contagious Diseases; modes of preventing spread of these Diseases; Sanitary Legislation; Duties of the Teacher.

Personal Hygiene (with the necessary minimum of Anatomy): Framework of the body; Spinal curvature, its causes. Digestive System; foods; care of Teeth; saliva. Physiology of respiration and circulation. Skin and other depuratory organs—hair, nails, bathing, clothing, etcetera. Muscles; the relation of exercise to health. Brain and nervous system; relation of mind to body; mental exercise; study; rules regarding mental work; irregular and overwork; mental strain and worry. Effects of Alcohol, Tobacco, etcetera, on organs and functions.

The Eye: Its physiology and hygiene; lighting; Myopia and Presbyopia; affections produced by improper accommodation; Colour blindness; tests for defective eyesight.

The Ear, the Nose, and the Throat: Their physiology and Hygiene; ear and throat troubles, causing dulness in pupils; tests for defective hearing and breathing.

Accident and Emergencies: First Aid in such cases as fainting, suffocation, drowning, hemorrhage, fractures and dislocations, venomous stings, poisoning, frost-bites, sunstrokes and heatstrokes, burns; bandaging.

Book of Reference.—Knight—Introductory Physiology and Hygiene.

XIX. *Physical Training.*

43.—The special object of the Course in Physical Culture is to enable the Teacher to make proper provision for the physical training of his Pupils. With Physiology and Hygiene (school and personal) as a basis it prescribes and directs rational forms of exercises for the attainment and maintenance of health, the development of a symmetrical body, and the formation of habits of grace and ease in muscular movement. To this end the Teacher-in-training should be made familiar with the German, Swedish, French (Delsarte), and American systems of Physical Training. The Course includes:—

Breathing Exercises: Running, hopping, quick walking.

Leg Exercises: Standing positions, fundamental stride, etcetera; standing with flexions of ankles and knees; fall-outs; charges; fencing positions and kneelings.

Arm Exercises: Starting position, hands at side, at shoulders, at thrust, at upward bend, at formal bend; movements of raising, swinging, rotation, circling, flexion, and intension.

Neck and Trunk Exercises: Flexion, extension, and rotation.

Free Exercises: All the simpler forms from fundamental positions; also compound movements of two parts in the same, opposite, and right-angled directions.

Tactics: Facings and steppings; marchings in various formations of rank, file, column, etcetera; fancy steps, following and changing steps, etcetera; running.

Special Exercises: For correcting the individual defects that may be found among children.

Recreative Gymnastics: Indoor and outdoor games.

XX. *School Law and Regulations.*

44.—The Ontario School Law and Regulations so far as they deal with the duties and obligations of Teachers and Pupils.

XXI. *Manners.*

45.—A Course in Manners. Especial care shall be taken that, while in attendance, the teachers-in-training shall observe the rules of Courtesy and social Etiquette.

Book of Reference.—Practical Etiquette.

SYLLABUS OF STUDIES AND REGULATIONS FOR KINDERGARTENS

Departments for the training of Kindergartners were opened at the Toronto Normal School in 1885 and at Ottawa in 1886.

THE KINDERGARTEN—ITS OBJECT AND PURPOSE.

1.—The purpose of the Kindergarten Course is to prepare Female Teachers in the theory and the art of organizing, governing, and instructing the **Pupils** of the Kindergarten.

The Kindergarten combines the nurture of the Home with the rational discipline of the School, and thus forms the necessary introduction to the Primary School. Through the Songs, Games, and Stories, ideals of right living on the plane of the child's life are made clear and self-compelling; and, through the Material, the intellectual powers are nourished, the senses are trained, interest is stimulated, constructive imagination is cultivated, and a basis is laid for the formation of good intellectual, moral, and physical habits. The Kindergarten thus preserves the freedom and play spirit of early childhood and at the same time prepares the child to be an intelligent, orderly, and industrious pupil of the school.

TRAINING SCHOOLS—THEIR SESSIONS AND TERMS.

2.—The Provincial Kindergartens for the training of Kindergarten School Directors are situated at Ottawa and Toronto. Any Public School Kindergarten may train Assistant Directors.

3.—The Session of the Kindergarten School will begin on the third Tuesday of September and end on the 30th day of June; and will consist of two Terms; the first from the opening of the School until the 22nd day of December, and the second from the 3rd day of January until the 30th day of June.

GRADES OF CERTIFICATES.

4.—The Education Department issues two grades of Certificates: Assistants' Certificates, valid for two years, and Directors' Certificates, valid during good conduct. No one without a Director's Certificate is eligible to take charge of a Kindergarten School.

Conditions of Admission for Assistant Kindergartners.

5.—(1) Application for admission to the course of training for Assistants shall be made to the Director in charge of the Kindergarten School not later than the second Tuesday of September. Each Applicant shall send with the application:

(*a*) A Certificate from competent authority that she will be at least eighteen years of age on or before the close of the Session.

(*b*) A Certificate of having passed the July Departmental Examination for Entrance into the Normal Schools.

(*c*) A deposit of $5, which will be returned to the Teacher-in-training before the end of October, but which will be forfeited if the Applicant fails to attend without giving satisfactory notice of withdrawal before the opening of the Training School.

(2) Each Applicant on presenting Herself at a Training School shall submit to the Director thereof:—

(*a*) A Certificate from the Principal of an Approved School that she has completed satisfactorily the subjects of the Lower School prescribed for the Normal School Entrance Examination. Failing this Certificate, she shall pass at a Normal School in September, immediately before the beginning of the session, the examination prescribed in the Normal School Syllabus of Studies.

(*b*) Proof that she is able to sing, and to play simple music at sight on the Piano or Organ.

(*c*) A Certificate from a Clergyman or other competent authority that she is of good moral character.

(*d*) A Certificate from a Physician that she is physically able for the work of a Teacher, and especially that she is free from serious pulmonary affection and from seriously defective eyesight and hearing.

(3) A Teacher-in-training who, in the opinion of the Director, is unduly defective in scholarship, or in natural aptitude, or whose progress, or conduct, is unsatisfactory, may be dismissed by the Director at any time during the Session from further attendance at the Training School.

Conditions of Admission for Directors of Kindergartens.

6.—(1) Application for admission to the course in training for Directors shall be made to the Deputy Minister of Education not later than the second Tuesday of September, on a form to be supplied by the Department of Education.

(2) Applicants must be the holders of Assistants' Certificates or have a Second Class Professional Certificate.

Certificates and Examinations.

Assistants and Directors.

7.—(1) Any person who attends a Kindergarten for one year and completes satisfactorily the Course prescribed for Assistants may, on the recommendation of the Director of such Kindergarten, endorsed by the Public School Inspector in whose inspectorate the Kindergarten is situated, be granted an Assistant's Certificate.

(2) The examination for Assistants shall include four Papers:—One on the Theory and Practice of the Gifts, one on the Theory and Practice of the Occupations, one on Songs, Games, and Stories, and one on Methods; each Paper valued at 300, and the book work at 1,200 marks.

(3) There shall be one Sessional Examination conducted by the Training Kindergartner, and a final examination conducted by a Committee of Directors appointed from the Kindergartners of the Province by the Education Department.

(4) The marks for each Paper at these examinations shall be divided as follows: One-fifth of the maximum for the Sessional examination, one-fifth for the Sessional records, and the remainder for the Final examination.

(5) Any Candidate who obtains 40 per cent. of the marks in each subject, and 60 per cent. of the total marks, shall be entitled to an Assistant's Certificate.

8.—(1) The holder of an Assistant's Certificate, or the holder of a Second Class Provincial Certificate, on attending a Provincial Kindergarten for one year, and on passing the prescribed examinations, may be granted a Director's Certificate.

(2) The examination for Directors shall include six Papers—Psychology and the Philosophy of Froebel as embodied in his teaching, History of Education, Theory and Practice of the Gifts and Occupations, Mutter and Kose-lieder, Nature Study, and Child Study and Methods, each valued at 500 marks.

(3) There shall be one sessional examination and one final examination conducted by the Staff and the Principal of the Normal School.

(4) The marks for each Paper at these examinations shall be divided as follows: One-fifth of the maximum for each Paper at the sessional examination, one-fifth for the sessional records, and the remainder for the final examination.

(5) The marks counted in estimating the final standing of the Teacher-in-training in Observation and Practice-teaching shall be those awarded her in these subjects during the Session, and more especially towards the close thereof, after an introductory Course of Lessons in each. The maximum marks for Practice-teaching and Observation shall be 900.

(6) In the case of Students taking the entire Course in one year a maximum of 1,200 may be awarded for Book-work.

(7) There shall be sessional examinations in Music, Art, and Physical Culture, each valued at 100 marks.

(8) Any Candidate who obtains 40 per cent. of the marks in each subject, 60 per cent. of the marks for teaching, and 60 per cent. of the total of the marks, may be awarded a Director's Certificate.

COURSE FOR ASSISTANTS.

I. KINDERGARTEN GIFTS.

9.—This Course shall include the following: A knowledge of the Gifts, their general objects as well as their specialties, how they are graded and why; their connection with other branches of Kindergarten work.

(1) *Symbolic Gifts, Including the First and Second Gifts.*

(A) *Theoretical Points for Discussion.*

(1) Description of each Gift.

(2) Analysis of the first Gift: Plaything; certain class of playthings; why colour, form, size, number, string; language.

(3) Analysis of the second Gift: Plaything; certain class of playthings; why form, size, number, string; language.

(4) Method of presentation and use: In the first gift: Play method, single object, classification of different possibilities. In the second gift: Play method, from one type to three general types, classification of different possibilities.

(5) Philosophical and pedagogical principles implied: Unity, self-activity, development, contrast, basis of experience, the concrete, the general to the particular.

(6) Mathematical basis: Why types; forms suggested by the play defined.

(7) Exercises suggested: Plays emphasizing activity; plays emphasizing imitation or analogy; plays emphasizing recognition of qualities; twirling games.

(8) Exercises originated by the students.

(9) Required Reading: Chapter on the Ball, Pedagogics of the Kindergarten, Froebel; Chapter on Infancy, Froebel's Education of Man; Chapter on Unity, Froebel's Educational Laws, J. L. Hughes; Chapter on Symbolism, Symbolic Education, S. E. Blow; the first and second songs in Blow's Commentaries of the Mother Play.

(B) *Practical Work.*

First Gift—Not fewer than six typical Songs that may be used in connection with the different classes of exercises suggested above, to be submitted in the Gift Book.

Second Gift—Not fewer than eight typical Songs that may be used in connection with the different classes of exercises suggested above, to be submitted in the Gift Book.

(2) *Building Gifts.*

(A) *Theoretical Points for Discussion.*

(1) Description of Building Gifts.

(2) Analysis: Discussion of building activities; race constructive activities; imitative play; organism in playthings; divisible material; number; measure as implied in building; decoration, etc.

(3) Method of presentation and use: Discussion of sequence; different illustrations of sequence in forms of objects and in forms of beauty, simple relationship, variation of one idea, memory sequence; different kinds of exercises, experimental, imitative, suggestive, memory, dictation, free invention.

(4) Philosophical and Pedagogical principles: Organic unity; relation of child and race; study of imitation; cause and effect; continuity; concept-making stage.

(5) Mathematical basis: Solid and surface forms defined; mathematical basis of building problems.

(6) Exercises suggested by the Director.

(7) Exercises originated: Building forms; decorative forms, borders, units.

(8) Required Reading and Quotations: Pedagogics of the Kindergarten: Chapters on the Third and Fourth Plays: Education of Man: Pages 71 to 79 and 108 to 111. Commentaries of the Mother Play: The Weather Vane, the Target, the Carpenter, the Bridge, the Little Artist.

(B) Practical Work.

Third Gift—Four original sequences in forms of life, not fewer than six forms in each sequence; three original sequences in forms of beauty, not fewer than six forms in each sequence.

Fourth Gift—Three original sequences in forms of life, not fewer than eight forms in each sequence; three original sequences in forms of beauty, not fewer than eight forms in each sequence.

Building problems for estimating dimensions, not fewer than four problems.

Exercises illustrating balance, surface representation, and communicated motion.

Fifth Gift—A list of original forms of life, not fewer than twelve; five sequences of beauty and of knowledge; developments of square and of triangular prisms.

Suggestions for different kinds of numerical exercises that can be given with the Fifth Gift.

Sixth Gift—A list of original forms of life, not fewer than six forms; two original sequences in forms of beauty, not fewer than three changes in each sequence; building problems, not fewer than six problems in the list.

Outlines of all exercises and sequences in the practical work with the Building Gifts to be placed in the Gift Book.

(3) Laying Gifts (*tablets, sticks, rings, and seeds*).

(A.) Theoretical points for discussion.

(1) Analogy or Symbolism.
(2) Picture representation.
(3) Decorative possibilities.
(4) Mathematical basis.

(B) Practical Work.

Seventh Gift (Tablets)—Derivation; definition; position of one Tablet; relative position of two Tablets to each other; mathematical figures that may be produced by combining two Tablets; mathematical figures produced by combining three Tablets; five life forms with two Tablets; five life forms with four Tablets; five life forms with eight Tablets; two life forms with sixteen Tablets.

All forms to be drawn in Gift Book. Each point in the development to be illustrated by any one form of tablet.

Decorative forms (symmetrical design)—Three designs emphasizing repetition, as in borders; three designs emphasizing units; two sequences, symmetrical designs; two designs emphasizing *all-over* repeats.

All forms to be drawn in Gift Book, illustrated by any one form of tablet.

Development of geometrical figures to three sizes:—Triangle, square, oblong, rhomboid, rhomb, trapezoid, hexagon, octagon; define each form; illustrate by any one form of tablet; comparison of geometrical figures formed by a given number of tablets of any one form.

Eighth Gift (Sticks)—Not fewer than three forms must be submitted with each of the following combinations:—Combination of sticks into life forms, using four sticks, even lengths; combination of sticks into life forms, using eight sticks, even lengths; life forms with sixteen sticks; life forms using sticks of any length.

All forms to be drawn in the Gift Book.

Decorative design:—Three designs emphasizing repetition, as in borders; three designs emphasizing units; two sequences, symmetrical design.

Ninth Gift (Rings)—Relative position of one large and one small ring to each other; exercise in the discovery of the relative position of the different sizes of rings to one another, one ring of each size; relative position of two half-rings to each other; relative position of one half-ring and one whole ring to each other; life forms with five rings, not fewer than three drawn; life forms with ten rings, not fewer than three to be drawn; life forms with four half-rings, not fewer than three to be drawn; miscellaneous forms of life with rings, half-rings and quarter-rings, not fewer than three to be drawn; symmetrical designs using rings, half-rings and quarter rings, not fewer than three forms; miscellaneous forms using rings, half-rings, quarter-rings, and sticks of any size, two forms.

II. KINDERGARTEN OCCUPATIONS.

10.—This Course shall include a knowledge of the Froebelian Occupations, and their connection with other branches of the work.

Theoretical points for discussion.

(1) Description of each Occupation. (3) Relation to race Activities.
(2) Fundamental basis of each Occupation. (4) Art basis.
(5) Relation of each Occupation to the harmonious growth of the child.

Practical work to be submitted in Occupation Book.

(1) *Sewing.*

Illustrations required in sequence of Sewing.

First Development—The square, the objective point.

(1) Straight lines of one length. (3) Variations in length.
(2) Variations in position. (4) Horizontal lines of one length.
(5) Horizontal lines, variations in position.
(6) Horizontal lines, variations in length.
(7) Right angles, repeat the order in numbers 1, 2, and 3, above.
(8) Square, repeat the order in numbers 1, 2, and 3, above.

Other forms of development:—Oblong, repeating the above order; square on the diagonal, oblique lines, first degree, repeating the above order; rhombus, oblique lines, second degree, repeating the above order; miscellaneous combinations, the student indicating the combination used, and repeating to the third point as above.

Sewing Inventions.—General Plan:—(*a*) From a centre; (*b*) a border; (*c*) an "all-over" design.

Forms of invention:—Vertical lines of one length following the general plan; one in vertical lines of all lengths following the general plan; one in vertical and horizontal lines of one length following the general plan in (*a*) and (*b*); one in vertical and horizontal lines of all lengths combined, following the general plan in (*a*) and (*b*); one in vertical, horizontal and slanting lines of one length, following the general plan in (*a*), (*b*), and (*c*); three inventions in any form using all the elements (vertical, horizontal and slanting lines of squares and oblongs), of any length, following each part of the general plan.

(2) *Drawing.*

Combine five vertical lines from one to five lengths into a triangle; repeat this triangle in four different positions; combine these four triangles into **(1)** a solid figure, (2) a hollow figure, (3) two intermediate figures; from the **solid** and hollow figures form four limbs: first limb, placing the lower half of the solid figure below the lower half of the hollow figure; second limb, placing the upper half of the solid above the upper half of the hollow figure; third limb, placing the right half of the solid to the right of the right half of the hollow figure; fourth limb, placing the left half of the solid to the left of the left half of the hollow figure; combine these four limbs into a large solid figure; reversing the position of the limbs, combine them into a large hollow figure; make from the four original triangles two twisting figures; make from these twisting figures two limbs, thus: by placing the right half of each figure to the left of the left half of the same figure; make two large figures by using each of the limbs twice. In the first figure the original solid will appear; in the second figure the original hollow will appear.

Apply these directions to any three of the following elements:—Horizontal lines, right angles, slanting lines of the first order, slanting lines of the second order, slanting lines of the first and second order, slanting lines of all orders, half circles, circles.

Drawing Inventions.—Types of Inventions:—Vertical and horizontal lines of one length, one form of life, and one form of beauty; vertical and horizontal lines of all lengths, one form of life, one form of beauty; slanting lines, first order, all lengths, one form; slanting lines, all orders, all lengths, one form; right isosceles triangles, all sizes, one form of life, two forms of beauty; equilateral triangles, all sizes, one form of beauty; two inventions in half circles, one border form; two inventions in circles, one border form; one invention in quarter-circles, half-circles, and circles combined, all sizes.

(3) *Art Work.*

Simple lines of pictorial composition to be applied to all work, *e.g.*, the paper on which a drawing is to be made should suit it in size and proportion; attention to be paid to variety in space-division.

The following mediums should be used:—Brush and ink, water colours, crayons, charcoal, and soft lead pencil.

Types of Work.—Nature drawing, including the drawing of grasses, sprays, of leaves and flowers, and fruit on the branch; landscape; figure pose; **animal studies**; still-life studies, including common objects, single and in groups; pictorial illustrations; design: (*a*) The decorative treatment of nature and other studies, making a clear distinction between this treatment and pictorial drawing; (*b*) the making of units of abstract "spots" and "spots" derived from nature, using in surface and borders; colour schemes from nature; colour harmonies and their discovery in nature; application of colour harmonies to design.

Colour Book.—The following classification of colour with definitions, to be shown with surface paper:—Scale of standard colours; **scale of tones of one** colour; scale of relative hues; contrasted, dominant, analogous, complementary, and perfected harmonies.

Illustrations to be mounted on grey cardboard.

Book of Reference.—Mark M. Maycock—A Class Book of Colour, Teacher's edition.

(4) *Weaving.*

Two movements in weaving:—(1) Following the line of the warp to give vertical effects; (2) varying from the vertical by a movement right or left, on the line of the warp, to produce diagonal effects.

First Series.—Vertical effects, regular combinations as one and two, three and two, two and four, etcetera.

Second Series.—Variations from this basis, producing stripe or bar, as two and one and one, three and one and one and one, three and three and one and one, not fewer than eight mats in the series.

Third Series.—Diagonal effects, using basis of first and second series for these, with possible variations in position, as right to left, left to right, etcetera, with not fewer than ten mats in this series.

Miscellaneous Mats.—Borders, four mats; all over repeats, four mats; units of design, two mats; conventional repeats, two mats.

NOTE.—Complementary, contrasted, dominant, and analogous harmonies should be used with these.

(5) *Folding.*

Salt-cellar ground form.—Salt-cellar, star, king's crown, queen's crown, paper box, satchel; an original sequence of life forms suitable for children four years of age; five or more inventions in life forms in the salt-cellar ground form; eight inventions in forms of beauty from the salt-cellar ground form; double salt-cellar ground form; cap, muff, boots, bobbin, shirt, trousers; inventions in life forms from the double salt-cellar ground form; table-cloth ground form; table-cloth, table handkerchief case, windmill, vase, boat with sail, chicken, double boat, boat with box, loose box, close box, picture frame, mirror, chinese junk; the table-cloth ground form, an original sequence of life forms suitable for children six years of age, not fewer than six; five sequences of forms of beauty, showing hexagons, trapeziums, in two positions, rhomboid, rhomb; original inventions from the table-cloth ground form, twelve or more; a series of forms from the triangular basis, not fewer than eight.

Encourage the repetition of one form in a mosaic.

(6) *Cutting.*

Forms—Right isosceles triangle, the ground form, a logical sequence of not fewer than eighteen figures; equilateral triangle, the ground form, a logical sequence of not fewer than twelve figures; freehand cutting, not fewer than twelve figures.

(7) *Pease Work.*

Forms—With one stick, a list of objects not fewer than five; simple life forms, using two, three, and four sticks, without enclosure of space; four life forms from each of the quadrilaterals; one or more life forms from each of the triangles; one or more life forms from each prism; one form of beauty from each of the following figures: Square, triangle, pentagon, hexagon, octagon.

(8) *Modelling.*

Typical forms, the other forms to be evolved in logical process from the sphere: Sphere, oblate spheroid, prolate spheroid, ovoid, cube, cone, frustum, conoid, cylinder; one form to be modelled from an object, based on each of the above types; one form, free invention, based on each of the above types; three miscellaneous inventions made large, such as a vase, a fruit basket, fruit, an animal.

III. SONGS AND GAMES.

11.—Songs and Games.—This course shall include a study of the general objects of the songs and games from Froebel's standard as indicated in the Mother Play, using the following songs as types:—The Taste, Naming the Fingers, The Bird's Nest, The Two Gates, The Little Gardener, The Carpenter, The Light Bird, The Knights, and the Good Child.

Theoretical Points for Discussion.

(1) The significance of gestures.

(2) The principles by which teachers should be guided in the selection of songs and games.

IV. STORIES.

12.—Candidates should be qualified to explain the value of stories, to classify them, and to show by what principles they should be guided in their selection.

V. NATURE STUDY.

13.—This Course includes the following:—A knowledge of the meaning of Nature Study and of its scope; the study of Froebel's Methods; (see commentaries on the Bird's Nest, The Two Gates, The Little Gardener); a review of the elementary Science course prescribed for the Lower and Middle Forms of the High School, for the purpose of a deeper sympathy and a clearer understanding of Nature through a study of the underlying laws of her development, such as adaptation of structure to habit and environment, the interdependence of things in Nature, etc.

Frequent excursions should be taken to suitable places where the materials of Nature Study can be observed and studied in their natural environment; and the habit of keeping records of observation should be established.

Book of Reference.—Hodge—Nature Study and Life.

VI. METHODS.

14.—This course includes an elementary explanation of the processes of mental development, with practical application to the exercises of the Kindergarten; and a study of the life of Froebel.

References.—E. Wiebé—Paradise of Childhood. Courthope Brown—Froebel.

NOTE.—The references to the Mother Play are not intended to cause the Assistants to make an intensive study of this work. They are merely suggestions to the trainer for developing Froebel's methods of teaching.

VII. PHYSICAL TRAINING.

15.—The special object of the course in Physical Culture is to enable the Teacher to make proper provision for the Physical Training of her pupils. With Physiology and Hygiene (School and Personal) as a basis, it prescribes and directs rational forms of exercises for the attainment and maintenance of health, the development of a symmetrical body, and the formation of habits of grace and ease in muscular movement. To this end the Teacher-in-training should be made familiar with the German, Swedish, French (Delsarte), and American systems of physical training.

Free Exercises: All the simpler forms from fundamental positions; also compound movements of two parts in the same, opposite, and right-angled directions.

Tactics: Facings and steppings; marching in various formations of rank, file, column, etcetera; fancy steps, following and changing steps, etcetera; running.

Special exercises for correcting the individual defects that may be found among children.

Recreative gymnastics, or gymnastic games; indoor and outdoor games.

COURSE FOR DIRECTORS OF KINDERGARTENS.

I. APPLIED PSYCHOLOGY AND THE PHILOSOPHY OF FROEBEL.

16.—The special object is to give a simple course in Applied Psychology with practical illustrations and to make the Student familiar with Froebel's educational principles. The Course includes the following Topics:—

(1) Aims of education; individual and social phases of education, their relation; the Froebelian ideal of Education.

(2) The educational process, its nature and relation to the end and means of education; development through self-activity; symbolic expression; play as an educational factor.

(3) Psychology: Field of Psychology; methods of psychological enquiry; the use of psychology to the teacher.

(4) Habit: Automatic and reflex action; primary instincts; development of reflexes; formation of habits and the development of motor control; the relation of habit to will; the intellectual and ethical aspects of habit.

(5) Attention: Nature of attention as a process; conditions of attention; forms of attention; discrimination; association; interest, its nature and relation to attention; methods of securing and retaining attention; obstacles to attention.

(6) Apperception and Retention: Meaning of the terms; their relation; mental assimilation, growth and development.

(7) Sensation: Distinctive characteristics of sensation; relation of sensation to knowledge; neural basis of sensation; classification of sensations.

(8) Perception: Distinctive characteristics of perception; genesis and development of perception; training of perception and formation of habits of observation.

(9) Imagination: Conditions of re-presentation; distinctive characteristics of imagination; relation of image to idea; mode of operation of imagination; reproductive imagination; productive imagination; training of imagination.

(10) Memory: Distinctive characteristics of memory; conditions of retention, recall, recognition; training and development of memory processes.

(11) Conception: Distinctive characteristics of conception; relation of concept and image; the function of language in the formation of concepts.

(12) Judgment and Reasoning: Distinctive characteristics of judgment; relation of concept and judgment; the distinctive characteristics of reasoning; training in judgment and reasoning.

(13) Affective elements of Consciousness: Elementary forms of affection; affection in its relation to sensation, perception, imagination, memory, and reasoning.

(14) Emotion: Distinctive characteristics of emotion; conditions of emotional development; classification of emotions; training of emotions.

(15) Development of the Will: Impulsive and volitional acts distinguished; distinctive characteristics of volition; definition of character; means of character development.

Books of Reference.—Betts—The Mind and its Education, $1.00. Horne—Philosophy of Education. Froebel—Education of Man. James—Talks to Teachers.

II. KINDERGARTEN GIFTS.

17.—The special object of this Course is to give a knowledge of the educational value of the Gifts and of their practical use in the Kindergarten. The Course includes the following topics:—

A study of the Gifts as a whole: Types of form, number, and relationship; relation of creative activity in form, number, and relationship; philosophy embodied in the Gifts; psychological study of Play.

Symbolic Gifts.—First and Second Gifts.

Study of child symbolism and racial symbolism; the meaning of play. *First Gift*—Application of symbolism to the education of little children; practical exercises with Students for classification of games; recording good typical exercises in Gift Books. *Second Gift*—Study of the four typical forms, a basis for classification, relation to crystalography, relation between force and form; place of the typical fact in the Kindergarten; the law of the Mediation of Contrasts and the method of application in the Kindergarten; the relation of the Second Gift to the child in activity games, in symbolic games, and in games emphasizing form, classification, and construction.

Building Gifts.—This Course includes a study of the following:—The investigative instinct in the race and in the child; the building instinct in the race and in the child; the history of the development of architecture in the race; relation of form, number and balance to creative work; correspondence between Building Gifts and organic development; correspondence between Building Gifts and mental development; method of using the Building Gifts; different types of exercises.

Laying Gifts.—This Course includes a study of the following:—Analysis of surface forms; picture making, its significance to the race and the child; psychological and philosophical significance of; method of using the Laying Gifts; different types of exercises.

Books of Reference.—1. Froebel—Pedagogics of the Kindergarten. 2. Froebel—Education of Man. 3. Snider—Play Gifts.

III. Industrial Occupations.

18.—The special object of this Course is to give the Students a knowledge of the educational value of the Occupations and of their practical use in the Kindergarten. It includes the following topics:—The instinct of creative self-activity, its place in the development of conscious individuality; the analysis of Play and Work, and the process of development from one to the other; study of the occupations as types of the Arts and Industries of the race; methods of expression, imitation, repetition, contrast, harmony; unity of Life the Goal, (*a*) the necessity of emphasizing a logical process, (*b*) law of contrast and mediation; discussion of methods in the Occupations; the supplementary Occupations, their value and limitations.

Occupation of Cutting.—Basis for Work:—Necessary elements, beauty, utility; sequence necessary to develop the idea of relationship; methods of expression: repetition, grouping, symmetry, harmony.

Different kinds of Cutting.—Froebel's sequence of Cutting, valuable for symmetry and sequence; nature and object Cutting, illustrating Songs, etcetera; free Cutting, its value and limitations.

Students work in.—Outline Cutting, with straight lines, with circular lines; Flowers, Seeds, etcetera, to be formed into borders; Leaf Cutting, freehand, of well known Leaves, these to be arranged into borders and symmetrical designs; typical Trees, used for artistic designing of borders and symmetrical designs; harmony work, dissimilarity united under a common thought, balance in every picture to be observed; Landscape Work: simple, Earth and Sky; with one dominant object; use of Trees.

Occupation of Sewing.—Sewing, a logical series of creations through lines and the combinations of lines; applications of method to Sewing; imitation, repetition, contrast, symmetry, and harmony in creation; two kinds of Cards, those used for Borders, those used for Figures; points to be noticed in the creation of a series, or sequence, spacing, proportion, colour, contrast to mediation.

Borders, how to evolve the series from the children:—Vertical lines, even spacing; vertical lines, broken spacing (grouping); vertical lines, uneven length (grouping); combining of vertical and horizontal lines to form a Border; combine these into objects of nature and forming them into a Border; the borderwork to be (pass through the same process as the vertical and horizontal); transforming these into objects of nature and forming them into a Border; the borderwork to be followed by symmetrical designing.

IV. Industrial Art.

19.—The special object of Art is to enable the Students to teach the Drawing and Colouring in the Kindergarten, to sketch sufficiently to be able to illustrate on Blackboard, or Paper, and to broaden their culture through an appreciation of the beautiful in form and colour. The Course includes the following topics:— Representation; Froebelian drawing, method of teaching; outline drawing, method of teaching; freehand drawing, method of teaching; how to use the various mediums: pencil, charcoal, crayons, ink with pen and brush; the drawing of flat objects such as leaves, grasses, etcetera; the drawing of common spherical, cylindrical and rectangular solids, illustrating the principles of freehand perspective; simple landscapes from nature and imagination; illustrations of Froebelian songs and games.

Water Colours: Theory of Colour; the Solar Spectrum; the six standard colours; the intermediate hues; the tints and shades of each colour in graduated scales; the pigmentary theory; primary, secondary, and tertiary colours; complementary colours; colour harmony: dominant, analogous, and complementary; the neutral value scale.

Decorative Design: Principles that determine the rhythm, balance, and harmony of tones, measures and shapes; borders and surface designs; outlining the development of architecture and ornament.

Picture: The critical study of a few masterpieces.

Books of Reference.—Froebel's Education of Man, pp. 75-78; 288-294. Prang's Text-books of Art Education, 7 books. Arthur W. Dow—Composition. Mark M. Maycock—A Class Book of Colour—Teacher's Edition.

V. Mother Play.

20.—The special object of the Course is a study of the educational principles and practice of Froebel as embodied in the "Mutter and Kose-Lieder." Throughout the course the relation between the Mother Play and other subjects of the curriculum, such as Psychology, Child Study and the practical work of the Kindergarten, should be constantly observed. It includes the following topics:—An analysis of the Mother Play as a whole; the history of its development; the educational aim of the book; its value in the Kindergarten and in the Training School; a detailed study of each typical song, its educational principles and practical application; the development of typical experiences through groups of songs.

Books of Reference.—S. E. Blow—Mottoes and Commentaries of Froebel's Mother Play. S. E. Blow—Songs and Music of Froebel's Mother Play. S. E. Blow—Letters to a Mother. S. E. Blow—Symbolic Education.

VI. Teaching by Means of Stories.

21.—The special object of the Course is to enable the Students to understand the value of stories, to make suitable selections, and to tell them successfully. It includes the following topics:—The educational value of stories; the study of the different classes of stories according to subject matter and suitability to the age of children; the analysis of selected stories; the necessary elements in valuable stories; discussions of the proper use of humour, the negative element, and rhymes; how to tell a story.

Each Student shall write two original stories, one subject to be selected by the Student and one by the Teacher; each Student to have a Book wherein will be kept lists of typical stories, classified according to the principles of Froebel's Mother Play, including stories for special festivals.

VII. HISTORY OF EDUCATION.

22.—The object of the Course in the History of Education is to widen the professional outlook and rationalize School practice through the discussion of the development and the merits and the defects of educational theories. It presupposes an historical background and discusses movements rather than individuals. The Course includes the following topics:—

Outline of the History of Education prior to the Fifteenth Century.—This should be a brief survey of those conditions and forces which were specially significant in determining later important movements. It should contain concise references to the following topics:—Education in its simplest forms among primitive peoples; the rise of the teaching class and the beginnings of School organization; the aim, organization, content and effect of Spartan, Athenian, and Roman Education; the educational theories of Socrates, Plato and Aristotle; the influence of Christian doctrines in educational thought and practice; the early Christian Schools; Monasticism and Education; the development of Scholasticism; organization and influence of the early Universities; the educational system of Chivalry; the influence of Saracen learning.

The Renaissance.—The leading tendencies of the Renaissance as a movement; the origin of these tendencies; conditions favouring the development of the movement; its history in Italy and in Teutonic Countries; the work of Petrarch, Boccaccio and the Byzantine Greek Teachers; the effects of the Renaissance in determining educational ideals and practice; the content and method of earlier and later humanistic education; educational leaders of the humanistic movement; the work and influence of Vittorino da Feltre, Erasmus, Ascham, and Sturm; the influence of the Renaissance on the organization of the Schools; typical humanistic Schools, the German Gymnasium, the English Public School and the Colonial Grammar School.

Reformation and Counter-reformation.—Relation of the Reformation to the Renaissance; the reformation movement in its relation to the development of elementary and secondary education in Europe; Luther and Elementary Education in Germany; rise of state supported and controlled Systems of Education; the educational tendencies of the counter reformation; the educational works of the Jesuit Order; subject matter, method and organization of Jesuit Schools; training of Teachers in the Jesuit Order; the Port Royal Schools: their aim, organization, Curriculum and methods; their influence; the Christian Brothers and Elementary Education in Roman Catholic Countries.

Realistic Education.—The development of Realism as an educational movement; its relation to Humanism; humanistic realism as represented by Rabelais and Milton; social realism as represented by Montaigne; sense-realism as represented by Ratich, Bacon, Mulcaster and Comenius; Bacon's "new method" for the discovery of truth; the influence of his theories on education; Comenius' conception of the purpose, content, method and organization of education, compared with modern ideals; brief account of his life and works; his place in education.

Disciplinary Conception of Education: Essential features of the modern disciplinary conception of education; its origin; strength and weakness of the theory; the educational theories of John Locke; his relation to disciplinary education and to later movements.

Education According to Nature: Relation of naturalistic tendencies in education to previous movements and to the condition of the times; history of the development of these tendencies; examination of Rousseau's educational theories as developed in the "Emile"; permanent results of his influence.

Modern Educational Theories: The Psychological ideal as represented in Pestalozzi; character and significance of the Pestalozzian movement; brief account of the life and works of Pestalozzi; formulation of his educational principles; his influence on education; the Herbartian movement; its relation to Pestalozzianism; Herbart's conception of the purpose, the means and the method of education; the doctrine of the correlation of studies; general characteristics of the Froebelian movement; brief account of Froebel's life and work; his educational theories as embodied in the Kindergarten; his influence on educational practice.

Scientific tendencies in education; theory of education as formulated by Herbert Spencer.

Book of Reference.—Munroe—Brief Course in the History of Education.

VIII. NATURE STUDY.

23.—The special object of this Course is to broaden the Student's culture by giving her a deeper knowledge of and sympathy with nature; and to enable her to present the subject of Nature Study in the Kindergarten according to Froebelian Methods. The Course includes the following topics:—The pedagogical view of the subject, including the character and scope of Nature Study; its adaptability to the tendencies and needs of the child; the special purpose to be kept in view in the treatment of the subject; the Froebelian idea of Nature Study as shown in The Mother Play, and in the Education of Man; the general method of presentation; the study of special topics dealing with the materials of Nature Study and illustrating methods of presentation in the Kindergarten; a study of plant and animal life from the standpoint of organic development for the purpose of understanding Froebel's parallel between the laws of nature and laws of mental development; a series of lessons on the Heavenly Bodies, observing the principal Constellations and tracing their movements throughout the Seasons; the preparation of Maps of the Constellations, to be seen during each Season.

Frequent excursions to be made to available localities where materials may be studied in their natural environment and relation; the making of collections of different kinds for extended observation and study; how to direct, as Teachers, the practical side of nature work.

School Gardening: Its relation to the general Nature Study Course; the pedagogical views of the subject; practice in planning and planting a Garden; the selection of suitable plants for School Gardens; growth and care of plants suitable for the School Room.

IX. CHILD STUDY.

24.—The special object of this Course is to aid the Teacher-in-training to study the development of the child definitely and systematically; to enable her to adapt intelligently her methods in each subject to the child mind at the different stages of its growth, and, by developing an intelligent sympathy, aid her in solving the problems of the management of the Kindergarten. The Course includes the following topics: The scope of Child Study; methods of investigation; importance of the interpretation as well as the discovery of the child's activities; formative influences in the development of character: nationality—the importance of the study of history in relation to child study, heredity, environment, and personality; mental types and variations from normal mental conditions; causes of, and methods of dealing with, unbalanced temperaments; the child's physical characteristics; children's motives and ideals; the study of children along the lines suggested in the Course of applied Psychology.

Child Study is to be closely connected with the work in Observation and Practice Teaching.

Books of Reference.—Kirkpatrick—Fundamentals of Child Study. Froebel—Education of Man. King—Psychology of Child Development. Tracy—Psychology of Childhood. Preyer—Infant Mind.

X. Methods of Teaching.

25.—The special object of this Course is to enable the Student to teach intelligently, to deal correctly with the problems of order and discipline, and to understand the principles involved in the construction of Programmes and Time-tables. The Course includes the following topics:

Programmes: The purpose and value of; the principles involved in their construction; the point of departure in Programme making, the child's essential experiences; the relation of the Mother Play to the Programme; continuity in the evolution of the child's ideals; unity; freedom and spontaneity; typical Programmes.

NOTE.—The Students during the latter part of the year are to construct the Programmes used in the practice Kindergarten, present them first in the Programme-class for discussion and revision, and afterward enter them in a Programme-book.

Time-tables: Their value; points to be observed in their construction.

Teaching: The meaning of Education through play; relation between play and work; characteristics of good teaching; evils of formalism; the Teacher's personality; characteristics of a good Lesson in matter and method; aim and value of questioning; characteristics of good forms of questions; value and limitations of typical forms of exercises; the meaning of good order; chief elements of governing power; analysis of successful methods; importance of right physical conditions; other helpful factors; ends and necessity of discipline, right conditions of, judicious and injudicious methods of.

NOTE.—Systematic observation and practice teaching to be continued daily throughout the year, the Students being divided into suitable groups and the observation and practice teaching supervised by the Staff and the results discussed at a suitable period.

Each Student-in-training shall be required, towards the end of the Course, to take charge of the practice Kindergarten for a week. She shall be notified of the subject and the scope of the work to be done, and shall present a plan of her method for each day of the week, for criticism.

XI. The Special Object of Music.

26.—The special object of the Course in Music is to train the Teacher in the use of Music as a means of self-expression and of aesthetic culture. The Course includes the following topics:

Tune: Practice in Singing from the staff and tonic-solfa modulators; intervals of moderate difficulty, contained in the major diatonic scales; modulation from any given key to its relative minor, and its dominant and subdominant.

Time: Practice in Singing rhythmical studies in simple, or compound duple, triple, or quadruple, times; the pulse as the unit of measurement in time, with its divisions into halves, quarters, or thirds in varied combination.

Ear Training: Development of the power to recognize by ear, and to transcribe the tonal and rhythmic elements of short musical phrases, when sung or played.

Voice Culture: Practice in correct tone production; vowel formation; enunciation of consonants; breath control; correct intonation; and the equalization of the various registers of the voice.

Songs: The study of songs suited to the requirements of pupils in all grades of Public and Separate Schools, with special attention to development of power in musical expression; the study of part songs of recognized merit, arranged for adult voices.

Notation: Elements of notation, both tonic-solfa and staff; the formation of the major and minor diatonic scales; elements of modulation and transposition.

Vocal Physiology: Comparison of abdominal, intercostal, and clavicular breathing; the larynx; action of the vocal chords in the production of the various vocal registers; influence of the mouth and nasal cavities on vocal resonance and vowel quality.

Methods: Concurrently with the foregoing Course, a practical knowledge of recognized systems of teaching the tonic-solfa and staff notations shall be acquired; also of the relative importance of the staff and tonic-solfa systems and the grading of musical studies.

FACULTIES OF EDUCATION IN THE UNIVERSITY OF TORONTO AND IN QUEEN'S UNIVERSITY, KINGSTON.

GENERAL INFORMATION IN REGARD TO THE FACULTY OF EDUCATION UNIVERSITY OF TORONTO.

The Faculty of Education was created by resolution of the Board of Governors of the University in December, 1906. Its first Curriculum was adopted in June, 1907, and it began its first session in October, 1907.

The Faculty of Education is the University's professional School of Education. It trains Candidates for Diplomas as special, or regular, Teachers, and in particular for Provincial Certificates as First-class Public School Teachers, High School Assistants, Specialists, and Inspectors. It also gives instruction looking towards post-graduate Degrees in Arts, and offers Courses for Degrees in Pedagogy.

The Students in Education may use the University's Library, Gymnasium, Athletic Fields, etcetera, under such conditions as obtain with other Students. In short, they enjoy all the privileges of University Students and are subject to the same Regulations.

Application for admission to the Faculty should be made to the Secretary of the Faculty before October 1st. All fees should be paid to the Bursar of the University.

Courses for Provincial Certificates.

(a) The General Course and the First Advanced Course, as the professional Courses for an Interim First-Class Public School and an Interim High School Assistant's Certificate.

(b) The Second Advanced Course, as the professional Course for an Interim High School Assistant's Certificate.

(c) The Special Courses for Specialists as the professional Courses for Interim Specialist's Certificates.

(d) The Special Course for Public School Inspectors, as the professional Course for a Public School Inspector's Certificate.

A Candidate for admission to the Faculty of Education shall submit with his application:

(1) A Certificate from a competent authority that he will be at least 19 years of age before the first of October.

(2) A Certificate from a Clergyman, or other competent authority, that he is of good moral character.

(3) A Certificate in detail from a Physician that he is physically fit for the work of a Teacher, and especially that he is free from serious pulmonary affection and from serious defects in eyesight and hearing.

(4) One or other of the following:

(a) His Certificate of graduation in Arts from the Registrar of any University in the British Dominions.

(b) His Senior Teacher's Certificate.

(c) Until the Session of 1910-1911, his Certificate from the Registrar of the Department of Education that he has passed the July Examination for Entrance into the Faculty of Education.

[After the Session of 1910-1911, in addition to his Certificate of having passed the July Examination for Entrance into the Faculties of Education, he shall be required, if a Candidate for a Certificate as Teacher in a Public School, to submit, endorsed thereon, the prescribed Certificate from the Principal of an Approved School that he has completed satisfactorily the Lower School subjects of the High School prescribed for Entrance into the Faculty of Education. Failing this Certificate, he shall pass at the University in September an examination in the following subjects of the Lower School Course of the High Schools, with 40 per cent. in each Examination Paper and 60 per cent. of the aggregate of the marks:

Reading, Spelling, Writing, Bookkeeping, and Business papers, Art, Biology, Geography, English Grammar, and Arithmetic and Mensuration.]

A General Course consists of three parts:

Part I.—1. The History of Education and Educational Systems, the Principles of Education, Psychology and General Method, School Management and School Law, and Special Methods in the subjects of the Public School Course, and the following subjects of the High School Courses:

English with History and Geography, Mathematics, Latin, and one of the following groups:

(a) Biology, Physics, Chemistry, and Mineralogy.   (c) Greek and French.
(b) French and German.   (d) Greek and German.

2. A review by the Student, from an academic standpoint, of the subjects of the High and Public School Courses.

Part II.—A Course of instruction, both academic and professional, in the Nature Study, Elementary Science, Music, Art, Commercial Work, Constructive Work, and Household Science (for women) of the Public School Course, and the Reading and Physical Training of both the High and the Public School Courses.

Part III.—Observation and Practice Teaching in the Public and the High Schools of Toronto, with Observation in ungraded rural Schools. The Observation will involve the equivalent of forty School Lesson-periods; and the Practice Teaching, the equivalent of twenty School Lesson-periods; or of more, in both cases, according to the experience, aptitude and progress of the Student.

In both the Observation and the Practice Teaching of this Course, the emphasis will be laid upon the work of the Public Schools and the Lower School work of the High Schools.

The First Advanced Course trains for Certificates as Teachers both in Public and High Schools, and consists of three Parts:

Part I.—1. The History of Education and Educational Systems, the Principles of Education, Psychology and General Method, School Management and School Law, and Special Methods in the subjects of the Public School Course and the following subjects of the High School Courses:

English with History and Geography, Mathematics, Latin, and one of the following groups:

(a) Biology, Physics, Chemistry, and Mineralogy.   (c) Greek and French.
(b) French and German.   (d) Greek and German.

The instruction in the History of Education and Educational Systems, the Principles of Education, and Psychology and General Method in this sub-section will be of a more advanced character than that given in the General Course, and will assume a knowledge of elementary Psychology and Ethics.

2. A review by the Students, from the academic standpoint, of the subjects of the High and the Public School Courses.

Part II.—A course of instruction, both academic and professional, in the Nature Study, Elementary Science, Music, Art, Commercial Work, Constructive Work, and Household Science (for women) of the Public School Course and the Reading and Physical Training of both the Public and the High School Courses.

Part III.—Observation and Practice Teaching as defined in Part III. of the General Course.

The Second Advanced Course trains for Certificates as Teachers in High Schools only, and consists of three Parts:

Part I.—1. The History of Education and Educational Systems, the Principles of Education, Psychology and General Method, School Management and School Law, and Special Methods in the following subjects of the High School Courses:

English with History and Geography, Mathematics, Latin, and one of the following groups:

(a) Biology, Physics, Chemistry, and Mineralogy. (c) Greek and French.
(b) French and German. (d) Greek and German.

The instruction in the History of Education and Educational Systems, the Principles of Education, and Psychology and General Method in this sub-section will be of a more advanced character than that given in the General Course, and will assume a knowledge of elementary Psychology and Ethics.

2. A review by the Student, from the academic standpoint, of the subjects of the High School Courses.

Part II.—1. A Course of instruction, both academic and professional, in the Reading and Physical Training of the High School Courses.

2. A Course of instruction in one of the academic departments for Specialists' certificates recognized by the Education Department. This Course of instruction is to be approved by the Faculty of Education as equivalent to the Public School subjects in Part II. of the First Advanced Course.

Part III.—Observation in the Public and High Schools and Practice Teaching in the High Schools of Toronto. The Observation will involve the equivalent of forty Lesson-periods, and the Practice Teaching the equivalent of twenty Lesson-periods, or of more in both cases according to the experience, aptitude and progress of the Student.

Special Courses include:

1. (a) Courses for Specialists under the Regulations of the Education Department of Ontario.

(b) A Course for Inspectors of Public Schools.

2. (a) In both the General and Advanced Courses, special training will be provided for Candidates for diplomas as Specialists.

(b) For a Public School Inspector's Diploma there will be an Examination in May, open to those who have fulfilled the conditions prescribed by the Education Department for Public School Inspectors' Certificates. The subjects of the Examination will be as follows:

Modern Systems and Tendencies in Education; History of Public Education in Ontario; School Administration and Law; School Inspection and Supervision, including the Supervision of Instruction in all subjects of the Public School Course.

REGULATIONS OF THE FACULTY OF EDUCATION.

1. Students in attendance who are Graduates in Arts before the beginning of the Session may elect the General Course or one of the Advanced Courses. All other regular Students, including Graduates in Arts who are exempt from attendance, shall take the General Course.

2. Students who complete the General Course, or an Advanced Course, will receive the Diploma of their respective Courses.

Students in the General Course or in an Advanced Course, who hold academic Certificates as Specialists, and who complete their special and their regular Courses, will receive Diplomas as Specialists.

Bachelors in Arts who obtain Honour standing in one of the Advanced Courses will be entitled to the Degree of Master of Arts under the conditions defined in Section 1 (d) of the Regulations respecting that Degree.

3. The standing of the Students in attendance in the General, an Advanced, or a Special, Course shall be determined by the combined results of the Term work and the May Examinations. The Term work shall consist of such exercises and tests as the Faculty may prescribe, in particular of mid-term Examinations which shall emphasize the academic aspects of the Public and High School subjects. The maximum marks for the Term work in any subject shall be forty per cent. of the aggregate of marks for that subject.

4. Part I. and Part II. Examinations are held in May, at Toronto, or at such local centres as may be selected by the Senate. Part II. Examinations may also be held at convenient periods during the Session. The percentage requirements for a Pass in the General and Advanced Courses are forty per cent. of the marks for each subject, and sixty per cent. of the aggregate of marks for each of Parts I., II., and III. The requirements in the Inspectors' Course are forty per cent. of the marks for each Paper and sixty per cent. of the aggregate of marks; in the Specialist Courses sixty per cent. of the marks in each subject. The requirement for Honours in the General, or Advanced, Courses or in the Inspectors' Course, is seventy-five per cent. of the aggregate of marks. Honours will be awarded only when all the Examinations of a Course are completed at one time.

5. A Candidate unsuccessful in Part III., or a Candidate who, while successful in Part III., has not obtained at least 35 per cent. of the marks for each subject in Parts I. and II., and at least 55 per cent. of the aggregate of the marks for each of said Parts, will be required to attend a second Session and pass in Parts I., II., and III. Unsuccessful Candidates who are not required to attend a second Session may complete their Courses by passing in Parts I. and II. at one subsequent Examination.

6. (a) Regular attendance in the General and the Advanced Courses is compulsory, except for such Students as are exempt from attendance under the Regulations of the Education Department of Ontario.

(b) Students who in the opinion of the Staff are unduly deficient in scholarship, or whose conduct, or progress, is unsatisfactory, may be dismissed from attendance at any time during the Session.

7. A Student preparing for a Certificate of qualification issued by the Education Department may take, in addition to the subjects of his Course in the Faculty of Education, a Course in a subject recognized by the Education Department for academic certificates, but only with the consent of the Faculty of Education; and no such Course shall be allowed to interfere with his regular Course as prescribed in the Faculty of Education.

8. Candidates for Specialists' Certificates under the Regulations of the Education Department shall have their academic standing approved by the Education Department before entering upon their special Courses.

9. Subject to the approval of the Minister of Education, the Faculty of Education may take such modifications of the scheme of optional groups in Part I. of any of the Courses as will suit the condition of Candidates who obtained their academic standing in Courses other than those recognized in the Regulations of 1904.

10. (*a*) The annual fee for the General, or the Advanced, Courses (with or without the Course for Specialists), which shall include the Library, Gymnasium, and Examination fees, shall be $15.00. The fee for the Examination in the General, or Advanced, Courses, when the Examination is not taken during the regular Session, shall be $15.00 or $10.00 for each Part when taken in Parts. The fee for the Specialists' Examination, when taken apart from the regular Course, shall be $5.00 for each **Examination Paper**. The fee for the Inspectors' Examination shall be $15.00. The fee for the University Diploma will be $2.00.

(*b*) All Students exempt from attendance, who are duly registered in the Faculty and who pay the annual fee of $15.00 (which shall not in this case include the fee for Examination), may receive from the Members of the Faculty such guidance in their Courses as may reasonably be given to Students not in attendance.

REGULATIONS OF THE EDUCATION DEPARTMENT.

1.—Certificates of qualification may be awarded by the Education Department on the results of the Examinations of the Faculty of Education as follows:

(1) *Interim High School Assistants' and Interim First-class Public School Certificates,* one or both, as the case may be.

(*a*) To Students who have attended regularly and have fulfilled the conditions prescribed by the Education Department for Candidates for Teachers' Certificates, and who have obtained in each of Parts I., II., and III. of their Courses 40 per cent. of the marks for each subject and 60 per cent. of the aggregate of the marks for the Term's work and final Examinations.

(*b*) To Students who are exempt from attendance and from the Examination in Part III., and have fulfilled the conditions prescribed by the Education Department for Candidates for Teachers' Certificates, and who have obtained at the Examinations in each of Parts I. and II. of their Courses 40 per cent. of the marks for each subject and 60 per cent. of the aggregate of marks.

(2) *Interim Second Class Public School Certificates,* valid for one year, to Students in the General and First Advanced Courses who have obtained at least 35 per cent. of the marks for each subject in Parts I. and II., and at least 55 per cent. of the aggregate of the marks for each of said Parts, and have passed in Part III.

(3) *Interim Specialists' Certificates*—(*a*) To Candidates in attendance who have fulfilled the conditions of the General, or the Advanced, Course, and who have obtained 60 per cent. of the marks assigned to the Term's work and final Examinations in the Special Course of their department.

(*b*) To Candidates who are exempt from attendance and who have obtained 60 per cent. of the marks assigned to Paper or Papers in their department.

(4) *Public School Inspectors' Certificates*—To Candidates who have obtained 40 per cent. of the marks for each Paper and 60 per cent. of the aggregate of marks.

2.—(*a*) Teachers who have been granted only Interim High School Assistants' Certificates may, without further attendance, obtain Interim First-Class Public School Certificates by passing at one Examination and with the usual percentages in the special Public School subjects of the General Course and by satisfying the Faculty by a practical test of their ability to teach Public School Classes.

(*b*) Teachers who hold First-Class Public School, or High School, Assistants' Certificates, interim, or permanent, may, without further attendance, obtain Interim Specialists' standing, provided they hold the necessary academic Certificate and pass in May the professional Examinations for such standing in the Special Courses prescribed by the Faculty of Education.

(*c*) Teachers who hold permanent Second-Class Certificates, with at least the academic standing prescribed for Entrance into the Faculties of Education, and who present Certificates of at least five years' successful experience from the Public, or Separate, School Inspectors under whom they have taught during that period, may write at the Examination for Interim First-Class Public School Certificates, taking Parts I. and II. together, or separately, but without taking the prescribed Session, or being required to pass in Part III. Such Candidates will be granted Interim High School Assistants' Certificates also on satisfying the Faculty, by a practical test, of their ability to teach High School Classes.

(*d*) Candidates who have attended a Session in any Course, and have obtained at least 35 per cent. of the marks for each subject in Parts I. and II., and at least 55 per cent. of the aggregate of the marks for each of said Parts, and have passed in Part III., may write at the examinations for Interim First-Class Public School, or High School, Assistants' Certificates without taking the Session over again, or being required to pass again in Part III.

3.—(*a*) An Interim First-Class Public School Certificate shall entitle the holder, if under 21 years of age, to teach in a Public, or Continuation, School only; and, if over 21 years of age, to teach in a High School also.

An Interim High School Assistant's Certificate shall entitle the holder, if over 21 years of age, to teach, as Assistant, in a High School, or a Continuation School.

Interim Certificates may be extended from year to year by the Minister of Education, on the report of the Public, Separate, Continuation, or High School, Inspector under whom the holder of the Certificate has last taught.

(*b*) After at least two years' successful experience as a Teacher, the holder of an Interim Certificate shall, on the report of the last Inspector concerned, be entitled to a permanent Certificate as a First-Class Public School Teacher, or as a High School Assistant, ordinary or special, according to the class of school in which the holder of the Certificate has taught, provided, however, that the holder of the Interim Certificate is then 21 years of age.

A Graduate in Arts in any University in the British Dominions, who holds a High School Assistant's Certificate, and who, as shown by the report of the High School Inspector, has taught successfully at least three years (two of which were spent in a High School or in a Continuation School with at least two Teachers) shall be entitled to a Certificate as Principal of a High School or Collegiate Institute or of a Continuation School with at least two Teachers.

General and Advanced Courses.

Part I.
History of Education, and Educational Systems.

General Course: Evolution of education in primitive society. Oriental education—Chinese, Hebrew and Hindu education as types. Educational ideals of eastern and western nations compared. Greek life and civilization. Old Greek education with Spartan education as its type. New Greek education with Athenian education as its type. The sophists and the great educational theorists, Socrates, Plato and Aristotle. The idea of a liberal education. Roman life and civilization. Roman educational ideals and practices contrasted with those of Greece. Great educational theorists, Cicero and Quintilian. The idea of a practical education. Life in the Middle Ages. Christianity and Education. The education of the monastery and the castle. Scholasticism and the rise of the universities. The Renaissance and the rise of humanism. Educational significance of the Renaissance. The work of Boccaccio, Erasmus, Vittorina Da Feltre, Ascham and Sturm. The Reformation and Counter-Reformation. Luther and elementary education. The Jesuits and the Teaching Orders. Realism and science in education. Types of realism represented by Rabelais and Milton, by Montaigne, by Ratich, Bacon and Mulcaster, and by Comenius. Education according to nature. Development of the new ideal in Locke, Rousseau and Basedow. The Pyschological ideal in education as represented in the work of Pestalozzi, Herbart and Froebel. The scientific movement. The sociological ideal. Present day tendencies in education. The development of public education in Germany, Great Britain, France, the United States, and Ontario.

References.—Monroe—A Brief Course in the History of Education. Davidson—A History of Education.

Advanced Course: The General Course repeated, with a detailed study of special periods.

References.—Monroe—A Brief Course in the History of Education. Davidson—Education of the Greek People. Woodward—Vittorino da Feltre and other Humanist Educators. Laurie—John Amos Comenius. Davidson—Rousseau and Education according to Nature. Pinloche—Pestalozzi and the Modern Elementary School. De Garmo—Herbart and the Herbartians. Hughes—Froebel's Educational Laws for all Teachers.

Principles of Education.

General Course: (1) A Course of Lectures dealing in the main with the following topics:—

Introduction: The meaning and aim of Education; statement and examination of typical theories; individual and social elements in Education: the School as an agency of social progress; its relation to other social Institutions, the Home, the Church, the State, the vocation, etcetera; the School as a means of individual growth and development; the problem of individual differences in children; the Curriculum as an expression of social values; its origin; phases of its growth; present day movements for reform of the Curriculum.

Physical Aspects of Education: The significance of infancy; the native physical endowment of the child; heredity and environment as factors in human development; instinct in Education; its relation to habit and intelligence; physical growth and development; motor activities in Education; their relation to mental and moral development; play as a factor in Education; the mental and moral bearings of Schoolroom Hygiene.

Mental Aspects of Education: The doctrine of self-activity; imitation and curiosity as factors in mental growth; the nature of the learning process; meaning of such terms as experience, knowledge, judgment, etcetera; place of analysis and synthesis, deduction and induction in the growth of experience.

Moral Aspects of Education: The Instinctive element in morality; the Social element in morality; the moral aspect of various School-room activities; the Curriculum as an agency in moral instruction and moral training; the Teacher as a factor in the moral life of the child.

(2) The Study in Class of certain educational classics selected from the following list: Milton, Tractate on Education; Locke, Thoughts on Education, and Conduct of the Understanding; Froebel, The Education of Man; Rein, Outlines of Pedagogics; Spencer, Education; Dewey, The School and Society, and Ethical Principles underlying Education.

References.—Raymont—Principles of Education. Horne—Psychological Principles of Education. Giddings—Elements of Sociology. Dewey—School and Society.

Advanced Course: 1. Lectures of a more advanced character upon the topics detailed in Part I. of the General Course, supplemented by the investigation of special topics by the students in the Course.

2. The Study in Class of Educational Classics selected from the list given in (2) above.

References.—Those of the General Course, and in addition: Mackenzie—Social Philosophy. Dewey—The School and the Child. The Educational Situation.

Psychology and General Method.

General Course: Relation of the mental to the physical. Inborn tendencies. Sensation. Perception. Attention. Memory. Imagination. Conception. Apperception. Judgment and Reasoning. Feeling and Emotions. Interest. Habit. Will. Character. Development of Motor Ability. Curiosity. Suggestion and Imitation. Heredity and Environment. Adolescence and Child Study. Meaning of Instruction. Instruction and Education. Psychologic Foundations of Method. General Principles. Function and Conduct of the Recitation, including a discussion of such topics as typical Lesson forms and teaching devices, planning for a Lesson, Class preparation for a Lesson, development of a Lesson, Lesson plans.

Advanced Course: Lectures of a more advanced character upon the topics of the General Course as outlined above with a study of special problems in Education.

References.—Titchener—Primer of Psychology. Angell—Psychology. James—Talks to Teachers on Psychology. Kirkpatrick—Fundamentals of Child Study. Thorndike—Principles of Teaching. Bagley—The Educative Process. McMurry—Method of the Recitation. Findlay—Principles of Class Teaching.

School Management and School Law.

(a) Moral and intellectual **purposes** of Schools. Physical training. Discipline. School habits. Incentives. Punishments. School Organization. Grading.

Course of Study and Time-Tables. Classification and promotion. Daily Programmes. Principles of teaching. Technique of Class Instruction. Recitations and questionings. Examinations and other tests.

(*b*) Problems in School Administration. Functions of various types of Schools. State and school. Forms of educational control. Executive and legislative functions of School Boards and School Officers. Relation of Principal to Teachers, and Teachers to Parents, Trustees and Caretaker. Business administration. Sites, Buildings and equipment. Class Room Decoration. School Sanitation and Hygiene. School Reports. Compulsory Education. Industrial Education. Schools for Delinquents and Defectives. School and Home. School and Society. Co-operation of Schools with other educational agencies. School Law and Regulations of Ontario.

References.—Landon—**Principles and Practice of Teaching and School Management.** Bagley—**Class Room Management. The School Law and Regulation of Ontario.** Shaw—**School Hygiene.**

The Courses in Special Method will deal with the selection and organization of the content of the various School subjects in the terms of the Curricula of the Education Department of Ontario, and will include a discussion of methods of instruction in each subject, together with an academic review of the subject itself. The following subjects will be discussed:

Part I.

(For further details see the Public and High School Courses of the Education Department of Ontario.)

English—Spelling, Composition, Literature, Grammar, and Rhetoric; History; Geography; Mathematics—Arithmetic, Mensuration, Algebra, Geometry, and Trigonometry; Latin; Greek; French; German; Science—Botany, Zoology, Physics, Chemistry, and Mineralogy.

References.—Text-books authorized for the Public and High Schools of Ontario. Chubb—**The Teaching of English.** Carpenter, Baker and Scott—**The Teaching of English.** McMurry—**Special Method in History, in the Reading of English, etcetera, etcetera.** Geikie—**Teaching of Geography.** Smith—**The Teaching of Elementary Mathematics.** Young—**The Teaching of Mathematics in Secondary Schools.** Bennett and Bristol—**The Teaching of Latin and Greek.** Report of the Committee of Twelve (on Modern Languages). Jespersen—**How to Teach a Foreign Language.** Lloyd and Bigelow—**The Teaching of Biology.** Smith and Hall—**The Teaching of Chemistry and Physics.** Ganong—**The Teaching Botanist.**

Part II.

Note.—While the same general purposes direct the Courses in the subjects of both Part I. and Part II., special emphasis will be placed upon the academic review in the Courses in the subjects of Part II.

(For further details consult the Curricula of the Education Department of Ontario.)

Nature Study and School Gardens: Character and Scope of Nature Study. Material for Nature Study. Content. Methods. Purpose of School Gardens. Preparation and Plans. Excursions and Collections.

Elementary Science: Botany, Zoology, Physics and Chemistry as prescribed for Fifth Forms and the Continuation Schools. Construction of Simple Apparatus. A Course in the Methods of Experimentation, and in the Manipulation of Apparatus.

Music: A Course both practical and theoretical to include Tune, Time and Rhythm, Ear-training, Voice-training, Singing, Tonic-Solfa and Staff-Notation, the Minor Mode etcetera.

Art: Freehand. Colour Work. Clay Moulding. Water Colour Sketches. Model and Memory Drawing. Freehand Perspective. Applied Design. Correlation with other subjects.

Commercial Work: Writing—Material, Position, Movement, Grouping and Practice. Bookkeeping. Business Forms. Stenography. Typewriting.

Constructive Work: Its Nature, Scope and History. Educational and Practical Values. Methods. Tools and Materials. The Workshop. Practice in the use of Paper, Cardboard, Raffia, Reed, Clay, Wood. Mechanical Drawing.

Household Science: Needlework. Cooking. Household Economics. Correlation with other subjects.

Reading: Its Scope and Processes. Voice Training. Phonics. Forms of Reading. Methods in Reading.

Physical Training: Breathing Exercises. Exercise for Legs, Arms, Neck and Trunk. Corrective Exercises. Games. Gymnastics. Calisthenics. Drill. Treatment of Emergencies. Personal Hygiene.

References.—The Text-book authorized for the Public and High Schools of Ontario. Silcox and Stevenson—Modern Nature Study. Hodge—Nature Study and Life. The Educational Music Course, Books I., II., III., IV. (Teachers' Edition). Art Education Drawing Book Course (Prang). McMurry—Special Method in Primary Reading. Penman's Art Journal.

Candidates for Diplomas as Specialists should familiarize themselves with the recent literature on the professional phases of their special departments.

Course for Public School Inspectors.

1. Modern Tendencies in Education and Modern Educational Systems (two Examination Papers).

Modern Tendencies in Education may be studied in current educational literature and in such works as Education and Interest (De Garmo), The Educational Situation and the School and the Child (Dewey), A Modern School (Hanus), The Children (Darroch), Among Country Schools (Kern), Moral Education (Griggs), The Place of Industries in Elementary Education (Dopp), School Sanitation and Decoration (Burrage and Bailey).

Modern Educational Systems, in particular the systems of Great Britain, Germany, and the United States may be studied in current educational literature or in portions of such works as the Educational Systems of Great Britain and Ireland (Balfour), The History of Education in the United States (Dexter), German Education, Past and Present (Paulsen, trans. Lorenz).

It is to be understood that all books mentioned in this sub-section, as in the other sub-sections of this Course, are suggestive, and in no sense obligatory.

2. History of Public Education in Ontario (one Examination Paper).

Candidates should have an intelligent conception of the Educational System of Ontario. This conception implies a knowledge of the System in its present forms, Higher, and in particular, Secondary and Primary, and in its historical development. References suggested here are the general Histories of Canada, or Ontario, portions of recent Reports of the Education Department of Ontario, the biographies of Strachan and Ryerson, Public Education in Upper Canada (Coleman), etcetera.

3. School Administration and Law (one examination Paper).

Candidates should familiarize themselves in general with the Public Schools Act, the High Schools Act, the Truancy Act, Department of Education Act, and the Regulations of the Education Department and in particular with the Law and Regulations in regard to the appointment and authority, qualifications and duties of Inspectors.

4. School Inspection, and Supervision in Public School Subjects (one Paper).

Candidates must show an intelligent appreciation of the duties and responsibilities of Inspectors; they must be acquainted with the best methods of School Management, and they must give evidence of a competency to instruct and to supervise instruction in any of the subjects of the Public School Courses of Study. The only reference suggested here is the School Law and Regulations of Ontario. For the rest the Candidate must rely upon his own knowledge of official practice in Inspection, and upon his own experience in School Management and in Class Instruction, supplemented by such reports and Books as he may deem pertinent.

Degrees in Pedagogy—General Information.

Recent Statutes have made important changes in the former Regulations as to the Degrees in Pedagogy. The fee schedules have been readjusted; the Courses themselves have been reorganized in sympathy with later movements in Education while they have also become more professional in purpose; and the Examinations have been divided into Sections to be taken in the same, or different, years; and, through the Staff of the Faculty of Education, the University will give assistance in the form of suggestions as to reading to all Candidates for the Degrees. It may be added that the Education Department of Ontario exempts the Holder of the Degree of B.Pæd. or D.Pæd. from one, or two (as the case may be), of the seven years of experience required of Candidates for Inspectors' Certificates.

The Degree of Bachelor of Pedagogy (B.Pæd.) is granted to Students in the Faculty of Education under the following conditions:

1. The Candidates shall hold (a) a Degree in Arts, not being an honourary Degree, from any University in the British Dominions; and (b) a First-Class, or High School, Assistant's Certificate granted by the Education Department of Ontario or a Certificate of equal value.

2. The Candidates shall pass an Examination in the History of Psychology and Ethics, in the Principles of Psychology, Ethics, and Sociology, with their applications to Education, in the Science of Education, and in the History and Criticism of Educational Systems.

3. Before he completes the examination for the Degree the Candidate shall submit Certificates of at least two years of successful experience in teaching.

4. The Candidate shall register in the Faculty of Education at least six months before he presents himself for Examination. The fee for registration is $10.

5. The Examination shall be held in May at the University of Toronto or in any other locality in the Province chosen by the Candidate and the Senate and under a presiding Examiner appointed by the Senate, provided the Candidate, or Candidates, thereat defray the cost of the local examination. The Candidate shall send notice not later than the 1st of April of his intention to take the examination and of the locality he has chosen for such examination.

6. The fee for the full examination is $10, or for each Section, if taken separately, $8. The fee for the Degree is $20. All fees shall be paid to the Bursar with the application for registration or examination as the case may be.

7. The work in each Section (A or B) may be taken and will be examined on separately. The standard for a Pass Degree shall be 50 per cent. of the marks assigned to each Section. The Candidate who obtains 50 per cent. of the marks of each Section and 66 per cent. of the aggregate of marks shall be awarded a Degree with Second Class Honours. The Candidate who obtains 50 per cent. of the marks of each Section and 75 per cent. of the aggregate of marks shall be awarded a Degree with First Class Honours.

8. Subject of Examination: (The bibliographies given below are not obligatory, they are suggestive only.)

A.

History of Psychology and Ethics (two Papers);
Principles of Psychology, Ethics, and Sociology (two Papers).

References.—Weber—History of Philosophy. Sidgwick—History of Ethics. Muirhead—Chapters from Aristotle's Ethics. Watson—Hedonistic Theories. Descartes—Method and Meditations (Veitch). J. S. Mill—Examination of Hamilton, and Utilitarianism. Wundt—Outlines of Psychology. Titchener—Outlines of Psychology. King—Psychology of Child Development. Thorndike—Educational Psychology. Mackenzie—Manual of Ethics. Giddings—Elements of Sociology.

B.

Science of Education (two Papers);
History and Criticism of Educational Systems (two Papers).

References.—Dickinson—The Greek View of Life. Monroe—Source Book of the History of Education for the Greek and Roman Period. Spencer—Education. Hall—Youth. Tyler—Growth and Education. O'Shea—Education as Adjustment. De Garmo—Secondary Education. Hanus—Educational Aims and Educational Values. Monroe—Text-book in the History of Education.

Candidates are recommended to read such additional works on the great modern educators (Comenius, Erasmus, Rousseau, Pestalozzi, Herbart, Froebel, Spencer, etcetera) as may be necessary to ensure an intelligent conception of their place and importance in the history of education. Specific advice as to Books will be given to those desiring it.

The Degree of Doctor of Pedagogy (D.Pæd.) is granted to Students in the Faculty of Education under the following conditions:

1. The Candidate shall hold a Degree in Arts, not being an honorary Degree, from a University in the British Dominions, with (*a*) Honours in a department or (*b*) a Provincial Certificate as specialist, or (*c*) the Degree of B.Pæd.

2. Before he completes the examinations for the Degree, he shall submit evidence of at least three years of successful experience as Teacher, or Inspector.

3. The Candidate shall register in the Faculty of Education at least six months before he presents himself for examination. The fee for registration is $10.

4. The Candidate shall pass an examination in the History of Psychology and Ethics, in the Principles of Psychology, Ethics, and Sociology, with their applications to Education; in the Science of Education, and in the History and Criticism of Modern Educational Systems, with special reference to Ontario. He shall also submit on, or before, April 1st a Thesis on some educational topic selected with the approval of the Faculty of Education. After the Examiners have reported in favour of the Candidate's answer Papers and Thesis, and before the Degree of D.Pæd. is conferred, the Candidate shall furnish the Registrar of the University with one hundred printed copies of the Thesis. The Thesis shall contain the report of the Examiners.

5. The examination, which may be taken as a whole, or separately, in Sections, shall be held at such times and under such conditions as to date of application, place of examination, division of the Examination, etcetera, as obtain with the Bachelor's Degree.

6. The fee for the whole Examination is $10, and for each Section when taken separately $8. The fee for the Degree is $25. All fees shall be paid to the Bursar with the applications.

7. Subjects of Examination: (The bibliographies given below are not obligatory; they are suggestive only.)

A.

History of Psychology and Ethics (two Papers);

Principles of Psychology, Ethics, and Sociology (two Papers).

References.—Höffding—History of Modern Philosophy. Windelband—History of Ancient Philosophy. Plato—Republic. Dewey—Leibnitz (Griggs series). The Philosophy of Kant, Watson's Selections. Wundt—Physiological Psychology. Seashore, Elementary Experiments in Psychology. James—Principles of Psychology. Stout—Analytical Psychology. Green—Prolegomena to Ethics. Bosanquet—Philosophical Theory of the State. Ward—Applied Sociology.

B.

Science of Education (two Papers);

References.—Harris—Psychological Foundations of Education. O'Shea—Dynamic Factors in Education. Harper—Trend of Higher Education. Fitch—Thomas and Matthew Arnold. Brown—The Making of our Middle Schools. Hall—Aspects of Child Life and Education. Welton—The Logical Bases of Education. Payne—Education of Teachers.

Candidates are recommended to read the more important educational works of Bacon, Locke, Rousseau, Pestalozzi, Herbart and Froebel, so far as to ensure an adequate knowledge of their influence on modern education. They will be expected, moreover, to make themselves familiar with the existing Educational Systems of Great Britain, France, Germany, United States and Canada, and with contemporary movements and tendencies in education by means of standard works and current educational literature. Specific advice as to Books, etcetera, will be given to those desiring it.

The Summer Session of the University of Toronto.

The Special Course for Candidates for Degrees in Pedagogy will take the form of a Seminar for the discussion of the more significant theories of Plato, Aristotle, Descartes, Leibnitz, Kant, Mill, Green, etcetera.

The examinations for First Class Public School and High School Assistant Certificates may be taken in May of each year. Candidates who hold Second Class Certificates and have taught successfully for five years are exempt from attendance in the Faculty of Education. Candidates who have attended and taken the Practical Examinations of the Normal College, or (under certain conditions) of the Faculty of Education, are also exempt from attendance. For all Candidates so exempt and for others who desire the training, Courses of Instruction are offered in the Summer Session. While the Lectures in these Courses are limited to specified subjects, it is intended that the work in education should include instruction and guidance in all subjects of the May Examinations.

The Courses in Art and Elementary Science are complex in character and are so arranged as to meet the requirements of the First Class Public School and High School Assistant Examinations and (in Art, at least) of the Art Specialist Examinations, and to meet in particular the demands that rise out of the new Regulations as to "Approved Schools."

While the Course in Physical Training covers the work prescribed for First Class Public School and High School Assistant Certificates it is offered primarily in response to recent tendencies in School practice.

In the Summer Session of 1909, Courses were offered in the following subjects: The Psychology and Ethics of the Courses in Pedagogy; the History of Education and Educational Systems; the Principles of Education; Applied Psychology and General Method; Elementary Science, Art, and Physical Training.

Information in Regard to the Faculty of Education, University of Queen's College.

Students in attendance in the Faculty of Education, apart from those who pursue Courses leading to Degrees in Pedagogy, shall be classified as Regular Students and Occasional Students. Regular Students shall be those admitted under the Regulations stated below.

All Classes except such as are directly practical are held in the Arts Building of the University, and every opportunity is given to the Students to share to the full in all phases of University Life. The Victoria Public School and the Kingston Collegiate Institute are used as Model Schools for observation and practice.

Intending Students should communicate with the Registrar at any time during August, or September, and must register for either the General, or the Advanced, Courses not later than October 5th. A Candidate for admission to the Faculty shall submit the following:

1. A Certificate from a competent authority that he will be at least 19 years of age before the first of October.

2. A Certificate from a Clergyman, or other competent authority, that he is of good moral character.

3. A Certificate in detail from a Physician that he is physically fit for the work of a Teacher and especially that he is free from a serious pulmonary affection and from serious defects in eye sight and hearing.

4. One, or other, of the following:

(*a*) His certificate of graduation in Arts from the Registrar of any University in the British Dominions.

(*b*) His Senior Teacher's Certificate.

(*c*) Until the Session of 1910-1911, his Certificate from the Registrar of the Department of Education that he has passed the July Examination for Entrance into the Faculty of Education.

[After the Session of 1910-1911, in addition to his Certificate of having passed the July Examination for Entrance into the Faculties of Education, he shall be required, if a Candidate for a Certificate as Teacher in a Public School, to submit, endorsed thereon, the prescribed Certificate from the Principal of an Approved School that he **has completed** satisfactorily the Lower School subjects of the High School prescribed for Entrance into the Faculties of Education. Failing this Certificate, he shall pass at the University in September an examination in the following subjects of the Lower School Course of the High Schools, with 40 per cent. in each Examination Paper and 60 per cent. of the aggregate of the marks: Reading, Spelling, Writing, Bookkeeping and Business papers, Art, Biology, Geography, English Grammar, and Arithmetic and Mensuration.]

Courses of Study.

The Courses of Study shall be a *General Course, Advanced Courses, Special Courses*, and the *Courses for Degrees in Pedagogy*.

A *General Course* shall consist of three parts:—

Part I.—1. The History of Education and Educational Systems, the Principles of Education, Psychology and General Method, School Management and School Law, and special Methods in the subjects of the Public School Course and the following subjects of the High School Course:

English, with History and Geography, Mathematics, Latin, and one of the following groups:—

(*a*) Biology, Physics, Chemistry and Mineralogy;
(*b*) French and German;
(*c*) Greek and French;
(*d*) Greek and German.

2. Such a review by the Student, from the academic standpoint, of the foregoing subjects, as is required for the High and Public School courses.

Part II.—A Course of instruction, both academic and professional, in the Nature Study, Elementary Science, Music, Art, Commercial Work, Constructive Work, and Household Science (for women) of the Public School Course, and the Reading and Physical Training of both the High and the Public School Courses.

Part III.—Observation and Practice Teaching in the Victoria School and Kingston Collegiate Institute, with Observation in ungraded rural Schools. The Observation will involve the equivalent of forty School Lesson-periods; and the Practice Teaching, the equivalent of twenty School Lesson periods; or of more, in both cases, according to the experience, aptitude and progress of the Student.

In both the Observation and the Practice Teaching of this Course, the emphasis will be laid upon the work of the Public Schools and the Lower School of the High Schools.

The First Advanced Course trains for Certificates as Teachers both in Public and High Schools, and consists of three parts, as follows:—

Part I.—The History of Education and Educational Systems, the Principles of Education, Psychology and General Method, School Management and School Law, and special Methods in the subjects of the Public School Course and the following subjects of the High School Course:

English, with History and Geography, Mathematics, Latin, and one of the following groups:—

(a) Biology, Physics, Chemistry and Mineralogy;   (c) Greek and French;
(b) French and German;   (d) Greek and German.

The instruction in the History of Education and Educational Systems, the Principles of Education, and Psychology and General Method, in this sub-section will be of a more advanced character than that given in the General Course, and will assume a knowledge of elementary Psychology and Ethics.

2. Such a review by the Student, from the academic standpoint, of the foregoing subjects, as is required for the High and the Public School Courses.

Part II.—A Course of instruction, both academic and professional, in the Nature Study, Elementary Science, Music, Art, Commercial Work, Constructive Work and Domestic Science (for women), of the Public School Course, and the Reading and Physical Training of both the High and the Public School Courses.

Part III.—Observation and Practice Teaching as defined in Part III. of the General Course.

The Second Advanced Course trains for Certificates as Teachers in High Schools only, and consists of three parts, as follows:—

Part I.—The History of Education and Educational Systems, the Principles of Education, Psychology and General Method, School Management and School Law, and special Methods in the following subjects of the High School Courses:

English, with History and Geography, Mathematics, Latin, and one of the following groups:—

(a) Biology, Physics, Chemistry and Mineralogy;   (c) Greek and French;
(b) French and German;   (d) Greek and German.

The instruction in the History of Education and Educational Systems, the Principles of Education, and the Psychology and General Method in this sub-section will be of a more advanced character than that given in the General Course and will assume a knowledge of elementary Psychology and Ethics.

2. Such a review by the Student, from the academic standpoint, of the foregoing subjects, as is required for the High School Courses.

Part II.—A Course of instruction, both academic and professional, in the Reading and Physical Training of the High School Course.

2. A Course of instruction in one of the academic departments for Specialists' Certificates recognized by the Education Department of Ontario. This Course of instruction is to be approved by the Faculty as equivalent to the Public School subjects of the First Advanced Course.

Part III.—Observation and Practice Teaching in the Kingston Collegiate Institute. The Observation will involve the equivalent of forty Lesson periods and the Practice teaching the equivalent of twenty Lesson periods; or of more, in both cases, according to the experience, aptitude, and progress of the Students.

Special Courses shall include:

1. (*a*) Courses for Specialists under the Regulations of the Education Department of Ontario;

(*b*) A Course for Inspectors of Public Schools;

(*c*) Such other special Courses as may be offered by the Faculty from time to time.

2. (*a*) In both the General and Advanced Courses, special training will be provided for Candidates for Certificates as Specialists.

(*b*) For a Public School Inspector's Diploma there will be an Examination open to those who have fulfilled the conditions prescribed by the Education Department for Public School Inspectors' Certificates. The subjects of the Examination will be as follows:

Modern Systems and Tendencies in Education; History of Public Education in Ontario; School Administration and Law; School Inspection and Supervision, including the Supervision of Instruction in all subjects of the Public School Course.

GENERAL REGULATIONS OF THE FACULTY OF EDUCATION.

1. Students who are Graduates in Arts before the beginning of the Session shall take one of the Advanced Courses. All other regular Students, including Graduates in Arts who are exempt from attendance, shall take the General Course.

2. Regular Students who complete the General Course, or an Advanced Course, will receive the Diploma of their respective Courses.

3. Students in the General, or in an Advanced Course, who hold academic Certificates as Specialists and who complete their respective Courses, will receive Diplomas as Specialists.

4. Regular attendance in the General and the Advanced Courses is compulsory, except for such Students as are exempt from attendance under the Regulations of the Education Department of Ontario.

5. Students are exempt from attendance only as follows:—

(*a*) Teachers who have been granted only High School Assistants' Certificates may, without further attendance, obtain Interim First Class Public School Certificates by passing at one examination, and with the usual percentage, in the special Public School subjects of the General Course, and by satisfying the Faculty by a practical test of their ability to teach Public School Classes.

(*b*) Teachers who hold First Class Public School, or High School Assistants', Certificates, interim, or permanent, may, without further attendance, obtain Interim Specialists' Certificates, provided they hold the necessary academic Certificates and pass the professional Examinations for such standing in the special Courses prescribed by the Faculty of Education.

(*c*) Teachers who hold permanent Second Class Certificates, with at least the academic standing prescribed for entrance into the Faculties of Education, and who present Certificates of at least five years' successful experience from the Public or

Separate School Inspectors under whom they have taught during that period, may write at the Examination for Interim First Class Public School Certificates, taking Parts I. and II. together, or separately, but without taking the prescribed Session, or being required to pass in Part III. Such Candidates will be granted Interim High School Assistants' Certificates also on satisfying the Faculty, by a practical test, of their ability to teach High School Classes.

(*d*) Candidates who have attended a Session in the General, or First Advanced, Course, and have obtained at least 35 per cent. of the marks in each subject in Parts I. and II. and at least 55 per cent. of the aggregate of the marks for each of said Parts, and have passed in Part III., may write at the Examinations for Interim First Class Public School and High School Assistants' Certificates without taking the Session over again, or being required to pass again in Part III.

6. All Students exempt from attendance who are duly registered in the Faculty and who pay the annual fee of $15.00 (which shall not in this case include the fee for examination) may receive from the Members of the Faculty such guidance in their Courses as may reasonably be given to Students not in attendance.

7. Students may be dismissed by Resolution of the Faculty, for negligence, incapacity, or any other sufficient cause.

8. A Student in the General, or First Advanced, Course may take, in addition to the subjects of his Course in the Faculty of Education, a Course in a subject recognized by the Education Department for academic Certificates, but only with the consent of the Faculty; and no such course shall be allowed to interfere with his regular Course as prescribed in the Faculty of Education.

9. Candidates for Specialists' Certificates under the Regulations of the Department of Education shall have had their academic standing approved by the Department of Education before entering upon their special Courses.

10. Subject to the approval of the Minister of Education, the Faculty of Education may make such modifications of the scheme of optional groups in Course I., Part I., in Course II., Part I., and in Course III., Part I., as will suit the condition of Candidates who had obtained their academic standing in Courses other than those recognized in the Regulations of 1904.

11. The annual fee for the General, or the Advanced, Courses (with or without the Course for Specialists), which shall include the Library, Gymnasium and Examination fees, shall be $15. The fee for the Examination in the General, or Advanced, Courses when the Examination is not taken during the regular Session, or when it is taken by Students not in attendance, shall be $15, or $10 for each of Parts I. and II. if taken in parts. The fee for the Specialists' Examination when taken apart from the regular Course shall be $5 for each Examination Paper. The fee for the Inspectors' Examination shall be $15. The fee for each Diploma shall be $2. For Special Courses, or any cases not provided for herein, the fee schedule shall be such as obtains in the Faculty of Arts.

Examinations in the Faculty of Education.

1. Candidates for Interim High and Public School Certificates in attendance in the Faculty of Education, who have passed in Part III. during the Session, shall take at their final examinations both Parts I. and II. of the General or of the Advanced Course, as the case may be.

2. The standing of the Students in attendance in the General, or in an Advanced, Course shall be determined by the combined results of the Term work and the May Examinations. The Term work shall consist of such exercises and other tests as the Faculty may prescribe, and the maximum of marks therefor in any subject shall be 40 per cent. of the aggregate of marks for that subject.

3. Examinations in Part I. are held in May at Kingston or at such local centres as may be selected by the Faculty. Sessional Examinations will also be held before Christmas, chiefly for the purpose of testing the Students' knowledge of the subjects of the Public and High School Courses.

Examinations in Part II. are held at convenient periods during the Session and in May at Kingston. The percentage requirements for a pass in the General, or Advanced, Courses are 40 per cent. of the marks for each subject and 60 per cent. of the aggregate of marks for each Part. The requirements in the Specialists' Course are 60 per cent. in each subject. The requirement for Honours in the General Course, or in an Advanced Course, or in the Course for Inspectors, is 75 per cent. of the aggregate marks.

4. An unsuccessful Candidate for a Diploma in the General, or an Advanced, Course may be required, and Candidates unsuccessful in Part III. of either Course shall be required, to attend a Second Session, and repeat both the Term work and the final Examinations. On the recommendation of the Faculty, Candidates who fail in Part I. of the First Advanced Course may be granted a Diploma in the General Course.

Details of Courses.

History of Education and Educational Systems.

General Course:

Evolution of Education in Primitive Society.

Oriental Education, Chinese, Hebrew and Hindu Education as types.

Educational Ideals of Eastern and Western Nations compared. Greek Life and Civilization. Old Greek Education with Spartan Education as its type. New Greek Education with Athenian Education as its type. The Sophists and the Great Educational Theorists, Socrates, Plato and Aristotle. The Idea of a Liberal Education.

Roman Life and Civilization. Roman Educational Ideals and Practices contrasted with those of Greece. Great Educational Theorists, Cicero and Quintilian. The Idea of a Practical Education.

Life in the Middle Ages. Christianity and Education. The Education of the Monastery and the Castle. Scholasticism and the Rise of the Universities.

The Renaissance and the Rise of Humanism. Educational significance of Renaissance. The work of Boccaccio, Erasmus, DaFeltre, Ascham and Sturm.

The Reformation and Counter-Reformation. Luther and Elementary Education. The Jesuits and the Teaching Orders.

Realism and Science in Education. Types of Realism represented by Rabelais and Milton, by Montaigne, by Raich, Bacon and Mulcaster, and by Comenius.

Education according to Nature. Development of the new ideal in Locke, Rousseau and Basedow.

The Psychological Ideal in Education as represented in the work of Pestalozzi, Herbart, and Froebel.

The Sociological Ideal.

The Development of Public Education in Germany, Great Britain, France, the United States and Ontario.

References.—Monroe—Brief Course in the History of Education. Davidson—A History of Education.

Advanced Course:

The General Course repeated, with a detailed study of special periods and movements.

References.—Monroe—Text-book in the History of Education. Davidson—Education of the Greek People. Woodward—Vittorino da Feltre and other Humanist Educators. Laurie—John Amos Comenius. Davidson—Rousseau and Education according to Nature. Pinloche—Pestalozzi and the Modern Elementary School. De Garmo—Herbart and the Herbartians. Hughes—Froebel's Educational Laws for all Teachers.

Principles of Education.

General Course:

A Course of Lectures dealing in the main with the following topics:

1. Introduction: The meaning and aim of Education; statement and examination of typical theories; individual and social elements in Education; the School as an agency of social progress; its relation to other social institutions, the Home, the Church, the State, the Vocation, etcetera; the School as a means of individual growth and development; the problem of individual differences in children; the Curriculum as an expression of social values; its origin; phases of its growth; present day movements for reform of the Curriculum.

Physical Aspects of Education: The significance of infancy; the native physical endowment of the child; heredity and environment as factors in human development; instinct in Education, its relation to habit and intelligence; physical growth and development; motor activities in Education, their relation to mental and moral development; play as a factor in Education; the mental and moral bearings of School-room Hygiene.

Mental Aspects of Education: The doctrine of self-activity; imitation and curiosity as factors in mental growth; the nature of the learning process; meaning of such terms as experience, knowledge, judgment, etc.; place of analysis and synthesis, deduction and induction in the growth of experience.

Moral Aspects of Education: The instinctive element in morality; the social element in morality; the moral aspect of the various school-room activities; the curriculum as an agency in moral instruction and moral training; the teacher as a factor in the moral life of the child.

2. The study in class of certain educational classics selected from the following list: Milton—Tractate on Education; Locke—Thoughts on Education and Conduct of the Understanding; Froebel—The Education of Man; Rein—Outlines of Pedagogics; Spencer—Education; Dewey—The School and Society, and Ethical Principles underlying Education.

References.—Raymont—Principles of Education. Horne—Psychological Principles of Education. Giddings—Elements of Sociology. Dewey—School and Society.

Advanced Course:

1. Lectures of a more advanced character upon the topics detailed in Part I. of the General Course, supplemented by the investigation of special topics by the students in the Course.

2. The study in class of educational classics selected from the list given in (2) above.

References.—Those of the General Course, and in addition: Mackenzie—Social Philosophy. Dewey—The School and the Child.

Psychology and General Method.

General Course:

Relation of the Mental to the Physical. Inborn tendencies, Sensation, Perception, Attention, Memory, Imagination, Conception, Apperception, Judgment and Reasoning, Feeling and Emotions, Interest, Habit, Will, Character, Development of Motor Ability, Curiosity, Suggestion and Imitation, Heredity and Environment, Adolescence and Child Study, Meaning of Instruction, Instruction and Education, Psychologic Foundations of Method, General Principles, Function and Conduct of the Recitation, including a discussion of such topics as typical lesson forms and teaching devices, planning for a lesson, class preparation for a lesson, development of a lesson, lesson plans.

Advanced Course:

Lectures of a more advanced character upon the topics of the General Course as outlined above, with a study of special problems in Education.

References.—Titchener—Primer of Psychology. Angell—Psychology. James—Talks to Teachers on Psychology. Kirkpatrick—Fundamentals of Child Study. Thorndike—Principles of Teaching. McMurry—Method of the Recitation. Findlay—Principles of Class Teaching.

School Management and School Law.

(*a*) Moral and Intellectual Purposes of Schools. Physical Training, Discipline. School Habits, Incentives, Punishments. School Organization, Grading, Course of Study and Time-Tables. Classification and Promotion. Daily Programme. Principles of Teaching. Technique of Class Instruction. Recitations and Questioning. Examinations and other Tests.

(*b*) Problems in School Administration, Functions of Various Types of Schools. State and School. Forms of Educational Control. Executive and Legislative Functions of School Boards and School Officers. Relation of Principal to Teachers, of Teachers to Parents, Trustees, and Caretaker. Business Administration. Sites, Buildings, and Equipment. Class-room Decoration. School Sanitation and School Hygiene. School Reports. Compulsory Education. Industrial Education. Schools for Delinquents and Defectives. School and Home. School and Society. Co-operation of Schools with other Educational Agencies. School Law and Regulations of Ontario.

References.—Shaw—School Hygiene. Landon—Principles and Practice of Teaching, and School Management. The School Law and Regulations of Ontario.

Special Methods.

The courses in Special Method will deal with the selection and organization of the contents of the various school subjects in the terms of the curricula of the Education Department of Ontario, and will include a discussion of methods of instruction in each subject, together with an academic review of the subject itself.

NOTE.—While the same general purposes direct the courses in the subjects of both Part I. and Part II., special emphasis will be placed upon the academic review in the courses in the subjects of Part II.

The following subjects will be discussed:

Part I.

(For further details see the High and Public School Courses of the Ontario Department of Education.)

English—Spelling, Composition, Literature, Grammar, and Rhetoric; History; Geography; Mathematics—Arithmetic, Mensuration, Algebra, Geometry, and Trigonometry; Latin; Greek; French; German; Science—Botany, Zoology, Physics, Chemistry and Mineralogy.

References.—The Text-books authorized for the Public and High Schools of Ontario. Chubb—The Teaching of English. Carpenter, Baker and Scott—The Teaching of English. McMurry—Special Method in History; In the Reading of English. Geikie—Teaching of Geography. Smith—The Teaching of Elementary Mathematics. Young—The Teaching of Mathematics in Secondary Schools. Bennett and Bristol—The Teaching of Latin and Greek. Jesperson—How to Teach a Foreign Language. Report of the Committee of Twelve. Lloyd and Bigelow—The Teaching of Biology. Smith and Hall—The Teaching of Chemistry and Physics. Ganong—The Teaching Botanist.

Part II.

(For further details consult the Public and High School Courses of Study.)

Part II. consists of Academic and Professional Courses of instruction in the following subjects:

Nature Study and School Gardens: Character and Scope of Nature Study. Material for Nature Study. Content. Methods. Purpose of School Gardens. Preparation and Plans. Excursions and Collections.

Elementary Science: Botany, Zoology, Physics, and Chemistry as prescribed for Fifth Forms and the Continuation Schools. Construction of Single Apparatus. A course in the Methods of Experimentation and in the Manipulation of Apparatus.

Music: A Course both practical and theoretical, to include Tune, Time and Rhythm, Ear training, Voice training, Singing, Tonic-Solfa and Staff Notation. The Minor Mode.

Art: Freehand, Color Work. Clay Modelling. Water-Color Sketches. Model and Memory Drawing. Freehand Perspective. Applied Design. Correlation with other Departments.

Commercial Work: Writing—material, position, movement, grouping and practice. Bookkeeping. Business Forms. Stenography, Typewriting.

Constructive Work: The Nature, Scope and History. Educational and Practical Values, Methods. Tools and Materials. The Workshop. Practice in use of paper, cardboard, raffia, reed, clay, wood. Mechanical Drawing.

Household Science: Needlework. Cookery. Household Economics. Correlation with other Subjects.

Reading: Its Scope and Processes. Voice Training, Phonics. Forms of Reading. Methods in Reading.

Physical Training: Breathing Exercises. Exercises for Legs, Arms, Neck and Trunk. Corrective Exercises. Games, Gymnastics. Calisthenics. Drill. Treatment of Emergencies. Personal Hygiene.

References.—The Text-books authorized for the Public and High Schools of Ontario. Silcox and Stevenson—Modern Nature Study. Hodge—Nature Study and Life. The Educational Music Course, Books I., II., III., IV. (Teachers' Edition). Art Education Drawing Book Course (Prang). McMurry—Special Method in Primary Reading. Penman's Art Journal.

Courses for Specialists.

Candidates for diplomas as Specialists should familiarize themselves with the recent literature on the professional phases of their special departments.

Course for Public School Inspectors.

1. Modern Tendencies in Education and Modern Educational Systems (two Examination Papers).

Modern Tendencies in Education may be studied in current educational literature and in such works as Education and Interest (De Garmo), The Educational Situation, and The School and the Child (Dewey), A Modern School (Hanus), The Children (Darroch), Among Country Schools (Kern), Moral Education (Griggs), The Place of Industries in Elementary Education (Dopp), School Sanitation and Decoration (Burrage and Bailey).

Modern Educational Systems, in particular the systems of Great Britain, Germany, and the United States may be studied in current Educational literature or in portions of such works as the Educational Systems of Great Britain and Ireland (Balfour), The History of Education in the United States (Dexter), German Education, Past and Present (Paulsen, trans. Lorenz). It is to be understood that all books mentioned in this sub-section, as in the other sub-sections of this Course, are suggestive, and in no sense obligatory.

2. History of Public Education in Ontario (one Examination Paper).

Candidates should have an intelligent conception of the Educational System of Ontario. This conception implies a knowledge of the System in its historical development, and in its present forms, with special reference to Secondary and Primary Education. References suggested here are the general histories of Canada, or Ontario, portions of recent Reports of the Education Department of Ontario, the biographers of Strachan and Ryerson, Public Education in Upper Canada (Coleman), etcetera.

3. School Administration and Law (one Examination Paper).

Candidates should familiarize themselves in general with the Public Schools Act, the High Schools Act, the Truancy Act, Department of Education Act, and the Regulations of the Education Department, and in particular with the Law and Regulations in regard to the appointment, authority, qualifications and duties of Inspectors.

4. School Inspection, and Supervision of Instruction in Public School Subjects (one Paper).

Candidates must show an intelligent appreciation of the duties and responsibilities of Inspectors; they must be acquainted with the best methods of School management, and they must give evidence of a competency to instruct and to supervise instruction in any of the subjects of the Public School Courses of Study. The only reference suggested here is the School Law and Regulations of Ontario. For the rest the Candidate must rely upon his own knowledge of official practice in Inspection, and upon his own experience in School Management and in Class Instruction, supplemented by such Reports and Books as he may deem pertinent.

Provincial Certificates.

1. The Education Department accepts the Courses of the Faculty of Education in the University of Queen's College as follows:

(*a*) The General Course and the First Advanced Course as the professional Courses for an Interim First Class Public School and an Interim High School Assistant's Certificate.

(*b*) The Second Advanced Course, as the professional Course for a High School Assistant's Interim Certificate.

(*c*) The Special Courses for Specialists as the professional courses for Interim Specialists' Certificates.

(*d*) The Special Course for Public School Inspectors, as the professional Course for a Public School Inspector's Certificate. (To come into effect after June, 1910.)

2. Certificates of qualification may be awarded by the Education Department on the results of the examinations of the Faculty of Education, as follows:

(1) Interim High School Assistants' and Interim First Class Public School Certificates, one, or both, as the case may be:

(*a*) To Students who have attended regularly and have fulfilled the conditions prescribed by the Education Department, and who have obtained in each of Parts I., II., and III. of their Courses 40 per cent. of the marks for each subject, and 60 per cent. of the aggregate of the marks for the Term's work and final examinations.

(*b*) On the recommendation of the Faculty of Education, to Students in attendance in the First Advanced Course who have obtained 40 per cent. of the marks for each subject of Part I. and 55 per cent. of the marks for said part, and who have fulfilled the conditions prescribed by the Education Department, and who have obtained of the examinations in each of Parts I. and II. of their Course 40 per cent. of the marks for each subject and 60 per cent. of the aggregate of marks.

(2) Interim Second Class Public School Certificates, valid for one year, may be given on the recommendation of the Faculty to Students of the General or First Advanced Course who have obtained at least 35 per cent. of the marks for each subject in Parts I. and II. and at least 55 per cent. of the aggregate of the marks in said Parts, and have passed in Part III.

(3) Interim Specialists' Certificates:

(*a*) To Candidates in attendance who have fulfilled the conditions of one of the Advanced Courses and who have obtained 60 per cent. of the marks assigned to the Term's work and final Examinations in the Special Course of their department.

(*b*) To Candidates who have obtained 40 per cent. of the marks in each Paper and 60 per cent. of the aggregate of marks.

3. (1) An interim First Class Public School Certificate shall entitle the Holder, if under 21 years of age, to teach in a Public, or Continuation, School only; and, if over 21 years of age, to teach in a High School also.

(2) An interim High School Assistant's Certificate shall entitle the Holder, if over 21 years of age, to teach, as Assistant, in a High School, or a Continuation School.

(3) Interim Certificates may be extended from year to year by the Minister of Education on the report of the Public, Separate, Continuation, or High School, Inspector under whom the holder of the Certificate has last taught.

Degrees in Education.

Degree of Bachelor of Pedagogy.

The Degree of Bachelor of Pedagogy (B.Pæd.) is granted to Students in the Faculty of Education under the following conditions:

1. The Candidate shall hold (a) a Degree in Arts, not being an honorary Degree, from any University in the British Dominions; and (b) a First Class, or High School Assistant's, Certificate granted by the Education Department of Ontario, or a Certificate of equal value.

2. The Candidate shall pass an examination in the History of Psychology and Ethics, in the Principles of Psychology, Ethics and Sociology, with their applications to Education, in the Science of Education, and in the History and Criticism of Educational Systems.

3. Before he completes the examination for the degree, the Candidate shall submit Certificates of at least two years of successful experience in teaching.

4. The Candidate shall register in the Faculty of Education at least six months before he presents himself for examination, and shall write such Essays and Exercises as may be prescribed. These will be read and returned with criticisms and suggestions. The fee for registration is $10, and for extra-mural assistance $5 for each Section.

5. The Examination shall be held in May at Queen's University, or in any other locality in the Province chosen by the Candidate and approved by the Senate, and under a presiding Examiner appointed by the Senate, subject to the usual fees and Regulations of the University regarding Extra-mural Examinations. The Candidate shall send notice not later than the 1st of April of his intention to take the examination and of the locality he has chosen for such examination.

6. The fee for the full Examination is $10, or for each Section, if taken separately, $8. The fee for the Degree is $20. All fees shall be paid to the Treasurer with the application for registration, or examination, as the case may be.

7. The work in each Section (A or B) may be taken, and will be examined on, separately. The standard for a Pass Degree shall be 50 per cent. of the marks assigned to each Section. The Candidate who obtains 50 per cent. of the marks of each Section and 66 per cent. of the aggregate of marks shall be awarded a Degree with Second Class Honours. The Candidate who obtains 50 per cent. of the marks of each Section and 75 per cent. of the aggregate of marks shall be awarded a Degree with First Class Honours.

A.

8. History of Psychology and Ethics (two Papers); Principles of Psychology, Ethics and Sociology (two Papers).

References.—Weber—History of Philosophy. Sidgwick—History of Ethics. Muirhead—Chapters from Aristotle's Ethics. Watson—Hedonistic Theories. Descartes—Method and Meditations (Veitch). J. S. Mill—Examination of Hamilton, and Utilitarianism. Wundt—Outlines of Psychology. Titchener—Outlines of Psychology. King—Psychology of Child Development. Thorndike—Educational Psychology. Mackenzie—Manual of Ethics. Giddings—Elements of Sociology.

B.

Science of Education (two Papers); History and Criticism of Educational Systems (two Papers).

References.—Dickinson—The Greek View of Life. Monroe—Source Book of the History of Education for the Greek and Roman Period. Spencer—Education. Hall—Youth. Tyler—Growth and Education. O'Shea—Education as Adjustment. De Garmo—Secondary Education. Hanus—Educational Aims and Educational Values. Monroe—Text-book in the History of Education.

Candidates are recommended to read such additional works as may be necessary to ensure an adequate knowledge of the place and importance of the great Educators in the History of Education, more particularly Comenius, Locke, Rousseau, Pestalozzi, Herbart, Froebel and Herbert Spencer. Specific advice regarding Books will be given to those desiring it, on application to the Registrar.

Degree of Doctor of Pedagogy.

The Degree of Doctor of Pedagogy (D.Pæd.) is granted under the following conditions:

1. The Candidate shall hold a Degree in Arts, not being an honorary Degree, from a University in the British Dominions, with (*a*) honours in a department, or (*b*) a Provincial Certificate as Specialist, or (*c*) the Degree of B.Pæd.

2. Before he completes the examination for the Degree, he shall submit evidence of at least three years of successful experience as Teacher, or Inspector.

3. The Candidate shall register at least six months before he presents himself for examination. He shall register as an intra-mural Student to take such University Classes as may be approved by the Faculty of Education, or he shall register as an extra-mural Student. In the latter case he will be required to write Essays and Exercises on such subjects as may be prescribed. These will be read and returned, with criticisms and suggestions. The fee for registration in the Course is $10 per Session, and for Extra-mural assistance $5 for each Section of the Course.

4. The Candidate shall pass an examination in the History of Psychology and Ethics, and Sociology, with their applications to Education; in the Science of Education, and in the History and Criticism of Educational Systems, with special reference to Ontario and the Nineteenth Century. He shall also submit (before April 1) a Thesis on some educational Topic selected with the approval of the Faculty of Education. After the Examiners have reported in favour of the Candidate's answer Papers and Thesis, and before the Degree of D.Pæd. is conferred, the Candidate shall furnish the Registrar of the University with one hundred printed copies of the Thesis. The Thesis shall contain the report of the Examiners.

5. The Examination, which may be taken as a whole, or separately, in Sections, shall be held at such times and under such conditions as to date of application, division of the examination, etcetera, as obtain with the Bachelor's Degree.

6. The fee for the whole Examination is $10, and for each Section, where taken separately, $8. The fee for the Degree is $25. All fees shall be paid to the Treasurer with the applications.

7. History of Psychology and Ethics (two Papers); Principles of Psychology, Ethics, and Sociology (two Papers).

References.—Windelband—History of Ancient Philosophy. Plato—Republic. Höffding—History of Modern Philosophy. Dewey—Leibnitz (Griggs series). The Philosophy of Kant (Watson's Selections). Wundt—Physiological Psychology. Seashore—Laboratory Course in Psychology. James—Principles of Psychology. Stout—Analytical Psychology. Green—Prolegomena to Ethics. Bosanquet—Philosophical Theory of the State. Ward—Applied Sociology.

Science of Education (two Papers); History and Criticism of Educational Systems (two Papers).

References.—Harris—Psychological Foundations of Education. O'Shea—Dynamic Factors in Education. Harper—Trend of Higher Education. Fitch—Thomas and Matthew Arnold. Brown—The Making of Our Middle Schools. Hall—Aspects of Child Life and Education. Welton—The Logical Bases of Education. Payne—Education of Teachers.

Candidates will be expected to make themselves familiar with the Educational Systems of Great Britain, France, Germany, the United States, and Canada, and with contemporary movements and tendencies in Education, by means of standard works and current educational literature. Specific advice regarding Books will be given to those desiring it, on application to the Registrar.

They are also recommended to read the more important works of such educators as Bacon, Locke, Rousseau, Pestalozzi, Herbart, and Froebel, so far as to ensure an adequate knowledge of their influence on modern educational thought and practice.

REGULATIONS OF THE EDUCATION DEPARTMENT FOR THE INSTRUCTION OF TEACHERS IN MANUAL TRAINING AND HOUSEHOLD SCIENCE.

Manual Training.

1. Subject to the conditions herein mentioned, the Macdonald Institute, Guelph, shall be the only Institution recognized by the Education Department for the training of Teachers in Manual Training.

2. The Macdonald Institute shall provide, to the satisfaction of the Education Department, suitable Courses of Study, as well as adequate accommodation, equipment and instruction for Students desiring to become Teachers of Manual Training.

3. Any person holding at least a Second Class Certificate from one of the Normal Schools, who completes satisfactorily a one year's Course at the Macdonald Institute, shall be awarded a Teacher's Certificate in Manual Training.

4. Any Graduate of the Normal College (New Faculty of Education) who completes satisfactorily a one year's Course at the Macdonald Institute shall be awarded a Teacher's Certificate as a Specialist in Manual Training.

5. Any person holding a Certificate from the Macdonald Institute as a **Teacher of Manual Training** shall be qualified to have charge of a department of Manual Training under any High, Public, or Separate School Board.

6. No grant shall be paid by the Government towards a department of Manual Training unless the Teacher who has charge of such department is duly qualified as herein provided.

7. A Certificate as a Teacher of Manual Training, or as a Specialist in the same department, shall give no qualification to teach any of the other subjects of the Public, or High, School Curriculum.

8. These provisions shall not affect any person who is now in charge of a department of Manual Training in any High, Public, or Separate School, or who may be appointed by the Board concerned before the 1st of September, 1904; it being understood that such persons shall have qualifications satisfactory to the Minister of Education.

HOUSEHOLD SCIENCE.

1. Subject to the provisions hereinafter mentioned, no Certificate to teach Household Science shall be awarded after September 1st, 1904, to anyone who does not hold at least Junior Leaving, or Junior Matriculation, standing.

2. All Institutions whose Graduates may be recognized as Teachers of Household Science shall provide, to the satisfaction of the Education Department, suitable Courses of Study, as well as adequate accommodation, equipment, and instruction, for Students preparing to become Teachers in this department.

3. Every Student who desires to become a Teacher of Household Science must take a two years' course of Study in the department, but any person holding, at least, a Certificate from one of the Normal Schools who completes satisfactorily a one year's Course shall be awarded a Teacher's Certificate in Household Science.

4. Any Graduate of the Normal College who completes satisfactorily a one year's Course at one of the recognized Institutions for the training of Teachers in Household Science shall be awarded a Teacher's Certificate as a Specialist in this department.

5. Any person holding a Certificate to teach Household Science granted by the Education Department shall be qualified to have charge of a department of Household Science under any High, Public, or Separate School Board.

6. Certificates as Teachers of Household Science shall give no legal qualification to teach any of the other subjects of the School Curriculum.

7. No grant shall be paid by the Government towards a department of Household Science unless the Teacher who has charge of such department is duly qualified as herein provided.

8. These provisions shall not apply in the case of Teachers already in charge **of the department of Household Science or to Students preparing to be Teachers** of the subject who have been enrolled before the date of these Regulations.

TEACHERS' TRAINING COURSES IN ELEMENTARY AGRICULTURE AND HORTICULTURE AND INDUSTRIAL ARTS.

Arrangements have been made by the Department of Education for the instruction of Teachers in Elementary Agriculture and Horticulture and Elementary Industrial Arts, at the Ontario Agricultural College, Guelph.

The Course in Elementary Agriculture and Horticulture is intended for those who pass the April Examinations for Second Class Certificates and fulfil the other conditions prescribed by the Department of Education.

The Course in Elementary Agriculture and Horticulture is intended primarily for rural school Teachers; that in Elementary Industrial Arts for Teachers of graded urban Schools. Students are not permitted to take both Courses, or parts of each Course.

The Term will be for ten weeks, commencing Thursday, April 21st, and closing Wednesday, June 29th.

No fees are charged for the Course. A contingency charge of $1.00 is payable at registration, covering cost of keys, etcetera. This is returned at the close of the Term, less any charges for losses, or breakages.

Students are, however, required to furnish their own working materials for art-work, plant collecting, etcetera, and to pay for Laboratory breakages. They should come prepared to purchase all necessary equipment for the work at the commencement of the Course. This will cost two, or three, dollars, and may be bought at Guelph.

The Department of Education will pay the travelling expenses of the Teachers-in-training to and from their homes; and board and lodging will also be provided free.

Applicants for the Course are required to pledge themselves to three years' service in teaching in Ontario Schools. Applications for admission are to be handed to the Principal of the Normal School not later than March the 22nd.

ELEMENTARY AGRICULTURE AND HORTICULTURE.
PRINCIPAL: PROFESSOR McCREADY.

The object of this Course is to train Teachers in Laboratory, Workshop, Garden, and Field. The theory and demonstration of the Lecture and Laboratory will illustrate the out-of-door practice; it will be elementary in character, the needs of Pupils in the rural School being kept always in view. Most of the instruction will be of a practical nature, and much of it will be given out-of-doors. There will be a relatively small amount of time given to Book work.

The whole College equipment of Garden and Orchard, Farm and experimental Plots, Stables, Workshops, Museums, Campus, Greenhouses, Laboratories, Forest Nurseries, experimental Wood Lot, and Dairy and Poultry Farms will be at the service of Students for observations.

The Course is for Teachers who have to deal with Public School Pupils and not for Students preparing to become experts in the Science of Agriculture. The subjects will be taken up from this viewpoint.

Special attention will be given to the subjects of School Gardening, Botany, Horticulture, Field Husbandry, Physics, and Entomology.

The following weekly Time Table shows the probable allotment of time for each subject:

Hours.	Monday.	Tuesday.	Wednesday.	Thursday.	Friday.
9.00–10.30...	Physics	Entomology	Physics	Entomology	Experimental Botany
10.30–12.00...	Chemistry	Botany	Field Husbandry	Botany	School Gardening Methods
1.30– 3.00...	Field Husbandry	Fruit, Vegetable or Landscape Gardening	Visits to College Depts. or Reading or Individual Work	Field Work in Botany and Entomology	Visits to local Industries or Field Work in Physics or Orchard
3.00– 4.30...	Botany	Floriculture	Do. do.	Do. do.	Do. do.

Certificate.

A Certificate in Elementary Agriculture and Horticulture will be granted to those Students whose work, as represented by regular attendance, garden practice, individual experiments, laboratory work, collections, written records and final tests, shows satisfactory progress and ability to carry out this work in the Schools.

Students whose work, or conduct, is unsatisfactory, will be asked to retire.

COURSE OF STUDY.

Farm Life and Allied Industries.

Lectures will be given by Institute Lecturers and others working for the improvement of conditions in the country—in School, Home, and Farm. Discussion will be held as to how the School and Teacher can help towards an improvement. (Evening Lectures.) In this connection visits will be paid to Country Schools; Students will also be made acquainted with the government publications and educational organizations.

Visits will be made also to local industries in Guelph to learn how urban activities are inter-related with those of the farm. (About four afternoons.)

Nature Study Literature.

Nature Study Literature: The interpretation of Nature by the greatest Writers; Nature literature in Ontario Readers; Canadian Authors. Scientific writings and Nature Literature compared. School Libraries; selections for rural Schools. Home Libraries; reading in the country Home. (Evening Lectures.)

School Gardening.

Brief sketch of the development of School Gardening in Canada and abroad; its aims as a School Study; laying out of a Garden; individual Plots; class Plots; Teacher's Plots; experimental Plots; forestry Plots; borders, keeping of Tools, Home Gardens; keeping of Garden records; observations in Gardens at Marden School and Macdonald School; School exhibits (10 Lessons).

Each Student will be provided with a Garden for practice and observation; she will visit it every day, and keep records of her work and observations in a Garden Journal. After the Gardens are planted the work in them will be carried on without special provision on the Time Table; in most cases the evenings will be found the most suitable time for this.

Botany in 50 Lessons.

1. Economic Plants: Examination, description, and classification of common Garden, Field, and Forest Plants.

2. Forest Botany: Identification of our Forest Trees; planting Seedbeds in School Gardens; work in College Nursery and in the experimental Bush; collection of Weeds, etcetera.

3. Weeds: Provincial Laws, Seed Control Act. Study and identification of the Seeds of common Weeds. Collection.

4. Plant Diseases: Study and identification of common Fruit, Vegetable and Grain diseases; laws regarding Barberry, Black Knot, etcetera; application of preventives and remedies. Collection.

5. Experimental: Students will be assigned simple experiments in Plant Physiology from the subjects listed below. These experiments they will demonstrate before the Class:

(*a*) The Seed: Testing the vitality; determining the condition necessary for germination; how the Seedling becomes established.

(*b*) The Root: How Roots grow, their function; how they absorb food and water; proof of their using air and giving out carbon dioxide; quantity of water absorbed.

(*c*) The Leaf: The function of Leaves, control and measure of transpiration; respiration; starch formation; behaviour in light and darkness.

(*d*) The Stem and Buds: Forms, structures and functions of Stem and Buds; influence of temperature, moisture, and light on growth; how the Sap circulates.

(*e*) The Flower and Fruit: The functions of the parts of Flowers; causes controlling the opening and closing of Flowers; pollination; formation of Fruits; devices for protecting and disseminating Seeds; cross fertilization; Plant Breeding in experimental Plots.

Horticulture in 25 Lessons.

1. Fruit-growing (8 Lessons): Development, importance, needs, and outlook for the Fruit industry; Governmental interest and action regarding shipping, marking, cold storage, fumigation of nursery stock; experimental stations; co-operation in shipping; adaptation of various Fruits to School Garden work; arrangement and planting of the same; Nursery practice in the propagation of Trees and Plants; principles of Orchard management; Pruning; Spraying; Cultivation.

2. Vegetable Gardening (4 Lessons): Choice of Vegetables for School Gardening; preparation of Soils; testing and planting of Seeds; general care and cultivation; preparation and use of Hot-beds and Cold-frames; use of Tools and Implements.

3. Landscape Gardening (4 Lessons): The principles of Landscape Gardening in relation to the laying out and beautifying of School and Home grounds, including a practical study of Trees, Shrubs, and ornamental features on the College Campus and neighbouring School and Home Grounds.

4. Floriculture (9 Lessons): Propagation and care of House and Window Plants; preparation of potting Soils; Bulb culture; making and planting of Flower Beds, annual and perennial Borders.

Field Husbandry in 20 Lessons.

Importance of Field Crops in the national economy; systems of Farming; Rotation of Crops, fertility of Soil; cultivation of the Land; Classes of Farm Crops; uses of Farm Crops; varieties of Farm Crops; selection of Plants; selection of Seeds; improvement of Crops by means of selection and hybridization; practical tests in connection with Experimental Union; study of work being done in experiments with Farm Crops in Canada and in the United States.

Examination of Field Crops on neighbouring Farms; the work on the experimental Plots; Farm Crops in the School Garden; the Agricultural Museum; Laboratory Study of the Root development of Farm Crops and of types of Seeds of Grains, Grasses, Clovers, Roots, and fodder Crops.

Soil Physics in 30 Lessons.

Applications of Physics in Farming; nature of Soils, Soil Moisture, Heat and Air; principles of Tillage and systems of Drainage and Cultivation; measurements of Fields with the chain; identification of samples of Soils; principles of Common Farm Machines; Meteorological records.

Entomology in 30 Lessons.

Losses through insects in agriculture and horticulture; Governmental interest; classification of insects and laboratory study of types; common beneficial and noxious insects; out-of-door study and collecting in field, garden, orchard, and forest; insecticides; a collection of insects properly mounted and labelled is required. Work of the Entomological Society of Ontario and the organization of local clubs in connection with it.

Soil Chemistry in 10 Lessons.

Agricultural Chemistry: Plant growth and composition, soils; manures and fertilizers.

Bacteriology in 5 Lessons.

Lectures and demonstrations exemplifying the work of Bacteria in Soil. Dairying. Plant diseases. An experiment on Soil inoculation in the School Garden.

The Books in the Reference Library.

The Books in the Reference Library will be kept for Students' use in Massey Library, or on the Laboratory Book Shelves. Government publications and the best Agricultural papers will also be available. These Books are specially selected, and Teachers should use the list as a guide in purchasing Books for School Libraries.

Farm Lands and School Gardening.—Nature Study and Life (Hodge), The Outlook to Nature (Bailey), Among Country Schools (Kern).

Botany.—High School Botany (Spotton), The Farm Weeds of Canada (published by Dominion Government, free), Experiments with Plants (Osterhout), Botany, an elementary text-book (Bailey), Agricultural Botany (Percival).

Horticulture.—Nursery Book (Bailey), Principles of Fruit-growing (Bailey), Vegetable Gardening (Green), Landscape Gardening (Waugh), Flowers and How to Grow them (Rexford).

Field Husbandry.—The Cereals in America (Hunt), Forage Crops (Voorhees), The Story of the Plants (Grant Allen), Agriculture (James).

Physics.—The Soil (King), Engineering for Land Drainage (Elliott), Surveying (Baker & Dickson), Meteorology (Davis).

Entomology.—Manual for the Study of Insects, Insects Injurious to Fruits (Saunders), Insects Injurious to Vegetables (Chiltendon), Insects Injurious to Staple Crops (Sanderson), Outdoor Studies (Needham).

Animal Husbandry.—Types and Breeds of Farm Animals (Plumb), Principles of Breeding (Davenport), Judging Live Stock (Craig).

Dairy Husbandry.—The Elements of Dairying (Decker), Cheese-making (Decker), Testing Milk and Its Products (Farrington and Woll), Canadian Dairying (Dean), Modern Methods of Milk Testing (Van Slyke).

Poultry.—First Lessons in Poultry Keeping.

Chemistry.—Sanitary and Applied Chemistry (Bailey), Chemistry of the Farm (Warrington, first five chapters), Fertilizers (Voorhees), Plant Life (Masters).

Bacteriology.—Agricultural Bacteriology (Conn), Bacteria in Relation to Country Life (Lipman).

Forestry.—A First Book of Forestry (Roth), Bulletin No. 24 (Forest Service, U. S. Dept. of Agriculture), Sylvan Ontario (Muldrew).

Farm Carpentry.—Woodworking for Beginners (Wheeler), Benchwork (Goss), Every man's Own Mechanic (Spon).

ELEMENTARY INDUSTRIAL ARTS.

PRINCIPAL: PROFESSOR EVANS.

The object of the Course is, by supplementing the work they have already taken up, to prepare a body of Teachers for organizing and carrying on Elementary Industrial Training in the Schools of the Province, in centres which are unable to provide well equipped Manual Training departments.

In the working out of the Course in Industrial Art great stress is laid on Drawing. "Every workman should for the most part be able to conceive clearly and accurately in his own mind the shape of everything he may have to make or to work with. This makes it the first condition of skill that he should master shape in his own mind, and that mastery requires him to be a Geometer."

The work outlined below is not completely covered in the ten weeks' Term. The examples and exercises selected will, however, illustrate general principles and lay sufficient foundations for working out practical Courses in the different Schools of the Province. It should be understood that the standing of a Specialist in Manual Training cannot be obtained in this Course; but the work done during the Session will be counted *pro tanto*.

The work will be taken at the Manual Training Department of the Ontario Agricultural College. This is located in Machinery Hall, which is equipped with

Class-rooms, a Drafting Room, a Wood Working Room, an Art Room, and all necessary Tools and appliances.

Visits will be made to local Schools to study Equipment, Organization, etcetera, and to local Industries to observe processes.

Students are required to provide their own equipment for Art and Drawing. They should bring with them any outfit they possess, as well as any Books dealing with the subjects of the Course. Materials used in the work will be provided at cost.

Teachers are requested to bring as far as possible the work in Drawing, Art, Basketry, etcetera, which they completed at the Normal Schools, so that the work in each branch may not be duplicated.

A Certificate in Elementary Industrial Arts will be granted to those Students who complete the Course satisfactorily and give evidence of ability to carry on this work successfully in the Schools. The daily record of Class Work under the observation of the Instructors, as well as the results obtained at the final examinations, will both be taken into consideration.

Students whose work, or conduct, is unsatisfactory will be asked to retire.

The following Time Table shows the probable allotment of time for each subject, provided the organization of the classes will permit it:

Hours.	Monday.	Tuesday.	Wednesday.	Thursday.	Friday.
9.00–10.30...	Drawing	Drawing	Drawing	Drawing	Drawing
10.30–12.00...	Constructive Work	Constructive Work	Constructive Work	Drawing	Pedagogics, Methods, Planning lessons, etc.
1.30–4.30...	Woodwork	Woodwork	Woodwork	Visits to local Industries	Woodwork

Course of Study.

Pedagogics, Etcetera.

(a) Manual Training as a factor in general education; (b) Sketch of the various Systems: Russian, Swedish, Sloyd, etcetera; (c) Progress of Manual Training in Canada; (d) Methods of Teaching, plans of Courses and Lessons; Organization, Equipment, Plans, estimates of Cost, etcetera; (e) Lectures dealing with industrial questions and the means of improving our opportunities; (f) Visits to local Industries and consideration of Industrial Development in Canada.

Drawing, Applied Art, and Design.

Emphasis will be laid on the practical application of Drawing to the Industries.

Drawing: (a) The use of Squares, Triangles, and Instruments; (b) Plane Geometry, practical Problems, Lines, Angles and Polygons; (c) Construction and use of plain Scales; (d) Orthographic projections of Solids—three or more views; (e) Cutting and oblique Planes and sections; (f) Isometric projection; (g) Working Drawing; (h) Machine Drawing; (i) Tracing—Blue printing.

Applied Art and Design: Observation of these in local manufactures and in common decorated objects, such as Wall Paper, Carpets, Furniture, Cloths, Jewellery, Iron and Brass work; practical applications in everything undertaken in the constructive work.

Wood Working.

(a) Bench exercises in making articles requiring joints, mortises, fastenings with dowels, pins, cleats, keys, wedges, glue, screws and nails, etcetera; (b) Calculation of the quantity of Lumber necessary for making the articles and estimation of cost; (c) Tools (5 Lessons), their construction, care, use and sharpening; (d) analysis of action of cutting Tools, cutting Angles, etcetera.

Finishing (2 lessons): (a) Staining, fuming, filling, shellacing; (b) Oil and wax polishing; (c) Pigments, priming coats; (d) Oils, driers, brushes; (e) Painting and Glazing.

Forestry and Lumber (4 lessons): (a) Forest preservation—propagation, time of cutting, pruning; (b) Trees—classes, structure, growth, seasoning, shrinking and warping; (c) Properties of Woods—durability, elasticity, stiffness, density; (d) Varieties of common Woods—peculiarities of each, colour, grain, identification; (e) Defects in Lumber—resin pockets, knots, shakes; (f) Decay and its causes—preservation; (g) Lumbering—Transportation, Sawmills, grading widths.

Constructive Work.

(a) Cardboard work—thin and thick boards (20 hours); (b) Modelling—Clay, Sand and Papier Mache (10 hours); (c) Simple Book Binding (10 hours); (d) Simple metal work (15 hours); (e) Knife work, such as can be carried on in the ordinary Class Room at the School Desk (10 hours).

REFERENCE LIBRARY.

Theory.—Theory of Educational Sloyd (Salomon), School and Society (Dewey), Education and the Larger Life (Henderson), The Place of Industries in Elementary Education (Dopp), Economics of Manual Training (Rouillon), Manual Training made Serviceable to the School (Goetz).

Drawing.—Bases of Design (Walter Crane), Line and Form (Walter Crane), Classroom Practice in Design (J. P. Haney), Principles of Design (Batchelder), Machine Drawing and Design (D. A. Low), Plane and Solid Geometry (Geo. Gill), Mechanical Drawing (Anthony).

Wood-working.—Educational Wood-working (J. C. Park), Elementary Sloyd and Whittling, Essentials of Wood-working (Griffith), Beginning Wood-work (Van Deusen), Problems in Wood-working (Murray), Problems in Furniture Making (Crawshaw).

Finishing.—Polishes and Stains for Woods (Upcott Gill), Natural Woods and How to Finish Them.

Lumber.—Primer of Forestry (Pinchot. U. S. Dept. of Agriculture), Timber (Hasluck), First Book of Forestry (Rothe), Our Native Trees (Keeler).

Constructive Work.—Seat Work and Industrial Occupations (Gilman I. Williams), Correlated Handwork, Cardboard Construction (Trybom), Paper and Cardboard Construction (A. H. Chamberlain), Story Telling with the Scissors (M. H. Beckwith), Practical and Artistic Basketry (L. R. Bradley), Occupations for Little Fingers (Sage & Cooley), Hand Loom Weaving (M. P. Todd), Clay Modelling (Holland), Clay Modelling (Unwin), Copper Work (Rose).

REGULATIONS OF THE ONTARIO DEPARTMENT OF EDUCATION FOR THE SUMMER SCHOOL FOR TEACHERS AT THE ONTARIO AGRICULTURAL COLLEGE, GUELPH.

Session—July 4th to July 30th.

Terms and Courses.

The term will be for four weeks, commencing July 4th, and closing July 30th.

Instruction will be given in five Courses, and Students may select any one of these; no Student will be permitted to take more than one Course, videlicet:

I. Nature Study.
II. Elementary Agriculture and Horticulture.
III. Art and Constructive Work.
IV. Woodworking and Mechanical Drawing.
V. Household Science.

Unless ten Students enter for a Course, a Class therein will not be formed.

Fees, Supplies, Etcetera.

No fee is charged Teachers resident in Ontario. Non-resident Teachers are charged a fee of Ten Dollars, payable at the opening of the Term.

Students are required to furnish their own working materials for Art, Plant Collecting, etcetera. Any materials supplied by the College to the Students and retained by them are furnished at cost price. Students will be required to pay for Laboratory breakages.

Faculty of Instruction.

The instruction given will be under the supervision of the President and the direction of the Heads of the College Departments.

Arrangements will be made for special Lectures by others interested in matters concerning Country Life and the Industrial phases of Education.

SYLLABUS OF STUDIES.

I.—Nature Study.

Method of Instruction.

The material that lies nearest to hand about the College will be used largely in the instruction. The first day of the Course will be spent in making a general survey of the College and Farm. Only occasionally will it be necessary to leave the College Grounds to prosecute Studies.

Students will be instructed in making collections of Weed Seeds, Grasses, Leaves of Trees, Insects, etcetera. Material for this work will be provided by the Students themselves or supplied at cost price at the College.

In general, the mornings will be devoted to work indoors and the afternoons to work in the Fields and Woods. When weather will not permit of field work,

Laboratory exercises will be substituted. Saturdays will be for all-day Excursions, or reviewing and arranging the week's work. Such Students as wish to spend their time in independent work along special lines will be encouraged to do so and given every possible assistance; Students of previous Classes especially will be helped in such work. Students will keep careful records of all their work.

Equipment.

Students should bring field or opera Glasses, Pocket Knives, pocket magnifying Glasses, and any Books which they possess and have found useful. As a considerable part of the work is taken in fields, gardens, and woods, Women Students should also provide themselves with stout boots, walking skirt, handy cap, garden gloves, etcetera.

Course of Study.

In the Nature Study Course, the chief object will be to make Students acquainted with the common objects about them with a view to teaching the children in the schools. The best methods of teaching will be taken up concurrently with the instruction.

The work will necessarily overlap in many subjects with the Course in Agriculture, and must be taken as the first Course leading to the Certificate in Elementary Agriculture and Horticulture. Teachers in Town or City graded Schools will find their needs best met in this Course. Lesson periods are as a rule either a whole forenoon, or afternoon, or half that length of time.

Plant Studies.

School Gardening (1 Lesson): Planning and keeping of Garden Plots (each Student will prepare and care for a Plot); keeping of Garden records; Studies of growth in different plants; garden weeds. After the Garden is planted each Teacher's gardening is carried on independently. She will visit her Garden daily to attend to the necessary work and make observations on the Plant growth.

Horticulture (4 Lessons): Visits to the College Orchards, small Fruit Gardens, Vegetable Gardens, and Flower Gardens, to learn of the best varieties of cultivated plants, methods of cultivation, spraying, pruning, etcetera.

Plant Propagation (8 Lessons): Practical lessons on propagation of Plants by cuttings, propagation of Bulbs, Potting, general care of House Plants. (Students will be permitted to take the Plants, which they propagate, to their Homes.)

Botany (12 Lessons): Collection, examination and identification of common Plants, such as: (1) Weeds of fields, gardens, lawns, and roadsides; (2) common diseases of Grains, Vegetables, and Fruits; (3) Grasses and cultivated Farm Crops; (4) flowering Plants in Gardens. Observation of College Woods and Campus to learn the characters and names of our common Trees; visits to the Forest Nurseries to learn how Trees are propagated; observation Plots of Tree Seedlings in the School Gardens.

Collection and study of common Weed Seeds.

Simple physiological experiments with Plants in Garden, or Laboratory.

Recognition of plant societies on Excursions.

Animal Studies.

Insects (4 Lessons): Collection, examination, and identification of common Insects found in the Gardens, Orchards, Fields, and Woods; instruction regarding the treatment of Insect Pests.

Pond Life: Collection of Animal Life from Streams and Ponds; observation of Snails, Clams, Crayfish, Fish, Tadpoles, etcetera, in Aquaria.

Birds (4 Lessons): Identification of Birds observed on Excursions, or about the College; studies of skins and mounted specimens in the Museum to become acquainted with the common Birds of Ontario.

Farm Animals (12 Lessons): Observation of the kinds of Horses, Cows, Sheep and Pigs kept on the Farm; their characteristics, uses and care. Visits to Poultry Department to learn about the varieties and care of domesticated Birds.

Physical Nature.

Physiography: Observation and recognition of Earth forms, the work of Streams, etcetera, to be seen on Excursions; study of Soils, Rocks, Gravel Pits, and Quarries.

Meteorology: Observation of Weather; keeping weather records; study of Weather Maps; making Weather Charts.

Astronomy (4 Lessons): Talks on elementary Astronomy; "star-gazes" to learn the best known Constellations and Stars; interpretation of Star-maps.

II.—ELEMENTARY AGRICULTURE AND HORTICULTURE.

Course of Study.

The object of this Course is to give Teachers a training in the elementary scientific principles and practices of modern Farming, so that the Country or Village School may adequately sympathize with and direct the life-interests of country Boys and Girls.

The Course is for Teachers who have to deal with Public School Pupils and not for Students preparing to become experts in the Science of Agriculture. The subjects will be taken up from this view-point.

School Gardening: The work of the Nature Study Course reviewed and continued.

Botany (8 Lessons): The Work of the Nature Study Course reviewed and continued. Simple experiments in Plant Physiology.

Field Husbandry (8 Lessons): Importance of Field Crops in the national economy; Systems of Farming; Rotation of Crops; fertility of Soil; cultivation of Land; classes of Farm Crops; uses of Farm Crops; varieties of Farm Crops; selection of Plants; selection of Seeds; improvements of Crops by means of selection and hybridization; practical tests in connection with Experimental Union; study of work being done in experiments with Farm Crops in Canada and in the United States.

Examination of Field Crops on neighbouring Farms; the work on the experimental Plots; Farm Crops in the School Garden; the Agricultural Museum; Grains, Grasses, Clovers, Roots and Fodder Crops; Laboratory Study of the Root development of Farm Crops; types of Seeds of common Farm Crops.

Physics (8 Lessons): Application of Physics in Farming; nature of Soils, Soil Moisture, Heat, and Air; principles of Tillage, and systems of Drainage and cultivation; identification of samples of Soils; Meteorological records.

Agricultural Chemistry (4 Lessons): Plant Growth and composition, Soils; Manures and Fertilizers.

Bacteriology (4 Lessons): Lectures and demonstrations exemplifying the work of Bacteria in Soil, Dairying, Plant and animal Diseases; an experiment on Soil Inoculation in the School Garden.

Entomology (8 Lessons): The work of the Nature Study Course reviewed and continued.

Losses through Insects in Agriculture and Horticulture; classification of Insects and Laboratory Study of types; common Beneficial and Noxious Insects; out-of-door Study and collecting in Field, Garden, Orchard, and Forest; Insecticides; a collection of Insects properly mounted and labelled is required; work of the Entomological Society of Ontario; organization of local clubs in connection with it.

Certificates.

To Students who complete satisfactorily two Summer Courses and a Winter Reading Course a Certificate in Elementary Agriculture and Horticulture will be issued by the Department of Education. The Course in Nature Study should be taken first, preparatory to the second summer's Course in Agriculture and Horticulture.

Elementary Industrial Arts.

The object of the Courses is to train Teachers in the elements of the Industrial Arts. Work in the Elementary Industrial Arts consists of two Courses: I. Art and Constructive Work, and II. Woodworking and Mechanical Drawing. Only one of these may be taken at a Session. Students who expect to attend two Sessions are advised to take Course I. first, as a preparation for Course II. Teachers of the higher grades will find Course II. more suitable for them. The instruction will, as far as possible, follow the departmental Course of Study outlined for Public Schools. The Courses will be taken up at the Manual Training Building, which is equipped with Drafting, Art, and Woodworking Rooms, as well as with all necessary Tools and Appliances. The best methods of teaching this subject will be taken up concurrently with the instruction.

The work covered will be accepted *pro tanto* towards securing a Certificate in Elementary Industrial Arts or Specialist's standing in Manual Training.

III.—Art and Constructive Work.

Equipment.

Students should bring with them any good Manuals that they may have on the subjects of the Course. The working outfit will include Tracing Paper, Carbon Paper, Drawing Paper (unglazed), Reeves' Water Colours Number 50 A, Crayons, Charcoal Sticks, Japanese brushes and a water cup. For material furnished by the College, the Students are charged the cost price.

Art.

Art Work: Blob, black and white, flat washes in Colour, Colour harmonies, Colour schemes; drawing of Plants, Flowers, and Insects.

Sketching: Representation of Simple Landscapes in pencil, crayon, and brush.

Applied Art and Design: Practical applications in everything undertaken in the constructive work.

Constructive Work.

Cardboard Work: Thin and thick boards.
Modelling: Clay, sand, and Papier-mache.
Simple Book Binding.
Simple Metal Work.
Knife Work: Such as can be carried on in the ordinary Class room at the school desk.

Industries.

Visits will be paid to local Industries to see modern industrial equipment and organization in operation and to learn how fundamental the Art and Constructive work of the School is, *e.g.*, Carpet Mills, Paper Box Factory, Piano Factory.

IV.—WOODWORKING AND MECHANICAL DRAWING.

Equipment.

Students should supply themselves with a set of good drawing instruments and a set of drawing pencils ranging in hardness from HHH to HHHHH. For material provided by the College, students are charged cost prices.

Woodworking.

Bench Work: Exercises in making articles requiring joints, mortises, **fastenings** with dowels, pins, cleats, keys, wedges, glue, screws, and nails.

Estimates of Cost: Calculations of the quantity of Lumber required for the articles and the cost.

Tools: Their construction, use, care, and sharpening.

Mechanical Principles: Analysis of the action of Cutting tools, cutting angles, etcetera.

Finishing: Staining, fuming, filling, shellacing, oiling, etcetera, as required in finishing the articles made.

Forestry and Lumber: Observation and consideration of the properties of the Lumbers used, their defects, their preparation in the Mills, care, etcetera.

Mechanical Drawing.

The Drawing will be closely related to the Woodworking. Every exercise will be worked out on Paper before the practical work at the Bench is commenced.

In the working out of the Course great stress is laid on Drawing. "Every Workman should for the most part be able to conceive clearly and accurately in his own mind the shape of everything he may have to make or to work with. This makes it the first condition of skill that he should master shape in his own mind, and that mastery requires him to be a Geometer."

In the preparation of the working Drawings the following branches of the subject will be practised:

(*a*) The use of squares, triangles, and instruments; (*b*) Plane Geometry—practical problems, lines, angles and polygons; (*c*) Construction and use of plain scales; (*d*) Orthographic projections of solids—three or more views; (*e*) Cutting and oblique planes and sections; (*f*) Isometric projection; (*g*) working drawing; (*h*) Machine drawing; (*i*) Tracing—blue printing.

V.—HOUSEHOLD SCIENCE.

The Classes will be held in the Macdonald Institute.

The course will include the following: 28 practical Lessons in Plain Cookery; 12 practical Lessons in Laundry; 12 Lectures on Home Nursing; 6 Lectures on Hygiene.

Students are required to bring with them two plain cotton dresses, at least two large white bib aprons, and two small hand towels for wear in the laundry and cookery lessons.

The Lessons will be distributed as noted in the following time-table:—

Hours.	Monday.	Tuesday.	Wednesday.	Thursday.	Friday.
8.45– 9.35...	Home Nursing	Hygiene	Home Nursing	Hygiene	Home Nursing
9.35–12.05...	Cookery	Cookery	Cookery	Cookery	Cookery
1.30– 4.00...	Laundry	Cookery	Laundry	Cookery	Laundry

No Certificate will be issued for this Course.

MACDONALD HALL.

The College Authorities have made arrangements to open Macdonald Hall for the use of the Teachers while in attendance at the Summer School. The Hall will accommodate one hundred and ten ladies, and Rooms will be reserved in the order in which applications are received.

Board and Room will be provided for the session, July 4th to July 30th, for fifteen dollars.

Each resident of Macdonald Hall will be expected to provide such personal matters as she may require.

REGULATIONS IN RESIDENCE.

1. Good health is a requisite for admission. Students showing signs of tubercular or nervous troubles will be asked to retire.

2. A disposition of cheerfulness and helpfulness is essential. Students who cannot help in promoting this will be asked to seek accommodation elsewhere.

3. Students are required to make good all breakages or damage to furniture, etcetera, used by them.

4. Simple rules regarding conduct in Hall, time of meals, study hours, etcetera, will be drawn up on consultation with the students when they arrive.

GENERAL INFORMATION.

The Hall will open on the first Monday in July, classes will be organized the following day, and the Hall will close on the last Saturday in July.

Certificates of attendance will be issued to those who show satisfactory application and proficiency.

No fee is charged Ontario Teachers. Non-residents will pay ten dollars.

All applications should be made to

G. C. CREELMAN, *President.*

AGRICULTURAL EDUCATION IN ONTARIO.

A PAPER PREPARED BY J. GEORGE HODGINS, M.A., LL.D.,

Deputy Minister of Education for Ontario and Honorary Secretary of the Education Convention held at the New Orleans Exhibition in 1884* and an International Juror at that Exhibition.

"Book farming," as it was often derisively called, was for a long time looked upon with contempt in this Province; and unfortunately, too, such an opinion was often held and freely expressed by the more energetic and successful farmers. The cause was not far to seek. It involved a knowledge of "agricultural chemistry" and kindred subjects, the very name of which was enough for such men, who, in the early times in this Province, knew very little beyond what their own experience and good sense taught them, and, therefore, despised "book learning," so far as it related to farming and agriculture.

It was not until some men of mark amongst us, such as the late well known and esteemed Honourable Adam Ferguson, and the late lamented Honourable David Christie, introduced scientific farming into this country with remarkable success that public opinion, especally amongst the Farmers themselves, began to change. The interest, too, excited in the farming community by the success of, and competition at, the county and provincial agricultural fairs, deepened the conviction—at all events in the minds of the younger generation of Farmers and Farmers' sons—that there was "something in it" after all, and that "book farming" was not to be despised.

The late Reverend Doctor Ryerson did all in his power to foster this better feeling in the country. In 1847, when the Government House and its spacious grounds in Toronto were under his control (for the purposes of Education Offices and Normal School), he freely placed these Grounds at the disposal of the Provincial Agricultural Association every year, for the purposes of their annual fair. In his Report, too, on a "System of Public Elementary Instruction for Upper Canada," published in 1846, he thus referred to the subject of Agricultural Education, which he included in the subjects of instruction which he proposed to introduce (at as early a date as possible) into the Public Schools. He said:

Agriculture—the most important department of human industry—has not yet been introduced in any form whatever as a branch of elementary education in our Schools.

---

*Prepared chiefly from material sent to the writer by Mr. James Mills, President of the Agricultural College, Guelph.

The Legislature has given some pecuniary assistance, and Societies have been formed with a view to encourage experiments and promote improvements in Canadian Agriculture; but experiments without a knowledge of principles will be of little benefit, and improvements in the practice of agriculture must be very limited until the science of it is studied. * * * The agricultural pupil should be made acquainted with the different kinds of soils and their characteristic qualities; the modes of qualifying and improving each; different kinds of manure and other improving substances; the effects of different kinds of soil on different crops; rotation of crops, and the best methods of producing and securing them; Agricultural Implements and the Machines which have been invented to save labour; different kinds of stock, the various modes of feeding them, with the economical advantages of each; the method of keeping full and accurate accounts, so that the Farmer may be able to ascertain precisely, not only his gross profits and losses, but the profit and loss in each detail of the system, and from each field of his farm. Of course, Specimens, Models, Pictures, or Drawings, should be used in teaching these elements of Agriculture, etcetera.

The Normal School for Upper Canada (Ontario) was established in the Autumn of 1847. In the Programme of Studies then drawn up it was provided that one of the Masters should deliver a course of Lectures to the students on "Agricultural Chemistry; comprehending the nature of the substances which enter into the composition of Vegetables; the sources from which those substances are derived; the origin and composition of Soils; the conditions necessary for producing a luxuriant vegetation, etcetera, etcetera." In the early Spring of 1848, and in addition to these Lectures, a portion of the Grounds attached to the Normal School (*i. e.*, the present Government House Grounds) was set apart for agricultural purposes and for agricultural experiments under the direction of a skilled Expert. A report of these experiments was regularly made to the Chief Superintendent of Education, and the Students were examined in the subject generally.

In 1849, when the seat of Government was removed from Montreal to Toronto (after the burning of the Parliament House in the former City), the Government House (in which the Normal School had been held) with the Grounds attached, was resumed by the Government. The experiments consequently ceased. But the Governor-General (Lord Elgin) was so impressed with the value of the instruction given to the Students in Agricultural Chemistry that he instituted two Prizes for proficiency in that subject. For some years these Prizes were continued, and much interest was manifested in the competition for them. A Chair of Agriculture was subsequently established in the University, but the number of Students who attended Lectures on the subject was not large.

For some years little was done to promote the study of Agriculture except the stimulus derived from agricultural publications and the successful agricultural Exhibitions, Fairs, and Farmers' Clubs, which gave a special prominence to the subject.

In 1870 the Chief Superintendent of Education, being desirous to carry out his original intention of making Agriculture one of the subjects of Study in the Public Schools, prepared a Manual on the subject, which he dedicated to the Board of Agriculture.* In the dedicatory preface he used the following language, striking and admonitory as it is:

---

*In his introductory note Doctor Ryerson intimated that his labour in preparing this work was entirely a gratuitous contribution to the cause.

Identified as I am by birth and early education with the agricultural population of this country, I regret to see so many of our agricultural youths leave the noblest of earthly employments and the most independent of social pursuits, for the professions, the counting room, the warehouse, and even for petty clerkships and little shops. * * * As a general rule the Sons of Farmers, as soon as they begin to be educated, leave the farm; this is a misfortune to the parties themselves, a loss to Agriculture, and to the country. * * * Politicians are accustomed to call Farmers "the bone and sinew of the land"; and bone and sinew they will remain, and never anything else, without education. It is a supreme law, illustrated by all history, that head rules muscle; and all Farmers who educate only their muscles, and not their heads, must occupy the inferior relation of muscle. * * * I know it may be said by some, "Our fathers were not educated, and yet were successful Farmers." But these very Farmers will bear witness that they would have done and felt much better had they been educated.

* * * * * * * * * * *

The first and great staple interest of our country requires young men who will devote to Agriculture their talents, their attainments, their fortunes, and their lives; and in no other pursuit is a wider and more inviting field of enterprise open to them.

In that year (1870) the distinguished President of the Agricultural Association for Ontario, the Honourable David Christie (Senator of the Dominion), in accepting, on behalf of the Association, the dedication of the "First Lessons on Agriculture for Canadian Farmers and their Families," by Doctor Ryerson, said:

My conviction is that the [teaching of Agriculture] must begin in our Common Schools; that is, elementary Agricultural and mechanical instruction should form a leading part of the teaching. Doctor Ryerson has published a valuable little work on Agriculture, which I hope to see made a Text Book in all the rural districts. * * * Doctor Ryerson has done good service to the country by compiling the Manual, * * * and I hope that he will see to it that the benefit which it is so well calculated to confer shall not be lost to the country. It is a good thing for the cause * * * that we have so able a coadjutor as the Chief Superintendent of Education. I feel convinced that he will soon make Agricultural and Mechanical instruction a leading feature in our Common-school teaching.

During the same year the Honourable John Carling, Commissioner of Agriculture for Ontario, in his Report, thus intimated the intention of the Government to promote elementary and higher education in Agriculture. He said in that Report:

What now appears to be more especially needed in carrying forward this great work is, in addition to the ordinary instruction in Common Schools, the introduction of elementary instruction in what may be termed the foundation principles of Agricultural and Mechanical Science. * * * Our enlightened and energetic Chief Superintendent of Education would, I believe, approve and help forward such a movement.

A special agent was sent * * * some months ago to visit the Agricultural Colleges of the United States, to ascertain and report upon the best and most successful system there adopted, with a view to the establishment of such an Institution in this Province. * * * The local Government has already determined upon introducing Agricultural teaching into our Common Schools, and also to establish an Agricultural College in this Province during the ensuing year.

The late lamented Mr. William Johnston, M.A., formerly President of the newly established Agricultural College (now situated at Guelph), thus continues the narrative of the establishment of the College. He says:—

PART XIV.   LECTURE ON AGRICULTURE IN ONTARIO.   317

During the winter of 1870, the Honourable John Carling, at that time Minister of Agriculture for Ontario, commissioned the Rev. W. F. Clarke, Editor of the *Ontario Farmer*, to visit some of the Agricultural Colleges of the United States and report on them, at the same time drawing up a scheme for the establishment of an Agricultural College in Ontario. Mr. Clarke's Report forms an appendix to that of the Commissioner of Agriculture for the year 1870. A farm at Mimico, seven miles from Toronto, was first purchased, but, on the advice of many Experts, whose reports form an appendix to that of the Commissioner of Agriculture for 1872, that Farm was sold and the present one at Guelph purchased in the fall of 1873.

AN OUTLINE OF THE PRESENT POSITION OF THE ONTARIO AGRICULTURAL DEPARTMENT.

The Ontario Agricultural College is situated on a farm of 550 acres, a mile south of the City of Guelph, in the County of Wellington. The College Building is 240 feet in length, of an average depth of 42 feet, and is of two storeys and a Basement. The centre portion has an additional storey. It contains the usual Public Lecture Rooms, Library, Reading-room, Museum and at the present time a small Laboratory. Connected with it, at the rear, are the Dining-rooms, Kitchens, Laundry, Matron's and servants' apartments. The Teaching Staff is composed of:

1. A President.
2. Professor of Agriculture.
3. Professor of Science.
4. Professor of Veterinary Science.
5. Mathematical Master.
6. Farm Foreman.
7. Horticultural Foreman.
8. Mechanical Foreman.

I. The Course of Study, which is of one or two years, includes the following subjects:

First Year.—Practical Agriculture, Veterinary Anatomy, Veterinary Materia Medica, Physical Geography, Chemistry, Botany, Zoology, English and Mathematics.

Second Year.—Agriculture and Horticulture, Veterinary Pathology, Veterinary Surgery and Practice, Agricultural Chemistry, Economic Botany, Entomology, Meteorology, Book-keeping, Leveling and Surveying, English Literature, and Political Economy.

And these are arranged under the departments of

1. Agriculture.
2. Science.
3. Veterinary Science.
4. English and Mathematics.

Connected with the Course of Study in the Class-rooms is, outside on the fields and in the yards, barns, stables, and shops,

II. The Course of Apprenticeship, which is divided into

1. The Field department.
2. The Live-stock department.
3. The Horticultural department.
4. The Mechanical department.

The terms of admission to the regular course is the educational standard requisite for entrance into the High Schools of the Province. The academic year is divided into two Sessions, the Winter one beginning on the 1st of October and ending on the 31st of March; and the Summer Session commencing about the 16th of April and closing on the 31st of August. The Library is still very small, as are also the Laboratory and the Museum. The Boarding-house will accommodate 140 Pupils. It is directly under the charge of the President, assisted by the Mathematical Master. The Farm is all under cultivation, except four Groves of woods, which are purposely left upon it. The farming is that which is generally known as mixed farming. More attention has been paid to the actual farming and stock-breeding than has been given to them in any other Agricultural College in America. There are herds of the improved shorthorn, Ayrshire, Hereford, Devon and polled Angus breeds of Cattle; flocks of the Cotswold, Border Leicester, Oxford Down, and Southdown breeds of Sheep; and of the improved Berkshire and small Suffolk breeds of Pigs. The latest implements and machines are used, including a steam Thresher and a steam Pulping Apparatus. The Horticultural operations are subsidiary, but on a sufficiently large scale, the Kitchen Garden covering six acres, and the Flower Gardens, Lawn, and Shrubbery extending over twenty-five more. The Mechanical department, which is also subsidiary, has confined itself hitherto to permanent improvements, in the shape of Fencing, Draining, and Building, with repairs and setting up of all implements and machinery. The students labour on a daily yearly average at least five hours a day—that is, the whole day during the Summer months, half the day during the Spring and Autumn months, and a shorter time during the Winter ones. Thus, leaving out the evenings, half the day, counting the whole year round, is taken up with the Course of Apprenticeship, and the other half with the Course of Study. The Students are allowed for skilled labour at a maximum rate of ten cents per hour. The Rules and Regulations need not be enumerated.

The whole expense is borne directly by the Provincial Legislature, there being no endowment fund. The cost of yearly maintenance is about $22,000; and at the close of this year the Province will have expended on capital account, in the shape of a farm, buildings, and other permanent improvements, very nearly $200,000. The proceeds of the Farm and Stock have hitherto been spent in building up the Farm. Fees have only been charged for a short time, Students from the Province now paying a tuition fee of $25 per annum, and from outside the Province, $50 per annum. The management of the outside is under the charge of the Farm Superintendent and Professor of Agriculture, that of the inside under the President, and the financial management of the whole under the Bursar. The whole Institution, and each and all of the Officers, are directly under the charge of the Commissioner of Agriculture, who is directly responsible to the Government, the latter to the Legislature. In conclusion allow me, in no boastful spirit, to point out that the Ontario Agricultural College excels in its basis any other on the continent of America, and in any part of Europe, or Germany, in these five cardinal points—points which, we have seen, lie at the foundation of the success that has been achieved by any in existence in teaching simply agricultural education:

1. It does not attempt anything but strictly agricultural education.

2. It is not a mechanical or general industrial college.

3. It is not in any sense a literary Institution, with a leaning to agricultural subjects.

4. It places as much importance on a Course of Apprenticeship as it does on a Course of Study.

5. It makes Manual Labour a reality as well as a name, causing its Students to perform the work of a Farm of 500 acres.

In his evidence before the Ontario Agricultural Commission (in 1880), the present able President of the Agricultural College at Guelph, Mr. James Mills, M.A., elaborates this statement of his predecessor, Mr. Johnston, and gives the fullest particulars as to the condition and great value of the College.

NOTE.—With a view to emphasise the importance of the practical character of the system of Education which is given at the Agricultural College at Guelph, I insert here the very popular "Lecture on the Importance of Education to an Agricultural People," which was delivered in several Counties of Upper Canada in 1856 by the Reverend Doctor Ryerson who therein described himself as "the Son of a Canadian Farmer, and having devoted some of my early years to agricultural pursuits." I have condensed the Lecture in many parts—leaving out local and other references so as to render it the more interesting and effective—such as it was when delivered more than fifty years ago.

AN ADDRESS BY THE REVEREND DOCTOR RYERSON ON AGRICULTURAL EDUCATION.

At the earnest request of the Provincial Board of Agriculture, the Chief Superintendent of Education sent to the Provincial Exhibition of 1856, from the Educational Museum, a number of articles which were of practical value to the Farmer, the Mechanic, as well as of special interest to School Trustees and others. These objects comprised among many other things the following articles, videlicet:—

A collection of Models of Agricultural Implements arranged in three groups. (1) A series of about forty models from the Kingdom of Wurtemburg, South Western Germany, which received the Gold Medal at the Paris Exhibition of 1855; (2) a similar series of about twenty Agricultural Models, from Austria, North Eastern Germany; and, (3), a similar smaller series of ten Models from Denmark, and a variety of most interesting Articles of practical value in the Farmer's daily life.*

The practical utility of such an exhibition of School Apparatus, Maps, etcetera, was felt by every one who witnessed it; and the multitudes who thronged to the Education Court and sought information and explanation of the varied objects which it contained showed how general was the desire of the public to avail themselves of the facilities provided by the Department to supply the Public Schools of Upper Canada with those indispensable adjuncts to the work of a successful Teacher,—those invaluable instruments of his profession, without which it is impossible, from day to day, to sustain a continued interest on the part of the pupils in the exercises and duties of the School Room.

In connection with the Exhibition the Chief Superintendent, at the special request of the Local Committee, delivered the following Address on the Importance of Education to an Agricultural People;—its Advantages to the Community, and the importance of making it an element in Common School instruction; by means of the use of visible illustrations and proper apparatus to facilitate its communication. He said:—

1. Man is endowed by his Maker with physical, intellectual and moral powers; he sustains a three-fold relation to the world around him, according to the three-fold class of powers with which he is endowed; he requires a corresponding preparation for the duties of that three-fold relation. That preparation is properly termed Education. It is our apprenticeship for the business of life. The rudiments of that apprenticeship are the same in all departments of life; but it varies in its more advanced stages according to the particular profession or employment which we may pursue, whether of law, or medicine, agriculture, commerce, or mechanics. What is rudimental, or elementary, in Education is essential to the successful pursuit of any one of the several departments of human activity and enterprise. All must learn to read, to write, to calculate, to use their native tongue,—the Farmer as well as the Lawyer, the Mechanic as well as the Physician; in addition to which each must learn that which will give him skill in his own peculiar employment.

---

* Most of these Models and other interesting Articles in our Educational Museum were, in 1881, gratuitously distributed by the Honourable Adam Crooks, the first Ontario Minister of Education, to the University of Toronto and the School of Practical Science.

2. Agriculture constitutes the most extensive, as well as most important, branch of human industry; and the importance of Education to an Agricultural people is the topic on which I am to address you.

3. But when I speak of Education in reference to Agriculture, I do not mean the same thing as when I speak of it in reference to Navigation, or Manufactures, or Commerce, or to the learned Professions. I mean such an Education as the successful pursuit of Agriculture requires—such an Education as the interests of an Agricultural people demand. The fact is, that the Education of Agriculturists has formed no part of the policy, or care, of Governments,—and especially of our own,—down to a very recent period. * * * But, wherefore the selection of different soils for different purposes—wherefore the different processes to which they were subjected—wherefore the rotation of crops and the various modes of cultivating them—wherefore the peculiar construction of the implements and machinery worked by them—wherefore the times and seasons of disposing of the fruits of their own labour to advantage, and how, and when to provide for it—what and wherefore the principles of trade—and how to make the requisite calculations, and keep the needful accounts to effect the advantageous disposal of agricultural productions and ascertain the results—and how the proceeds of these might be applied for the promotion of personal, domestic and social enjoyment,—all these branches of knowledge were not, until lately, considered important enough to provide specially for their being specially made the subject of education. * * * But in Germany and France the Public Systems of Education have respect to Agriculture, as well as to the Professions and Trades. Patriotism and the progress of popular principles of government are doing in England what revolutions have prompted on the Continent, and what experience is creating in the United States of America; and the proposition introduced into our Legislature to establish an Agricultural School and Model Farm in connexion with the improved Grammar School of each District, is an important step in the same direction.*

4. In Canada, proprietorship in the soil is almost co-extensive with its culture; and every Farmer should embody in his own person the practical knowledge possessed in Europe by the proprietors, their agents, or middlemen, their overseers and labourers—for he performs the offices of all these, although on a limited scale, in his own little domain. In the temperate climate and appropriate seasons, the varied and fertile soil, the undulating, or level, surface, if not in its geographical position, Divine Providence has especially marked out Upper Canada for Agriculture, and has destined the mass of its inhabitants to be "tillers of the ground." We have not the cotton fields of the Southern States, or the vineyards of France, or the foreign inland trade of Germany, or the mineral treasures of England,—although in some of these we are not altogether deficient, and we may yet be found to abound in others;—but we have inexhaustible mines of virtuous wealth in our fields and forests, and the development of that wealth must constitute the leading employment and controlling interest of Upper Canada. The Agriculturists are likely to continue to be, as they now are, the people of Canada. The commercial and manufacturing interests are mere offshoots of the agricultural; extend them as you please, and the wider the better, and they cannot ever employ a twentieth of the population; magnify them as you may, they will be small fractions of the mass, depending both for their character and existence upon the agricultural population. The increasing tens of thousands who are migrating to and growing up in our Country will be chiefly agricultural. Its laws will be given, its commerce and manufactures will be regulated, the character of its government will be determined, and its interests will be decided by an agricultural population. Our Counties will give laws to Towns, and not Towns to Counties; and whether patriotism, or faction, prevail in the councils of the Government, or whether quietness, or commotion, reign throughout the land, will depend upon the

---

* This was one of the features of a University Bill introduced into the House of Assembly by Sir John Macdonald as early as in 1847. In this he was greatly in advance of the times.

Farmers of Canada; and they will be the arbiters, whoever may be the originators, of our Country's destinies. * * *

5. An educated Lawyer, rich in mental treasures, refined in taste, honest in principle, sound in judgment, eloquent in speech, with active faculties and habits, is undoubtedly an ornament, a safeguard, a blessing to any country; but he is so, not because he is a Lawyer, but because he is a man of knowledge, talent and virtue—endowments which if equally possessed by the Farmer, or Mechanic, will make him equally a guardian, an honour to, and benefactor of his country. It is the *man* and not the *profession* which constitutes the character. And it is the mind—in the largest sense of the term, including the conscience and the affections, as well as the understanding—which makes the man; and it is the culture of this which makes the difference between savage and civilized nations—between the boor and the scholar, the statesman and the peasant—between Bacon, when he was learning his A-B-C's, and Bacon after he had made the circle of the Sciences—between Newton when he was keeping sheep, and Newton when he was explaining the Laws of the Universe—between the least educated Farmer in Canada and the Head of the Government. Mind is the gift of God, and to the Farmer, not less than to the philosopher; but the development of mind in the different departments of human knowledge and human industry, is the work of man. And the power of each individual, or of each class of individuals in a community, is in proportion to their intellectual and moral development. It is this which makes the Bar the guides of public opinion and rulers of the land, though constituting less than one per cent. of the population; it is the absence of this which leaves the Agriculturists almost without a representative in the administration of civil affairs, though constituting nine-tenths of the entire population. Ought this so to be? Ought not the positive as well as negative power of Farmers in public affairs to be in proportion to their numbers and wealth? This doubtless ought to be; but it cannot be until the education of Farmers generally is equal to that of other classes of the community. And this is the first ground on which I urge the importance of education to an agricultural people, that they may occupy their appropriate position of power and influence in comparison with the other classes of the population.

6. Another ground on which I would urge the education of Farmers is, that they may enjoy the contentment and happiness of which agricultural life is susceptible. To be born, to eat, to drink, to grow up, to toil, to decay and die, is the mere life of animals; and human beings that do and know no more rise not above the animal tribes. * * * To such a state there is a tendency in a rural community, the members of which are sparsely settled, isolated from each other, and wholly occupied in providing for physical wants. Their views, their feelings, their enjoyments are thus liable to become materialized; and, what they shall eat and drink, and wherewithal they shall be clothed, to form the limits of their ambition and pursuits. * * *

7. It is not, indeed, to be supposed, nor is it to be desired, that the sons of agriculturists should, in all cases, follow the business of their fathers, as was required by law in regard to all the professions and trades in ancient Egypt, and as is still the case among some nations of Asia. This principle of *caste*, is not compatible with civil freedom, nor with the free scope of individual enterprise, or with the essential conditions of public prosperity. In a free state of society where Agriculture has unrestricted and profitable intercourse with all other interests, it is to be expected that peculiar talents, inclinations and circumstances will prompt many changes from agricultural to commercial, manufacturing and professional life. And it is well that all other pursuits should thus be connected with the farm-house. * * * But such changes should be dictated by the same considerations which govern the scions of noble families to pursue arms, or law, or commerce, or agriculture. And this will be the case, provided the farm-house be equally with the house of the Merchant, or Manufacturer, or Lawyer the abode of intelligence and rational enjoyment, and, therefore, of respectability and honour. And when the farm-house is thus the abode of moral and intellectual wealth, as well as of material

plenty, few will be disposed to exchange its virtuous quiet for the chances and turmoil of other pursuits. Let the Farmer's fireside be the place of reading, reflection and conversation, such as appertain to intelligent and improving minds, and where is there a scene more attractive? * * * I think there is no secular employment to which one becomes so much attached, and which affords such increased pleasure in its pursuits, as Agriculture, carried on scientifically and to the best advantage. Other employments are chosen and followed with view to their profits, and are usually abandoned as soon as a fortune is amassed; but every step in the progress and improvement of Agriculture adds a fresh charm to its pursuit, while its results present fresh beauties to the eye, and create new sources of physical and intellectual enjoyment. The hand of industry will add ever growing beauties and attractions to the cottager's acre and the landlord's domain. In the chemistry of his soils and manures, in the botany and vegetable physiology of his garden, fields and forests; in the animal physiology of his stock and poultry, in the hydraulics of his streams and rivulets, and the geology and mineralogy of their banks, in the mechanics of his tools, and the natural philosophy of the seasons, and the application of this varied knowledge to the culture of his lands, the care of his flocks, and the improvement of his estate, he finds exhaustless subjects of inquiry, conversation and interest, and all connected with his own possession, associated with his own home, and involved in his own prosperity. Thus, by observation, experiments and labours, each field and forest, each orchard and grove, each garden and walk, each hill and vale, each rock and rill will become endeared by a thousand pleasing recollections and delightful associations, from youth to old age, and thus will the **Canadian Farmer's place of abode** be his earthly paradise; and no Highlander will sing with more enthusiasm of his native hills and glens than will the educated **Farmer of Canada** contemplate his native or adopted home. It is well known that General Washington, after he had succeeded in founding the American Republic, devoted himself to the cultivation of his farm at Mount Vernon. He had attained high military distinction in being the first, as well as last, successful opposer of British power and prowess, and in establishing a new system of Government; but, in his last and ripest years, this remarkable man stated the results of his own experience in the following words:—" The more I am acquainted with agricultural affairs, the more I am pleased with them; insomuch that I can nowhere find so great satisfaction as in those innocent and useful pursuits. In indulging these feelings I am led to reflect how much more delightful to the undebauched mind is the task of making improvement on the earth, than all the vain glory which can be acquired from ravaging it by the most uninterrupted career of conquest. And I know of no pursuit in which more real and important services can be rendered to any country than by improving its agriculture."

8. But there is another ground on which the importance of education is commended to the most earnest attention of Farmers: It is the advantage which it gives them in pursuing their business in the most economical and profitable manner; it contributes to their gain, as well as to their happiness. It is power created and labour saved. In manufactures and commerce, the application of science is felt to be essential to success in this age of improvement and keen competition. Old modes of manufacture would be ruinous, as would old modes of travelling and trans-shipment. The cotton gin, by employing a new mode of separating the seed from the material which adheres to it, has added one-third to the value of all the cotton-growing lands of America and other countries; the spinning-jenny and power-loom have reduced the expense on all wearing apparel two-thirds, so that the people of this age can clothe themselves for one-third the expense incurred by their forefathers; the invention and improved application of machinery have reduced the average prices of Sheffield hardware and cutlery more than sixty per cent. since 1818; steam has superseded animal power, and even the winds of heaven have brought distant continents into convenient neighbourhood with each other; men travel by steam, print newspapers and books by steam, and talk by lightning. And the employment of these and innumerable other inventions and improvements is absolutely essential to the least success in both commerce and manufactures. * * * An

agricultural education will be as advantageous to the Farmer as a professional one to the Lawyer, or a commercial and mechanical one to the Trader or Engineer. Take two or three examples, out of a multitude which might be adduced, did time permit.

9. First, in reference to the *soil*, on the productiveness of which depends the Farmer's interests and hopes, and as to the application of *chemistry* to its cultivation and improvement. Let Sir Humphrey Davy speak on this point:—

" It is scarcely possible to enter upon any investigation in Agriculture without finding it connected, more or less, with doctrines, or elucidations, derived from chemistry.

" If land be unproductive, and a system of ameliorating it is to be attempted, the sure method of obtaining the object is by determining the cause of its sterility, which must necessarily depend upon some defect in the constitution of the soil, which may be easily discovered by chemical analysis. Some lands of good apparent texture are yet sterile in a high degree; and common observation and common practice afford no means of ascertaining the cause, or of removing the effect. The application of chemical tests in such cases is obvious; for the soil must contain some noxious principle which may be easily discovered, and probably easily destroyed.

" Are any of the salts of iron present? They may be decomposed by lime. Is there an excess of silicious sand? The system of improvement must depend on the application of clay and calcareous matter. Is there a defect of calcareous matter? The remedy is obvious. [The application of vegetable matter.] Is an excess of vegetable matter indicated? It may be removed by liming and burning. Is there a deficiency of vegetable matter? It is to be supplied by manure.

" A question concerning the different kinds of limestone to be employed in cultivation often occurs. To determine this fully in the common way of experience would demand a considerable time, perhaps some years, and trials which might be injurious to crops; but by the simple chemical tests the nature of a limestone is discovered in a few minutes; and the fitness of its application, whether as a manure for different soils or as a cement, determined."[*]

10. Respecting the errors arising from an ignorance of the mode in which lime operates in fertilizing land, and from not knowing why its application would be as injurious in one case as it would be beneficial in another, Mr. Falkner, an eminent English Agriculturist, remarks, that " the application of this manure is most suitable when soils contain a great quantity of rough vegetable matter, which quick lime breaks down, or decomposes, and thus renders a portion of it soluble in water. Though this operation is understood by some, they are not aware that in this case a portion is taken up by the lime, from which it cannot afterwards escape, and is therefore lost to the use of vegetation as soluble matter or manure. This is, however, an unavoidable condition of the benefit afforded by lime under such circumstances. But the ignorance of this operation leads often to a great misapplication. The author has often seen Farmers mix quick lime with dung, or half decomposed manure, and even put it upon land recently folded with sheep, which is obviously improper, as the lime in this case unites with a portion of the soluble manure and destroys it."[†]

11. The distinguished Author of the work on British Husbandry has observed, in regard to the application of manures from the farm-yard to different kinds of soil, " that warm and cold soils require manures of a contrary nature. An advance stage of their fermentation is in some cases less favourable to vegetation than in others; and in the instance of potatoes, it is well known that horse stable dung is employed with more effect alone than when mixed. It may, therefore, be advisable that horse litter, in particular, should be separately kept in yards, not merely for the purpose just mentioned, but that, as being of a hotter nature than any common dung, it may be mixed with that of other cattle in such proportions as may be thought best adapted to the purposes for which the compost is required."

---

[*]Davy's Agricultural Chemistry.
[†]British Husbandry.

12. On this subject Sir Humphrey Davy has remarked,—" There has been no question on which more difference of opinion has existed than the state in which manure ought to be ploughed into the land; whether recent, or when it has gone through the process of fermentation; but whoever will refer to the simplest principles of chemistry cannot entertain a doubt on the subject. As soon as dung begins to decompose, it throws off its volatile parts, which are the most valuable and the most efficient. Dung which has fermented, so as to become a mere soft cohesive mass, has generally lost from one-third to one-half of its most useful constituent elements; and that it may exert its full action upon the plant, and lose none of its nutritive powers, it should evidently be applied much sooner, and long before decomposition has arrived at its ultimate results."†

13. These remarks and authorities, which I have introduced in reference to soils and one or two kinds of manures—illustrative of the necessity and great advantage of some knowledge of chemistry in the most profitable culture and judicious application of each—might be indefinitely extended to the various modes of culture, and various kinds and applications of manures, to the elements and offices of both air and water, of light and heat, and the importance of a knowledge of them to the Farmer; but these must suffice on this point.

14. If we turn from the soil to the seed, the plants, the trees, and the fruits, and from thence to the flocks and herds, which altogether constitute the Farmer's productive wealth and his constant care, we can scarcely conceive of any knowledge more useful, as well as interesting to him, than that of the vegetable physiology of the former and the animal physiology of the latter, together with the best modes of cultivating the one and rearing the other. How great is both the advantage and enjoyment of the instructed over the uninstructed man in these departments of Agriculture? It is as great as the advantage of the educated anatomist and physician over the uneducated quack—as great as that of the mariner skilled in the science of navigation over the sailor who knows nothing beyond the ropes and helm of the ship—as great as that of the scientific mechanic over the journeyman who knows nothing of the principles of mechanics, and whose knowledge extends not beyond making smooth boards, joints and mortices, as directed by another. Farmers can never cultivate their gardens, plant and improve their orchards, till their fields, adorn their premises, and rear their flocks to advantage, without knowing the why and wherefore of each step of their procedure, any more than can the Mathematician, in demonstrating a theorem, or the Statesman in governing a kingdom. The pecuniary loss sustained by an ignorant Farmer is not easily estimated, and is only equalled by his loss of pleasure and satisfaction, arising from an acquaintance with the constitution and laws of those parts of the Creator's works with which he has to do; and the elementary knowledge preparatory to which should form a part of our system of agricultural education.

15. But the Farmer has also to do with implements and machinery of different kinds, and with various applications of animal and mechanical power in the prosecution of his work. The Honourable J. Buel, late President of the Agricultural Society of the State of New York, in an excellent work called the " Farmers' Instructor," remarks, on this point, that " many of our farm implements have undergone improvement; yet there are others which have been either partially introduced, or are hardly known, that are calculated to abridge labour and to increase the profits of a farm. There exists a great disparity in the quality of implements. In ploughs, for instance, there is a difference which eludes superficial observation, particularly in regard to the force required to propel them, that is worth regarding. I have seen this difference in what have been termed good ploughs, amounting to nearly fifty per cent., or one-half." * * * A little knowledge of the elements of mechanics—such as should be taught in every good Common School—will save the Farmer from much loss, and secure to him much gain, both in the construction of agricultural implements and the application of power in the use of them.

†Davy's Agricultural Chemistry.

16. Nor will it be less advantageous and interesting to the Farmer to possess (as he might do in a short time) such a knowledge of mensuration as to be able to measure his fields; and so much skill in Linear drawing as to be able to present to the eye his erections, his implements, the interesting animals and objects on his farm, or which might fall under his observation; and such a knowledge of accounts as will enable him to transact his business in trade with ease and correctness, and ascertain, in order and separately, the expenditure and profits connected with the cultivation of each field, each kind of vegetable, and grain and stock, and, by thus balancing the profit and loss of each, to ascertain not only the gross results, but the results in detail, and to modify his plans and labours accordingly. Such a mode of procedure is not only interesting as a recreation and matter of curiosity, and as furnishing many pleasing topics of conversation, but is useful as a habit, and highly important as a remedy against losses and a means of economical and profitable labour. It is thus that the skilful dealer, by keeping an accurate account of the profit and loss of each leading article of his trade, knows how to vary his selections from time to time, so as to secure the earliest and largest returns for the least expenditure of time and money. Nor should the Farmer be less prudent and skilful than the Trader.

17. Now the elementary knowledge involved in such an education extends not beyond our mother tongue, and may be taught in our Common Schools, within the period during which farmers' sons are usually sent to them. And then the development and practical application of that knowledge will be indefinitely promoted by suitable circulating Libraries in connection with Common Schools. I trust in less than a twelve-month the Provincial Board of Education will select books for such Libraries and ascertain and provide the cheapest methods of procuring and rendering them accessible to all parts of the country,* so that every Farmer and his family can have access to a hundred volumes of appropriate and entertaining books per annum for less than as many pence. But the preparatory instruction of the School is requisite to invest the perusal and study of even Agricultural Books with the interest and benefit they are calculated to impart.

18. I, then, earnestly and affectionately put it to the Farmer, whether the attainment of the practical, and appropriate, and, I may add, accessible, education above indicated, is not essential to the maintenance of their position in society, to the enjoyment of the domestic satisfaction and social happiness for which their situation and pursuits are so favourable, and for the success of their labours and the advancement of their best interests? Permit me to say that I speak as a native of Canada—as the son of a Canadian Farmer, and as having devoted some of my early years to Agricultural pursuits—and as most fervently desirous of conferring upon the rising and coming generations of Canada advantages which the Country at large could not afford to Agricultural youth in my own school-boy days. * * *

19. I cannot conclude this part of the subject without making two additional remarks. The first is, that what I have said respecting the education of Farmers and Farmers' sons is equally applicable and equally important in reference to the education of Farmers' Wives and Farmers' Daughters—those lights and charms of the domestic circle—without whose co-operation and intelligence, industry and virtue, the Farmer's labours would be in vain; his Home would be homeless and his life a scene of perplexity and toil. The variation between the education of Farmers' Sons and Daughters is confined to a few particulars— the leading features and the solid branches are the same; and the botany of the garden and fields, and the chemistry of the kitchen and dairy, the natural history of the pastured inhabitants of the Farm, together with the whole circle of domestic accounts, appertain peculiarly to the Matron and Daughters of the farm-house, besides the other ordinary and general knowledge which adorns and elevates the sex; in which I may mention what I hope to see taught to the Sons and Daughters of our entire population—vocal music—an art and accomplishment which often converts the domestic fireside into paradise, refines and promotes social feelings and enjoyments, and blesses

---

*This was done soon after this lecture was delivered.

the Churches of the land. But let it not be imagined that I would wish to see Farmers' Wives and Daughters lay aside country plainness and simplicity of manners and attempt city fashions and vanities. * * * On this point I can both adopt and endorse the following words of an intelligent American: "How important in a country Home is a studious, a cultivated, a refined and sensible Mother; a Mother capable of winning and keeping the confidence of her children; of securing honour from both Sons and Daughters as they rise to manhood and womanhood. * * * Delightful instances occur to my mind where the working Father and Mother have been surrounded with Sons and Daughters, versed not only in all common education, but in the histories and classics of their native tongue; where, not distant from the plough and the spinning wheel, the most liberal studies have been pursued, and the most refined conversation enjoyed; scenes which intercourse with other countries and many cities, and with the refined and intelligent of the highest classes has not cast into the shade."*

20. My second and last remark is, that the Education to which I have had reference in the foregoing observations, and which I believe to be essential to the well-being of an agricultural population, is *Christian*—using the term in the sense of the Scriptures, from which it is derived, as embracing what Christians of every form of worship hold in common, without reference to the peculiarities of any. I do not regard any instruction, discipline or attainments as Education which does not include Christianity. * * * It is the cultivation and exercise of man's moral powers and feelings which forms the basis of social order and the vital fluid of social happiness; and the cultivation of these is the province of Christianity. The extent and application of this principle in our Schools I have explained at large in my " Report on a System of Public Elementary Instruction for Upper Canada ";† and I will conclude what I have now to say in the expressive words of the President of Amherst College, in the United States: " A more Utopian dream never visited the brain of a sensible man than that which promises to usher in a new golden age by the diffusion and thoroughness of what is commonly understood by Popular Education. With all its funds, and improved School-houses, and able Teachers, and grammars, and maps, and blackboards, such an education is essentially defective. Without moral principle at bottom to guide and control its energies, education is a sharp sword in the hands of a practised and reckless fencer. I have no hesitation in saying that, if we could have but one moral and religious culture. it is even more important than a knowledge of letters; and that the former cannot be excluded from any system of popular education without infinite hazard. Happily the two, far from being hostile powers in a common domain, are natural allies, moving on harmoniously in the same right line, and mutually strengthening each other. The more virtue you can infuse into the hearts of your pupils, the better they will improve their time, and the more rapid will be their proficiency in their common studies. The most successful Teachers have found the half-hour devoted to moral and Religious Instruction more profitable to the scholar than any other half-hour in the day; and there are no Teachers who govern their Schools with so much ease as this class. Though punishment is sometimes necessary, where moral influence has done its utmost the conscience is, in all ordinary cases, an infinitely better disciplinarian than the rod. When you can get a School to obey and study because it is right, and from a conviction of accountability to God, you have gained a victory which is worth more than all the penal statutes in the world; but you can never gain such a victory without laying great stress upon Religious principle in your daily instructions."‡

---

*American Institute of Instruction, Vol. V., page 53.
†See pages 140-2 of the sixth Volume of the Documentary History of Education in Upper Canada.
‡Lecture before the American Institute for Instruction, at Boston, 1843.

THE AGRICULTURAL COLLEGE AND THE MACDONALD INSTITUTE AND HALL, GUELPH.

The Ontario Agricultural College was established by the Ontario Government in 1874. The objects of the Institution were twofold: First, to train young men in the science and art of improved Husbandry; and second, to conduct Agricultural experiments and publish the results.

In 1875 the President said in his first Report:—

"It is evident to the most cursory observer that Canada depends, and will be obliged for many years to depend largely, if not exclusively, on her raw produce for her national wealth. And amongst the various forms of raw material none are so valuable as those included under the head of Agricultural Produce. To the observant statesman, it is plain that the readiest manner of increasing the national wealth is by increasing the quantity and quality of that produce. But though plainly seen, it is not so easily accomplished. Precedent, prejudice, and general conservatism stand in the way. Throughout the Province there is a powerful minority of intelligent, enterprising, and successful Farmers pursuing the improved system of cultivation; yet the great majority are depending solely on increased acreage for increased returns."

Since the time the College was established it has gradually endeavored to overcome the prejudice against Book learning, until at the present time between 30,000 and 40,000 Farmers visit the College each year with the object of getting information that will help them on their own Farms. Last year there were 1,298 Students in attendance. We have now a well equipped Women's department, where practical instruction is given to Farmers' Daughters in Cooking, Sewing, and Laundry work; also in Dairying, Horticulture, and management of Poultry.

GUELPH, 22nd February, 1910.   G. C. CREELMAN, *President*.

The College is beautifully situated on an elevation directly south-east of the City of Guelph in the County of Wellington. The location (1,138 feet above sea level) is in the midst of pleasant scenery and healthful surroundings, for which this part of the Province is widely known Being a mile and a half from the City of Guelph the College is remarkably free from those things which at many Colleges are wont to distract the attention of Students and to dissipate their energies.

BUILDINGS AND EQUIPMENT.

The Men's Residence: The residence is recognized as the main building. It is built of grey limestone, and, although no particular style of Architecture was followed in its construction, it presents a venerable appearance, expressive of power and repose. It comprises a central portion five storeys high, and two wings extending on either side, and behind these are other extensions. It is situated on the highest point of College Heights, and faces the south-west. The building provides Bedroom and Dining-room accommodation for 218 Students, and a small portion is reserved as a contingency Hospital.

A large, comfortable Parlour and a Reading Room are at the convenience of those who care to use them between study hours.

MAIN BUILDING, ONTARIO AGRICULTURAL COLLEGE, GUELPH.

The whole of the building is well ventilated, and is heated by steam, Radiators being placed along the Halls and Corridors, and in every Room. A Bathroom containing cold and hot water baths, shower baths, etcetera, and a Lavatory fitted up after the most modern and approved methods are at the disposal of the Students at all hours.

The Massey Hall and Library, an abiding expression of the generosity of the late Mr. Hart A. Massey, is a handsome red brick building. The Hall occupies the ground floor. This is semi-circular in shape and provides seating accommodation for about four hundred and fifty people. It is used for Roll-call, Sunday Chapel Service, Literary Society meetings, concerts, etcetera. Overhead is the Library, consisting of a Reference Library, a Lending Library, and two Magazine Rooms. Accommodation is provided for eighty thousand Volumes.

MACDONALD HALL, THE WOMAN'S RESIDENCE OF ONTARIO AGRICULTURAL COLLEGE, GUELPH.

Biology and Physics: The building devoted to Biology and Physics is a commodious, substantial, red brick structure, with Class Rooms and Laboratories well fitted up for instruction and research work in the Biological and Physical Sciences. The ground floor is used as a Museum. Here are to be found some excellent collections of interest to the Botanist, the Ornithologist, the Geologist, the Zoologist, the Entomologist, and others. Here, also, is to be seen a collection of waxwork replicas of nearly all the different species and varieties of Fruit and Vegetables grown in Canada. The models show the difference in size, shape, colour, and general appearance of the objects which they most faithfully represent, thus providing an excellent key to the many and varied products of the Orchard and Garden, illustrating the desirable and undesirable qualities of these products.

Horticulture: The department building is equipped with Classroom, Workroom and Offices. It has in connection a large glass Laboratory for practical work in propagation, grafting, seed testing and sowing, methods of tree planting, etcetera.

In addition, two large Greenhouses are attached for experimental work in Vegetable forcing, and two for the propagation and growing of a large collection of flowering and decorative Plants for practical demonstrations in Floriculture.

The Chemistry Building is situated to the south-east of the Main College Building, facing the Massey Library. It contains Lecture Rooms, Laboratories for regular Qualitative, Quantitative, and Organic analysis; Laboratories for experiment station analyses and research work; and a specially equipped Room

THE CONSOLIDATED SCHOOL, ONTARIO AGRICULTURAL COLLEGE, GUELPH.

for investigating wheat and flour problems. All Laboratories have the most up-to-date arrangement of Tables, with Sinks, Fume Closets, Down Drafts, etcetera.

The Gymnasium is a substantial Building, and the whole of the floor space is available for Drill and Sport. All the necessary fittings for Gymnastic work are in evidence. The floor is marked out for baseball and basketball. In the basement are shower baths and a large swimming bath.

Agriculture: This is a large two-storey structure, erected on the lower part of the College Campus. The Building contains an Office, an Agricultural Museum, three large work Rooms, a tool Room, a dark Room for photography, and six or seven Basement Rooms, all for the use of the Field Husbandry Department; Offices for the Department of Animal Husbandry; an Office, a private Laboratory, a Work Room, and a Students' Laboratory for the Department of Bacteriology; a Class Room for practical instruction in Live Stock and a Lecture

Room for the use of the Professors of Field Husbandry, Bacteriology, and Veterinary Science.

Judging Pavilion: This is a round, white brick building, located on the lower part of the Campus, immediately in the rear of the Agriculture building. The Pavilion has a 50-foot Ring, with a seating accommodation for 300 persons, and is used especially for practical work in Live Stock. Into this Ring all classes of Horses, Beef Cattle, Sheep, and Swine are brought.

Machinery Hall: This is a new two-storey building, 146 feet long by 64 feet wide. The north-west wing and the central portion are devoted to Manual Training and Farm Mechanics. In the basement of this wing is the Forge Room, well equipped for instruction in metal work and blacksmithing. The Basement of the central part provides accommodation for the storage of farm machinery and implements. On the first floor are situated the Machine Shop, Offices, and Store-rooms.

THE CONSOLIDATED SCHOOL AND ITS CONSTITUENTS, ONTARIO AGRICULTURAL COLLEGE, GUELPH.

Across the corridor is Machinery Hall, to be used for demonstration purposes in farm mechanics. It also contains an unique collection of domestic utensils and farm implements and machinery of early pioneering days. The second floor is taken up with class rooms for Woodworking, Drawing, and Primary School work, offices and store-rooms. The south-west wing of the Building is occupied by the farm Carpenter, Blacksmith, and Painter.

Dairy: The Buildings of the Dairy are used for instruction work in Cheesemaking and Farm Dairy. In another Building are located Lecture Rooms, Office, Dairy Library, Rooms for Students and Instructors, the Butter-making and Milk-testing branches of the Dairy, Store-room, etcetera.

Poultry: The buildings connected with this department are well equipped, and have sufficient accommodation for 700 laying hens. The houses are of several designs, many of them being for experimental purposes. Colony houses have been established for the purpose of rearing young chicks, a Brooder House, and a fattening house. The main Building contains the Head Office of the department, a large Lecture Room, an experimental Incubator Room, Feed Rooms, etcetera.

Macdonald Hall is a fine, large, imposing brick Building, in the Elizabethan style of architecture. It was erected in 1904, at a cost of $100,000, and is the generous gift of Sir William C. Macdonald, of Montreal, as is also Macdonald Institute. It comprises everything that experience could suggest as necessary for the purpose of a residence for Girls; is commodious, substantial in appearance, and complete in appointments. The building has apartments for 110 boarders, together with a large Gymnasium, Dining Room, Reception Room and Parlour.

The Macdonald Institute is a fine building, large and imposing in its general outline, commodious in its internal arrangement, and elegant as regards the quality and finish of the inside work. Its equipment and accommodation is ample to furnish long and short courses in Home Economics and Nature Study. The Home Economics Course is for Farmers' Daughters and other young women who desire to learn the theory and practice of Cooking, Ventilation, general Housekeeping, Laundry work, Sewing, Dressmaking, Millinery, Home Decoration, etcetera.

The Departments and Equipment of the College.

Animal Husbandry: In this department considerable time is spent in practical work in judging Horses, Cattle, Sheep, and Swine. In addition to the practical work, Lectures are given on the Feeding and Management of Stock, the principles of Breeding, and the history and characteristics of the different breeds. The Student is also given instruction on Herd Books, etcetera.

Bacteriology: No other science comes nearer the everyday life of the Farmer than that one which teaches of Bacteria, Yeasts and Moulds, and their relation as causative agents to the common practices of the farm and home. The chemical changes in the soil and the manure heap whereby the unavailable plant food is changed into a form assimilable by plants; the proper handling of Milk, fermentation of Vinegar, the making of Bread, the canning of Fruit, the preservation of Meats, the avoidance of disease, etcetera. It is the aim of the Department of Bacteriology, by means of Lecture and Laboratory Courses, to familiarize the Student with the nature of Micro-organisms and methods of dealing with them as met with in the farm and home pursuits, that he may render harmless those that are inimical and make use of those that are beneficial. The equipment of the department consists of the requisite apparatus for giving instruction along agricultural, horticultural, dairy, and domestic science lines, and for research.

Botany: A Lecture Room and two large Laboratories are made use of for this work, and Glass Houses for physiological work have been erected. In addition to Microtomes, Paraffin Baths and Physiological apparatus for advanced and research work, the Laboratories are supplied with Microscopes and general apparatus for the use of students. The Herbarium connected with the department contains an almost complete collection of Ontario plants, as well as many foreign ones, and an extensive collection of Fungi, which can be used for reference. The Museum, which is in connection with the department, contains many interesting and instructive botanical specimens and an extensive and valuable collection of Minerals and Rocks. These can be made use of for purposes of study by the students.

Chemistry is intimately connected with the proper understanding of the principles of Crop and Animal production, consequently this department is equipped to analyse Soils, Fodders, Dairy products, etcetera, in addition to the regular qualitative, Gravimetric and Volumetric work. Two Laboratories are fitted with modern Tables, with Fume Closets, and Down Draft connections; two more are especially arranged for Quantitative analyses and for Organic preparations; a fourth Room is reserved for the analyses of Dairy Products, a fifth for Nitrogen determinations, and two for the ordinary experiment station analytical work and for research work. There are also two Lecture Rooms, a large one for the Junior classes, and a smaller one for the Senior and Household Economic Classes. The building also contains a Room equipped with a reduction mill, Electric oven, and all the most modern apparatus for testing Wheat and Flour and for studying problems in relation to these materials. In addition, the building contains Offices, Store-rooms, etcetera.

PARTIAL VIEW OF EXPERIMENTAL GROUNDS, ONTARIO AGRICULTURAL COLLEGE, GUELPH.—FARMERS EXAMINING THE PLOTS.

Dairy: The cheese-making apparatus is located in the Dairy building. The Milk vats consist of three 300 lb. Vats, two 800 lb. Vats, and one 3,000 lb. Vat, for holding Milk to be used in the manufacture of cheese. Curd knives, curd mills, gang press, etcetera. Instruction is given in the methods of making Canadian Cheddar and the leading varieties of soft cheese. The Creamery is located in a Building in which are the Milk-testing Laboratory, Class-rooms, Office, Library, Reading Room, Coat Room, etcetera. The apparatus in the Creamery consists of two power Cream separators, (one Turbine and one Belt), Pasteurizers, a Carbon-dioxide ice machine, milk and cream Coolers, two combined Churns and Butter Workers, Vats, Skim-milk weigher.

The Farm Dairy is equipped with the leading makes of hand Cream Separators. There are also Barrel churns, Lever Butter workers, and a full set of appliances for teaching practical Butter-making on the Farm. The testing of Milk with Lactometer and Babcock Tester is also a part of the practical teaching in the Farm Dairy.

Home Economics: The work of this department is arranged to give instruction in problems of current economic, social, and public interest; to prepare students to participate intelligently in the molding of public opinion; and to direct their attention towards a broad and unbiased view of the debatable questions of the day; in short, to assist them to perform to the fullest degree the duties of citizenship.

English: The Course in English extends over the four years of the College Course. It consists of Classes in Public Speaking, in practical Composition, and in the study of English Authors. Public Speaking: By means of the Literary Societies and the various Class Societies, many incidental opportunities are afforded the Student for acquiring a certain measure of familiarity with the public platform. In order to supplement these opportunities, regular Classes have been organized for practice and instruction in Public Speaking. Each member of the Class is given an opportunity to prepare and to speak on a subject, and a few minutes of each period are devoted to common-sense criticisms of the Speeches, criticisms on the Student's manner, voice, choice of words, and choice, or treatment, of the theme. Practical Composition: Many of the Students will be expected, after they leave the Institution, to contribute occasionally to the columns of Agricultural Journals. English Authors: During the four years of the Course many selections from various Authors are read.

Entomology and Zoology: Elementary and advanced Courses are given in Systematic and Economic Entomology, Vertebrate and Invertebrate Zoology, Histology and Physiology. Special attention is given to practical work in the Laboratory and Field. The Entomological Cabinets contain, in addition to many exotic Insects, specimens of a large proportion of the more common species of Ontario. The collection includes many sets of specimens illustrative of the life-histories, habits and work of Insects. The Laboratory is also supplied with Breeding cages, Aquaria, Terraria, Microscopes, Photographic apparatus, Spraying machinery, and Electrical Lantern, and a large number of views for illustrating Lectures. An Insectary affords facilities for special investigation in the study of life-histories of Insects, and for experiments in Economic Entomology. The equipment of the Zoological Laboratory consists of Microscopes, Microtomes, Aquaria, Terraria, Bird-skin Cabinets, and collections of preserved Animals for Class work. The Museum contains a very complete collection of mounted and classified Birds, and a number of Birds' Nests and Eggs. Other Cabinets contain the life-histories and work of Insects, and many Mammals also. The large collections of Insects belonging to the Entomological Society of Ontario occupy a portion of the Museum, and are available for reference and study.

Farm: The Farm proper consists of about 345 acres, and is well tilled and well managed. It is composed of nearly every variety of soil, and is well suited for Grain, Roots and Pasture. The equipment consists of large and commodious Farm Buildings with all modern improvements, up-to-date implements and machinery, and good specimens, of seven breeds of Cattle, four of Sheep, three of Swine and one of Horses.

Field Husbandry: This department has a Class-room for Students. The Laboratory is supplied with specially constructed Seed sorting Tables, finely graded Screens, Germinators, Balances, apparatus for testing hardness and weight per bushel of Grains, etcetera. The Agricultural Museum in connection with the department contains dried specimens and Seeds of many leading varieties of Farm Crops, arranged in such a way as to show their comparative value as determined by actual experiment on the College trial grounds. In this Museum are also cases containing seeds, etcetera, arranged to show the exact results of many valuable experiments in selection of Seed, sowing at different dates, methods of cultivation, etcetera. The department also has fifty acres of land, devoted entirely to experimental work with Farm Crops, and Students are required to spend much of their time in this field during the Autumn term, examining the Crops, and noting the methods of conducting experiments and the results.

Forestry: In this department instruction is primarily intended to aid the Farmer in the care and establishment of Woodlands on the Farm, besides giving the Student an intelligent conception of the forestry problems from a national standpoint. Three College Woodlots present conditions which are typical of the Ontario Woodlot, and lend themselves for practical illustrations of work given in Lecture Rooms.

About twenty-five years ago several plantations were made in various parts of the Farm, and these show interesting results, of value in the study of formation of plantations. In connection with the Government co-operative plan of assisting Tree-planters, a College nursery has been established to produce nursery stock, where the Student will be able to obtain practical knowledge of Forest nursery work.

Landscape Gardening and Floriculture: The object of this department is to stimulate in our Students an appreciation and love for the beautiful in Nature; to show by precept and example how such beauty may be made contribute to our every-day enjoyment in the beautifying of the Home and home surroundings. The equipment of the department includes sixty acres of the College Campus and Grounds, with an interesting and varied collection of ornamental Trees, Shrubs, and Vines; flower borders of hardy Annuals and Perennials; Greenhouses and Laboratories for practical demonstrations in Floriculture; and a large and varied collection of lantern Slides for illustrating Lectures at the College, and at Public Meetings throughout the country.

Manual Training: This department aims to supply and provide a training necessary for, and beneficial to, every agricultural Student. The Forge Room is fitted with ten down draft Forges connected with a Blower and an Exhaust Fan, each power driven, together with Anvils, Swage Blocks, Grindstone, and all necessary Tools and appliances. Instruction is given in tempering, welding, drawing and pointing, bending and shaping, cutting, breaking, flattening, twisting, etcetera. The Machine Shop contains two Screw Cutting Lathes, Power Drill, Power Hacksaw, Grindstone, Benches for chipping, filing and fitting, soldering and brazing outfit, together with the necessary tools In Machinery Hall there are three Gasoline Engines, and numerous Tools and implements for demonstration purposes in Farm Mechanics. In the Woodworking Room each Student is provided with a Bench and set of Tools. In addition to these there are distributed in different parts of the Room on racks and in cupboards a complete kit of Woodworking Tools. In the Drawing Room complete Plans are made before the Models are commenced. The Benchwork consists of instruction in making various useful objects, such as Hammer and Axe Handles, Whiffletrees, Joints, etcetera, the care, use, Sharpening,

Grinding and adjustment of Tools. The Drawing Room is equipped with typical Geometrical Models, Casts, Tables, Blackboards, Drawing Boards, and apparatus for making working drawings of the Objects to be made in the Workroom.

Physics: The work of the department of Physics is included under the following heads: General Physics, Soil Physics, Meteorology, Climatology, Mechanics, Hydraulics, Drainage, Surveying and Levelling. The equipment for General Physics consists of apparatus for the elementary study of Hydrostatics, Heat and Electricity, such as Pumps, Variscope, Barometer, Equal Pressure apparatus, to illustrate Capillarity and Surface Tension, Specific Heat, Latent Heat, expansion of Metals and Liquids, Electroscopes, Condensers, Galvonometers, Induction Coils, X-Ray outfit, Telephone, Telegraph, Motors and Dynamos. The Soil Physics outfit consists of a plant for the physical Analysis of Soils, together with

MANUAL TRAINING AT THE ONTARIO AGRICULTURAL COLLEGE, GUELPH.

apparatus for studying the Physical Properties of the Soil, such as specific Gravity, Specific Heat, Capillary Capacity, rate of Percolation of Water through different types of Soil, Aeration of soils, etcetera. For the study of Meterology we have two outfits, one for student practice, the other for the official records of the department, each consisting of Maximum and Minimum and "Wet and Dry bulb" Thermometers, Rain Gauge, Barometer and Soil Thermometers. A complete set of Pulleys, Levers, and Winclasses is provided for the study of the Mechanics of simple machines; and some apparatus for illustrating the elementary principles of the Flow of Water. Surveying and levelling is taken up extensively enough to enable any Student to make a survey of his own Fields for Drainage purposes and to plan and lay out the Drains. The equipment for this work consists of Surveyor's Chains, Tapes and Levels; enough to accommodate a larger class of Students.

Pomology: The equipment of this department comprises various plantations of Orchard and small Fruits, as well as an excellent Vegetable Garden. These are largely used as sources of supply for the residence Schools. They serve also as demonstrations and Object Lessons of a practical nature, and, in this capacity, are instructive alike to Students and Visitors. The department possesses a full line of Orchard and Garden Implements and appliances, and also Storage Houses for Fruits and Vegetables. A Cold Storage plant affords facilities for lengthening the season of many Fruits and Vegetables, and an excellent collection of Fruits and Vegetables, modelled in Wax, gives likewise an opportunity for identification and study of a large number of varieties.

Poultry: This department is located near the Dairy. Portions of the Horticulture and Farm departments are used for rearing the young Stock. Twenty-five Incubators of many makes, together with Brooders, cramming machines, Fattening Crates, etcetera, form a portion of the equipment. There are 25 varieties of Poultry, representing Fifteen Breeds, which are kept for illustrating the Lectures, and for the practical instruction of students.

Veterinary Science: The department is furnished with a Skeleton of a Horse and a full supply of the Bones of ordinary farm Animals for illustration of the Veterinary Lectures; and the Live Stock Class-room is used by the Veterinary Surgeon for demonstrations in "practical horse," that is, for handling Horses in the presence of the Class, judging them by points, examining them as to soundness, and freedom from blemishes, administering medicine, and showing Students how to perform various Surgical Operations, etcetera. When an animal dies from disease or injury, it is dissected and the cause or causes of death sought for and pointed out in the presence of the Students.

Ontario Veterinary College, Toronto: The Council of the Agricultural and Arts Association was by Act of Parliament empowered to establish a Veterinary College for the instruction of pupils by competent and approved Teachers in the science and practice of the Veterinary art, and examine pupils in Anatomy, Physiology, Materia Medica, Therapeutics, Chemistry, and as to the breeding of domesticated Animals; and upon proof to the satisfaction of the Council that such pupils possess the requisite qualifications, to grant. Diplomas certifying that they are competent to practise as Veterinary Surgeons.

University of Toronto: In 1862-1863 a course of Lectures on Veterinary Medicine was given in the connection with Professor Buckland's Agricultural Class. The Course was attended principally by Agricultural students. In 1866 three of them graduated. Many of the Students came from the United States.

Other Subjects Taught: Lectures are given in the various subjects throughout the term, together with, in Geology and Apiculture, practical Laboratory work, Field Excursions and Class Room demonstrations.

Advantages of the Agricultural Course.

The Course of Study and apprenticeship is especially adapted to the wants of young men who intend to be Farmers. The Lectures in the Class-room, the work in the outside departments and the Laboratories of the Institution, the experimental work, the debates in the College Literary Society, the surroundings, the atmosphere of our College life, all tend to awaken, stimulate, develop and brighten the minds of the Students; to teach them the use of their eyes and hands, give them a taste for reading, increase their respect for the pursuit of farming, and make them more intelligent workers and better citizens.

The Various Courses in the Agricultural College.

1. Department of Agriculture: (a) Four Years' Course. leading to Degree of B.S.A.; (b) Two Years' Course—Associate Diploma; (c) Factory Dairyman's Course, 12 weeks; (d) Farm Dairy Course, 12 weeks; (e) Poultry Course, 4 weeks; (f) Stock and Seed Judging Course, 2 weeks; (g) Fruit Growing Course, two weeks.

2. Department of Home Economics: (a) Normal Course in Domestic Science, 2 years; (b) Housekeeper Course, 2 years; (c) Home Maker Course, 1 year; (d) Short Course in Domestic Science, 3 months; (e) Short Course in Sewing, 3 months.

3. Department of Manual Training: Teachers' Normal Course, 1 year.

4. Department of Nature Study: (a) Teachers' Normal Course, 1 year; (b) Short Course for Teachers, 3 months.

From this it will be seen that there is at Guelph a College equipped for educating young men on practical lines; stirring them up to observe, read, and think for themselves, making them more intelligent workers, giving them information and training which will be of use to them in their efforts to make a living, and developing in them a love for work and life on the farm.

The College Scholarships, Prizes and Medals.

Four Scholarships of $20 each will be awarded on the first year's work, of theory and practice. The awards will be made on the following groups of subjects:

Agriculture: Animal Husbandry, Apiculture, Dairying, Field Husbandry, Poultry, Veterinary Science.

Biological Science: Botany, Pomology, Zoology.

English and Mathematics: English, Mathematics.

Physical Science: Chemistry, Geology, Manual Training, Physics.

To obtain one of these Scholarships, the Candidates must take 40 per cent. of the marks for each subject in the year's work, and 75 per cent. of the aggregate number of marks allotted to the subjects in the group.

No Student shall receive more than one of these scholarships.

Mr. George Chapman, of Guelph, has generously offered the sum of twenty dollars ($20.00), to be expended in Books, as a prize in English of the first two years. The three divisions of the work under the English department will be taken into consideration in awarding the prize, namely, English Literature, English Composition and Public Speaking.

Three prizes of the value of $10.00 each in Books, to be selected by the winner, will be given as follows:

One to the second year Student who shall compose and read before a Committee the best essay on a subject assigned for the year. The subject for 1910-11 is: The Ontario Pioneer in Agriculture.

One to the Student who shall stand first in general proficiency on the first and second year's work; theory and practice.

One to the Student who shall rank highest in general proficiency and who shall obtain first-class Honours in his major subjects of the fourth year.

The Governor-General's Silver Medal is awarded each year to the second year Student who has ranked highest in general proficiency in the first and second year's work.

The Gold Medal for the Senior Year of the intrinsic value of $25, to be awarded to the Student of the senior year who, by vote of his Classmates, approved by the Staff, is declared to be the best "all round" man in his year.

Messieurs H. Barton and R. S. Hamer, Graduates of the class of '07, have offered to donate each year for five consecutive years a Gold Medal to that Member of the International Live Stock Judging Team who shall secure the highest number of marks in the Students' Judging Contest held annually at Chicago.

Diplomas admitting to the status of "Associate of the Ontario Agricultural College," are granted to all Students who comply with the following conditions:

1. Are in attendance at lectures for two years, unless in special cases where the candidate's scholarship and practical training warrants a slight departure from this rule.

2. Complete the work of the regular two years' Course of Study.

3. Pass satisfactorily all prescribed Examinations both on the subjects contained in the Curriculum and on the work of apprenticeship.

4. Compose an acceptable Thesis on some subject in the Course of Study, or connected therewith.

Short Courses in Practical Work.

Any person—man, woman, boy or girl—may come to the College at any time for practical work, with more or less instruction from the man in charge; in one or more departments, say in Poultry, Horticulture, or dairying.

Terms.

The scholastic year consists of one Session, which is divided into two Terms:
Fall Term: 20th of September to 22nd of December.
Winter Term: 4th of January to 15th of April.

The Terms are arranged in this way to enable students to get home for seeding, haying, and harvest.

Examinations.

Associate Examinations: All first and second year students are required to pass two regular examinations during each year; one in December on the work of the fall term, and one in April on the work of the winter term, including Classroom and Laboratory work, Farm Management, experiments.

Examinations are held at the conclusion of the Lectures on each particular subject, and these are considered final.

Examinations for Degrees: Examinations for the Degree of B.S.A. are held annually, at the close of the fourth year, in the month of May. These Examinations are conducted, and the Degrees conferred, by the University of Toronto.

Course of Instruction for an Associate Diploma.

This Course extends over a period of two years, and is intended specially as a preparation for work and life on the Farm. It embraces a Course of Study of Apprenticeship.

SPECIAL STUDENTS.

In case a Candidate for an Associate Diploma does not rank high enough in the work of the first two years to admit him to the Third Year standing, but wishes to continue his studies in certain departments for a few months longer than the regular Associate Course permits, with a view of preparing himself more fully for Farm management, or for any particular work which he may have in view, he may return to the College, and spend a few months at Agriculture and Live Stock, Dairying, Agricultural Chemistry, Geology, Botany, Entomology, Horticulture, or any other subject in the Course, provided he attends faithfully to his work and puts in the full number of hours per day on the subjects selected.

CANDIDATES FOR THE B. S. A. DEGREE.

The College is affiliated with the University of Toronto for advanced Examinations and Degrees.

LENGTH OF COURSE.

The Course for the Degree of Bachelor of the Science of Agriculture (B.S.A.) extends over a period of four years.

The work of the first two years is embraced in the Course prescribed for the Associate Diploma and the work outlined below proceeds from the Associate standing, and extends over a period of two years.

The Examinations of the third year work are conducted by the College. The final Examinations at the end of the fourth year are conducted by the University of Toronto.

ADMISSION TO THIRD YEAR STANDING.

An Associate of the College is admitted to the third year standing and allowed to proceed with the work of third and fourth years :—

Provided he has taken rank in his Associate Course satisfactory to the College Staff, 60 per cent. of the marks in English and 50 per cent. in general proficiency.

NOTE.—In addition to the above, Candidates intending to take "Agriculture Option" must present satisfactory evidence of having spent at least two years at practical work with a good Farmer; those entering for the "Dairy Option" must have spent one season at practical work in a Cheese Factory and one in a Creamery, or have spent one season in a Cheese Factory or Creamery and have taken the full course (Cheese and Butter) in a Dairy School; and those entering for the "Horticulture Option" must have spent at least one year at practical work with a good Fruit-grower, Market Gardener, or Florist.

A Graduate, or Undergraduate in Arts, or Science, of any reputable University, having had the necessary training in Farm Work, may proceed to the Degree, upon presenting Certificates of standing satisfactory to the Head of the department to which the Certificate relates, and approved by the President, and passing examinations on subjects not covered by his Certificates.

The work done previously by such a Candidate will be accepted *pro tanto* for any part of the work prescribed for the Degree, provided he submits to the President all credentials and records of standing from other Institutions.

Third Year (for the B.S.A. Degree).

Attendance and Term Work for Third and Fourth Years.

Note.—Any Candidate before being passed on any examination must have attended at least seventy-five per cent. of the Lectures and seventy-five per cent. of the Laboratory periods in each subject, and must have obtained at least fifty per cent. of the marks for Term work in each department and sixty per cent. in all departments together. "Attendance" and "Term Work" rank as separate subjects.

The Course of Study.

Botany—Cryptogamic, Plant Physiology. Chemistry—Inorganic Qualitative Analysis, Organic Quantitative Analysis. Economics. English—Composition, Literature. Entomology. French or German. Geology. Physics—Heat, Cold Storage, Meteorology. Nature Study.

Outline of Work in Nature Study.

For Third Year Students, being a Substitution for the Six Weeks' Course of the Spring.

1. Collections: Each student will present on September 24th, at the time of the practical examination, a collection of 50 plants properly pressed, mounted and named (if possible). These are to represent different types of plants illustrative of third year Cryptogamic Botany; i.e., Ferns, Mosses, Liverworts, Lichens, Algae, Fungi. No collection of Insects is required.

2. Nature Study: Note Book—Each student will keep a record of observations on the natural phenomena of the locality in which he spends the Summer, e.g., the Birds, Insects, Trees and Flowers discovered in his walks; reports on Insect outbreaks; injury to Crops by Fungous Diseases; Weather conditions; physical characters of the Soil, Rocks, Rivers, and Land Surfaces.

The records will be made systematically (daily or weekly) in a special book (or in loose-leaf note book if the student prefers). This also will be handed in at the time of the examination.

3. Examination: An examination will be held on September 24th, 1910, to test the Student on his ability to recognize and explain the habits, etcetera, of the common Insects, Trees, Shrubs, Weeds, Wild Flowers, Birds, etcetera. In the case of Students who have spent the Summer outside of Ontario, special provision will be made in the examination.

Books that may be found suitable guides for the work.—*Birds*—Bird Guide, Part 2 (Reed), or Birds of N. E. North America (Chapman). *Insects*—Manual (Comstock). *Trees*—Sylvan Ontario (Muldrew). *Flowers and Weeds*—H. S. Botany (Spotton). *Cryptogamic Plants*—Plant Structures (Coulter).

Each Student is required to prepare a brief report for the Biological Department on the principal Insect and Fungus pests of his particular neighborhood.

Fourth Year (for the B.S.A. Degree).

One of the following options:—(1.) Agriculture, (2.) Bacteriology, (3.) Biology, (4.) Chemistry and Physics, (5.) Dairy, (6.) Horticulture.

Thesis.—Each fourth year student is required to prepare a Thesis on some branch, or department of the work in his special Course, under the direction of the Professor, or Instructor, in whose department the work is done. . . . The Thesis must be based chiefly on original investigation, and will be followed by an oral examination before a Committee of the Staff appointed for the purpose.

Agriculture Option.

The Course on Economics offered the graduating Class deals almost entirely with Agricultural organization and the problems arising therefrom. The study of Markets and Transportation. Local Co-operative Associations are studied critically and comparisons drawn between Canadian methods of co-operation and those of the leading co-operative countries, such as Denmark, Germany and France. The difficulties attending organizations are dealt with in this course, and the student is instructed with regard to the formation and successful operation of a Society. The Farmer's position as compared to that of the Manufacturer; his need of business training; his financial problems—means of obtaining credit, commercial transactions, etcetera, are given as much attention as the time allotted to the course will permit.

French: Grammar and easy sight Translation.

Poultry: Buildings, feeding and management; principal breeds. Each student shall be required to operate at least one incubator, to rear one brooder of chicks to four weeks of age, to feed and care for one pen of laying hens for one month, and to crate, fatten, kill and dress one dozen Birds. Reading, as assigned.

Botany: (a) Systematic botany—Grasses, Weeds and Forage Crops; (b) Fungi and Fungous Diseases. Collections—50 specimens (25 of which are to be grasses or forage plants, and 25 to be fungi, representing the diseases of vegetables and cereal crops'; specimens to supplement the collections of the second and third years, and not to repeat them.

Bacteriology: A course of forty Lectures extending throughout the year, on infectious Diseases of animals, modes of infection, prevention and eradication; Bacterial diseases of plants; the role of Micro-organisms in the Soil; the relation of Bacteria to the handling of Milk; and other phases of Bacteriologic Science as met with upon the Farm.

Fourth Year (for the B.S.A. Degree).

Bacteriology Option.

Majors:

1. Microscopical Methods: A study of the Morphology of Micro-organisms by the examination of living cultures and various staining methods; preparation of morbid specimens, embedding of tissues and section cutting.

2. Cultivation Methods: Apparatus, principles of sterilization, preparation of culture media, and various means employed in the cultivation of different types.

3. Physiologic Bacteriology: Chemical composition, nutrition, circumstances affecting growth products of growth, chromogenic, zymogenic, toxic and pathogenic bacteria. Studies in symbiosis, metabiosis and antagonism. Studies in enzymes.

4. Examination of Air, Water, Soils and Foods.

5. Hygienic Bacteriology: Infectious diseases; anthrax, symptomatic anthrax, tuberculosis, glanders, typhoid fever, hog cholera, diphtheria, actinomycosis,

pyemia, fowl and insect diseases; toxins and antitoxins, susceptibility and immunity, attenuation of virus, protective inoculation; serum-therapy.

6. **Fermentation Bacteriology**: Micro-organisms of fermentation; enzymes; fermentations—alcoholic, acetic, lactic, butyric, ammoniacal, putrefactive, nitrification, denitrification.

7. **Agricultural Bacteriology**: Relation of micro-organisms to tillage of the soil; management of the compost heap; bacteria and the farm water supply; disposal of sewage; bacteria and pure milk production; principal diseases of animals.

8. **Dairy Bacteriology**: The relation of micro-organisms to dairying; the fermentations of milk; pure culture system in butter and cheese making; pasteurization and sterilization; the bacteriological analysis of milk, butter and cheese; sanitary milk production; diseases conveyed by dairy products.

9. Chemistry of Fruits, Vegetables and Fermentations.

Reading: As assigned.

Thesis: As already outlined.

MINORS:

1, English; 2, Economics; 3, German; 4, Botany; 5, Zoology; 6, Chemistry.

FOURTH YEAR (FOR THE B.S.A. DEGREE).

Biology Option.

MAJORS:

1. Botany:

(*a*) Systematic: Lectures and Laboratory work on the chief orders of Flowering plants; including Grasses and the identification of Grass, Clover, and other seeds. A mounted collection of 50 plants and 50 specimens of weed seeds.

(*b*) Structural and Histological: Lectures and Laboratory work on the organs of the plant; mounting, examining, and drawing vegetable cells and tissues.

(*c*) Physiological: An advanced Seminary and Laboratory course in which each student investigates for himself the main life processes of Plants.

(*d*) Fungi and Plant Pathology: Laboratory Course with occasional lectures, in which are studied the injurious fungi affecting orchard, garden, greenhouse, and farm crops.

(*e*) Cryptogamic: Laboratory study of the chief types covering the Thallophytes, bryophytes and pteridophytes.

Reading: As assigned.

2. Zoology:

(*a*) Invertebrate: A systematic study of the lower animals with reference to structure, function, development and relationship, the Student using as types the amœba, paramecium, vorticella, sponge (commercial and grantia), fresh water hydra, corals, campanularian hydroid, tape-worm, liver fluke, starfish, earth worm, crayfish, spider, grasshopper and mussel.

(*b*) Vertebrate: This is a continuation of course A, the student using as types the fish, the frog, the snake, the turtle, the pigeon, and the cat or rabbit.

(*c*) Economic: A Laboratory and Lecture Course on the identification, habits and life histories of animals, giving special attention to Ontario forms.

Reading: Bulletins and Reports of United States Department of Agriculture, and Ontario Fish and Game Association.

(d) Vertebrate Histology: In this subject instruction is given in the theory and use of the Microscope and its accessories, in Photo-micrography and Vertebrate Histology. The study of the animal cell, its multiplication and contents. The methods of preparing microscopical sections of tissues and the normal histology of the various tissues and organs of the body.

(e) Insect Histology and Morphology: In this subject instruction is given on the fine gross anatomy of the Insect.

Reading: Riley's "Notes on Histology."

(f) Physiology: The study of the functions of the different organs and parts. Lectures and demonstrations are given on the cell, blood, circulation, respiration, digestion and absorption, secretion and excretion, general metabolism and animal heat and force.

3. Entomology:

(a) Systematic: A Laboratory course in the identification and classification of Insects. Each student is required to collect and mount at least 200 Insects representing as many orders as possible.

(b) Economic: A special study of injurious and beneficial Insects. The life histories of many species to be worked out in the Insectary.

Reading: As assigned.
Thesis: As outlined.

MINORS:

1. English.
2. Economics.
3. French or German.
4. Bacteriology: A Laboratory Course in the study of Morphology and cultural characters of micro-organisms, and their relation to water supply, soil, dairy products, plant and animal diseases, and fermentation industries.

Reading: As assigned.

5. Chemistry of Insecticides and Fungicides.

FOURTH YEAR (FOR THE B.S.A. DEGREE).

Chemistry and Physics Option.

MAJORS:

1. Chemistry:

(a) Inorganic Chemistry: Advanced Course.

(b) Soil Chemistry: Atmosphere, soils, reactions occurring in soils, fertilizers, the plant, its characteristics and relation to soil and atmosphere.

(c) Organic Chemistry: Lectures and preparation of Organic compounds. —Organic Chemistry.

(d) Animal Chemistry: Foods, their composition and digestibility; food constituents and their function; physiological value of the nutrients; selection and compounding of rations.

(e) Chemistry of Insecticides and Fungicides: Short course dealing with the Chemistry and the preparation of the principal insecticides and fungicides.

(f) Chemistry of Fruits, Vegetables and Fermentations.

Laboratory Work: (1) Qualitative Analysis; (2) Volumetric Analysis; (3) Polariscope and Sugar Determinations; (4) Analysis—of Water, Soils, Fertilizers, Fodders, etcetera; (5) Preparation of Organic Compounds.

Reading: As assigned.

2. Physics:

(*a*) Climatology: A general study of conditions that influence Climate; particular study of Canadian Climate, climatic factors in relation to Agriculture; climate limits in Canada for the agricultural and horticultural products.

(*b*) Soil Physics: Movements of air and water in the soil; soil temperatures; conditions affecting tilth; analysis and microscopic examinations of types.

(*c*) Tillage and Drainage: Spring and Autumn tillage; relation of various implements to air, moisture, warmth and tilth of soil; management of different types of soil; principles of drainage; preliminary surveys; systems of drainage; preparing plans for drainage; principles and methods of irrigation.

(*d*) Logarithms and Thermodynamics.

(*e*) Electricity: Telephones, principles, installation and care; Telegraphy, metallic circuit and wireless; generators, direct and alternating; transmission of electricity; motors, direct and alternating; electric lighting; wiring, installation of plants for farm use.

(*f*) Light and Sound.

(*g*) Cold Storage: Principles, methods and results.

3. Thesis: As already outlined.

MINORS:

1, English; 2, Economics; 3, French or German; 4, Field Husbandry.

FOURTH YEAR (FOR THE B.S.A. DEGREE).
Dairy Option.

MAJORS:

1. Dairy Husbandry:

(*a*) Farm Dairy work and milk-testing, theory, practice and lectures.

(*b*) Lectures, in the winter term, with "Principles and Practice of Buttermaking," "Testing Milk and its Products," "Science and Practice of Cheesemaking."

(*c*) Laboratory course of experiments in Cheese-making, butter-making, cream separators and milk-testing, relating to the latest practices in dairy operations. Time, amounting to two days a week, throughout the year, one being Saturday, will be devoted to this experimental work.

Reading: As assigned.

2. Bacteriology: Dairy bacteriology, and such general Bacteriology as is necessary for a thorough understanding of the work of dairying.

Reading: As assigned.

3. Chemistry:

(*a*) Dairy Chemistry: (a) A Chemical study of milk, butter, cheese, and the by-products of the dairy; (b) Laboratory work, analysis of the products of the dairy, preservatives, adulterants, water and coloring material.

(*b*) Animal Chemistry: As outlined in the Chemistry and Physics Option.

Reading: As assigned.

4. Thesis: As already outlined.

MINORS:

1, English; 2, Economics; 3, French or German; 4, Soil Chemistry; 5, Field Husbandry—Advanced course in field crops emphasizing hay, pasture and fodder crops. Lectures and laboratory work.

FOURTH YEAR (FOR THE B.S.A. DEGREE).
Horticulture Option.

MAJORS:

1. Horticulture:

(*a*) Pomology: Lectures—The theory and practice of Nursery work and Fruit growing. Systems of handling and selling. Systematic classification of Canadian fruits and identification of varieties. Manufacture of fruit by-products, canned and evaporated stock, vinegars, fruit juices, etcetera. Practical work—Stratification and planting of seeds and pits; budding, root and cleft grafting; making cuttings; pruning and spraying; picking, grading; packing; selection of fruit for exhibition purposes; judging; studies of varieties and commercial packages at exhibitions.

(*b*) Vegetable Gardening: Lectures—Theory and practice of truck gardening under glass and out-doors; greenhouse construction and management. Canning factory crops and methods of canning. Seed growing. Spraying, fumigating, etcetera. Practical Work—Selection and testing of seeds; preparation of vegetables for exhibition and market; judging; greenhouse management.

(*c*) Floriculture: Lectures—Theory and practice of commercial plant and flower production; cutting, storing and shipping flowers; handling decorative and bedding plants. Practical Work—Propagation and culture of special florists' crops; greenhouse management; making and planting flower beds and borders; visits to leading commercial establishments.

(*d*) Landscape Gardening: Lectures—History and development; principles underlying rural and civic improvement; planning public and private grounds, etcetera. Practical Work—Surveying; preparation of plans; studies of home and school grounds.

(*e*) Plant Breeding: Lectures—Studies of theory and practice of plant improvement with special reference to fruits, flowers and vegetables.

Reading: As assigned.

2. Biology:

(*a*) Plant Pathology: Identification and classification of diseases affecting orchard, garden and greenhouse crops, prevention and remedies. A collection of 50 injurious fungi required.

(*b*) Economic Entomology: Special study of injurious and beneficial insects affecting fruit, vegetable and greenhouse crops. Life histories and treatment. Each student is required to collect at least 100 specimens of different species of insects of economic importance, to be arranged in systematic order, and to be neatly mounted and labelled with date and place of capture.

3. Thesis: As already outlined.

MINORS:

1. Systematic Botany: Lectures and laboratory work on the chief orders of flowering plants, with special reference to cultivated forms. A mounted collection to be made of 50 cultivated plants.

2. Physics: Climatology.

3. Bacteriology: A Laboratory Course with supplemental Lectures in fall Term on bacterial diseases of plants, Bacteria as related to the canning industry, bacteriological analysis of soils, etcetera.

4. Soil Chemistry.

5. (a) Chemistry of Insecticides and Fungicides; (b) Chemistry of Fruits, Vegetables and Fermentations.

Reading: As assigned.

6, English; 7, Economics; 8, French or German.

THE MACDONALD INSTITUTE.
Home Economics Department.

The Home Economics Department of the Macdonald Institute has two objects in view. The one to bring to the vocation of home making the same kind of help which the Ontario Agricultural College brings to the business of farming; the other, to provide for the adequate training of Home Science Teachers for our Public Schools.

Three Home-maker Courses are offered, two continuing three months, and the other for one year. The one year Course, which may be broadened and extended over two years, is planned for the Girls who are able to live in their own homes, and desire to better fit themselves for the duties of the home-maker. The home-maker, from the very nature of the work, is thrown very largely on her own resources, and should be capable of dealing intelligently with difficulties as they arise. The Course, therefore, aims to give the student, by means of many lessons and much individual practice work, a good foundation in the different branches of ordinary household work: such as Cookery, Sewing, Laundry, etcetera, to introduce her to some of the Housekeeper's administrative problems; and, above all, to awaken her interest in the wider questions of sound bodies, wholesome dwellings, and real homes. The Short Course in Domestic Science is an abbreviation of the longer Home-maker Course, but is thorough as far as it goes. The Short Course in Sewing is in no sense professional, but aims to help a girl to deal intelligently with the family Sewing.

The Normal Course is the outgrowth and continuation of the work of the Ontario Normal School of Domestic Science and Art in Hamilton. In 1903 the Hamilton School was closed, and its Students and Staff transferred to the more satisfactory surroundings of the Agricultural College at Guelph. The Course continues two years, the first being devoted chiefly to study of the subject matter, and the second chiefly to study of the problems, and practice in the methods of presenting the subject to Public School Classes. The Class is fortunate in having four classes from the Guelph Public Schools as a field of observation and practice, and also in being permitted to observe the Domestic Science teaching in the Macdonald Consolidated School and Guelph Central Public School. Every effort is made to train the students to study the problem; to use the subject as a means of developing intelligent power in the children; and to teach good elementary Domestic Science. It is left to other Schools to train the special Teachers necessary for demonstration and advanced Cookery Classes. The object of the Course will be achieved when its Certificate stands for women who will intensify our Schoolgirls' interest in home and home affairs.

A housekeeper Course is offered to a limited number of older women, who wish to study systematic methods of Housekeeping, with a view to becoming professional Housekeepers.

Optional Courses are also offered to students who cannot secure the desired training in any regular Course, or who cannot take a full Course. The elective subjects, however, render the regular Course elastic, and students are advised to enter regular Courses if possible.

Macdonald Institute offers no Courses in Music, Painting or Languages.

The Home Economics department occupies the first floor of Macdonald Institute, and most of the ground floor.

The equipment consists of two class Kitchens, with individual equipment for lessons in Cookery, etcetera; a practice kitchen with individual equipment for practice in cookery and house work, or for experimental work of various sorts; a small dining-room for lessons in table-setting and waitress work; a pantry, three cold storage rooms, and a large stock room; several lecture rooms; a class laundry, with individual equipment, steam dryer, mangle, etcetera; a dress-making room, fully equipped, a fitting room, a room for plain sewing and millinery; three locker rooms for students; seven offices; and a small apartment of two Bedrooms, Bathroom, Living Room, Kitchen and Pantries for practical work in Housekeeping.

Macdonald Institute is provided with a Library and Reading room suited to the special needs of the Home Economics students, which supplements the larger collections of Massey Hall.

A large Assembly Hall at the top of the building is used for Prayers, General Meetings, and Lectures.

Macdonald Hall is under the personal care of an experienced Superintendent. The Hall and Institute are situated side by side, just north of the campus and overlooking the City of Guelph.

The Macdonald Consolidated Rural School for Ontario stands on an adjoining site.

The School year opens September 15th and closes June 25th. It is divided into three terms, beginning respectively in September, January and April.

Normal Course in Domestic Science.

The Normal Course in Domestic Science aims to lay a thorough foundation for the special work of teaching Domestic Science in the Schools of our country. The Institute cannot make the Teacher; it furnishes opportunities and favorable conditions to earnest students; the rest lies with the student.

The Course opens in September, and continues two years. Students passing the examination satisfactorily are awarded the Macdonald Institute Teacher's Certificate in Domestic Science.

Candidates who are Graduates of the Ontario Normal College, or who hold a professional Second-class Teacher's Certificate in Ontario, are eligible for entrance to the senior year of this Course. Experienced Teachers are thus able to try the final examinations after one year's attendance.

The Ontario Agricultural College is affiliated with the Toronto University, and the work of the Normal Classes will be acceted *pro tanto* in the Courses leading to the University degree in Household Science.

THE HOUSEKEEPER'S COURSE

Is designed to aid those women who desire to become professional or skilled Housekeepers. It offers training in practical work, in household organization, in the sciences closely related to the problems of the housekeeper. The students will be given as much practice as possible. . . .

The Course opens only in September, and continues two years. Students doing the required work, and passing the examination satisfactorily, are awarded the Macdonald Institute Housekeeper Certificate. . . .

Candidates for this course must be mature women in sound health, with executive ability, with sufficient education to master the necessary marketing and clerical work and with considerable experience in practical housework. . . .

Graduates of this course who complete six months successful housekeeping in an institution will be granted a Professional Housekeeper's Certificate. . . .

THE HOME-MAKER COURSE

Affords opportunity for training in the subjects which specially concern the Home-maker. It is designed for young women with little or no experience in household affairs. One short year of work and study will not make expert Housekeepers of them. . . .

The Course opens only in September, and continues one year. Students doing the required work and passing the examinations satisfactorily are awarded the Home-maker Diploma of Macdonald Institute. . . .

SHORT COURSE IN DOMESTIC SCIENCE.

The short Course in Domestic Science is planned for those who cannot spend more than one Term at the Institute. It does not aim to cover the ground of the long Courses, and provides training chiefly in practical work, but is thorough as far as it goes.

Three short courses are given each year, one each term.

Candidates for this Course must be at least 17 years of age, and have a good elementary education. Preference will be given to Farmers' Daughters.

Students already proficient in plain Sewing may present Garments made by themselves, in proof of proficiency. If credited with plain Sewing they will be permitted to join a more advanced Sewing class, or elect another subject.

Students who have had satisfactory experience of general Housework will be given partial credit for Home-practice and be allowed to substitute an elective subject.

Following are the subjects prescribed: Plain Cookery, Plain Sewing, Laundry, Foods, Sanitation, Home Nursing and Hygiene, Care of the House, Home Ethics, House-Practice.

The Short Course in Advanced Sewing is planned to meet the demand for a short Course devoted chiefly to Dressmaking and allied subjects; but is in no sense a professional Course. It is very practical, and will give a thorough training as far as it goes.

Candidates for this Course must be at least 17 years of age; have had a good elementary education, and be possessed of good eyesight. Each Candidate must send with her application for admission a satisfactory shirtwaist of her own cutting and making as evidence of her ability to carry out the work of the course.

Following are the subjects prescribed: Dressmaking, Millinery, Embroidery, Textiles, Color and Design, Laundry, Home Ethics.

Optional courses are offered to a limited number of students, who do not wish to take full regular Courses, or who wish to take a group of subjects fitting their special needs.

Candidates for these Courses must be at least 17 years of age, and give evidence of fitness for the work undertaken.

REGULATIONS—HOUSEHOLD SCIENCE.

Approved by Order-in-Council.

1. Subject to the provision hereinafter mentioned, no certificate to teach Household Science shall be awarded to anyone who does not hold at least Junior Leaving, or Junior Matriculation, standing.

2. All Institutions whose Graduates may be recognized as Teachers of Household Science shall provide, to the satisfaction of the Education Department, suitable Courses of study as well as adequate accommodation, equipment and instruction, for students preparing to become Teachers in this department.

3. Every Student who desires to become a Teacher of Household Science must take a two years' Course of Study in the department, but any person holding, at least a Certificate from one of the Normal Schools, who completes satisfactorily a one-year Course, shall be awarded a Teacher's Certificate in Household Science.

4. Any Graduate of the Normal College who completes satisfactorily a one-year Course at one of the recognized Institutions for the training of Teachers in Household Science shall be awarded a Teacher's Certificate as a Specialist in this department.

5. Any person holding a Certificate to teach Household Science, granted by the Education Department, shall be qualified to have charge of a department of Household Science under any High, Public, or Separate, School Board.

6. Certificates as Teachers of Household Science shall give no legal qualification to teach any of the other subjects of the School Curriculum.

7. No grant shall be paid by the Government towards a department of Household Science, unless the Teacher who has charge of such department is duly qualified as herein provided.

8. These provisions shall not apply in the case of Teachers already in charge of a department of Household Science, or to students preparing to be Teachers of the subject, who have been enrolled before the date of these Regulations.

MACDONALD HALL OF THE ONTARIO AGRICULTURAL COLLEGE.

Officers:—G. C. Creelman, B.S.A., LL.D., President; S. Springer, Bursar; Mrs. K. T. Fuller, Superintendent; Miss Ethel Tennant, Housekeeper.

Macdonald Hall is on the north side of the Campus, on the highest point of the College Heights, and is especially designed for the comfort and well-being of the women Students of Macdonald Institute. The Superintendent will control the Students in residence, will direct the social life, and will do her utmost to make the Hall a real home.

TEACHERS' TRAINING COURSES.

MANUAL TRAINING DEPARTMENT.

There are three distinctive Courses:

1. A Course for Agriculture Students in Wood-working, Metal-working and Farm Mechanics.

2. A Normal Course for the training of Instructors in Manual Training.

3. Optional Course in Wood-work, Wood-carving, Art Metal, Basketry, etcetera.

The instruction does not aim at the production of finished articles, though all exercises are embodied as far as possible in complete objects, but to inculcate principles emphasizing the reason for doing work in the particular way which is the result of practical constructive experience. These principles involve exercises having values only as they have rendered educational service in the process of construction, or in their manipulation. In this way the student not only acquires conception of skill as such, but also the idea that correct results are attained only by the skilful application of a plan clearly thought out. The endeavour is to find the best plan and the reason for its preference. In changing conditions of the thing in hand during its construction, there is a constant necessity for creating new means to meet new requirements and directive skill, and logical processes thus evolved to make manual training rise to the level of scientific or mathematical studies as a means of intellectual development.

The Teacher's Normal Course of One Year: This course affords a comprehensive study of the subject as related to the needs of both the specialist and the regular grade Teacher, and will deal with those forms of industrial work that are most practical and significant. Only Teachers holding permanent Certificates are eligible for entrance.

DEPARTMENT OF NATURE STUDY.

This Department was organized and equipped for the training of Canadian Teachers in the knowledge of the common forms and forces of nature, as a means of training children in observation, expression and sympathy.

Courses of Instruction.

1. Spring Course: This is a ten weeks' Course for Graduates from the Provincial Normal Schools. Applications for it are made through the Department of Education. The work is to prepare Teachers for special service in the Rural Schools. It leads to a College Certificate in Elementary Agriculture and Horticulture.

2. Summer Course: This is a four weeks' course held in July. Teachers in Rural Schools may receive the Certificate in Elementary Agriculture and Horticulture by attending two Summer Sessions and taking a Winter's Reading Course. For Teachers in graded Schools the work is specially adapted, emphasizing the Nature Study rather than Elementary Agriculture.

3. Normal Course: A more advanced Course of a similar nature, and extending over a full year, is given to Teachers who wish to qualify as Specialists in this department. The work is of a selective character, special Courses being taken from the different College Departments, with emphasis placed on Field Husbandry, Horticulture, Entomology and Physics. It leads to a Special Teachers' Certificate in Agriculture and Horticulture. The aim is to provide instructors fitted to carry on the work of Elementary Agriculture and School Gardening in Normal Schools, in a group of Rural Schools, in a Consolidated School, or in High Schools.

Forestry.

Development of Forestry work in other Countries; value of lumbering industry; Canada's conditions and needs; Laws and Regulations regarding re-forestation and forest preservation; the establishment, care and protection of wood lots. Identification of our forest Trees; planting Seed-beds in School gardens; work in College nursery and in the experimental Bush; collection of weeds, etcetera.

Farm Carpentry, Etcetera.

Exercises in making articles needed in Garden work. Instruction in the care of Tools and the general repairing to be done about a School, or Home, such as mending gates and fences. Instruction in making working drawings of simple articles. Observation of approved and up-to-date methods of Stabling, Fencing, Road-making, supplying water, etcetera.

Work in Summer Courses.

Nature Study and Elementary Agriculture: The work taken during July is divided into two branches. For all Teachers who have not previously taken a Course, the Nature Study side of the work is emphasized. Excursions are taken to learn the common Trees, Weeds, Birds, Insects and Rocks. Studies are made of the Physiography of the neighbourhood. Studies are also made of the Heavens, in order to become acquainted with the well known Stars and Constellations. Some time is devoted to Art Study and to Nature Literature; students also receive instruction in School Gardening and Horticulture.

For Teachers taking a second Session the work is a modification of the regular ten weeks' Course already outlined. The course in Nature Study is preparatory to this.

MANUAL, OR INDUSTRIAL TRAINING, IN THE EARLY DAYS OF UPPER CANADA.

Although there was in the early days in Upper Canada no facilities for the establishment of Manual, or Industrial, Education, yet it became frequently a popular topic for discussion in the Legislature and among the Ratepayers in Cities and Towns.

After one of these educational Episodes (of discussion) in the House of Assemblage, in 1832, Mr. Mahlon Burwell, a Pioneer Educationist, presented a Report to the House, in which the subject of Elementary Scientific Education was advocated. The Report stated:—

"That the situation of the Province in wealth and commerce and in its demand for superior attainments in the various professions is very different from what it formerly was; and that unless opportunities are furnished by the establishment of superior Schools for the instruction of our youth in branches of science, we must fall behind the age in which we live."

What was thus put forth as a local thought, but yet as an educational axiom, by these educational Pioneers of Upper Canada, upwards of seventy years ago, is thus forcibly and beautifully amplified by the President of the British Association in 1887. Speaking generally, and contrasting the educational policy of the colonies and that of the Mother Country, he said:—

"The Colonies, being young Countries, value their raw materials as their chief source of wealth. When they become older they will discover it is not in these, but in the culture of scientific intellect, that their future prosperity depends. . . . Jules Simon tersely puts it: 'The nation which most educates her people will become the greatest nation, if not to-day, certainly to-morrow.' Higher education is the condition of higher prosperity, and the nation which neglects to develop the intellectual factor of production must degenerate, for it cannot stand still. . . . The illustrious Consort of our Queen was not the first Prince who saw how closely Science is bound up with the welfare of States. . . . How unwise it is for England to lag in the onward march of Science, when most other European powers are using the resources of their States to promote higher education and to advance the boundaries of knowledge [She] alone fails to grasp the fact that the competition of the world has become a competition of intellect. . . . A nation in its industrial progress, when the competition of the world is keen, cannot stand still. . . . I contend that in public education there should be a free play to the scientific faculty, so that the youths who possess it should learn the richness of their possession during the educative process. . . . Science has impressed itself upon the age in which we live; and as Science is not stationary, but progressive, men are required to advance its boundaries, acting as pioneers in the onward march of States. Human progress is so identified with scientific thought, both in its conception and realization, that it seems as if they were alternative terms in the history of civilization."

In giving these extracts so fully I have done so for two reasons: First, I desire to do honour to the zeal and to acknowledge the forethought and prescience of those Members of the House of Assembly who, in 1832, placed so strong an emphasis upon the value of "the instruction of our youth in branches of science"; and, secondly, to point out, in the weighty words of Sir Lyon Playfair, the immense importance (in the light of past experience) which he and other leaders of thought in regard to England's Industrial life and practical progress attach to the teaching of Elementary Science in the Schools. He touches upon this point in another part of his Address, in pointing out the absurdity of requiring all Pupils to study the same subjects. He says:—

"In a School a Boy should be aided to discover the class of knowledge that is best suited to his mental capacities, so that in the upper forms of the School, and in the University, knowledge may be specialized in order to cultivate the powers of the man to the fullest extent. . . . The adaptation of Public Schools to a scientific age does not involve a contest as to whether Science or Classics shall prevail, for both are indispensable to true education. The real question is, whether Schools will undertake the duty of moulding the minds of Boys according to their mental varieties."

LATER OPINIONS ON THE NECESSITY FOR MANUAL TRAINING IN OUR SCHOOLS.

So deeply impressed was I of the immense importance of this subject, and of the necessity of providing in our School System for a practical solution of the question which was then, and is now, of pressing importance—Manual Training in our Schools—that in 1876 I prepared and delivered an Address on the subject, in various parts of the Province. The Address was founded on the Industrial Lessons taught to us so impressively at the Centennial Exhibition, Philadelphia, in 1876.* These Lessons, in their educational aspects, were even more forcibly impressed upon me at the great Industrial Exhibition held in New Orleans, in 1885. Having been there six weeks, as an Educational Juror, on behalf of the United States Bureau of Education, I had abundant and admirable facilities for studying the whole question, and for seeing how it was being worked out (more or less effectually) in the various national school systems which came under review during that enquiry—especially in France. Thus the French school law of 1882 provides that " primary education includes [among other things] the elements of the natural, physical and mathematical sciences, and their application to agriculture, to hygiene, and to the industrial art; manual work, and the use of tools of the principal trades, the elements of drawing, modeling, etc." Apprenticeship schools have also been established, the object of which is to form workmen, as distinguished from foremen, and in which various trades are taught. An official report, published by the United States Bureau of Education in 1882, states that the apprentices of these schools "find employment readily after they have left the workshops, at wages, it is said, varying from five to even as much as eight francs per day."

In discussing this question in the lecture to which I have referred, this passage occurs:—

"It is not assumed that every Pupil in our Schools is qualified, or that he should be compelled, as a matter of course, to engage in the study of elementary science or practical drawing. Far from it. But what I do say is, that those pupils who exhibit a taste for any of the various subjects of natural history, elementary science or practical mechanics, should have an opportunity in the Public and High Schools (of cities and large towns) of learning something about them. In an address by Mr. Gladstone on this subject, he stated that the boys of the English schools, and it is so in our schools, had not yet had fair play in the study of elementary science and natural history. . . .

"There are few schools in which there are not boys possessing talent—scientific, inventive, or industrial talent—or constructive genius, which is never evoked, much less aroused or stimulated. As to the question whether for the few the country should be put

---

* I hope to be able to insert the Address on this subject in a future Volume. The Title of the Address is : " A Plea for Elementary Science and Industrial Training in Our Schools," based upon the results of my Experience at the noted Centennial Exhibition at Philadelphia in 1876.

to the expense of their special training, I answer it in the words of Professor Huxley, who says:—

"'To the lad of genius, even to the one in a million, I would make accessible the highest and most complete training the country could afford. Whatever it might cost, depend upon it the investment would be invaluable. I weigh my words when I say: that if the nation could purchase a potential Watt, or Day, or Faraday, at the cost of a hundred thousand pounds down, he would be dirt cheap at the money. . . . It is a mere commonplace and an every-day piece of knowledge to say that, what these three men did, (in their special departments of practical science), has produced untold millions of wealth for England and the world, speaking in the narrowest economical sense of the word.'"

The educational mind of the United States, as well as Europe, is being constantly directed to the consideration of this interesting practical subject. Magazines and reviews, as well as educational journals, freely discuss it. One of the most useful articles on "Manual Training in the Public Schools" will be found in the *Andover Review* for October, 1888. The United States Bureau of Education has also published various reports and papers on the subject. One of the most valuable is an elaborate report on "Industrial Education in the United States," published in 1883. Some of the railways in that and in this country have also established Training Schools for their Employès.

DEPARTMENTAL REGULATIONS IN REGARD TO MANUAL TRAINING.

(Approved by Order-in-Council.)

1. Subject to the conditions herein mentioned, the Macdonald Institute, Guelph, shall be the only Institution recognized by the Education Department for the training of Teachers in Manual Training.

2. The Macdonald Institute shall provide, to the satisfaction of the Education Department, suitable Courses of Study as well as adequate accommodation, equipment and instruction for Students desiring to become Teachers of Manual Training.

3. Any person holding at least a Second Class Certificate from one of the Normal Schools, who completes satisfactorily a one-year's Course at the Macdonald Institute, shall be awarded a Teacher's Certificate in Manual Training.

4. Any Graduate of the Normal College, who completes satisfactorily a one-year's Course at the Macdonald Institute, shall be awarded a Teacher's Certificate as a Specialist in Manual Training.

5. Any person holding a Certificate from the Macdonald Institute as a Teacher of Manual Training shall be qualified to have charge of a department of Manual Training under any High, Public, or Separate School Board.

6. No Grant shall be paid by the Government towards a department of Manual Training unless the Teacher who has charge of such department is duly qualified, as herein provided.

7. A Certificate as a Teacher of Manual Training, or as a Specialist in the same department, shall give no qualification to teach any of the other subjects of the Public, or High, School Curriculum.

8. These provisions shall not affect any person who is now in charge of a department of Manual Training in any High, Public, or Separate School; it being understood that such persons shall have qualifications satisfactory to the Minister of Education.

MANUAL TRAINING, HOUSEHOLD SCIENCE, AND SPECIAL TECHNICAL INSTRUCTION.

1. The plans of every Building hereafter erected or of any Room adapted for the purpose of Manual Training, Household Science or Special Technical Instruction shall be submitted to the Minister of Education, and be subject to his approval, and a copy of such plans shall be filed in the Department of Education.

2. Subject to the Regulations, every School maintaining a Manual Training department shall be entitled to the following annual grants:—

(*a*) A fixed grant of $350.

(*b*) 10 per cent. of the expenditure over $600 for Teacher's salary or salaries, but so as not in any case to exceed $100.

(*c*) 20 per cent. of the cost of equipment for each of the first five years, and thereafter of the annual renewals and additions.

3. Subject to the Regulations, every School maintaining a department for Household Science shall receive annually:—

(*a*) A fixed grant of $200.

(*b*) 20 per cent. of the expenditure over $500 for Teachers' salaries, but so as not to exceed $50.

(*c*) 20 per cent. of the cost of equipment for each of the first five years, and thereafter of annual additions and renewals.

4. Any School under the control of a Public, Separate, or High School Board, or Board of Education, or of a recognized Technical School Board, which is specially organized and equipped for giving instruction in the theory and practice of the Mechanical and Industrial Arts and Sciences, shall be entitled to receive out of any Legislative appropriation therefor, in addition to such sums as they may be entitled to receive under Sections 2 and 3 hereof, such further sum as the Minister of Education may approve, based upon inspection and report, but so as not in any case to exceed $750. To be eligible for this Grant the Building in which instruction is given, equipment, Courses of Study, and qualification of the Staff shall be approved by the Minister of Education.

5. In apportioning the Legislative Grants on equipments, the maximum value recognized shall be (*a*) for Manual Training $500, (*b*) for Household Science $300, but no Grant in respect of equipment shall be paid where such equipment has been donated to the School Board.

6. The Course of Study, and the qualifications of every Teacher hereafter employed, shall be subject to the approval and Regulations of the Education Department.

7. The unit of distribution of the Legislative grant for Manual Training and Household Science shall be the time of one Teacher for five hours on each of five days per week.

8. The Grants mentioned in the foregoing Sections shall be subject to such pro-rata increase or reduction as the Legislative appropriation therefor will permit.

9. No Manual Training, or Household Science, School, or department, will be recognized as efficiently equipped that is provided with accommodation for less than 12 or more than 25 Students, at any one time, for practical work.

PART XV.

MISCELLANEOUS EDUCATIONAL INSTITUTIONS, COMPRISING THOSE OF AGRICULTURE, ART, MUSIC, TELEGRAPHY, BUSINESS AND TECHNICAL TRAINING, ETCETERA.

REGULATIONS AND COURSES OF STUDY FOR THE AGRICULTURAL DEPARTMENTS OF THE HIGH SCHOOL AT ESSEX, AND THE COLLEGIATE INSTITUTES AT GALT, COLLINGWOOD, LINDSAY, PERTH, AND MORRISBURG.

1. Pupils who take the regular two years' Special Course in Agriculture, or a partial Course therein, in a High School, shall be admitted in accordance with the Regulations that govern the admission of other High School Pupils.

2. To the Courses held throughout the County, such persons may be admitted as, in the judgment of the Teacher of Agriculture, are competent for the work, whether, for example, Farmers, or farmers' Sons, or Daughters, or Pupils of Public Schools or of other High Schools. A list thereof and their reported attendance shall be kept by the Principal of the School; but they shall not be enrolled as regular High School Pupils unless they have been admitted to a High School as provided above.

3. The Teacher of Agriculture in a High School shall hold the Degree of B.S.A. from the University of Toronto, or a Certificate of qualification from the Ontario Agricultural College. Such Teachers may also take part in the Science work of the School at the discretion of the Principal, provided such work does not in any way interfere with their special work as Teachers of Agriculture.

4. Like the other Members of the High School staff, the Teacher of Agriculture shall be generally subject to the authority of the Board and Principal of the High School, the latter of whom shall control his Time-table and have the general direction of his movements.

5. With a view to bringing the Department of Agriculture into closer touch with the farming community and of making it more directly beneficial to them, the Teacher of Agriculture shall also act as the local agent of the Department of Agriculture for the district, as follows:

(*a*) He shall visit from time to time the various parts of the County and report upon their special requirements.

(*b*) He shall take charge of an Office situated in the High School district, where he may meet the Farmers, giving them aid and advice, supplying them with the Bulletins of the Department of Agriculture and such other Farm Literature as may be useful, and discussing with them the latest experimental results of the work of the Ontario Agricultural College.

(c) He shall keep in touch with local Agricultural Associations, Farmers' Institutes, etcetera, and shall act in concert with the Staff of Lecturers, Demonstrators, and Professors of the Ontario Agricultural College.

(d) Where practicable, he will arrange for Excursions for Students and others to the Agricultural College in the month of June, and shall take special charge during such visits of those who have been in attendance on his Classes.

(e) He shall attend the Winter Fair and annual meeting of the Experimental Union, held yearly in Guelph for one week in December.

6. A suitable Laboratory and the Equipment necessary to carry out the work as outlined under Chemistry, Physics, and Biology.

Experimental Grounds, separate from the ordinary School Grounds, for illustration purposes in the growing of various classes of Farm Crops and training in experimental work. The area of the Grounds will be determined by local conditions; one acre might be sufficient.

A list of suitable equipment from which Boards may select has been prepared and may be obtained on application to the Educational Department.

7. The Agricultural Department of each High School or Collegiate Institute shall be inspected at least once each year by an Officer of the Ontario Agricultural College deputed for this purpose by the Minister of Education. This Officer shall report to both the Department of Education and the Department of Agriculture.

8. The regular Special Course in Agriculture in a High School shall be the two years' one, as defined below. Partial Courses may also be provided in the High School for regular High School Pupils or for such occasional Pupils as may desire them.

9. Regular High School Pupils taking the special Course in Agriculture shall take in addition the subjects which are obligatory upon all High School Pupils, namely, Geography, Arithmetic and Mensuration, English Grammar, Writing, Reading, English Composition, English Literature, and History, with such suitable modifications of this Course, and with such additional subjects, as may be deemed expedient by the Principal and the Parent, or Guardian, of the Pupil.

10. It is not intended that all the work outlined in the Course below shall be covered in two years. The outline is suggestive rather than obligatory, and the amount of work to be taken up shall be determined by the needs of the community, and the nature of the special subjects selected. In some districts, Horticultural subjects, for example, will receive special emphasis; in others, Dairying, and, in others again, Stock raising, and so on.

11. In addition to the regular Special High School Course, partial Courses shall be provided, when needed, in the High School and in other parts of the county, of such duration and character as may meet the needs of the farming community. These may include short Courses in Horticulture; Soils, Seeds, Weeds; Farm dairying, Poultry keeping, etcetera, as well as Demonstrations and Lectures in particular subjects (Stock judging, Seed judging, etcetera) at one or more

meetings at suitable centres. In these courses the Teacher of Agriculture will be assisted, when necessary, by Members of the Staff of the Ontario Agricultural College, and he will be supplied by the College with abundant material for demonstration purposes.

12. High School Pupils who take the two years' Special Course herein provided, and whose competency is attested by the Principal of the School and the Teacher of Agriculture, shall be eligible for entrance to the Second Year work of the Ontario Agricultural College.

REGULAR TWO YEARS' SPECIAL COURSE.

13. The following is the regular two years' Special Course, to be organized in accordance with the requirements of each locality:

(1) Field Husbandry: History of Agriculture; different Systems of Farming; different kinds of Soil; rotation of Crops; Farm Crops in their relation to Drainage; application of Manures; Green Manuring; preparation of the Land for the different Crops; methods of cleaning, testing, and selecting Farm Seeds; study of Cereals, Roots, Fodder Crops, Grasses, Clovers, and other Farm Crops; Sowing, Harvesting, Preserving, Marketing.

Experimental Grounds near the School will be used for illustrative experiments with varieties of Cereals, Grasses, Root Crops, and in Seed selection, methods of cultivation, Rotation of Crops, and the use of various kinds of Fertilizers.

(2) Animal Husbandry: A study of the history and characteristics of the principal Breeds of Live Stock, including light and heavy Horses, Beef and Dairy Cattle, Sheep, and Swine; feeding and management; principles of breeding; registration of pedigrees; market requirements.

Visits to Local Farms, and practical work in judging Stock.

(3) Dairy Husbandry: The Herd; formation, care, and management of a Dairy Herd, rearing of Calves; Dairy Stables: lighting, cleaning and ventilating; individual cow records. The Milk: care of Milk, elementary Chemical and Bacteriological study of Milk. The Home Dairy: running of hand Separators and care of Dairy Utensils; manufacture, packing, and marketing of Butter.

Visits to local Creameries and Cheese Factories, and a study of Factory methods of Manufacture, Packing, and Marketing.

(4) Poultry: The most valuable Breeds and varieties of Hens, Ducks, Geese and Turkeys, their characteristic points and peculiarities; various methods of housing Poultry; incubation, brooding, and rearing of Chickens; general methods of feeding and management; market conditions; the fattening and dressing of Poultry for Home and Foreign Markets.

(5) Horticulture: Treatment of Fruit Plantations: Cultivation, Grafting, Spraying; value of Cover Crops; methods of growing and caring for Vegetables; selection of varieties; study of Insect and Fungus Diseases affecting Fruits and Vegetables; care, storing, and marketing of Fruit.

(6) Forestry: Forestry as related to the Farm; classification of the common Forest Trees; the establishment, care and protection of the Woodlot; varieties and methods for roadside Planting and Shelter Belts.

(7) Agricultural Botany: Identification and eradication of Weeds and Weed Seeds; Seed Control Act and its application; experiments to show Seed Germination and Growth of Plants; the relation of Plants to Soil, Air, Light, Temperature, and Moisture; systematic study of the structure of Cereals, Grasses, Legumes, and Roots; Plant Diseases: Smut, Rust, Mildew, etcetera; how to recognize and combat them; Collecting, Pressing, and Mounting of Weeds, Grasses; Weed Seeds for samples in identification.

(8) Entomology: A practical Course in economic Insects, identification, habits, and life histories; a close study of the more important Insects, by means of Breeding and Rearing Cages; Insecticides; collecting of Injurious and Beneficial Insects and samples of their work.

(9) Agricultural Physics: Soil: Classification and physical examination, origin, and mode of formation; Soil forming, soil forming Rocks and Minerals; behaviour towards moisture. Surveying and Drainage: Measurement of Fields and Farms with the Chain; calculating areas and drawing Plans; use of various Instruments for determining Levels, preparing Plans for Drainage; methods of Digging, laying of Tile, and filling of Trench; calculations concerning required size of tile and cost of various systems. Conservation of moisture by Drainage, Mulching, and cultivation; Capillarity and its relation to Plant Growth. Water capacity of different Soils. Mechanics: Principles of Farm Machinery; principles of Ventilation, Lighting and Heating.

(10) Agricultural Chemistry: Chemical composition of Soils; elements used by Plants; availability and assimilation of Plant Food in the Soil; application of Fertilizers; absorption and retention of important constituents, as Nitrogen, Phosphoric Acid, and Potash; Insecticides and Fungicides; their composition and proper mixture.

EASTERN DAIRY SCHOOL, KINGSTON.

The Eastern Dairy School was established and maintained by the Ontario Government under the authority of an Act of the Legislature passed in 1910. Director of the School, Mr. G. A. Putnam, B.S.A.; Superintendent, Mr. G. G. Publow, with a staff of twelve Officers and Teachers.

Programme of Instruction in the Dairy School.

Dairy Lectures: Lectures on the science of Dairying, including Feeds and Feeding; Care and Management of the Dairy Cow; Diseases of Dairy Cattle; Building up of the Dairy Herd; Production and Care of Milk; Milk and its Products; Factory or Co-operative Dairying; Manufacture, Care and Marketing of Dairy Products; Locating and Planning of Factories, etcetera.

Dairy Bacteriology: A thorough Course of Lectures will be given upon the principles of Bacteriology and their application to dairying. The Lectures will be illustrated by means of Photographs, Lantern Slides and Cultures. A knowledge of Bacteriology is essential to success in present-day dairying.

Chemistry: A Course of Lectures in Chemistry, with special reference to the chemistry of milk and its products, will be given in the Chemical Lecture Room of the School of Mining of Queen's University, and will be fully demonstrated by the Lecturer as he proceeds. Lectures will be supplemented by the students being required to take up work in the chemical laboratory.

Miscellaneous Subjects: Soldering and Pipe-fitting will be taught in a Room specially fitted for this purpose. Lectures upon and instructions in the handling and care of Boilers and Engines will be given by a competent Engineer.

This Course covers comprehensively all the practical and scientific phases of the manufacture of dairy products.

At the close, written and practical examinations will be held, embracing the following subjects: Dairy Lectures, Cheese-making, Separators and the creaming of milk, Butter Making, Milk Testing, Dairy Bacteriology, Dairy Chemistry, Miscellaneous Subjects.

Candidates for Certificates must obtain at least 33 per cent. of the marks in each examination subject. Those who secure an average of 60 per cent. to 74 per cent. will be given second class honors, and those averaging 75 per cent. or over first-class honors.

A short Course in Mathematics and Bookkeeping with special regard to their application to the Secretary's work of Cheese Factories and Creameries will be given Long Course students.

Discussions: In addition to the morning Lectures afternoon Lectures will be given daily, excepting on Saturday. These afternoon Lectures will partake of the nature of discussions, led by one or other of the Instructors and taken part in by the Class, and will cover the practical work of the different departments.

For practical work the Class will be divided into Sections, one Section going to the Cheese-making, another to the Butter-making, and a third to the Milk-testing department.

ONTARIO VETERINARY ASSOCIATION, TORONTO.

At a meeting of graduated Veterinary Surgeons held on the 24th of September, 1874, for the purpose of forming an Association of qualified Veterinarians, the purpose and object of the Association was stated to be to deal with the subject of the ailments of animals, and to suggest and provide the best means of treating such cases. It also had for its object the mutual improvement of its members in those branches of knowledge pertaining to their profession and the advancement of the position and interests of Veterinary Surgery and treating of the diseases of animals.

Interesting papers have been read at the meetings of the Association and discussed. Addresses on various topics have been had, and proceedings have taken place with a view to the advancement and success of the Association in matters connected with the profession.

At the meeting held on the 24th of September, 1874, the following officers were elected: Professor W. Smith, President; Mr. Hagyard, First Vice-President; Mr. Wilson, Second Vice-President; Mr. C. H. Sweetapple, Secretary, and Mr. Cowan, Treasurer. (A number of Directors were also appointed.)

It was resolved that this Association shall be composed of duly qualified Veterinary Surgeons of Ontario, holding Diplomas from some recognized Veterinary College.

At a meeting held on the 4th of October, 1910, the following Officers and Directors were elected:

Mr. C. E. S. Baird, President; Mr. W. Mole, First Vice-President; Mr. H. E. Hurd, Second Vice-President; Mr. C. Heath Sweetapple, Secretary and Treasurer; Mr. J. R. Fowler, Assistant Secretary.

Directors.—Messieurs G. Coulton, C. Elliott, W. Steel, T. H. Lloyd, T. E. Watson, and T. Babe. Auditors, Messieurs J. H. Reid and C. Elliott.

TORONTO, October 5th, 1910.   C. HEATH SWEETAPPLE, *Secretary.*

BUSINESS COLLEGES IN ONTARIO.

These Colleges are practically a most useful feature in our Educational System. They give a Business training that can be best obtained in this special class of educational Institutions. Their object is to fit young men and women for the various departments of mercantile life.

These Colleges are all conducted upon a similar basis, and pursue somewhat analogous Courses, though these are possibly more varied in some Colleges than in others. The following details of subjects taught will give an idea of the work carried on: Spelling, Dictation, Business Arithmetic, Mental Arithmetic, Penmanship, Business Correspondence, Business Paper, Commercial Law, Book-keeping; Business Department, comprising Buying, Selling, Correspondence, Banking, etcetera; Telegraphy, Type-writing, Shorthand, etcetera.

THE BRITISH AMERICAN BUSINESS COLLEGE.

The British American Business College was established in Toronto in 1860, and is the oldest Commercial School in Canada. The Founder of the School was Professor Isaac Bates.

At that time young people who were desirous of entering business life found it necessary to serve a long apprenticeship in the business, or factory, such as the case might be. They had to start in without any definite knowledge of the requirements of the position they were supposed to fill. To meet these conditions, and to make it possible for young people to go into commercial life with a reasonable knowledge of the subjects to be handled, the College was established. From the beginning its work was most successful and many men now prominent in business and financial life in Toronto and other important centres received their early training at the College.

In 1868 the School was amalgamated with the Bryant and Stratton Business College, Messieurs J. D. O'Dell and Edward Trout being joint Managers. Seven years later it was removed to larger premises at numbers 112-114 King Street West, opposite the Rossin House, and subsequently to the Yonge Street Arcade, Confederation Life Building, and then to its present location, the Y.M.C.A. Building at the corner of Yonge and McGill Streets.

The Ownership of the School in 1895 passed into the hands of a Joint Stock Company composed of a number of prominent financiers and Business men of Toronto, and six years later (1901) became a member of the Federated Business Colleges, of Ontario, from whom it was purchased by the present Principal, Mr. T. M. Watson, in 1909.

The British American Business College, Limited, is owned and controlled by its former students, and a new and important era in the existence of this old and favourably known institution has been entered upon. An important feature in connection with the College is its Alumni Association, which is composed of its Teachers, ex-Teachers, Students and ex-Students. Although organized less than a year ago this Association has already secured a large membership and is growing very rapidly. Its object is to promote the best interests of the Members by business, social, educational and other means.

THE ONTARIO BUSINESS COLLEGE, BELLEVILLE.

The Ontario Business College was established in the City of Belleville in 1870. For the past thirty-four years Mr. J. W. Johnson, President of the Institute of Chartered Accountants, and at present Member for West Hastings in the Ontario Legislature, has been its Principal. The Institution is well known throughout all the Provinces of Canada, and elsewhere. From several Countries there are Students in attendance each year. The Text Books of the College, of which Mr. Johnson is the Author, are generally used elsewhere. They are: " The Canadian Accountant," " Joint Stock Company Bookkeeping," and " Promissory Notes and Drafts." The Principal is assisted by a competent Staff, each Member of which is highly educated, and has had practical experience in business careers. The great success which has attended the Ontario Business College has been well earned by the extent and thoroughness of the work done. The College has proved by the successful careers of its thousands of Graduates that technical Schools of Commerce, of which the Ontario Business College is one of the best examples, have proved their right to exist and are fully and finally accepted.

TECHNICAL EDUCATION AND INDUSTRIAL SCHOOLS.

In promoting Education in the early days of Upper Canada the settlers had to be content with such efforts as they could put forth to establish elementary schools for their children. No provision was made, nor could then be made, for the establishment of industrial, or purely technical, education, for such of the youth of the country as sought to obtain a higher education which would fit them for a professional, or business life. It was not until 1870 that the Government issued a Commission to the Editor of this volume and Doctor MacHattie of London, to proceed to the United States and obtain information in regard to the extent to which technical education was provided for in that country, and report upon some scheme by which it could be introduced with success into Upper Canada. The result was the establishment of the College of Technology in the City, but which was afterwards transferred to the Queen's Park, and named the "School of Practical Science," now the Faculty of Applied Science and Engineering of the University of Toronto.

It was found impossible to introduce even any elementary form of industrial education into the Public, or Common, Schools until provision had been made for Training Teachers to perform that duty. At length that object was accomplished, and in the Agricultural College at Guelph a Department has been established for the preparation of Teachers to act as Experts in Manual Training, and in the teaching of Industrial arts in the Public and Separate Schools of the Towns and Villages.

With a view to promote coherence in dealing with these several topics, and to give a due prominence to each of the Institutions devoted to the special subjects which I have enumerated, I shall deal with them separately.

TECHNICAL EDUCATION IN A POPULAR FORM.

Some years ago there was organized in the City of Toronto a School of Technology for the giving of Lectures, both daily and in the evenings, to such as chose to attend. The success of the School was assured, and the Managers of it have issued the following information on the subject:—

The City of Toronto in 1891 organized Evening Classes in a Hall, on the north side of College Street, opposite McCaul Street, under the name of the Toronto Technical School. The growing demand for Technical Education and the necessity for securing another Building induced the City Council in 1900 to purchase a Site for a Building on College Street, opposite University Crescent. In 1901 Day Classes were added to the Evening Classes. In 1904 the Technical School Board, the High School Board and the Public School Board were amalgamated, forming the present Board of Education, and under this Board the Day Classes of the Toronto Technical School were organized into the Technical High School.

The Board of Education has recently purchased additional property, on which a new and well-equipped school building will soon be available for the rapidly growing needs of technical education. Owing to the congestion in the present Building the Board will erect a new Building in which they will establish a number of mechanical and other laboratories, with the most modern equipment.

The purpose of the Day Classes is:—

1. To provide systematic instruction for those intending to enter upon a Business career as Office Assistants, or later in some managerial capacity.

2. To prepare Students for entrance to the School of Applied Science, or other Schools of Engineering.

3. To provide a Training in Science and Art for those purposing to enter upon the industrial side of life as Assistants, or later as Foremen, or Superintendents.

4. To provide a Course in Home Economics for those desiring to become more proficient in the care of the Home.

5. To give all regular Students a good general training in English and Mathematics, with options in Science, Art or Modern Languages, in addition to the regular subjects of their course.

6. To make provision for special Students desirous of taking a limited Course of one or more subjects in Drafting, Freehand Drawing, Design, Modeling in Clay, Wood Carving, Physics, Chemistry, Household Science, or Household Art.

Students who have High School Entrance standing will be admitted to any of the regular Classes. Students who wish to take a Special Course of one or more subjects will be admitted on application, subject to such conditions as may be defined from time to time.

The following are the Courses of the Day Classes, from which Students may make a selection:—(1) Business Course; (2) Matriculation Course (School of Applied Science); (3) General Scientific Course; (4) Art Course; (5) Home Economics Course; (6) Special Courses.

The following are the Departments of Teaching in the Day Classes:—(1) Department of Commerce and Finance; (2) Department of Industrial Art; (3) Department of Physics; (4) Department of Chemistry; (5) Department of Mathematics; (6) Department of Language and History; (7) Department of Household Science and Art.

The first year is free in all regular Courses. The second year fee is $3 per Term, except in the Home Economics Course, which is free. The third year fee is $5 per Term. (Three Terms in the year.)

The fee for Special Students is $2 per subject per Term; for three subjects or more the fee is $5. The following are excepted from the above:—The subjects in Household Art—Sewing, Millinery, etcetera, free; in Cookery, for each Course over and above three Courses, an extra fee is charged; Modeling in Clay, Advanced Electricity, Advanced Chemistry, and Fancy Cookery are each $4 per term; the fee for the Nurses' Course is $12, and for the Housekeepers' Course, $10.

The Evening Classes provide Scientific, Artistic, and Practical training for Apprentices, Journeymen, Foremen, Clerks, Salesmen, and others, who are engaged in industrial, or commercial, pursuits during the daytime, and who desire supplementary instruction in the application of Science and Art to the Trades, Manufactures, and other occupations. While regular Courses are defined for the Students of the Evening Classes, no restrictions are enforced. Each student is permitted to select those subjects which will best help him to make progress in his particular trade, or business.

The Session commences on the first Monday in October and closes on March 31.

Applicants for registration in the Evening Classes must be at least fifteen years of age, except under special circumstances, when the Principal may admit applicants under fifteen years of age provided that such applicants are deemed capable of profiting by the work of the Classes.

In Drafting, the use of a Locker may be had by depositing 50c. for a key. In Chemistry, an extra deposit of $2 is required for the use of Apparatus and Locker. These deposits, less deductions for losses and breakages, are refunded at the close of the session.

Year Cards will be granted to such Students as have been regular and punctual in their attendance and are deemed worthy of a standing in their Session's work. Diplomas will be awarded to such Students as have completed a Course in any department and are deemed worthy of a standing in the work of that Course. Examination tests will be held in all the subjects; in the final year of any Course, the Candidate for a Diploma must pass with a standing of at least Class II.

The Evening Classes give instruction in Mathematics, Applied Mechanics, Electricity, Steam Engineering, Chemistry, Architecture and Building Construction, Machine Drawing, Sheet Metal Drawing, Freehand and Design, Modelling in Clay, Wood Carving, Estimating cost of building, Cookery, Home Nursing, Sewing, Millinery, Embroidery, etcetera.

The Committee recommend that the following be added to both Day and Evening Courses:—Carpentry and Joinery, Wood Turning, Pattern Making, Plumbing, Sheet Metal Work, Printing, Foundry Practice, Machine Shop Practice, Forging, Design as applied to Textiles, etcetera.

That, with the added practical work, the Courses be extended to four years, and that the class unit be twenty for Shop and Laboratory work, and forty for Academic work.

The Committee recommend that the Toronto Technical High School keep closely and constantly in touch with the various industrial interests, and that such subjects and Courses be added from time to time as may be necessary to promote the welfare of these industries themselves and of all parties connected therewith.

ELEMENTARY INDUSTRIAL ARTS IN PUBLIC AND SEPARATE SCHOOLS OF VILLAGES AND TOWNS.

The following are the regulations on this subject:—

1. The Public, or Separate, School Board of Trustees in a Village, or a Town, that provides and maintains a department for teaching the Elementary Industrial Arts, employs a teacher with a Departmental Certificate in these subjects, and provides accommodations and equipment satisfactory to the Minister of Education, shall be paid by the Minister an initial grant not exceeding $50 and a subsequent annual grant of $30 for each school approved by the Minister, from any appropriation made by the Legislature for instruction in these subjects.

2. These provisions shall not apply to any School Board receiving grants for Manual Training. Manual Training can be satisfactorily carried out only where preparatory training is given in the Elementary Industrial Arts, and the grants made for Manual Training under Regulations cover both Elementary Industrial Arts and Manual Training.

3. The School Board shall provide the necessary Tools, Materials, and other Requisites, and suitable Classroom accommodation for carrying on the instruction.

4. The accounts of the Course in Elementary Industrial Arts shall be kept separate from the general School Expenditure, and the grants made must be expended solely for this Course.

5. Much of the work of the Course in Elementary Industrial Arts may be done out of School hours, but a definite place must be provided for it in the Time Table, satisfactory to the Inspector of Technical Education.

6. On the report of the Inspector of Technical Education that the organization and the teaching are satisfactory, an annual Grant of $30, in addition to the regular salary paid by the School Board, will be paid by the Minister, out of any appropriation made by the Legislature for this purpose, to each legally qualified Teacher who holds a Certificate in Elementary Industrial Arts, and who gives instruction in accordance with the Regulations of the Department of Education.

The following is a summary of the general aims of the Courses in the Elementary Industrial Arts:

1. To stimulate intelligent appreciation of Industrial life and processes.

2. To develop at an early age habits of industry, respect for labour, and a love for productive and constructive work.

3. To encourage the spirit of co-operation on which depends not only the success of the modern Shop, but also the success of every individual life.

4. To bring the life and interests of the School more closely into touch with the working life to be lived after School days are over.

5. To reveal to the Pupils to some extent their peculiar bent, so that the choice of an occupation may be the more intelligently made.

6. To give ability to read and make working Drawings such as are used in the Industries.

7. To give facility in the handling of common Tools, and ability to put and keep them in good working order.

8. To give accurate ideas of the cost of Labour and value of material.

Organization of Work.

Suitable forms of work should be taken in every grade, being carefully planned so as to make adequate preparation for that of the next higher. Where practicable, one Teacher, or where necessary two Teachers, should take the whole of this subject, moving from Class to Class. In this way the Teachers will be able to keep in view the final purpose and to regulate instruction and methods so as best to achieve it. Where the organization renders the employment of two Teachers necessary, frequent conferences should be held between them so as to harmonize instruction and methods.

If there are a number of large Boys in the School, the Carpentry may well expand within a year, or two, so as to include building a small Shop on the School Grounds and fitting it up for working purposes.

Under specially favorable circumstances it will not be difficult to include in the Course the making of plans for the construction of Farm Buildings of the simpler sort. Exercises may be given in the Sewing of Leather and in the splicing of ropes, finding practical application in the Mending of Harness, Making of Halters, etcetera, as the necessities of the Farm and Home may require. Some exercises in Painting and Glazing may also be given, and opportunities are not lacking for applying the knowledge thus gained on the School, or Farm, Buildings.

As the work is intended to have special reference to the Industries of the district, specimens of the Articles manufactured, both complete and in process, should be collected, and thus the nucleus of a live Museum formed, which would provide a valuable aid to the instruction given. Manufacturers are usually willing to donate specimens for this purpose.

Employers and Manufacturers should be invited to give periodical Talks to the Pupils on the particular Trades in which they are engaged, the articles they manufacture, the processes they undergo, the materials from which they are made, and the Countries from which they come. The information thus obtained should be afterwards used for composition exercises, etcetera.

Every opportunity should be taken to show the Pupils by practical examples that the work they are doing is calculated to be of industrial service to them. When working in any material, references to the Trade in which it is employed should always be made. The Pupils who show special aptitudes along these lines should have special facilities offered them to induce them to stay a year longer in School in order to take up advanced work.

Visits to Shops, Buildings, Factories, etcetera, should be undertaken under guidance. Before these Visits the Pupils should be given some information about the particular Trade concerned, and receive some instruction regarding the vital points of the Industry. After a Visit of this kind the Pupils should always be required to reproduce in intelligible form the information gained.

Periodical Exhibitions will do much towards increasing the interest of the Parents and thus securing their co-operation. The local press should also be made use of in this connection. In the preparation of work for an exhibition the Teacher should guard carefully against the temptation to actually perform any of the operations. Every Pupil should be able to say, with truth, that the whole of the work is the product of his own hands. It should always be remembered that the training of the Pupil, and not the making of the object, is the final end in view.

Accommodation and Equipment Provided.

In the higher grades the provision of the necessary space will no doubt be found to be the most pressing problem. It is highly desirable that a separate Room be provided. If the School possesses a Basement, it can often be fitted to carry on the work, though a basement should not be chosen if other space is available. Individual benches are recommended where space is available.

In the primary grades no addition to the furniture of the ordinary Classroom is necessary, though a large flat-top table will always be found to be of great service.

For the necessary Tools, a small Box, or Tray, should be provided.

Where industrial work is done, as it will be in the majority of cases, at the ordinary School Desk, it is advisable to provide a sheet of stout mill board in order to protect the top.

Where single benches cannot be installed, a long narrow bench fitted to the wall of the Classroom will best meet the conditions. This should be provided with one or more vises, according to the space available and the number of Pupils to be accommodated. Such a bench should be rigid and be provided with a smooth-working vise. It should also be provided with as many sets of Tools as there are Pupils working at any one time.

A collection of Woods grown in the neighborhood of the School should be made. Each specimen should be so prepared as to show horizontal, tangential, and transverse sections, and should be labelled by number and not by name so that the collection may be used for exercises in identification. Attention should also be paid to the growing Tree, so that it may be recognized by its Shape, Leaves, Bark, etcetera.

The pupils should be encouraged to fit up where possible a Home Workshop in the Basement, or Shed.

Details of the Course.

Drawing: It should be kept in view first and always that Drawing lies at the base of every industry. Every object and every Building, whether it be a simple Cottage or a gorgeous Cathedral, begins with a plan, and the successful carrying out of the project depends on the plan being faithfully followed. "First plan your work and then work your plan." The individual who can draw with ease and accuracy can gain skill in any kind of manual industry much more quickly than would be possible without such power.

At first, objects will be drawn full size, with ruler, and afterward to a simple scale. The measured drawing is a valuable exercise. Doors, Gates, Classrooms, Cupboards, Yards, Gardens, Tables, etcetera can all be measured and a simple scale worked out. As the pupil advances, simple Plans, Elevations, and Sections will be introduced, care being taken to explain every term required, and to teach the correct method of using the necessary Instruments. Measurements should be carefully inserted, and from the first the greatest attention should be paid to accuracy.

From the third form up, the common Drawing Instruments should be introduced and their correct use insisted upon. Together with this use of instruments the practice of free hand Sketching should be largely made use of. The ability to sketch rapidly and accurately any piece of construction is of great educational value as well as of direct industrial value.

The common Geometrical Terms and Figures and their construction should be carefully taught and frequently practised, as no progress in Mechanical Drawing can be made until they are thoroughly known. Simple Tracings and Blue Prints, as used in the ordinary shop, are also most important.

At the end of the Course every Pupil should be able to read and to make such Working Drawings as are used in the local Industries.

Paper and Cardboard Work: This work will include the common Geometrical Figures, type solids, and objects based on them. As the work advances the paper will be replaced by thin cardboard and this by stouter.

Here the Working Drawing has to be made on the actual material. Errors in the drawing will plainly show in the finished object, unless corrected. All the typical solids should be made in cardboard, and these and the other objects constructed may be used afterwards, with good effect, for rapid sketching.

In all the practical work throughout the School, every effort must be made to economize time in the distribution of Tools and material. Unless care be taken, and a systematic method adopted, there will be much waste.

Clay Modeling: Clay may be used in the manufacture of common objects, such as Plates, Cups, Saucers, Flower Pots and Simple Vases. Grace and beauty of form are all-important. Much attention must be paid to the condition of the Clay.

There are two main phases of Clay work:

1. Representation, including Animal and Plant forms, Architectural details, etcetera.

2. Clay Modeling, as an industry including the various products made in Ceramic manufacture. In this Course the subject should be largely taught from a practical standpoint, and household utensils should be the subject of the exercises.

After a year or two of this work, a simple kiln for burning clay models might be built in the School yard.

Knife Work in Thin Wood: This forms an excellent introduction to ordinary Bench Work in Wood.

The Tool exercises involved in the various articles in this Course should include whittling with the grain, across the grain, and oblique, convex and concave whittling, sawing across the grain, sandpapering, boring with gimlet, and fastening pieces together with glue and nails. This work should prepare the Pupils for the more advanced work in thin Metals and wood to be given in the upper grades. Each Pupil should make his own drawing, but, for variety and practice in reading, he may occasionally be allowed to work from a carefully dimensioned and prepared Blackboard drawing, or a Blue Print. Twigs and small branches from the Trees may be sometimes used with good effect.

Bent Iron and Thin Metal Work: This is a useful form of work, especially valuable from the point of view of design. It can be carried on at the ordinary Bench with very few additional Tools. Very occasionally a piece of heavier iron may be needed, and this can be obtained from the blacksmith's shop. Norway iron is best, as it can be bent cold without breaking. Strips of wood can be used for some purposes, and blackened when finished. When wide bands are required, they may be of sheet tin.

Much practice should be given with the C. and S. curves, as many designs are formed from these and their combinations and modifications. The object to be made should be sketched, care being taken to keep the design simple. Strength and beauty of construction always depend on a few bold lines. After the sketch has been criticized, corrected and accepted, a full sized drawing should be made on heavy Manilla paper. The object of the working drawing is to enable the Pupil to see the exact size and shape of each piece of iron as it is being formed. The work should be constantly placed on the drawing as a test. Such objects as the following afford useful exercises:—Letter rack, vase mount, match holder, candlestick, photograph frame, flower pot holder, tea pot stand, wall bracket, candle bracket, cake dish frame, hanging vase holder, grille, newspaper rack, lantern, etc. Many beautiful and useful objects may be made out of thin sheet copper.

Bench work Selection of objects for this work is different, as the choice is so wide. They should be well within the capacity of the Pupil, as correct workshop methods should always be employed.

A fair amount of accuracy should be insisted upon. "According to drawing" should be the test. Attention should be given to "repairing" as well as "making." Objects might be allowed to be brought from Home for this purpose, and the School itself will often provide opportunities.

In this and other parts of the Course the cost of the material in bulk should be given, a money value set on the time of the Boy and the total cost of the finished object worked out. The problem of the modern Shop is time and cost, and no Pupil should complete this Course without some knowledge of both.

Much attention should be directed to the mechanical features of construction —joints, various methods of fastening, etcetera—to be found in Buildings, Bridges,

Doors, Windows, Drawers, Boxes, etcetera—and the Pupil encouraged to examine from a structural point of view every object he meets with.

There are many forms of work other than those mentioned, and every effort should be made to give the work as wide a bearing as possible.

One of the leading features of modern Shop practice is "division of labour," and this principle should be applied to one or two problems during the School Course. A large project should be selected, each part of which is to be constructed by a different Student. During its process the Pupil learns that he must fit in to the general scheme of things, and that his work must be well done or it will spoil the whole when the parts are brought together. The possibilities of this method, from an Industrial and Educational point of view, are great, and they should be carefully worked out. Labour-saving devices should be used as far as possible in order to reduce cost and bring conditions as close as possible to those prevailing in the Shop.

The extent to which Industrial work or vocational Training may be correlated with ordinary School subjects is very great. The making of Scientific Apparatus adds life and vitality to Science Teaching. Descriptions of Tools and processes are practical exercises in composition. Calculations of Time, Cost and Material provide a kind of Workshop Mathematics that will prove most valuable. The study of the growth of Timber, Seasoning, Warping, etcetera, offer practical Nature Study, and in fact the points where this subject may touch and help other Studies are only limited by the resourcefulness of the Teacher.

Trade papers, catalogues, and magazines should be constantly in use, and Books on practical subjects added to the School Library. A partial list follows: These should be gradually purchased as opportunity offers:

Theory.—Among Country Schools (Kern), Industrial Social Education (Baldwin), Place of Industries in Elementary Education (Dopp. University of Chicago Press), Working with the Hands (Booker Washington), Educational Foundations of Trade and Industry (Ware).

Drawing and Design.—Prang's Text Books of Art Education (Eight numbers. Geo. M. Hendry Co.), Lettering (Steeley), Principles of Design (Batchelder), Design, The Making of Patterns (Hatton), Mechanical Drawing (Cross), School of Art Geometry.

Paper and Cardboard.—Correlated Handwork (Trybom and Heller), Busy Hands (Booker), Industrial Work for Public Schools (Holton and Rollins), Seat Work and Industrial Occupations (Gillman and Williams), Paper Sloyd for Primary Grades (Rich), Pretty Pursuits for Children, Pleasant Pastimes for Children, Manual Training Schedule (New York Board of Education, free), Paper Modeling (Swannell).

Clay.—Clay Modeling for Little Ones (Pearce), Clay Modeling (Gordon), Clay Modeling (Holland), Plaster Casts and How They are Made (Frederick), Clay Work (Lester).

Knife Work.—Wood Work in the Common School (Hinckley), Knife Work in the School Room (Kilbon), Easy Woodwork (Field), Elementary Knife Work (Hammell), Advanced Knife Work (Hammell).

Metal Work.—Copper Work (Rose), Bent Iron Work (Erskine), Metal Work (Leland), Venetian Iron Work.

Bench Work.—Art Crafts for Beginners (Sanford), Joints (Cristy), Woodworking for Beginners (Wheeler), Mechanics' Own Book, Picture Frame Making for Amateurs (Lukin), Handyman's Book (Hasluck), Elementary Woodwork (Forster), Primer of Forestry (Pinchot. Bulletin 24, Agriculture Department, U. S. A.), Our Native Trees (Keeler), Educational Woodwork for School and Home (Park),

Supply of Teachers, Elementary Industrial Arts.

By arrangement with the Minister of Agriculture, the Minister of Education has established a Course at the Ontario Agricultural College, Guelph, in order to provide Teachers with second-class Certificates, competent to give instruction in Elementary Industrial Arts, in addition to the ordinary subjects of the Public and Separate Schools. Application to the Deputy Minister of Education may be made, who will supply a list of such Teachers with their addresses.

INDUSTRIAL SCHOOLS IN THE CITIES AND CHIEF TOWNS OF ONTARIO.

In 1868, a Public Meeting was held in Toronto, with a view to consider and deal practically with a class of Vagrant Children, which were becoming too numerous in the City. After a good deal of discussing, it was decided that the only successful way in which they could be dealt with was to send them to an Industrial School. As the result of this meeting an appeal was made to the School Board of the City of Toronto to establish such a School, but the Board considered that it had no legal authority to do so. However, in 1871, a comprehensive School Act having been passed by the Legislature, provision was made in it to enable School Boards in Cities and Towns to establish Industrial, Manual Labour, Schools in these Municipalities. The City Board, having taken the matter up, thought that the best and most effective way in which it could deal with the question was to appoint a Committee to make enquiries as to the best and most effective manner in the United States in which such Schools were established and conducted.

The Committee appointed by the Board having visited the United States and collected a great deal of information on the subject presented the following Report to a special committee of the Board of Trustees:—

Your Committee has received from the Deputation appointed by the Board to visit the States of New York and Massachusetts a full and comprehensive Report in regard to the form and working of Industrial and Reformatory Schools in those portions of the above States that were visited.

It will be in the recollection of the Board that the subject of Industrial Schools is not now brought forward for the first time. On the 19th of April, 1868, a very large and influential Meeting of citizens was held, with a view to the establishment of Schools of this class for reclaiming Vagrant Children of both sexes, and a series of very important Resolutions were passed by the Meeting, which were afterwards transmitted to the Board of School Trustees with a request for their joint co-operation.

The plan proposed was based on voluntary aid to be given by the citizens, who were to supply the Food and Clothing to the Scholars, the educational part of the system to be under the control of the School Board. The Committee on School Management, in their Report, declining to recommend the adoption of the plan proposed,—owing to the then existing state of the School Law,—expressed their opinion that two things were vitally important to the success of such Schools:—1st. The entire separation, through the night as well as the day, of these juvenile Vagrants, for a period longer, or shorter, according to circumstances, from all association with the corrupt sources by which they are surrounded, and, of course, influenced, as experience has fully proved that nothing short of complete isolation can, or will, meet the question; and 2nd. The securing of the object in view by a Compulsory Attendance.

At the last Meeting of the Legislature, the School Law was amended by 34 Victoria, Chapter 33, and Section 42 of the amending Act provides that,—

"The Public School Board of each City, Town, and Village, may establish one, or more, Industrial Schools for otherwise neglected children, and make all needful Regulations and employ the means requisite to secure the attendance of such children, and for the support, management, and discipline of such School, or Schools."

The same Act gives the right to all children to attend School and introduces the principle of Compulsory Attendance.

The Board, by the passage of the above Act, being now in a position to deal with the subject legally and effectually, it is but right that Toronto, the Capital of Ontario, should take the lead in providing for her Vagrant population that training and that kind of education which they so greatly require, and from which they are debarred it may be by the extreme poverty, ignorance, vice, greed of gain, or indifference of their Parents, or Guardians; a System of Education and Industrial Training that will convert what would otherwise be the costly inmates of our Gaols and Penitentiaries into industrious citizens, capable of working for the common good, and with honour to themselves and those connected with them. The necessity for these Schools is,

1st. To reach a class not yet provided for by our City Schools and complete the system of national education. Although our Schools are Free to all, still experience has shown that the Vagrant Class and the children of Parents too poor to provide them with Clothes, or whose employment is thought necessary for the family sustenance, seldom, or ever, find their way into our Schools. In the year 1863 a School Census was taken under the authority of the Board, when it was found that no less than 1,165 Protestant children of School age were not attending any School, or receiving any kind of Education. This number in the year 1868 had risen to 1,600 children, and with our growing population the number may now be taken to be considerably larger than this. How important, then, to provide at once for these poor children growing up in our midst in ignorance and neglect.

2nd. To enable the Board properly and efficiently to carry out the Truant system, or compulsory attendance at our Schools, and thus ensure the education of all at the expense of all.

Were the Board at present to put in force the power given them to enforce attendance at our Schools, the first difficulty to be overcome would be, where to send children of the class referred to? To send them to our Schools in the condition in which they would most likely be found, without the necessary clothing, dirty, and with all their wild untutored habits, must tend to demoralize our present Schools and impair their efficiency. Proper Accommodation must, therefore, at once be found in the shape of an Industrial School, or allow the School Law to remain a dead letter.

3rd. As a matter of self-defence and gain, to add to the wealth of the community by rendering the vagrant and neglected class industrious, teaching them to earn an honest livelihood, and thus lessen the expenditure required to keep them from doing us harm, or punishing them for harming us.

The truth of this proposition is so universally recognized as to require but few remarks. It has been conclusively proved that the more remunerative the employment, the less incentive there is to crime, and the greater the self-respect. In Industrial Schools the inmates are taught different branches of Trade, so that, on leaving the School for active life, they find themselves able at once to command employment at remunerative wages, being educated and skilled Workmen, and the increase of "self-respect" enables the delinquent to look back on his former life with fear and trembling, and to be avoided in future.

Lastly. As a matter of philanthropy, to house the homeless, reclaim the vagrant, elevate the debased, reform the vicious, and prevent pauperism, from which this Province is so happily free.

From the above statement and facts your Committee would recommend,—

1. That the system of Compulsory Attendance be put into operation in the City of Toronto, and a Truant Officer appointed in the Eastern and Western divisions of the City to see that the same is properly carried out.

2. That the establishment and equipment of an Industrial School is desirable.

3. That the School partake of the Reformatory and Voluntary character, so happily combined in some of the Institutions in the United States, due provision being made for the classification of the inmates.

4. That such amendments be asked for to the existing School Law, if necessary, as will give the Board the power of detention in the School of the children committed to their care during minority, or until such time as the Board may consent to their discharge.

5. That a special application be made through the Education Department to the Legislature for a Special Grant from the School Fund towards the establishment of the said School, to cover the expenses over and above that which would be incurred, for purely educational purposes.

TORONTO. 26th December, 1871. W. BARCLAY MCMURRICH, *Chairman of Committee.*

THE WORK DONE BY THE INDUSTRIAL SCHOOL, TORONTO.

An Industrial School Association having been formed at the Alexandra School for Girls, Toronto, the annual meeting of the Association was held in June, 1909. The gathering was large and the excellent work being done by the Ladies among the Girls at the Alexandra School was freely commented upon, and was a matter of congratulation.

His Honour the Lieutenant-Governor presided at the meeting. He spoke of the interest he had taken in the Alexandra School since its inception, when he was a member of the Ontario Government. He referred to the devotion of Miss Wilkes to the Cause of the Girls, and he knew that a great deal of good, useful work was being done in the institution of which she had been one of the founders. He was pleased that the old-time punitive methods, as applied to boys and girls in such institutions, were disappearing, and he was gratified to note an absence of anything like restraint at the Alexandra School.

The annual report of the Alexandra School for Girls, which was read by Miss Josephine Parrott, the Superintendent, stated that in the year ending April 30 there had been sixty girls in the school, their average age being 14 1-2 years. Some had been placed in employment and some had returned to their homes. The methods of management were mentioned, and it was pointed out that the girls were taught woman's work, so that they would be enabled to take their proper place in the world. Out of fifty girls who had left, only one was a complete failure.

In addition to the reports of the Alexandra School, reports of the Victoria Industrial School for Boys, Mimico, were read. Superintendent C. Ferrier gave an interesting account of the good work being done among the 241 boys at the Mimico institution, where boys are being trained to become useful citizens.

NOTE.—The idea of establishing an Industrial School in Toronto first suggested itself in 1868, and the plan was then largely discussed. In 1871 the School Act authorized Public School Boards of Cities, Towns and Villages to establish one or more such Schools. An Industrial School for Toronto was erected near the

Village of Mimico, seven miles from the City, the Ontario Government having given a plot of eight Acres, and leased forty-two in addition.

The Act passed in 1884 defines an "Industrial School" to be: A School in which industrial training is provided, and in which children are lodged, clothed and fed, as well as taught, shall exclusively be deemed an Industrial School within the meaning of this Act.

INDUSTRIAL SCHOOLS AMONG THE INDIANS.

In addition to the Schools which are maintained by the Dominion Government among the Indians on the Reserves, there are special ones maintained by some of the Churches, such as the excellently managed Mohawk Institution at Brantford. There is also the Mount Elgin Institute at Munceytown. These Schools, as they should be, are Industrial, as well as Literary. There are also the Shingwauk Home for Boys and the Wawanosh Home for Girls, both situated at Sault Ste. Marie, District of Algoma. They owe their origin to the indefatigable efforts of the Principal, the Reverend Edward F. Wilson. The Shingwauk Home was named after an Indian Chief (Little Pine), and was first opened at Garden River in 1873. Near the close of that year the Home was destroyed by fire, but was re-erected at Sault Ste. Marie during the following Summer—the Corner-stone having been laid by the Earl of Dufferin on the 30th July, 1874—and the School was opened on August 2nd, 1875.

The Wawanosh Home for Girls, also named after an Indian Chief, (Sailing Gracefully), was opened, with a number of Indian Girls as Pupils, on August 19th, 1879.

Training.—The Girls are thoroughly trained in Housework, Cooking, Baking, and Laundry work; and the Boys, after spending about two years steadily at School, in their third year commence learning a Trade, and during the last two years of residence rank as Apprentices. . . . . Carpentering and Printing are taught within the precincts of the Institution, but for instruction in other branches of Trade the Boys are sent to the Village near by.

These Homes are supported mainly by voluntary contributions, the annual grant from the Indian Department being insufficient for their support. Most of the individual children are provided for by weekly contributions made in Canadian Sunday Schools of the Church of England. There are nearly eighty children in the two homes.

NOTE.—A number of Indian Schools exist in various parts of the Province. They are under the management of the Dominion Government, but, for purposes of inspection, are under the supervision of the Ontario Education Department.

MOUNT ELGIN INSTITUTION, MUNCEY TOWN.

This Institution was so called, in honour of the late Earl of Elgin, who was Governor-General of Canada at the time it was established. A number of Indians were settled at Muncey and lived there as Pagans. A young man who was a Teacher near by, at Westminster, became interested in these Indians, and repeatedly visited their Camp. At his fourth visit he offered to teach the Indian Children to read and write like the white man. To this the Indians objected, for, they said, that the White Man " used reading and writing to deceive and cheat the Indians." After much persuasion, two families consented to send their children to his School; he persevered in his persuasion to other Indians until he had eight Indian Children in his School. The Teacher, Mr. Carey, lived for five months near the Camp at his own expense. This was the beginning of the Mount Elgin Institution, where at the time three different Indian dialects were taught.

The Reverend Thomas Hurlburt, who was a great friend of the Indians, was appointed to Muncey Town in 1828. He says: " I took charge of the Missions and of the School and had also the Pastoral charge."

On July 17th, 1849, the Corner Stone of the new Industrial Indian School was laid at Muncey by the Reverend Doctor Richey, President of the Conference. The Reverend S. D. Rice was Principal of the Institution at the time of the Corner Stone ceremonies. Some years afterwards, when the Reverend Thomas Cosford was in charge of the Institution, (from 1875 to 1880). he wrote the following account of it. He says:

The object of this Institution is to Christianize and elevate the Indian Youth of our Country, to teach the Boys useful Trades, such as Carpentering and Cabinet Making, as well as the correct principles of Farming; and the Girls Sewing, Knitting and Spinning, and General House Work. In these pursuits many of the Boys and Girls make very creditable proficiency and become good workers. Quite a goodly number are now employed in Teaching School, others are Assistant Missionaries, while many have obtained greatly improved ideas and skill as well as Industry in farming, and the Girls are also equally benefited, being greatly improved in their modes and efficiency of House Keeping, as well as in their general intelligence, taste and acquirements.

Not less than six hundred and fifty of these Indian Youths have, up to this time, been educated at this Institution, and many of them have been enjoying these advantages during a period of two, three, four and five years. They are taken into the Institution, boarded, clothed and educated, under the most judicious and watchful care, to promote their happiness and physical health, social habits and general deportment, while the most untiring efforts are made to promote their moral and religious interests; and further, the greatest care is taken to inculcate habits of industry and frugality, which are essential in the future prosperity and happiness of the Indian race. With these efforts they will become well-to-do, while without them they must be poor.

The Farm of the Institution is in a good state of productiveness. It contains about 226 acres of rich land. The Buildings are ample, and in a good state mainly. All the Departments of the Institution are in a state of creditable prosperity. We now supply the Institution with all the necessary Farm products, and have from $600 to $800 worth to sell. We raised in 1878, 836 bushels of Wheat, 700 of Oats, 285 of Peas, 17,000 of Indian Corn and 750 of Carrots. There were 86 Waggon loads of Hay, and about 25 loads of other Cattle feed, besides a large quantity of Wheat, Oats and Pea Straw for Cow-house and Stable. We have seven Horses and two Colts, twenty-five Cows, seventy Sheep, fifteen Calves, ten Yearlings, six two-year-old and six three-year-old. Have sold four four-year-old for $140. We have twenty-five fat Hogs, and expect thirty next year. Have had 6,000 pounds of Pork per year for the last three years, besides fat Sheep and Cattle.

It is but proper to observe that, in 1845, the late Reverend Peter Jones collected money in England and Scotland for the laudable purpose of educating the Indians. The amount realized in all was about $7,500.

The cost of labour, Salaries, Farm Implements, Blacksmithing, Clothing, Shoemakers and Wages amounted in one year, with cost of extra Stock, etcetera, to $27,256.80, towards which there was realized from Sales of various kinds of work and the present value of Stock, etcetera, $21,887.49. The Government makes a Grant of $5,035 towards the expenditure.

Muncey, or Mount Elgin, Industrial Institution, like similar Institutions, is conducted in such a manner as harmonised with the views of the late Reverend Peter Jones. We take the following from the Report of Commissioners who were appointed by the Government to collect information relative to Indian Affairs. Mr. Jones says:

The Credit Indians live in a Village, and some of them have to go a mile, or two, to their Farms. Before their conversion very few of them raised even Indian Corn, but now many of them grow Wheat, Oats, Peas, Indian Corn, Potatoes and their Vegetables. Several cut Hay and have small Orchards.

The best mode of promoting religious improvements among the Indians is to combine Manual Labour with Religious Instruction, to educate some of the Indian youths with a view to their becoming Missionaries and School Teachers, as it is a well-known fact that the good already effected has been principally through the labour of Native Missionaries.

Considering that they are taught in a strange language, Indian Children show as much aptitude as White children.

The best mode of promoting the moral, intellectual and social improvement of the Indians is to establish among them well-regulated Schools of Industry, and the congregating of the several and cultured tribes into three, or four, settlements, which would be a great saving to the Government and to Missionary Societies; at the same time, it would afford greater facilities for their Instruction in everything calculated to advance their general improvement.

I know several Indians who have become pretty good Mechanics with little, or no, instruction. At the Credit River Mission there are two or three Carpenters and a Shoemaker. At Muncey we have one Blacksmith and some Carpenters and Sailors.

The condition of the Indians would soon improve if Schools of Industry were established among them. Agricultural Societies should be formed in each settlement and rewards offered to such as might excel in any branch of Farming.

The History of the Ojibway Indians, by the Reverend Peter Jones, contains much valuable information which I have not seen elsewhere.

Industrial Institutions are in the course of erection—two, I think, in the Northwest, under the care of the Methodist Church. A new establishment is also in course of erection at Muncey.

TORONTO.   (Reverend) EDWARD BARRASS.

THE SHINGWAUK AND WAWANOSH HOMES.

In submitting this short sketch of the Shingwauk and Wawanosh Homes, I do so, hoping it may be what is required in the work you are preparing; also I will do so in a manner knowing that all are not acquainted with the Homes and their beautiful situation.

The Homes are situated on the beautiful River St. Mary, just one mile below the Town of Sault Ste. Marie. There is in connection with the Home Ninety-three acres of land, which is mostly suitable for gardening and other purposes, such as Hay, Grain, Pasture, etcetera. This season we have harvested a fine lot of first quality Hay, and we have just taken into our large Barn some of the finest Oats I ever saw, and the sample of Grain was excellent. There being so much to do the first year, we were late in getting some of the land broken up. After clearing and draining it, we sowed it to Oats and Peas for green fodder for feeding our cows. In the Garden we have hundreds of fine Cabbages and Carrots, Turnips and Potatoes. We intend planting small fruits, such as Strawberries, Currants, etcetera. We hope to build a Green House on a small scale, so that we may begin to support our Homes, and in this way we may with the grant from the Indian Department pay off the present deficit, and then begin to improve the Homes generally.

The Building consists of the Main Block, 185 x 40 feet, with various wings and the Principal's Residence.

A little way from the Main Building is the Drill Hall, a large two-storey Building, 60 x 30 feet. The ground floor is a Drill Hall and Play Room in stormy and wet weather. The Upper Storey is used as a School Room.

Besides these Main Buildings we have a very nice little Hospital, a Laundry and Farmer's Cottage, Horse Stable and large Hay Barn, with Cow Stable.

The Factory, situated near the River, is well equipped, and our boys like to work there, and are allowed to make toy Boats by way of recreation. We have, with the help of the Boys, just finished two Rowboats, and the pleasure derived from them is the life of the play time for both Boys and Girls.

The Children go to School for the first Session of School each day. The older ones go in the morning, while part of them alternately work in the morning and then they change, and those who have been at School in the morning go to the different kinds of work in the afternoon. The younger pupils go to School both Sessions each day.

We are teaching the Boys to Farm, Garden, and work in the Woodwork at the Factory, caring for the Horses and Cattle, Painting, Kalsomining, etcetera.

The Girls do Housekeeping, Laundry and Cooking.

We are working with reduced numbers of both Children and Staff. During the last Term we had only forty, with a Staff of five Teachers and at present only four.

The reduced plan was proposed by our Bishop and Home Committee, so that we might with rigid economy keep from falling behind. We have done so, and more than that, we have cleared off nearly one half of the deficit and hope to be all right in another year or so.

In School our Scholars compare very well with those in the Public Schools. The Inspector said that he gave them exactly the same work, and they did remarkably well.

We have had no call from any Doctor as yet, and that is something to be thankful for. Mrs. Fuller has treated all the sick cases, so far. Some cases of hurts, etcetera, such as boys are subject to, were serious enough. We are, indeed, thankful to all who have helped the Home, in money and material, and they are many.

Thanking you for your kind consideration,

SAULT STE. MARIE, September, 1910.   BENJ. P. FULLER, *Principal*.

PROMOTION OF INDUSTRIAL EDUCATION BY THE UNIVERSITY.

At a meeting of Engineers in Toronto in January, 1910, representatives of the Canadian Manufacturers' Association were present and were very hearty in their appreciation of the work done by the University, as a factor in the industrial development of Canada.

Mr. A. D. Campbell, in proposing "Canadian Industries," indicated the relation of the University to the various industrial activities.

On all hands the effort to bring the Provincial University into closer touch with all the industrial activities of the country was approved and commended, and the industrial waste which prevails could be cured only through thorough and systematic technical education, and the practical application of the scientific knowledge of the universities to the industries of the country.

President Falconer, responding for the University, urged the necessity for the work of applied science in developing the natural resources of Canada, and pointed out how not one department alone, but the entire work of the University, has to do with solving the real problems of Canada.

Doctor J. A. Macdonald warned against evils and abuses which must be taken out of the way if Canada is to come to her own and if the Empire is to remain united and strong. He emphasized specially the economic waste of natural resources. He also argued for the better industrial education of the farmers, and urged that the foundations be well laid in the public schools. Mr. J. P. Murray of Toronto made a plea for the use of the Schools in country places and villages for extending industrial education among those who could not attend the University. He illustrated the growing value of scientific knowledge by reference to the textile industry.

THE COMMISSION ON INDUSTRIAL TRAINING AND TECHNICAL EDUCATION, OCTOBER, 1910.

From the information thus far obtained by the Royal Commission on Industrial Training and Technical Education in the visits of the Commission to various Cities and Towns in Ontario, it is clear that public opinion has been strongly expressed in favour of the elements of both Industrial Training and Technical Education having a prominent place in the Curriculum of Study in the Public Schools and Collegiate Institutes of the Province. I have made a selection from the opinions expressed at various public meetings which the Commission has held on the subject. So far as reported in the Toronto *Mail and Empire* of the 21st of October, the Commission has heard over six hundred Witnesses.

The report says that "Workmen, Employers of Labour and Educationists bear testimony as to the great desirableness of having existing means for the preparing of Skilled Workers improved by the co-operation of the Public Schools in preliminary and supplementary work."

The fact brought out in the testimony of several witnesses that apprentices and workmen are making use of the opportunities given them by Correspondence Schools carried on in the United States is an indication that there is room for more work on the part of the Public Educational System of this Country. Mr. C. Waterous, of the Engine Works, Brantford, said that he understood one of these Schools was drawing about $8,000 a month from Ontario mechanics.

The more that education bears on industry the more does it exalt industry and teach pupils pride in it. There is no question but that the Workman who knows something about the Science of his technical methods is more contented, as well as more efficient, than the man who works in submission to rules of which he does not understand the principle. The Plumber who has been led to study the laws of Gaseous expansion and who has had some instruction in the theory of Heat will take pleasure in his daily work, and is almost sure to develop inventive power. If our Public Schools did no more than inculcate an admiration for present-day achievements in subordinating the powers of Nature to the service of industry, their influence to increase the general respect for labour would be immense. It cannot be denied that there is need for teaching that will make young people hold the Mechanic Arts in higher honour. It is not the wish of intelligent employers of skilled labour or of Artisans who have developed skill along with manual facility—that the Public Schools be turned into workshops and process buildings. All that is required of the Public Schools is that they respond more readily to the ruling conditions in the pursuits by which the great mass of the people make their living. As we are all by nature consumers, most of us are by necessity producers, and the schooling we get in our youth should go some distance towards qualifying us to be breadwinners. That the Schools can do much to form the tastes and habits of workers in their pupils is undoubted. They can at least interest the young in the modern wonders of industrial production. Nearly every occupation in which the wage-earner is engaged is now an applied Science. The underlying principles are proper subjects for School treatment, and very young pupils can be led to take an interest in simple Mechanical, Chemical and Physical facts underlying the everyday callings of life.

Some of the witnesses before the commission dwelt on the importance of having boys kept at school until they were 16—that is, boys who were intended for mechanical pursuits. In the latter period of their School term some instruction to subserve rather definitely the business of the youth's life as a worker might be given.

At Chatham the suggestion was advanced by Captain J. S. Black that the Federal Government should combine Military Training with Technical Education, and met with great approval. The scheme outlined was to make Drill Sergeants Experts in some technical branch of education and require them to give free instruction to men of the Regiments, thus educating them and encouraging them to join the Militia.

Charles Cornelius told of actual results obtained in Grand Rapids, Michigan, as the result of the introduction of Manual Training in the Public and High Schools. At present the most valued men in his factory are men who received such training in the Public Schools in the States.

Mr. W. R. Landon, of the Chatham Wagon Company, was convinced that workmen in the factories would avail themselves of an opportunity to attend a night school for the purpose of receiving technical training. The Schools to-day, he said, do not fit boys to accept positions in his factory. He would be willing to allow beginners in his factory to attend a Technical School for a few hours each day at the company's expense.

At St. Thomas, T. W. Crothers, K.C., M.P., gave valuable information regarding the education of Boys and of farm help, and an appeal was also made for a domestic science school here for Girls by the Inspector of Schools.

Mr. M. L. Gardner, Assistant Superintendent of apprentices on the New York Central Lines and M. C. R. at St. Thomas, stated that between thirty and forty young people were now taking up Technical Education under the different master mechanics in the Michigan Central shops alone. It was made clear that a Technical School was badly needed in St. Thomas. All the railroads promise to support the School.

Technical Education in Europe.—A gentleman, Mr. King, who had taken part in proceedings on Technical Education in Europe, in reply to inquiries on the subject by the Reporter, said: " I was greatly impressed by the important part that Industrial Training and Technical Education are playing in all trades and industries, and by the important place assigned to this branch of instruction by the State in the several Countries visited. The Conference at Brussels was composed chiefly of a body of Experts, who were concerned mainly with a consideration of the Curricula of Institutions having to do with the higher branches of technical training. By meeting with members of this Conference I was enabled to enlist the sympathy of many present, and of the Governments represented, in the work of the Canadian Commission, and I think that we may feel that, when the Members of the Royal Commission on Industrial Training and Technical

Education visit Great Britain and other European Countries they will be afforded every facility for observation and information by the Governments of the several Countries and those directing their Technical Schools and Colleges."

A School for Chefs is the latest scheme of the London County Council. It is to be a branch of the Westminster Technical Institute, and as a beginning fifteen boys from 14 to 16 years of age will soon start a three-years' course in cooking. At the end of that time they will be placed as assistant chefs at large restaurants or hotels or private houses, where it is hoped they will in time qualify as chief cooks, and thus meet the foreigner on his own ground. The boys who enter must have passed the sixth standard at school. Their instructor will be a French chef, who will teach them how to judge food in buying it, the proper storage of dry and perishable articles, the care of refrigerator and larder, the management of cooking apparatus, the care and cleanliness of cooking utensils, and the whole art of preparing food, from the making of soup stock to the concoction of the most delicate sauce or souffle.

Household Economy in Germany.—At Berlin, in Germany, what is at once a new occupation for women and a new feature of German social policy is being established in Southern Germany by the employment of women as travelling Teachers of Household Economy for the agricultural population. The first School for the training of the Teachers has been founded at Miesbach, in Bavaria. The Course of Instruction occupies a year and a half, and includes instruction in all departments of urban and rural Housekeeping. Fruit culture, Vegetable growing, and Kitchen gardening in general, the treatment of Fruit, Poultry raising, and Agriculture, Sewing and Needlework are also taught. The student must, in addition, become an expert in Physical exercises, Singing, and First Aid to the Injured. The theoretical instruction deals chiefly with the Chemistry of Food, Bookkeeping, Hygiene, and the intellectual nourishment proper for the class among whom the students will have to work. As Teachers they will have to visit all small Towns and Villages. The system is expected to do much to raise the standard of comfort, health, and education among German peasants.

Trades for Girls.—At a proposed meeting of the National Society for the Promotion of Industrial Education, to be held in Boston in November, it is intended to devote an entire day to the consideration of ways and means of securing more adequate preparation for Girls who enter the trades. At another meeting the topic will be " Demands and Opportunities for Girls in Trades and Stores," and also " The Training of Teachers for Girls' Trade Schools."—*Toronto Globe.*

Technical Education in Dublin.—This subject attracts a good deal of attention in Dublin, and, in a late Lecture on the subject, Mr. Fennehy devoted attention to the necessity of more attention being given to correct Drawing. He said that he would like to see Drawing made an essential element in every Primary School. In an interesting Address, illustrated by numerous Drawings, he shewed that perspective was the grammar of the art of objective drawing. It was not the art of drawing, but the science which dealt with the principles of the art.

THE HAMILTON SCIENTIFIC ASSOCIATION.

This Society was organized in 1857. It has therefore been in existence fifty-three years, which gives it a place with the oldest Scientific Societies in Canada. The founders of this Institution, having faith in the worth of knowledge, and zeal for its diffusion, associated themselves for mutual improvement, and more especially to study the Physical Geography, Geology, Flora and Fauna of the Niagara peninsula. This, the main object of the Association, was made effective by a fee for membership, by holding monthly meetings, and by making occasional Scientific Excursions into localities deemed best fitted to make known the natural beauty, abundant life, and characteristic features of the Niagara district.

By mutual agreement it became the duty of each member to promote the welfare of the Society by collecting specimens of Natural History objects, by the reading of carefully prepared papers on scientific research, or by rendering other relevant service to his Associates. Some time after the Society was organized, in furtherance of its plans for future usefulness, a Charter of incorporation was obtained from the Provincial Legislature. Since that date its collection of Books, Periodicals and Natural History specimens has become the nucleus of a scientific Library and Museum, and its proceedings are received in exchange by Scientific Societies in many parts of the world.

Few Societies accomplish all that their founders anticipate, and to that rule the Hamilton Association is no exception. But, if in some respects it has fallen short of the ideals of its promoters, it has, in other aspects, surpassed their expectations. From time to time working sections of the Society have been established for the study of Astronomy, Geology, Biology, Linguistics and Photography as an art. An analysis of the Reports of these Sections, and of the Cabinets of the Museum, show that the energy of th Association has been directed to many fields of useful knowledge.

Two or three items of such work deserve mention. Several years ago the Association sent to an English and to a French Exposition prepared specimens of the Forest Trees of Ontario, suitable for export timber of industrial importance. Afterward that service was supplemented by a list of Plants which, subjected to repeated revision, remains an authoritative Conspectus of the Flora of the Niagara district. In 1886 the Association first published in its Journal sketches of the "Birds of Ontario," a volume of three hundred and forty pages, which is still quoted by Ornithologists, and was at the time the best account of Ontario Birds. The Author of that work, the late Mr. Thomas McIlwraith, was a member of the Society, and a well-known Ornithologist. Professor Hall, when Palæontologist of the State of New York, often wrote in commendation of the Society's Geological collections. And recently the Siliceous Sponges and Fossil Grapholites of the Hamilton escarpment, collected by Mr. Walker, and by Colonel Grant, Members of the Association, have been gladly taken into their Cabinets by Curators of American and European Museums of distinction.

The Hamilton Association has on its roll of Membership about two hundred and fifty names, and has fair claims to be considered a local focus for the concentration and subsequent diffusion of current Scientific opinion. The admirable system of University extension Lectures of late years has aided the Society's efforts to popularize Scientific knowledge, and both the present and last preceding Provincial Governments have recognized its public usefulness by a yearly grant of $400.

Apart from its local Members, the bead-roll of the Society contains many well known names. Among these is that of the noted Arctic explorer, Doctor John Rae, who received ten thousand pounds, sterling, for his discovery of the fate of Sir John Franklin. Doctor Rae was the second president of the Hamilton Association, and during the current year the Professor of Anthropology and Biology at Jena, Ernst Hæckel, sent to the Secretary of the Society an account of his famous museum with the request that it be printed in the Society's Journal, and that his name be added to its list of Members.

HAMILTON, October, 1910.   H. B. WITTON, SR.

THE HAMILTON TECHNICAL AND ART SCHOOL.

The Hamilton Technical and Art School, established in 1909, holds a unique position among the Educational Institutions of the Province.

Always noted for the extent and variety of its industrial work of recent years Hamilton, by reason of location, shipping facilities, and the energy and enterprise of its citizens, has attracted a number of the manufacturing establishments in the Country.

In order to meet more fully the educational requirements of a population so largely devoted to industrial pursuits, the Board of Education established the "Hamilton Technical and Art School" at an expense of $100,000 for the Building and its equipment, the whole of which was defrayed by the municipality.

The School is a large, four-storied Building, situated on Stinson Street. It contains Workshops, an Electrical Laboratory, a Drafting Room, Art Studios, Class Rooms and Rooms especially equipped for teaching dressmaking, cooking and printing.

The Shops, which are a prominent feature of the School, afford facilities for practical instruction in Woodworking and Iron-working. The Woodshop is equipped with Benches and Tools sufficient for thirty pupils, as well as Lathes for woodturning, Power Saws and other machines; the Forge shop contains sixteen Forges, a full complement of small Tools, while in the Machine Shop may be found seven Engine Lathes, a Planer, a Shaper, and a Milling Machine, besides smaller Machines and a full line of Tools. The Electrical Laboratory is equipped with Generators and Motors of various types for running tests, as well as Apparatus for experimental work of a more elementary character. The Shops and the Electrical Laboratory each covers from 2,400 to 3,000 square feet of floor space.

In the department of Household Science there are Classes in Cooking and Dressmaking. Classes in Millinery will be added in the near future.

The Drafting Room provides accommodation for fifty pupils in Architectural and Mechanical Drawing.

In the Fall of 1909 the Hamilton Art School, an Institution with a record of over twenty years' successful work, was taken over by the Board of Education and combined with the Technical School. The upper Floor was fitted up specially for the new department, which now teaches almost every branch of fine and applied Art.

As the Technical and Art School is contiguous to the Collegiate Institute, and both institutions are under the control of the Board of Education, the Physics and Chemistry Laboratories of the latter School are open to pupils of the former.

Instruction is provided in both day and evening Classes. The day Classes are composed partly of regular pupils and partly of occasional pupils. The former are chiefly Boys, who intend later to enter industrial life. They devote approximately two-fifths of their time to the study of English, Mathematics and Science, two-fifths to Shop and Laboratory work, and the remaining one-fifth to Mechanical and Freehand Drawing. The occasional pupils, who are drawn principally from the Collegiate Institute and the Commercial classes of the Public Schools, devote part of their time to work in the Technical School, the Boys being taught Woodworking and Iron-working, and the Girls Household Science and Drawing.

The students of the evening Classes are for the most part, (to the extent of over eighty per cent.), engaged in some industrial employment during the day.

The total enrollment in these Classes last year was 385, of whom 253 were men and 132 women. The School is open three evenings a week, from 7.30 to 9.30, for six months. The subjects taught are Mathematics, Physics, Chemistry, Architectural Drawing, Mechanical Drawing, Woodworking, Forging, Machine Shop practice, Electricity, Art, Cooking, and Dressmaking. Printing and Millinery will be added to the list in the near future.

The Staff, under the principalship of Mr. J. G. Witton, is composed of nine full time and six part time Teachers.

Such, in brief, is the first Technical School to be established in the Province of Ontario. That it has a promising field of work is abundantly proved by the evidence taken before the Royal Commission on Industrial Training and Technical Education, at whose Sessions both Employers, Superintendents and Workmen testified to the many advantages to be derived from the instruction of our young Artisans along the lines of their work. As Canadians we are all concerned with the development of the magnificent material resources of our Country, and, therefore, with the efficient industrial training of our young workmen.

The Hamilton Board of Education has initiated an educational movement of prime importance, and its efforts have been warmly commended in high quarters. At the closing Session of the Royal Technical and Industrial Commission in the City of Hamilton, the Chairman, Doctor James W. Robertson, said: " I wish to express my appreciation of Hamilton. We found in this city, for the first time in our travels, a Technical School provided by the people and maintained jointly by them and the Government. We did not find before we came here a School with any account of its mode of conducting classes for young men and women. We appreciate the fact that Hamilton has recognized the need of the people, and has made a successful effort to meet it.

HAMILTON, October 11th, 1910.　　　　　　　　　　　J. G. WITTON, *Principal*.

THE QUEEN'S COLLEGE SCHOOL OF MINING, KINGSTON.

Up to 1893 very little had been done for mining education in Canada. While several Canadian Universities had mining Courses in their Calendars, it cannot be fairly stated that there was anywhere in the Dominion any equipment for that department of engineering education. The School of Mining was founded in that year with a separate Charter and a Board of Governors of its own. The funds at first available were (1) a subscription list of about $35,000, and (2) an annual grant of $5,000 from the Ontario Government. For several Sessions all the departments were housed in Carruthers Hall, but in 1894 there was built the Mining Laboratory, with funds provided by the Government of Ontario. In 1900 the School of Mining had grown to such an extent that, an appeal being made to the Ontario Government, the Legislature voted $112,500 to erect two large buildings (Ontario Hall and Fleming Hall) for the departments of Mineralogy, Geology and Physics, and for Civil, Mechanical and Electrical Engineering.

In 1895, the University constituted its Faculty of Practical Science and built a Mechanical Laboratory which was available for the Students of Mining as well as for those of other branches of Engineering. The two Institutions co-operated informally until the year 1900, when they were amalgamated as the School of

Mining, which then became a College of Applied Science affiliated to the University. The teaching Staff has grown until it now numbers ten Professors, three Associate or Assistant Professors, four Lecturers, and nine Demonstrators, twenty-six in all. Last Session, (1905-6), there were 192 Engineering Students enrolled.

One feature of work of the Mining School is Summer work in Mining Camps, (with a view to stimulate the study of elementary Mineralogy and Geology), also to take part in railway surveys, electrical works, and in machine shops, and thus spend at least part of the Summer holidays. Students have found it to be very useful and interesting, if not stimulating.

In the Report for 1908-09, it is stated that at a recent meeting of the American Institute of Mining Engineers, held in Cobalt, Mr. John Hays Hammond, the Leader among Mining Engineers, said that Canadians need not go outside of Canada for Mining Engineers so long as the Kingston School of Mining was providing such graduates. At the banquet of the Canadian Mining Institute in Montreal recently, Earl Grey gave that School the first place among such Institutions in Canada. In referring in the Legislature to the Grant for buildings, Sir James Whitney said (in part): " I am unable to express in detail the great and lasting advantage that this Institution is to the Province. No appropriation given under the auspices of the Government gives us more satisfaction."

The outlook is encouraging. Canada is growing fast. Increase in population means new Railroads, new Power development, and other Engineering structures requiring the services of Engineers. Development and application of Electrical Power are expanding in importance, and Canada, on account of the amount and wide distribution of Water Power, will lead the world in this, and thus provide employment for large numbers of Civil, Electrical and Mechanical Engineers and for those who take our new course in Power Development. In working up our immense stores of raw material there will be plenty of employment for Metallurgists and Chemists. If we add to all these the work opening up for our Mining Engineers, it is plain that the young Engineer may look forward to a bright career in Canada.

Science Research Scholarships, instituted by Her Majesty's Commissioners for the Exhibition of 1851, have been awarded to a number of Queen's University graduates since 1894.

THE DOMINION SCHOOL OF TELEGRAPHY AND RAILROADING, TORONTO.

The Dominion School of Telegraphy and Railroading, of Toronto, was established in 1900, in order to meet the growing demands of an Institution devoted entirely to Railway Station work. The Course covers instruction in Railroad and Commercial Telegraphy, Freight, Ticket and Baggage work, applicable to Canadian Railways, and specially prepared to meet the immediate demands of the Grand Trunk, Canadian Pacific and Canadian Northern and other Dominion Railways.

The Officials of these Railways were quick to recognize the advantages of an Institution devoted entirely to this work, and the thoroughness in which it was carried on, and to show their appreciation in some tangible way, they supply their regular Report Forms for practical use in the School.

In addition to this, the School has the unique distinction of being the only one with the Grand Trunk and Canadian Northern main line Telegraph wires, which pass into the School for the benefit of giving the Students the practical work.

Mr. Joseph Edward Cassan, President of the School, is the Author and Originator of the "Railroad Agent's Course," and he has the distinction of being the first one to prepare such a Course of Study. He has had a general railroad experience, having spent years with the C.P.R. in the various capacities of Telegrapher, Freight and Ticket Clerk, Cashier and Agent, being employed by the Grand Trunk Railway in Toronto Union Ticket Office, and has had seven years' experience with the largest Technical School in the world.

Specially Prepared Text-Books for Railroad Study.

In order to properly cover the Station work of Canadian Railways it was found necessary to prepare special Instruction Papers, and to this end the President was fortunate in securing the assistance and co-operation of Railway Officials in the different departments. After the work was put into manuscript form, it was then carefully checked over by practical Railway men, so that no information would be given except that which would have a real practical application in every day Railroad routine. The President then personally consulted Railway Officials, and visited the different Stations, in order to secure such information as was necessary to bring the work up to its present standard.

The Mail Department was organized in July, 1908, for the express purpose of teaching branches of the work by correspondence, in order that Students who are unable to attend the Railroading Day School could devote their spare time to this practical course of training. The purpose of the School is to qualify young men as Agents, Telegraphers, Freight and Ticket Clerks and Baggagemen.

The School is situated at 91 Queen Street East, Toronto, not far from the Union Station. Students attend from various parts of Ontario, Manitoba, British Columbia, Nova Scotia, New Brunswick, Quebec, Newfoundland, England, Scotland and the United States.

Instruction is given in the Day and Night School, and also by correspondence. Between 200 and 300 Students are enrolled on an average each year.

The demand for the Students of this School is continuous. They are often called to take positions before they finish their Course.

Arrangements have been made for opening a Class for "First Aid to the Injured," as the Managers of the School feel that many lives may be saved if the Employees first on the scene in cases of accident know just what to do in the emergency.

Toronto, October 6th, 1910.　　　　　　　　　　　　J. E. Cassan, *President.*

THE CANADIAN HOROLOGICAL INSTITUTE, TORONTO.

The Canadian Horological Institute was established by its present Director, Mr. H. R. Playtner, in Toronto in 1890.

It is a Trade School for Watchmakers, the object being to turn out thoroughly competent practical and technically trained workmen, for the Watchmaking and kindred Trades. There are no watch-movement factories in Canada, and the sense in which the word "watchmaking" is used refers more particularly to Watch repairers, but as a first-class watch repairer is able to make any part of a watch the name "Watchmaker" is still used and so held by the trade. Students of good character are admitted either with, or without, previous experience. The Course outlined requires two years continued attendance. There are shorter Courses for those with previous experience. The shortest of these is six months, but experience has shown that all should take the full Course, as previous training was often of a kind which lacked real value.

The students come mostly from all parts of Canada, some come from the various States of the Union, and a few from England and elsewhere. It is a Day School only, open eight hours per day during eleven months each year. Under three broad headings the work of the School consists of:

Lectures, four hours per week.

Technical Drawing, four and one-half hours per week.

Bench Work, thirty-five hours per week.

All three branches of the work are very closely related.

The lectures deal with the natural laws governing Timekeeping mechanisms, their intelligent application in practice, and the mathematical calculations required for the complete calibres of Watches, Chronometers and Clocks.

Mechanical drawings in plan and elevation of the various mechanisms are made from the calculations, as taught at the Lectures.

In Bench Work Students take up the actual repairing of Watches, the Trade send in especially difficult work, and the Students are engaged thereon for the time of thirty-five hours per week.

Especially apt Students construct a complete Watch movement of the highest class, not two being alike, during the second year, from their own plans and calculations, as their masterpieces, which they own when completed. Only those who complete this work can enter for the School's Diploma. From this it follows that not only are the Students fitted as Watch repairers, but they may also hold positions as Bench men, Foremen and Designers in Watch and Clock Factories.

The School is well equipped and occupies its own Building, corner of Church and Wellesley Streets, erected especially for the purpose three years ago.

TORONTO, October 13th, 1910. H. R. PLAYTNER, *Director*.

PROVISION FOR THE PROMOTION OF SCIENCE AND A PROVINCIAL OBSERVATORY.

As early as in 1805, a bill was introduced into the House of Assembly, "For appropriating a certain sum of money for the purchase of Philosophical Apparatus for the use of this Province." This Bill failed to pass at that Session, but it became Law in 1806, and Four hundred pounds ($1,600), were expended in the purchase of the desired Apparatus, and it was placed in charge of the Reverend Doctor Strachan, who used it in illustrating Elementary Science in *The Old Blue School,* and in Popular Lectures.* In 1833, this proceeding of the Legislature, and the reason for it, was introduced to the notice of the House of Assembly in

---

*See the First Volume of the Documentary History of Education in Upper Canada, pages 51, 56 and 132.

the following Resolution, proposed by Mr. Mahlon Burwell, seconded by Mr. Hugh C. Thomson:

Resolved, That, in 1806, the Legislature, to show that something more was even then required than Grammar Schools, passed an Act providing from their limited means a small Apparatus for the instruction of youth in Physical Science, that they might enter the world with something more than a common District (Grammar) School Education.

Among Petitions, which incidentally touched upon subjects of a kindred nature, was one from the York Literary and Philosophical Society (of which Archdeacon Strachan was President, Mr. Thomas Mercer Jones, Secretary, and Mr. James G. Chewett, Curator), presented to the House of Assembly on the 7th of December, 1832, praying for a grant of money:—

To be applied in the appointment of persons duly qualified to investigate, thoroughly and scientifically, the Geology, Mineralogy and General Natural History of the Province, as well as to procure and report every kind of information tending to promote Science, and an acquaintance with the characteristics of the Country, such as the more prominent features of Land and Water, and the capabilities of communication between different parts of the same.

Another Petition was presented to the House of Assembly from the Mechanics' Institute of York in February, 1834. It prayed the House of Assembly to grant it Two hundred pounds ($800), for the purchase of Chemical, Philosophical and Astronomical Apparatus. The grant was not made in either case, however.

In the same month Doctor William Rees—then well-known in Toronto— petitioned the House of Assembly for aid to publish a Work on "The Medical Topography and Climate of North America." As such a work would go far to remove the prejudice, founded on ignorance, that the Climate of British North America is unhealthy. Later he Petitioned the House for a grant for the establishment of a Museum and Zoological Gardens, etcetera.

The Topographical labours of Mr. Joseph Bouchette, in producing Maps of the Country, were recognized by the House of Assembly in February, 1834, and the following Resolution on the subject was passed:

Resolved, That the sum of One hundred and seventy-one pounds, ($684), be granted to enable the Clerk of this House to purchase copies of the Maps and Topographical work of Mr. Joseph Bouchette, Surveyor-General of Lower Canada, for the uses of the Government officer, etcetera.

In addition, the House of Assembly passed Resolutions, on which were founded Addresses to the Lieutenant-Governor, recommending that a copy of the Hudson Bay Company's Charter be obtained, and that an Exploration of the Country north of Lake Huron be made.

On the Petition of Mr. John Harris of Woodhouse,* praying for the establishment of an Observatory, the House of Assembly reported in favour of doing so,† and added:

---

* Mr. Harris here spoken of was a Cousin, by marriage, of the Reverend Doctor Ryerson. In his "Loyalists of America," Volume II., page 228, Doctor Ryerson thus refers to him: Mr. Harris "was an active and scientific Officer in the Royal Navy, having been employed with the late Admirals Bayfield and Owen in the Survey of the Canadian Lakes and Rivers by the Admiralty during the years 1815 to 1817. . . . After a few years' residence in Kingston, Mr. and Mrs. Harris (née Amelia Ryerse), returned to a beautiful homestead on Long Point Bay, (near Mrs. Harris' Father's Home). . . . . Mr. Harris was . . . . selected by the Government of the day to be the recipient of various Government offices. During the years 1837-38 he took an active part in quelling the Rebellion.

† The Toronto Observatory was established in 1839. An account of it is given in this Volume.

And here it is not out of place for your Committee to express their high respect for the scientific attainments of that gentleman, Mr. Harris, and his incessant exertions, since his first coming into the Province, to promote the dissemination of the higher branches of Mathematical knowledge, even at the expense of some great personal sacrifices, and now he gives an example to other scientific men, of which numbers are to be found in the Province, to come forward and express their desire that means may be afforded the youth of Upper Canada to acquire that instruction in Literature and Science which is not denied the youth of any enlightened community whose population is not one-sixth of that of this Colony.

THE MAGNETIC AND METEOROLOGICAL OBSERVATORY, TORONTO.

(*Under the Direction of the Dominion Government.*)

In the year 1838 the British Association for the Advancement of Science, in a Memorial addressed to Her Majesty's Government, solicited their attention to the expediency of extending, by means of fixed Observatories, the researches regarding the geographical distribution of magnetic force to certain stations of prominent magnetic interest within the limits of the British Colonial Dominion.

Canada was named as one of the stations, and a further suggestion was made that the observations should include meteorological as well as magnetical phenomena, and that the stations might be placed under the superintendence of the Master-General and Board of Ordinance.

These suggestions, which were approved by the Royal Society, were acted upon, and Lieutenant Riddell, of the Royal Artillery, was sent out as the officer to take charge of the Canadian Station, with instructions to work under the directions of the Master-General, or Major Edward Sabine, one of the leading spirits in magnetic research of the day, who had charge of the head office for the surveys at Woolwich. He examined several localities, and at last selected Toronto. A grant of two and a half acres of land was offered by the Council of the University of King's College, with the sole condition that the buildings to be erected should not be appropriated to any other purpose than that of an Observatory, and should revert to the College when the Observatory should be discontinued. The sanction of the Governor-General having been obtained, in January, 1840, the building was begun in the spring, and ready for occupation in September. The Observatory is situated in latitude 43′39′25′, and longitude 79′21′30′ W, at a height of 107.9 feet above the level of Lake Ontario, and 342 feet above the level of the sea.

In 1841, on Lieutenant Riddell's return to England, the Observatory was placed in charge of Lieutenant Younghusband, who remained the Director until near the end of 1843, except for a few months during which Lieutenant Lefroy—now General Sir John Henry Lefroy, R.A., F.R.S., etcetera—had charge

He was a resident of Toronto for nine or ten years, in charge of the Royal Observatory. He was then a captain in the Royal Artillery, and ranked high as an eminent meteorological observer. He spent a winter within the Arctic circle collecting information. He became Director-General of the Ordinance, and commandant of the Royal Arsenal at Woolwich. He was for five years Governor of Bermuda, and on leaving there paid a short visit to Toronto in 1884, when the British Association met in Canada. He was afterwards for some time Governor of Tasmania.

During his early stay in Toronto he was instrumental in founding the Canadian Institute, and was one of its earliest presidents, if not its first president. His portrait hangs on the walls of the Institute.

His career was distinguished by high scientific attainment and excellent administrative ability. He will be long remembered by those who knew him as a faithful friend, an intellectual companion, and a pure-minded Christian gentleman. His first commission was in December, 1834; Lieutenant-Colonel September, 1855, and Colonel February, 1865. His son, Mr. A. Fraser Lefroy, is a member of the Toronto bar.

Sir John Beverley Robinson, speaking in the Canadian Institute upon the occasion of Captain Lefroy's departure from Toronto, conveyed a well expressed and accurate summary of his character. The Chief Justice said:—

It is not merely that his familiarity with rather a wide range of scientific subjects qualified him for taking much more than an ordinary part in the proceedings of the Institute, but his eager thirst for knowledge, his ardent devotion to the interests of science, his indefatigable industry, his strong religious sense of the obligation which we all lie under to the common family of mankind; and, as much as all these, his hopeful turn of mind, which made it always difficult for him to believe that anything would be found impracticable by which great public good might be attained; these all made him an invaluable fellow-worker with you, especially in laying the foundation for your future system of proceeding. Some portion of his spirit inevitably communicated itself to those with whom he was associated, and thoroughly unselfish and disinterested as he was seen to be in all his aims, he proved to be an efficient applicant on behalf of the association whenever an occasion offered, being a suitor whom all were reluctant to disappoint and all willing to oblige.

Sir Henry Lefroy was the last of these warrior scientists in charge of the Observatory. The first civil Director was Professor Cherriman, and he was followed by Mr. Kingston, who in turn was succeeded by Mr. Charles Carpmael. Mr. R. F. Stupart is the present Director of the Observatory.

In the year 1850, the Chief Superintendent of Education, the Reverend Doctor Ryerson, at the suggestion of Colonel Lefroy, R.A., submitted to the Government a plan for the establishment of meteorological stations throughout what was then known as Upper Canada, at every Senior County Grammar School.

The Duties of the Observatory Service.

The duties of the service are:

1. To collect trustworthy statistics and to see to their arrangement in forms convenient for application to the solution of either strictly climatic questions or of other questions into which the climatic enters as an element.

2. To exercise by visitation and correspondence a general supervision over all Meteorological Stations that receive any aid from the Government, as well as other private Observers who may place themselves in connection with it.

3. To advise Observers in the selection of their instruments and the method of observation; to issue the necessary forms, and to determine the time for reporting.

4. To receive and compile Meteorological returns and to publish them or deduct from them from time to time.

5. To receive Telegraphic Weather Reports from Telegraph Stations and to despatch to various points by wire Probabilities founded thereon.

Time is also exchanged at regular intervals between the other Observatories and Toronto. Clock and Chronometer comparisons and Transit Observations having been sent in they are examined and correct time is furnished to the City and to Railway and Telegraph companies.

Instruments in Toronto Observatory.

The Telescope is fixed in the dome chamber, which is 18 feet in diameter, on a stone pedestal 48 feet in height, six feet in diameter at the basement and three feet at the apex. This block af masonry is protected from the bottom to the top of the building by a wooden framework, which shields it from external pressure and prevents any possible vibration, or oscillation. The mounting is a monument of ingenuity and skill. It is on the German or Frauschofer's system. The axis instead of being vertical is inclined to the horizon at such an angle that it points to the Pole. The Telescope is attached to a pivot, which turns on the polar axis and is so adjusted as to be at right angles to it. It thus moves in a plane parallel to the axis, and sweeps along the Meridian. A graduated circle is affixed to the lower end of the axis, and serves to give the right ascension and declination of any object, the graduations on it reading from one to twenty-four hours. A dividing Clock regulated to keep sidereal time forms part of the mechanism. There is no difficulty in the matter of adjustment, and, once fixed, the telescope remains constantly directed to the object without any alteration. Its Object Glass is six inches in diameter and its focal length eight feet, but the surface of the lens can be decreased at the will of the observer by what is known as the "pack of cards" motion. The Telescope is furnished with a Spectroscopic attachment and Micrometer. It is a beautifully balanced instrument, fully equipped with all modern appliances.

The Transit Instrument is quite effective for its purpose. By means of a single observation with this Instrument the place of any Star can be fixed—its polar distance, declination and right ascension. It is by observations such as may be made with this Telescope that the places of all the Stars have been noted and catalogues compiled giving their true positions. In the eye-piece of the Telescope there are nine equidistant parallel wires, and, by noting the time of the star passing over each and taking the mean, the true time can be taken more exactly than by one observation taken singly. The axis of the instrument is at right angles to the Meridian, and the tube points to a great circle passing through the North Pole. Much care has to be exercised in placing the instrument so that the Star can be observed as it crosses the Meridian. The time occupied in its transit is registered by means of an electric current in the clock-room. The afternoon was cloudless, but there was a haze over the sky. The sun shone brightly. Reference to the chart showed that the Star Orionus E. would then pass the Meridian at an altitude of 45.05. It was a Star of the second magnitude and might, or might not, be visible, I was told, to the inexperienced eye. The Telescope, however, clearly revealed its path. Like a ball of fire set on wheels of flame, it rolled at a terrific pace over the wires and disappeared from view.

In the Transit department are two clocks with electric attachment, and by means of them a daily record is kept of rate and error. One Clock gives the Sidereal time and the other the Mean time. The registration is performed by means of a Chromograph operating on a cylinder driven at a uniform rate of speed. The Stylographic Pen is carried on armatures and rests upon the paper which covers the Cylinder. The electric contact with each Clock is made by means of a small steel disc attached to the Pendulum, which rolls over an agate plain, kept entirely free from friction. Every second of time is marked by the electric current. Among the other furnishings of the Transit Room is a Star Chart—the Stars set in altitude for every hour of the twenty-four.

There are also instruments in the Meteorological and Magnetic departments of the Building. One of the most wonderful is the Thermograph, an Instrument for recording automatically the variations in the Temperature. In the results obtained by its means air, light, reflecting mirrors and mercury play a part. The Magnetic Room is a fine, airy chamber. It is fitted up with instruments for measuring horizontal and vertical force—inclinators and declinators—Magnets of the most sensitive character, one being hung by a fibre of raw silk. The "Bifilar Suspension" and the "Torson Balance" are amongst the terms that are used in description. These terms indicate differences in the construction of instruments employed to measure the intensity of Terrestrial Magnetism. The "eye readings" are taken from these instruments at 6 and 8 a.m. and at 2, 4, 10 and 12 p.m. daily. The process of the mapping of the lines of force in the magnetic field surrounding the earth is not easy to understand or to explain. The direction of magnetic force at any place is known when the declination and inclination have been measured by means of the Declinometer and Dipping Needle. The total force with which a unit Magnetic Pole would be moved along a line of terrestrial magnetic force may be resolved into a horizontal and vertical component. When the horizontal component of the force and the Dip are measured at a place the total force may be calculated, for it is equal to the horizontal force divided by the Cosine of the Dip. To determine the horizontal component an ordinary Declination Needle is allowed to oscillate about its position of rest. On counting the number of oscillations per second at different places the Observer is able to calculate the relative amounts of the horizontal force, just as the rates of the vibration of a Pendulum at different places determine the relative amounts of the force of gravity. Thus are what are called the Magnetic elements of the place calculated, and these, it may be stated, are found to vary considerably. The barometer naturally takes an important place among the instruments, but the method by which it measures the weight of air and the variations of its pressure is known to everybody. Down in the basement, the magnetographs are kept. They register by photography the variations in the terrestrial magnetic elements. They are removed as far as possible from violent fluctuations of temperature, and nobody is allowed to approach them with an umbrella or pocket-knife, for these would disturb the sensitive parts of the instruments.

THE PRACTICAL DAILY WORK OF THE TORONTO MAGNETICAL OBSERVATORY.

Mr. R. F. Stupart, the Director of the Observatory, and his Staff of eighteen assistants, receive the Weather Reports from 312 Observation Stations scattered throughout the whole Dominion, and from 36 stations in the United States, map out the varying conditions of storm, or sunshine, on the daily Weather Map, diagnose the situation generally, and prophesy what the next 36 hours will bring forth, meteorologically, in all the Provinces of Canada. It shows the care and knowledge required in making the diagnosis, that in the whole history of the Observatory there is not to be found two of these daily maps exactly alike. Every morning and every evening present new problems for solution. Winds are moving in different directions in different parts of the country; the areas of high and low pressure are never

PART XV.   PROVINCIAL METEOROLOGICAL OBSERVATORY, TORONTO.   393

exactly the same at the same hour on different days; where there was rain here yesterday, it is sunshine to-day. Hence the " clerk of the weather " cannot work by routine and precedent. He must bring into play his theories of " cause and effect"; analyze wind movements, temperatures, high and low pressures, and, partly by science and experience, partly by pure guess work, predict what is going to happen next. Hence the man who blames " Old Probs " for the few mistakes he makes is decidedly inconsiderate. As a matter of fact, our local weather predictions are right nine times out of ten—and in the tenth instance they are usually partly right.

The Observing Stations.

Each of the Observing Stations throughout the Dominion is equipped with a Mecurial Barometer, two Thermometers (a maximum and a minimum Thermometer), an Anemometer to measure the velocity of the wind, a Wind Vane and a Rain Gauge. From 234 of these Stations the Reports are sent in voluntarily. At 40 of the Stations, mostly in the Territories and in the Gulf of St. Lawrence district, small gratuities are given. At the other stations a regular salaried Official makes his daily observations at stated intervals and telegraphs daily, in code, the weather particulars to headquarters.

Here is a sample of one of the despatches received: " Toronto tureen lushburg sacrum essence weeping currency charade." Not very intelligible is it? But to Mr. Stupart it announces that the Barometer reads 90 minutes, the temperature 74 Degrees, one-tenth inch of rain has fallen, the weather is fair, the Wind northwest, the Wet Bulb Thermometer reads 70 degrees, etcetera.

These Reports are filed from the Telegraph Offices at 8 a.m. and 8 p.m. every day, 75th meridian time. By 8.30 a.m. all Reports from the Atlantic to the Pacific have been received at the local Observatory. At 9 o'clock, the United States Reports are received via Buffalo. The Weather Map is immediately made out, and, after a careful study of the Chart, the " probabilities " for the next 36 hours in the various Provinces are printed. These " probabilities " are ready by 10 a.m. The Telegraph wires quickly transmit the results of the local diagnosis back to the various Stations, and by noon the Dominion knows what sort of Weather to expect up to eight o'clock on the evening of the following day. Reports are also sent to various United States points. Some 85 Weather Charts are also sent to the local newspaper offices, the Board of Trade and other places in Toronto where they may be seen by the public.

The Storm Signals.

If a storm is brewing on the Lakes, or on the Atlantic, or Pacific, Storm Signals are sent out. At the various Harbour Ports Mariners may know by looking at the Signal Mast whether there is peril on the deep that day or not. Drums and Cones are the Signals used. The Cone displayed alone means a moderate gale; the Drum and Cone mean a heavy gale; the peak of the Cone downward means a southerly, or easterly, Wind; the peak of the Cone upwards means northerly or westerly Winds.

The Official Time-Keeper.

Another function of the Meterological Office is to regulate the Watches and clocks of the Dominion. At exactly 11.55 a.m. every day the Fire Hall Clocks in Toronto are rung by electrical communication with the Observatory. At noon daily comparisons are made with Montreal, and residents of Quebec and St. John know by the dropping of the time balls that it is 12 o'clock, noon. At Vancouver and Ottawa a gun is fired. r

Practical Uses of the Reports.

In Toronto alone the Observatory 'phone is kept busy all day with queries from business men and others who wish to know how the Weather is going to affect their plans. Fruit dealers, especially, are constantly ringing up during the Fruit Season for weather information to guide them in making shipments. Live stock men often postpone their shipments on the strength of unfavourable weather predictions. Steamship companies are largely guided by the " probs" in stocking their commissariat department.

Some Weather Facts.

A few facts may be noted as regards general Weather conditions which affect us here. Storms usually come to Toronto from the south, or southwest. Atmospheric movements are generally from the west to east. The low pressure being in the west, or southwest, the wind consequently sets in from the east, or northeast. Hence an easterly wind is usually the precursor of Storm. Inversely, a west wind usually denotes that the area of low pressure is receding and Fair Weather is coming.

The rings around the Moon, contrary to general supposition, are not at all reliable indications of rain, or snow. There is, however, some ground for the popular belief. These rings usually denote the formation of a certain kind of clouds which frequently produce rain, but cannot always be relied upon to do so.

In Mr. Stupart's opinion, sun spots have more to do with our weather conditions than have the rings around the moon.

Snowless Christmases.

The official records show some curious facts about our local weather. It is a peculiar fact that only once in eighteen consecutive years have the sleighs been running in Toronto on Christmas Day. On the whole, the local weather Experts believe that the settled parts of Canada, and especially Ontario, lead nearly all the other countries in the general average of fine, sunshiny, healthful weather.

Curious Contrivances of Observers.

Most people are ignorant as to just how the weather Observers note the changes of weather, the varying temperatures, the amount of rainfall, barometric pressure, etcetera. They do not have to keep vigil all night and all day marking down the risings and the fallings of the mercury. Photography, electricity and various mechanical devices do the work instead. Man only does the brain work and compiles the statistics. The velocity of the wind, the temperature, the humidity, earthquakes and nearly all other regular meteorological phenomena are marked down on paper, as they occur, by means of the various instruments in the Observatory.

The Thermogram, for instance, makes an exact diagram of the temperature and humidity, and gives, so to speak, a photograph of how hot and how cold and how damp the weather is. It is one of the most interesting Instruments at the Observatory. An upper black irregular line marks the variation of the Mercury in the Dry Bulb Thermometer; a lower irregular line marks the variation of the Mercury in the

Wet Bulb Thermometer, i.e., the Thermometer kept at a constant degree of humidity. Consequently the space between the lines marks the varying humidity. As the Mercury in the two Thermometers rises and falls light filtered through an Air Bulb falls on to a slowly revolving film of bromide paper, thus taking a sort of moving picture of the day's progress of the Mercury. These films are developed each day and furnish an exact record for statistical purposes.

Photographing an Earthquake.

The seismograph is an Earthquake recorder. It may be news to most people that on the average about eleven earthquakes per month in one year were recorded in Toronto. Since the local instrument was established in September, 1897, there have been 469 earth tremors recorded. Every earthquake in any part of the globe sends out its ripples similarly as a stone thrown into water sends out ever-widening ripples. And it takes only a score or so of seconds for these ripples to travel all around the globe and be recorded by every Seismograph doing business. The apparatus is somewhat complicated. In brief, it consists of a thin steel boom affixed at one end to a stone Shaft sunk into the earth, and with the other end suspended by a silk cord. The slightest tremor of the earth vibrates the boom and these vibrations are photographed much after the same principle as is applied to the thermogram. The filtered light upon the photographic film is interrupted by the vibrating disk on the end of the Boom, thus marking the irregular shadings in the photograph.

In connection with the Observatory in Queen's Park there is also a magnetic observatory at Agincourt, a few miles out of the city. There all local magnetic disturbances are noted, and from the statistics recorded local compasses are properly adjusted. When the Observatory was first installed the Compass Needle pointed 1 degree west of north. Now it points 5 degrees west of north. At Victoria, B.C., it points 25 degrees east of north.—*Compiled from the Toronto News Report.*

THE OTTAWA OBSERVATORY.

The Observatory, which has been established at Ottawa, was placed in charge of Doctor W. F. King as Astronomer Royal. It does good service.

The Observatory is intended to be for Canada what Greenwich is to Great Britain, Paris to France, and Berlin to Germany—the initial Meridian to which all future Longitude determination in Canada will be referred. The Zero Meridian for the world is by international agreement Greenwich. One of the immediate practical functions of the Observatory will be the determination of the exact geographical position of various points throughout the Dominion to which the various surveys may be joined and the country properly delineated. It will also furnish accurate standard time to all parts of the Dominion. Amongst the more specially scientific works to be carried on will be Pendulum observations for the determination of the forces of Gravitation, and the figure of the Earth, a work of international interest and importance.

Magnetic Observations.

Then there will be systematic Magnetic Observations distributed over Canada and the elements determined of the magnetic force, upon which depends the navigation of the Seas and Lakes and much exploratory work.

By means of the great Telescope worlds beyond ours will be studied; the Stellar Universe and depths will be sounded; the Stars will be made to reveal their nature, and of what they are composed, whither they are drifting and what is their stage of evolution.

An Equatorial Telescope 19½ feet long, with a lens of 15 inches diameter, has been installed in the Ottawa Observatory, the foundations of the Telescope extending from the lowest point in the Building. By an ingenious clock-work arrangement the Telescope moves with the revolution of the Earth, so that the particular Planet, or Star, which may be in the field of the Telescope for the time being remains there.

THE ROYAL ASTRONOMICAL SOCIETY OF CANADA, TORONTO

In 1884 Mr. Andrew Elvins, with two or three others, founded the Astronomical and Physical Society of Toronto, which six years later became an incorporated Society. The objects of the Society were: (a) To advance and popularise in Canada the study of Astronomy and cosmical physics; (b) to diffuse a practical knowledge of these branches of Science; and (c) to acquire real and personal property, mainly for these objects, including a Library and Instruments.

In 1900 the name was changed to the Toronto Astronomical Society, but the objects remained the same.

In response to a Memorial dated the seventh of January, 1903, addressed to the Governor-General, permission was granted, by His Majesty the King, to the Society to adopt the title the Royal Astronomical Society of Canada.

In 1898 accommodation was obtained in the Canadian Institute Buildings on Richmond Street East. When the Canadian Institute moved to College Street, the Society accompanied it, where it still remains.

In 1908 a new Constitution was adopted. The distinguishing feature of the new order of things was the provision for the organization of meetings outside of Toronto. Article VII. reads as follows:

"When, at any Centre, a sufficient number of Members of the Society desire to organize regular meetings, the Council may by Resolution authorize such meetings. These shall be known as meetings of the Royal Astronomical Society of Canada, and shall be under the control of the Council, which shall make an annual appropriation to defray the cost thereof."

Under this provision flourishing centres have been established at Ottawa, Peterborough, Hamilton and Regina.

The Society is open to all who are interested in Astronomy or Astronomical Physics, and the annual fee is $2.00. The membership is now about 500.

The first volume of Transactions was published in 1890; and the publication of yearly volumes continued until in 1907, when the *Journal of the Royal Astronomical Society of Canada* was begun. It is an illustrated bi-monthly Magazine, containing papers presented at the Society's Meetings, notes of observation, and work in progress at the Dominion Astronomical Observatory, Ottawa, and in the Meteorological Service, as well as other interesting features. It is sent to the members and to practically all the learned societies, observatories and important libraries in the world.

TORONTO, October, 1910. J. R. COLLINS, *Secretary.*

CONSERVATORIES AND COLLEGES OF MUSIC.

The Toronto Conservatory of Music.

Among educational Institutions of Ontario the Toronto Conservatory of Music takes a high place. It was established in 1886, and is now one of the leading Schools of Music. Prior to the year 1886 Doctor Edward Fisher, who had been a resident of Canada for ten years, brought forward a comprehensive scheme, which resulted in the establishment of the institution known as the Toronto Conservatory of Music, which is the pioneer Institution of its kind in Canada. Doctor Fisher, by reason of his reputation as a Musician, was able to interest the best class of citizens in his project, and from the incorporation of the Conservatory, in November, 1886, until the present time, the progress of the Institution has been most satisfactory. In September, 1887, the School opened with an attendance of about two hundred pupils. Success at once crowned the efforts of the Directorate, and for ten years the growth of interest on the part of the public and the yearly increasing number of students became very noted.

In 1897, a Site was purchased, and suitable Buildings were erected at the corner of College Street and University Avenue. In less than ten years again, the purchase was made by the Conservatory of a large brick Residence to the West of the Main Building. Other additions were also made from time to time, including a Residence for young lady Students. The Music Hall, furnished with a fine modern Organ and seating about six hundred people, is one of the most popular and artistic recital halls in Canada. Throughout all these buildings are found to-day the most modern and complete appliances that can be brought together to ensure the comfort, health and pleasure of both Teachers and Students.

It became affiliated with Trinity University in 1888, and also in 1896 with the University of Toronto. The Degrees of Bachelor and Doctor of Music are attainable by passing the prescribed Examinations as set forth in the Calendar of the University. Its Curriculum requirements are on a high plane and the Faculty includes many noted Musicians and Specialists in the art, from Europe and the United States, as well as Canada. In addition to the Voice, Piano, Organ and Theory, all orchestral instruments are taught and free Scholarships are annually offered in various branches of Orchestral work. In 1898, the Conservatory adopted the plan of holding outside Examinations in local centres throughout Canada, which has resulted in a commendable impetus in this direction, the Examiners being leading Members of the Faculty, and the standard of the Local Examinations being the same in every respect as that of the Toronto Examinations. At the present time there exist eighty-nine of these Local Centres, twenty of which are in the North-West Provinces. The Faculty has increased to the large number of one hundred and nine. The number of Students during the past year was upward of eighteen hundred, drawn from various parts of the Dominion and from other Countries. Two years ago the Conservatory formed a much-needed Alumni Association, which includes graduates and former pupils. The Teachers' Course and Post-Graduate Course for Artists are both widely in demand, so highly esteemed is the training received at the hands of the talented Instructors who compose the Faculty.

The position achieved by the Toronto Conservatory of Music is one calculated to awaken sentiments of patriotism and admiration among loyal Canadians who may confidently point to this home institution offering a thorough and artistic musical education. Many causes have contributed to such success, but there is no doubt that thanks are due mainly to the genius and discernment of its Founder and present Musical Director, Doctor Edward Fisher; to the earnest co-operation of the many eminent Instructors on its teaching Staff, and also to the enterprise and public spirit of the gentlemen comprising the Board of Governors of the institution, whose names are as follows: Sir John Alexander Boyd, K.C.M.G., President; Doctor J. A. Macdonald, 1st Vice-President; W. K. George, Esq., 2nd Vice-President; Messieurs James Henderson, D.C.L., E. A. Scadding, W. R. Wadsworth, George Edward Sears, Elmes Henderson, Herbert C. Cox, W. P. Gundy and G. T. Somers.

TORONTO, October, 1910.   *Communicated and Condensed.*

THE TORONTO COLLEGE OF MUSIC.
IN AFFILIATION WITH THE UNIVERSITY OF TORONTO.

The Toronto College of Music was founded by Doctor F. H. Torrington in 1888, incorporated by the Legislature in 1890. The first Musical Institution recognized by affiliation with the University of Toronto, the Toronto College of Music has from its inception proved to be an effective agency for Musical development in the Dominion.

Graduates of the Toronto College of Music are afforded the highest advantages of the University of Toronto, being exempt from all the University Examinations in Music except the third, or final, when qualifying for the Degree of Bachelor of Music. The faculty of the Toronto College of Music are thorough musicians, and the teaching representative of the best methods of Germany, France, Italy, England and the United States.

The equipment of the College is complete in every department; the three Manual Organ in the Concert Hall for practice, the Choir and Oratorio Chorus training under Doctor Torrington's personal direction, affording vocal and instrumental Graduates opportunities for public introduction in both Oratorio and Concert work. No means are neglected which will further the musical education of Students, and the advanced work of the College is shown in the character of the Programmes presented at the Recitals given in the College Hall, and in the numbers played with full orchestral accmpaniment at the Annual Concert in Massey Hall.

The College is situated on Pembroke Street (just above Shuter Street), on one of the most attractive residential streets in Toronto; quiet, beautifully shaded, and leading directly to the Allan Gardens.

To Doctor Torrington is due the establishing of Musical Festivals in Toronto. At the first of these, given in June, 1886, with one thousand voices in the Chorus and one hundred Performers in the Orchestra, he conducted the great Oratorios *Israel in Egypt* (Handel), *Mors et Vita* (Gounod), and miscellaneous Programmes. This Festival was very successful, and had a lasting influence on the musical life of the city, a variety of musical organizations resulting therefrom, one in particular being the Toronto College of Music.

The College Course of Training.

The object of the Toronto College of Music being to educate the Student upon a well regulated and scientific plan, the study of Music has been divided into the following courses: Kindergarten Music; Primary; First (Junior and Senior); Second; Third, or Graduate; Post-Graduate.

Kindergarten Teachers' Course: Lectures and demonstrations under Miss Westman's personal supervision are given in the College, and cover a period of five weeks. On completion of this Course a Teacher's Certificate can be obtained which makes the holder a Kindergarten Graduate of the Toronto College of Music (K.G.T.Coll.M.).

Teachers from out of Town can arrange to take this course by correspondence.

Primary: This Course is intended to impart a technical training from the first stages, the Teachers in this grade being thoroughly qualified for their work. Students may enter at the earliest age, and the foundation then laid ensures correctness of technique and style.

An examination is held covering the Primary work, which leads to the three higher grade examinations of the College Course, and Students, in Pianoforte, are strongly advised by the Musical Director to try this examination before entering for the First.

First (Junior and Senior) Second and Third: Students are guided through a Systematic Course of Study, and prepared for professional work both as Teachers and Artists.

The College Graduate Course covers a period of at least three years. The second Piano Examination has been divided into Junior and Senior Grades. Pupils are graded according to proficiency upon entering, and may complete the Course in less than the specified time.

The Post-Graduate Course is intended to provide for the study of music in its higher branches, and to prepare Students for professional work.

Normal Training of a practical nature is provided—" Method of Teaching," " Harmony at the Keyboard," " Accompanying," " Solfege," " Choir and Chorus Training."

Testimonials are awarded to Candidates who pass examinations in the several subjects leading up to Teacher's Certificates, and the different Diplomas.

Testimonials for examinations passed in other recognized Musical Institutions covering the same work will be accepted by the College in lieu of first, second or third year in the several subjects.

" Teachers' Certificates in Piano " are granted to Students who pass the Three Practical Examinations, as outlined in the College Syllabus, Senior Rudiments, First and Second Theory and Normal Training.

" Teachers' Certificates in Organ " are granted to Students who pass the Three Practical Examinations (Honours being necessary at the Third Examination), as outlined in the College Syllabus, Senior Rudiments, First and Second Theory and Normal Training.

" Teachers' Certificates in Vocal " are granted to Students who pass the Three Practical Examinations, as outlined in the College Syllabus, Senior Rudiments, First Theory, and Normal Training.

Certificates in Violin, Violoncello, or in any other Orchestral Instrument, will be granted to Students who pass the Three Practical Examinations, as outlined in the College Syllabus, Senior Rudiments, First Theory and Normal Training.

Piano Diplomas are granted to Candidates who pass the Senior Rudiments, First Theory (First History, First Written Harmony, First Piano Harmony), and the Three (Course) Piano Examinations (First-Class Honours being necessary at the Third Examination); after they have given a Public Recital and played a Concerto with full orchestral accompaniment. Candidates for Diplomas must obtain First-Class Honours in the Third Piano Examination before giving graduating recital.

Candidates for Piano Diploma are required to attend the Toronto College of Music for at least one month before playing with the Orchestra.

The playing for this Diploma must be up to the standard set by the College, and played under the personal direction of the Musical Director.

Candidates preparing Concertos to be played with orchestral accompaniment must send in the name of their Concerto to the Secretary by November 15th. The charge for orchestral parts, when supplied by the College, is two dollars ($2.00).

Vocal Diplomas are granted to candidates who pass the Senior Rudiments, First Theory (First History, First Written Harmony, First Piano Harmony), and Three (Course) Vocal Examinations (First Class Honors being necessary at the Third Examination); after they have given a Public Recital and sung a selection with full orchestral accompaniment.

The programme for the Recital and the selection to be sung with orchestral accompaniment must be up to the standard set by the College, and sung under the personal direction of the Musical Director. The charge for orchestral parts, when supplied by the College, is two dollars ($2.00).

Theory Diplomas are granted to Candidates who pass the Three Theory Examinations (First, Second and Third, Written Harmony, First and Second History, and Piano Harmony, First and Second Counterpoint, Canon and Fugue, Instrumentation, Elementary Acoustics, Musical Form and Analysis); after they have given proof of their practical knowledge of the piano, organ or some orchestral instrument.

Organ and Violin Diplomas, or Diplomas for other instruments, are granted to Candidates who pass the Three (Course) Examinations in the Practical Work (First Class Honors being necessary at the Third Examination), Senior Rudiments, and First Theory.

College Diplomas are granted to Candidates who pass the required Examinations in Vocal, or Instrumental, work, in addition to the Three Examinations in Theory; and after they have given, under the Musical Director, a Public Recital and a Selection with orchestral accompaniment, which must be up to the standard set by the College.

Candidates winning this Diploma are entitled to use the letters F.T.Coll.M. —Fellow Toronto College of Music.

Artists' Diplomas (Post-Grad.): Candidates for the Post-Graduate examination must attend the College for at least one year while preparing their work. They must hold a Diploma of the College (or its equivalent from a recognized Musical Institution), and the Second Theory Testimonial. Candidates will be required to give two Public Recitals of Compositions selected from, or equal in difficulty to, the lists given in the Syllabus. Each Programme must be entirely different from the other, and of sufficient length to occupy not less than one hour in performance. The programmes must be submitted for approval one month before the Recital. Programmes submitted and accepted by the College must not be changed.

Graduating Recitals: Candidates intending to give Graduating Recitals may send in their names and submit their Programmes after November 2nd, but not later than April 4th, in order to have their Recitals arranged. All Recitals must be given before May 13th. Programmes submitted and accepted by the College must not be changed.

Ensemble Work: Ensemble playing (two or more pianos with orchestral accompaniment) under Doctor Torrington's direction, is a great advantage to students who desire to take up the study of "Chamber Music" of the classical and modern composers, in order to attain a higher standing as Pianists.

The Degree of Bachelor of Music (Mus. Bac.) and Doctor of Music (Mus. Doc.) will be conferred by the University of Toronto upon Students of Music who comply with the requirements of the Curriculum in Music which is from time to time prescribed by the University Senate.

The Toronto College of Music Testimonials for First and Second Year Theory will be accepted *pro tanto,* by the University in lieu of their First Year Examinations, for Degree (Mus. Bac.).

The Toronto College of Music Diploma, awarded to Students who pass the Practical and Theoretical Examinations, will be accepted *pro tanto* by the University, in lieu of their First and Second Year Examinations, for Degree (Mus. Doc.).

Medals: The Toronto College of Music Gold Medal for Piano is awarded to the Student who has the highest all round standing upon completion of the College Course, practical and theoretical. The Torrington Gold Medal for Piano is awarded for excellence in piano playing. The Toronto College of Music Gold Medal for Voice is awarded to the Student who obtains the highest all-round standing in the Vocal course and pre-eminence in Solo singing. The Torrington Gold Medal for Voice is awarded for excellence in Solo singing.

Scholarships: The Heintzman and Company Scholarship for Piano (value $50.00) is competed for annually by Students of the College. The Mason and Risch Scholarship for Piano (value $50.00) is competed for annually by Students of the College. Neither of these Scholarships is awarded *twice* to the same Student, and no student can hold both at the same time. A number of Partial Scholarships are from time to time granted to talented Students in all grades, and the conditions governing these Scholarships are that the Student winning the Scholarship shall continue his, or her, studies for at least one year, taking not less than one full hour lesson a week for forty weeks, and no Student may hold more than one Scholarship at the same time.

Cash Prizes for Composition: A cash prize of $10 is offered for a Composition which may take the form of a Scherzo, Minuet, March, or Polonaise, written either for Piano, or Organ, or a Song with Organ, or Piano, accompaniment

This Composition may be performed at a public Concert of the College. A Cash Prize of $25 is offered for a Composition for chorus and orchestra (similar in form to "Spring's Message"—Gade), or Overture for full orchestra. This composition may be performed at a public Concert of the College.

Examinations: Examinations covering the practical work and Rudiments are held twice a year. The first of these Examinations at the end of the second College Term, in February; and the second Examination at the end of the fourth Term, in June. First, Second and Third Theory Examinations are held in June only.

The College Library contains a large collection of Books relating to the subject of Music in all of its forms.

The Toronto College of Music provides, for students of Music, a comprehensive system of instruction, giving them a thorough technique, and leading them to an artistic performance of the works of the best Schools of Pianoforte Music.

Recitals in which all College pupils may take part are given in the College Hall, on Saturday afternoons, before the pupils and their friends, and the Musical Director gives particular attention to the Recitals by the Junior pupils. From these Recitals are drawn the students who take part in the public Evening Recitals, held also at the College, and the more talented instrumental and vocal students are chosen from these for concert work in public halls.

An important part of the College training is the advanced work of the graduate pupils—Chamber Music: Piano and Strings, Concerto playing, with full orchestral accompaniment. Choir training, including Solo Singing, under the personal direction of Doctor Torrington, and public performance at the College Concerts before large audiences.

TORONTO, October 6th, 1910.   *Communicated and Condensed.*

THE LONDON CONSERVATORY OF MUSIC AND SCHOOL OF ELOCUTION.

The London Conservatory of Music and School of Elocution was founded by Mr. Cavan Barron, after his return from Leipzig in 1892.

Besides the Conservatory proper, branches have been started in various parts of the City. These branches are governed by the same Rules and Regulations as the Conservatory, and are under the guidance and direction of capable Teachers. The departments of inspection embrace all Instruments usually taught in Musical Institutions, as well as Vocal training and all Musical Theoretical subjects.

The School of Elocution is in charge of a graduate of the Leland Powers School, Boston.

The Conservatory of Music has many free advantages to its students. Lectures, Recitals, Vocal and Orchestral Practices are being arranged continually throughout the year, for the benefit of Students. Several medals and valuable scholarships are offered, to be competed for every year. In 1909 Mr. Barron retired from the Conservatory, and the work has since been carried on by Mr. F. Linforth Willgoose, a Musician of repute and a Musical Bachelor of Durham University, England. He is, like his predecessor, a Graduate of the Leipzig Conservatory. Under his direction the London Conservatory of Music has maintained steady growth, begun under the guidance of Mr. Barron, and from present indications a prosperous future is promised for this the most Western of the large musical institutions of Ontario.

LONDON, October, 1910. *Communicated.*

ONTARIO SOCIETY OF ARTISTS.

The Ontario Society of Artists is the oldest Art Society in the Province, being instituted in the year 1872. From its Members, and with their advice, the Duke of Argyle and Her Royal Highness Princess Louise, founded the Royal Canadian Academy. This Society in the early days conducted the Art Union and founded the Ontario Art School. The officers are: Mr. E. Wyley Grier, President; Mr. C. W. Jefferys, Vice-President; Mr. Robert F. Gagen, Secretary.

The Annual Exhibition of new works is held during the month of March, and under the Canadian National Exhibition Association this Society manages the Fine Arts Department.

One of the earliest objects of the Society was the establishment of an Art Museum for Toronto, and largely through its efforts is due the present Association, which has now every prospect of founding that much needed Institution.

The Graphic Arts Club and Toronto Society of Applied Art are both doing good work, and together manage those branches of Art at the Canadian National Exhibition.

TORONTO, October 6th, 1910. *Communicated and Condensed.*

ART SCHOOLS.

CENTRAL ONTARIO SCHOOL OF ART AND DESIGN.

The Government Art School in Toronto is the Central Ontario School of Art and Design, established under its present title in 1891. It has opened for the present year at Number One, College Street.

The principal Classes are for Painting, Drawing from the Antique and from Life, Drawing for Reproductive Purposes and from Life, Design, under highly competent Instructors.

The School year consists of three Terms of Ten weeks each. During the last year there were 126 Students in attendance.

TORONTO, October, 1910. *Communicated.*

OTHER ART SCHOOLS.

Other Art Schools are affiliated with the Ontario School of Art, Toronto. The following Art Schools have been established:—The London Art School, 1878; The Ottawa Art School, 1879; The Kingston Art School, 1884; The Hamilton Art School, 1886.

Every Art School incorporated under an Act of Parliament, and complying with the Regulations of the Education Department respecting the Equipment, Accommodation and Teachers required for Art Schools, shall be entitled to receive out of any moneys appropriated by the Legislative Assembly for Art purposes a fixed grant, and such additional sums for proficiency in Art studies as may be determined by the Regulations of the Education Department respecting final examinations.

By an Act passed in 1885, the Education Department was empowered to make Regulations for the organization and management of local Art Schools; to prescribe a Curriculum of Studies for such Schools, and, on examination, award Certificates valid in any Municipality in the Province.

COURSES OF STUDY FOR COMMERCIAL AND ART SPECIALISTS.

(Prescribed by the Education Department.)

Any person who passes the examination in the subjects set forth in Courses for Commercial and Art Specialists, and who is holder of a High School Assistant's Certificate, shall be entitled to an Interim Commercial, or Art Specialist's, Certificate.

COMMERCIAL COURSE.

Theoretical Book-keeping: Single and double entry; general merchandising, commission business, and the various forms of books necessary for the different kinds of business. (One paper.)

Practical Book-keeping: Making the proper records and financial statements from given data. (One paper.)

Penmanship: Theory and practice of penmanship; position and movement. (One paper.)

Mercantile Arithmetic: Interest, discount, annuities certain, sinking funds, formation of interest and annuity tables, the application of logarithms, stocks and investments, partnership settlements, partial payments, equating or averaging accounts, exchange, practical measurements, and the metric system. (One paper.)

General Commercial Knowledge and Business Lands: Also Auditing, Commercial Economics, Stenography, History of Commerce and Transportation.

ART COURSE OF INSTRUCTION.

The Art Course of Instruction includes (1) Freehand Drawing, (2) Clay Modeling, (3) Coloured Drawing, (4) Industrial Design, (5) Geometrical and Mechanical Drawing, (6) Drawing on the Blackboard, (7) History of Art, including an outline of the origin and development of Architecture, Sculpture and Painting, with some knowledge of the life and works of the great artists of each of the leading periods.

THE ENTOMOLOGICAL SOCIETY OF ONTARIO.

In the year 1863, a number of students of Practical Entomology (under the Presidency of the late Doctor H. Croft, Professor of Chemistry in the University of Toronto) formed the Entomological Society of Canada. Their proceedings were published in the *Canadian Journal,* issued by the Canadian Institute.

MILITARY INSTRUCTION OF HIGH SCHOOL CADET CORPS.

In accordance with the provisions of the High Schools Act, 1896, any High School, or Collegiate Institute, Board may establish Classes in Military Instruction, and shall be entitled to an annual grant under conditions and regulations as to examination and inspection prescribed by the Education Department.

The Minister of Education, after consultation with the High School Inspectors and the Officers of the Militia Department, has issued the following regulations on the subject:

1. High School Cadet Corps may be formed for instruction in military drill and training in the High Schools, or Collegiate Institutes, but such corps shall on no account be employed in active service.

2. Application for permission to form a Company shall be sent to the Minister of Education for Ontario for transmission to the Minister of Militia and Defence.

3. Certain equipments will be supplied to each company, free of charge, by the Department of Militia, on application through the Minister of Education.

4. The Board of Trustees shall make itself responsible by a written undertaking for the value of the Arms and Accoutrements to be entrusted to it, and shall return them in good order to the Department of Militia when required to do so.

5. The Board of Trustees shall provide a suitable room, fitted with lock-up arm Racks, to be used as an Armory, and shall satisfy the Department of Militia that the Arms and Accoutrements will receive proper care.

6. The company shall consist of not fewer than twenty-five young men, over sixteen years of age, actually attending the High School or Collegiate Institute.

7. On or before the first day of October, the Board of Trustees shall send to the Minister of Education a roll, signed by the then existing members of the Company. On this roll shall be designated one suitable member of the company as captain, and two other suitable members as lieutenants.

8. The Board of Trustees shall see that the members of its company are provided with a uniform forage cap, or other military head dress, as may be preferred. The uniform, or any part thereof, provided, shall be subject to the approval of the Minister of Militia.

9. The company shall be instructed in the Course contained in the sections of the authorized Infantry Drill and Rifle Exercises as prescribed below. This instruction shall form part of the regular course in the High School or Collegiate Institute.

10. The Board of Trustees shall permit the inspection and examination of the arms and accoutrements, and of the Cadet Company, at any time, by any officer who may be detailed for that duty by the Minister of Militia.

11. The instructor of each Cadet Company shall be a regular member of the High School, or Collegiate Institute, Staff, holding at least either a second class B Military School Certificate or a High School Cadet Instructor's Certificate.

12. The Course of Instruction to be taken up by each company of the Ontario High School Cadet Corps shall be as prescribed by the Militia Department.

13. Inspection: In May or June of each year, an Officer, detailed for this duty by the Minister of Militia, shall examine and inspect each Company and its arms and accoutrements, and shall report the result to the Adjutant General of Militia. On the report of the Minister of Militia to the Minister of Education for Ontario, that such inspection and examination have been satisfactory, the Minister of Education shall pay the sum of $50 for the current year to the Board of Trustees concerned.

High School Cadet Instructor's Certificates: In order to afford High School Teachers an opportunity of qualifying themselves to act as instructors of Cadet companies, a special course of instruction will be provided in Toronto, lasting about one month. At the close of the Course, Teachers in attendance, and such other Teachers as may present themselves, will be examined by an Officer of the Department. Each successful candidate will be granted a special certificate to be called "High School Cadet Instructor's Certificate." The course of instruction for the Certificate shall be as prescribed.

Candidates at the Examination will be required not only to show themselves proficient in the different exercises prescribed, but also to be able to instruct a Company or Squad thereon.

EX LIBRIS
DEPARTMENT OF MUNICIPAL AFFAIRS
ONTARIO
THIS BOOK MUST NOT BE REMOVED